AF478219

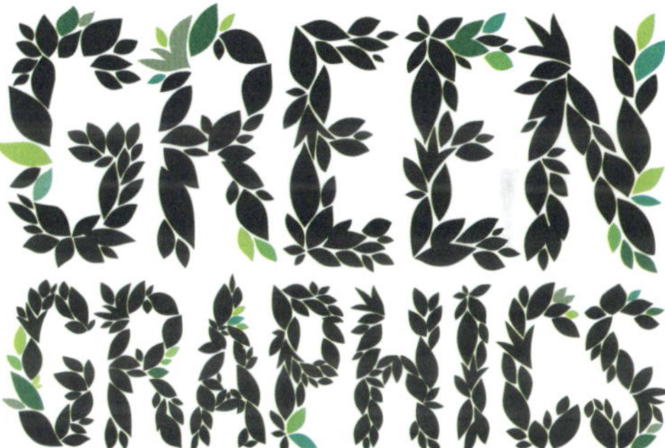

GREEN
GRAPHICS

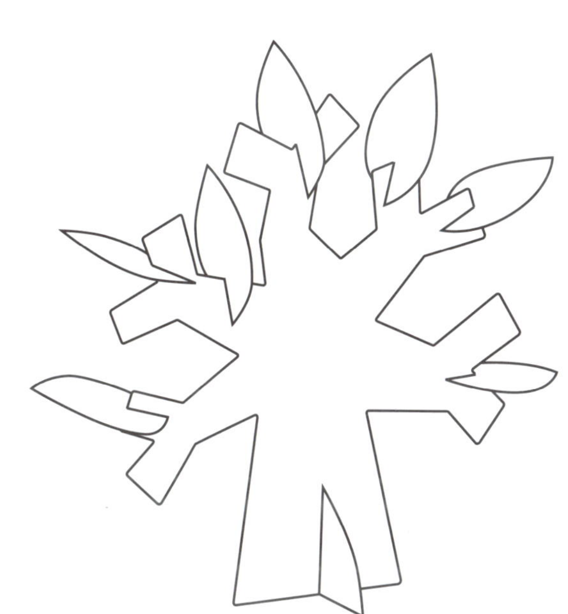

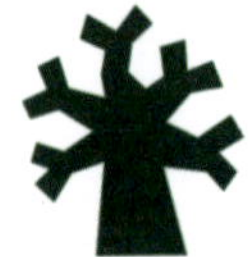

IMPRESSUM

GREEN GRAPHICS
Copyright © 2011
Index Book SL
Consell de Cent 160 local 3
08015 Barcelona - Spain
Phone: (+34) 93 454 55 47
Fax: (+34) 93 454 84 38
ib@indexbook.com
www.indexbook.com

Publisher: Sylvie Estrada
Authors: Vicky Eckert, Efrén Zúñiga, Ana Freixas
(www.estudio-ez.com)
Art direction: Vicky Eckert, Efrén Zúñiga
Page layout: Ana Freixas
Translation: Timothy Barton (www.timtranslates.com)

ISBN: 978-84-92643-54-7

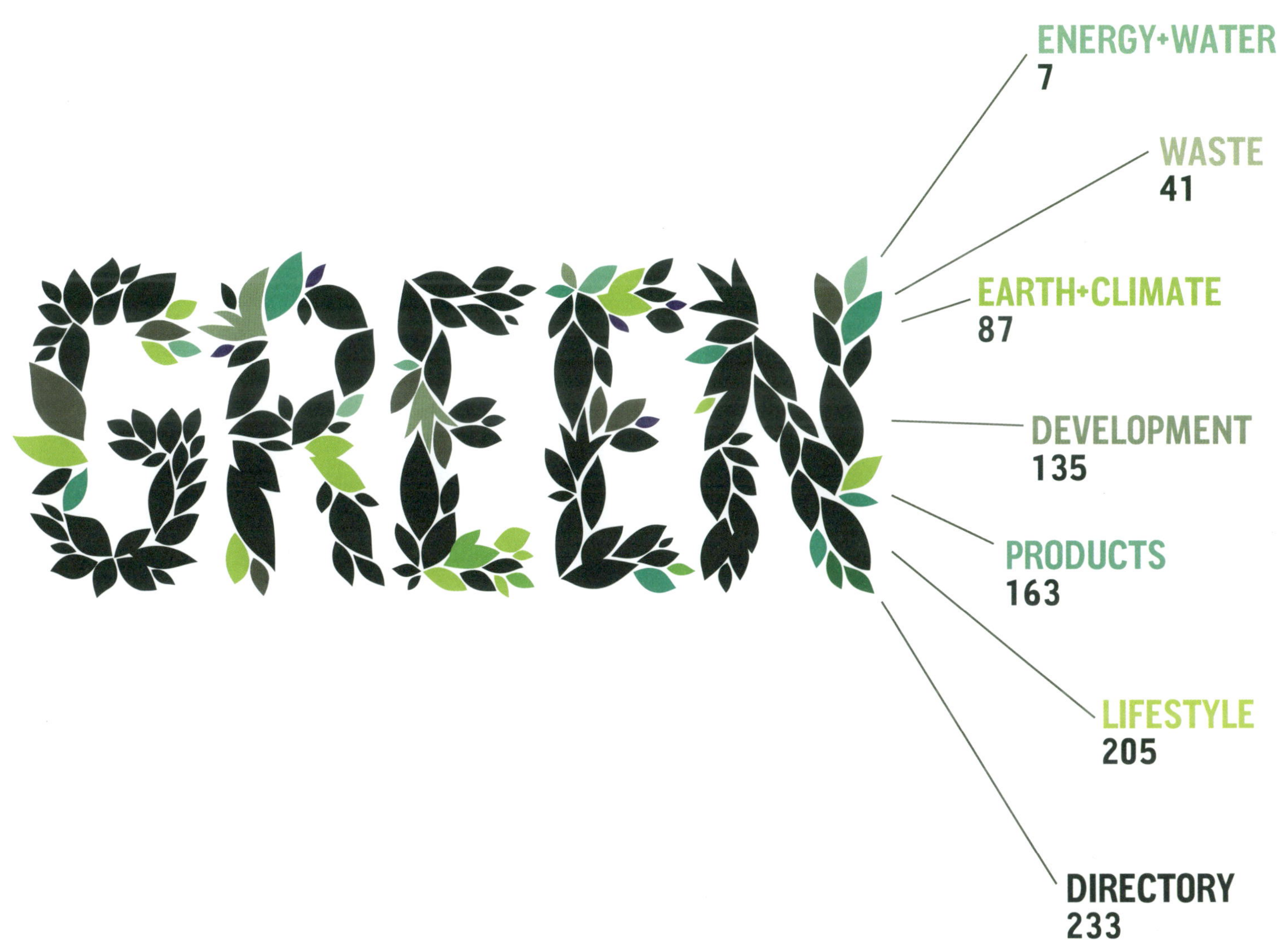

ENERGY+WATER
7
WASTE
41
EARTH+CLIMATE
87
DEVELOPMENT
135
PRODUCTS
163
LIFESTYLE
205
DIRECTORY
233

Fortunately, over the past few years there has been an increase in the number of environmentally friendly products available. Companies are making ever greater efforts to offer items produced using environmentally sustainable methods, including energy-efficient processes, renewable energy sources, and recyclable or recycled materials. Businesses are now proud to take the health of our planet into consideration in one way or another, which has become essential for the company image. We are therefore becoming accustomed to seeing technological advances on the news, publications on eco-design and new professions such as that of the eco-designer. All this shows the high level of activity and the change of focus in industrial design.

While advances in materials and technologies are highly visible, little attention seems to be given to the graphical communication needed to publicise these advances. Yet graphical communication is a powerful tool to change people's mentality, increase awareness and report on the problems and challenges of climate change.

For this reason, we have focused our interest on graphic design related to environmental issues, with graphical language playing the lead role. We have found a wide variety of styles and focuses, and have seen that there is great concern among graphic designers for the environment, since many of the initiatives were conceived by the designers themselves. At the same time, this selection of designs reveals the efforts made by associations and public bodies to promote a change of mentality.

These educational campaigns, exhibitions, events, corporate images, experiments and small gestures aim to get people thinking: each is a small contribution, and collectively they reflect the wide variety of aspects and solutions that the environment has in common with graphic design. These aspects and solutions are presented through six key themes.

The first chapter embraces both **energy and water**, since efficient, responsible use of these two resources is important. A central theme is mobility, which has a major environmental impact. There are various ways of reducing this impact, whereas for water there is practically only one direct message: save water.

There are many aspects to the topic of **waste**: generation, collection and processing of various types of materials, and the possibilities of recycling or reusing waste; simple initiatives to lengthen the life cycle of materials; full awareness and educational campaigns; and most importantly, waste-reduction strategies.

Earth + climate is the chapter on the things directly affected by climate change (the "patients"): the flora, fauna, natural resources, ecosystems, etc.

While the other chapters deal with specific actions or problems, the chapter entitled "Green **development**" covers how to conceive and plan future developments. Basically it discusses the jigsaw of sustainable development as a whole, rather than the individual pieces.
This chapter therefore comprises projects that simultaneously cover various sustainability topics related to sustainable development as a whole. The topic of architecture does not only concern a lifestyle; it is also related to energy, water, insulation, the direction a house faces, new materials, urban planning, etc. Similarly, there are conferences, campaigns and institutions that deal broadly with sustainable development (Agenda 21, economy, ecology).

For the "Green **products**" chapter, we looked for products whose producers took into account things like avoiding waste, reusing materials and using original concepts, as well as using packaging and promotional material that was able to communicate these concepts.

The creative, often entertaining, proposals in the chapter "Green **lifestyle**" convey the idea that a more eco-aware lifestyle is very appealing and that a change to a more responsible form of consumption is, far from being a punishment, enriching.

Finally, we would like to mention the "little treasure" that is the directory at the end of this book. We encourage you to visit the websites of the participants. These are a gateway to the complex topic of environmental sustainability, and contain many links. They are also a gateway to the abundant aspects, opinions, research and actions of the environmental movement and regarding the change in mentality that has begun in many parts of the world we share.

Thank you to all those who have participated in this book.

In biodiversity and in the ecological system, nothing works well unless everything works well together.

Joaquín Araujo, naturalist and environmental communicator

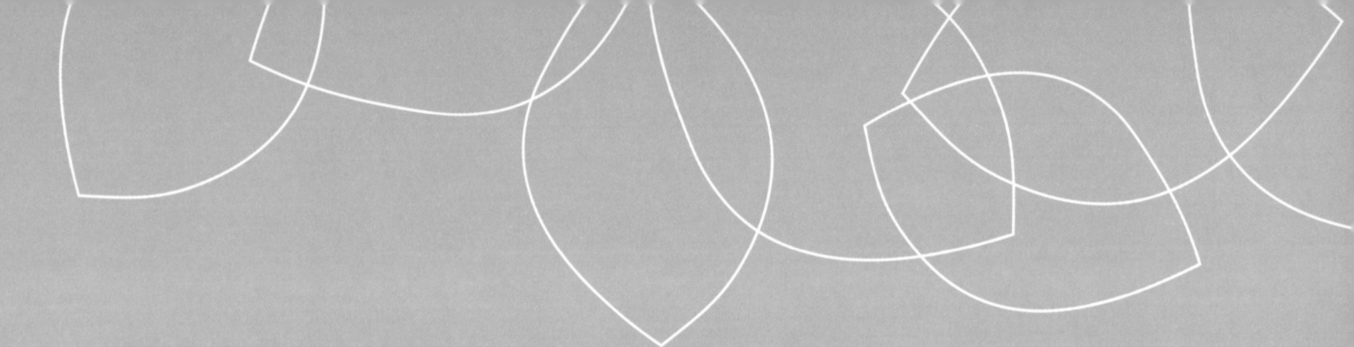
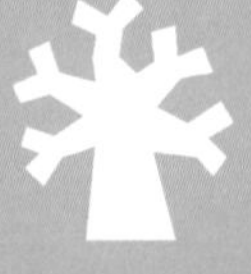

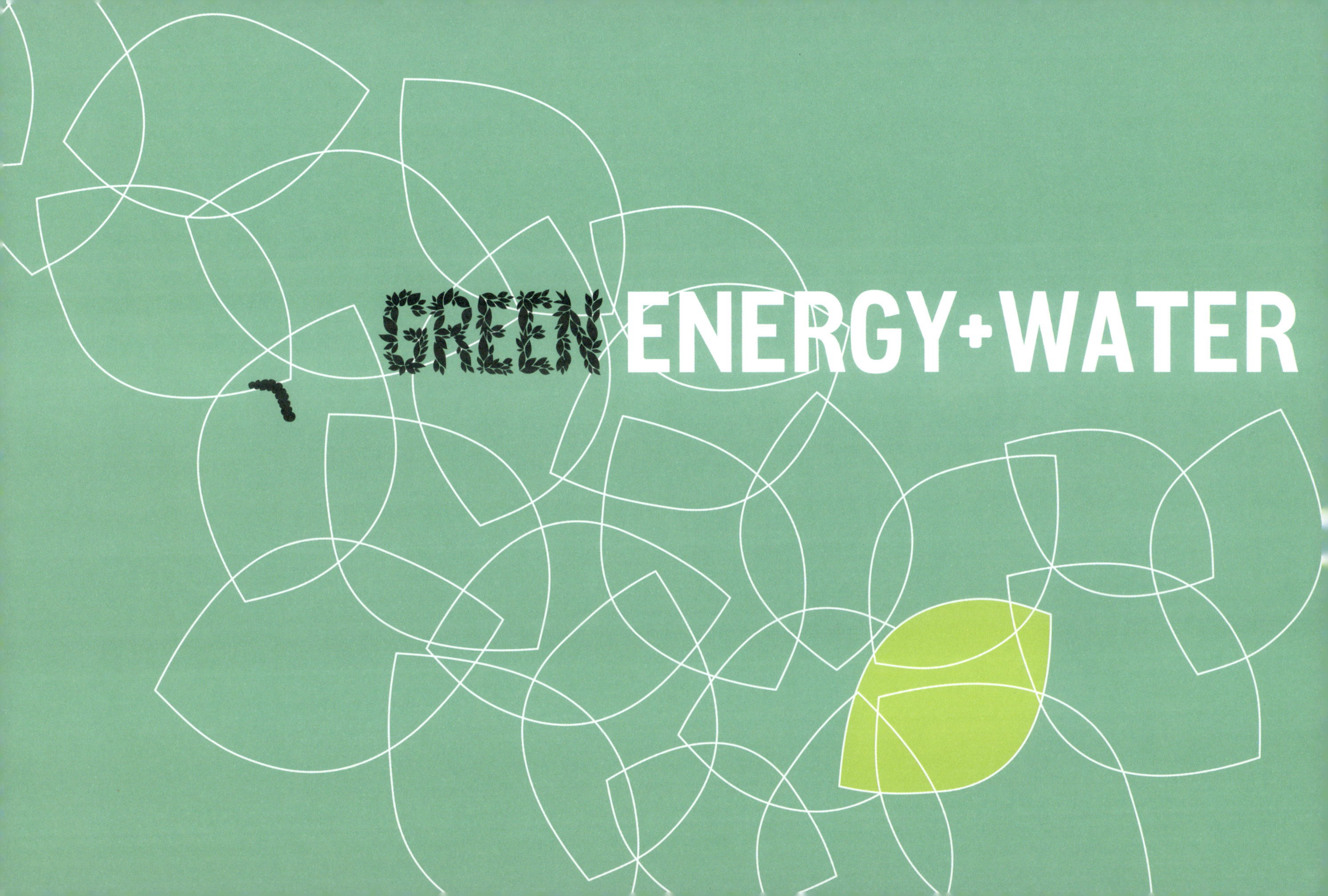

GREEN ENERGY+WATER

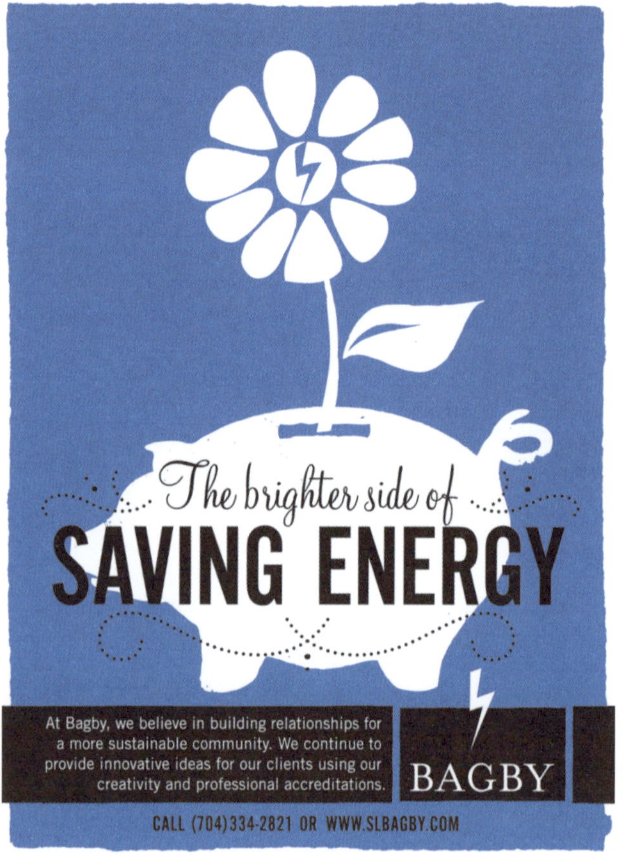

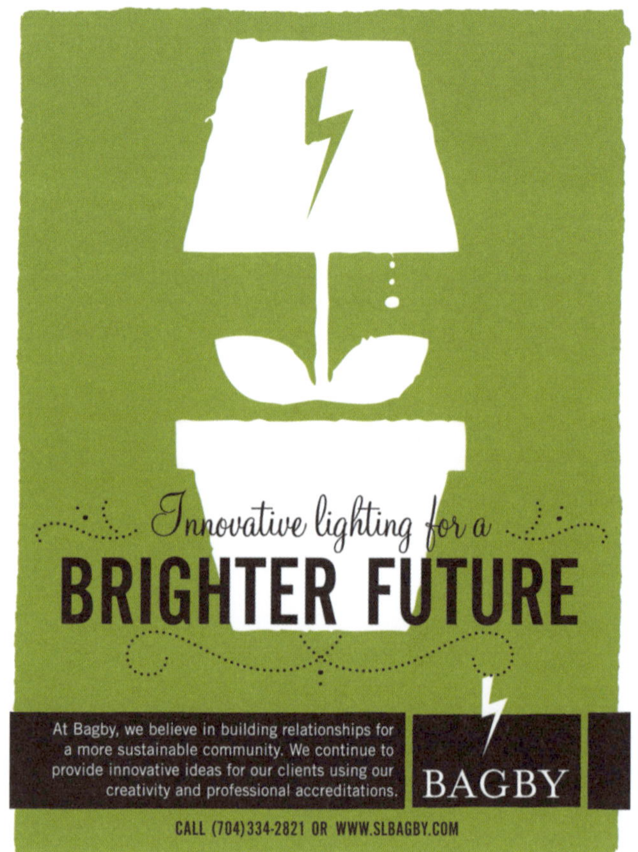

agency/studio: **A3 Design** / project: campaign for a company that offers energy-efficient lighting solutions. / client: Bagby Lighting / country: USA

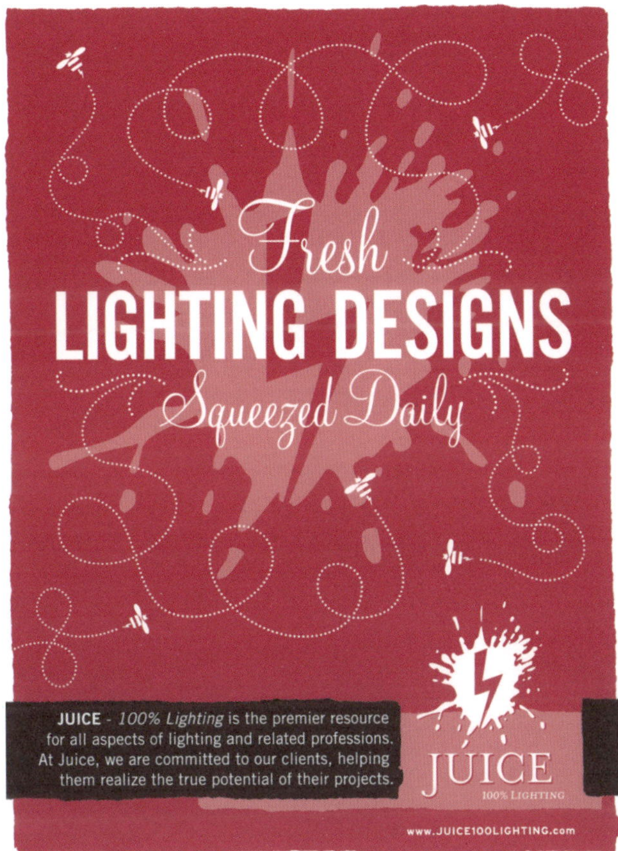

agency/studio: **A3 Design** / project: Fresh lighting designs squeezed daily. Image of Bagby's sister company that focuses on custom-designed solutions. / client: Juice 100% Lighting / country: USA

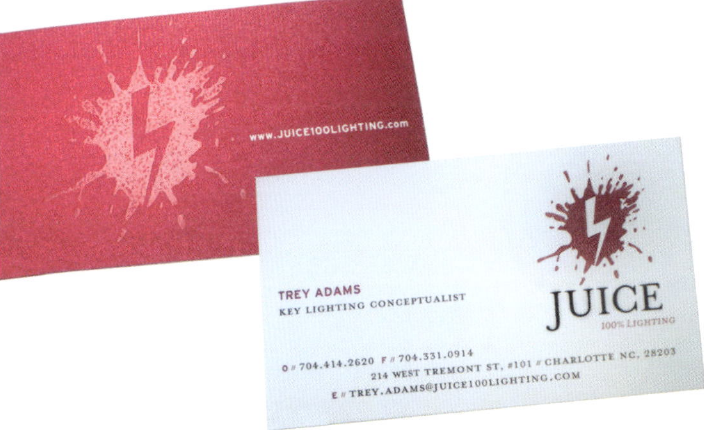

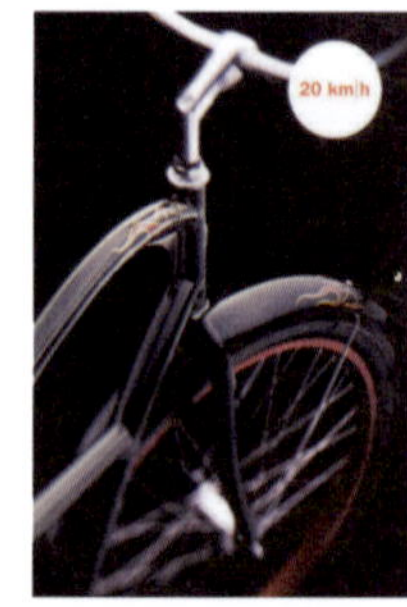
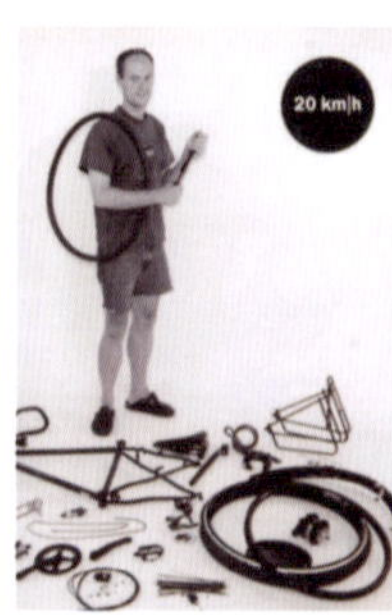
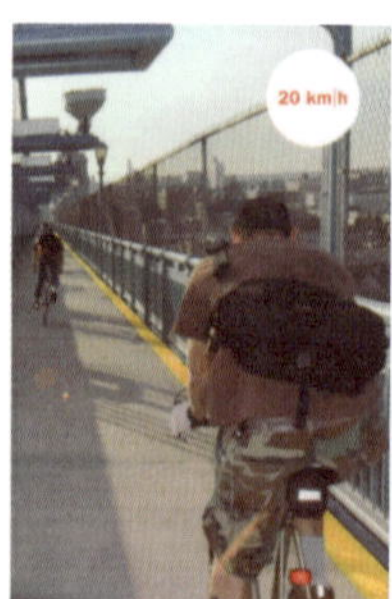
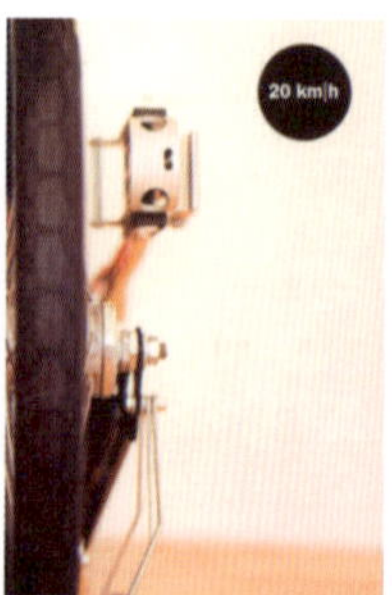
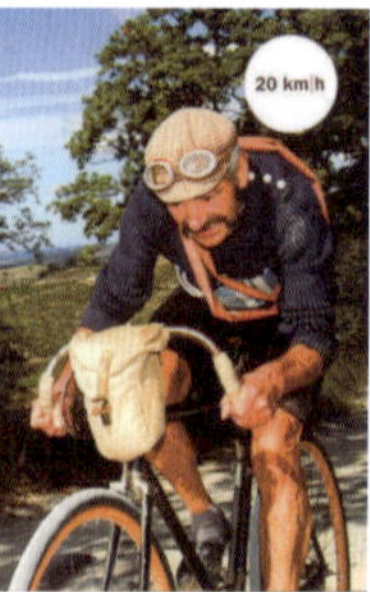
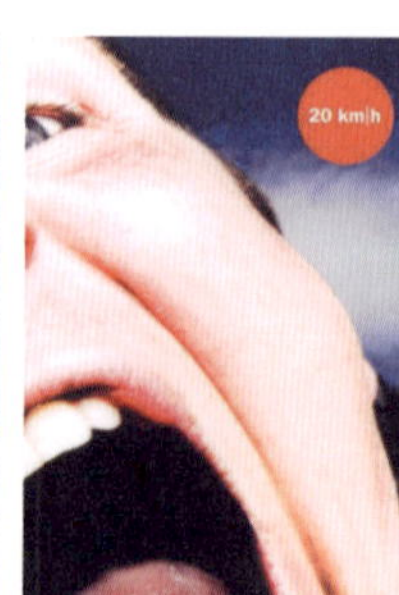
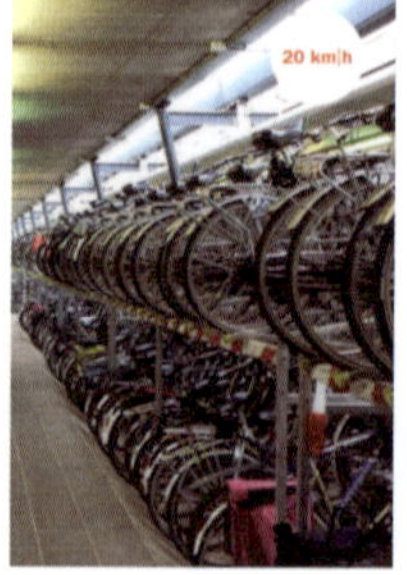
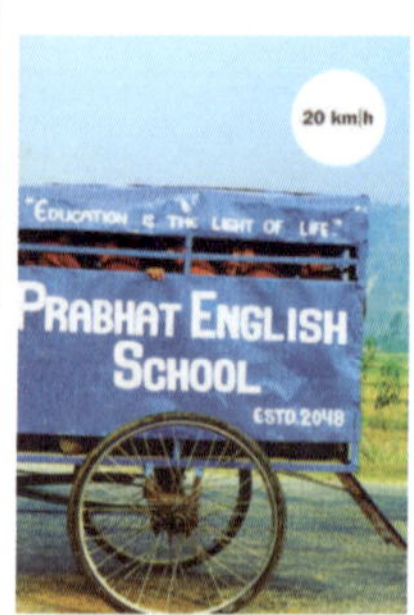

agency/studio: **David Torrents** / project: 20 km/h. Magazine about urban cycling. / client: bike tech / country: Spain

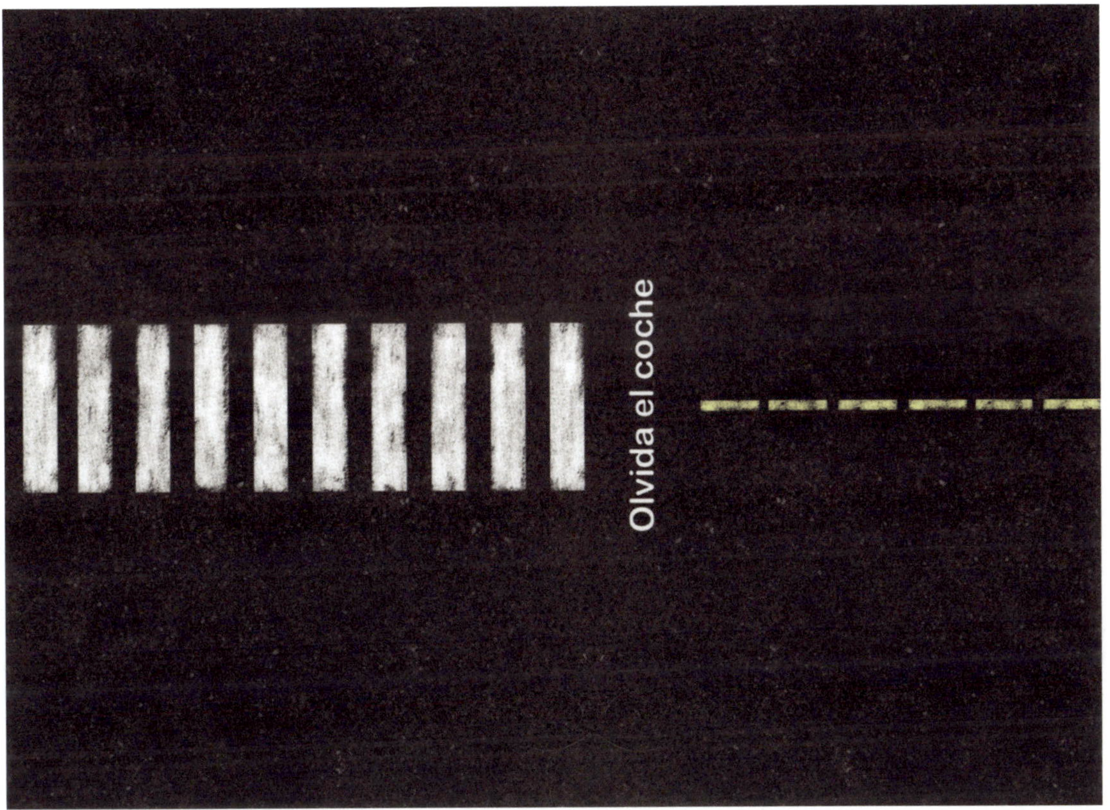

agency/studio: **Daniel Borrego** / project: Olvida el coche (forget about the car). The winning entry for the "Olvida el coche" poster competition. / client: Ecologistas en acción (Environmentalists in action) / country: Spain

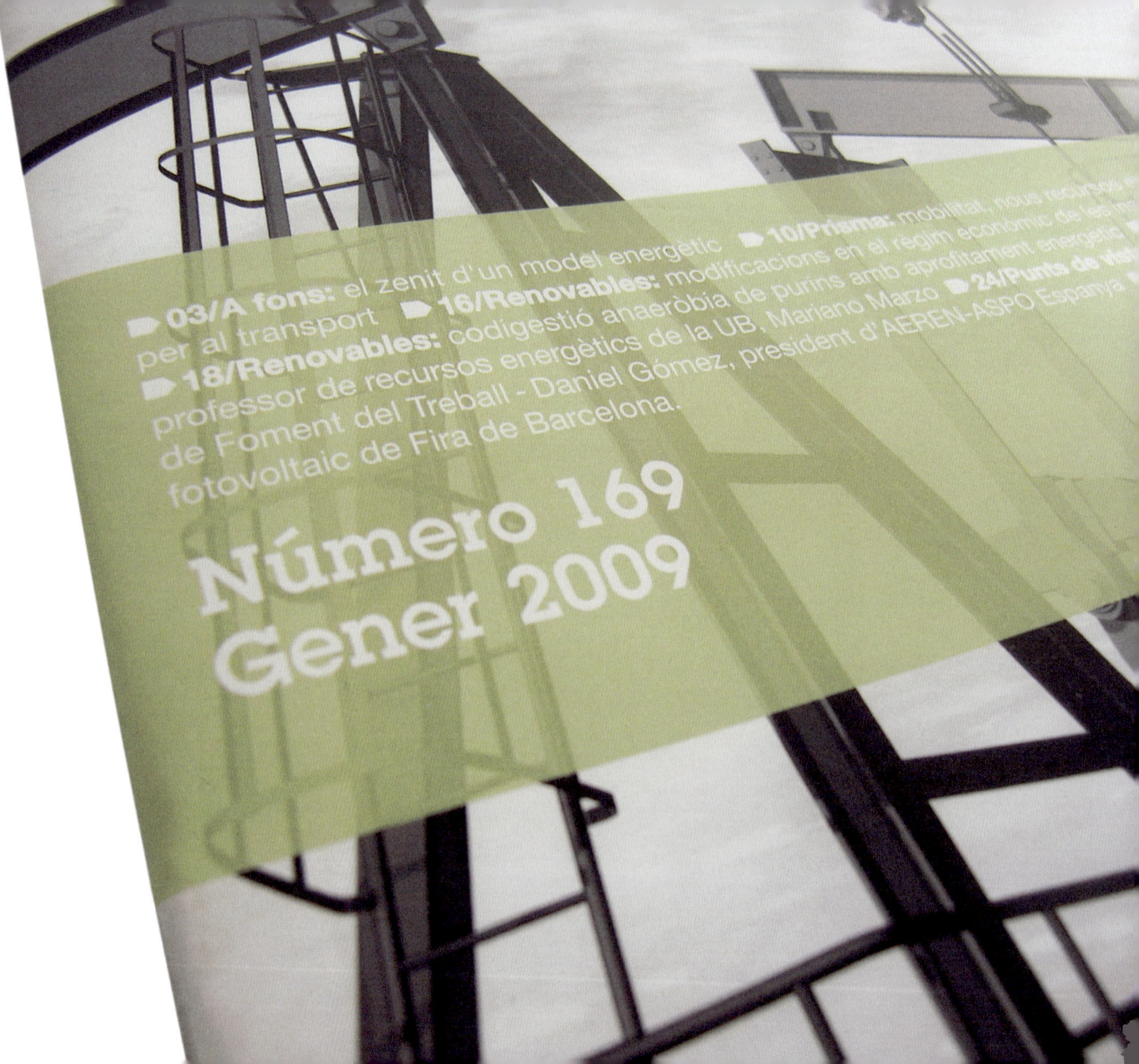
03/A fons: el zenit d'un model energètic 10/Prisma: mobilitat, nous recursos
per al transport 16/Renovables: modificacions en el règim econòmic de les instal·lacions
18/Renovables: codigestió anaeròbia de purins amb aprofitament energètic
professor de recursos energètics de la UB, Mariano Marzo 24/Punts de vista
de Foment del Treball - Daniel Gómez, president d'AEREN-ASPO Espanya
fotovoltaic de Fira de Barcelona.

Número 169
Gener 2009

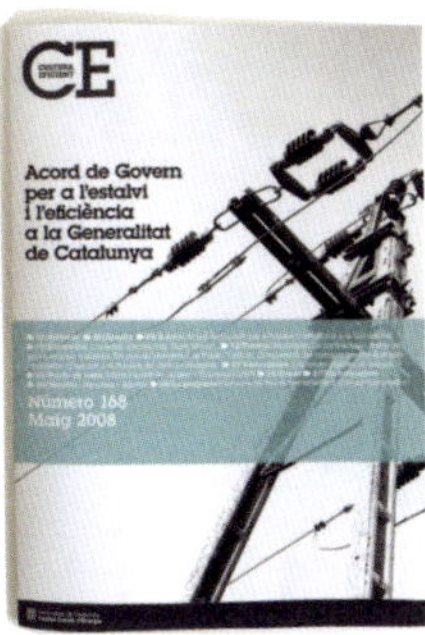
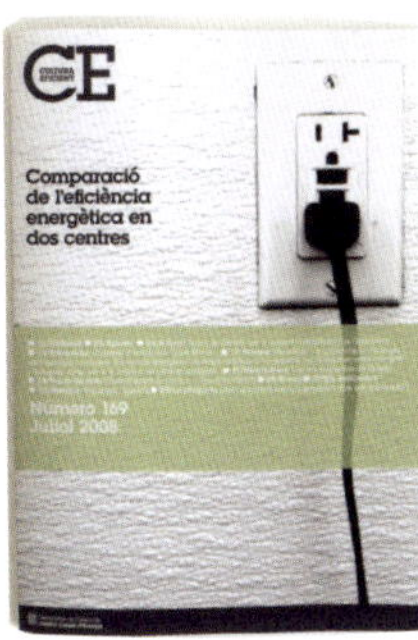
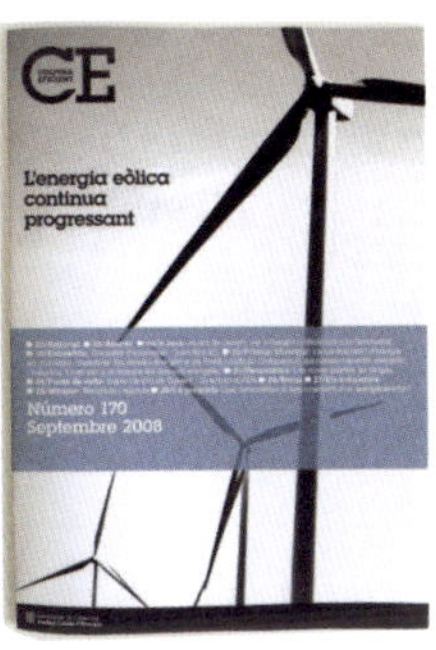
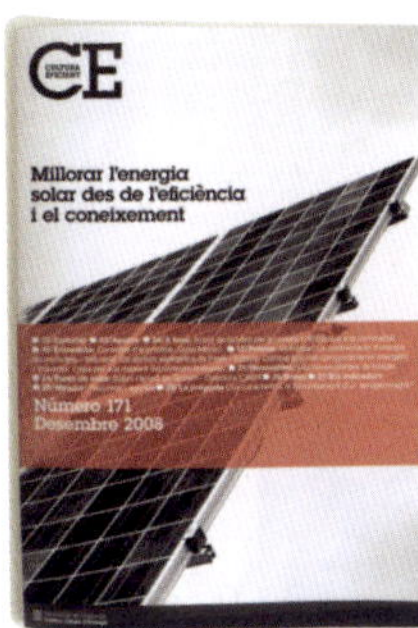

agency/studio: **Oxigen** / project: "Cultura Energètica" magazine, a quarterly publication by the Catalan Energy Institute about progress made in the areas of energy saving, energy efficiency and renewable energies. / client: ICAEN / country: Spain

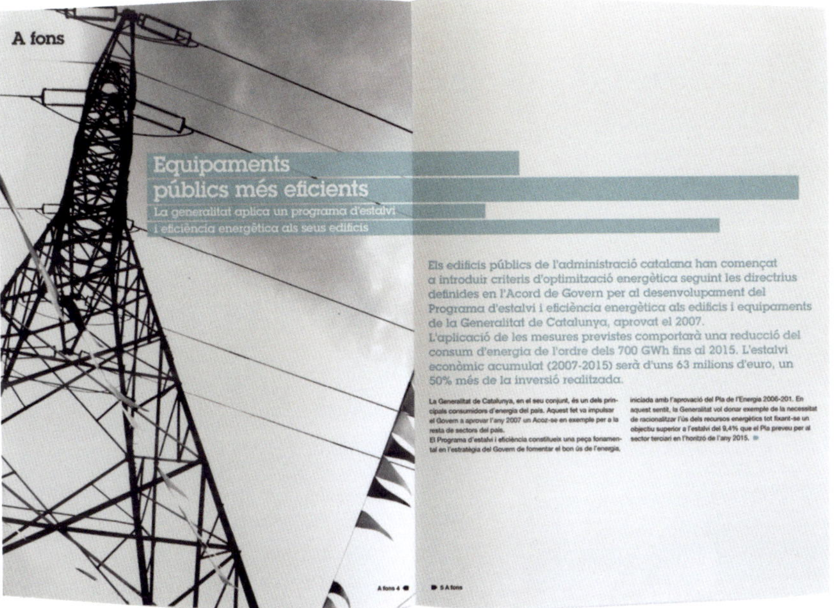

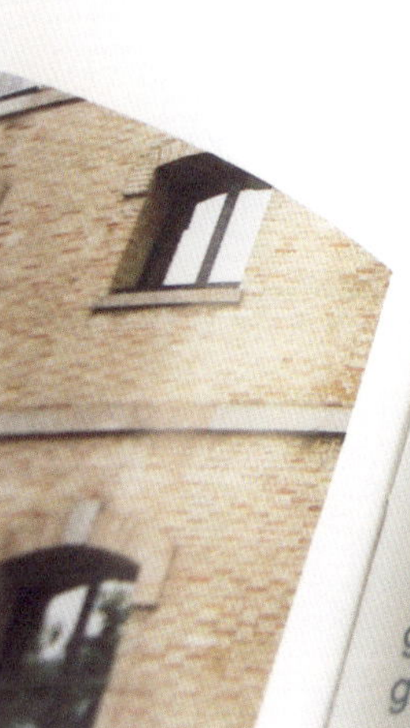

agency/studio: **Sonsoles Llorens** / project: felicitación 2010. Access to water will be one of the major challenges for much of the world's population in this new decade. The graphics aim to highlight the need not to waste natural resources. But they also have a more personal message: "Do not waste a drop". / client: Sonsoles Llorens design studio / country: Spain

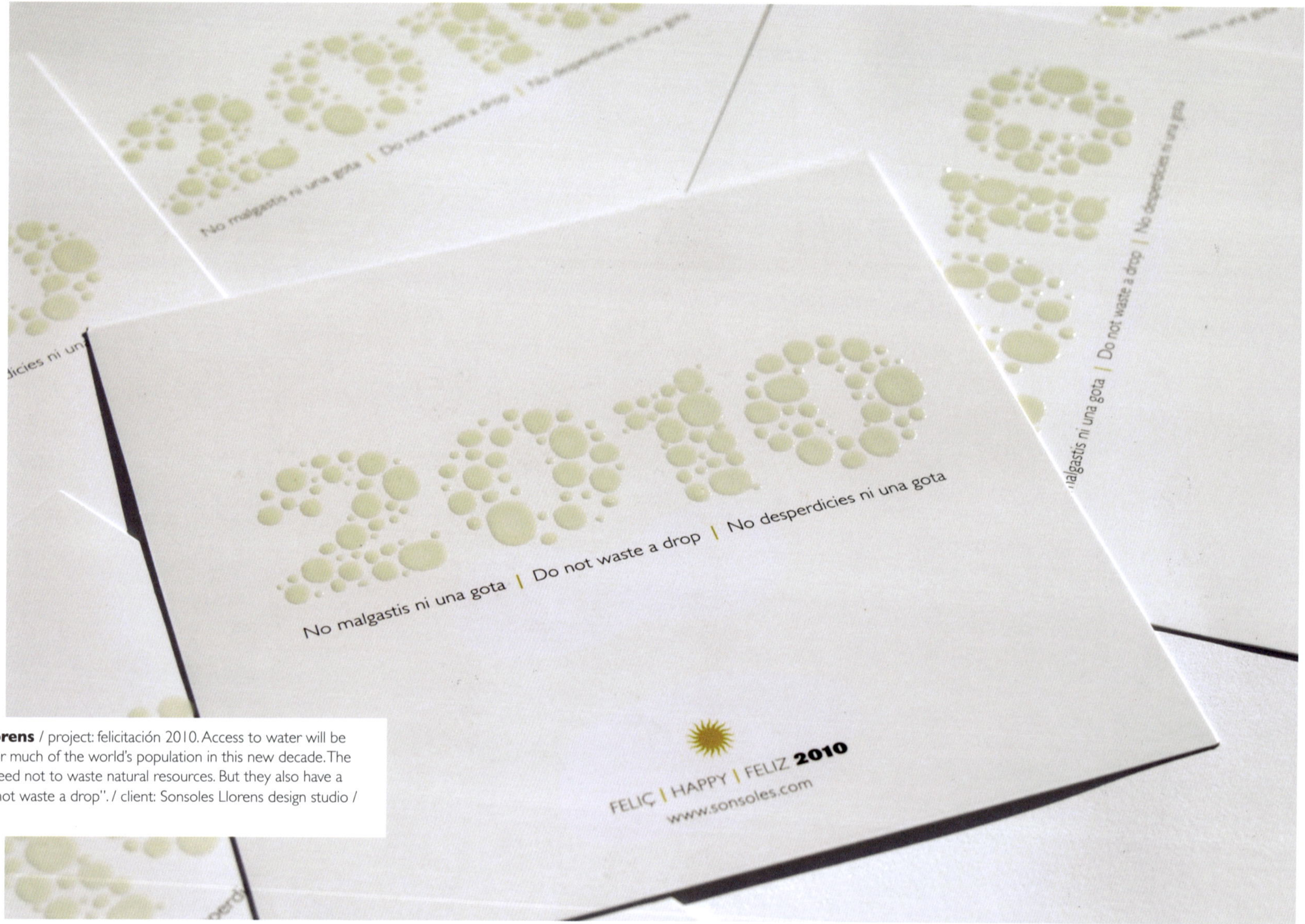

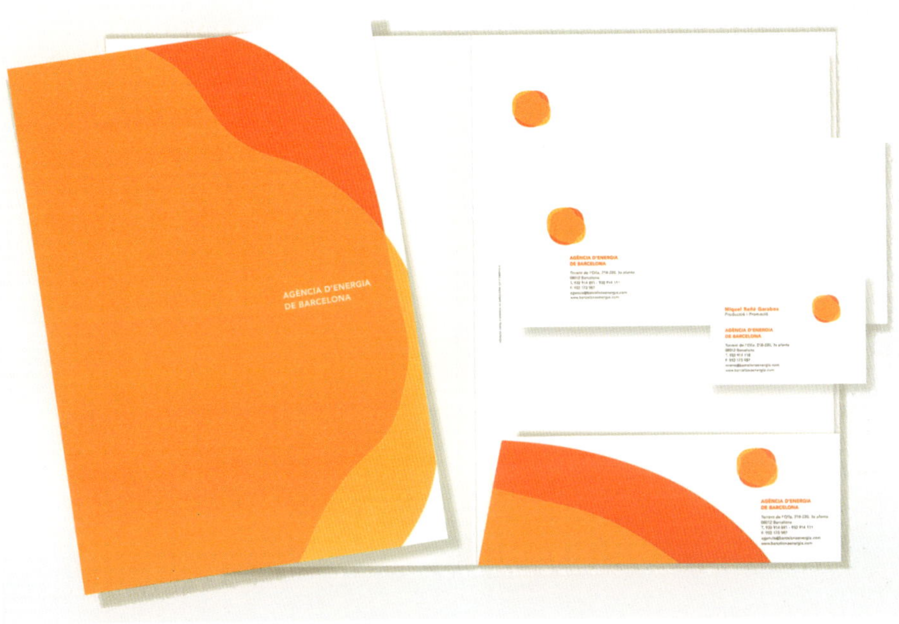

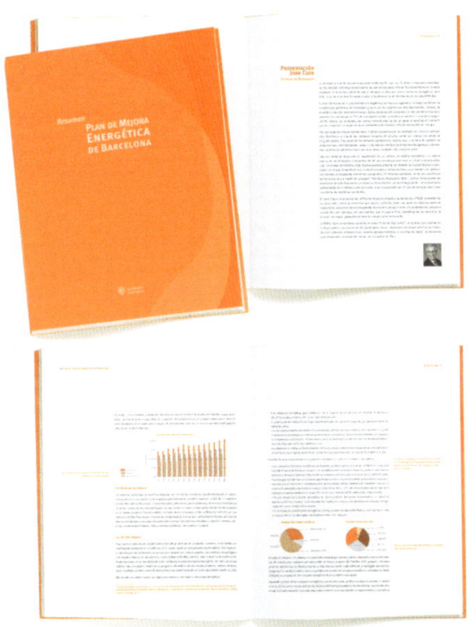

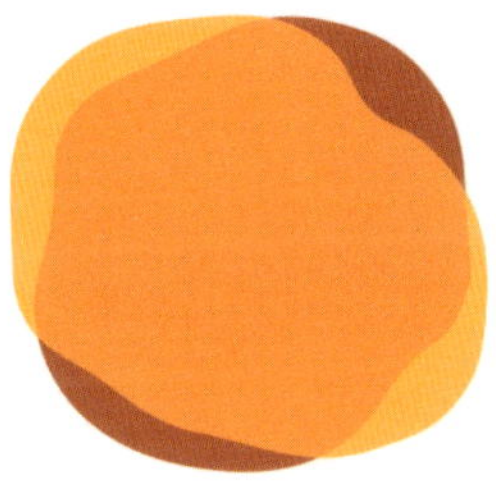

AGÈNCIA D'ENERGIA
DE BARCELONA

agency/studio: **Sonsoles Llorens** / project: Barcelona Energy Agency. The colours used and the reference to the sun connote the energy for which the agency is responsible, from an environmentally friendly, sustainable perspective. / client: Barcelona Energy Agency / country: Spain

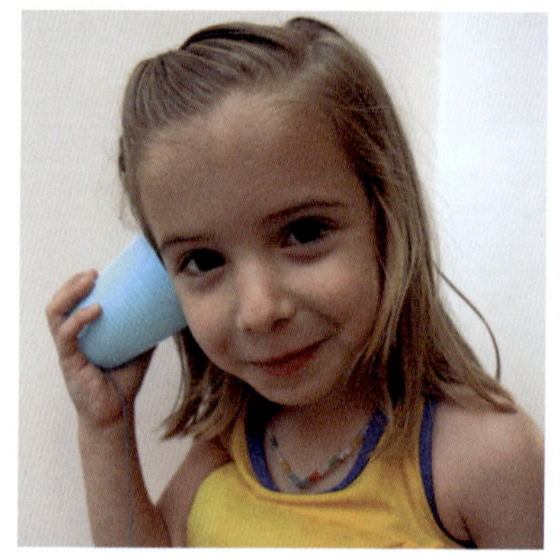

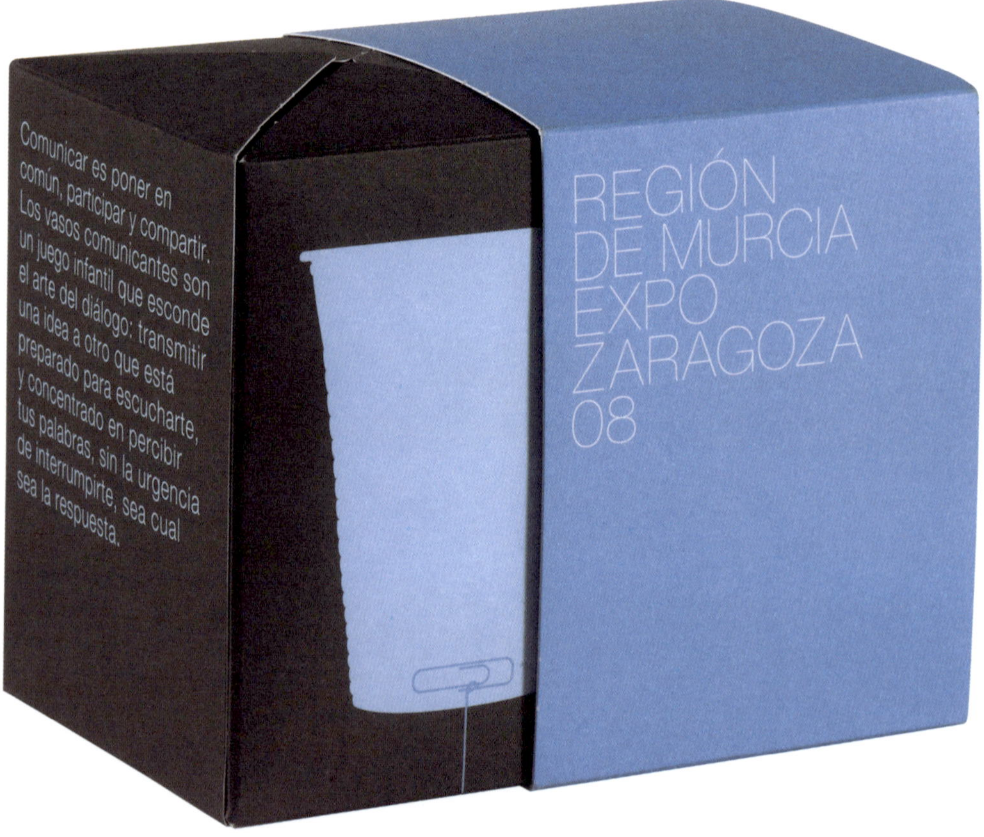
Comunicar es poner en
común, participar y compartir.
Los vasos comunicantes son
un juego infantil que esconde
el arte del diálogo: transmitir
una idea a otro que está
preparado para escucharte,
y concentrado en percibir
tus palabras, sin la urgencia
de interrumpirte, sea cual
sea la respuesta.

REGIÓN
DE MURCIA
EXPO
ZARAGOZA
08

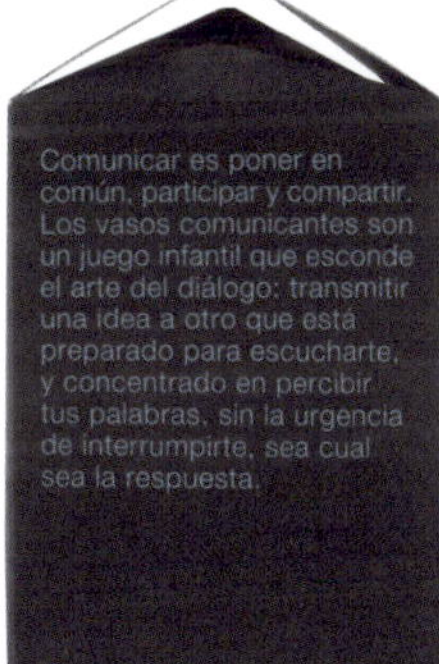

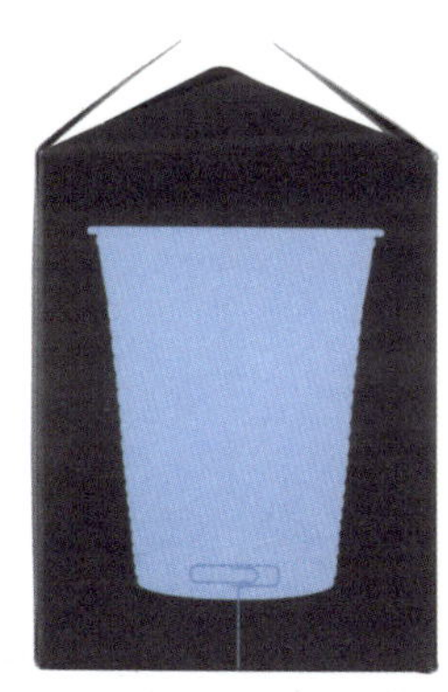
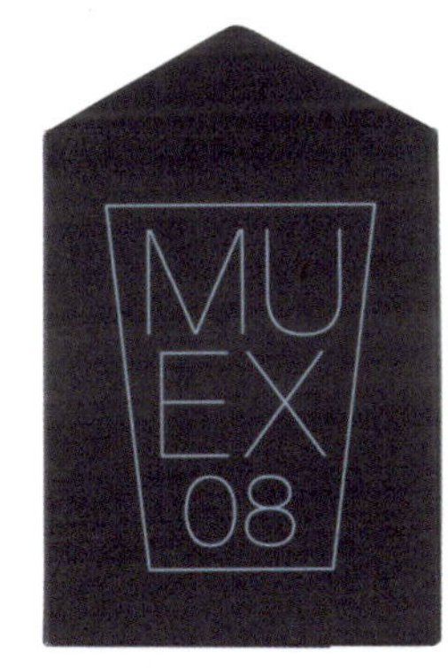

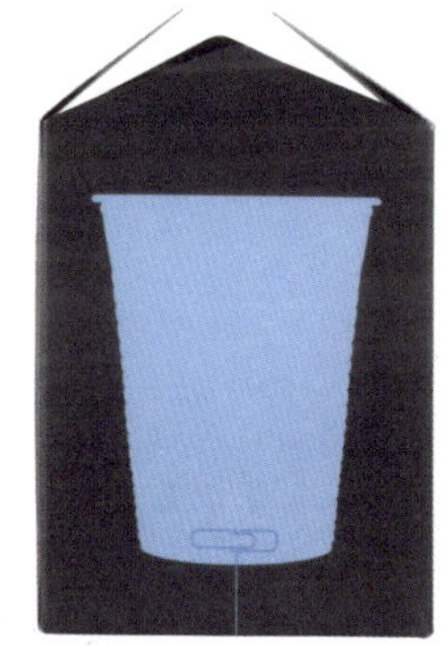
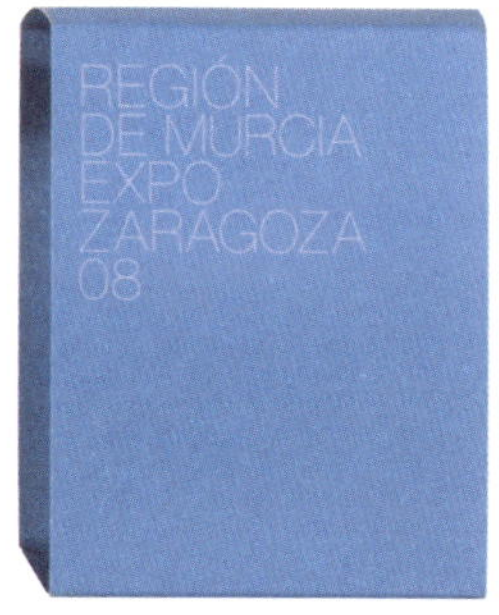

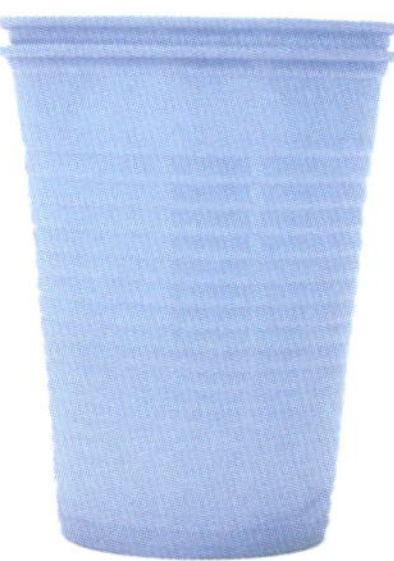

agency/studio: **Eduardo del Fraile** / project: Identity to promote the Region of Murcia at the Zaragoza International Exhibition. The comunication vessels are thought to encourage dialogue between two regions with great disagreements in terms of water policy. / client: Region of Murcia / country: Spain

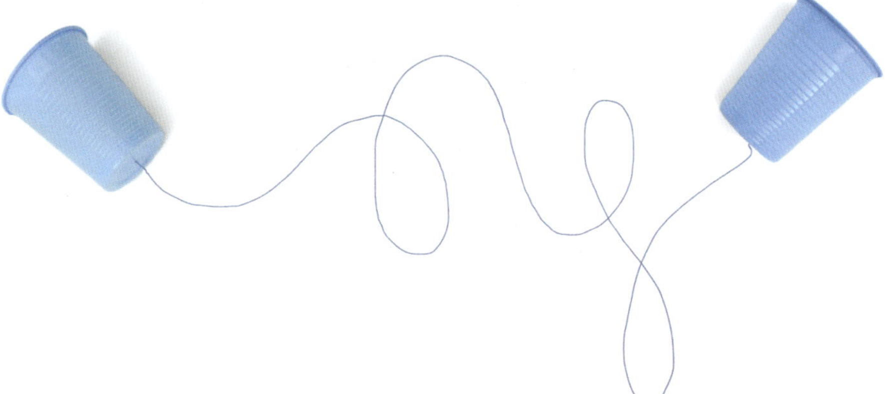

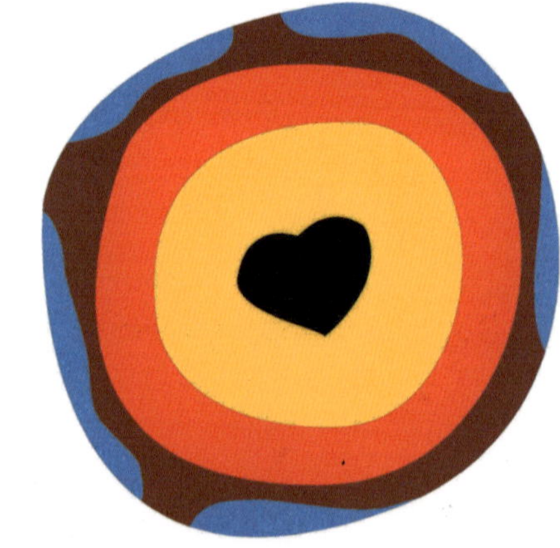

agency/studio: **Gorka Aizpurua** / project: logo for El Faro, the pavilion at Expo Zaragoza 2008 dedicated to water-related challenges. / client: El Faro, Citizens' Initiative Pavilion, Expo 2008 Zaragoza / country: Spain

el faro

pabellón
de iniciativas
ciudadanas

Consume con moderación. Es tu responsabilidad. 25^{w}

author: **Alejandro Rubens** / project: Consume moderately. Poster promoting energy-saving. / country: Spain

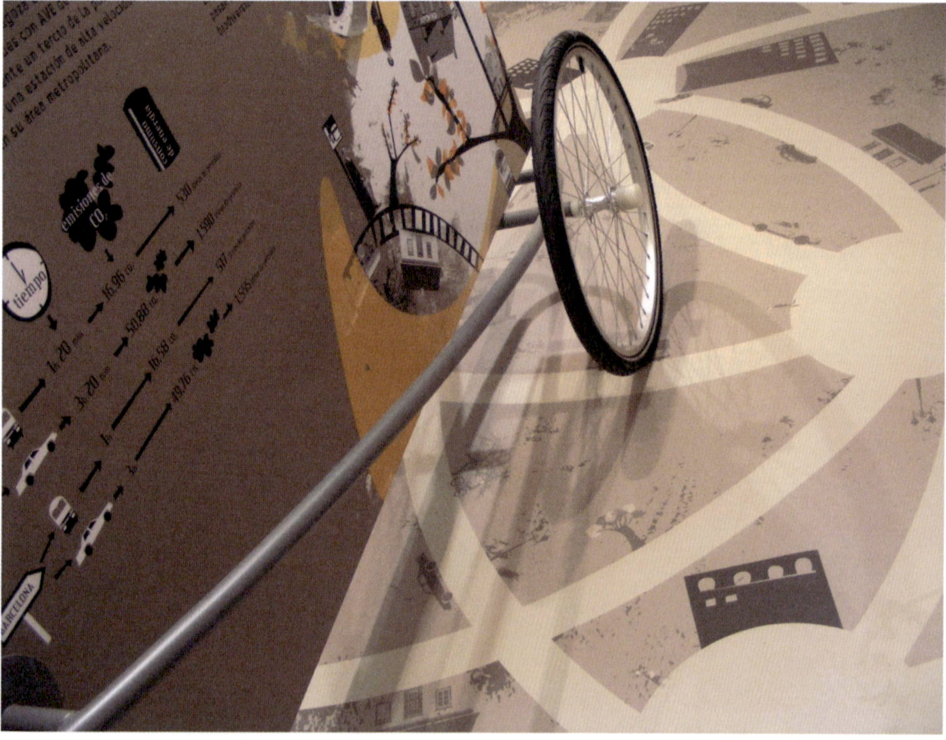

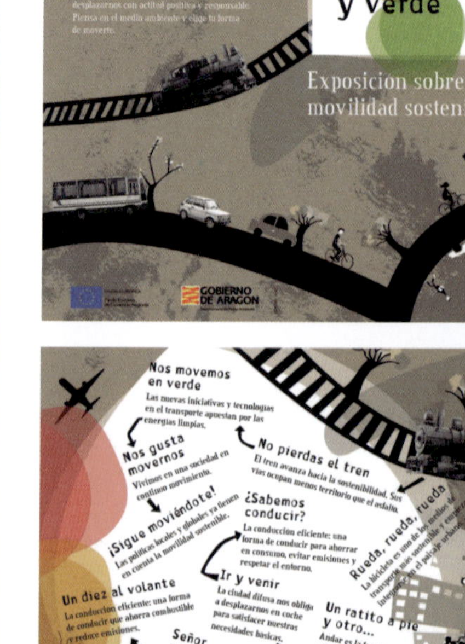

agency/studio: **lavola** / project: a travelling exhibition on sustainable mobility. / client: SODEMASA / country: Spain

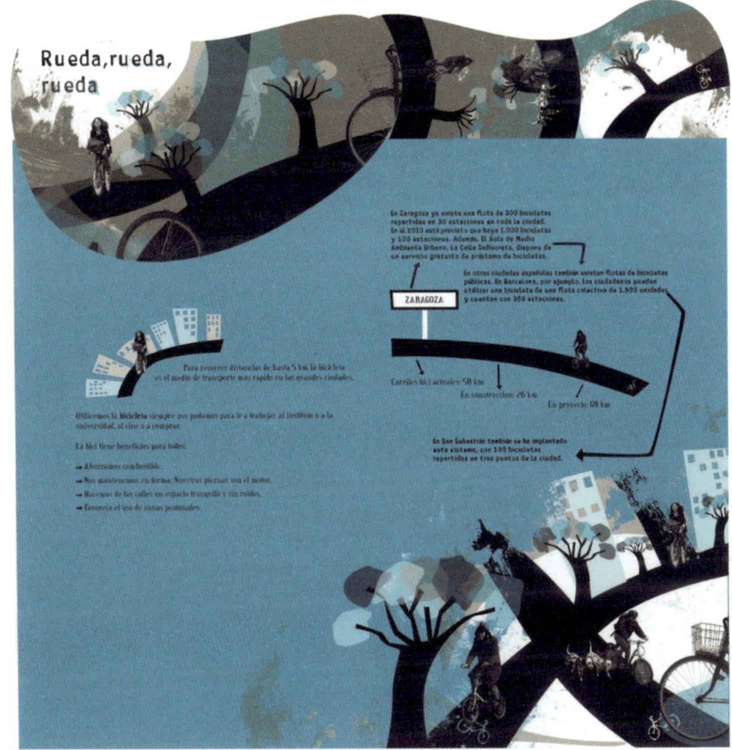

Rueda, rueda, rueda
Para recorrer distancias de hasta 5 km la bicicleta es el medio de transporte más rápido en las grandes ciudades.
Utilicemos la bicicleta siempre que podamos para ir a trabajar, al Instituto o a la universidad, al cine o a comprar.
La bici tiene beneficios para todos:
→ Ahorramos combustible.
→ Nos mantenemos en forma. Nuestras piernas son el motor.
→ Hacemos de las calles un espacio tranquilo y sin ruidos.
→ Favorece el uso de zonas peatonales.
En Zaragoza ya existe una flota de 300 bicicletas repartidas en 30 estaciones en toda la ciudad. En el 2010 está previsto que haya 1.000 bicicletas y 100 estaciones. Además, El Aula de Medio Ambiente Urbano, La Calle Indiscreta, dispone de un servicio gratuito de préstamo de bicicletas.
En otras ciudades españolas también existen flotas de bicicletas públicas. En Barcelona, por ejemplo, los ciudadanos pueden utilizar una bicicleta de una flota colectiva de 1.500 unidades y cuentan con 359 estaciones.
ZARAGOZA
Carriles bici actuales: 58 km
En construcción: 26 km
En proyecto: 69 km
En San Sebastián también se ha implantado este sistema, con 100 bicicletas repartidas en tres puntos de la ciudad.

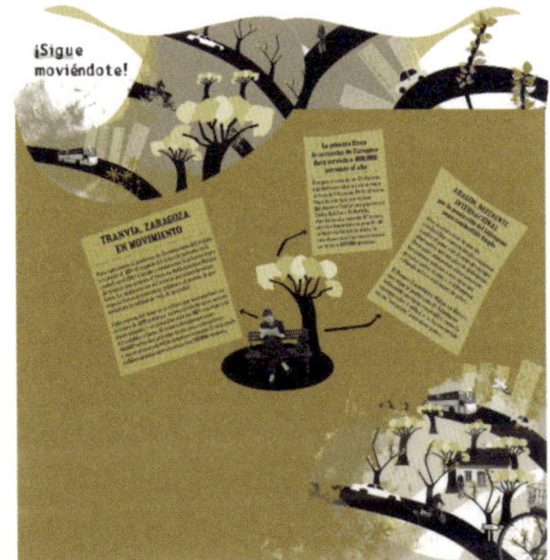

¡Sigue moviéndote!
TRANVÍA, ZARAGOZA EN MOVIMIENTO

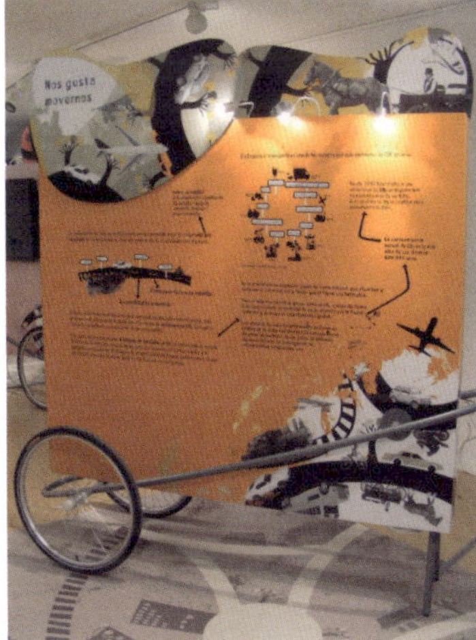

Nos gusta movernos

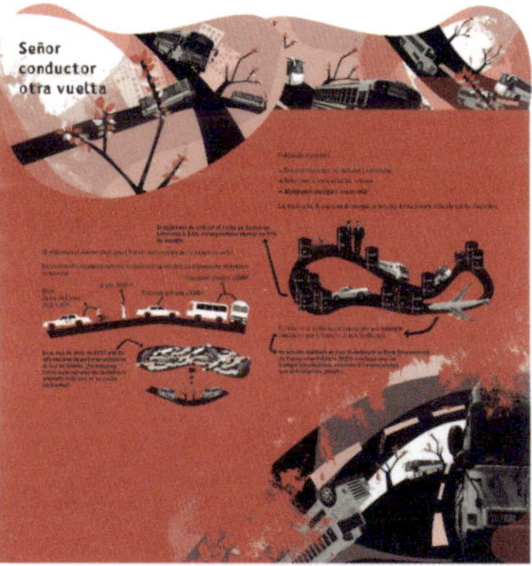

Señor conductor otra vuelta

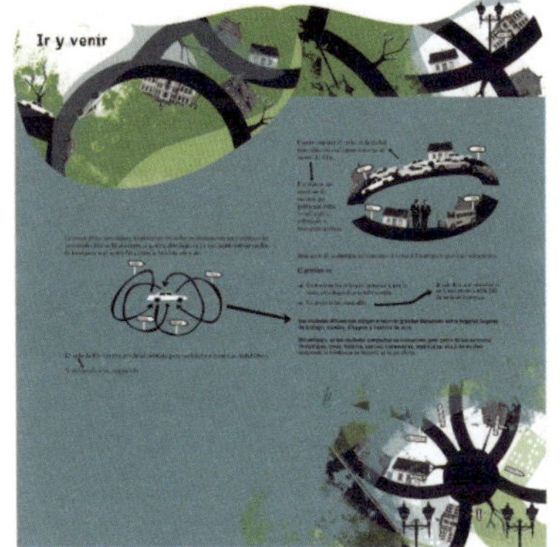

Ir y venir

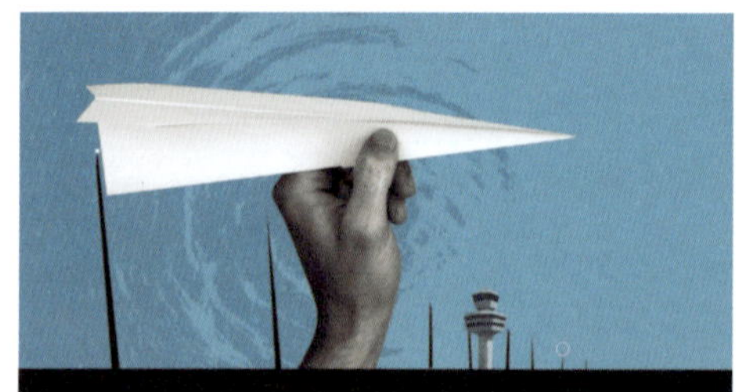

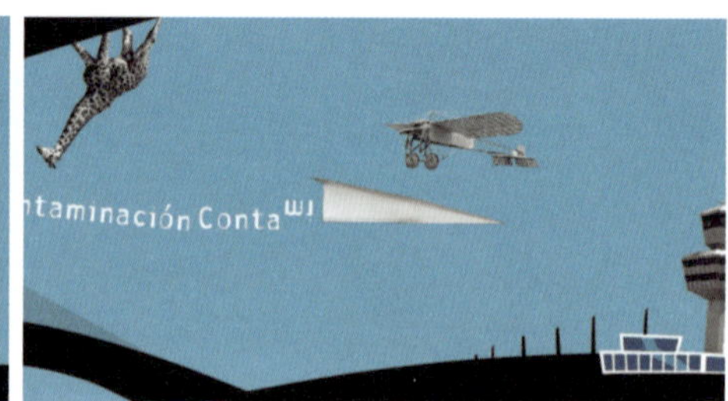

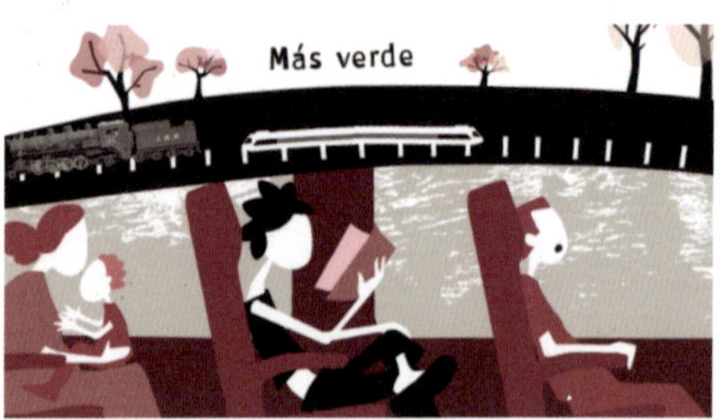

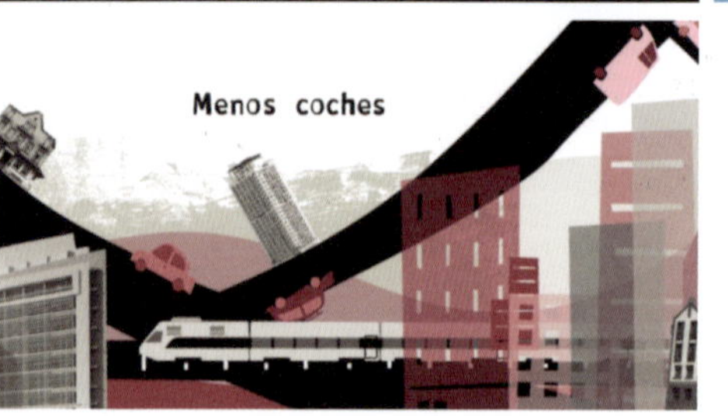

authors: **Doro Vogel / lavola** / collaborators: Pep Rimbau, Frank Neumann / project: a travelling exhibition on sustainable mobility. The five-minute video considers the advantages and disadvantages of each of the main methods of transport used in the Spanish region of Aragon. / client: lavola for SODEMASA, a public company owned by the Government of Aragon / country: Spain

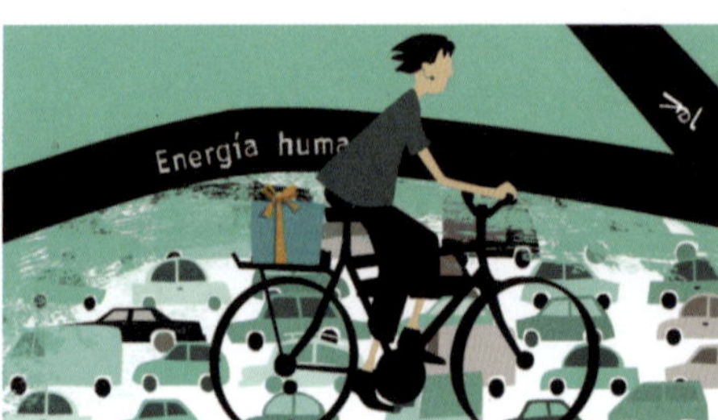

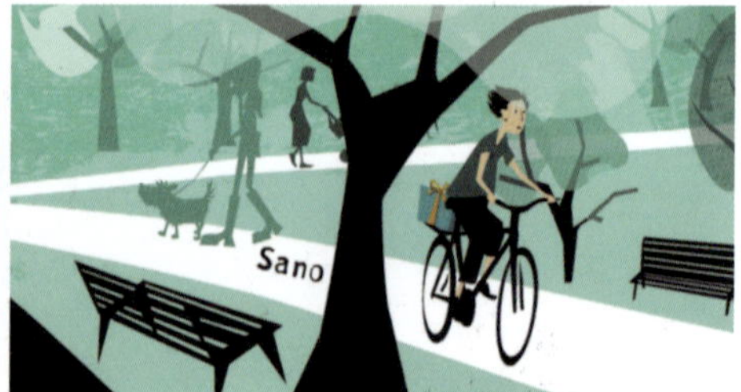

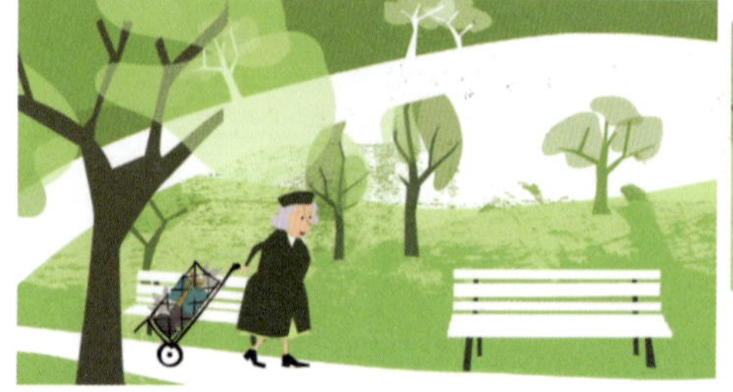

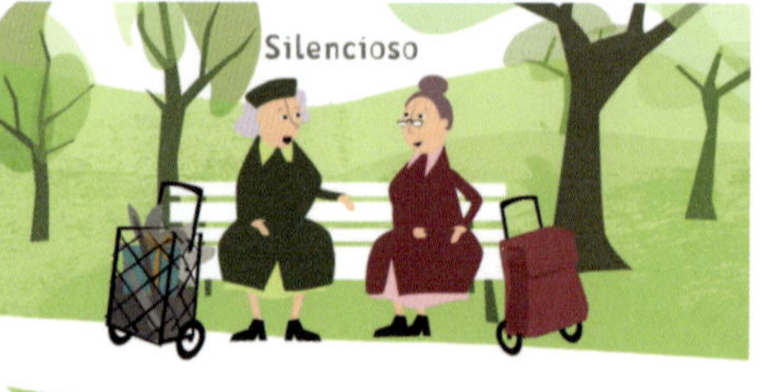

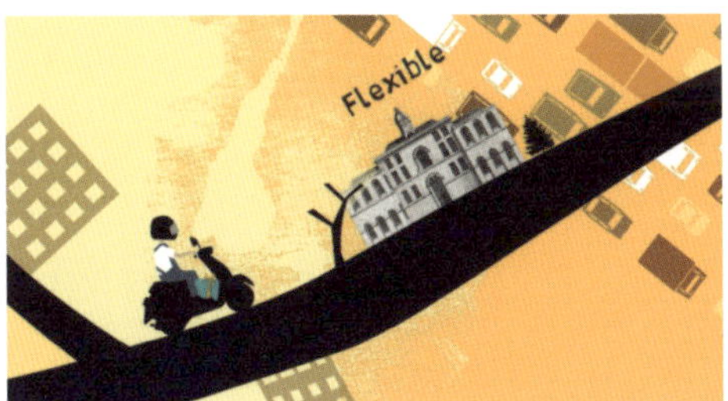
Flexible

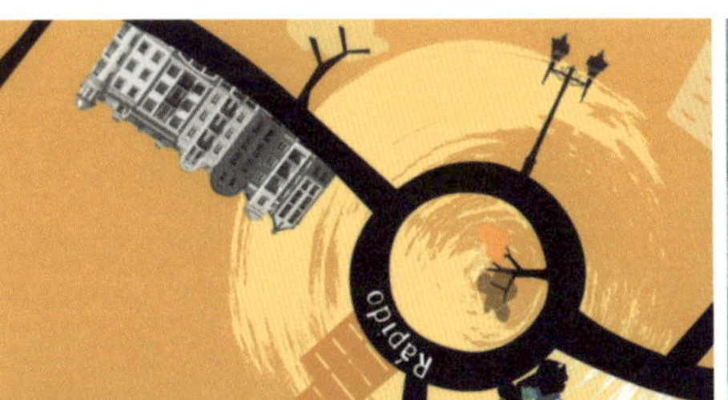
Rápido

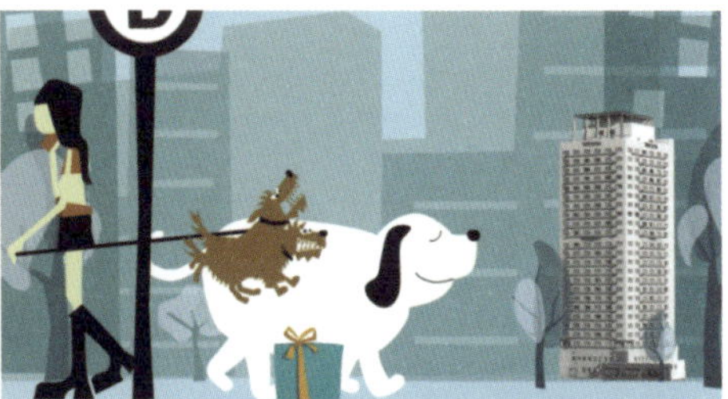

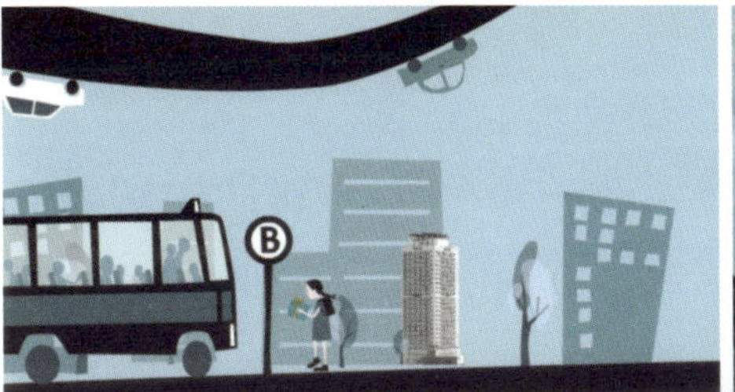

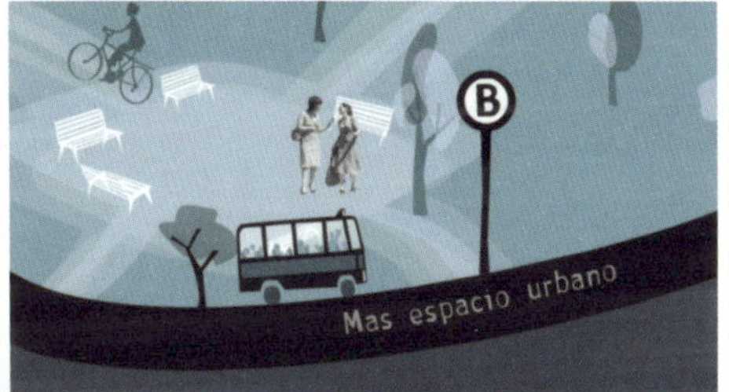
Mas espacio urbano

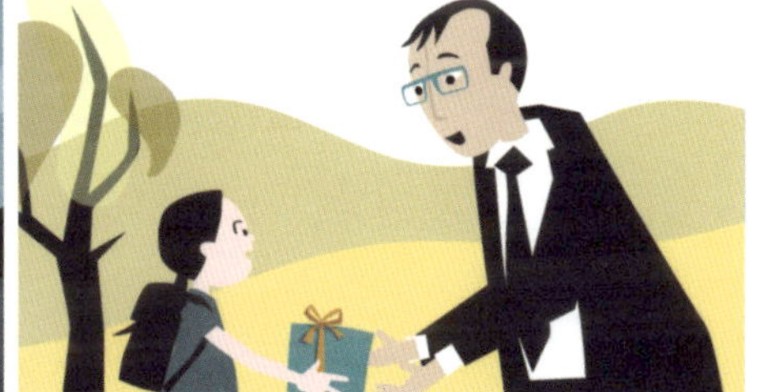

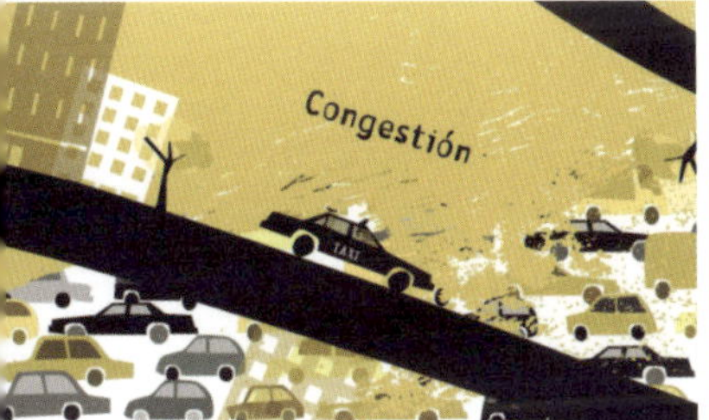
Congestión
TAXI

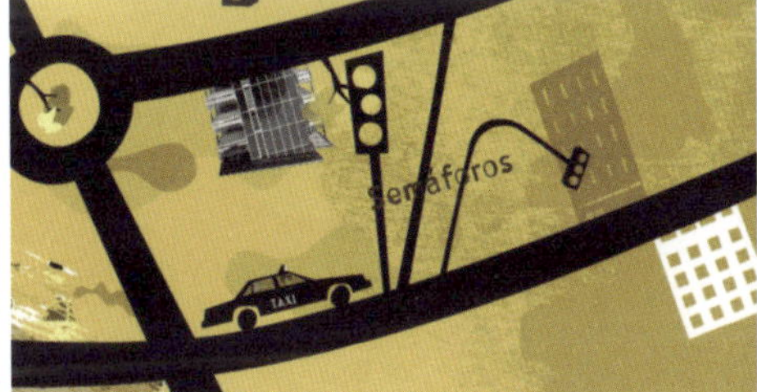
Semáforos
TAXI

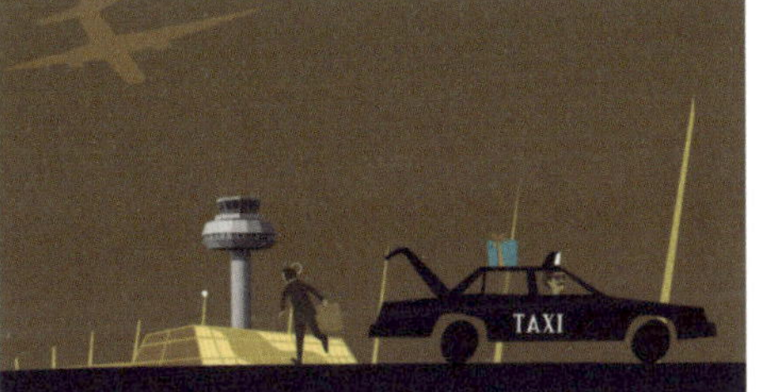
TAXI

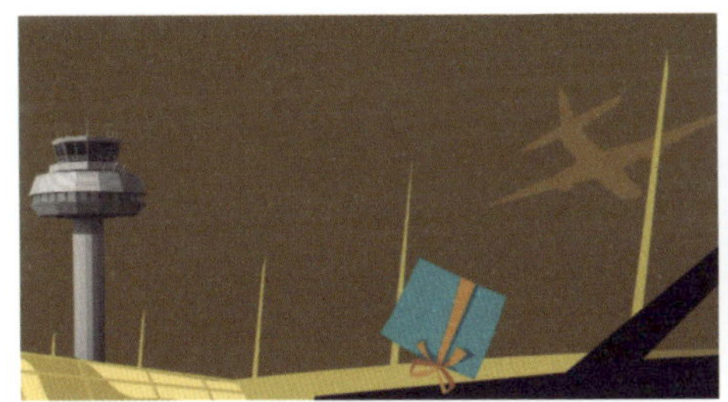

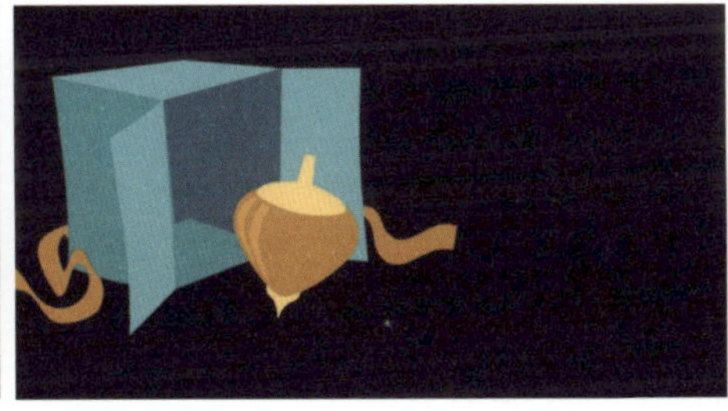

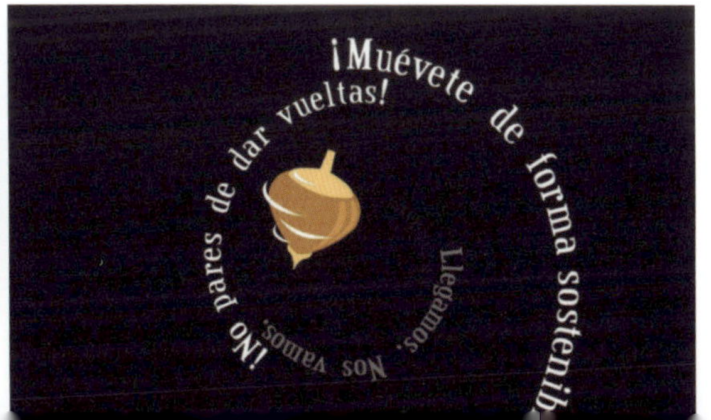
¡Muévete de forma sostenible!
¡No pares de dar vueltas!
Llegamos. Nos vamos.

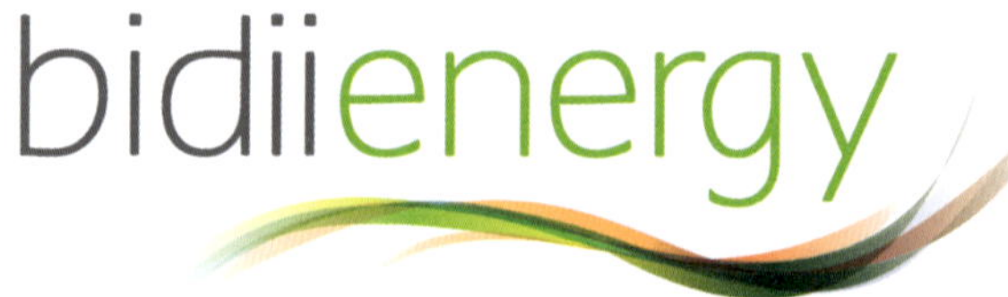

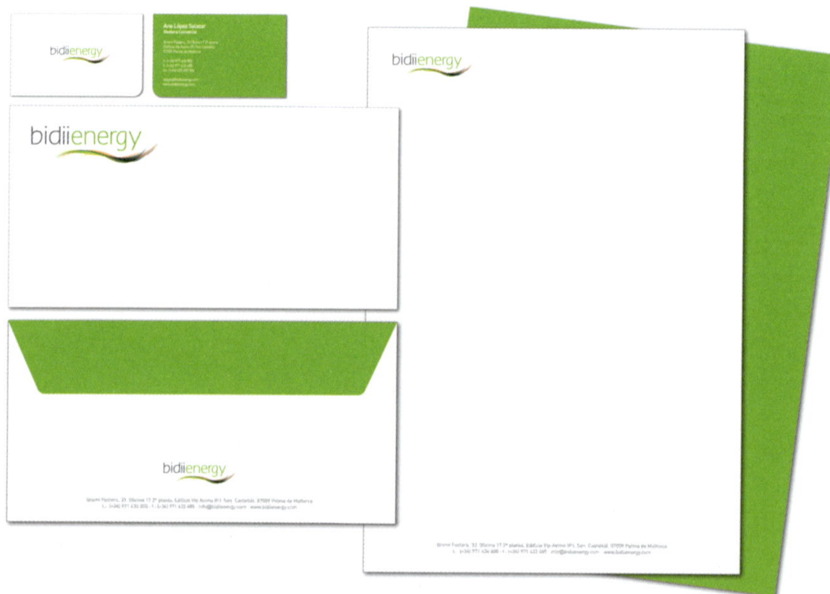

agency/studio: **Grupo Visualiza** / project: corporate identity for Bidii Energy, a company that carries out studies into reducing electricity bills. / client: Bidii Energy / country: Spain agency/studio: **Oxigen** / project: identity for Ahidra, a company dedicated to the energy-recovery and water-treatment technologies. / client: Ahidra / country: Spain

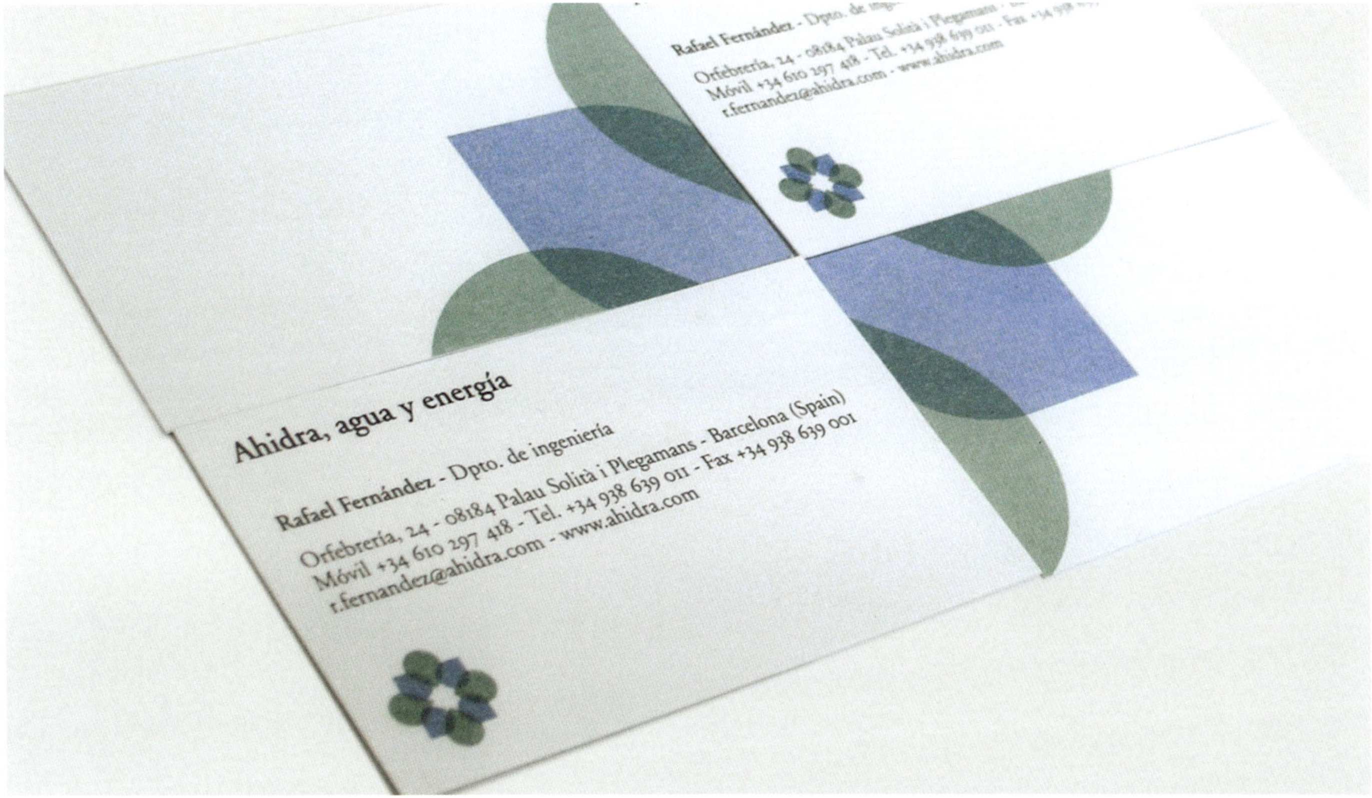

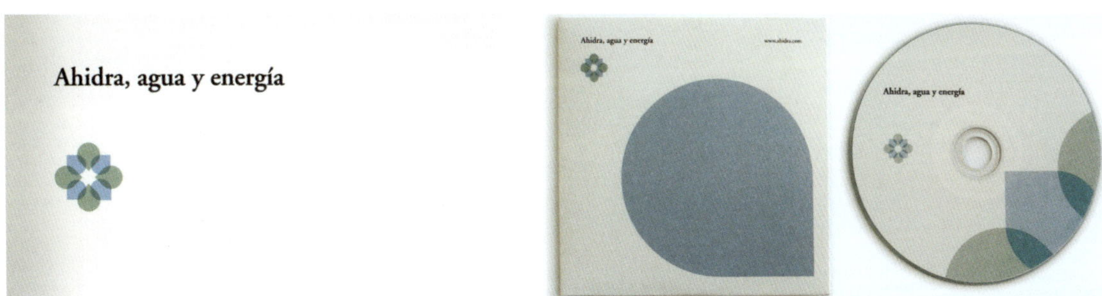

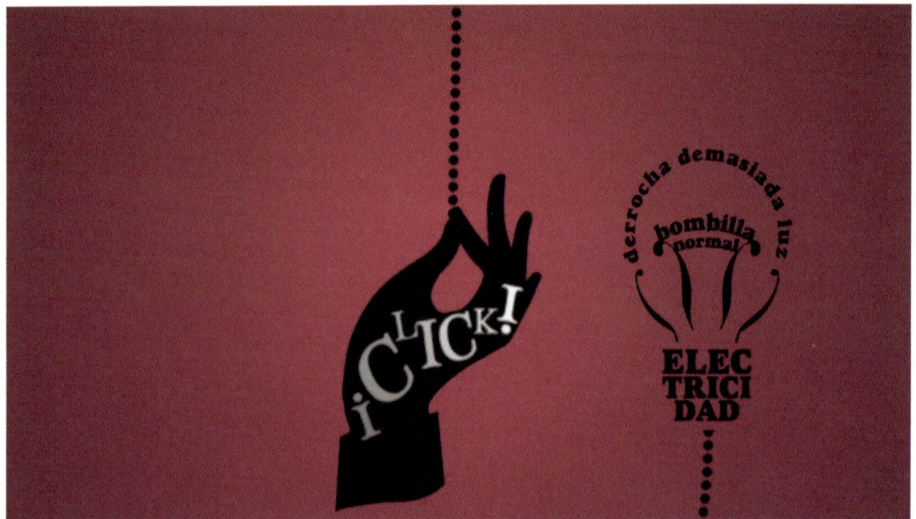

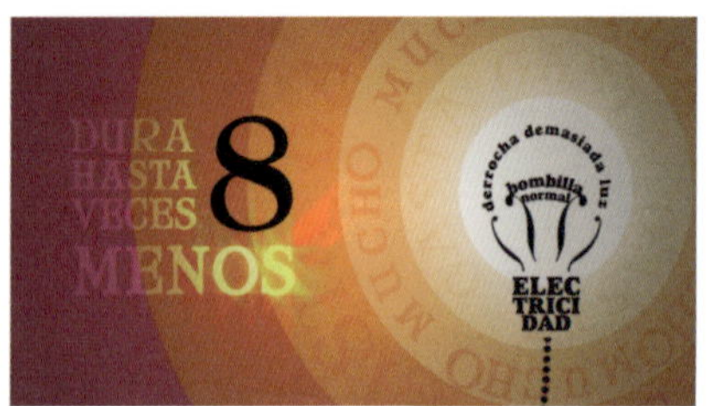

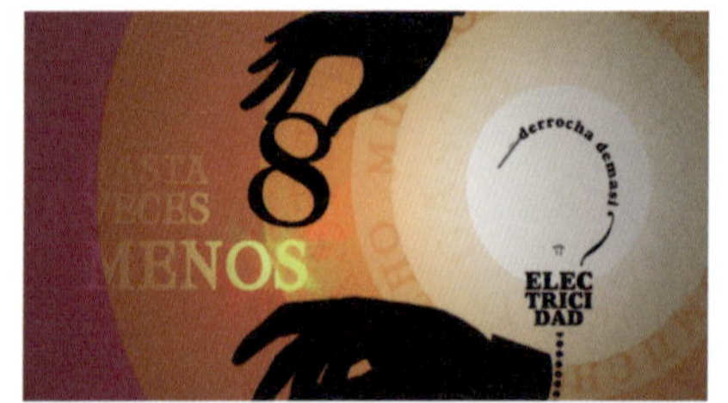

agency/studio: **Estudio Alejandro Gil** / project: a series of animations giving simple tips on looking after the environment. /
client: Radiotelevisión Canaria / country: Spain

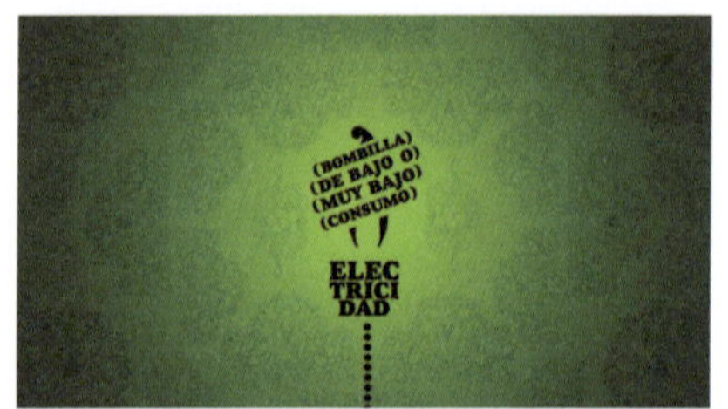

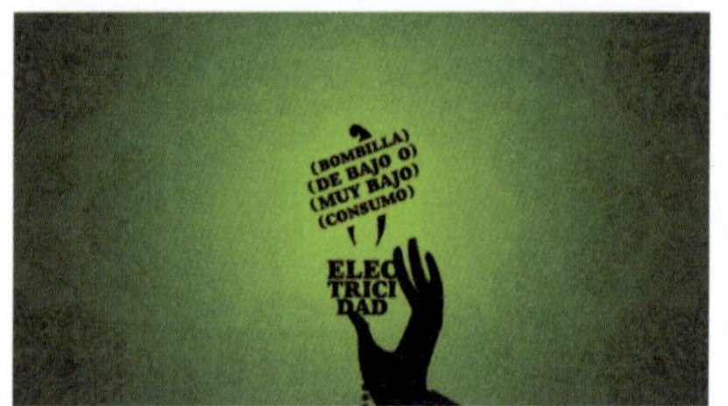

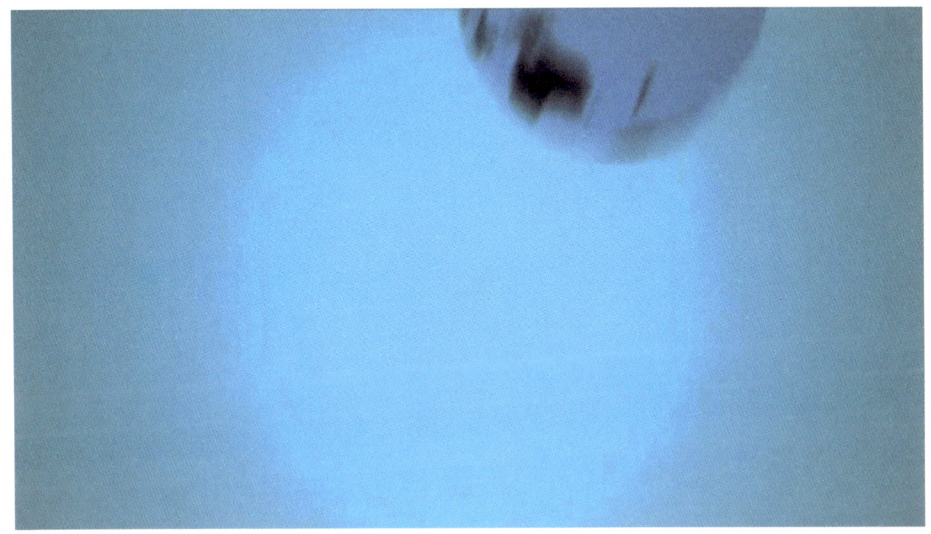

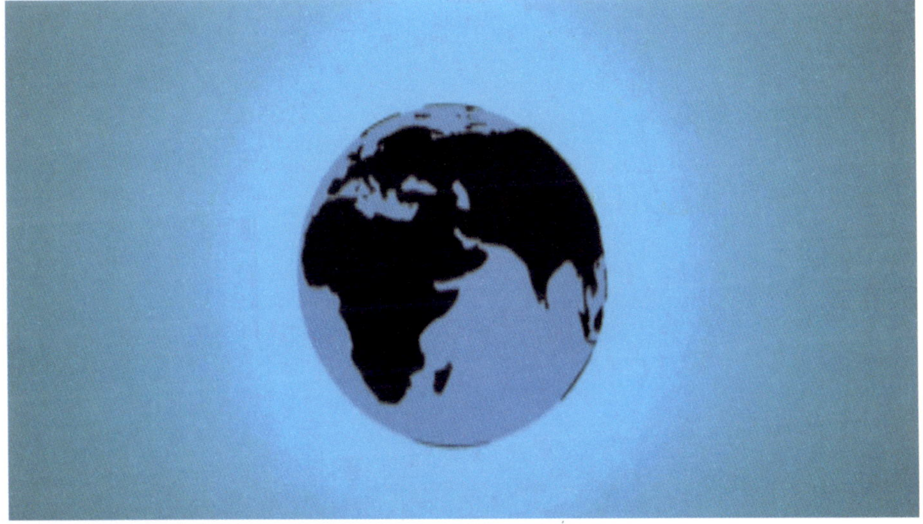

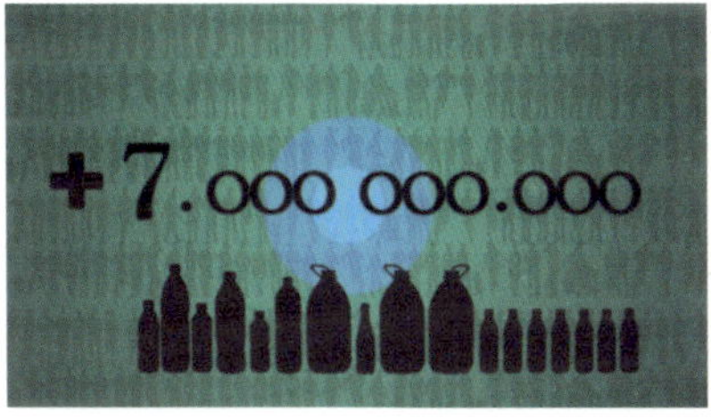
+7.000 000.000

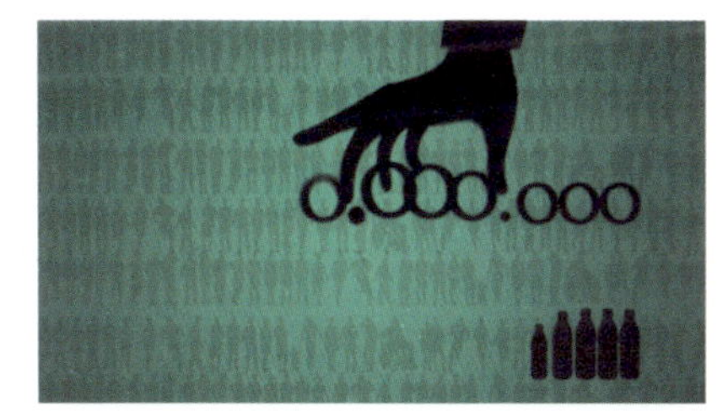
0.000.000

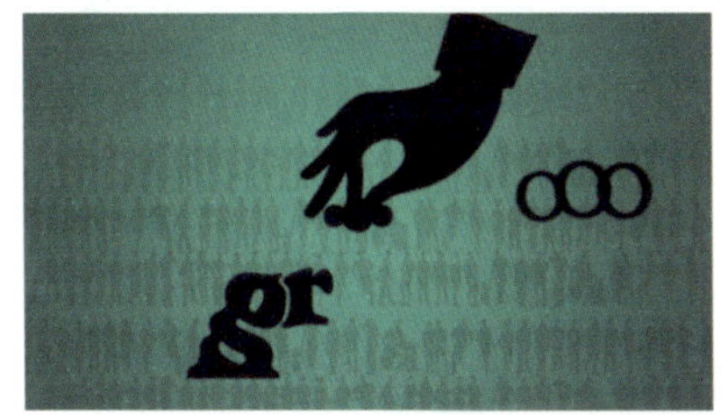
000
gr

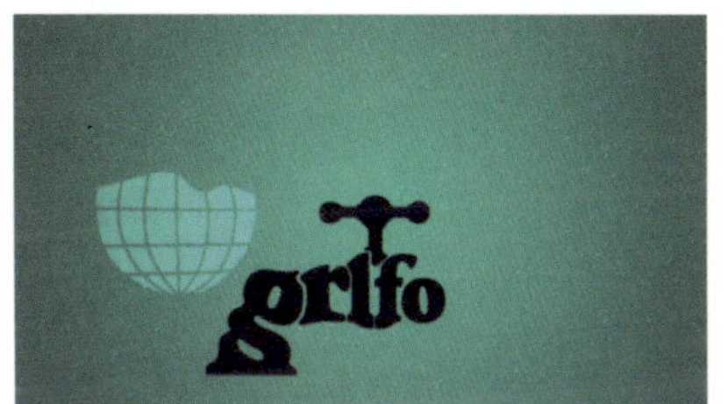
grifo

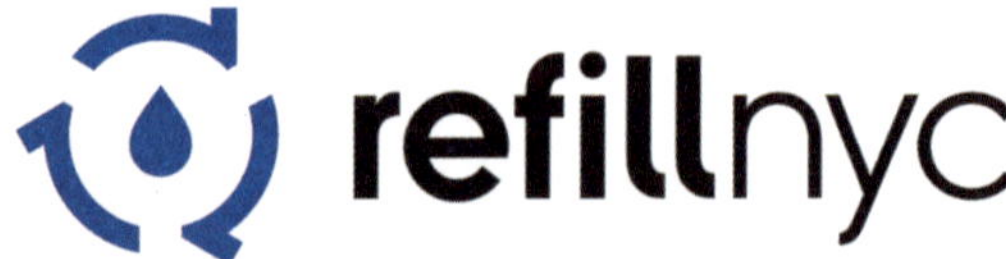

author: **Jesse Kirsch Design** / project: Refill NYC is a campaign to end the idea that bottled water is better for you than tap water. A guerilla-marketing approach displays surprising facts and figures on bright green labels to get people to start refilling reusable water bottles. / country: USA

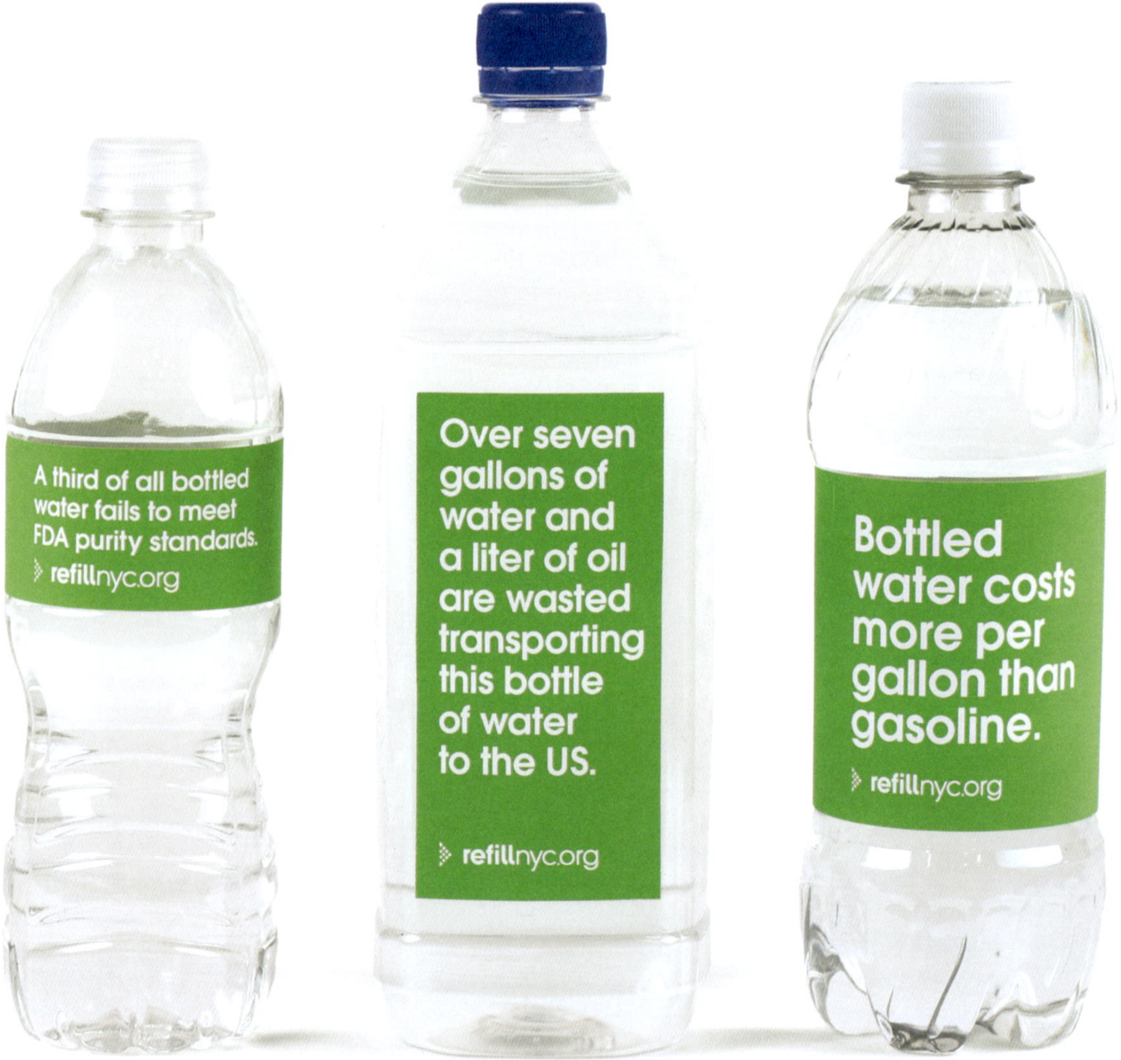

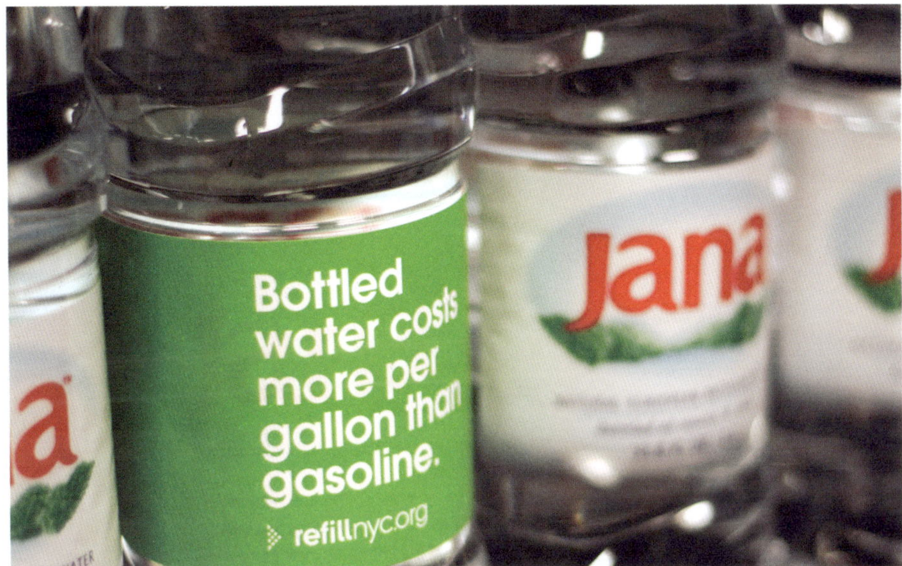
Bottled
water costs
more per
gallon than
gasoline.
refillnyc.org
Jana

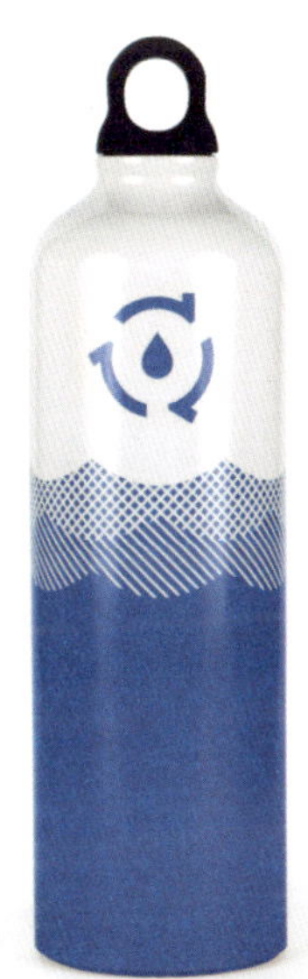

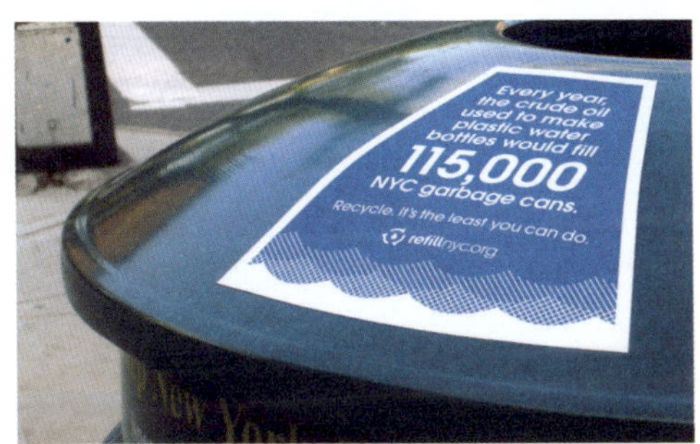
Every year,
the crude oil
used to make
plastic water
bottles would fill
115,000
NYC garbage cans.
Recycle. It's the least you can do.
refillnyc.org

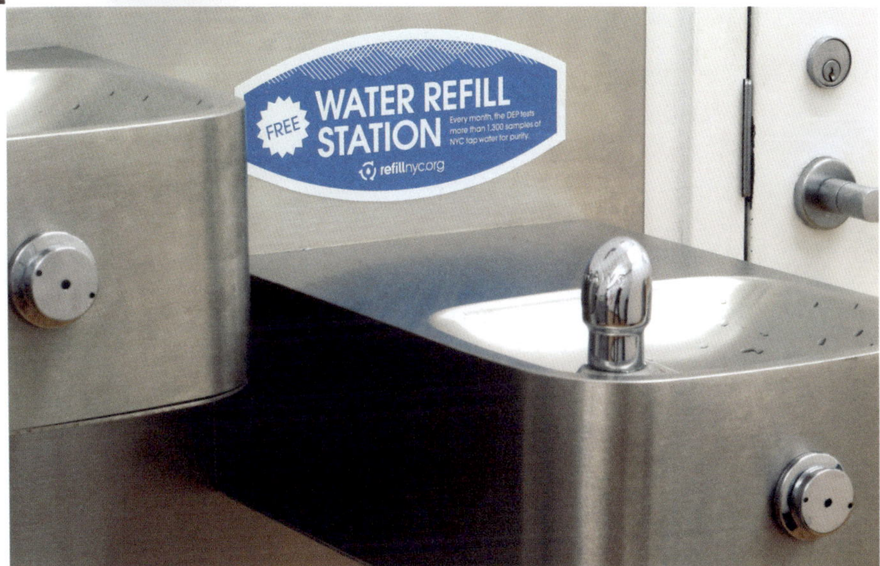
FREE
WATER REFILL
STATION
Every month, the DEP tests
more than 1,300 samples of
NYC tap water for purity.
refillnyc.org

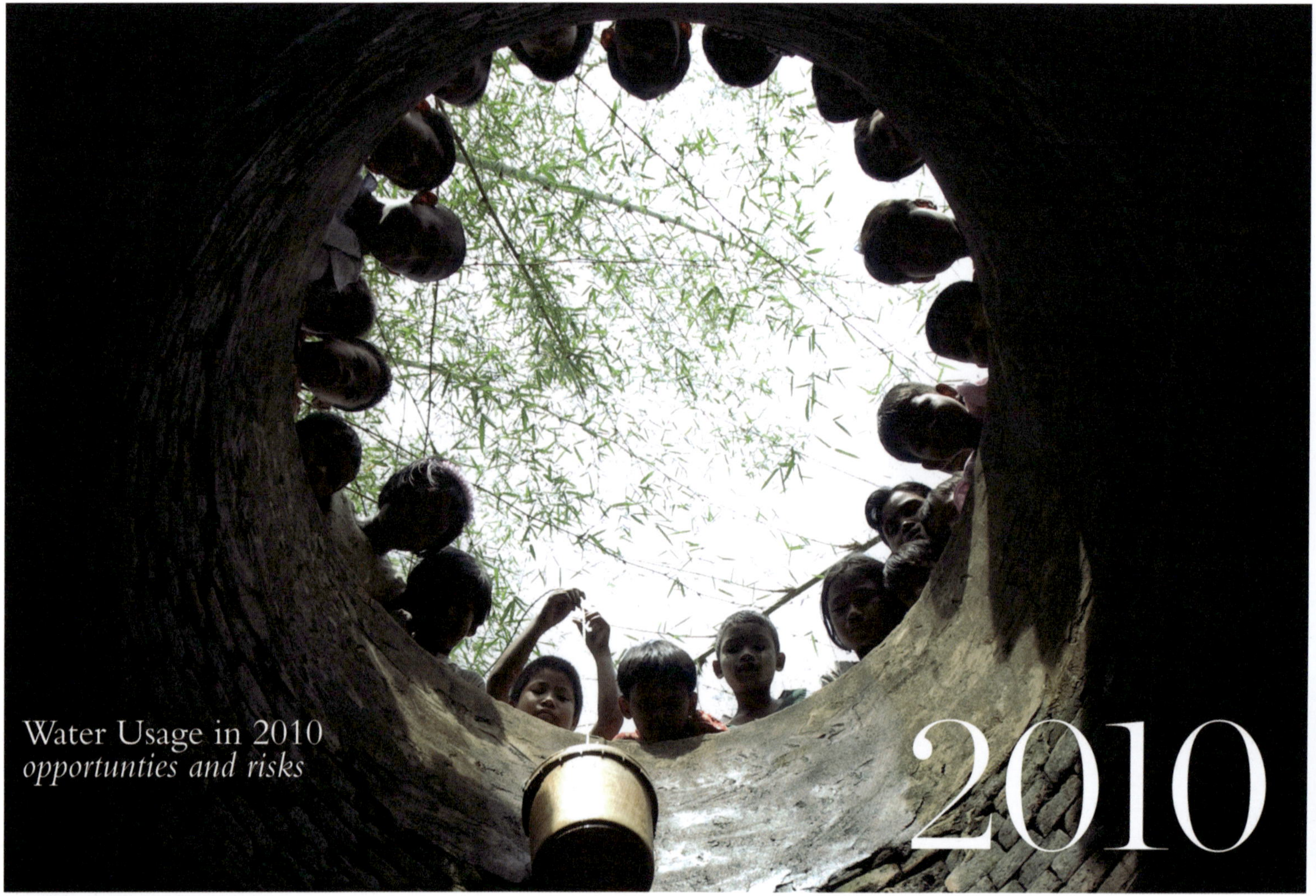

Water Usage in 2010
opportunties and risks

2010

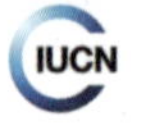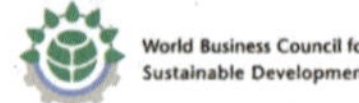
World Business Council for
Sustainable Development

Published by Entico Corporation in association with IUCN and World Business Council for Sustainable Development

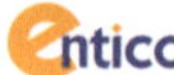

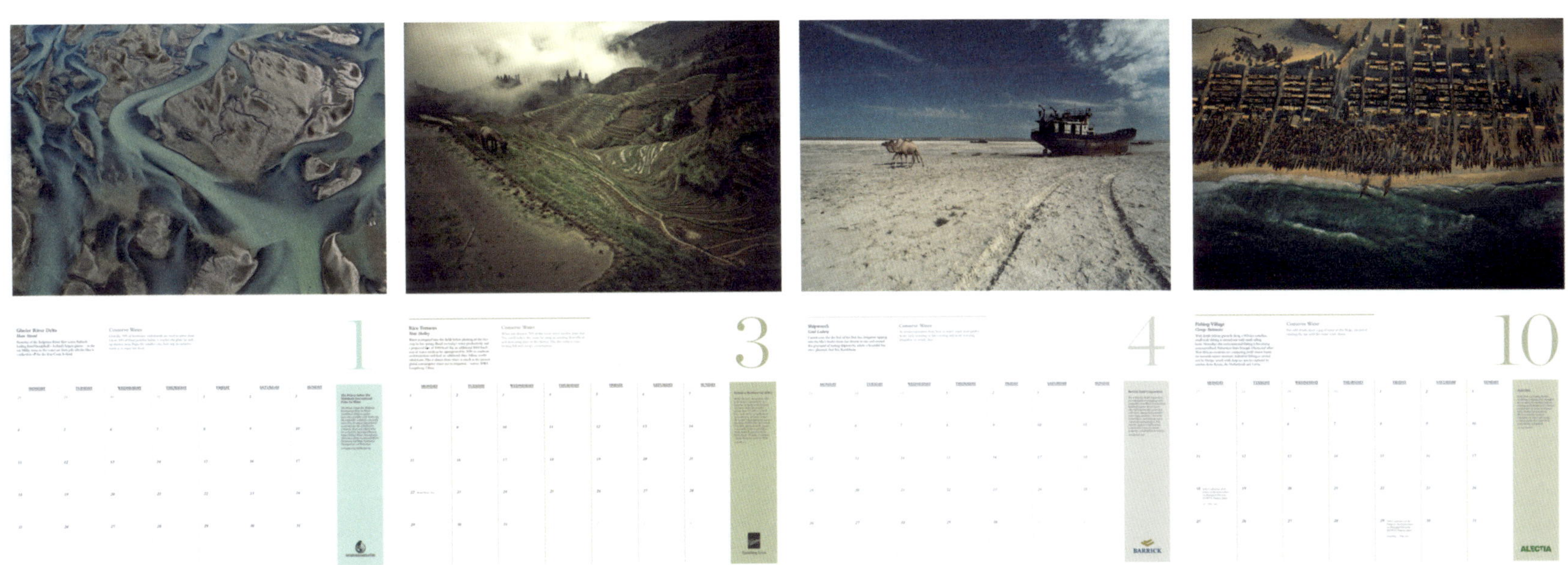

agency/studio: **Deep LLP** / project: "Water Usage in 2010: Opportunities and Risks" calendar; 2010. A calendar that highlights the problems of climate change. / client: United Nations / country: United Kingdom

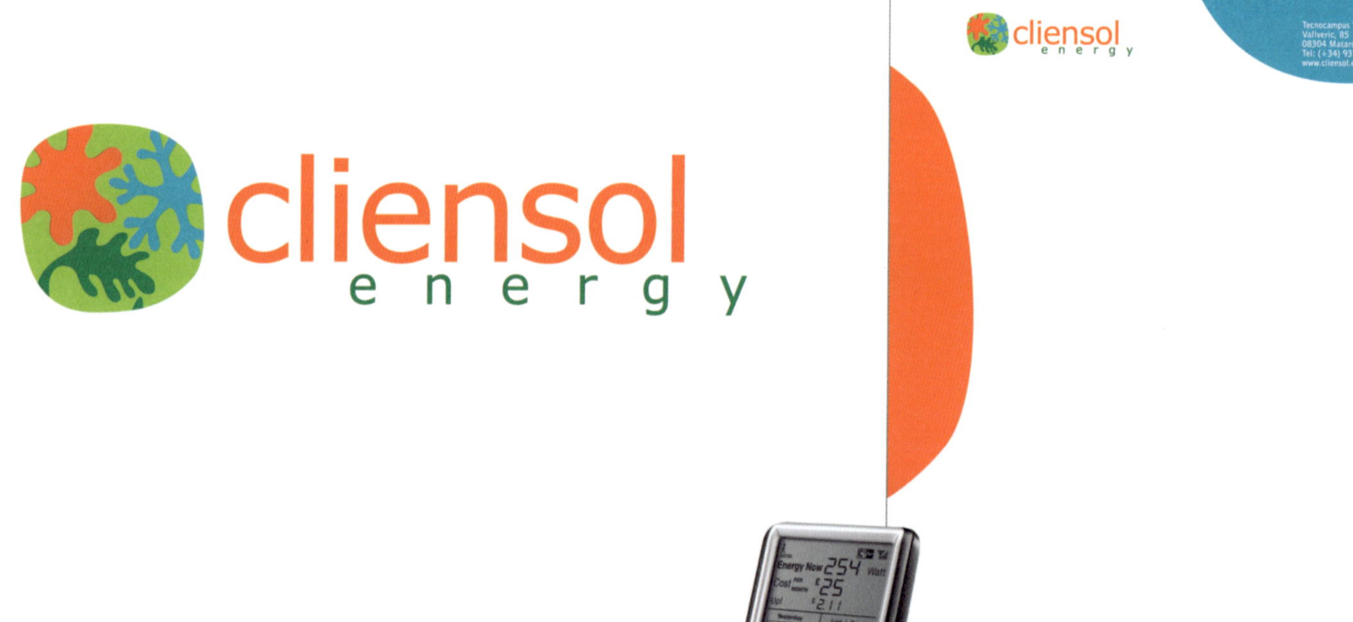

agency/studio: **Estudio Eckert+Zúñiga** / project: corporate image for
a company offering energy-efficiency services and products. / client: Cliensol
Energy / country: Spain

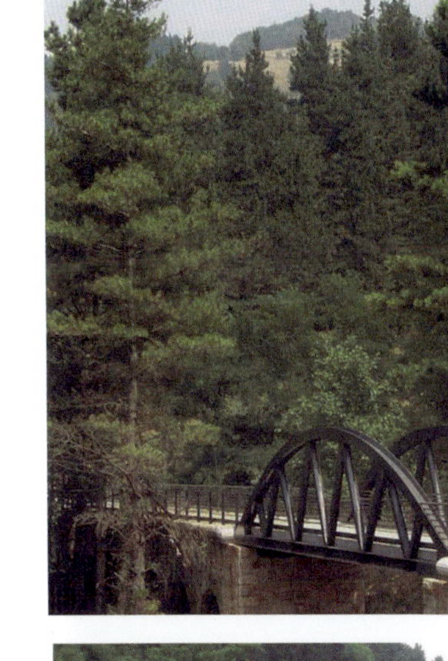

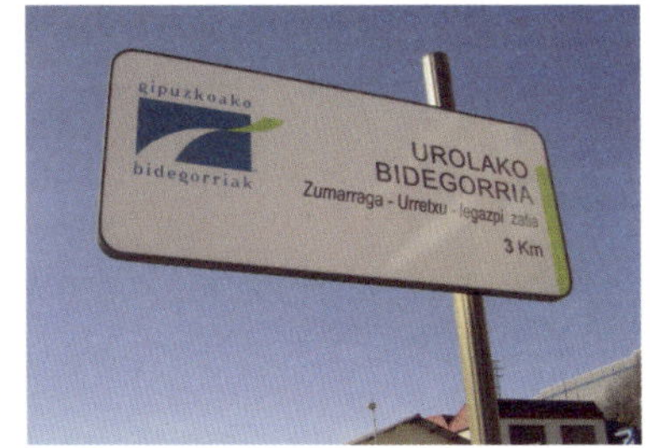

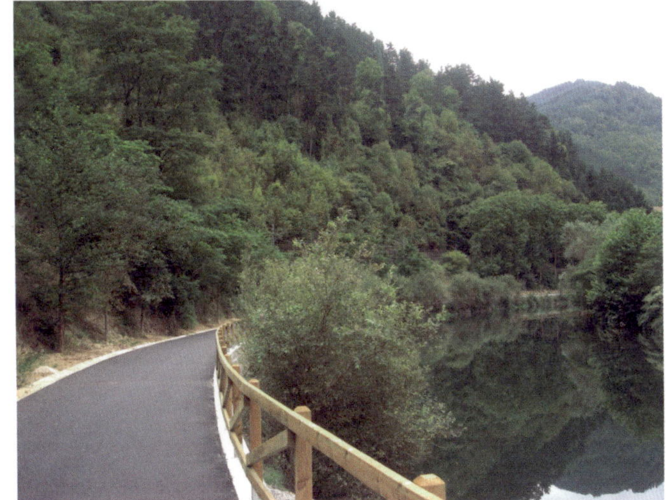

gipuzkoako
bidegorriak

agency/studio: **Tráfico Gráfico** / project: logo and signs for cycling routes in the Gipuzkoa region of the Basque Country. / client: Gipuzkoako Foru Aldundia (Regional Government of Gipuzkoa), Directorate General of the Environment / country: Spain

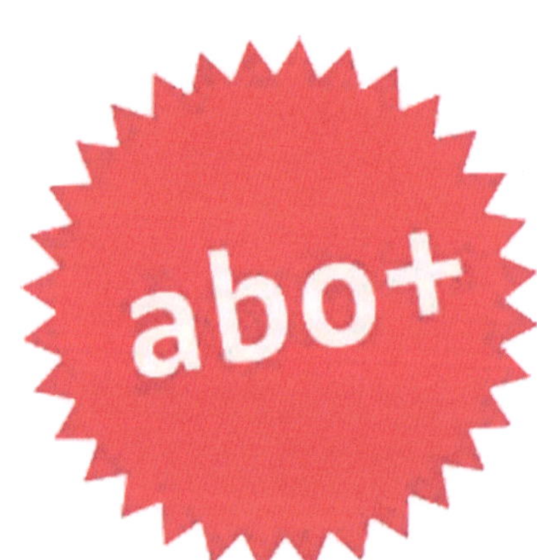

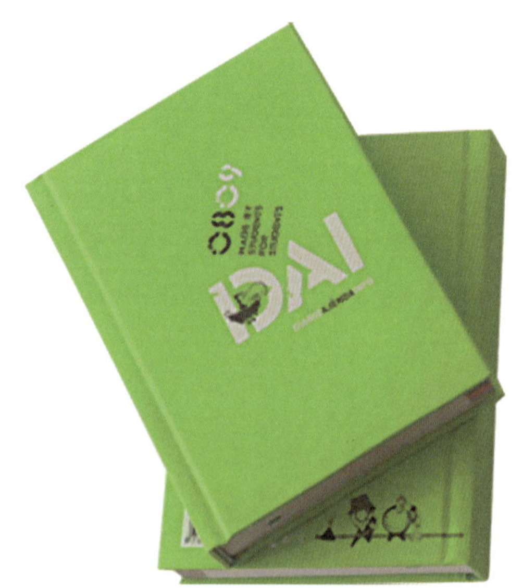

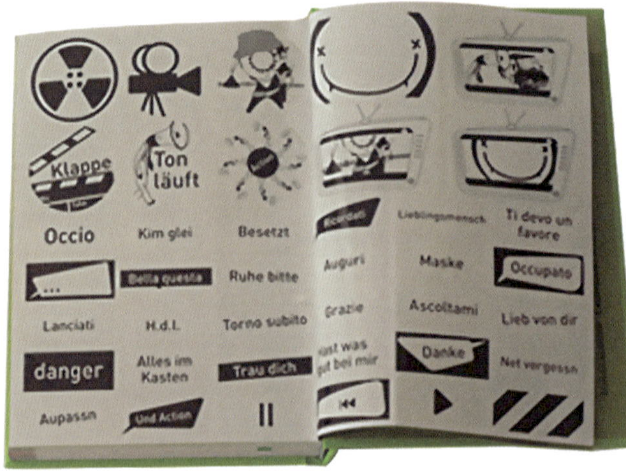

agency/studio: **helios** / project: "ABO+" is a marketing campaign to promote public transport for pupils and students. The number of subscribers of traffic tickets has increased from 4,500 to over 12,000 since it was launched in 2005. The campaign centres around funny characters who have achieved cult status. In the last campaign, the characters came to life, with professional actors re-enacting famous film scenes with them. / client: Autonomous Province of South Tyrol, Department of Human Resources, Tourism and Mobility / country: Italy

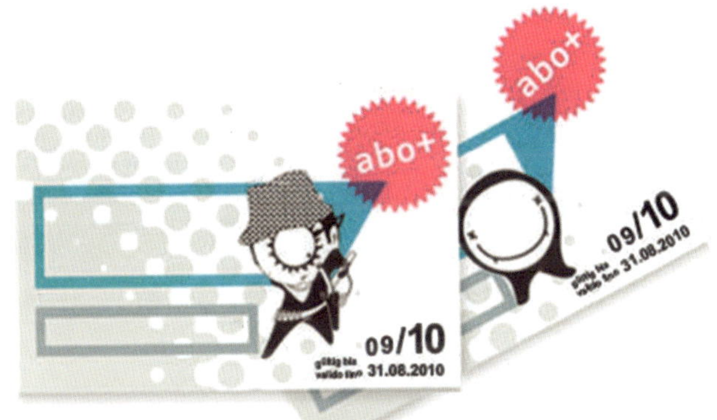

abo+
abo+
09/10
09/10
gültig bis
valido fino 31.08.2010
gültig bis
valido fino 31.08.2010

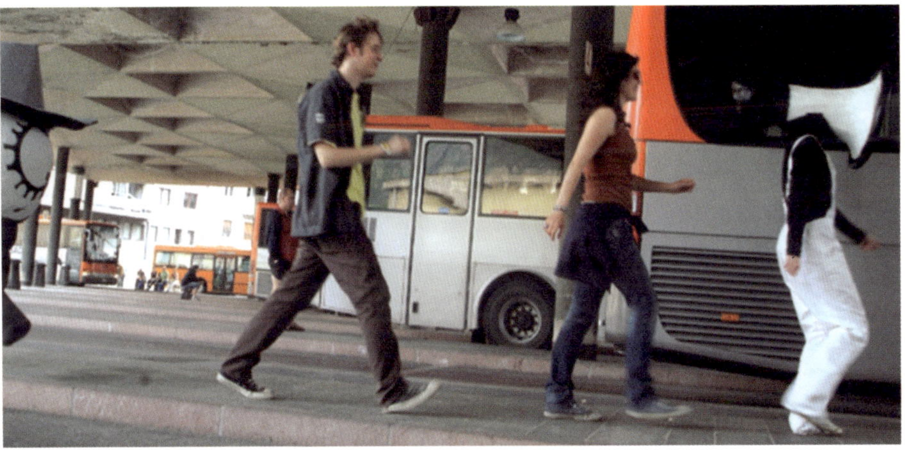

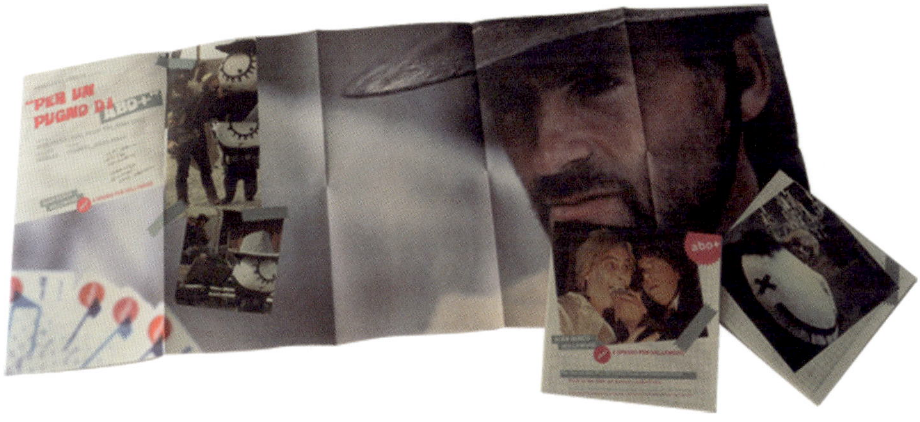

"PER UN
PUGNO DA abo+"

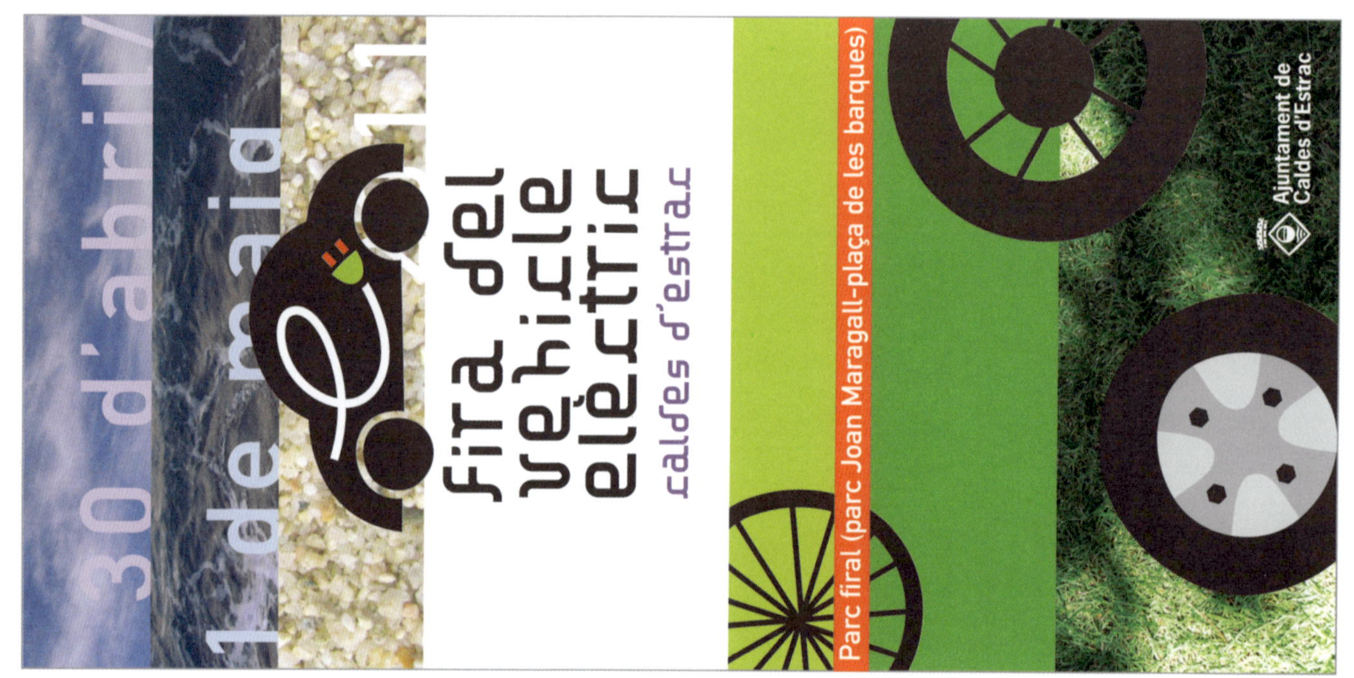

agency/studio: **Estudio Eckert+Zúñiga** / project: logo and poster for the electric vehicle show held in the town of Caldes d'Estrac, near Barcelona. / client: Caldes d'Estrac Town Council / country: Spain

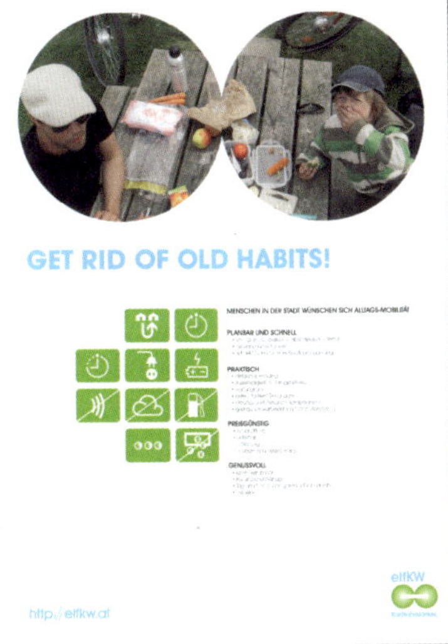

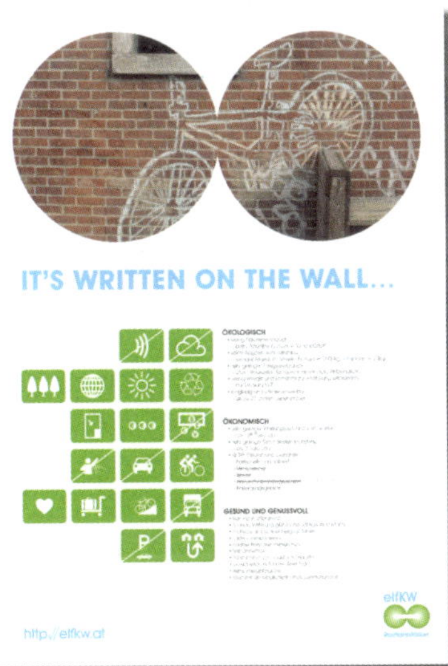

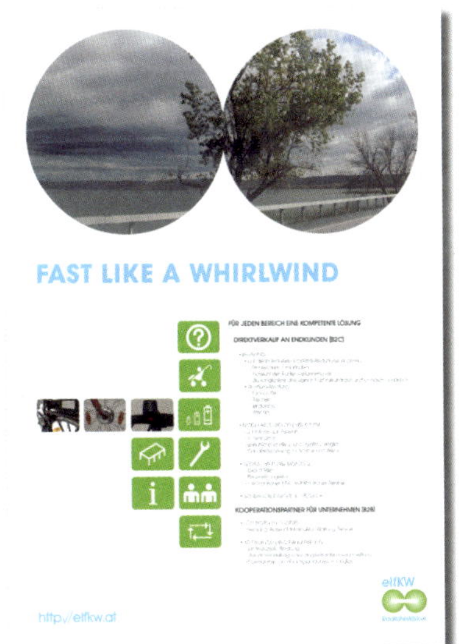

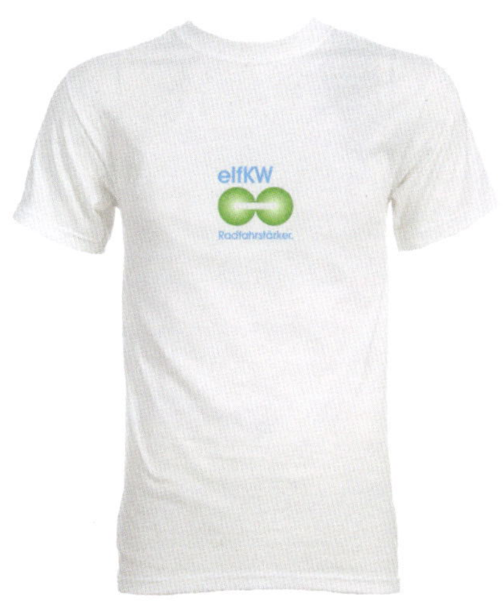

agency/studio: **Isebuki** / project: elfKW, sustainable individual transport. Corporate design for a Viennese company that converts regular bicycles into motorised bicycles. / client: elfKW / country: Austria author: **Lisa Stanzel** / project: Virtual Water: a short film about virtual water and how much water we really use each day. / country: Germany

VIRTUAL WATER
SHORT FILM

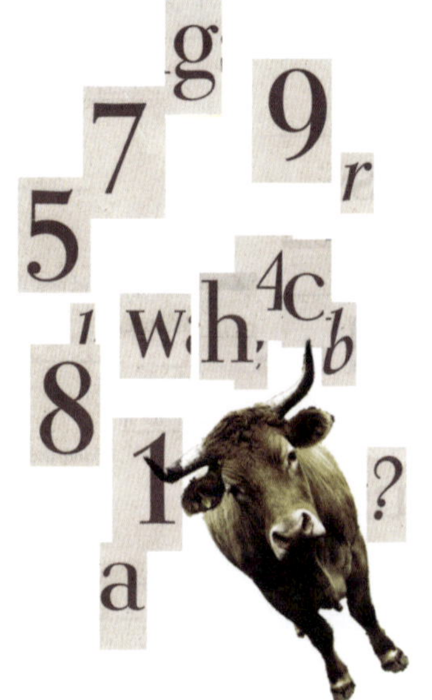

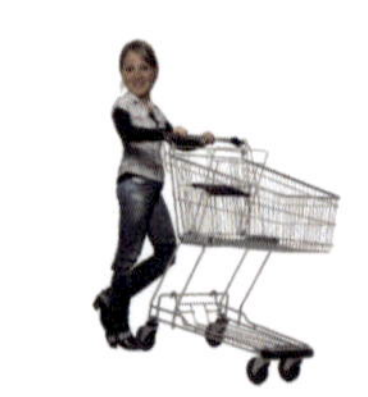

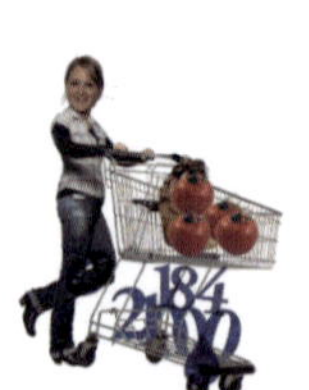

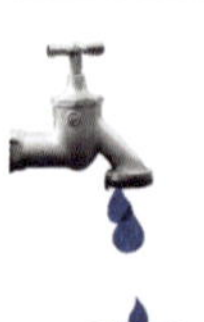

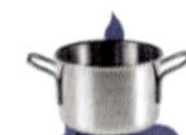

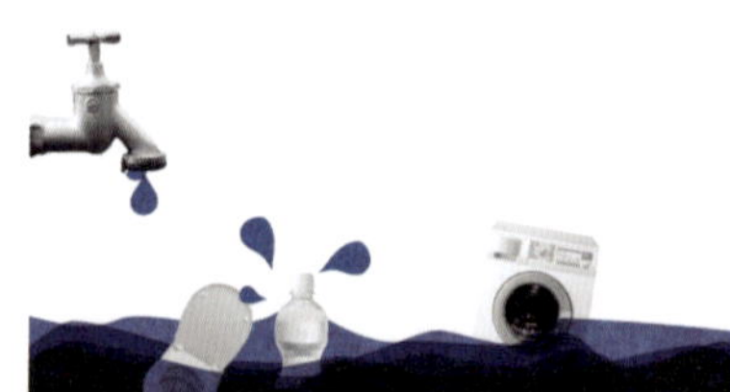

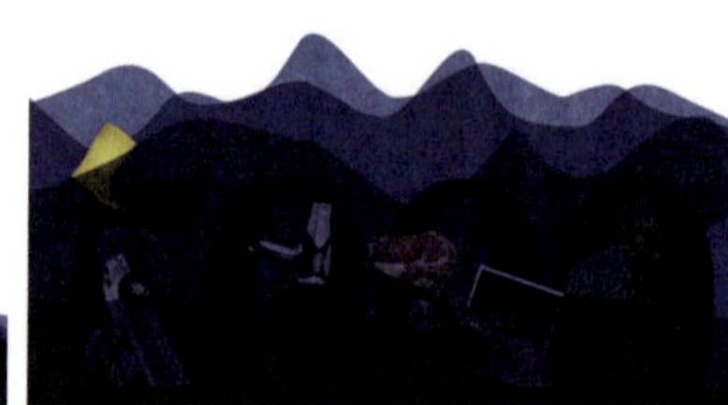

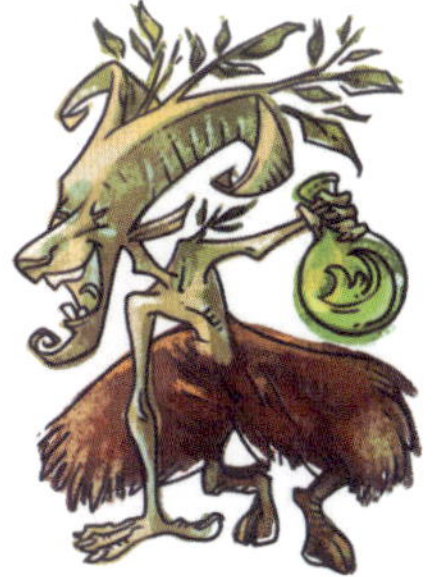 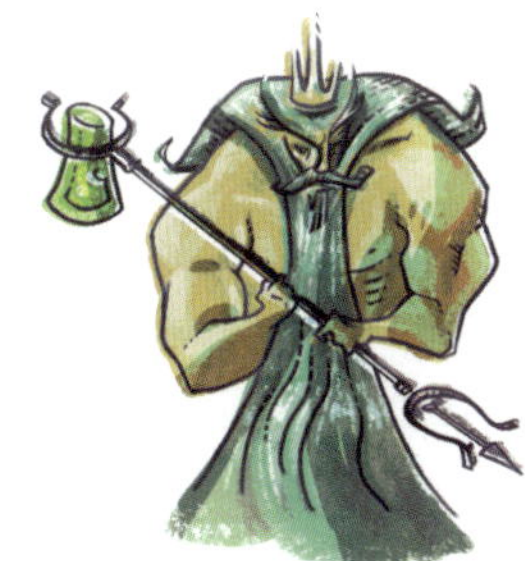 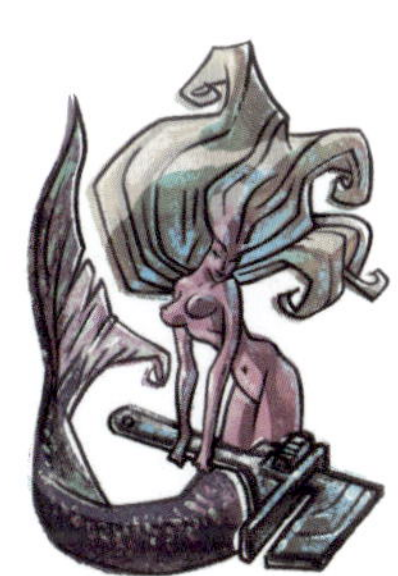

author: **Hans-Jörg Brehm** / project: Green scores. Trump cards (king, queen and knave) for a card game promoting the client's water-cleaning and -processing technologies. The images marry archaic "nature-spirits" with modern tools. / client: Aqua Terra Bioprodukt GmbH / country: Germany

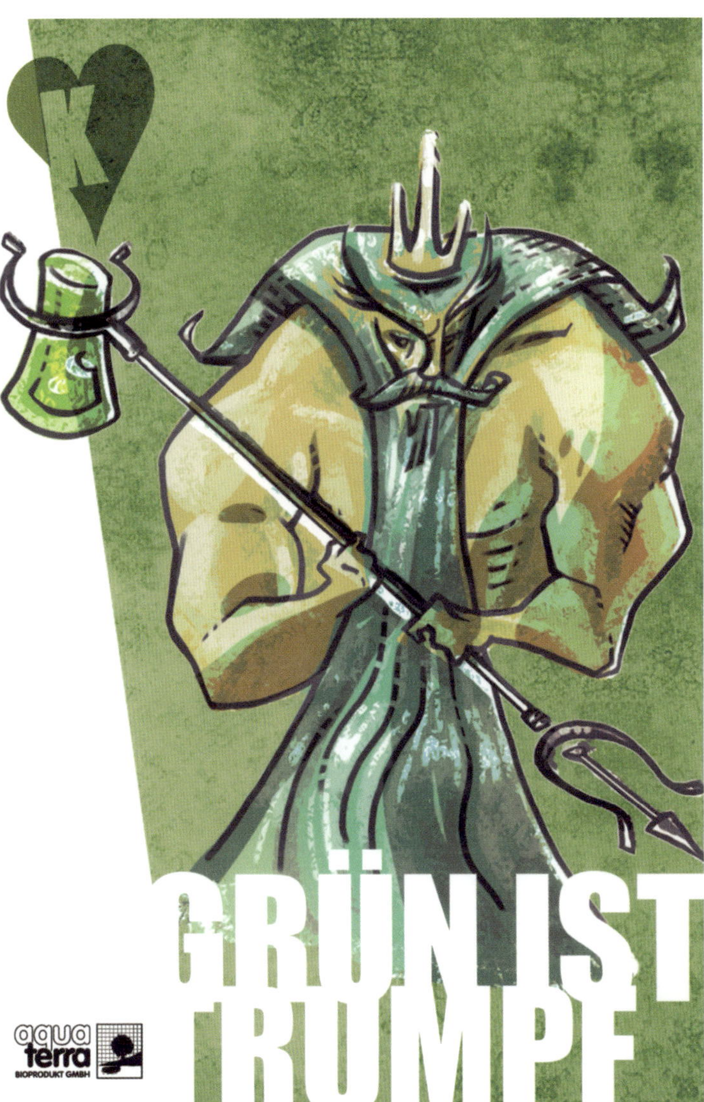

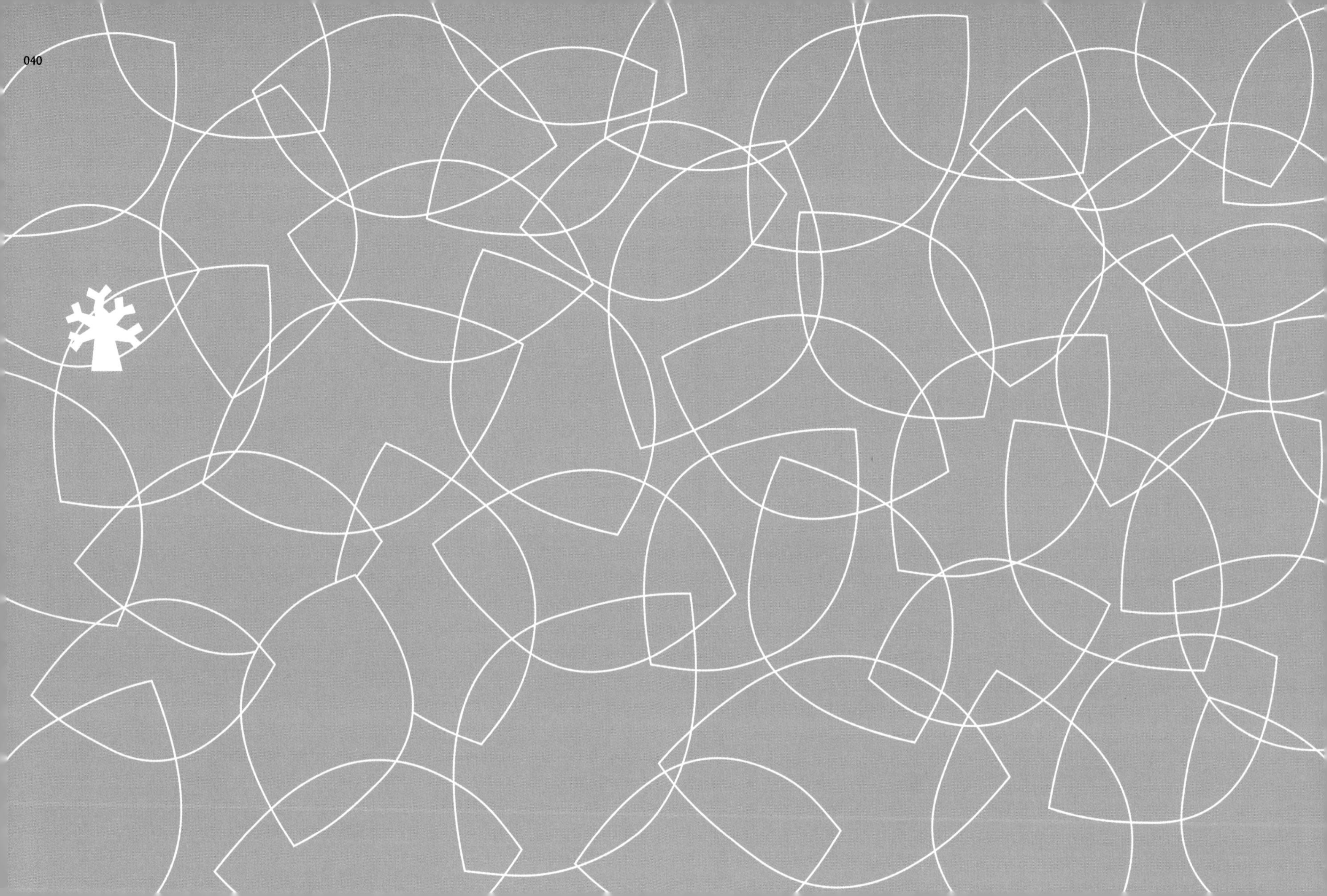

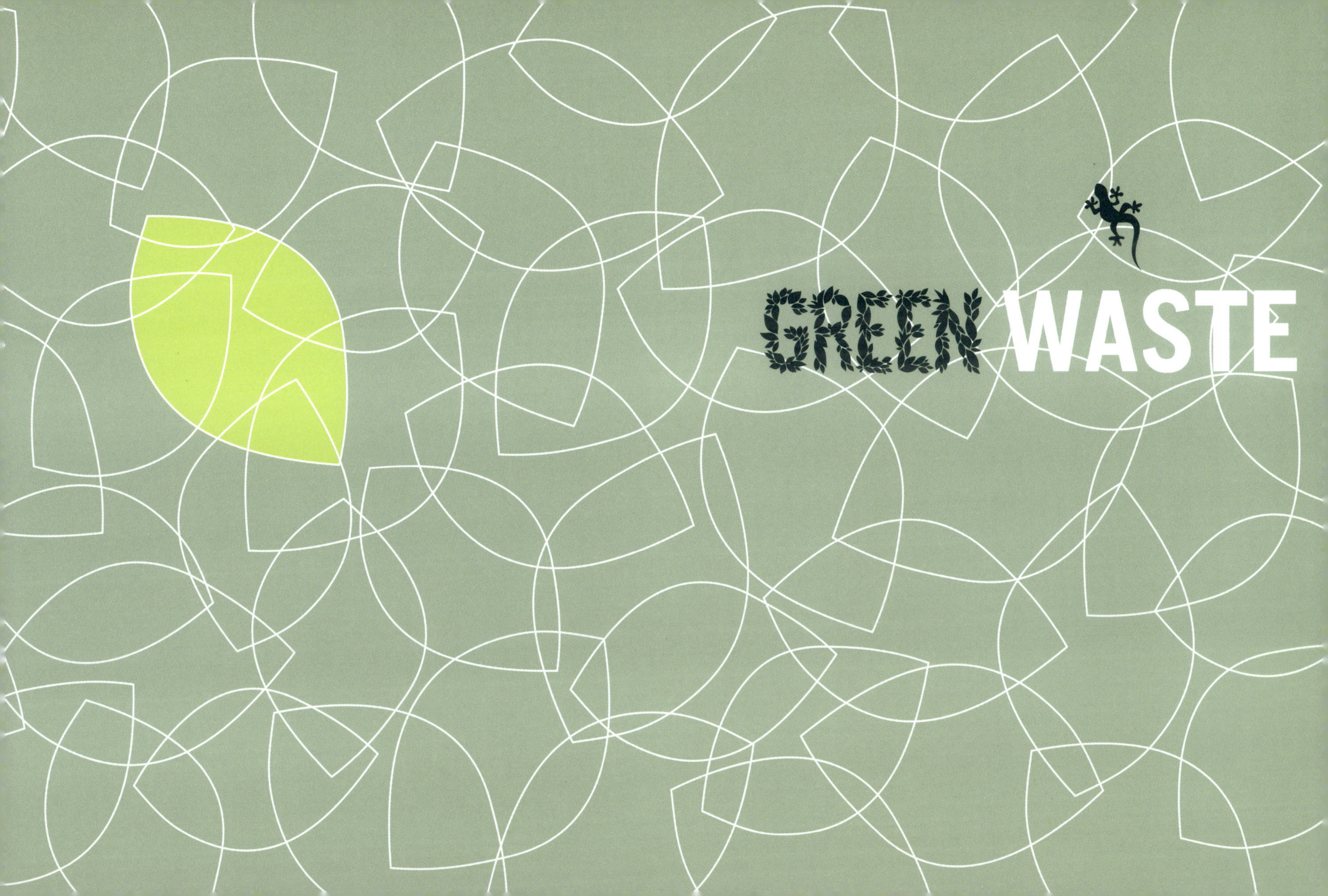
GREEN WASTE

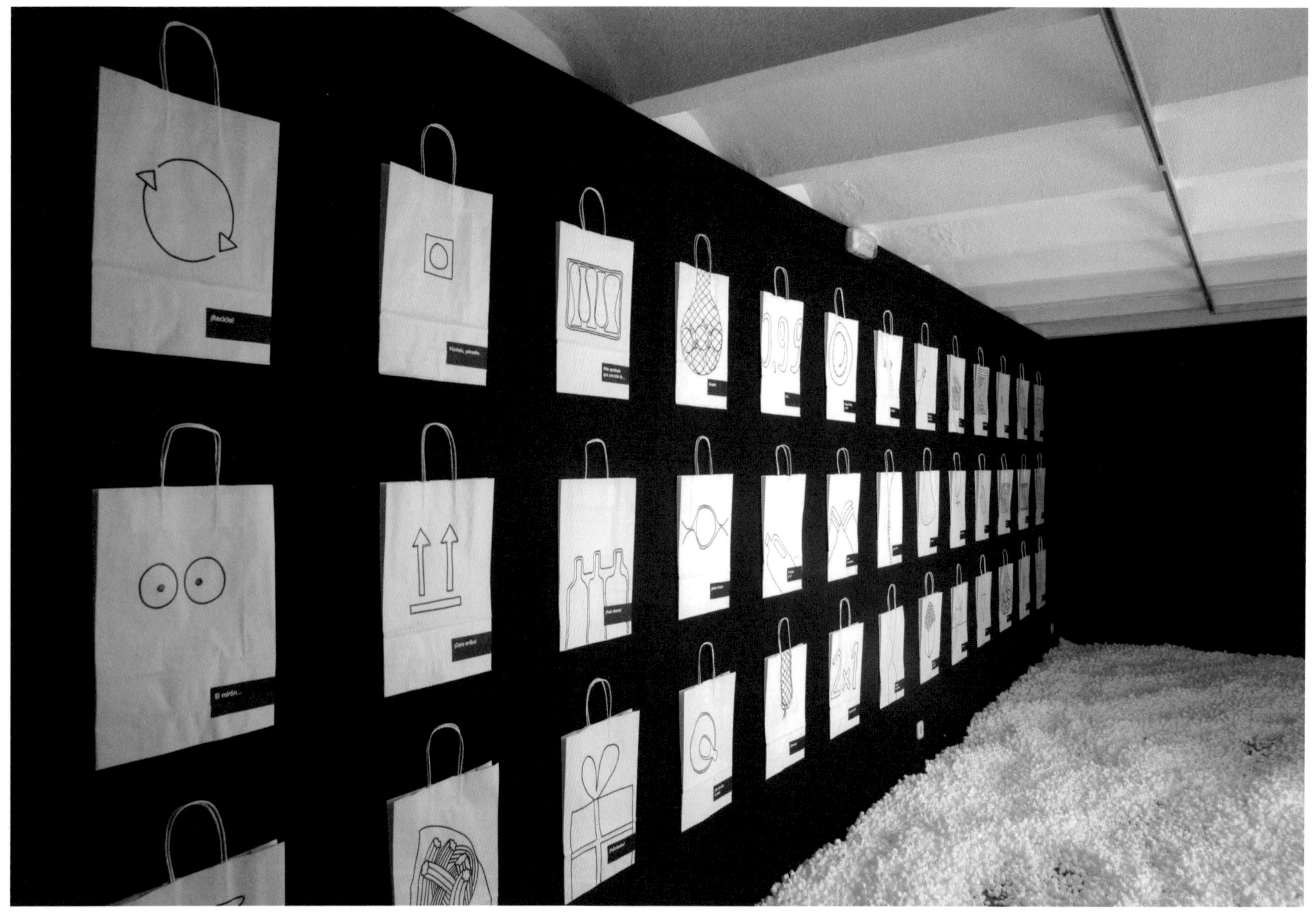

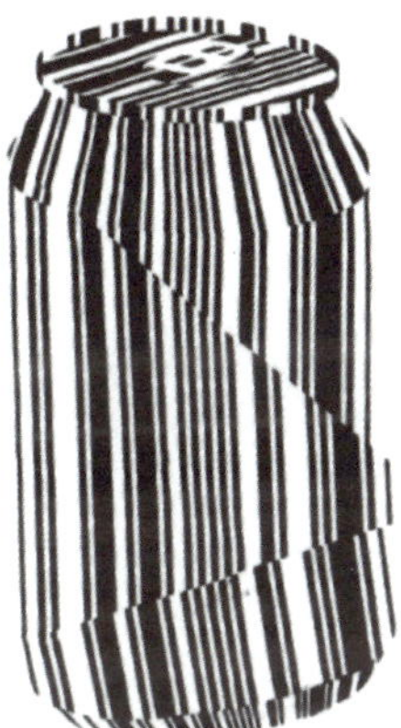

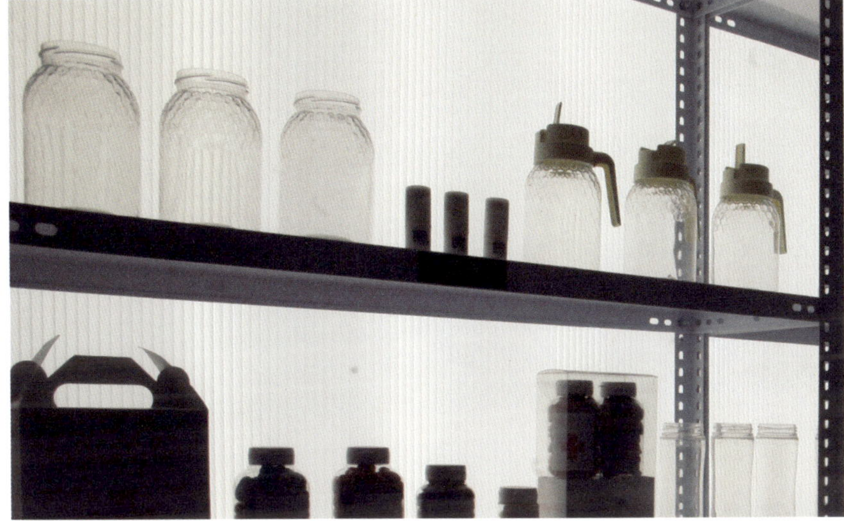

exhibition commissioning and design: **Lagranja Design** / graphic image: **Eduardo del Fraile** / project: Produce Consume Recicla (Produce Consume Recycle). An exhibition involving a set of installations that make us reflect on the life cycle of objects created to wrap, protect, contain and communicate products for mass consumption. / client: DDI (Spanish Public Corporation for the Development of Design and Innovation) and the Círculo de Bellas Artes / country: Spain

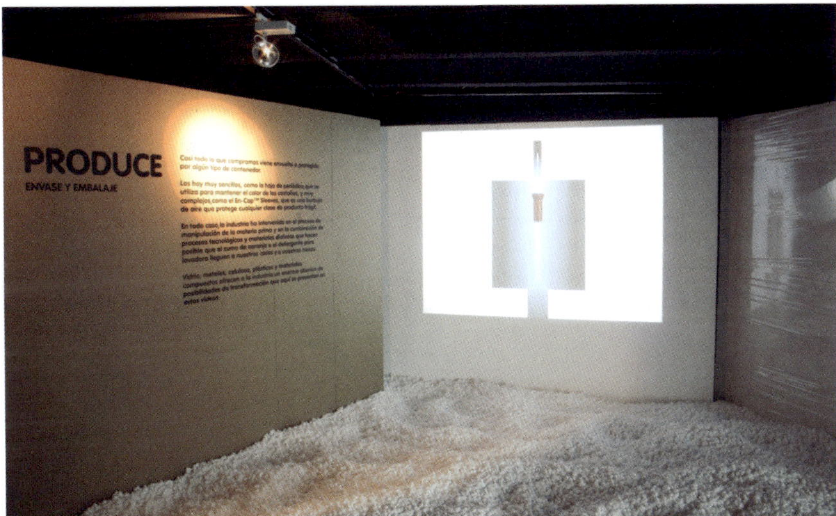

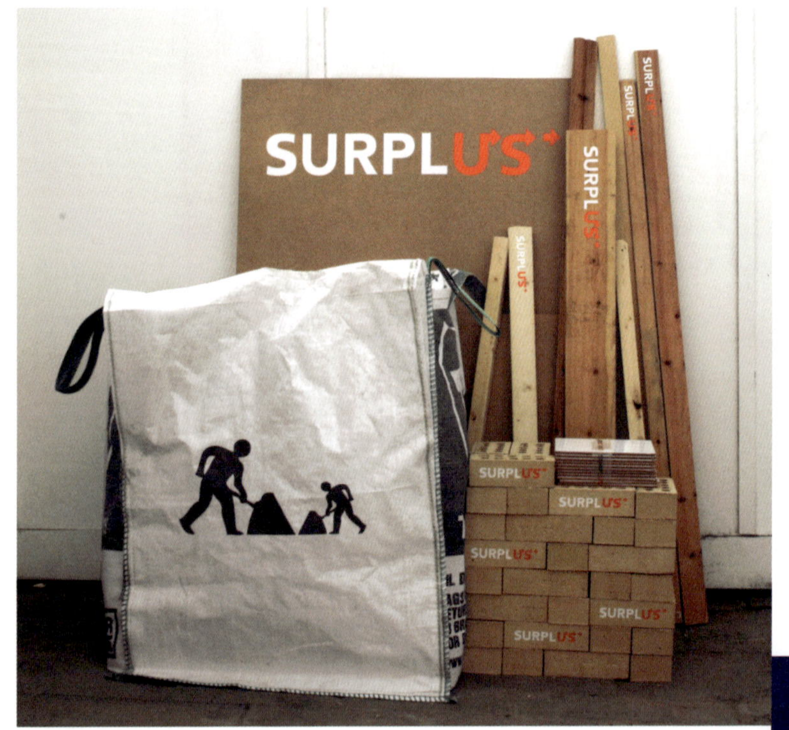

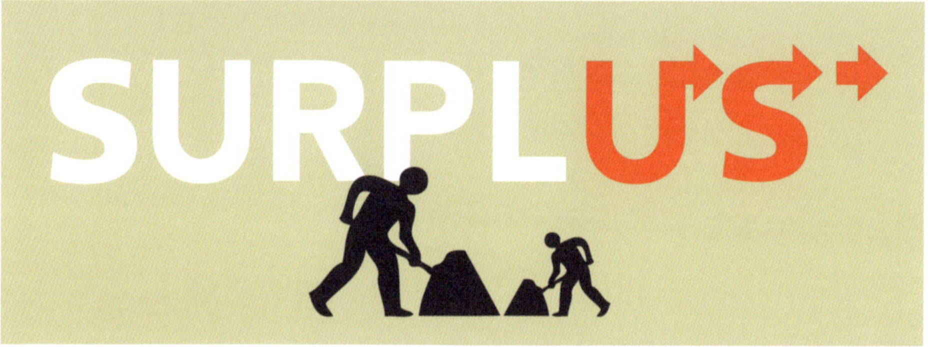

agency/studio: **Hannah, Sarah & Jo** / project: identity and website for a network linking the construction industry to the general public to pass on surplus material. / client: RSA / country: United Kingdom

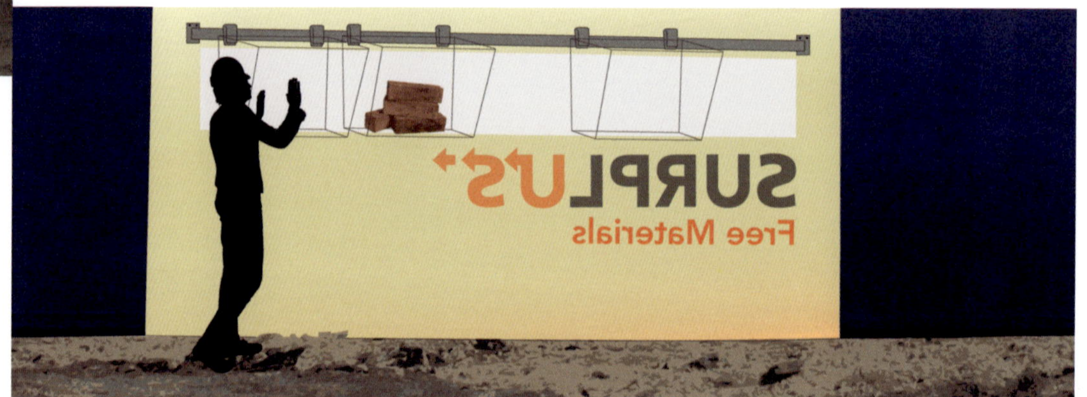

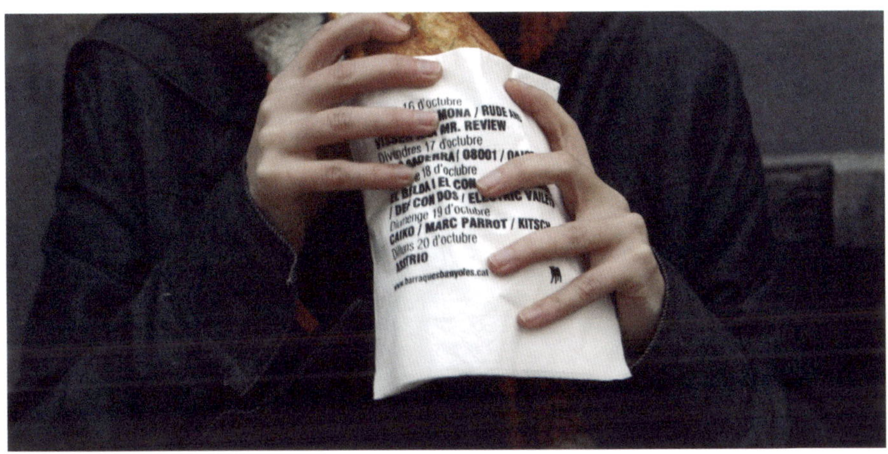

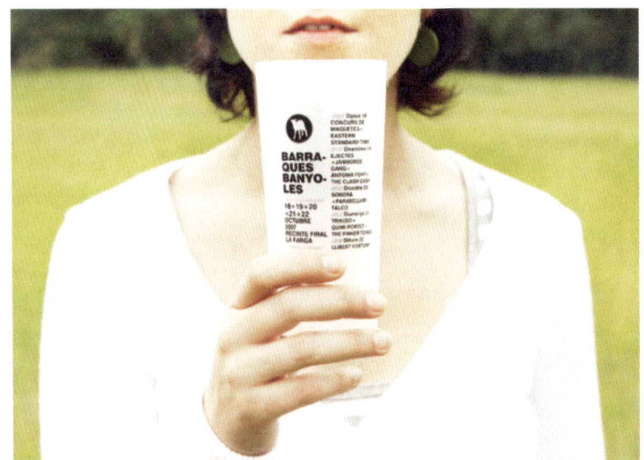

agency/studio: **Anna Pigem** / photos by Elisabet Serra / project: serviette and reusable glass printed with the programme of the Barraques de Banyoles series of concerts that will take place as part of the annual festival of the town of Banyoles. / client: Agrupació de Barraques / country: Spain

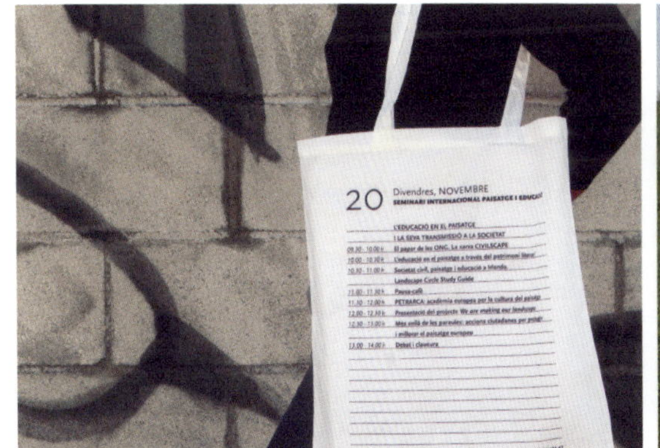

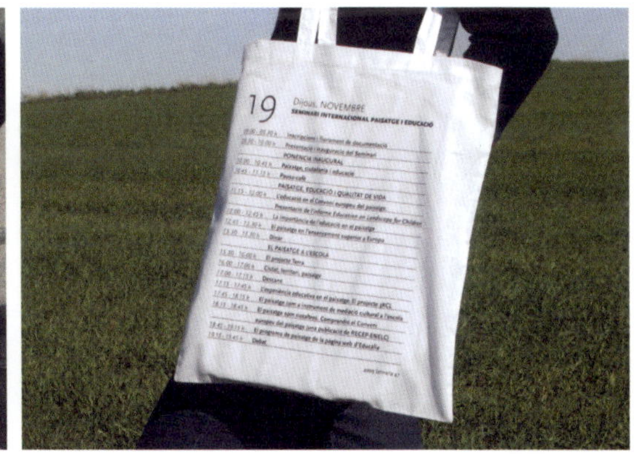

agency/studio: **Anna Pigem** / photos by Elisabet Serra / project: Clothes bag printed with the two-day programme of the International Seminar on Landscape and Education. One side of the bag has the programme for 19th November, and the other for the 20th. / client: Landscape Observatory of Catalonia / country: Spain

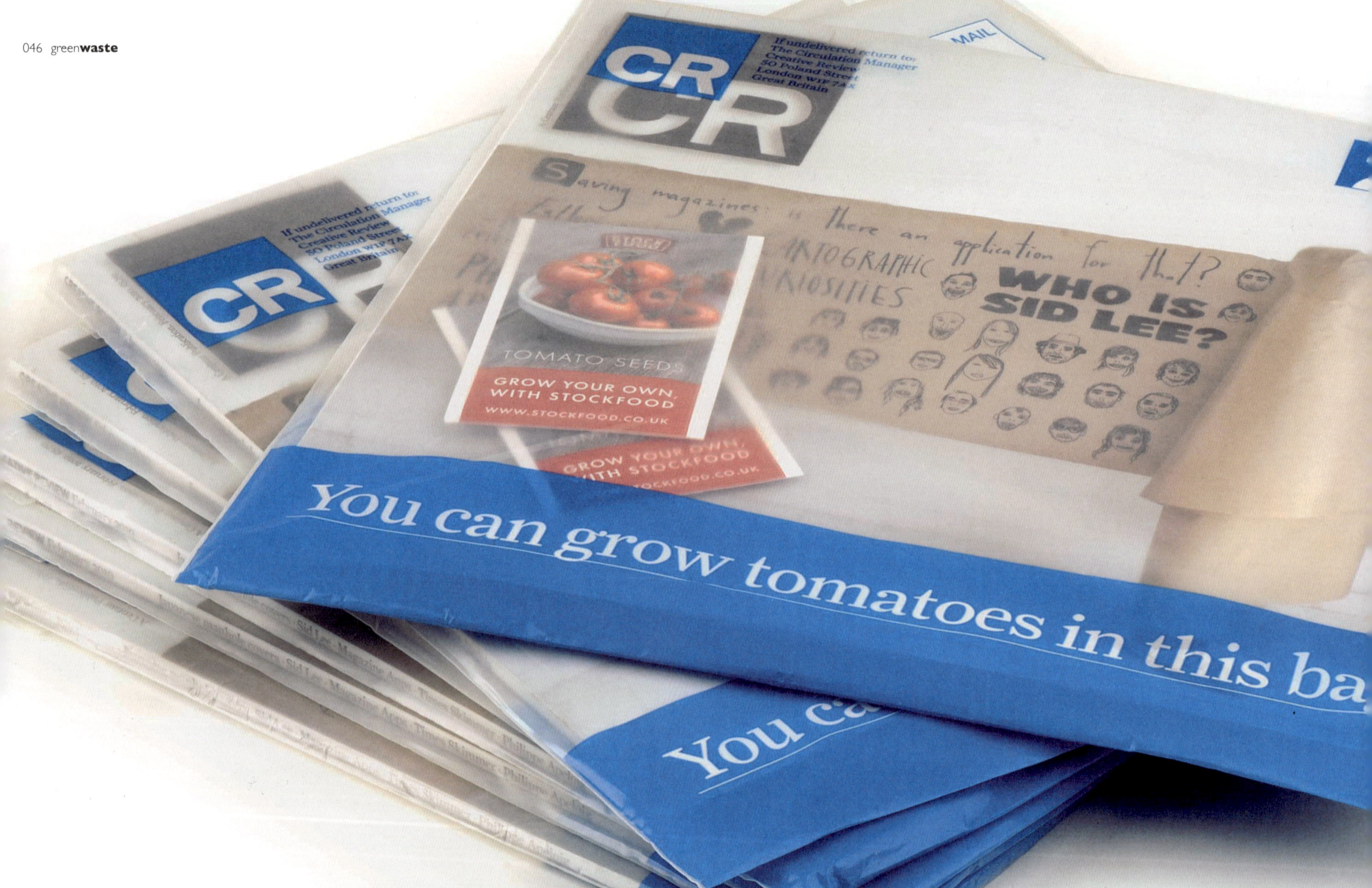
MAIL
CR
CR
If undelivered return to:
The Circulation Manager
Creative Review
50 Poland Street
London W1F 7AX
Great Britain
Saving magazines is there an application for that?
PHOTOGRAPHIC CURIOSITIES
WHO IS SID LEE?
TOMATO SEEDS
GROW YOUR OWN, WITH STOCKFOOD
WWW.STOCKFOOD.CO.UK
GROW YOUR OWN, WITH STOCKFOOD
STOCKFOOD.CO.UK
You can grow tomatoes in this ba
You ca

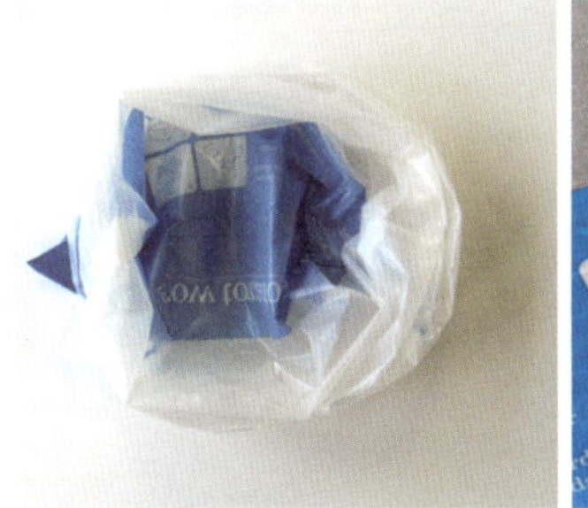

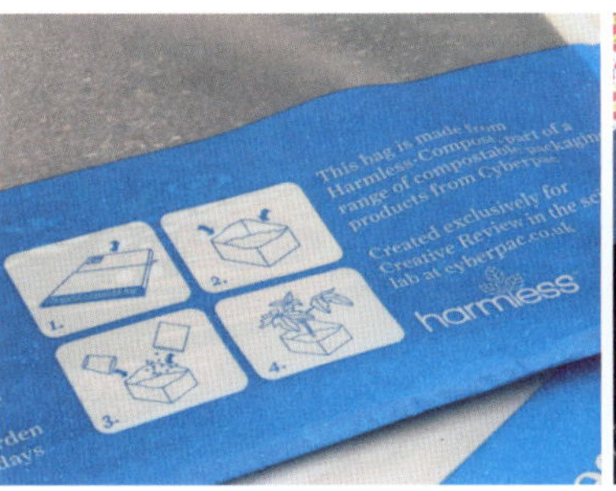

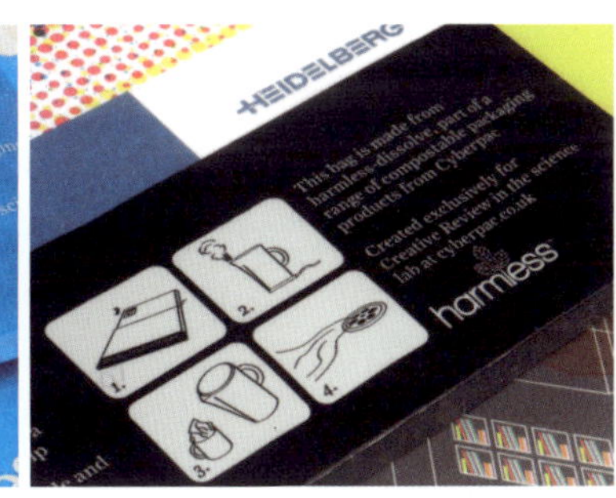

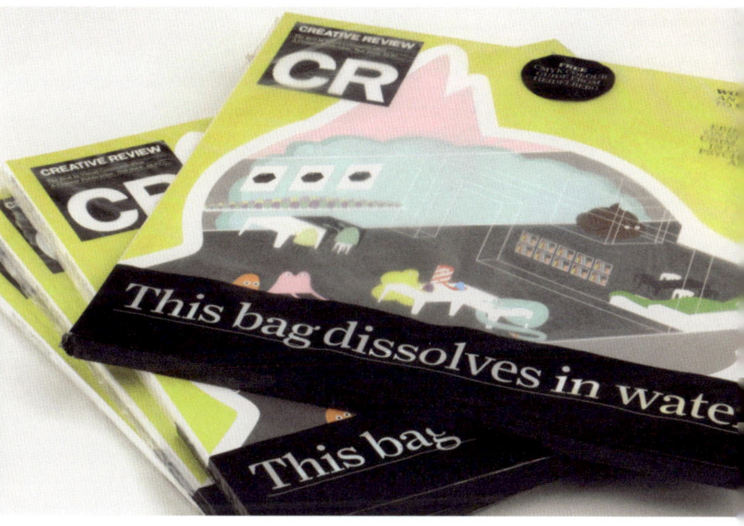

agency/studio: **Cyberpac** / project: Harmless Packaging is a range of compostable packaging sourced ethically, produced efficiently and sold responsibly. The monthly publication "Creative Review" turned to Cyberpac to provide a series of innovative, environmentally friendly packaging options for the magazine. The first issue showcased an industry first, dissolvable bag produced using "Harmless Dissolve", subsequent issues were released in compostable bags, with one encouraging readers to grow their own tomatoes using the packaging. / country: United Kingdom

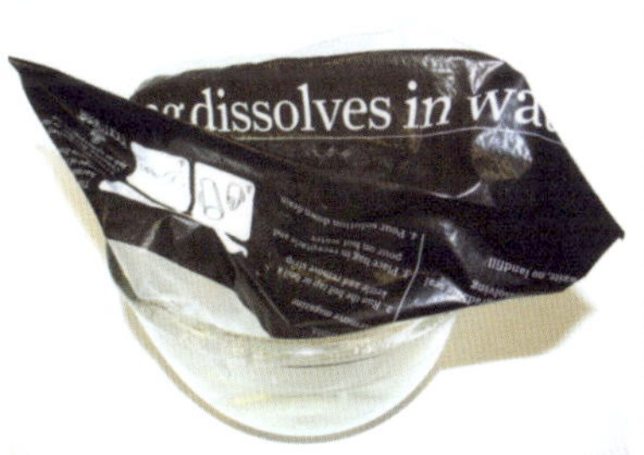

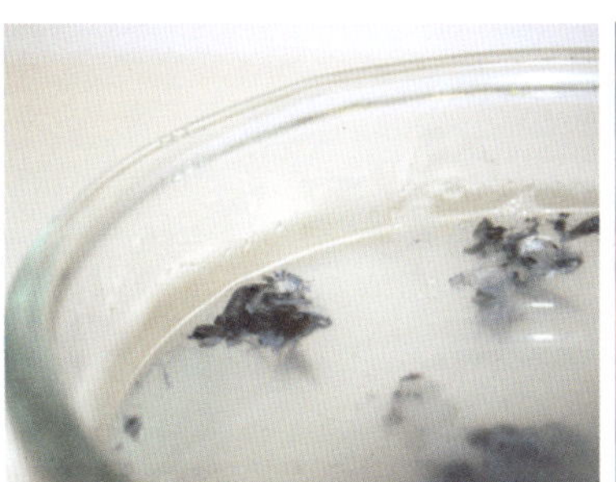

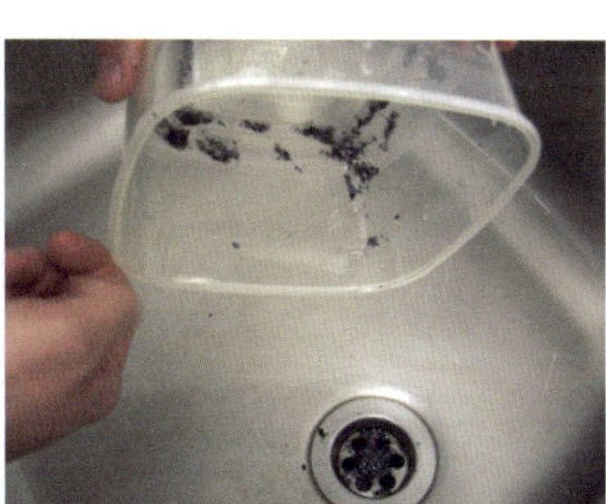

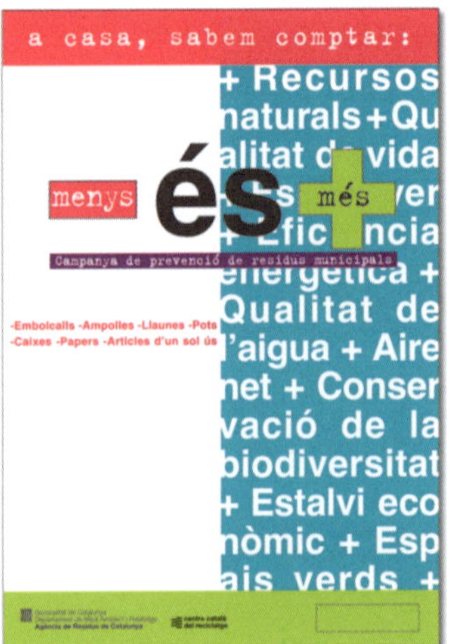
a casa, sabem comptar:
+ Recursos
naturals +Qu
alitat de vida
s   més ver
+ Efic ncia
energética +
Qualitat de
l'aigua + Aire
net + Conser
vació de la
biodiversitat
+ Estalvi eco
nòmic + Esp
ais verds +
menys és més
Campanya de prevenció de residus municipals
-Embolcalls -Ampolles -Llaunes -Pots
-Caixes -Papers -Articles d'un sol ús

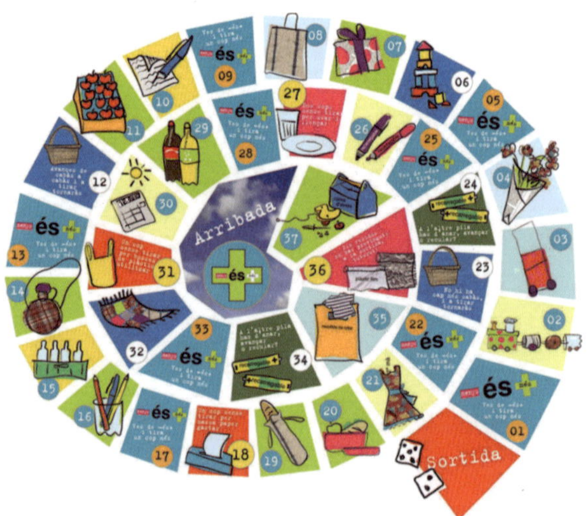
Arribada
Sortida
és

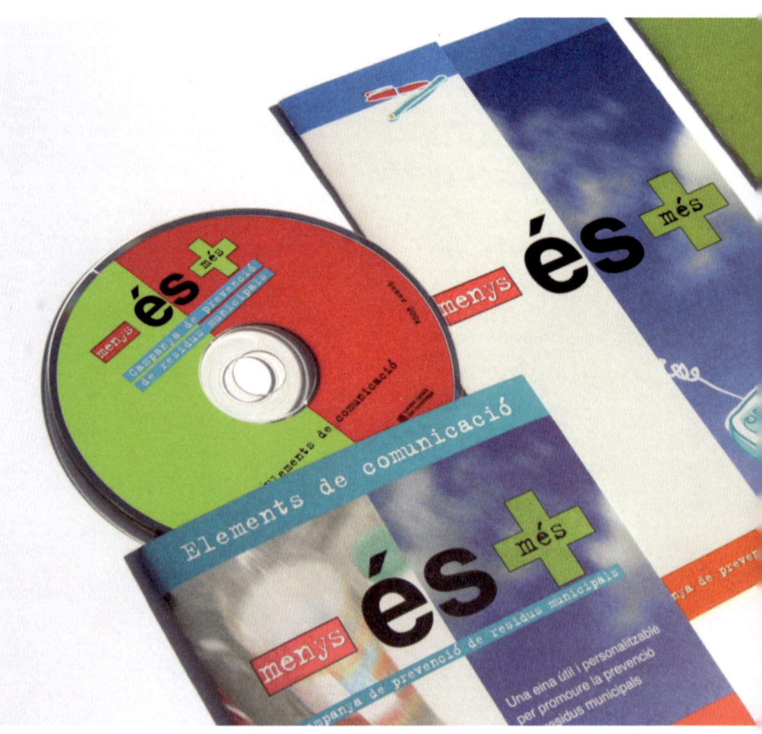
menys és més
Elements de comunicació
menys és més
Campanya de prevenció de residus municipals
Una eina útil i personalitzable
per promoure la prevenció
de residus municipals

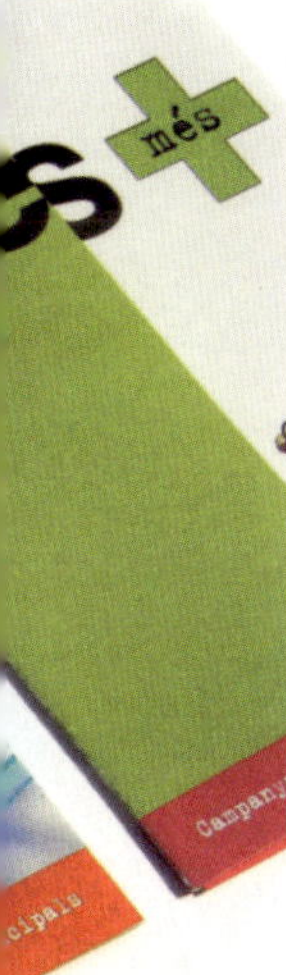

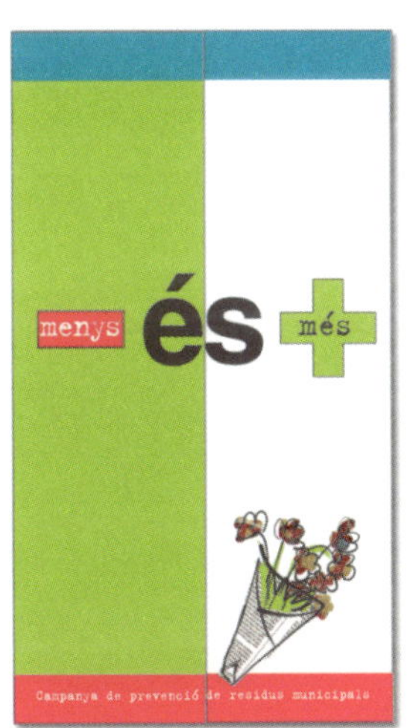

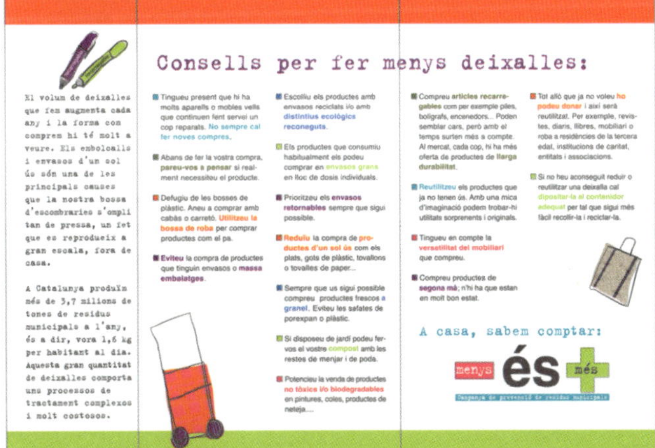

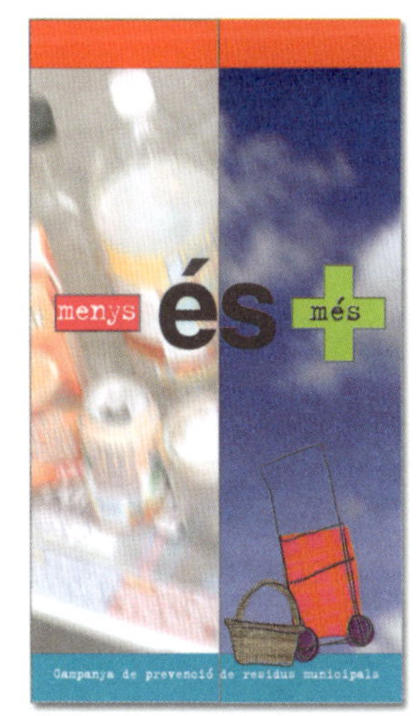

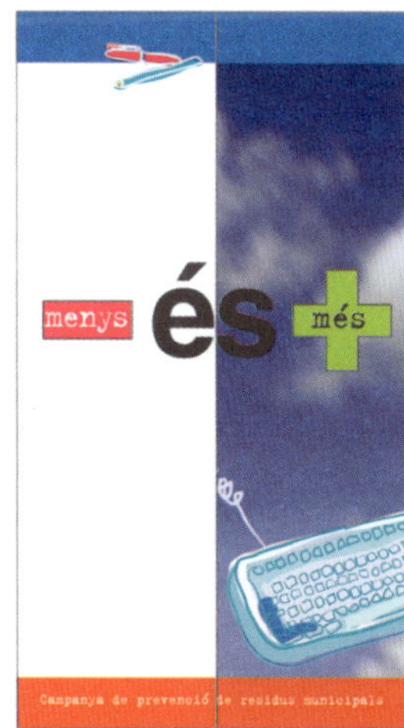

agency/studio: **Estudio Eckert+Zúñiga / lavola** / project: design of a set of customisable elements offered by the Government of Catalonia to local councils to carry out municipal waste-reduction campaigns. / client: lavola for the Catalan Waste Agency / country: Spain agency/studio: **Visual Think** / project: Plastic doesn't biodegrade. Albatross carcasses are being found on beaches around the world filled with hundreds of plastic pieces. This public service announcement encourages consumers to bring a bag or a bottle and reduce their use of plastic. / client: University of Utah (non-profit) / country: USA

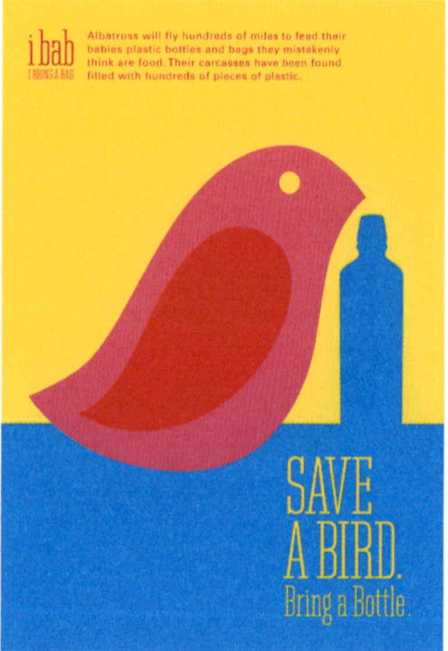

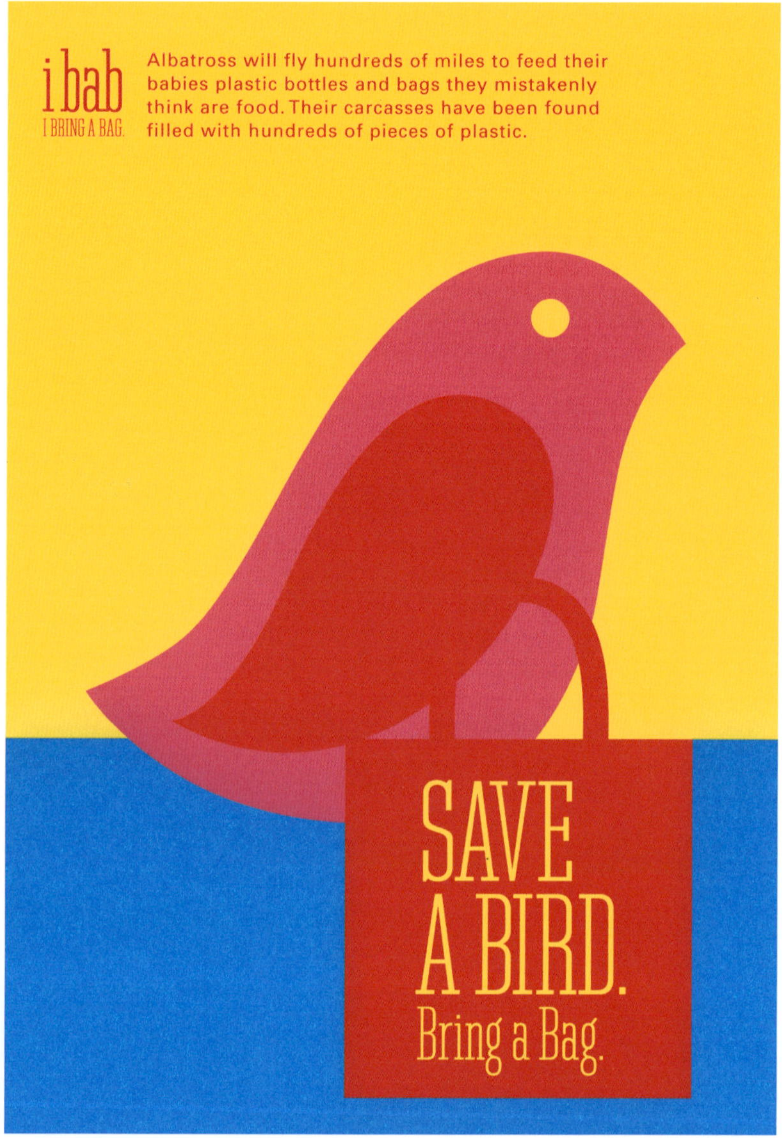

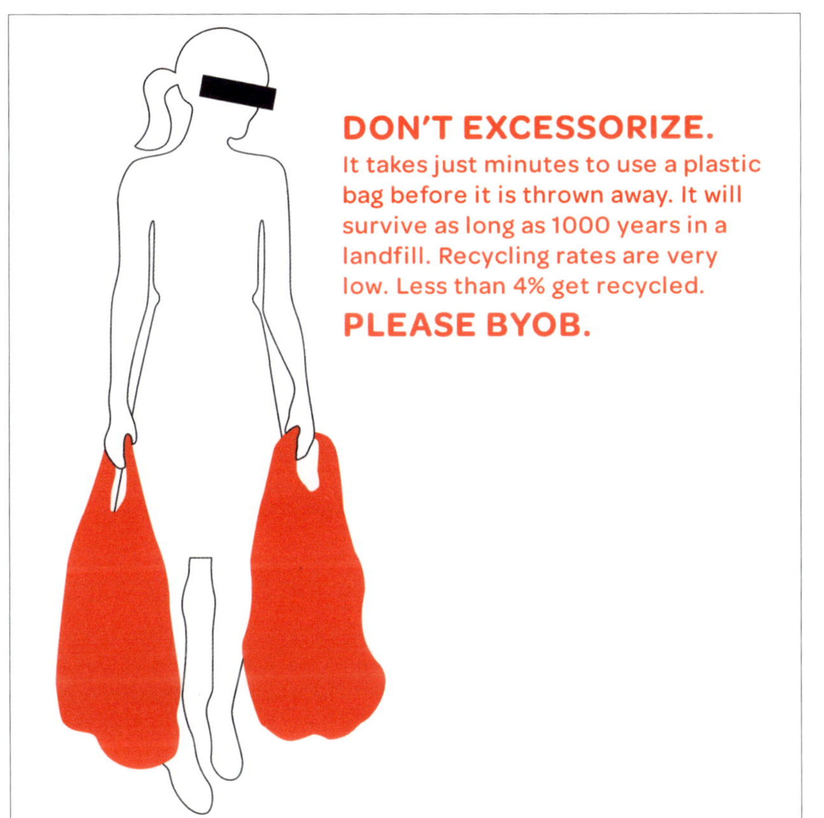

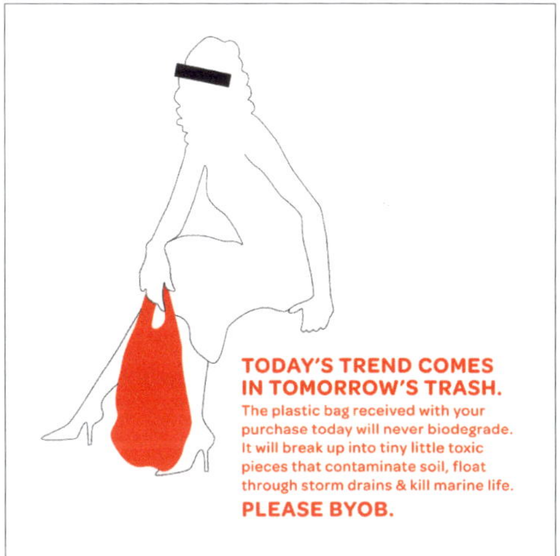

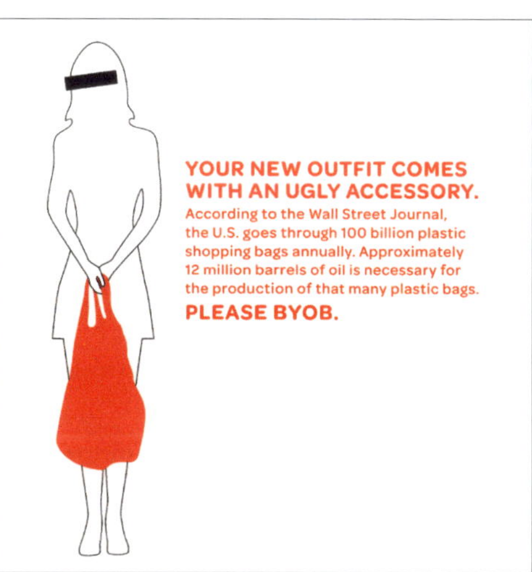

agency/studio: **Visual Think** / project: campaign against the use of plastic bags. / client: University of Utah (non-profit) / country: USA

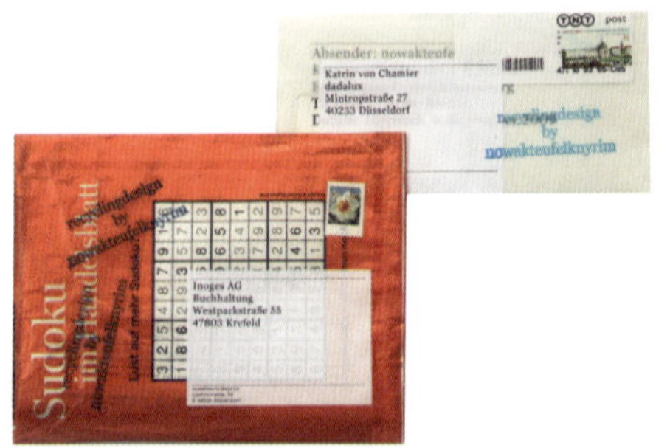

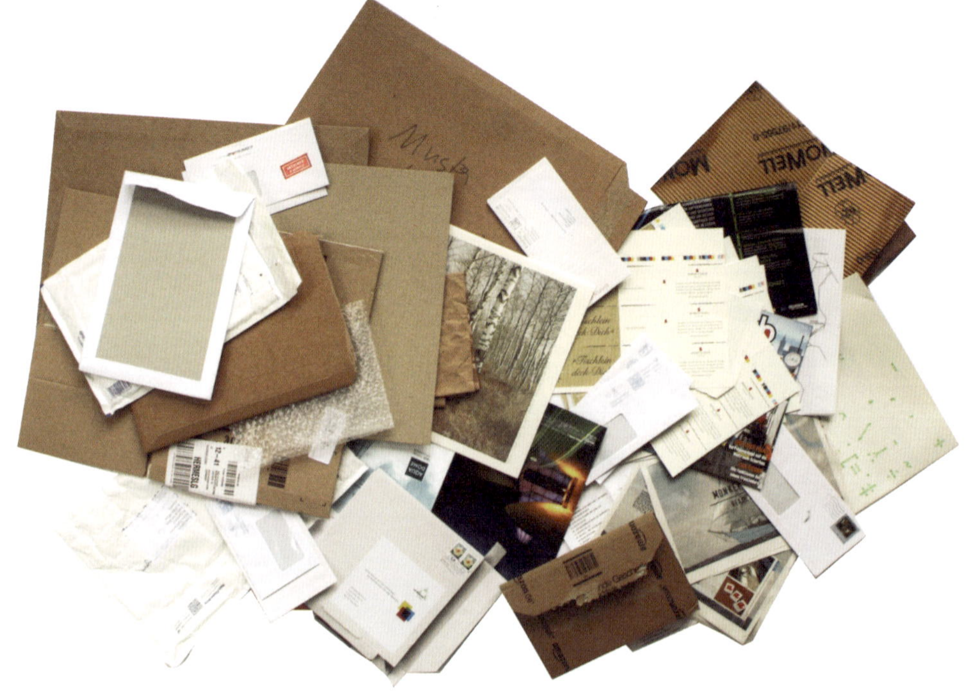

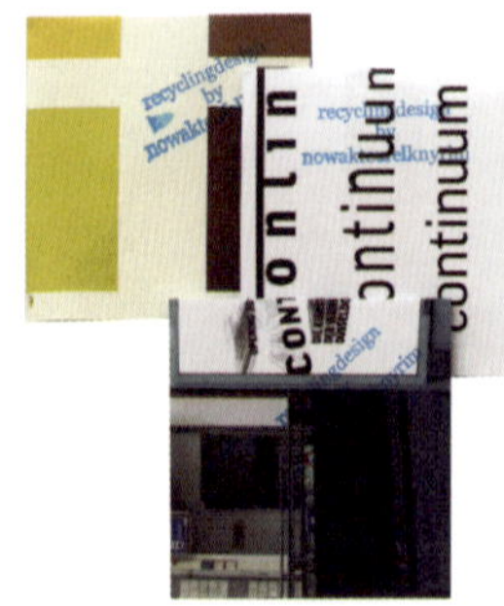

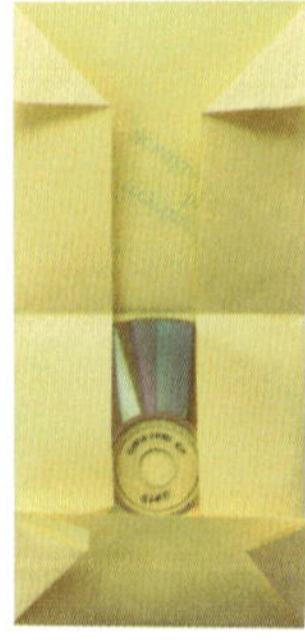

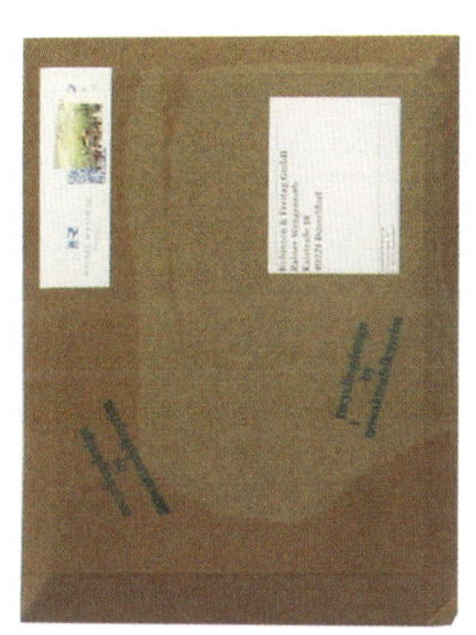

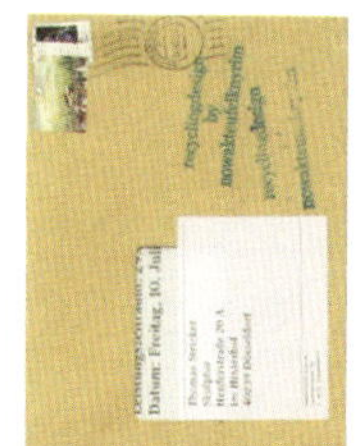
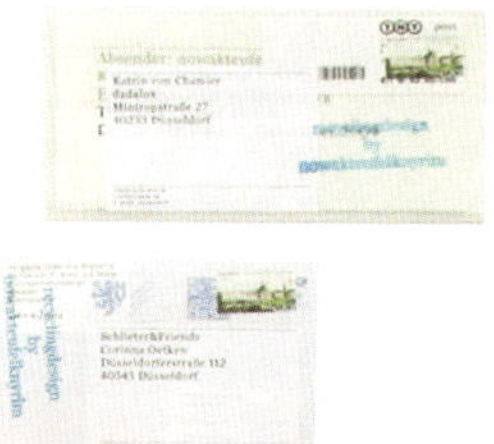
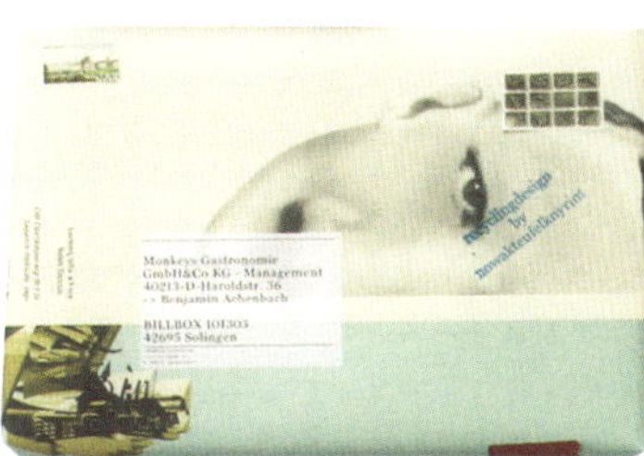
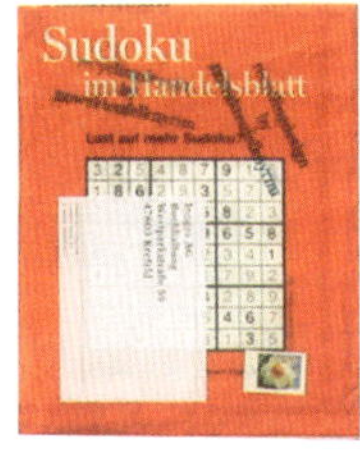
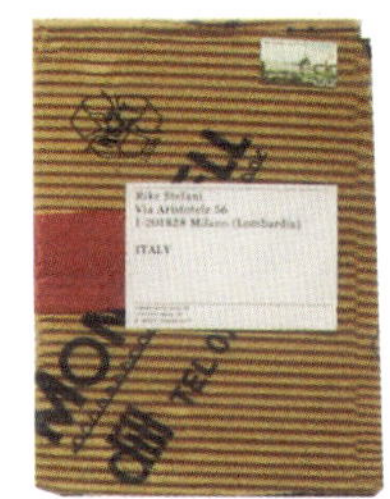
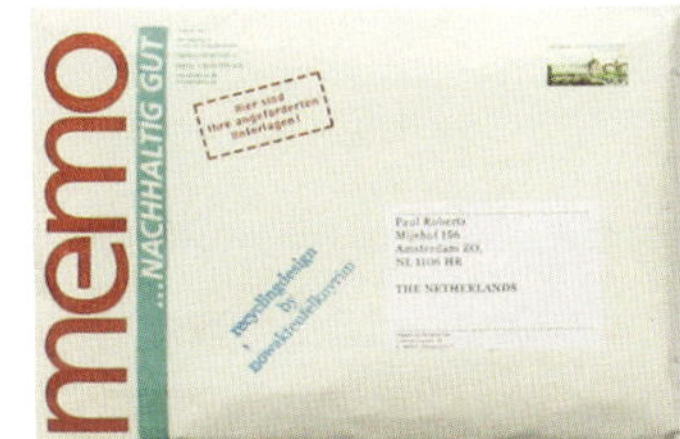
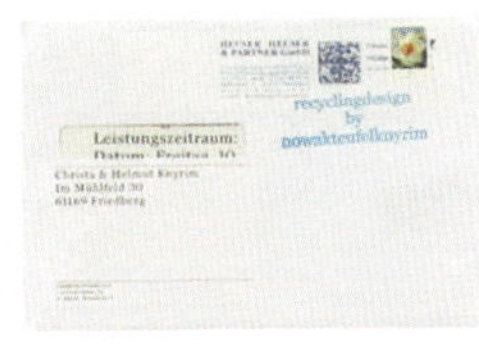
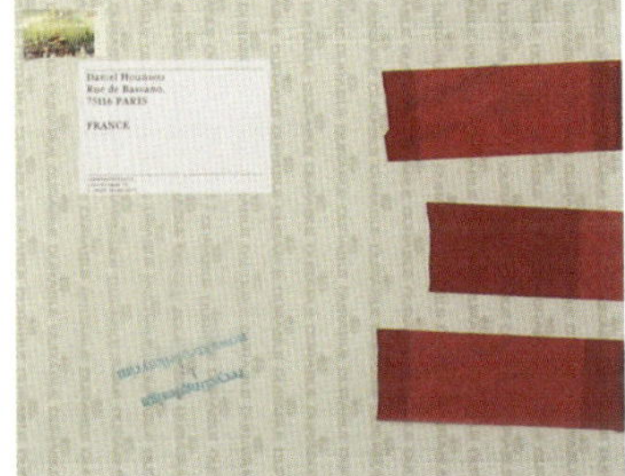
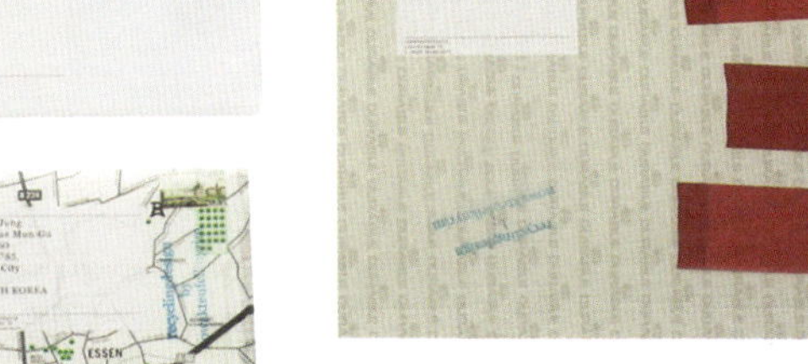
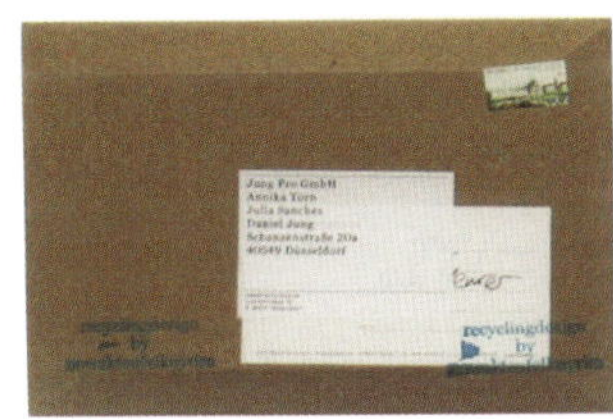

agency/studio: **Nowakteufelknyrim** / project: This design firm recycles old envelopes and packaging for its daily correspondence. It also makes sketchbooks out of used paper and dustbins out of old posters. A rubber stamp is used to mark the pieces as "recyclingdesign". / client: Nowakteufelkynrim / country: Germany

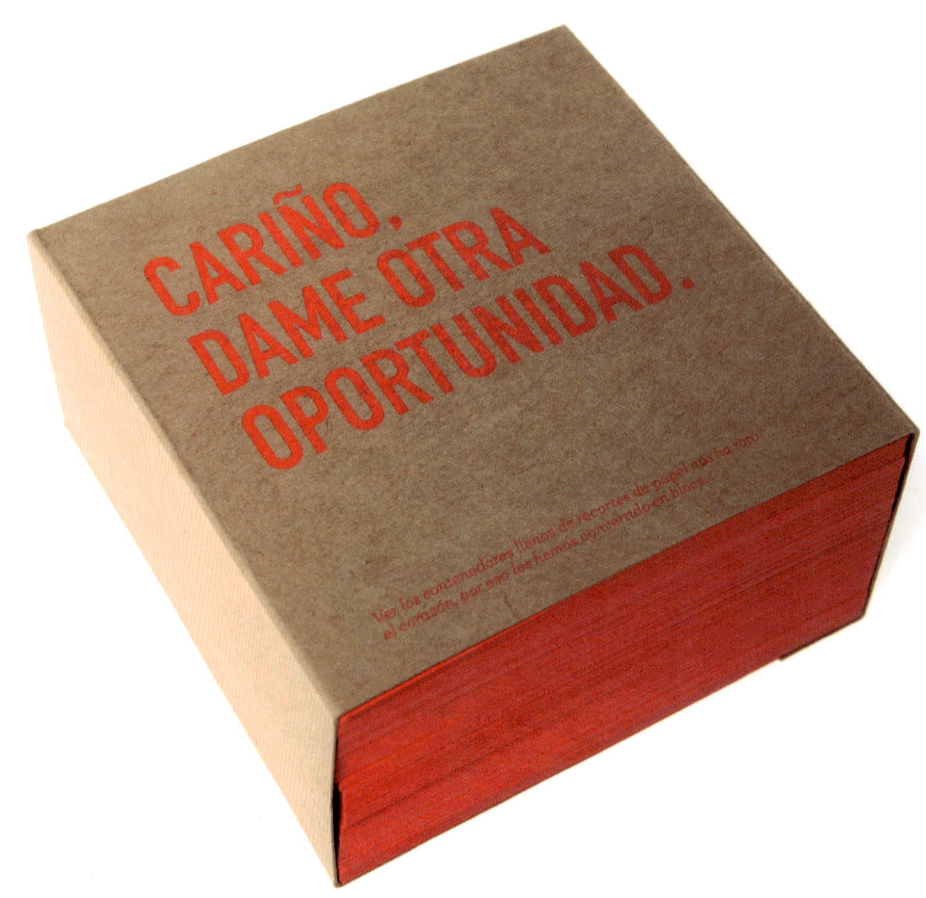

agency/studio: **Xurxo Baca** / project: notepad made from scrap paper as a gift for the clients of a publishing house.
/ client: Imgrafor / country: Spain

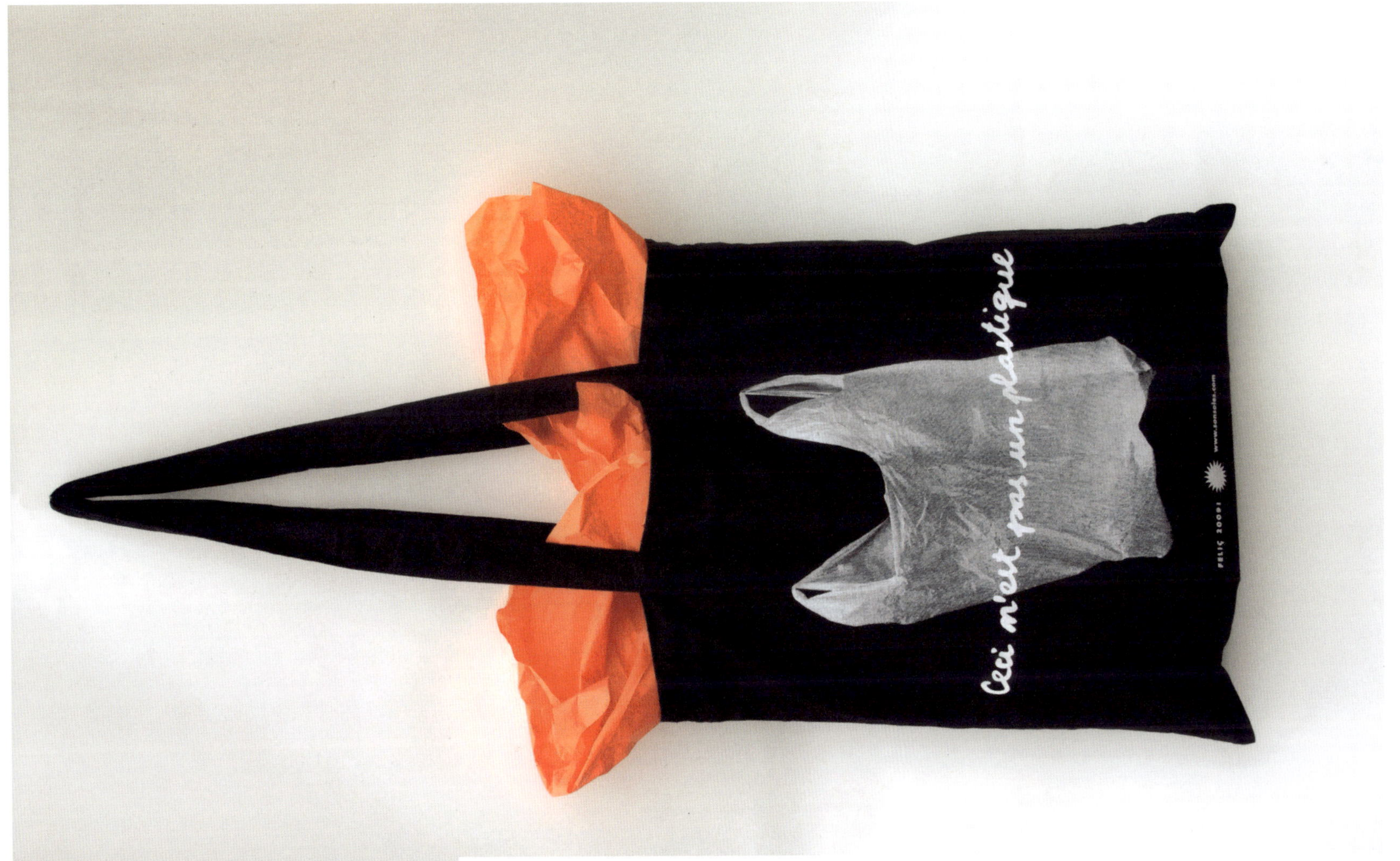

agency/studio: **Sonsoles Llorens** / project: felicitación 2009. Paraphrasing Magritte… a hint to encourage the reader to reuse bags and avoid generating unnecessary plastic waste. / client: Sonsoles Llorens design studio / country: Spain author: **Martijn Oostra** / project: 400 trees a year for paper coffee cups. In the Netherlands, 16 million paper coffee cups are used every year. That requires 270,000 kg of paper made from 400,000 kg of wood. One tree produces 1,000 kg of wood. That means 400 trees - almost a forest - are cut down to produce paper coffee cups. Use your own coffee cup! / country: Netherlands

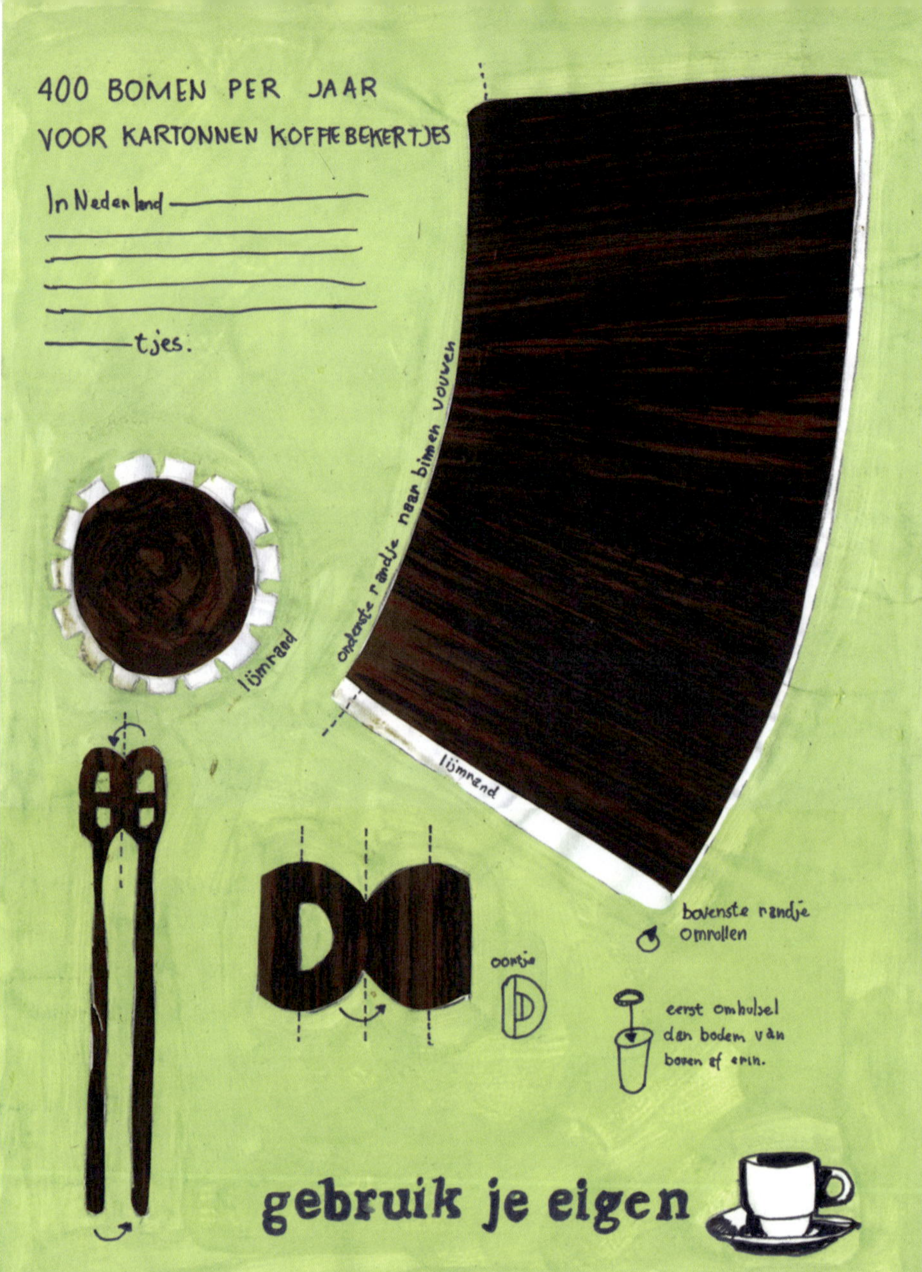

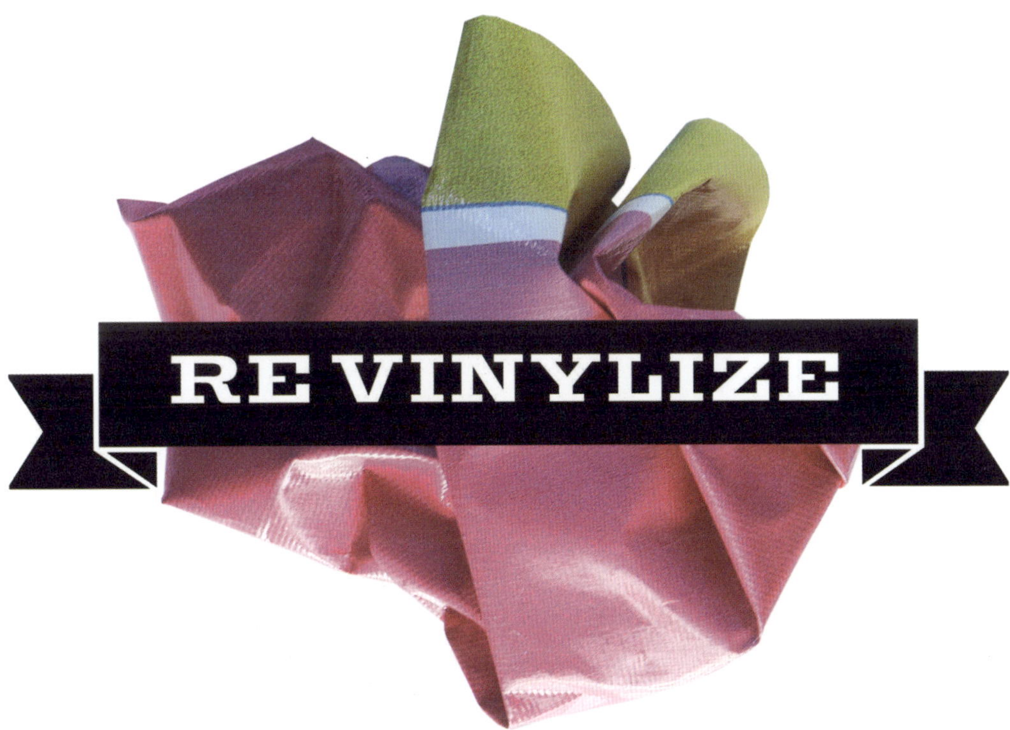

agency/studio: **Visual Think** / project: The Revinylize Project promotes and encourages social awareness with the power of creativity. By reclaiming local billboard material, the once giant images are transformed into smaller works of art in the form of unique vinyl bags and accessories. / client: AIGA Salt Lake City / country: USA

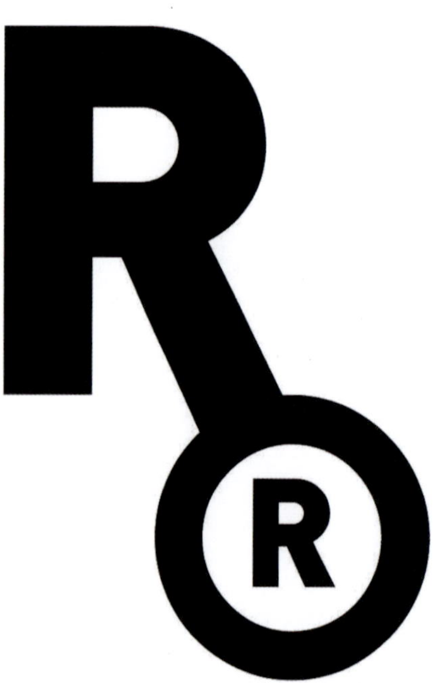

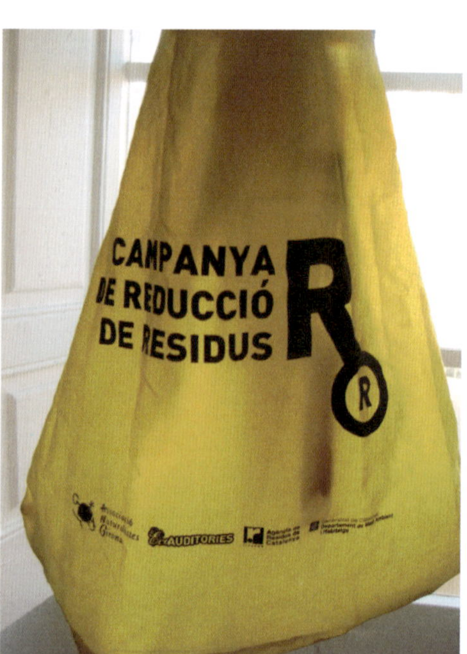

agency/studio: **Oriol Piferrer** / project: logo for the reusable bags of a waste-reduction campaign. / client: Girona Association of Naturalists (ANG) / country: Spain

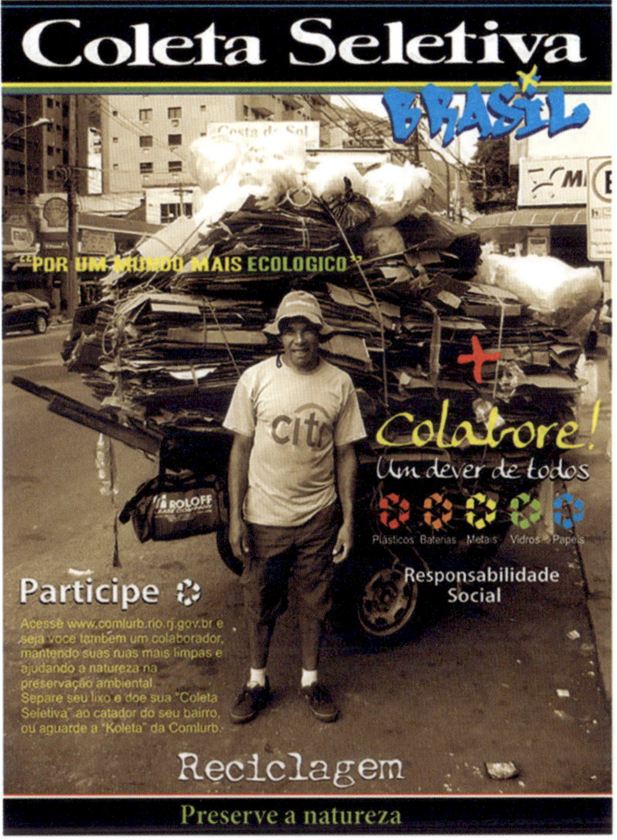

author: **Nordicoart+EStudio** / project: This poster was part of an awareness campaign on the importance of separating rubbish and giving it to the "catadores", or rubbish collectors, in the neighbourhood. The aim of the campaign is to change passive habits and behaviour patterns into proactive ones. / country: Brazil

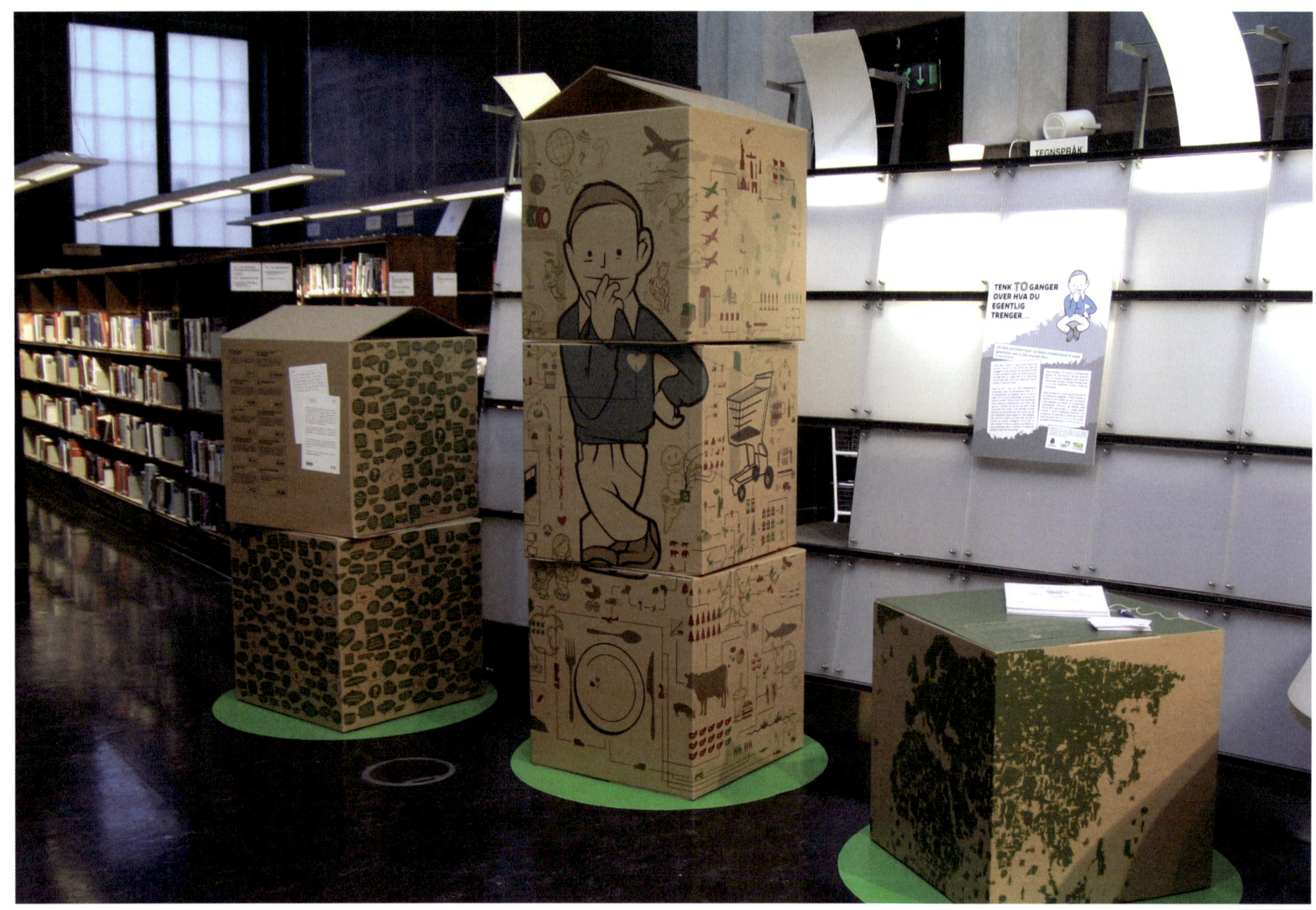
TENK TO GANGER
OVER HVA DU
EGENTLIG
TRENGER...

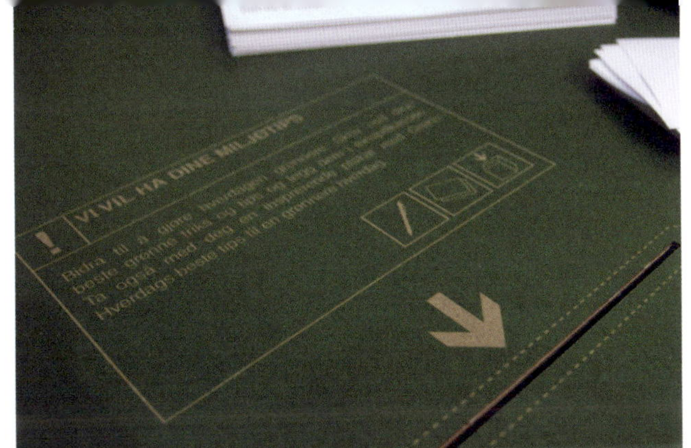

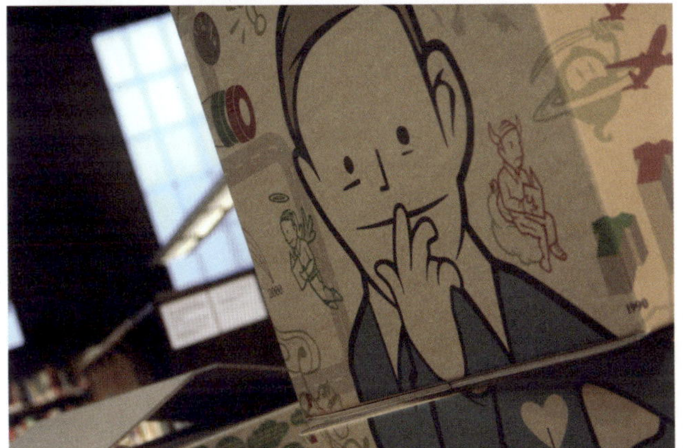

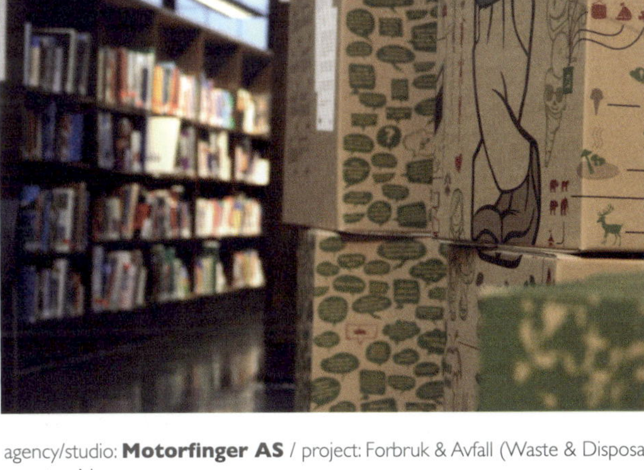

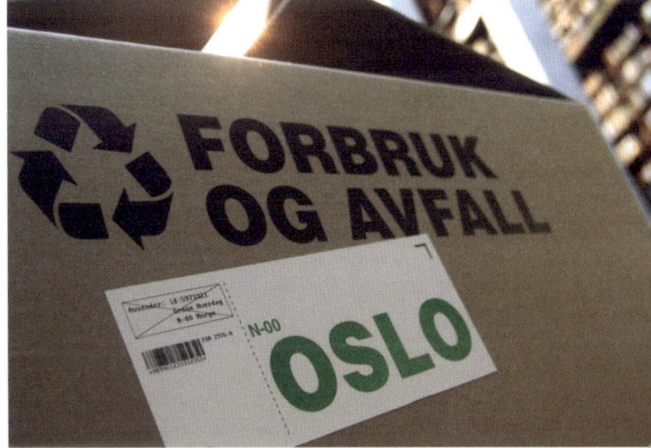

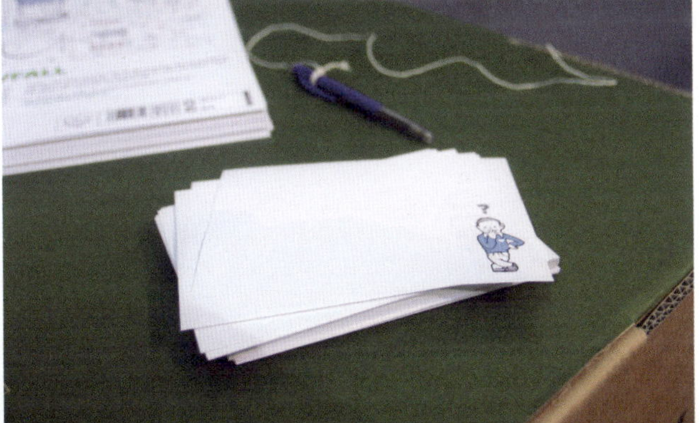

agency/studio: **Motorfinger AS** / project: Forbruk & Avfall (Waste & Disposal). Mobile exhibition on consumption and waste. / client: Grønn Hverdag /
country: Norway

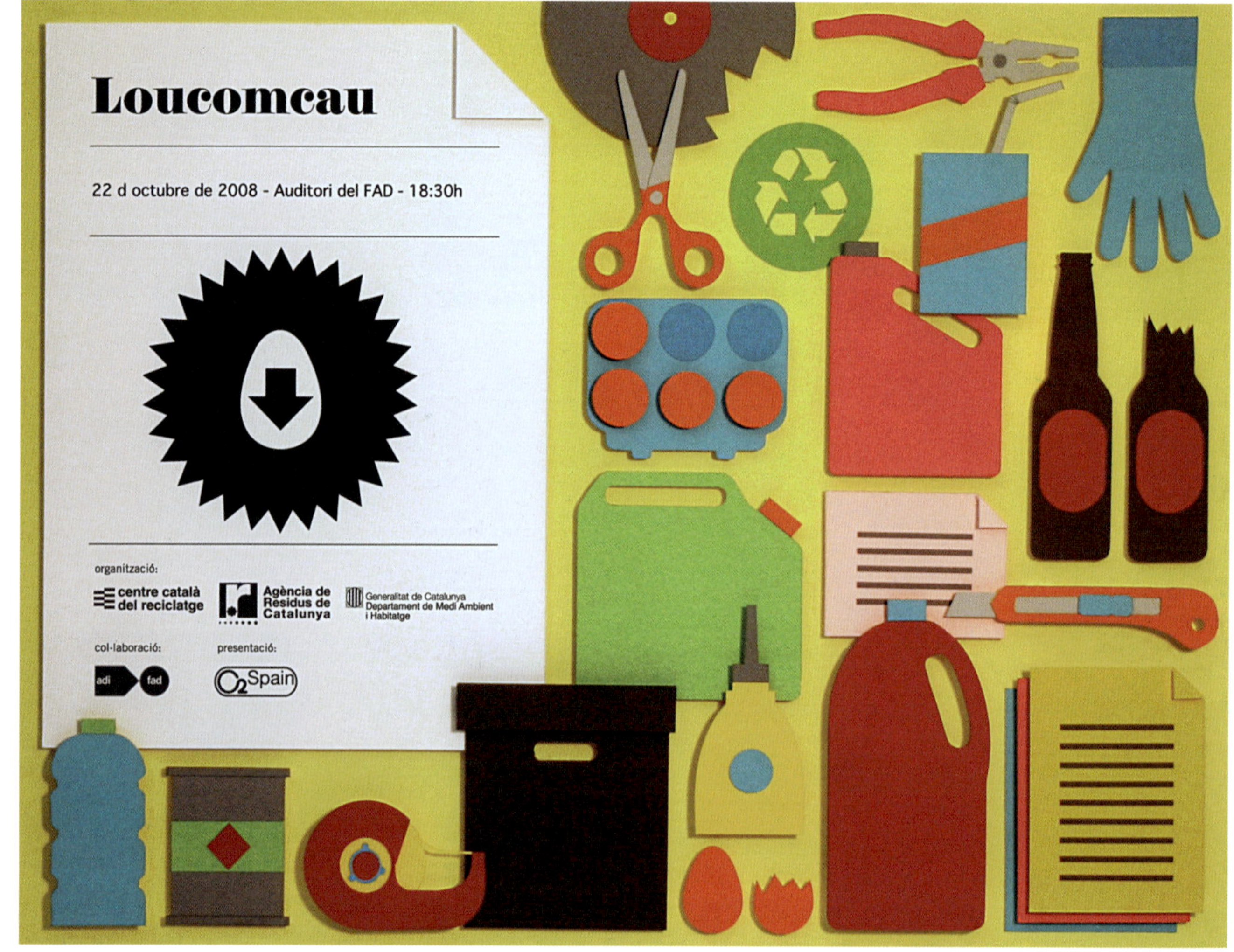

agency/studio: **Home de Caramel** / project: Loucomcau. Poster for the activities prior to the presentation of the 2009 Design for Recycling Awards. / client: Catalonia Waste Agency, O2Spain / country: Spain

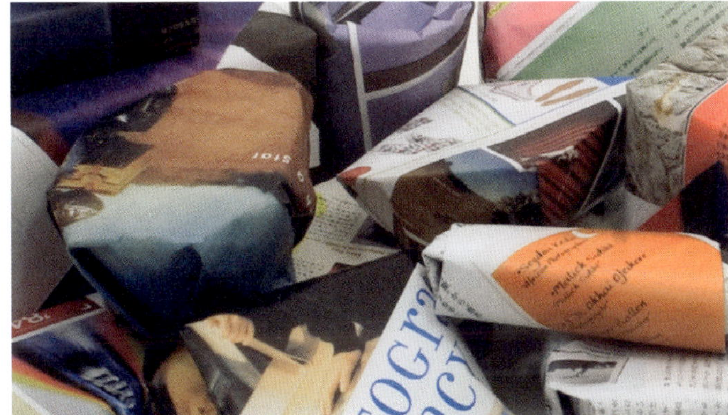

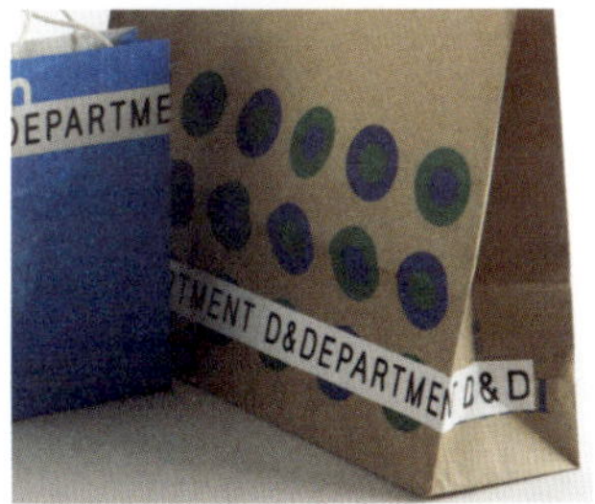

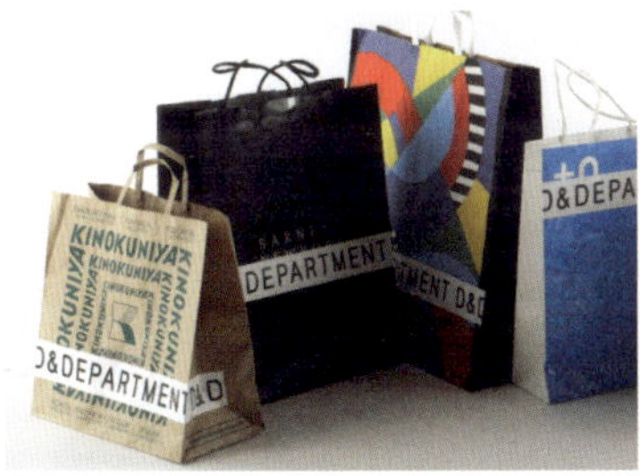

agency/studio: **D&Department Project** / project: D&Department's shopping bags are made by reusing unnecessary paper bags collected by its customers. / country: Japan

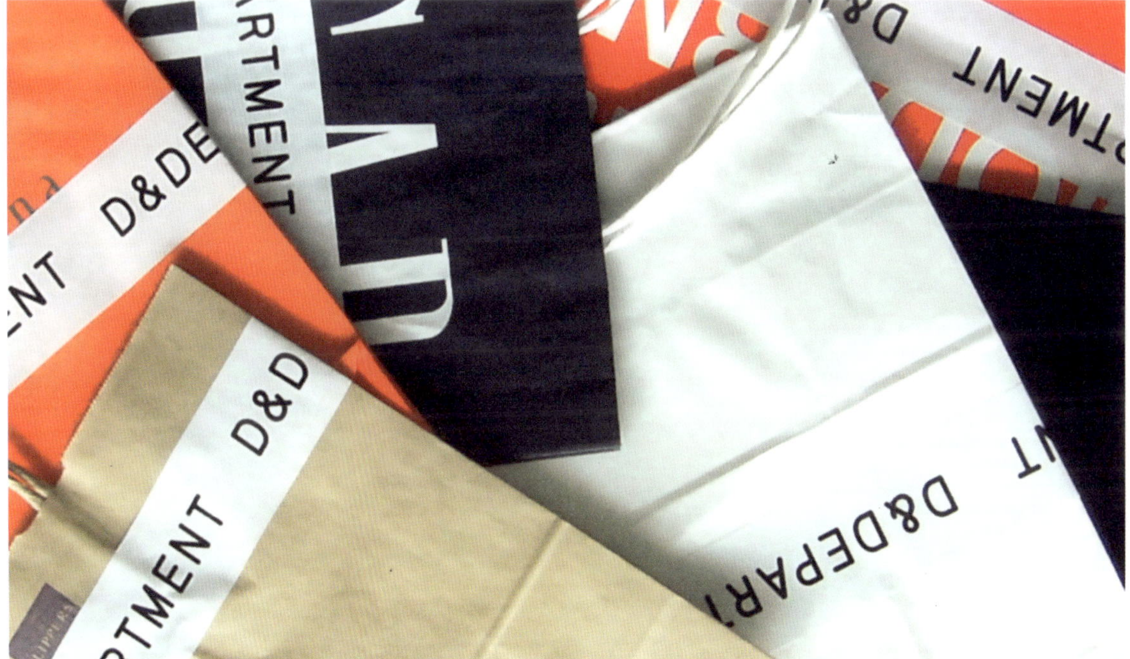

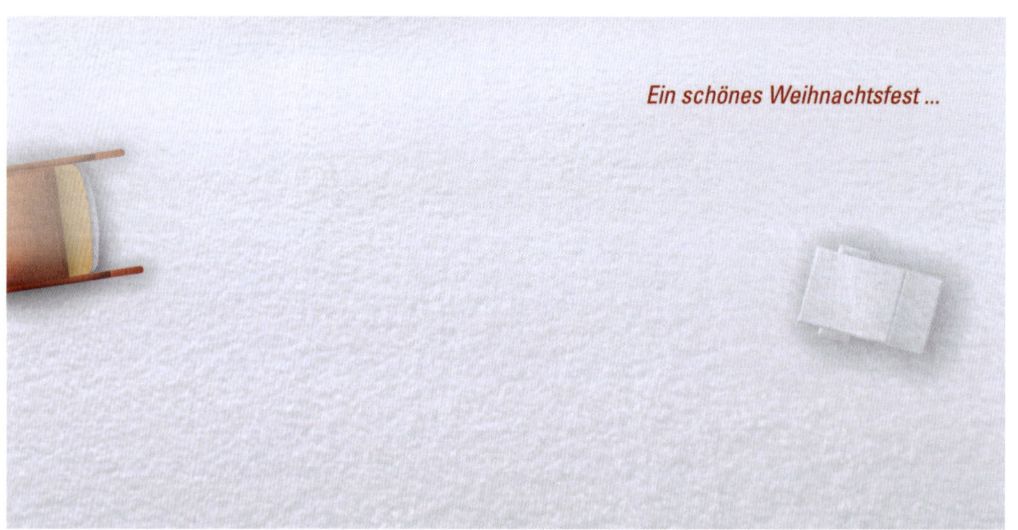

agency/studio: **Lichtenberg - Agentur für Mediendesign** / project: Christmas greeting cards for a waste disposal company to mail out to their clients. Without using any of the seasonal cliché visuals, it communicates the fact that, even while extending best wishes, this firm quietly does its job, being a reliable service provider. / client: Vetter's Container Service / country: Germany.

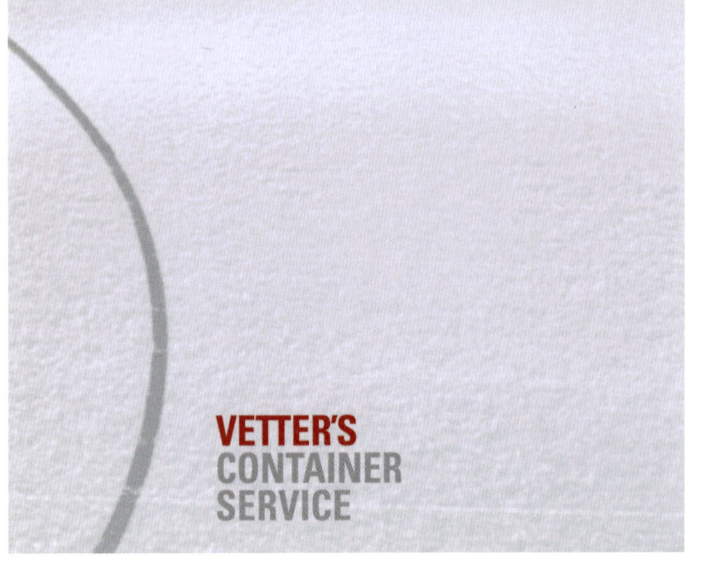

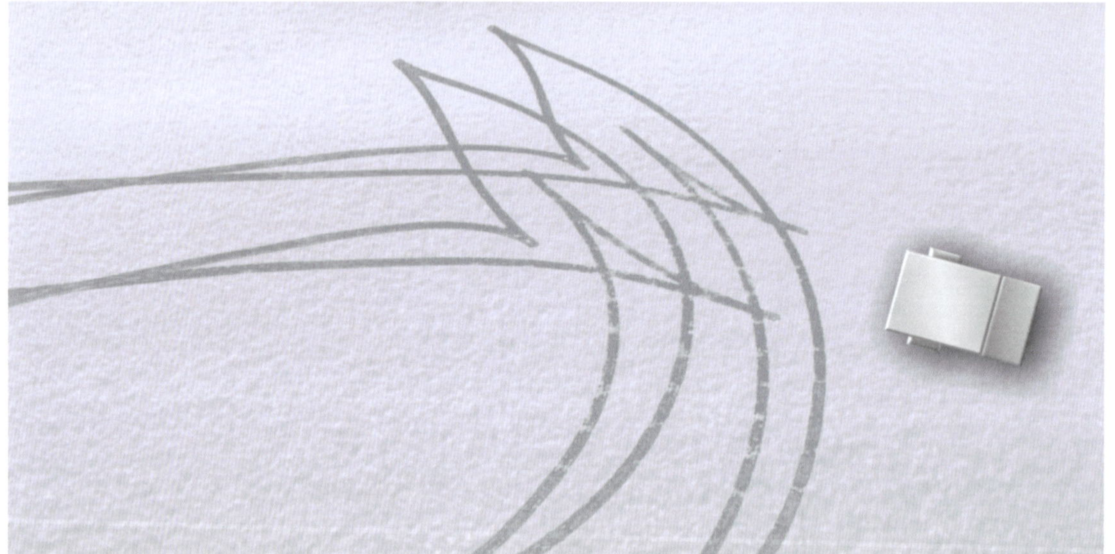

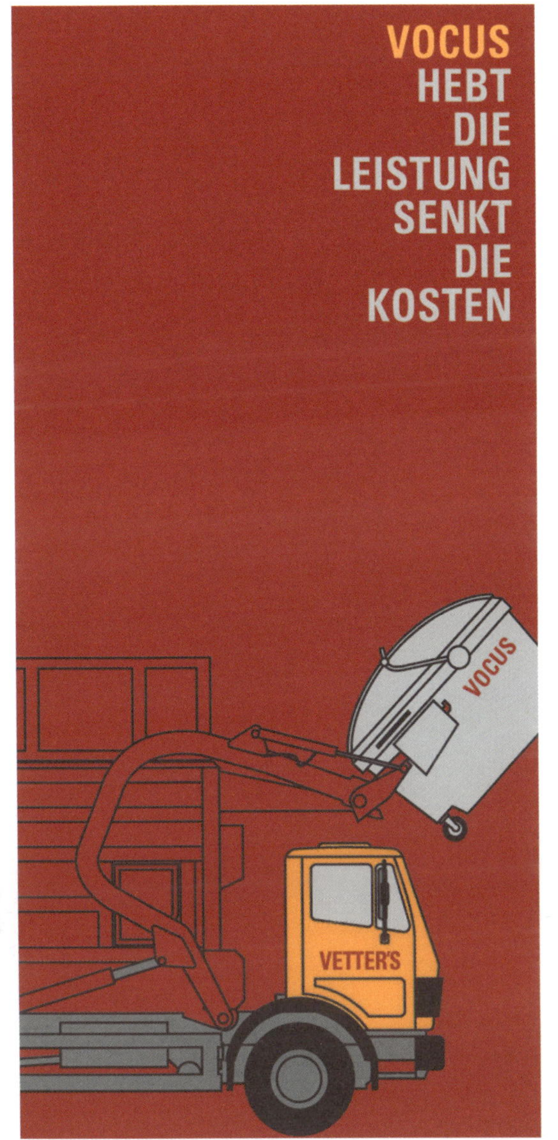

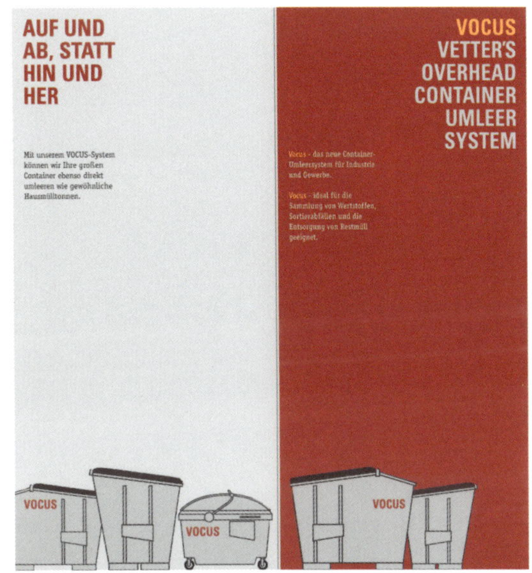

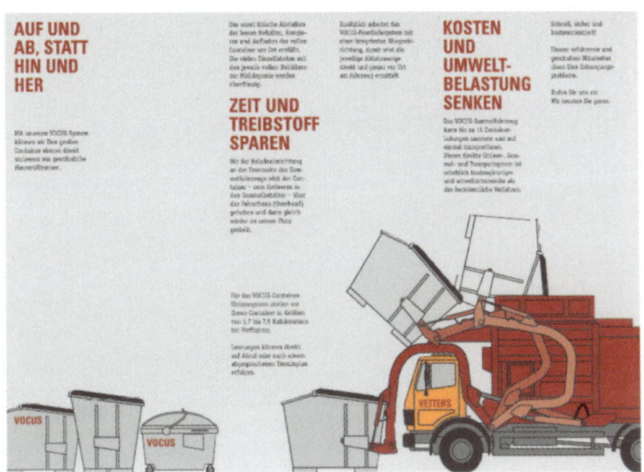

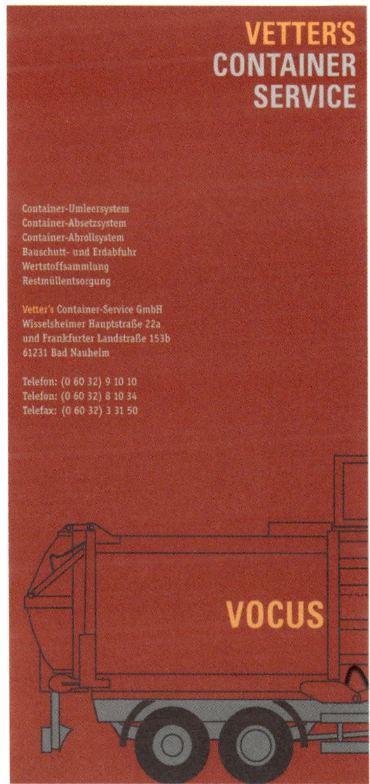

agency/studio: **Lichtenberg - Agentur für Mediendesign** / project: Folder about the new loading system of a waste disposal company. The system reduces costs by using front loaders. The truck empties large recycling bins into the hopper, instead of hauling them to the rubbish dump and returning the empty containers. / client: Vetter's Container Service / country: Germany

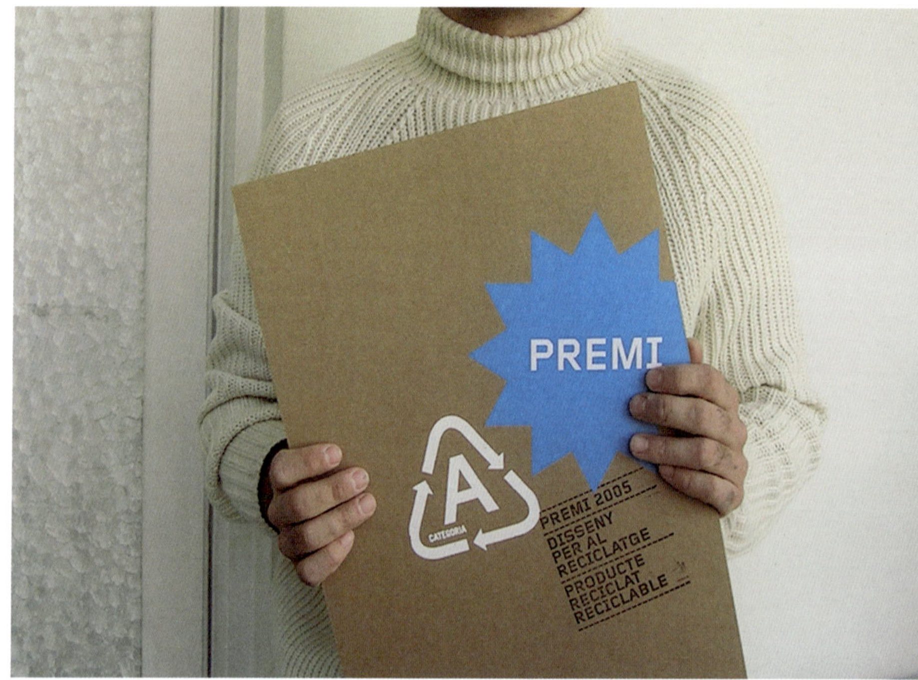

agency/studio: **extra!** / project: Design and graphic application for the "Design for Recycling: Recycled/Recyclable Product" exhibition held in Catalonia in 2005 and built using cardboard. A versatile, coherent system was created, with the event's philosophy based on the application of graphic design with rubber stamps and stickers. These were applied directly onto the cardboard. / client: Catalan Waste Agency / country: Spain

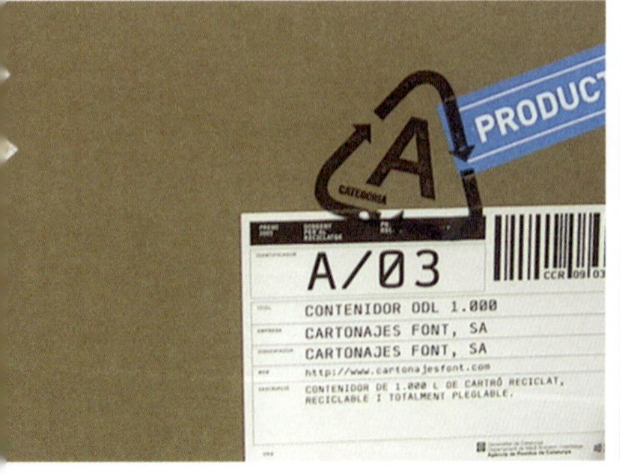

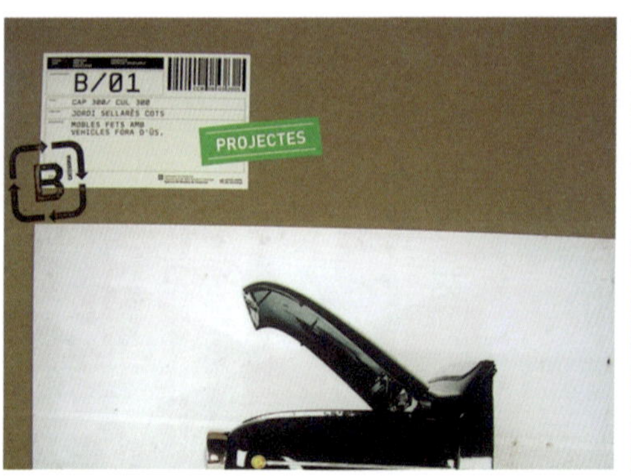

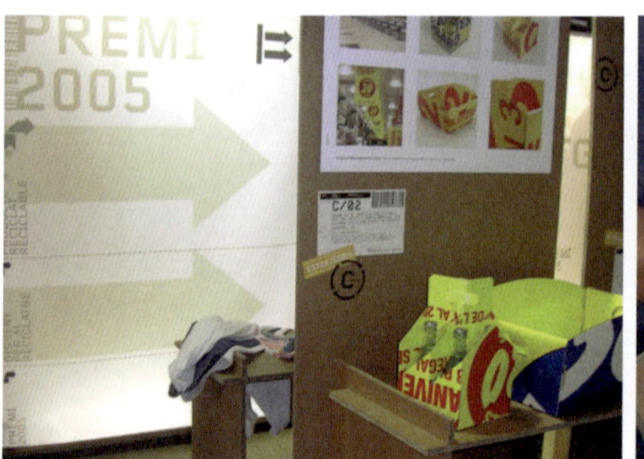

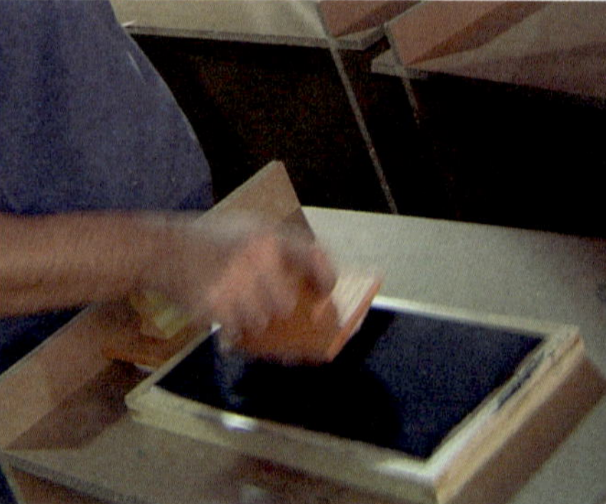

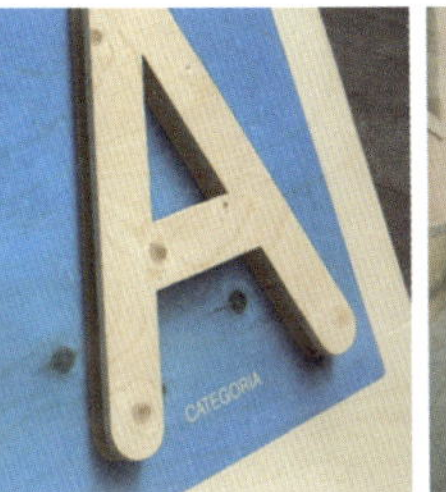

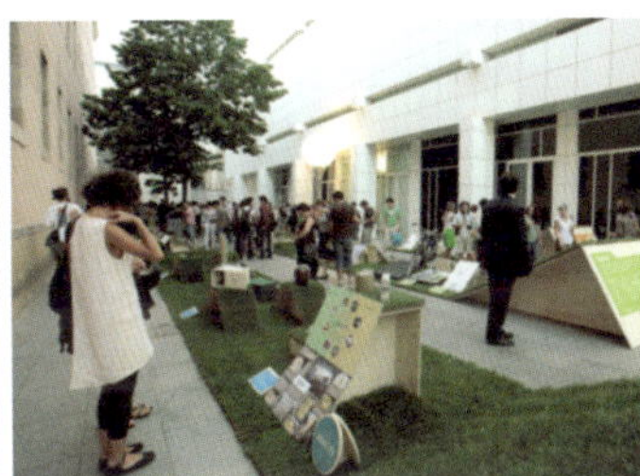

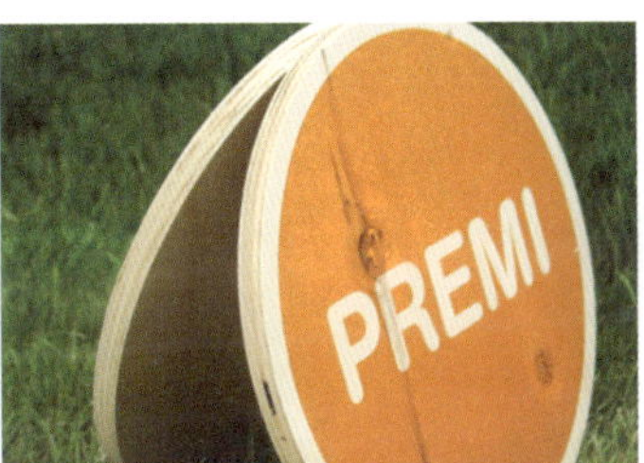

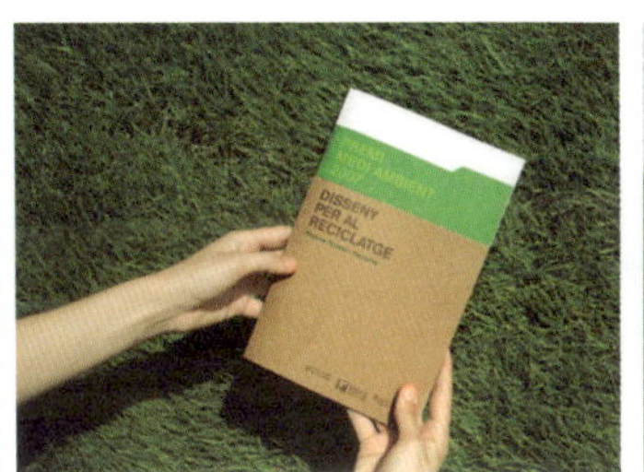

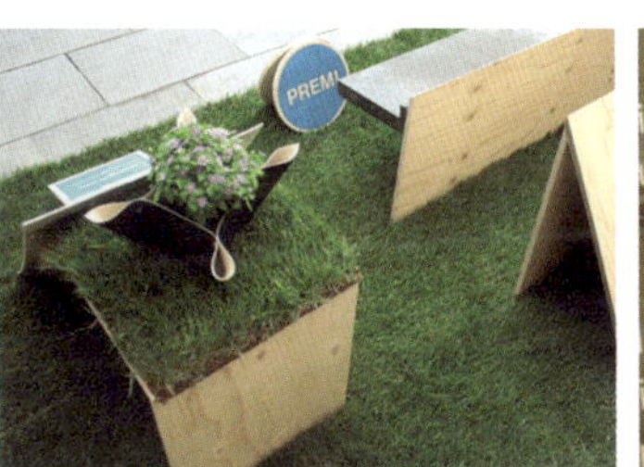

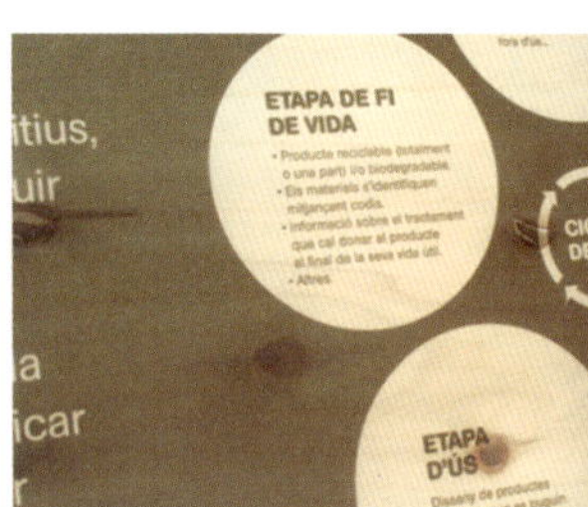

agency/studio: **extra!** / project: Concept, design and graphic application for the ephemeral exhibition "2007 Environment Prize". A pleasant, 100% recyclables support was created using roles of turf and wooden modular pieces that gave the design great versatility for a travelling exhibition. / client: Catalan Waste Agency / country: Spain

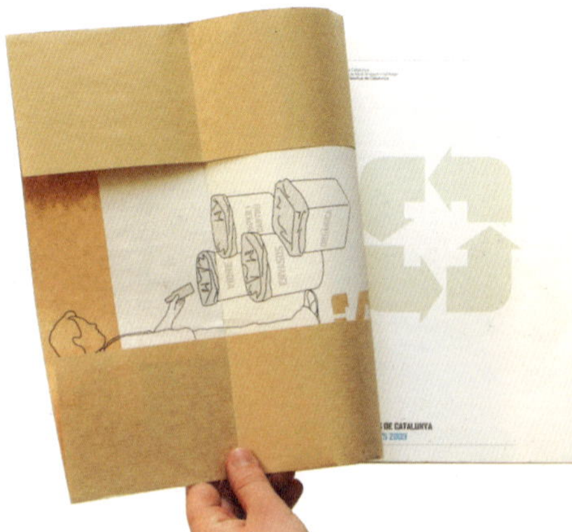

agency/studio: **extra!** / project: Annual report of activities. The publication aims to be coherent with the philosophy and objectives of the institution. Minimisation and reuse are key concepts that are transmitted through the simple, elegant ordering of information. The covers become an informative poster providing advice on waste reduction and recycling in the work environment / client: Catalan Waste Agency / country: Spain

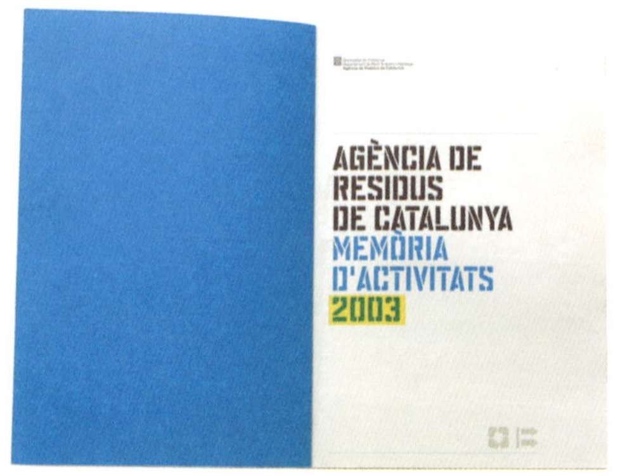

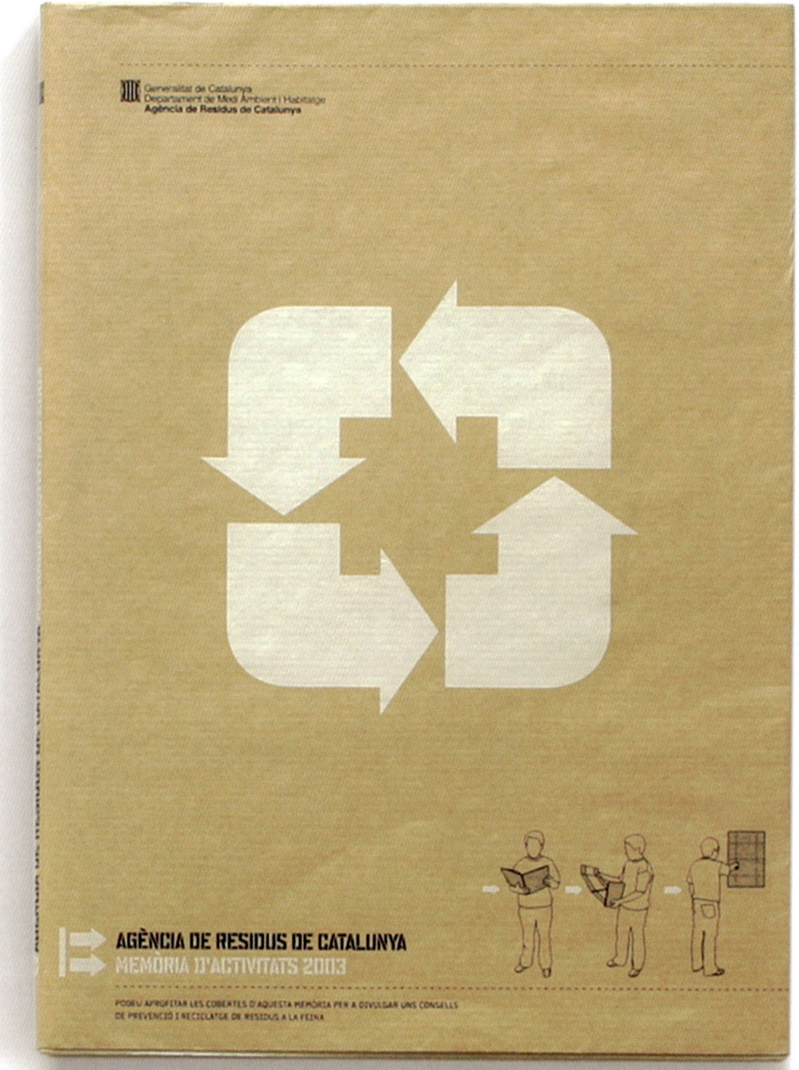

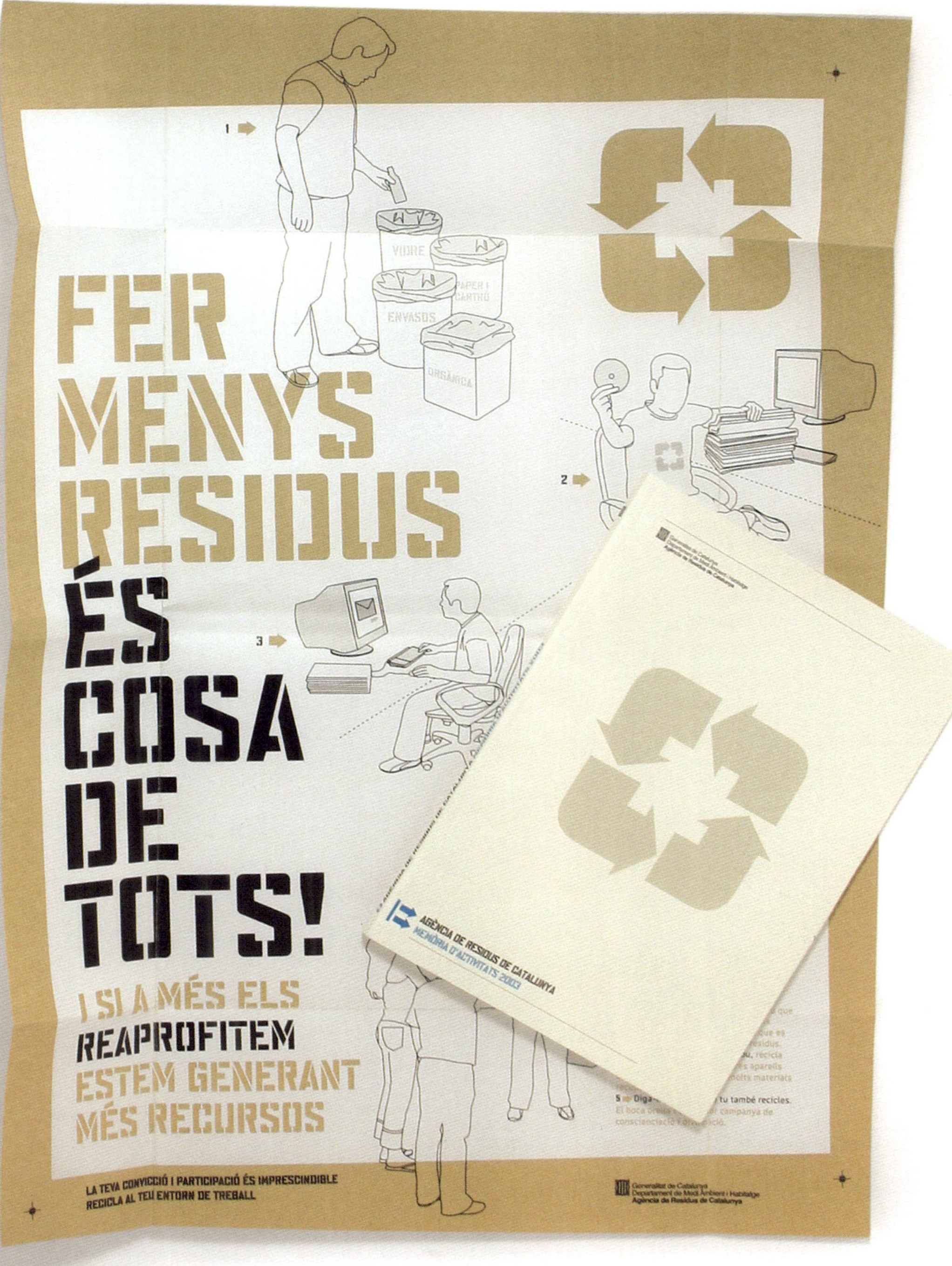
FER
MENYS
RESIDUS
ÉS
COSA
DE
TOTS!
I SI A MÉS ELS
REAPROFITEM
ESTEM GENERANT
MÉS RECURSOS
LA TEVA CONVICCIÓ I PARTICIPACIÓ ÉS IMPRESCINDIBLE
RECICLA AL TEU ENTORN DE TREBALL
VIDRE
PAPER I CARTRÓ
ENVASOS
ORGÀNICA
AGÈNCIA DE RESIDUS DE CATALUNYA
MEMÒRIA D'ACTIVITATS 2003
Generalitat de Catalunya
Departament de Medi Ambient i Habitatge
Agència de Residus de Catalunya

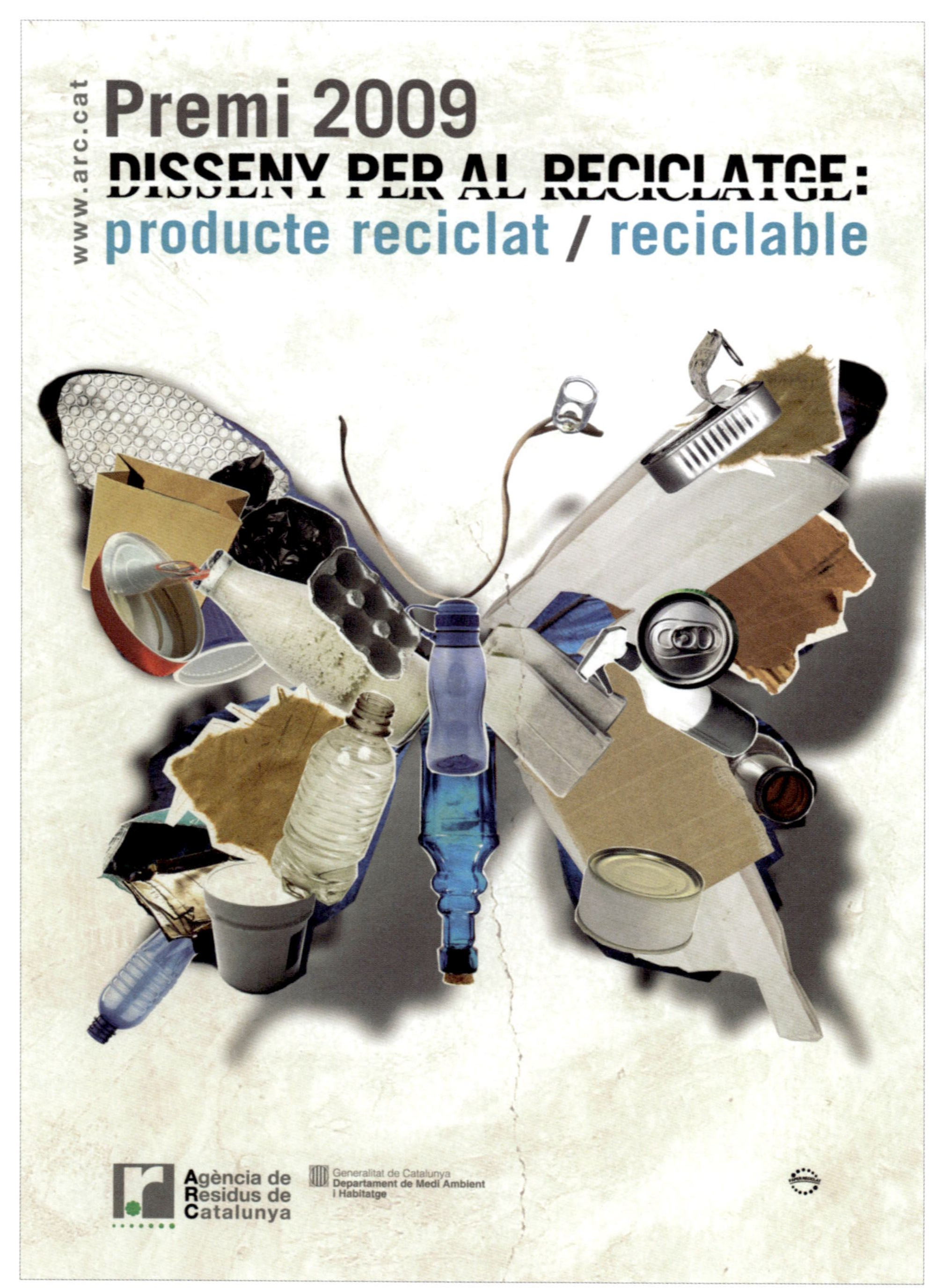
www.arc.cat
Premi 2009
DISSENY PER AL RECICLATGE:
producte reciclat / reciclable
Agència de Residus de Catalunya
Generalitat de Catalunya
Departament de Medi Ambient
i Habitatge

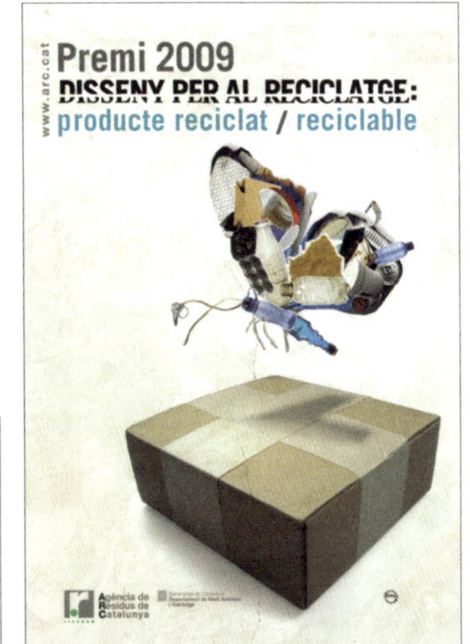

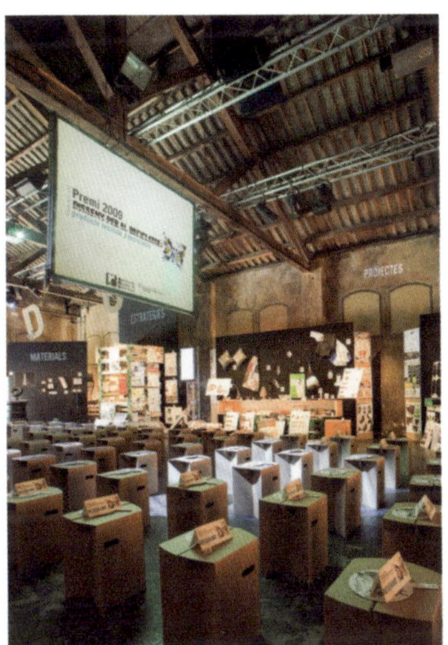

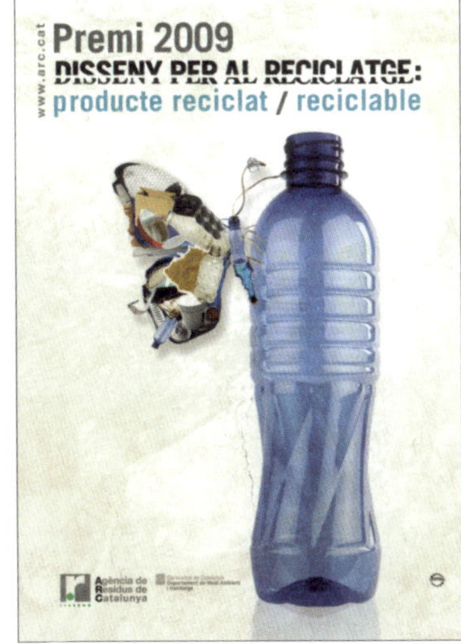

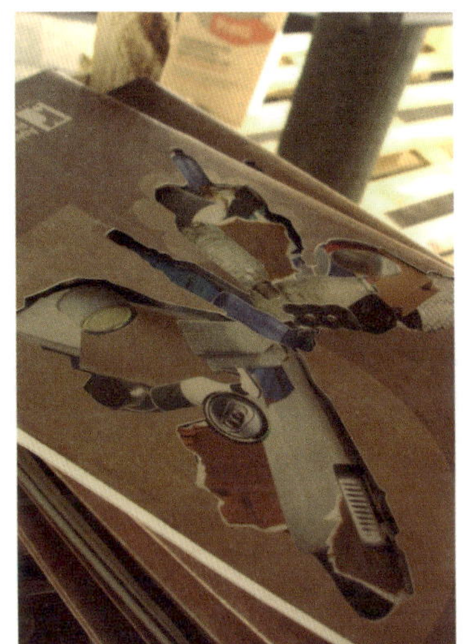

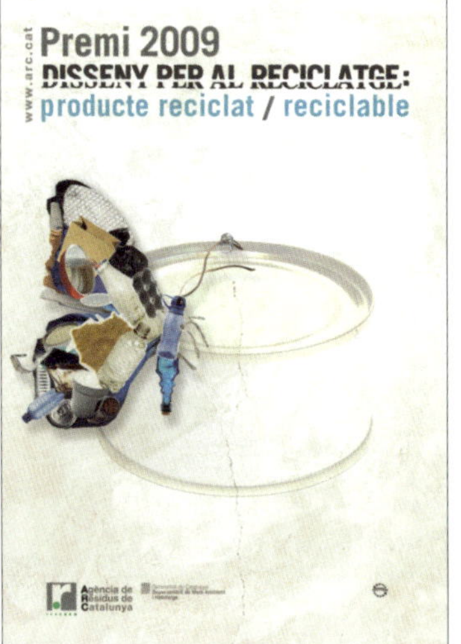

agency/studio: **C'est la vie** / project: Branding of the 2009 Awards Design for recycling. The project includes design and implementation of the 2009 awards ceremony and the design of a travelling exhibition of the 2009 winners / client: Catalan Waste Agency / country: Spain

Making recycled paper instead of new paper uses 64% less energy and uses 58% less water.

Recovered paper can be made into newspapers, magazines, printing paper and cardboard.

Paper products make up the largest part (approximately 40%) of our rubbish.

agency/studio: **Deep LLP** / project: recycling posters. Internal communications to encourage recycling / client: Lend Lease / country: United Kingdom

The energy saved by recycling 1 bottle will power a computer for 25 minutes.

There are about 1,000 milk jugs and other bottles in a recycled plastic park bench.

Making one aluminium drink can from raw materials uses the same amount of energy that it takes to recycle 20.

The energy saved by recycling 1 aluminium drink can is enough to run a television for three hours.

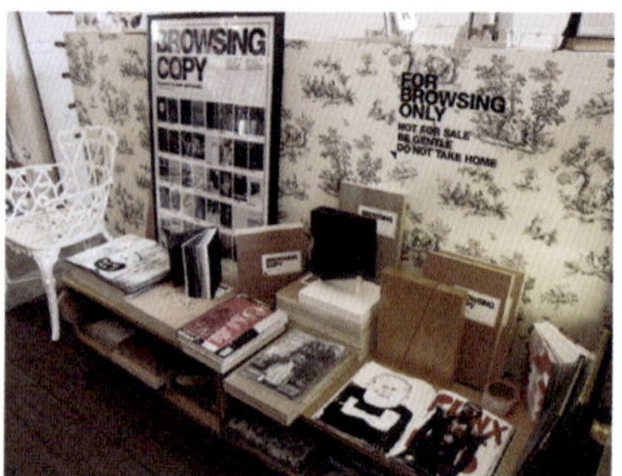

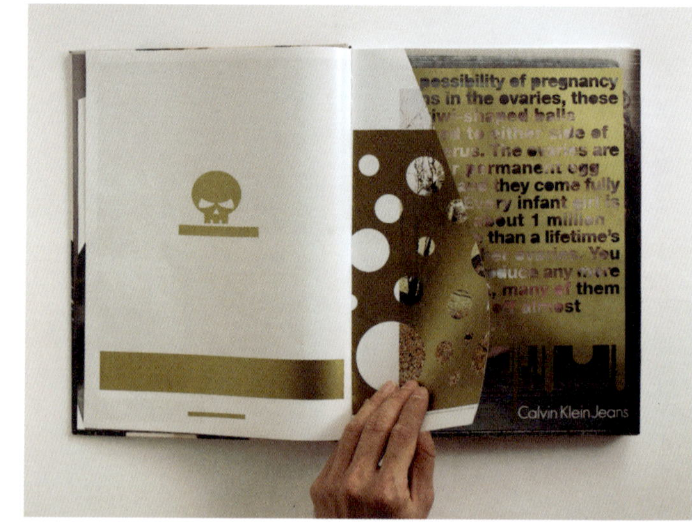

agency/studio: **Beautiful** / project: Browsing Copy: a project to save used books Designers and artists are invited to use the donated books as a canvas for their creativity. / client: A Beautiful Exhibition / country: Singapore

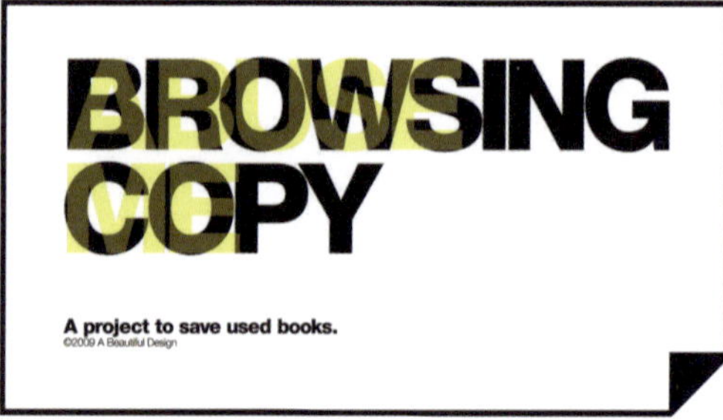

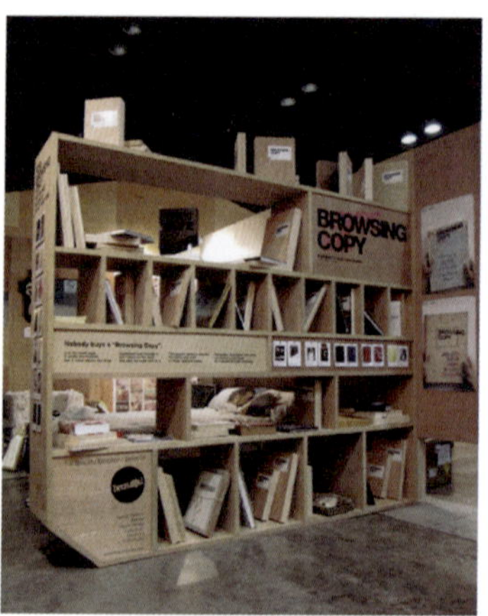

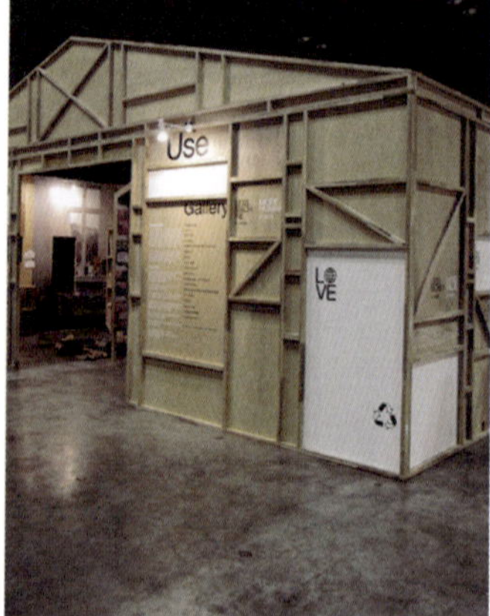

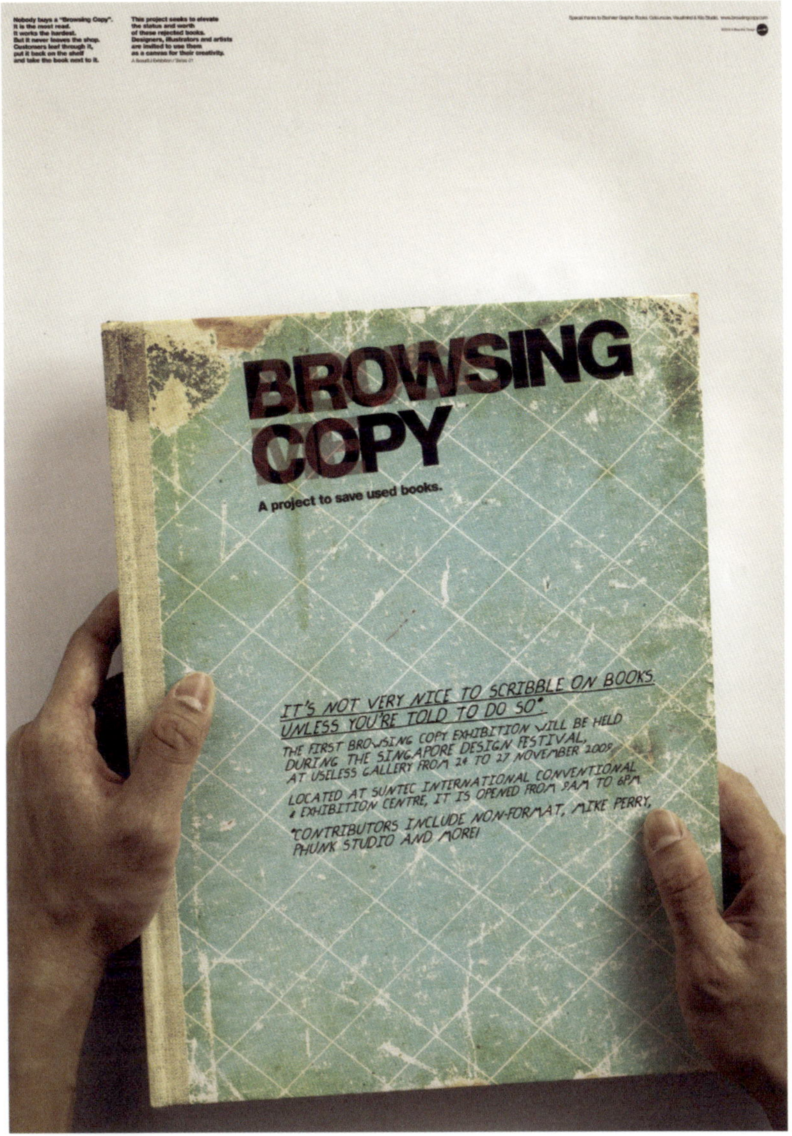

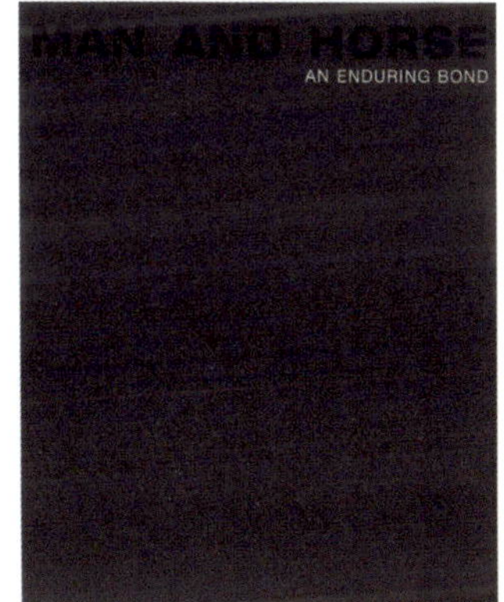
MAN AND HORSE
AN ENDURING BOND

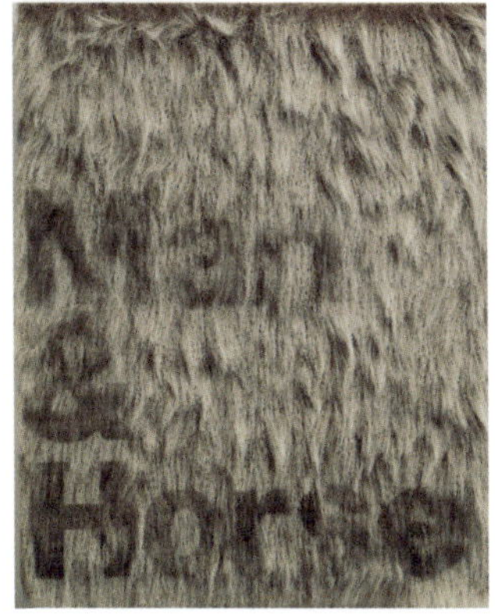
Man
&
Horse

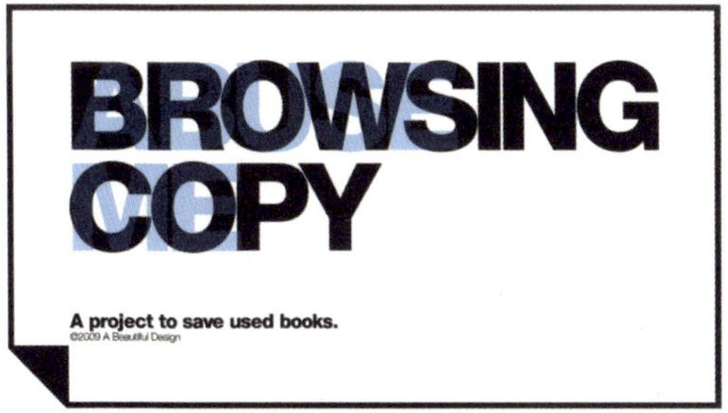

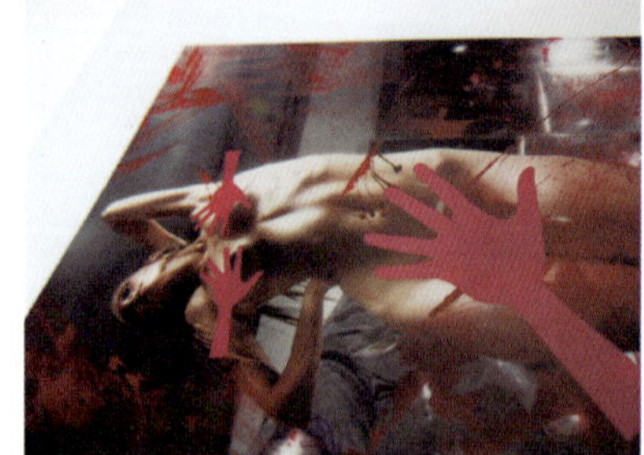

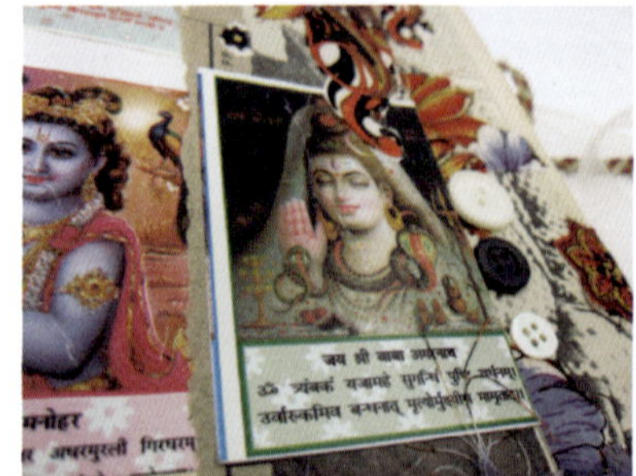

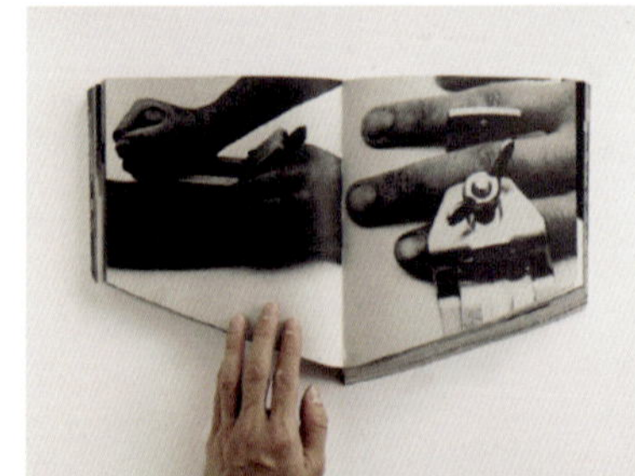

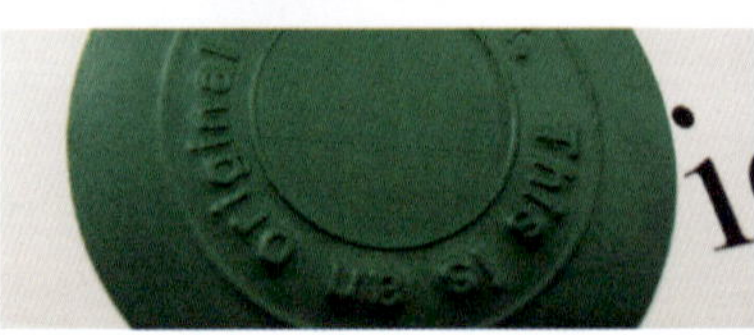

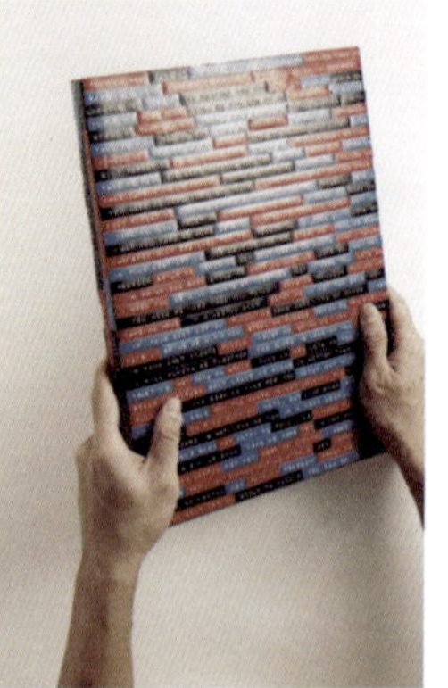

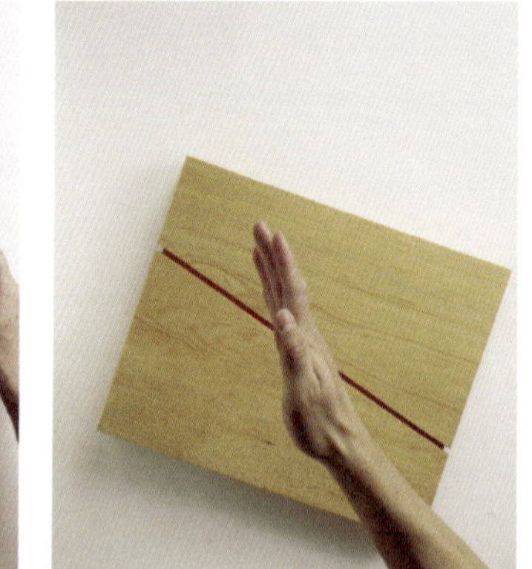

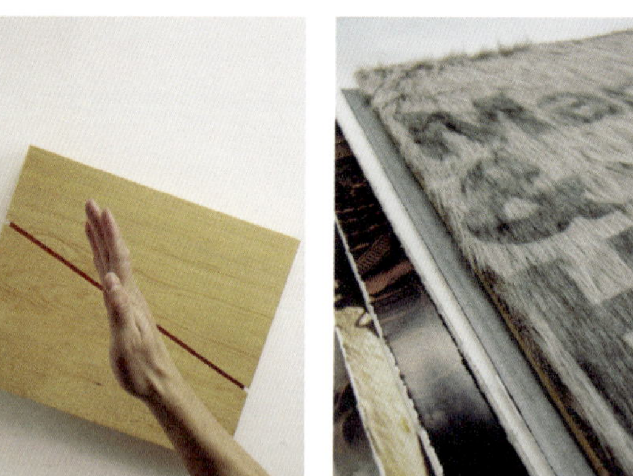

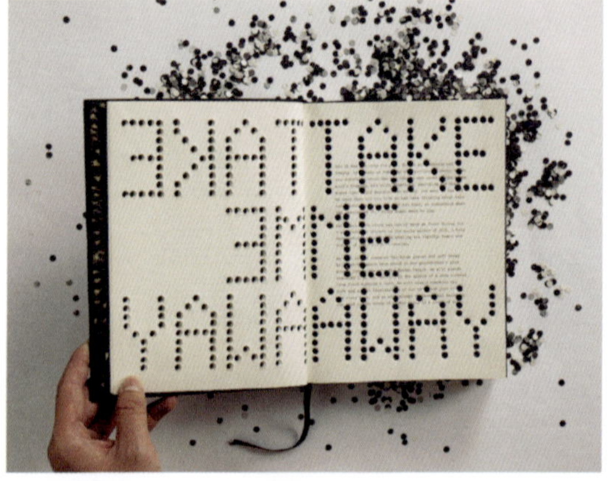
TAKE
ME
AWAY

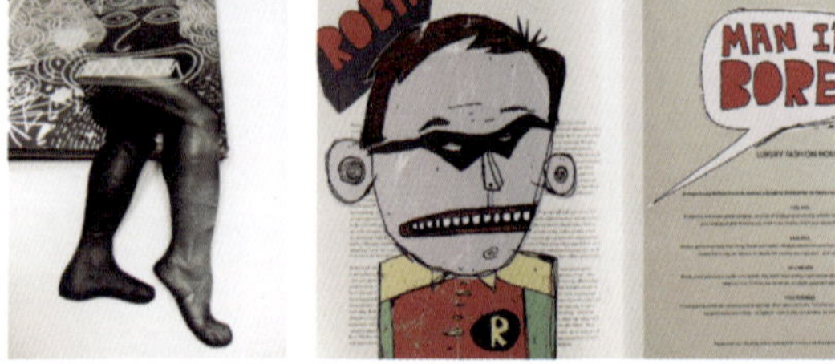

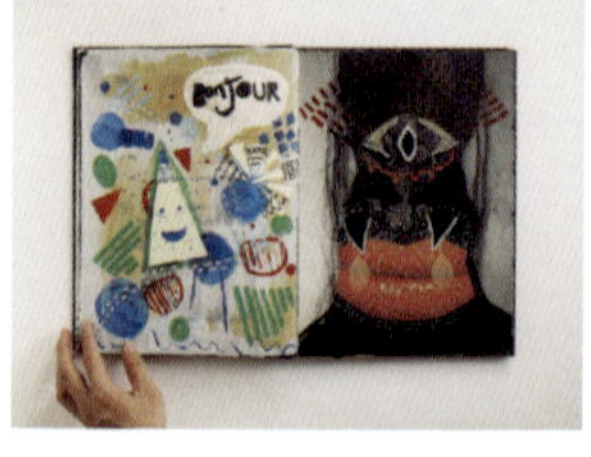

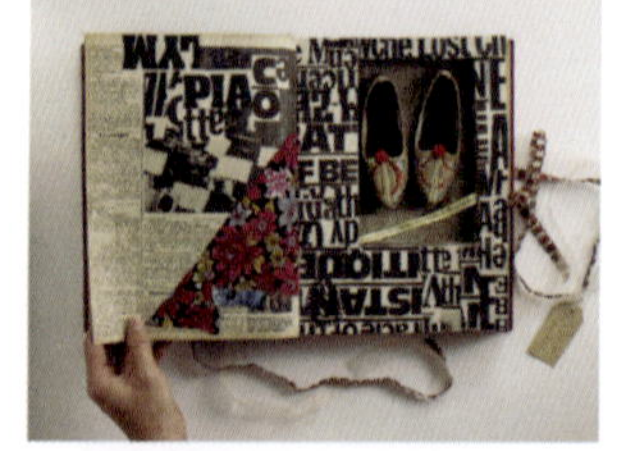

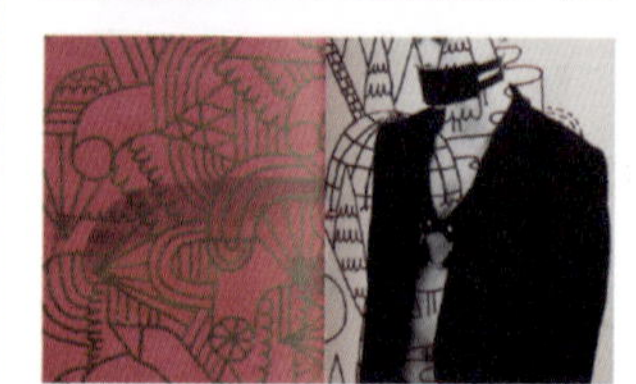
ROBIN
MAN I
BORE

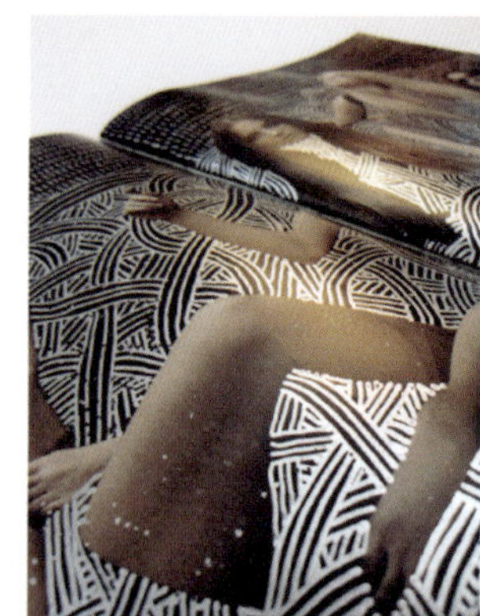

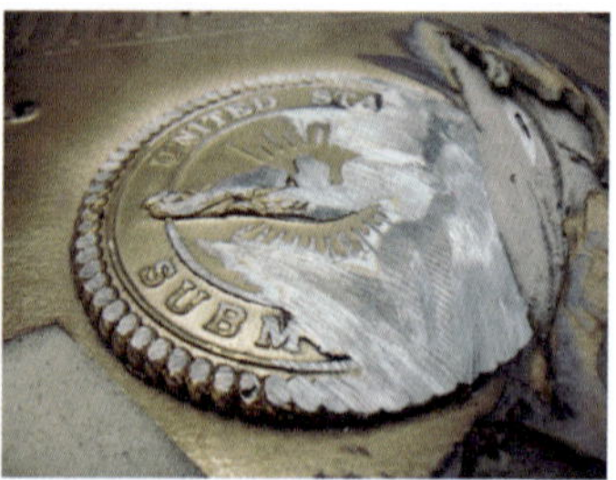

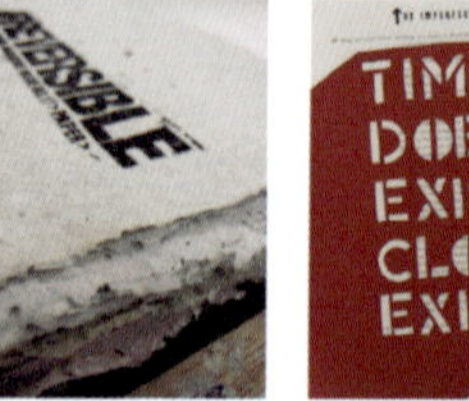
TIME
DOESNT
EXIST
CLOCKS
EXIST

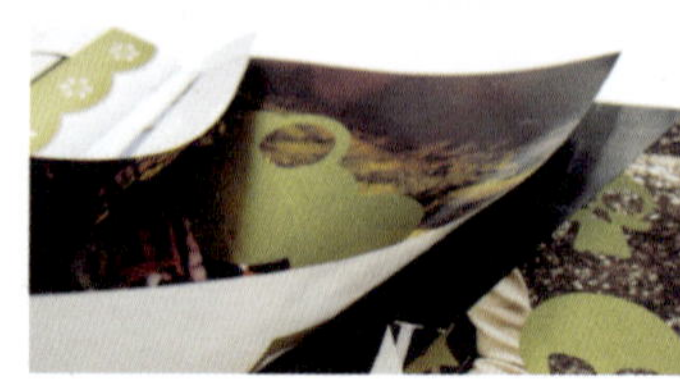

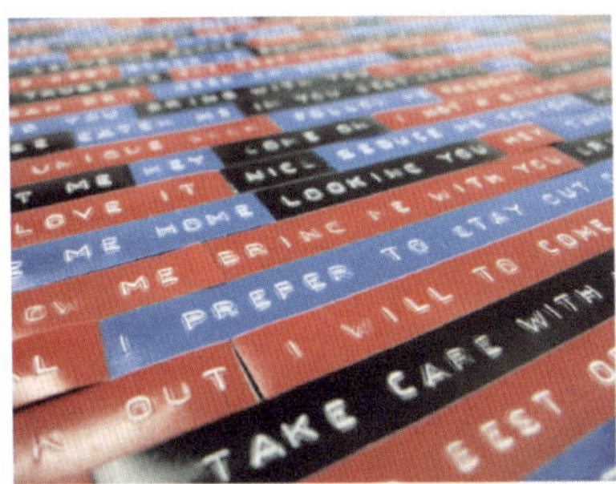
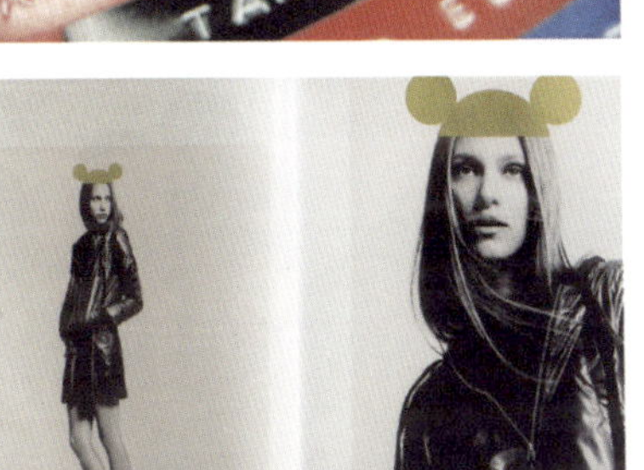
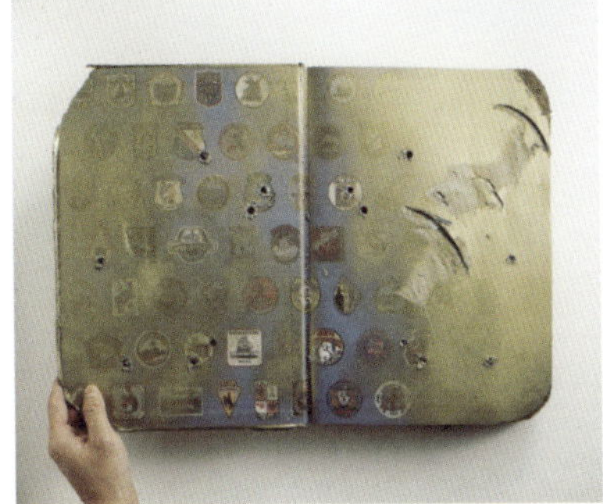
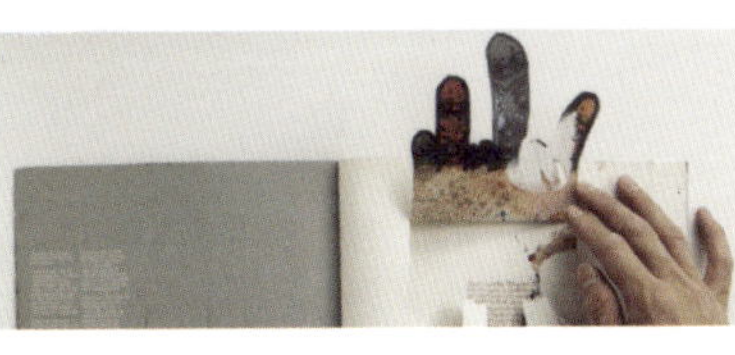
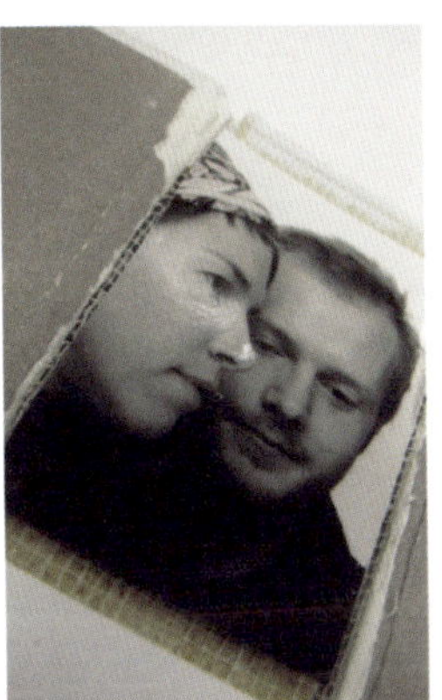
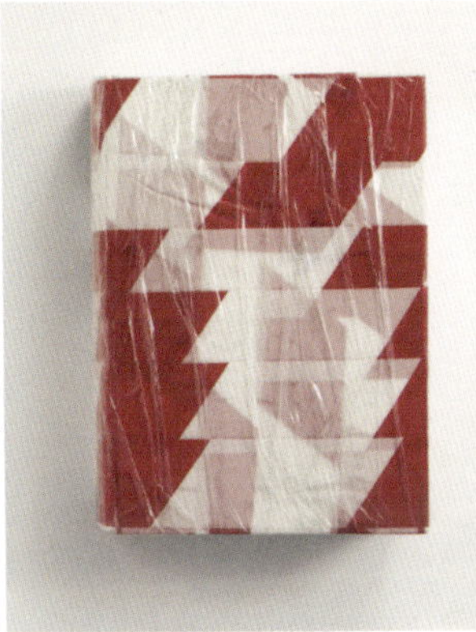
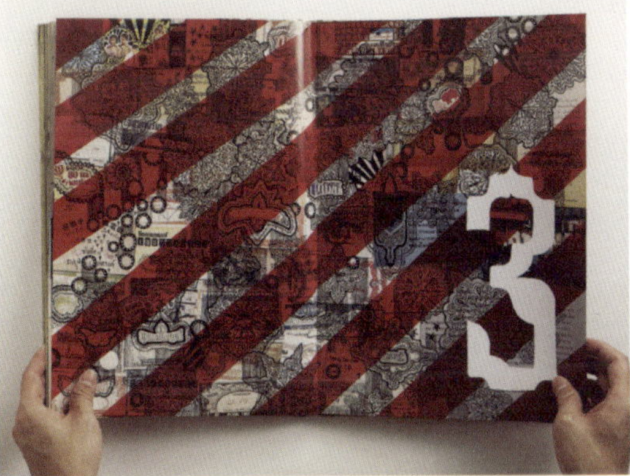
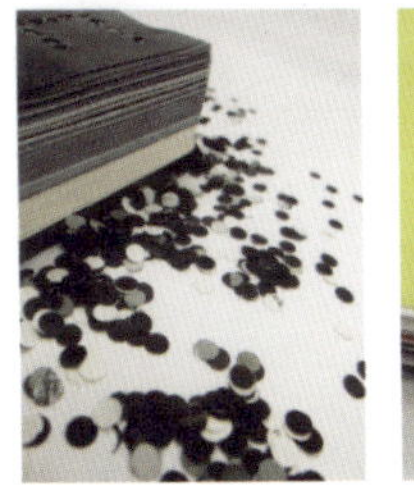
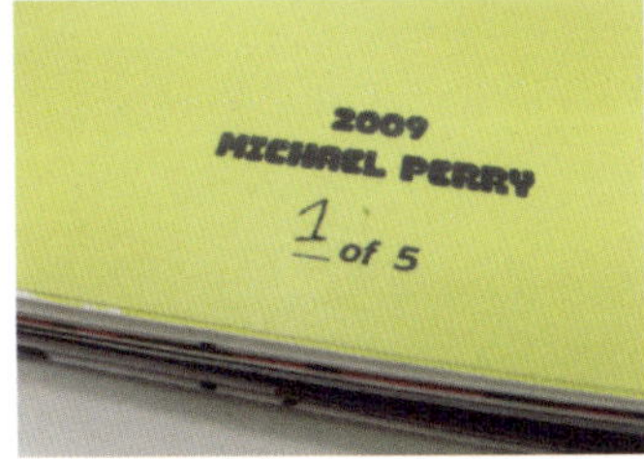

2009
MICHAEL PERRY
1 of 5

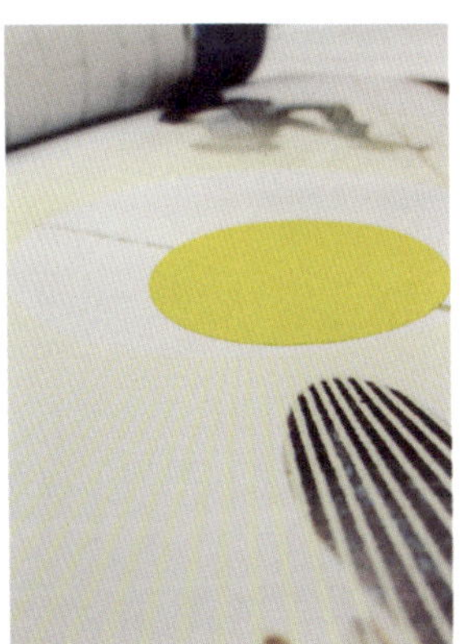
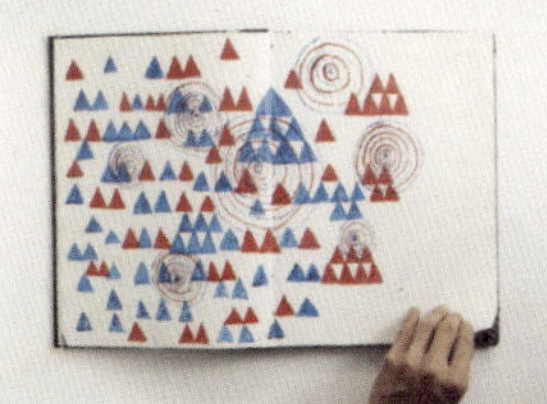
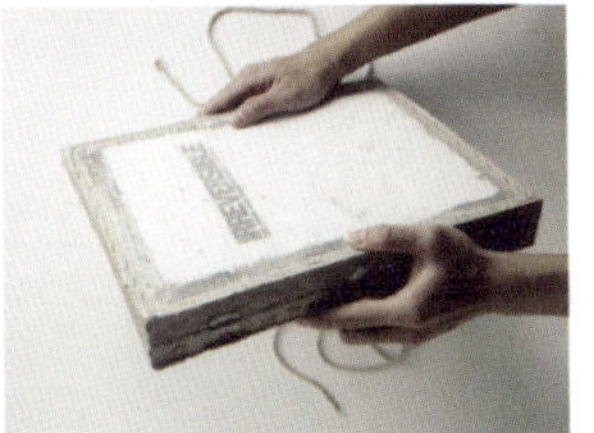
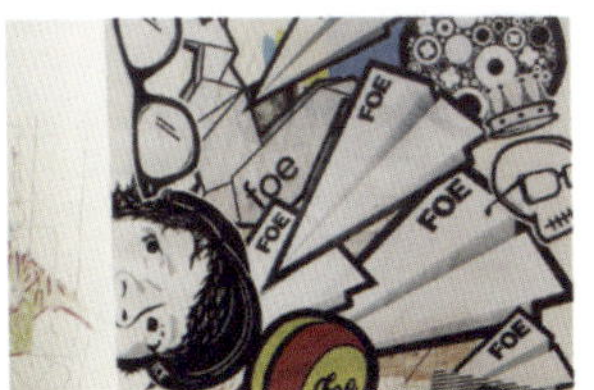
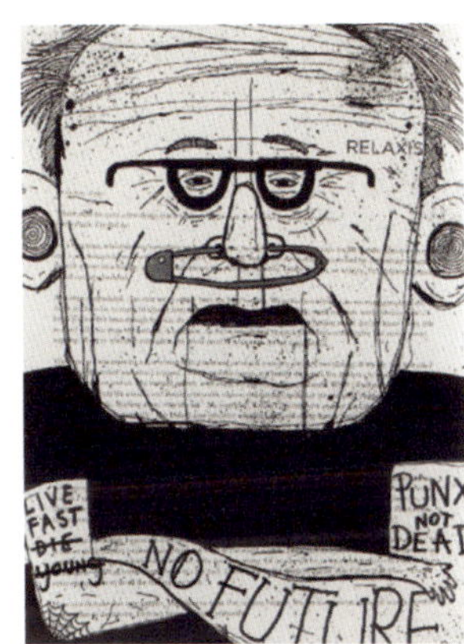

RELAXIS
LIVE FAST DIE YOUNG
PUNX NOT DEAD
NO FUTURE

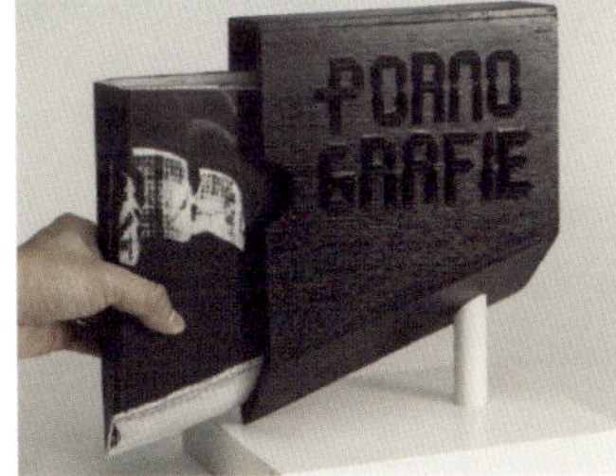

PORNO GRAFIE

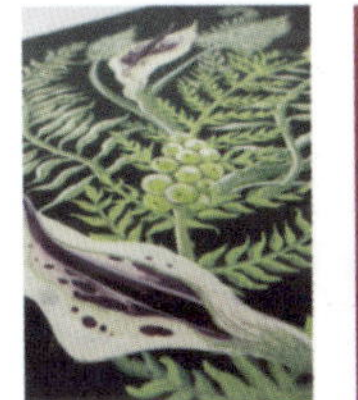
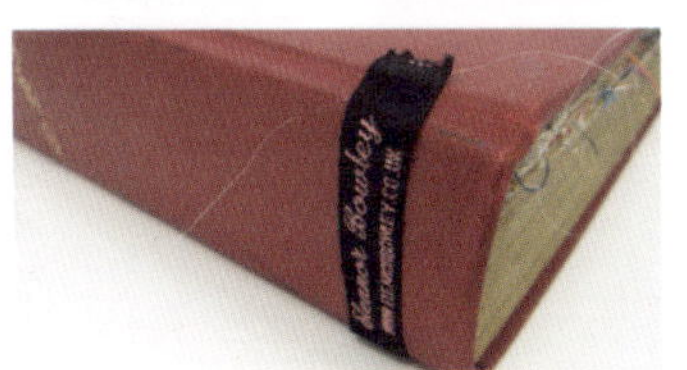

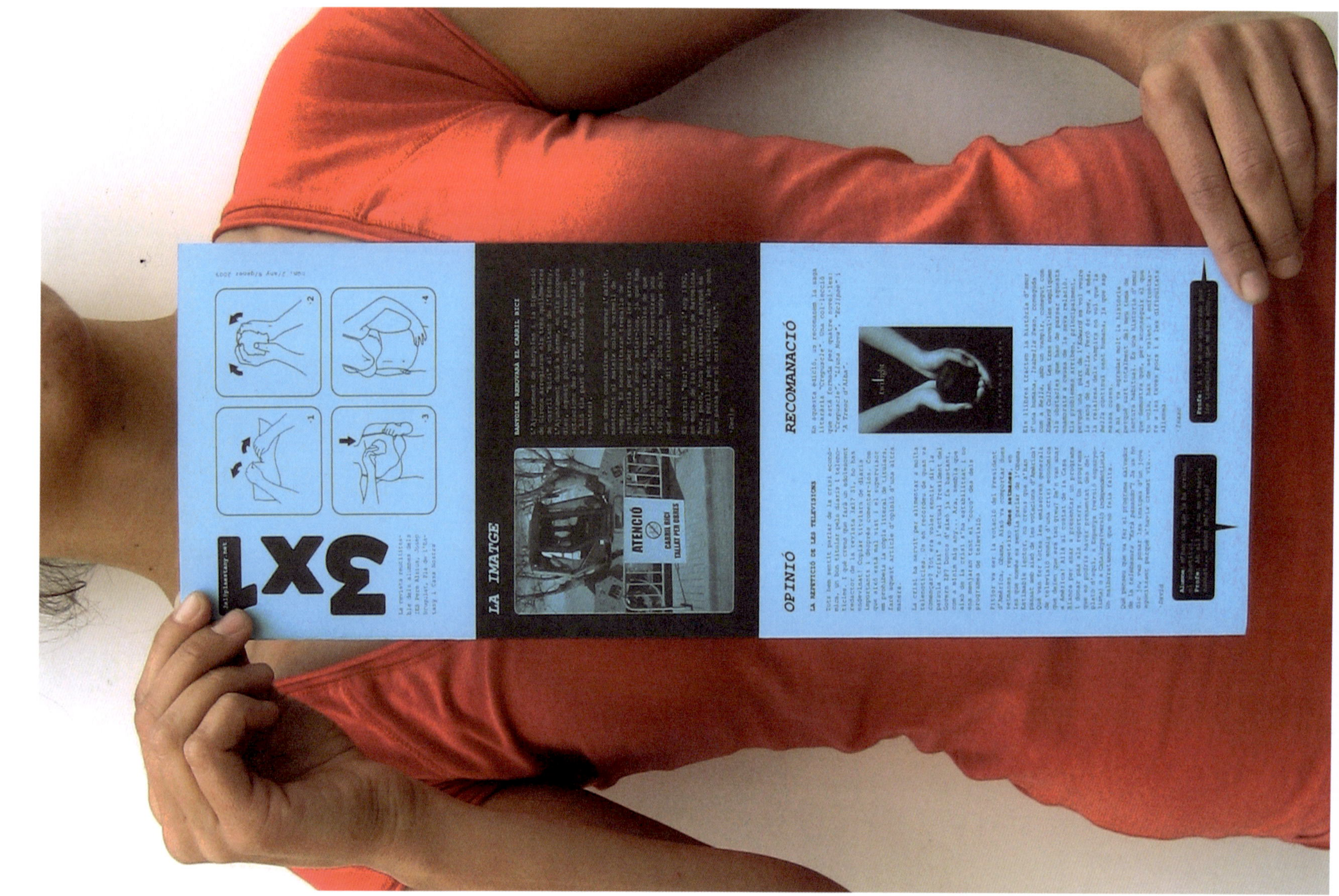

3x1
help1xetlong.net
LA IMATGE
ATENCIÓ
CARRIL BICI
TALLAT PER OBRES
OPINIÓ
RECOMANACIÓ

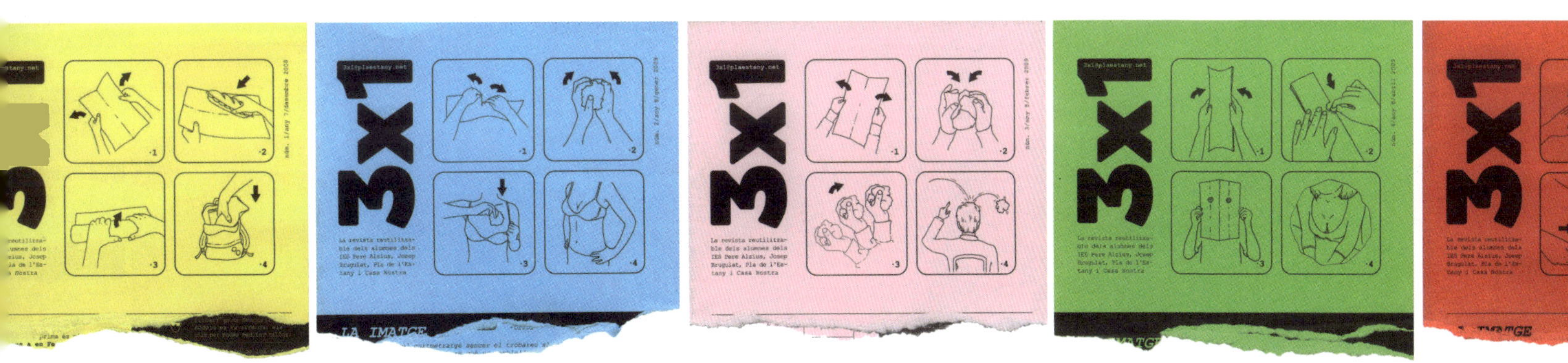

agency/studio: **Nifava** / project: 3x1. Reusable magazine produced by secondary-school students in the Pla de l'Estany area of Catalonia. Each edition proposes a new idea for recycling the magazine's paper based on the hypothetical needs of its readers. / client: Banyoles Town Council and Pla de l'Estany Country Council / country: Spain

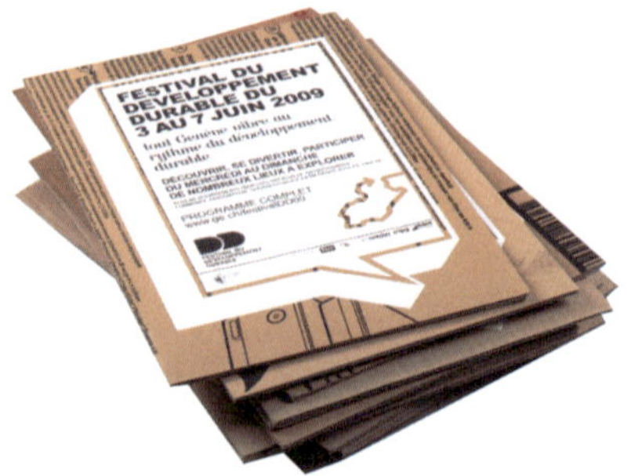
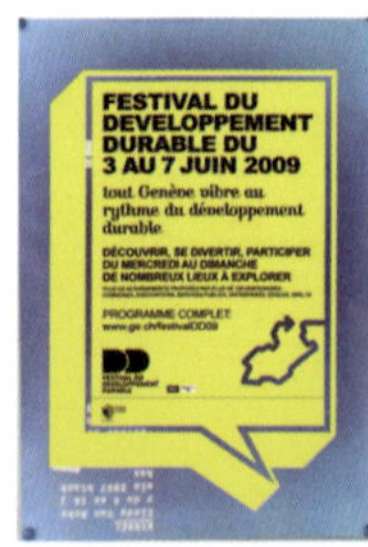
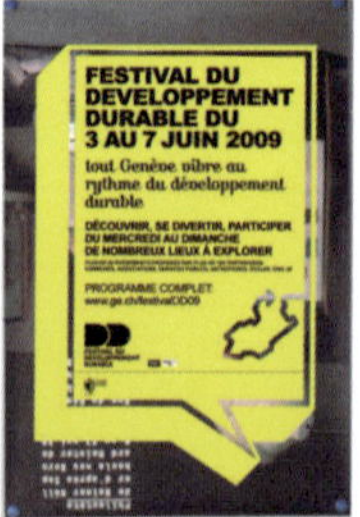
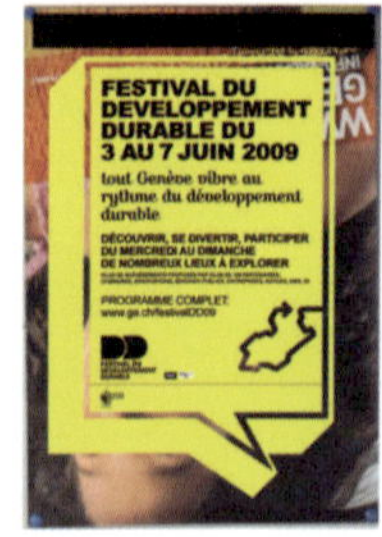
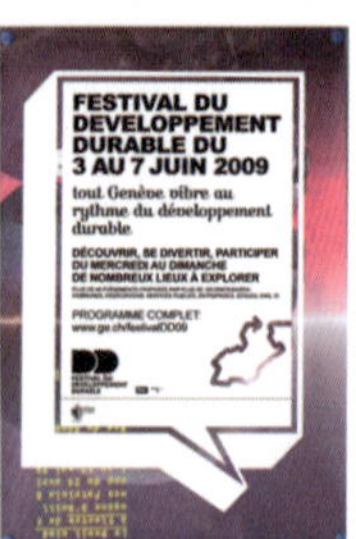
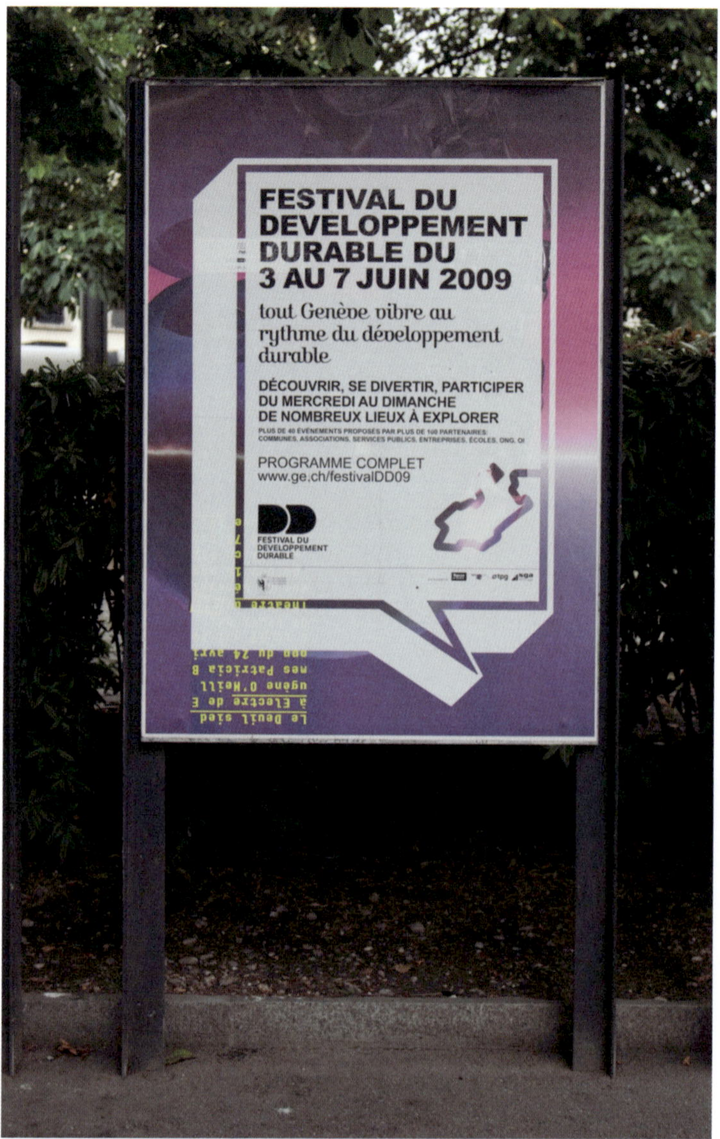

agency/studio: **Superposition** / project: A campaign for the Sustainability Festival which took place in June 2009 in Geneva. The strategy was to reduce the impact of the festival by reusing paper and cardboard for the posters and public transport boards. The used posters were overprinted using two-colour screen printing. / client: State of Geneva / country: Switzerland

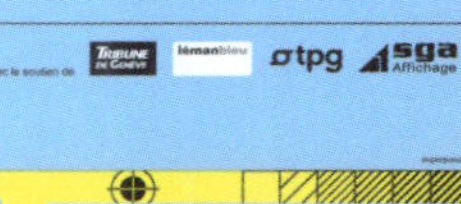
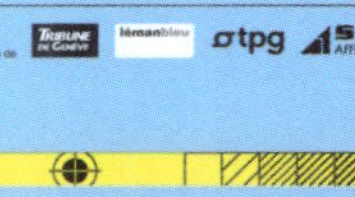
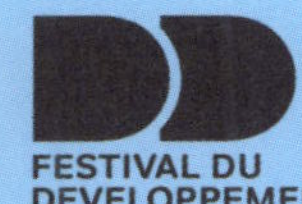
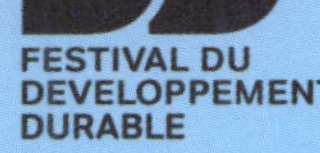
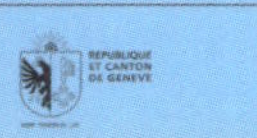

FESTIVAL DU
DEVELOPPEMENT
DURABLE DU
3 AU 7 JUIN 2009
tout Genève vibre au
rythme du développement
durable
DÉCOUVRIR, SE DIVERTIR, PARTICIPER
DU MERCREDI AU DIMANCHE
DE NOMBREUX LIEUX À EXPLORER
PLUS DE 40 ÉVÉNEMENTS PROPOSÉS PAR PLUS DE 100 PARTENAIRES:
COMMUNES, ASSOCIATIONS, SERVICES PUBLICS, ENTREPRISES, ÉCOLES, ONG, OI
PROGRAMME COMPLET
www.ge.ch/festivalDD09
DD
FESTIVAL DU
DEVELOPPEMENT
DURABLE
RÉPUBLIQUE ET CANTON DE GENÈVE
avec le soutien de
otpg
sga Affichage
SUPERPOSITION
ROUTE DES ACACIAS 43
1227 LES ACACIAS
INFO@SUPERPOSITION.INFO
WWW.SUPERPOSITION.INFO
022 300 67 78
09.05.08
205x218.ind

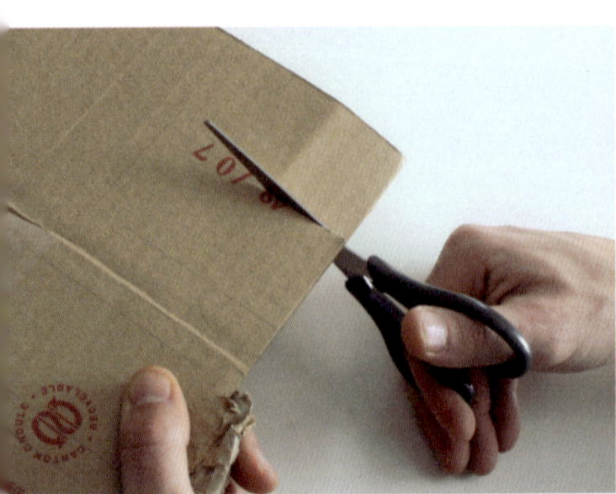
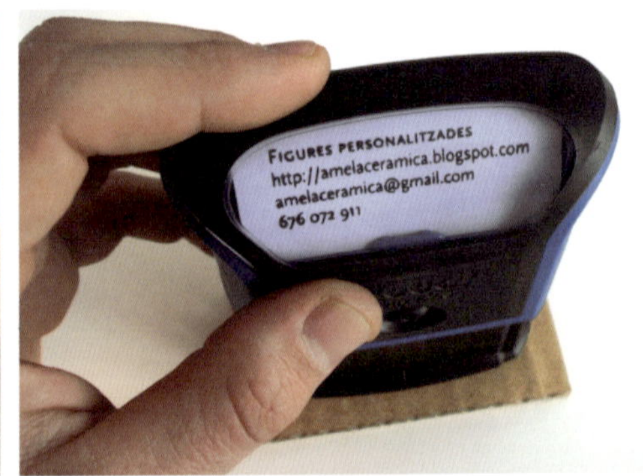

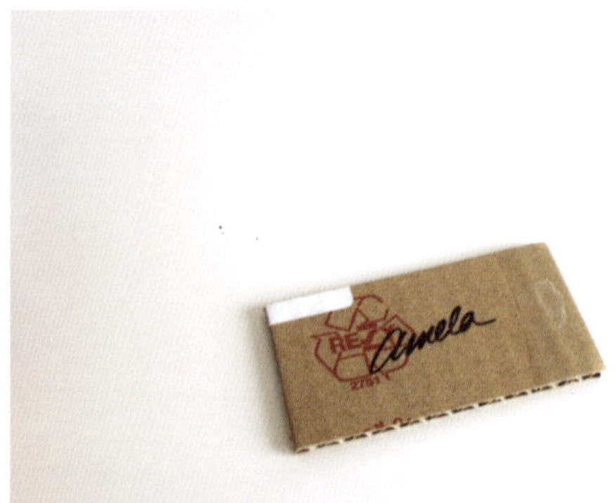
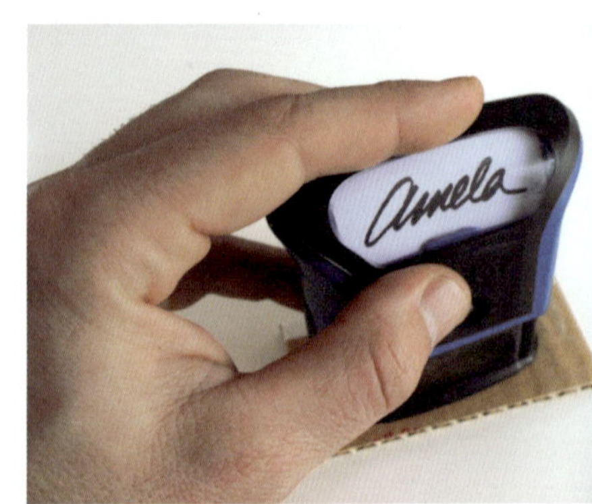

agency/studio: **Nifava** / project: Cards for an artisan specialising in producing customised ceramic figures. The cards were made on reused cardboard and the graphics were made using rubber stamps and coloured stickers. / client: Isabel Amela / country: Spain

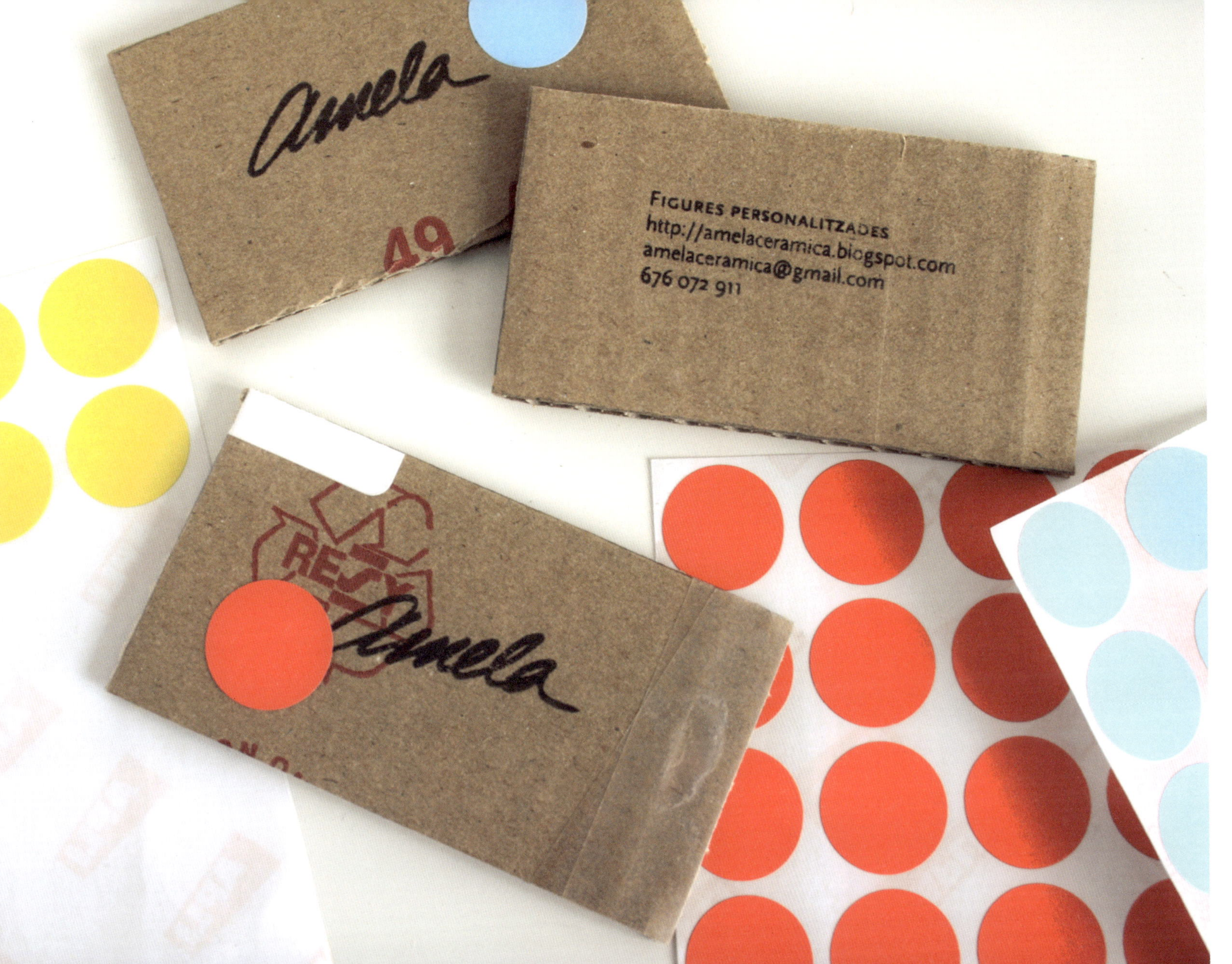

Amela
49
FIGURES PERSONALITZADES
http://amelaceramica.blogspot.com
amelaceramica@gmail.com
676 072 911
Amela

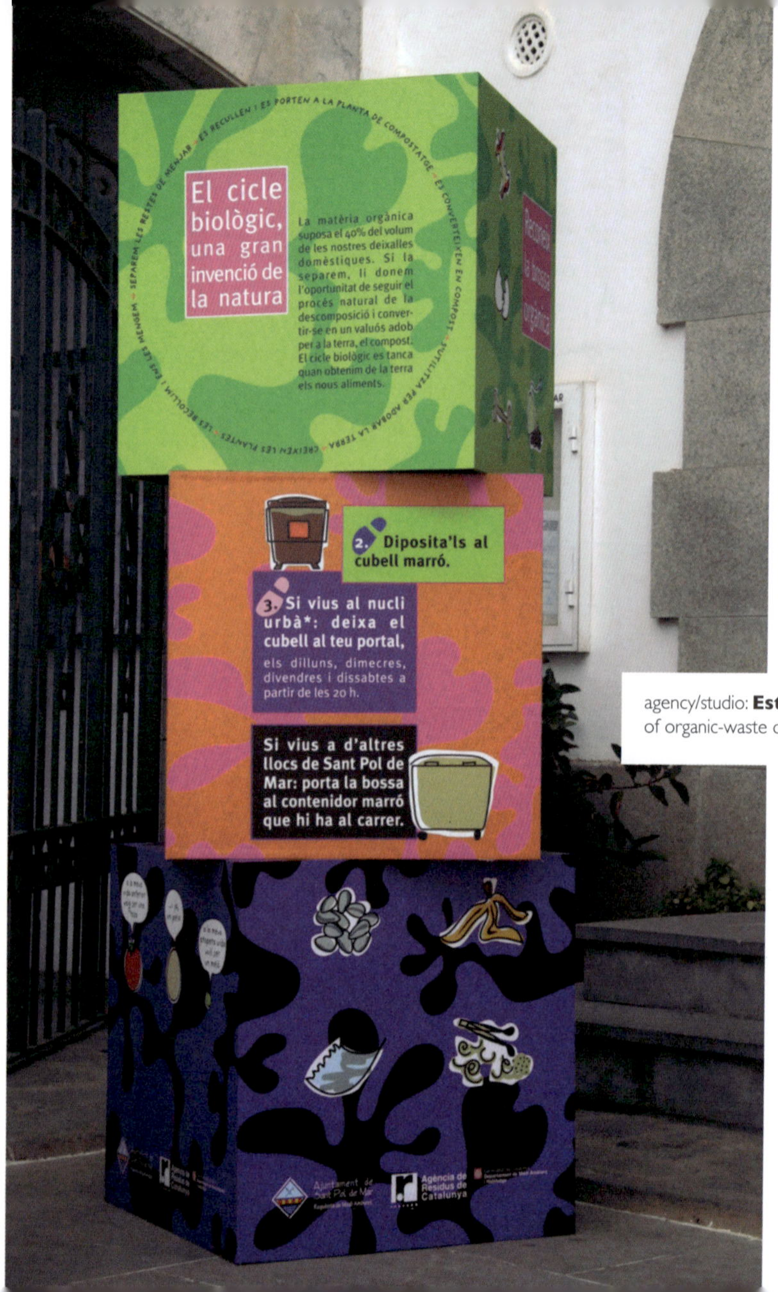

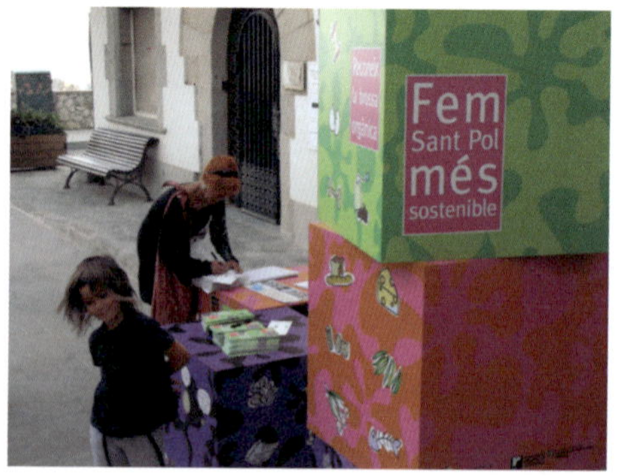

agency/studio: **Estudio Eckert+Zúñiga** / project: concept, design and graphic application of the campaign for the introduction of organic-waste collection in the town of Sant Pol de Mar / client: Sant Pol de Mar Town Council / country: Spain

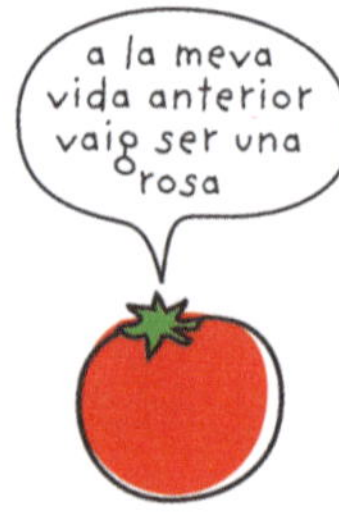

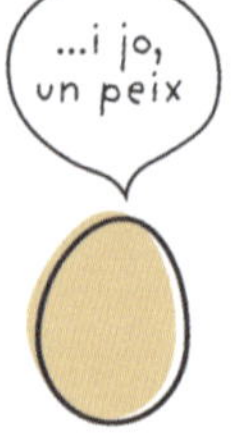

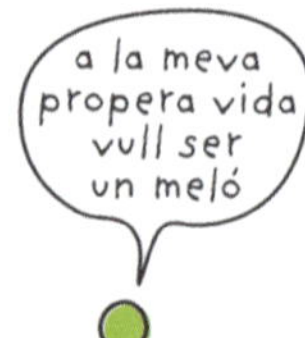

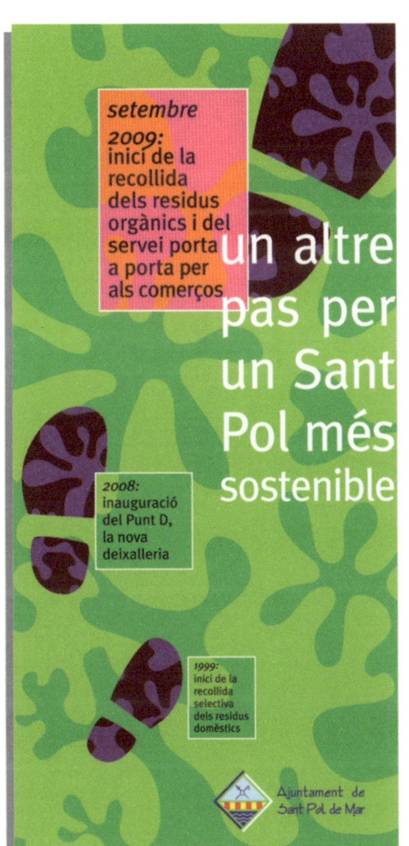

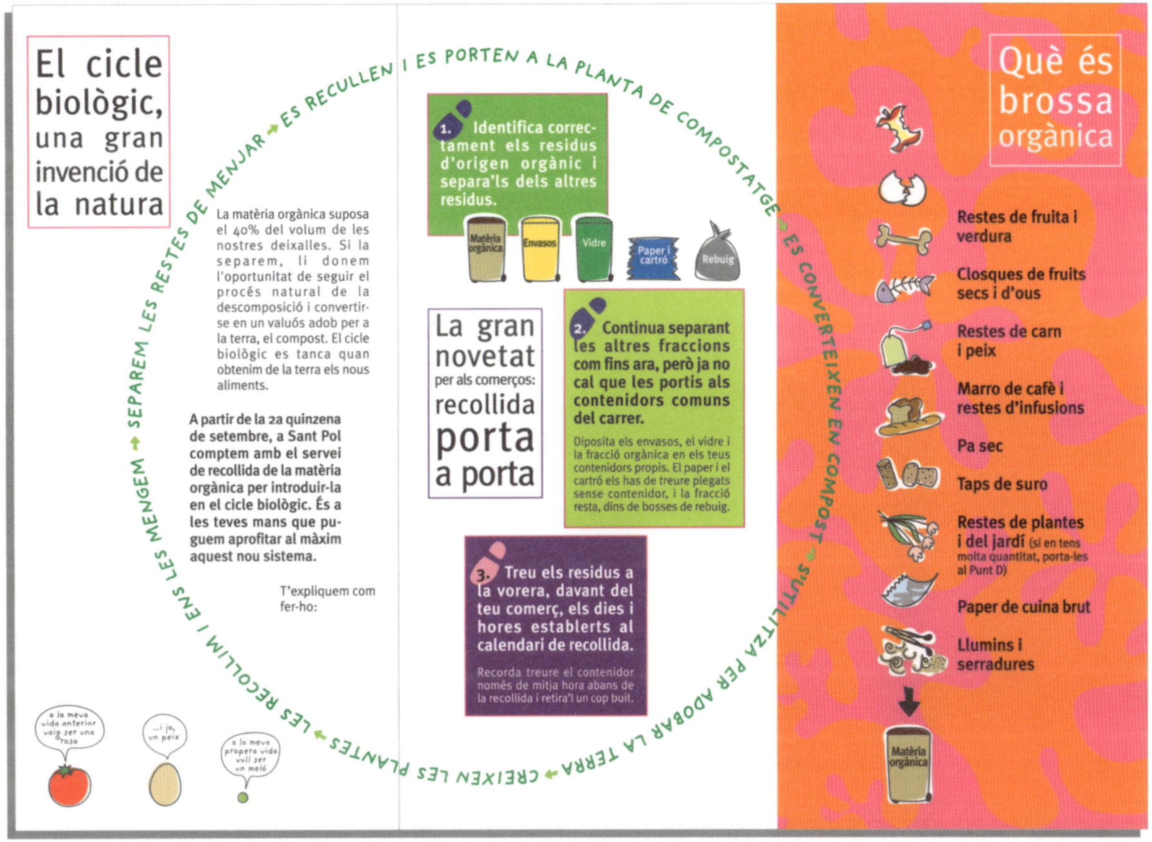

El cicle biològic, una gran invenció de la natura

La matèria orgànica suposa el 40% del volum de les nostres deixalles. Si la separem, li donem l'oportunitat de seguir el procés natural de la descomposició i convertir-se en un valuós adob per a la terra, el compost. El cicle biològic es tanca quan obtenim de la terra els nous aliments.

A partir de la 2a quinzena de setembre, a Sant Pol comptem amb el servei de recollida de la matèria orgànica per introduir-la en el cicle biològic. És a les teves mans que puguem aprofitar al màxim aquest nou sistema.

T'expliquem com fer-ho:

1. Identifica correctament els residus d'origen orgànic i separa'ls dels altres residus.

La gran novetat per als comerços: recollida porta a porta

2. Continua separant les altres fraccions com fins ara, però ja no cal que les portis als contenidors comuns del carrer.

Diposita els envasos, el vidre i la fracció orgànica en els teus contenidors propis. El paper i el cartró els has de treure plegats sense contenidor, i la fracció resta, dins de bosses de rebuig.

3. Treu els residus a la vorera, davant del teu comerç, els dies i hores establerts al calendari de recollida.

Recorda treure el contenidor només de mitja hora abans de la recollida i retira'l un cop buit.

Què és brossa orgànica

- Restes de fruita i verdura
- Closques de fruits secs i d'ous
- Restes de carn i peix
- Marro de cafè i restes d'infusions
- Pa sec
- Taps de suro
- Restes de plantes i del jardí (si en tens molta quantitat, porta-les al Punt D)
- Paper de cuina brut
- Llumins i serradures

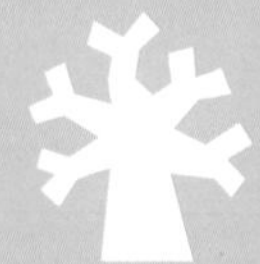

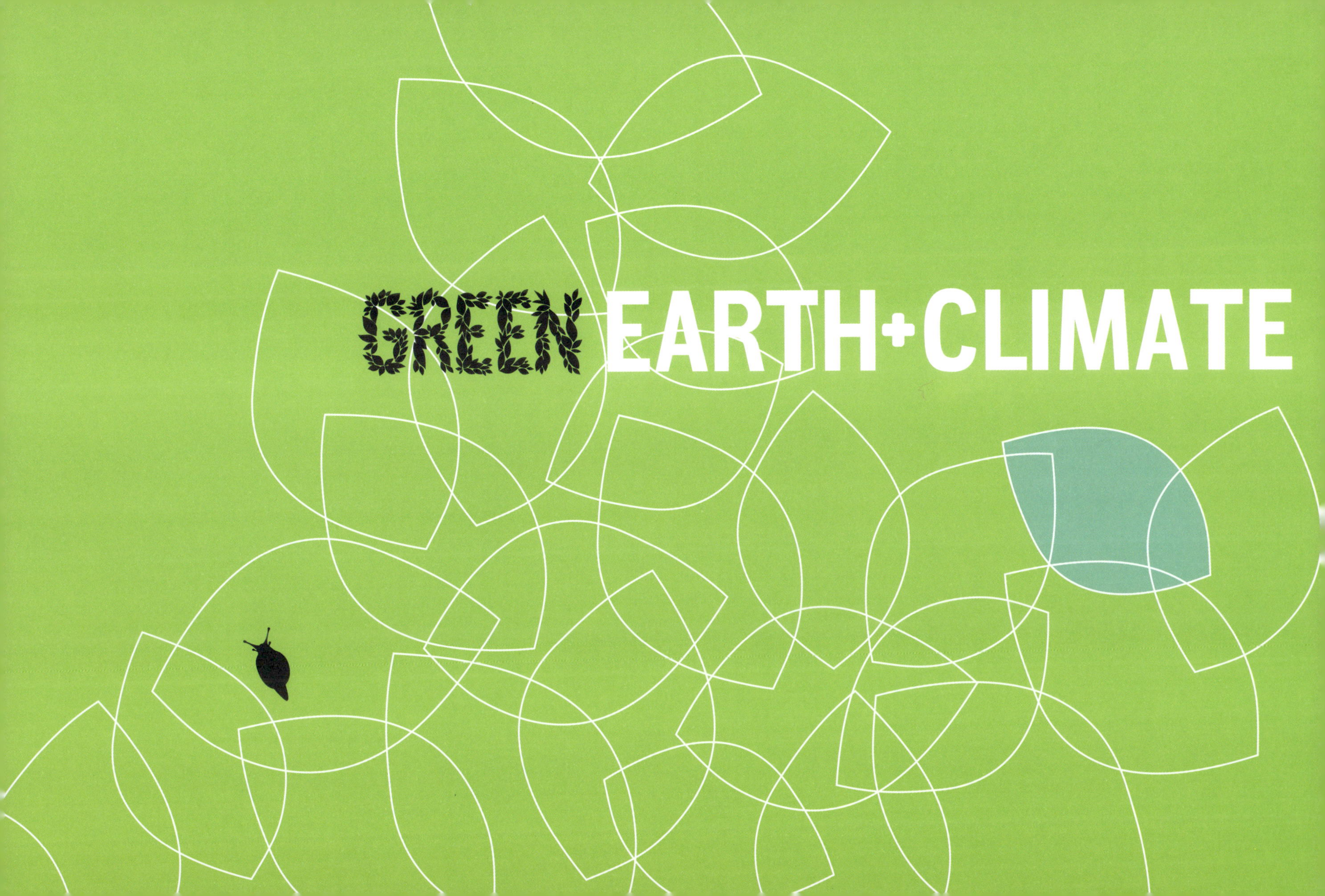

GREEN EARTH+CLIMATE

author: **Angieneering** / project: Planet Earth - directions for use. A medical box, including four leaflets (atmosphere, biosphere, hydrosphere, lithosphere/pedosphere). These leaflets explain how to use our planet correctly. / country: Austria

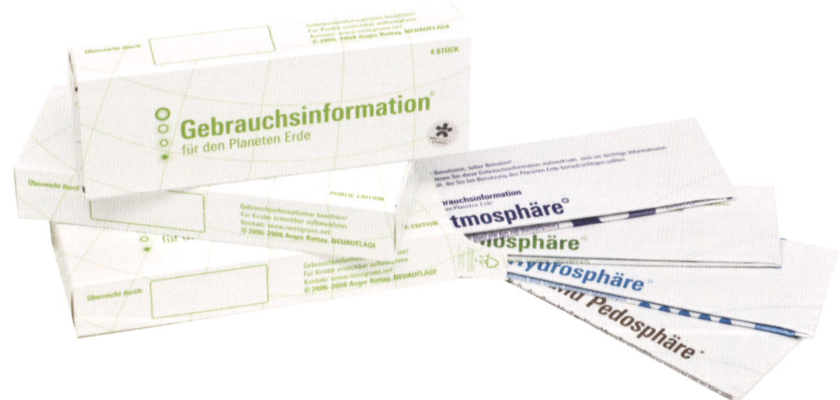

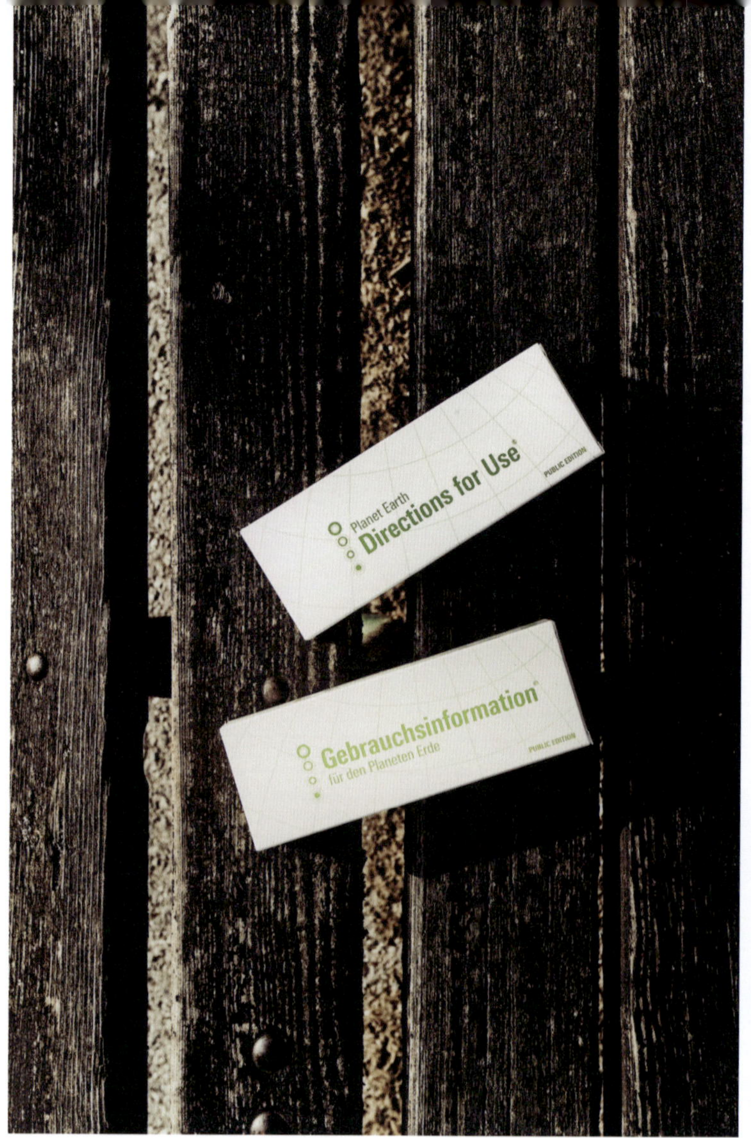

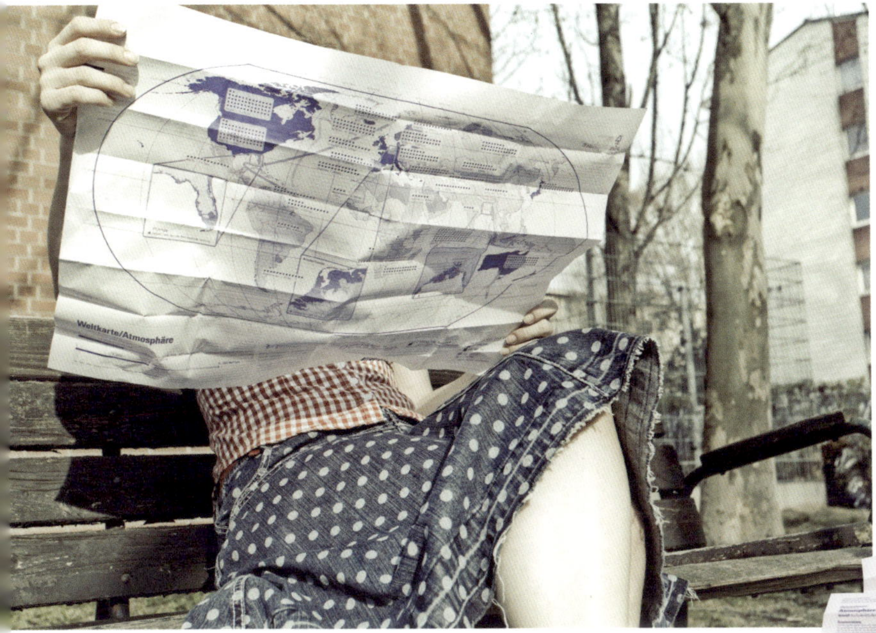

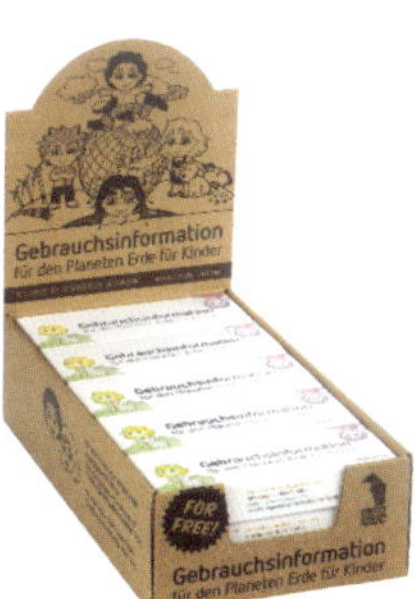
Gebrauchsinformation
für den Planeten Erde für Kinder
FOR FREE!
Gebrauchsinformation
für den Planeten Erde für Kinder

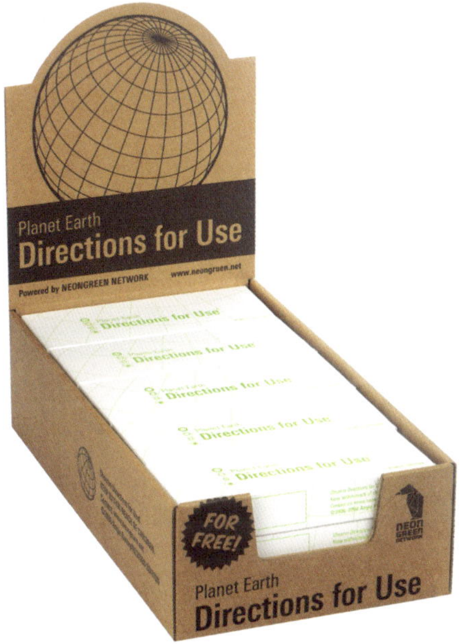

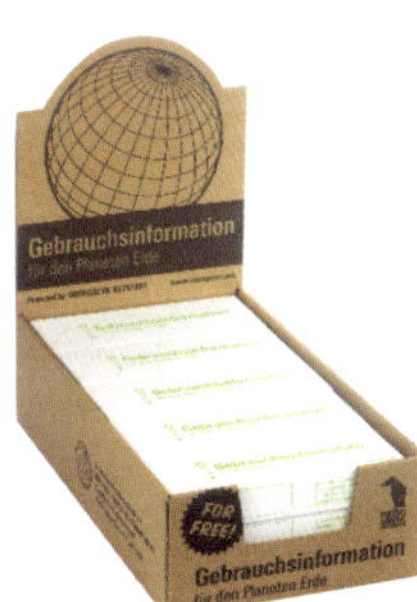
Gebrauchsinformation
für den Planeten Erde
FOR FREE!
Gebrauchsinformation
für den Planeten Erde

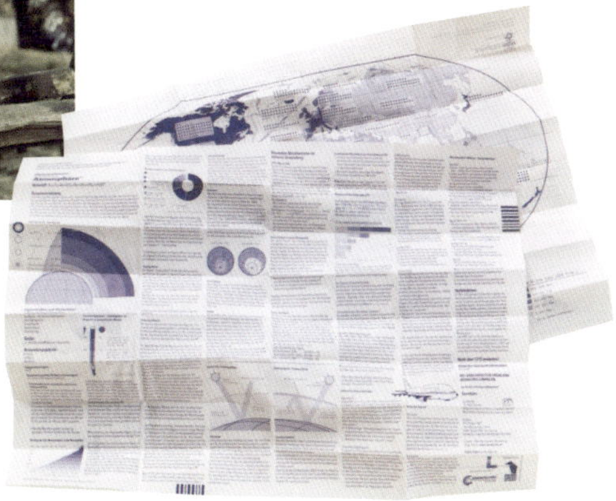

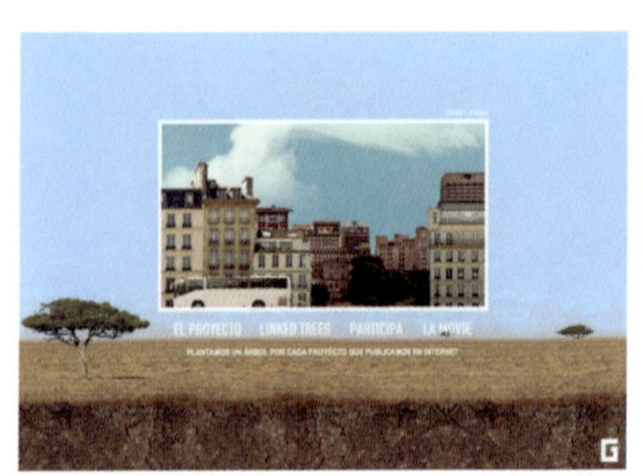
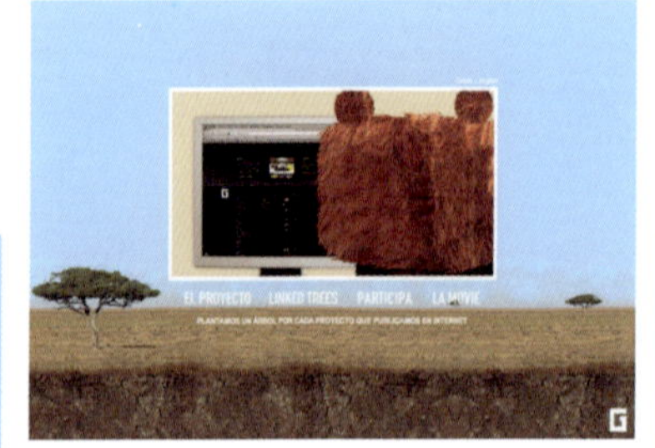
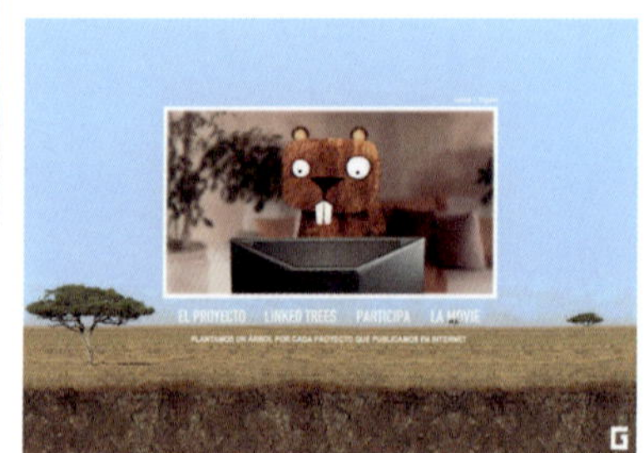
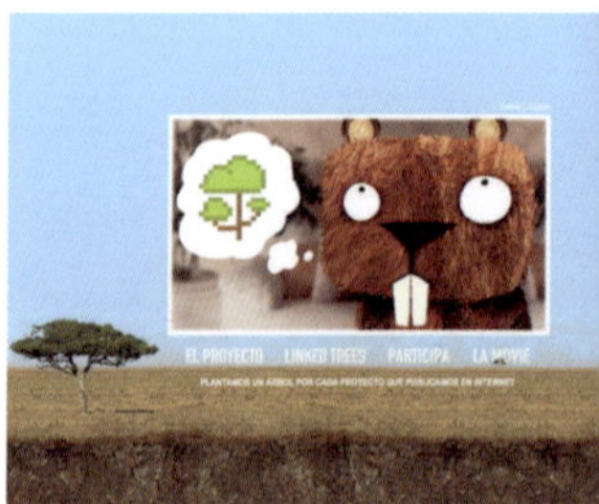

agency/studio: **Grapa.ws** / project: Link a Tree. Plant a tree for each project we publish on the Internet. Pure romanticism or environmental awareness? A bit of both. / client: Grapa.ws / country: Spain

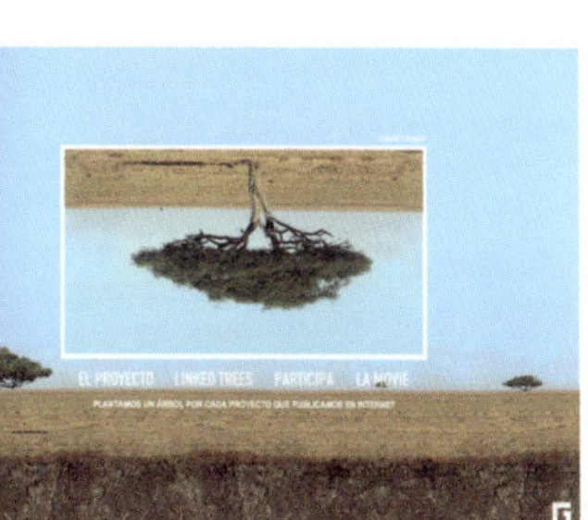

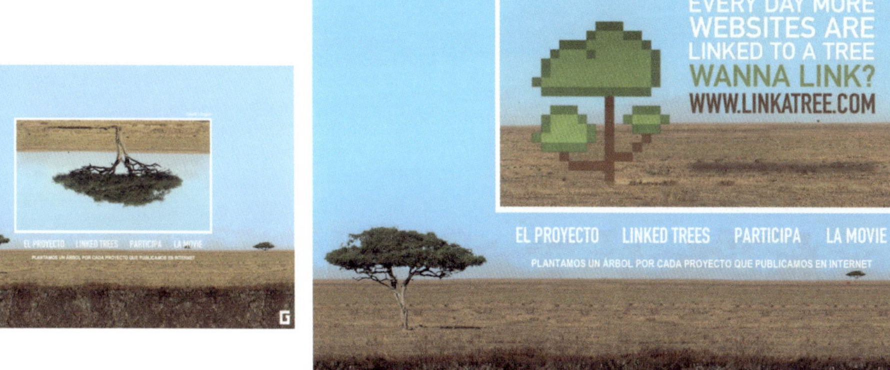
EVERY DAY MORE
WEBSITES ARE
LINKED TO A TREE
WANNA LINK?
WWW.LINKATREE.COM
EL PROYECTO   LINKED TREES   PARTICIPA   LA MOVIE
PLANTAMOS UN ÁRBOL POR CADA PROYECTO QUE PUBLICAMOS EN INTERNET

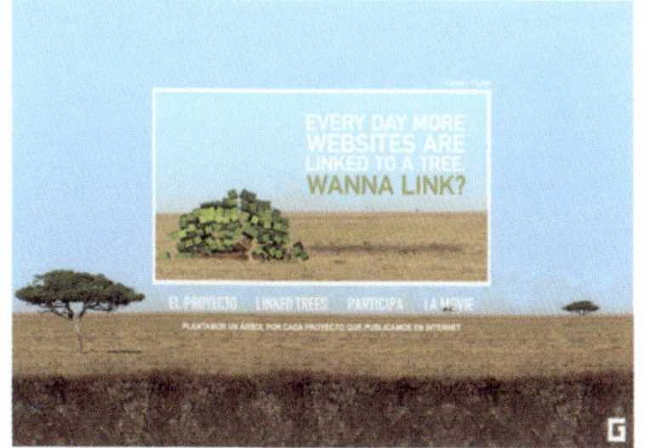
EVERY DAY MORE
WEBSITES ARE
LINKED TO A TREE
WANNA LINK?

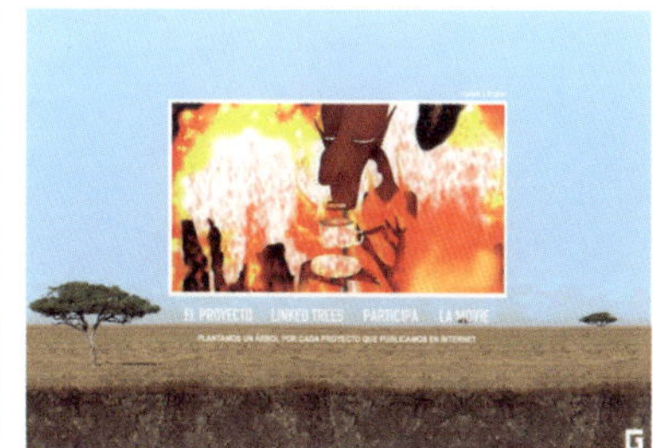

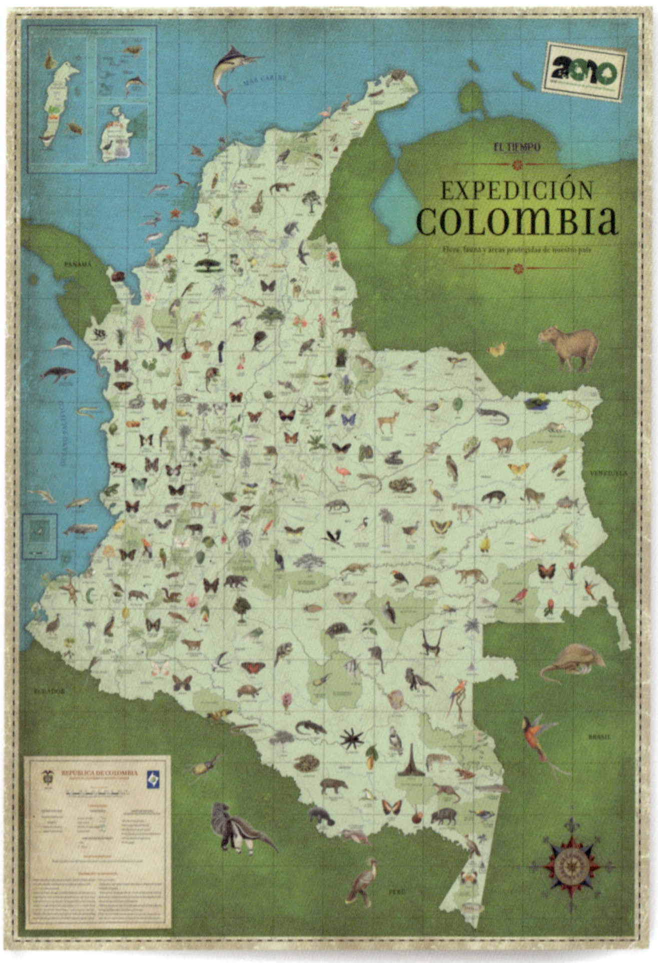

author: **Sandra Restrepo** / project: Expedición Colombia. A book with stickers and a map on biodiversity in Colombia. / client: El Tiempo / country: Colombia

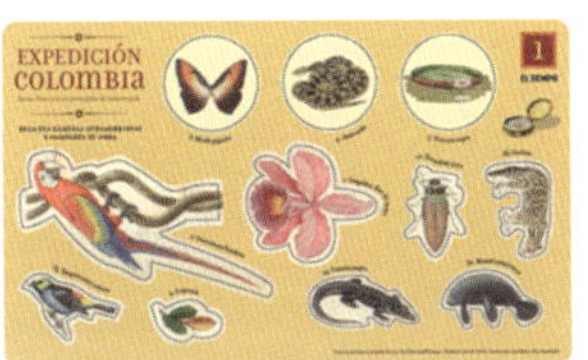
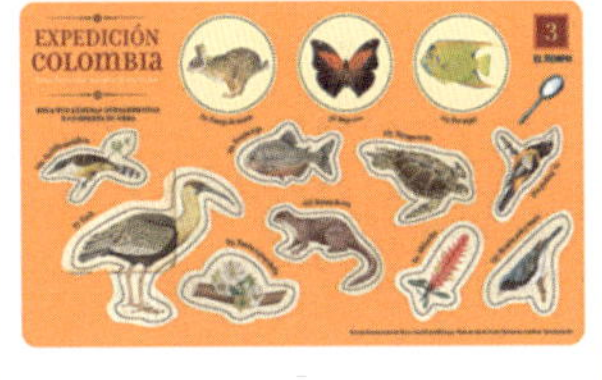
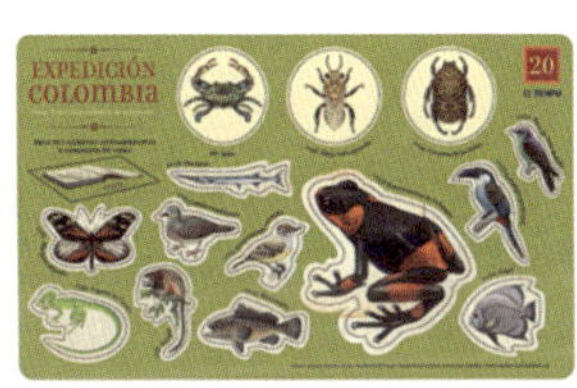
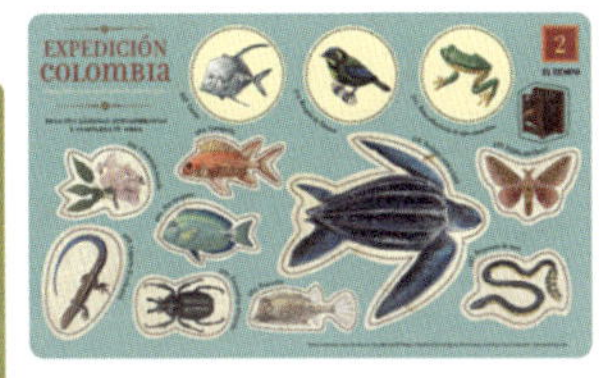
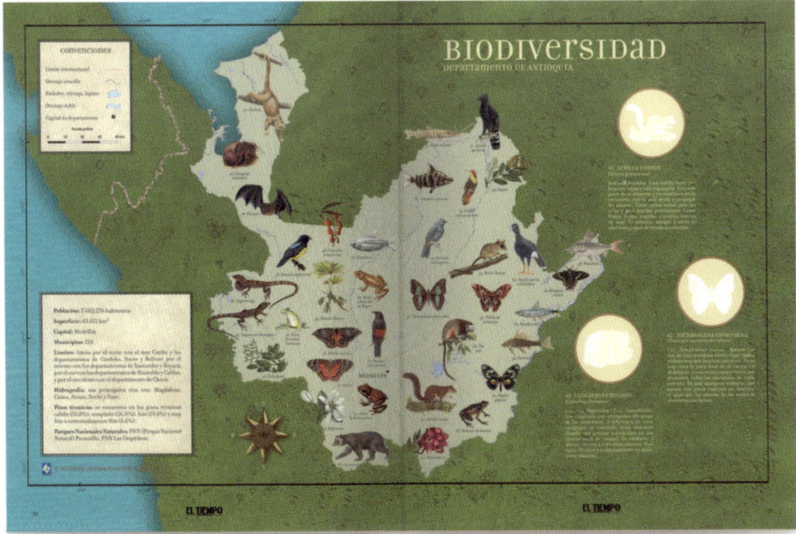
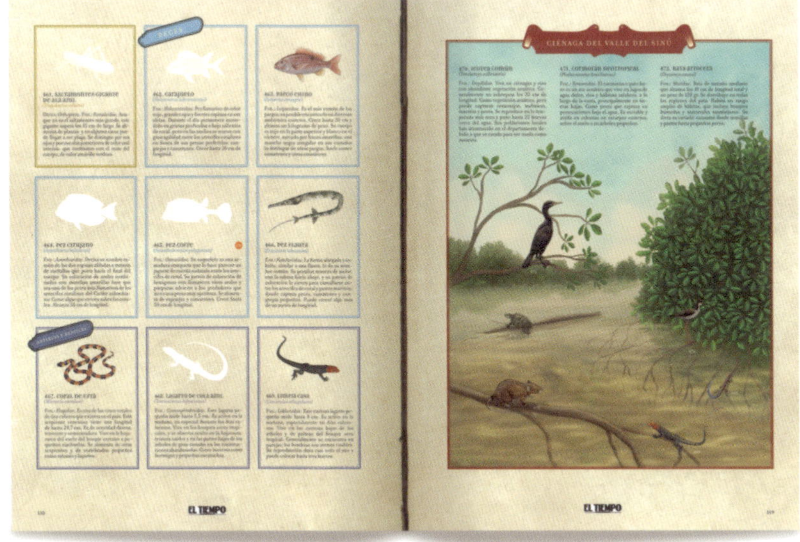

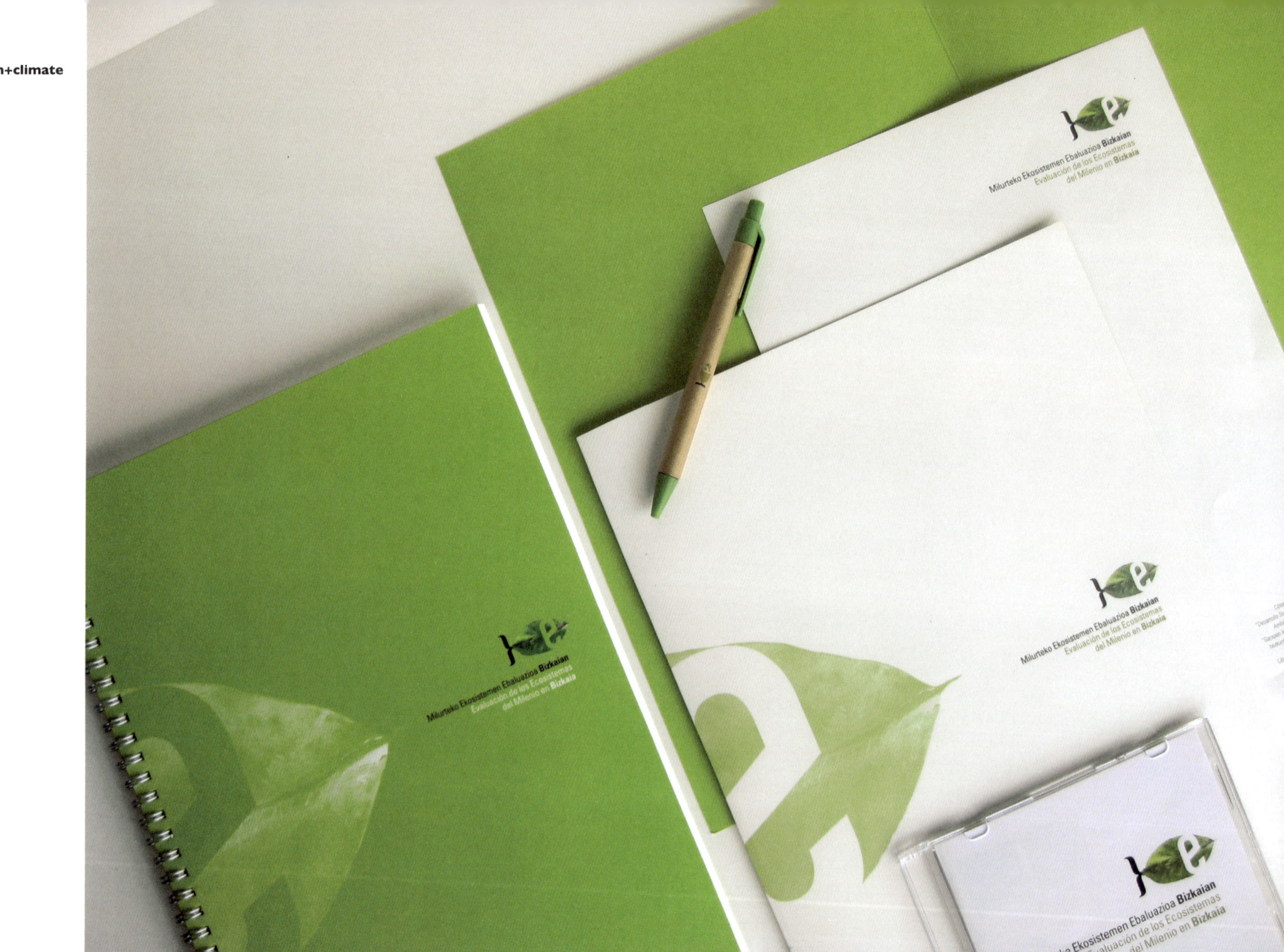

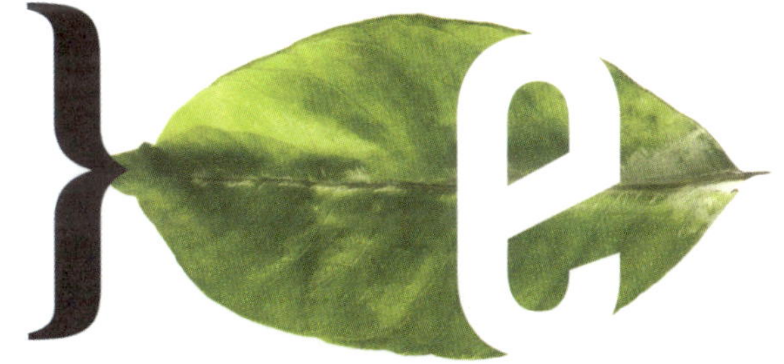

Milurteko Ekosistemen Ebaluazioa **Bizkaian**
Evaluación de los Ecosistemas del Milenio en **Bizkaia**

agency/studio: **Aerredesign** / project: visual identity of Evaluation of the Millenium Ecosystems in Biscay. / client: University of the Basque Country Unesco Chair of Sustainable Development / country: Spain

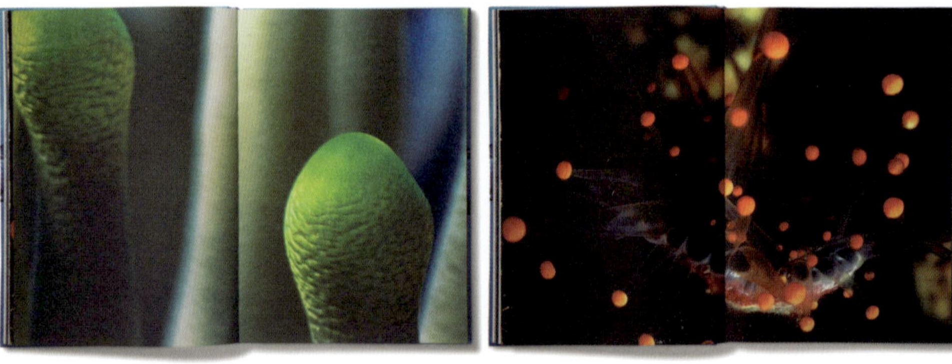

agency/studio: **Blok Design** / project: Eco. A photography book on at-risk underwater species that urges responsibility and action in protecting the beauty and diversity of Mexican seas. / client: ING / country: Mexico

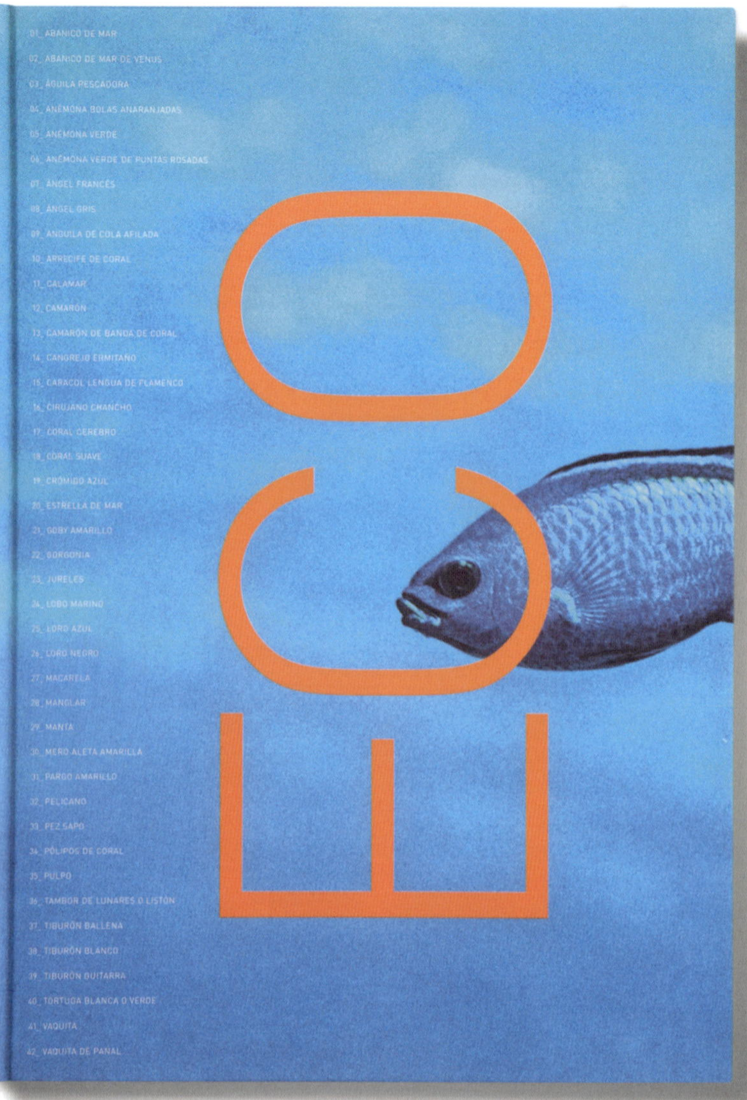

FINALIDAD DE COLABORAR EN SU PRESERVACIÓN Y AGRADECERLE A LOS MEXICANOS SU CONFIANZA Y PREFERENCIA AL ATRAER SU ATENCIÓN Y PROMOVER LA EDUCACIÓN CON RESPECTO A CÓMO PUEDEN CONVERTIRSE EN CONSUMIDORES RESPONSABLES E INFORMADOS./ EN ESTA EDICIÓN SE CONCENTRA NUESTRA ATENCIÓN EN LAS ESPECIES MARINAS, AUNQUE SON SÓLO UN EJEMPLO DE LAS RIQUEZAS NATURALES DE LOS DIFERENTES ECOSISTEMAS EXISTENTES EN NUESTRO PAÍS./ LA CREACIÓN DE ECO, NO HABRÍA SIDO POSIBLE SIN EL TRABAJO Y LA ESTUPENDA LABOR REALIZADA POR EL FOTÓGRAFO MANUEL LAZCANO, QUIEN NOS PERMITE VER A TRAVÉS DE SU LENTE PARA ENTENDER LA MAGNITUD DEL PROBLEMA Y ADMIRAR LA BELLEZA DE NUESTRO ENTORNO./ EN NOMBRE DE ING MÉXICO Y DEL MÍO PROPIO, CONSIDERAREMOS QUE NUESTRO PROYECTO HABRÁ SIDO EXITOSO SI LOGRAMOS INTERESARLOS EN EL TEMA PARA QUE HOY QUE TIENEN ESTA OBRA EN SUS MANOS ACTÚEN Y CONTRIBUYAN CON NOSOTROS EN EL CUIDADO DE NUESTRO ENTORNO. LA PARTICIPACIÓN DE TODOS ES NECESARIA PARA PRESERVAR EL GRAN TESORO NATURAL DE MÉXICO./ CARLOS MURIEL, PRESIDENTE Y DIRECTOR GENERAL DE OPERACIONES DE SEGUROS Y PENSIONES DE ING LATINOAMÉRICA.

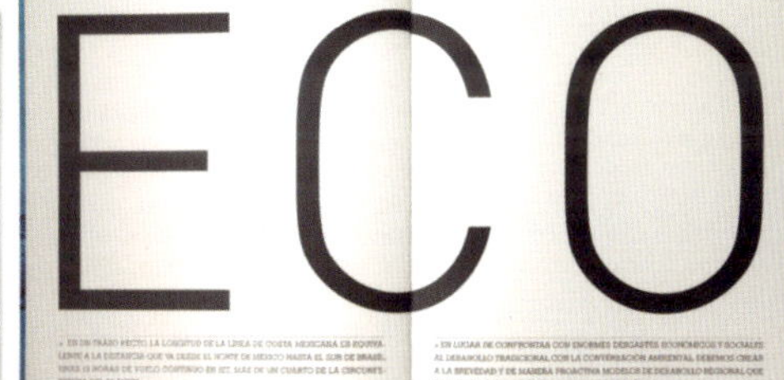

EN UN TRAZO RECTO LA LONGITUD DE LA LÍNEA DE COSTA MEXICANA ES EQUIVALENTE A LA DISTANCIA QUE VA DESDE EL NORTE DE MÉXICO HASTA EL SUR DE BRASIL. UNAS 13 HORAS DE VUELO CONTINUO EN JET. MÁS DE UN CUARTO DE LA CIRCUNFERENCIA DEL PLANETA.

EL MAR - SUS AGUAS, SUS RECURSOS PESQUEROS, SU FLORA Y SU FAUNA - A PESAR DE LOS ABUSOS QUE HEMOS COMETIDO, BIEN MANEJADO TIENE UN GRAN POTENCIAL DE RECUPERACIÓN. POCO TIEMPO DESPUÉS DE CUIDAR UNA ZONA MARINA, LA ABUNDANCIA DE VIDA RETORNA, LA PESCA EN SUS ALREDEDORES SE FORTALECE, LOS PECES SON MAYORES.

TODO LO QUE DESTRUYAMOS SERÁ PARA SIEMPRE, ESTAREMOS QUEMANDO LOS PUENTES, NO HABRÁ RETORNO. EN CAMBIO TODO LO QUE CONSERVEMOS CON SALUD AMBIENTAL DE LA ZONA COSTERA SERÁ LA BASE NATURAL PARA UNA ECONOMÍA SANA Y SUSTENTABLE.

EN LUGAR DE CONFRONTAR CON ENORMES DESGASTES ECONÓMICOS Y SOCIALES AL DESARROLLO TRADICIONAL CON LA CONSERVACIÓN AMBIENTAL DEBEMOS CREAR A LA BREVEDAD Y DE MANERA PROACTIVA MODELOS DE DESARROLLO REGIONAL QUE RESPONDAN A UNA VISIÓN PROFUNDA Y COMPROMETIDA.

DE ACUERDO A DATOS OFICIALES DE LA COMISIÓN NACIONAL PARA EL CONOCIMIENTO Y USO DE LA BIODIVERSIDAD, EL INVENTARIO CORRESPONDIENTE A LA ZONA COSTERA Y OCEÁNICA DE MÉXICO COMPRENDE UN TOTAL DE ESPECIES, CATEGORÍAS INFRAESPECÍFICAS, ESPECIES CITADAS Y PROTEGIDAS, DE LAS CUALES SON ENDEMISMOS O ESPECIES ÚNICAS EN EL MUNDO.

VIVIMOS UNA COYUNTURA. LA SIMETRÍA EN EL PODER, LA FUERZA DE LA NATURALEZA ANTE EL HOMBRE SE HA MANIFESTADO. NUEVOS CÓDIGOS SE DESARROLLAN. EMPEZAMOS A COMPRENDER EL SENTIDO DEL LENGUAJE DE LOS ANIMALES, DE LOS ECOSISTEMAS. UN NUEVO PRÓLOGO HA COMENZADO.

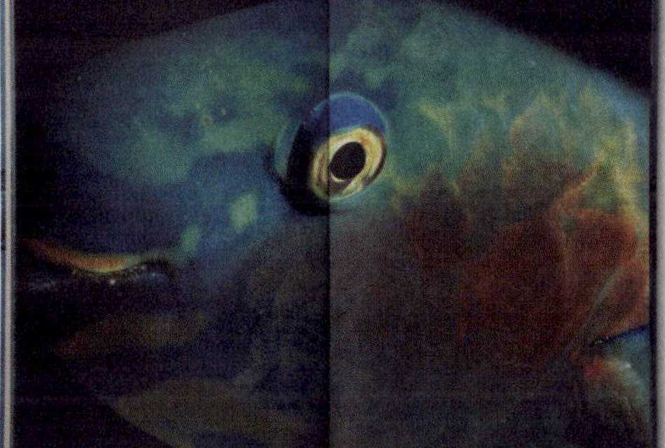

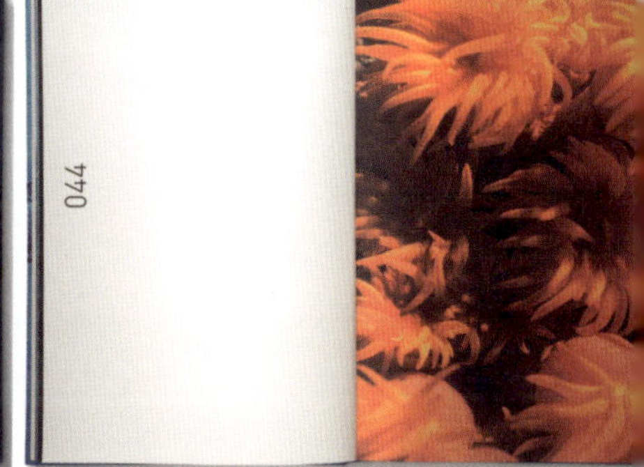

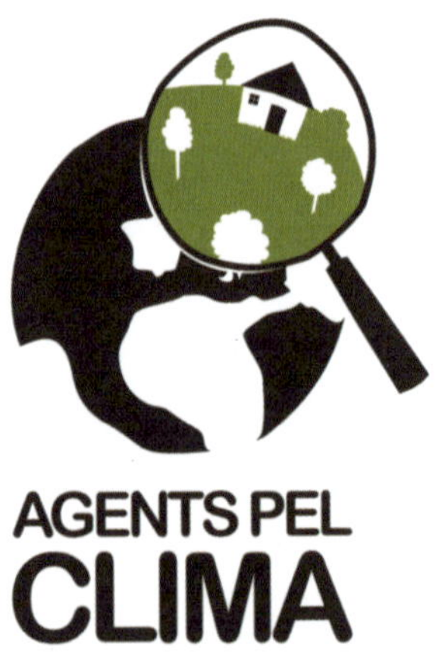
AGENTS PEL
CLIMA

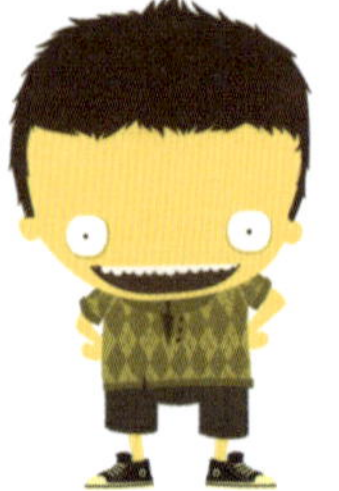
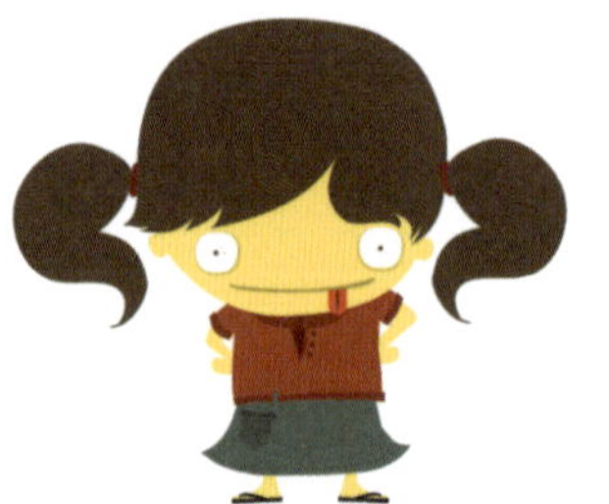
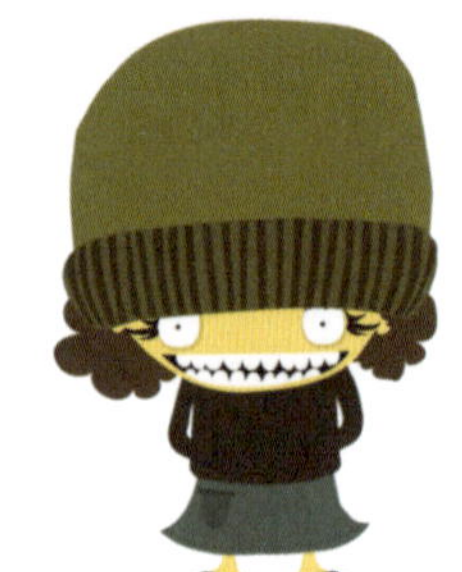
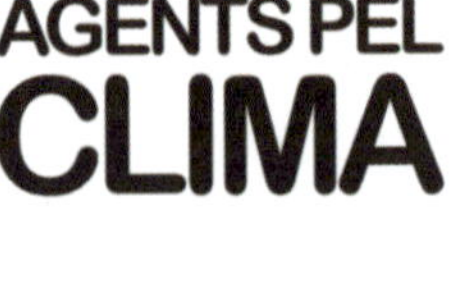
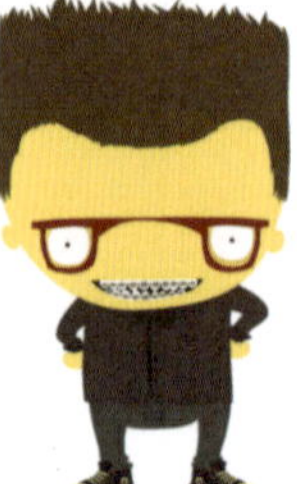
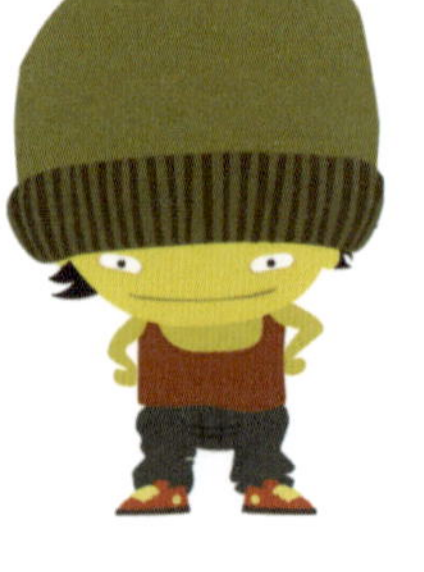
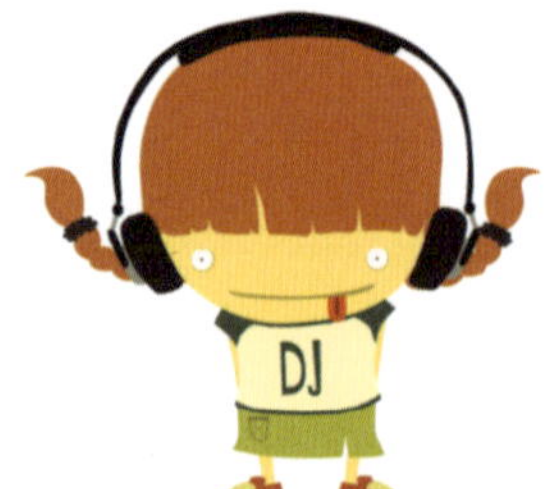
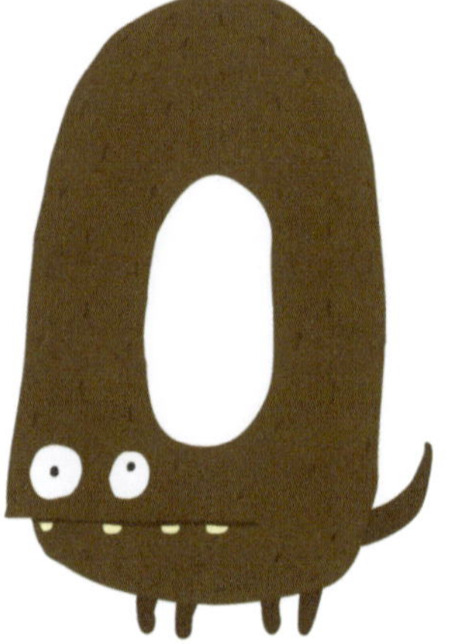
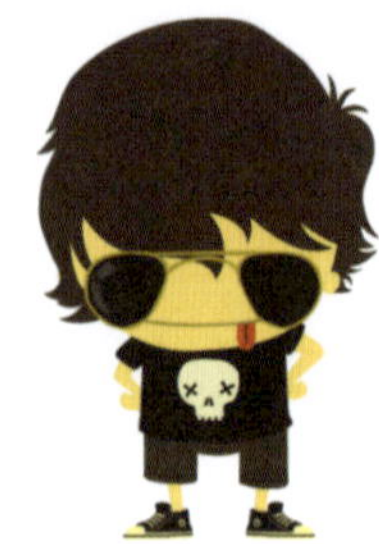
DJ
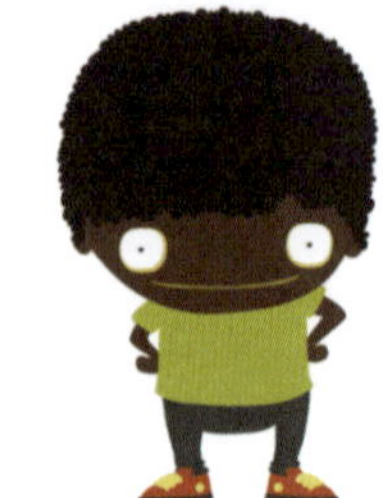
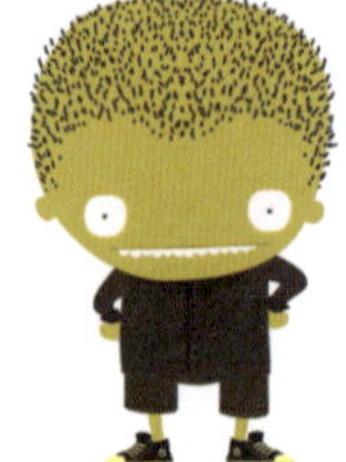

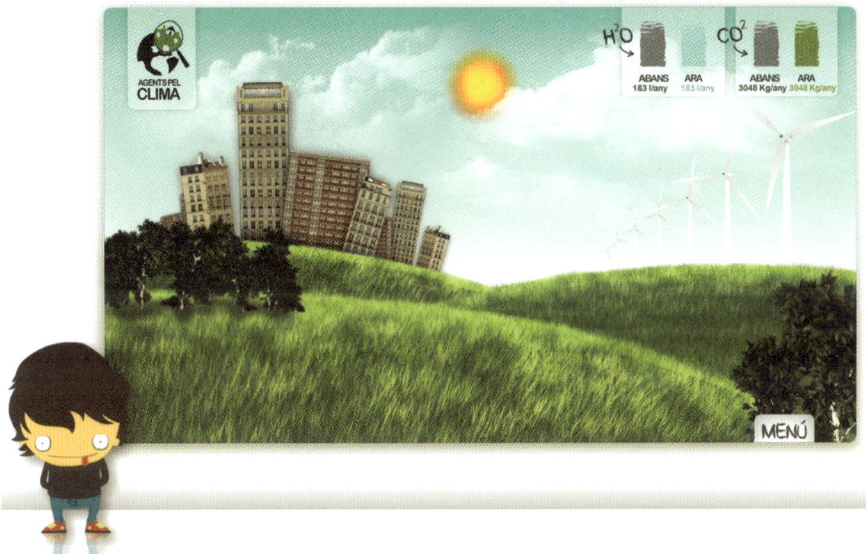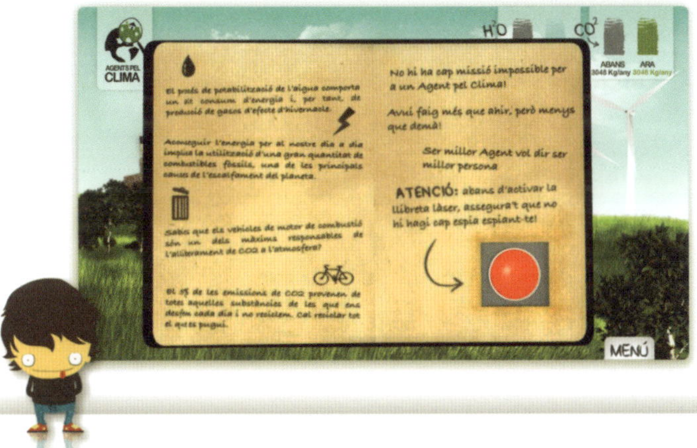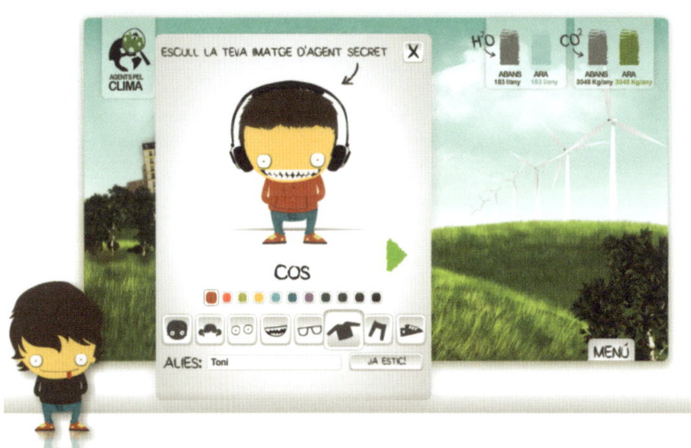

agency/studio: **Grapa.ws** / project: agentspelclima.cat strives to promote and reinforce environmental values in children through classroom dynamics. Children are encouraged to make small changes in their daily routine to reduce the environmental impact. / client: Acciónatura (NGO) / country: Spain

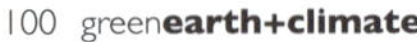

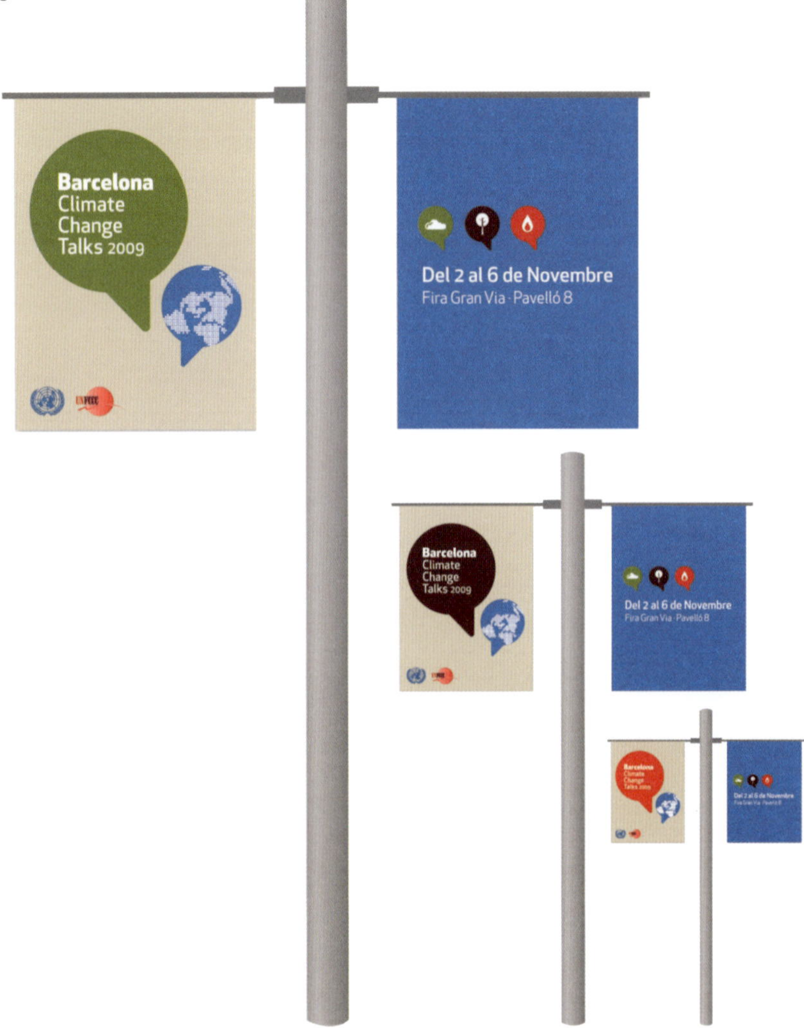

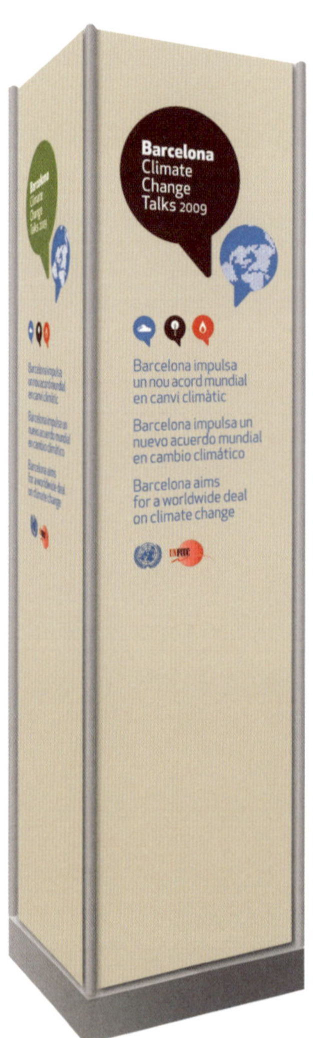

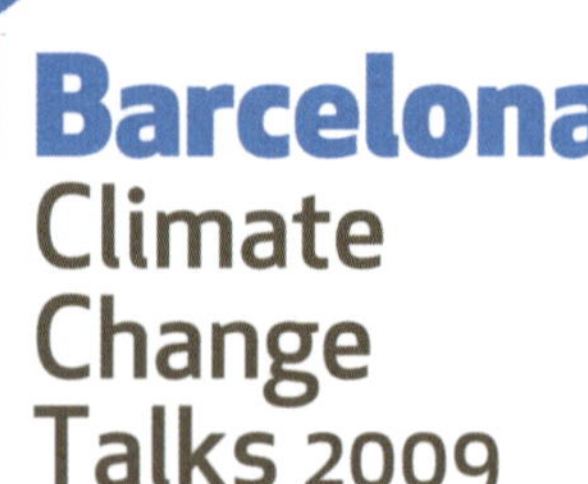

agency/studio: **Estudi Virgili** / project: graphic image of the Barcelona Climate Change Talks in 2009 / client: Barcelona City Council / country: Spain

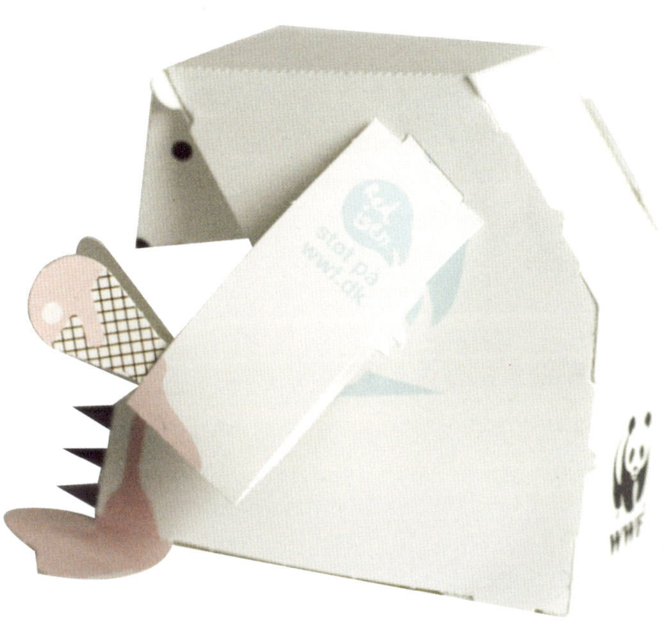

agency/studio: **Kenn Munk** / project: "Save the Ice" polar bears / client: WWF Verdensnaturfonden (Denmark) / country: Denmark

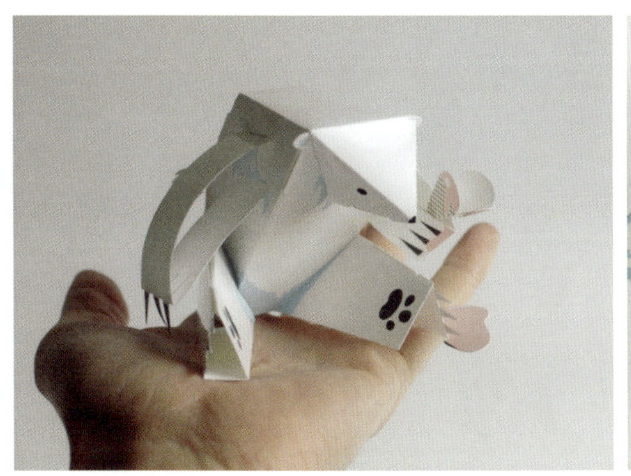

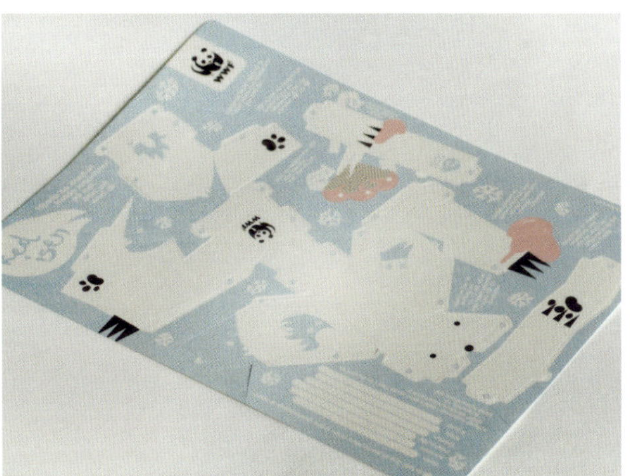

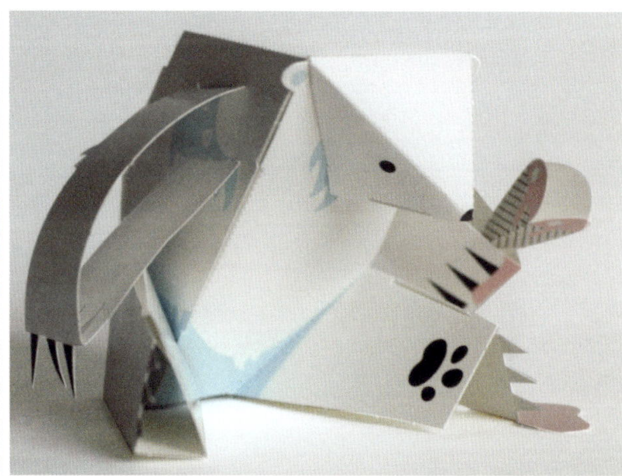

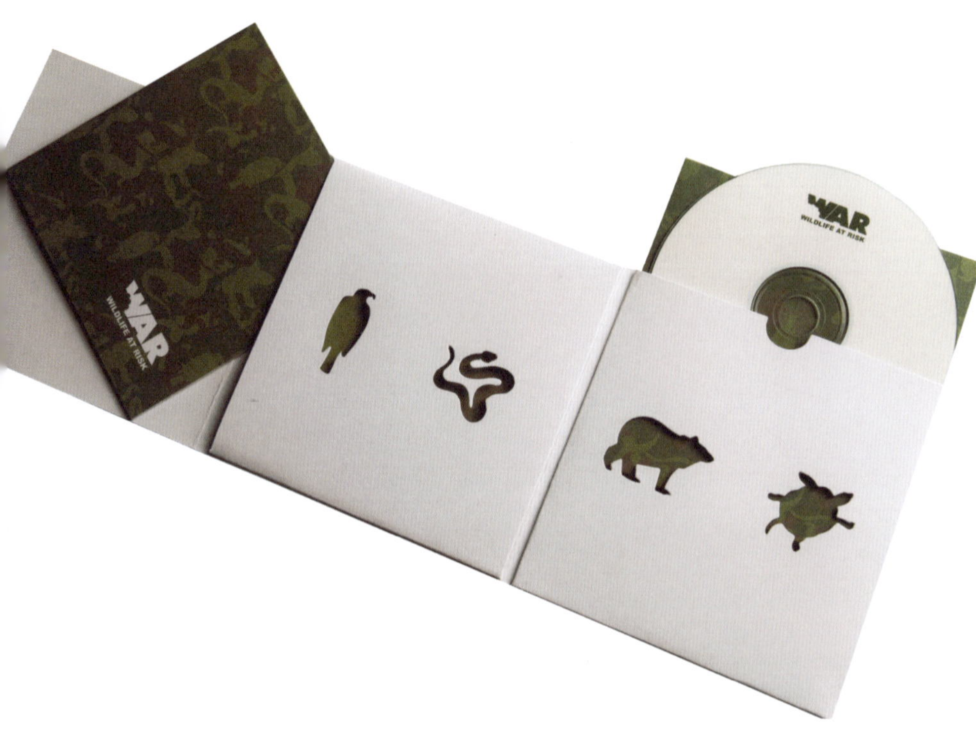

agency/studio: **Design Positive** / project: Wild animals are becoming harder to spot in Vietnam. Campaign for the Wildlife Rescue Centre in Vietnam that rehabilitates animals with the aim of placing them back in the wild. / client: Wildlife At Risk / country: Vietnam

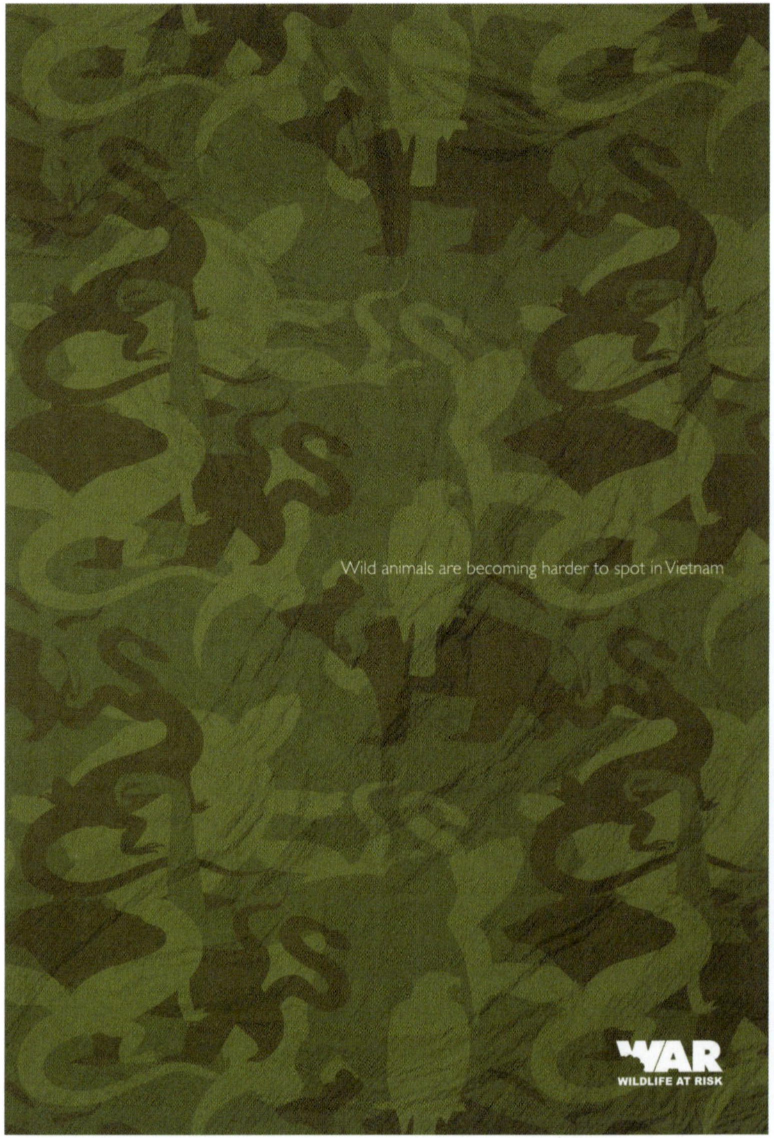

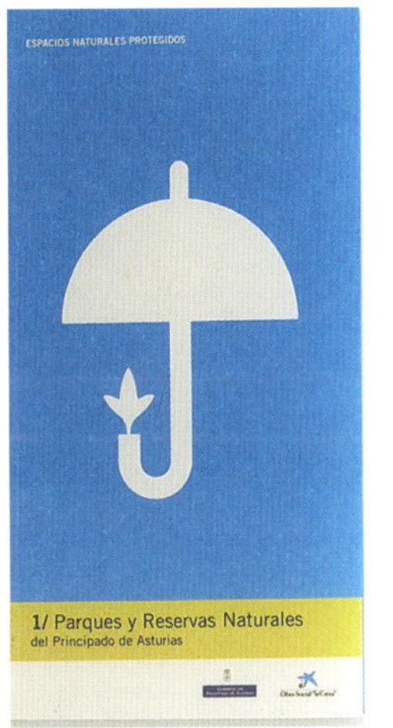

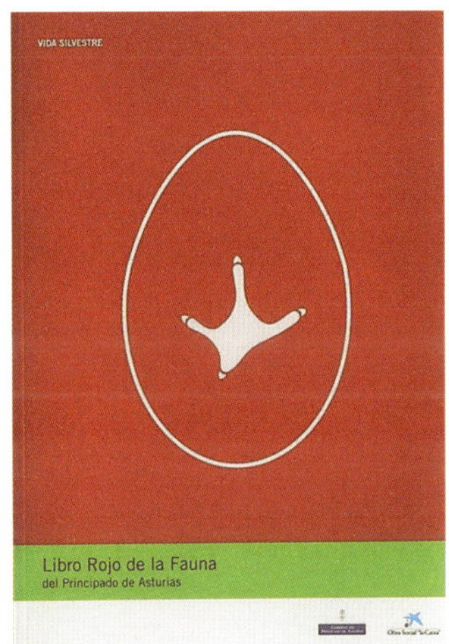

agency/studio: **Forma** / project: a collection of covers designed for a series of publications on protected natural areas, wildlife and environmental education. / client: La Caixa and the Council of Environment of the Principality of Asturias / country: Spain

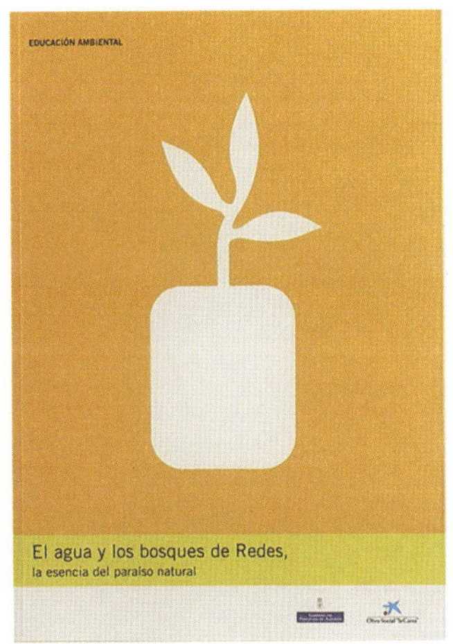

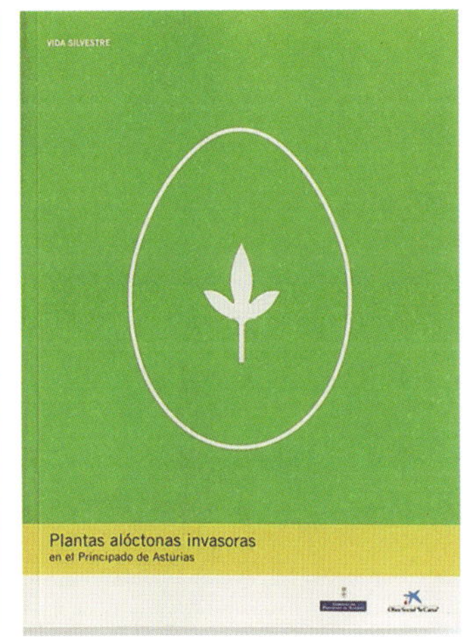

Groen! wenst je
een energiek 2008!

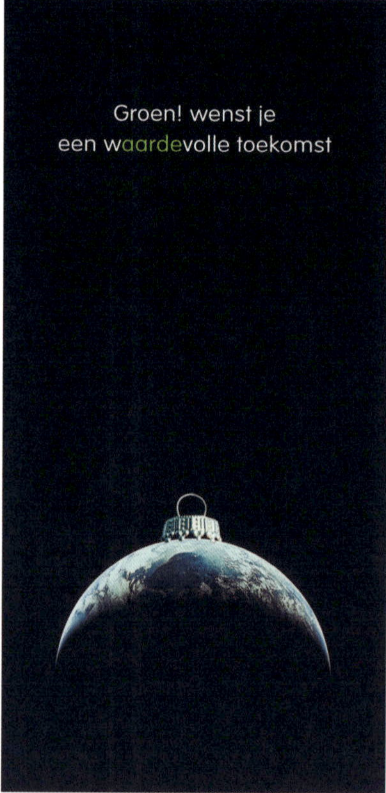

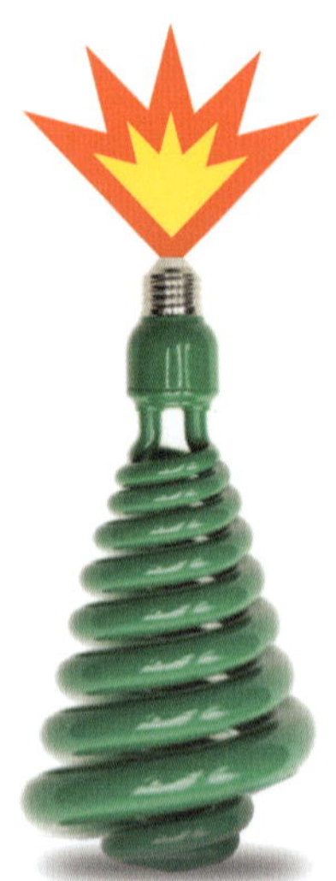

agency/studio: **K&TKW Ghent** / project: New year greeting cards and party political broadcast for the Belgian general election. / client: Groen! / country: Belgium

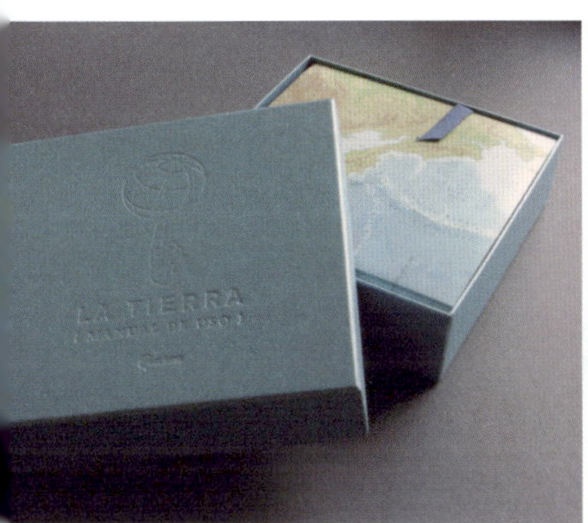
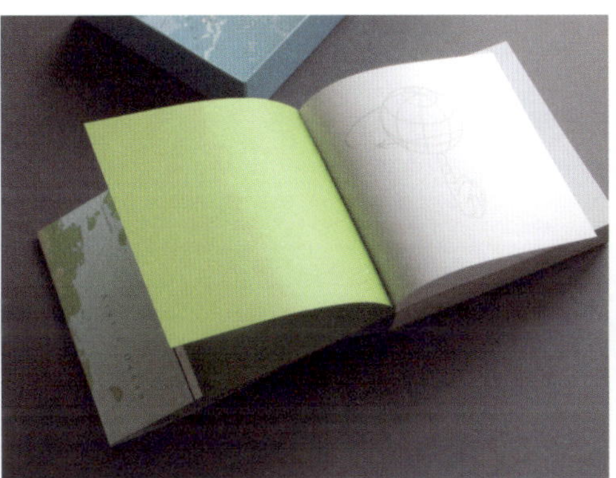
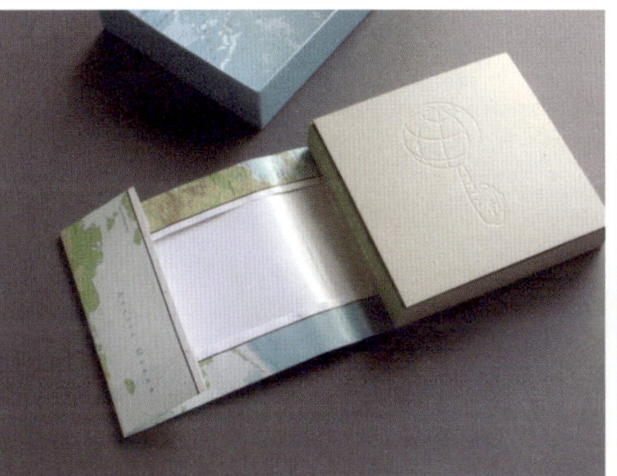
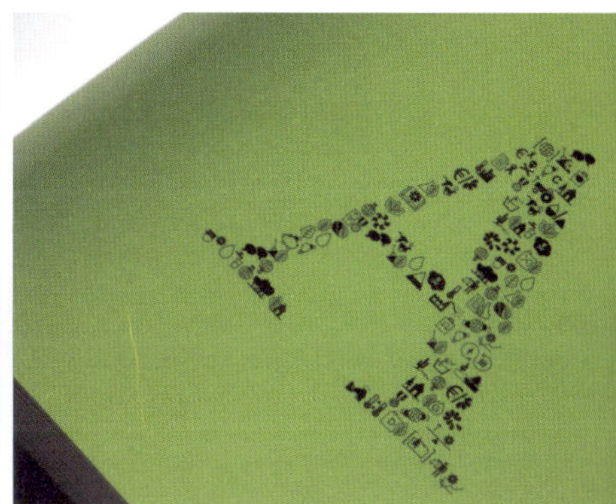

agency/studio: **Estudio Pérez Medina** / project: La Tierra (Manual de uso). For this publication, whose title translates as "The Earth (User Manual)", internationally renowned experts were asked to evaluate the situation of the Earth from a range of strategic viewpoints (art, philosophy, science, demography, etc.). / client: Acciona, McCann Erickson, La Fábrica Editorial / country: Spain

agency/studio: **Shailesh Khandeparkar** / project: Save nature. Save ourselves. Poster campaign about the
dependence between man and nature. / client: WWF / country: India

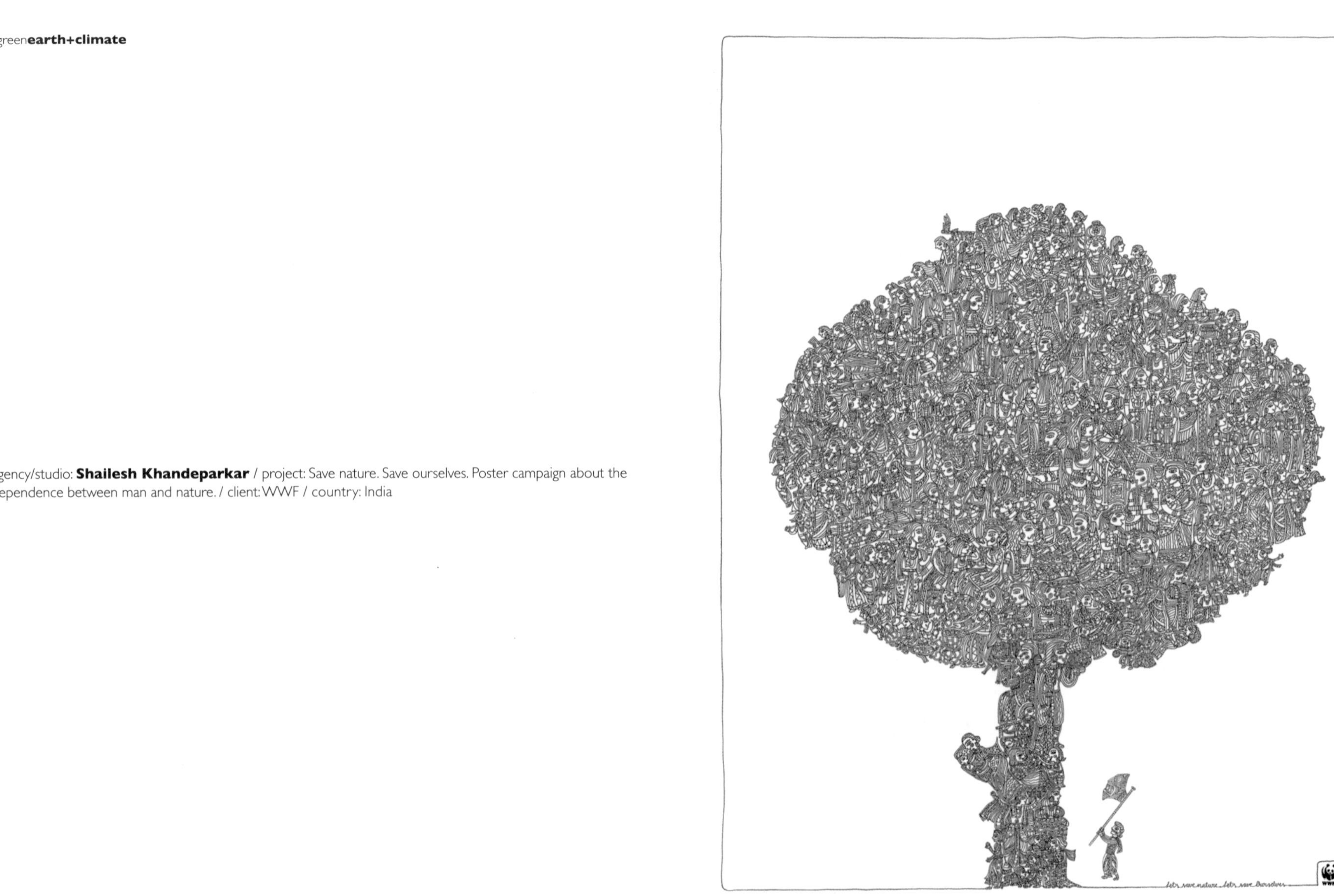

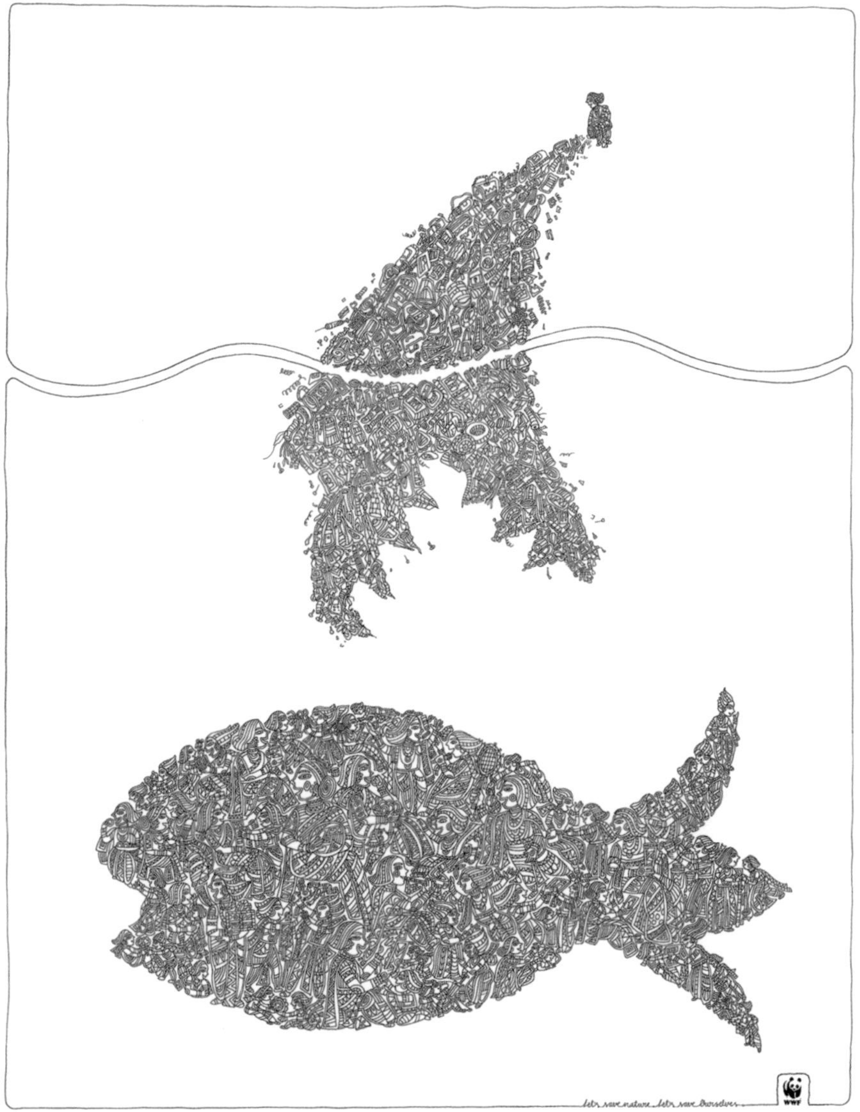

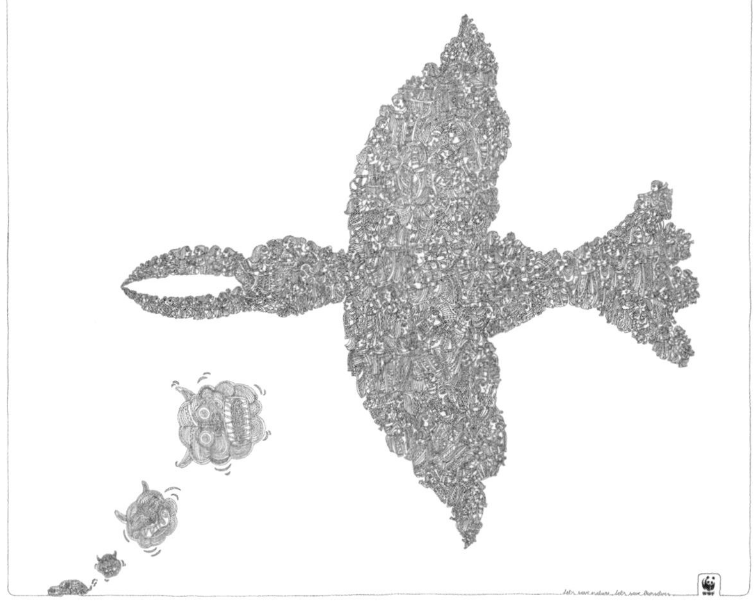
let's save nature...let's save ourselves...

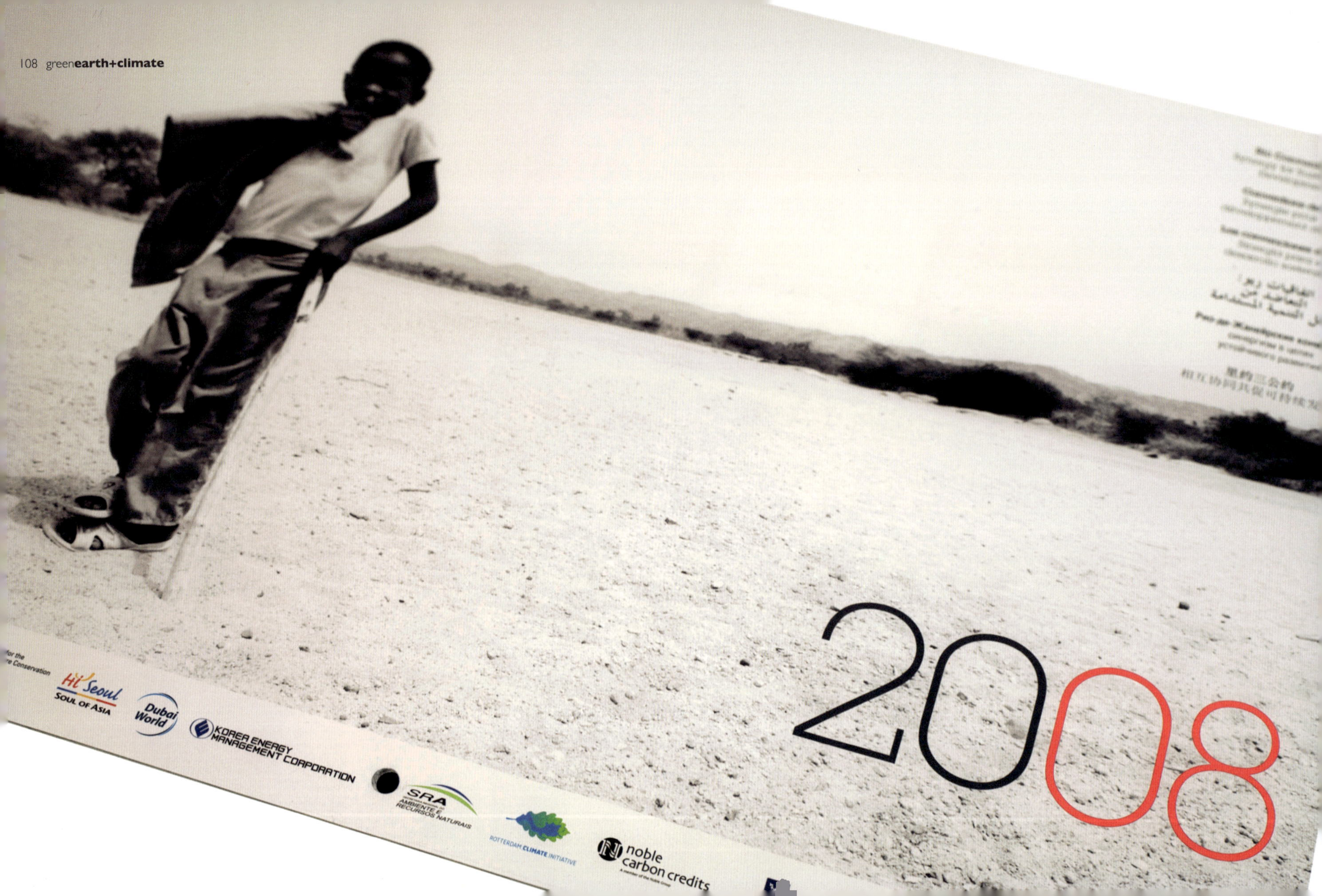
Hi Seoul
SOUL OF ASIA
Dubai World
KOREA ENERGY MANAGEMENT CORPORATION
SRA
AMBIENTE E RECURSOS NATURAIS
ROTTERDAM CLIMATE INITIATIVE
noble carbon credits
A member of the Noble Group
2008

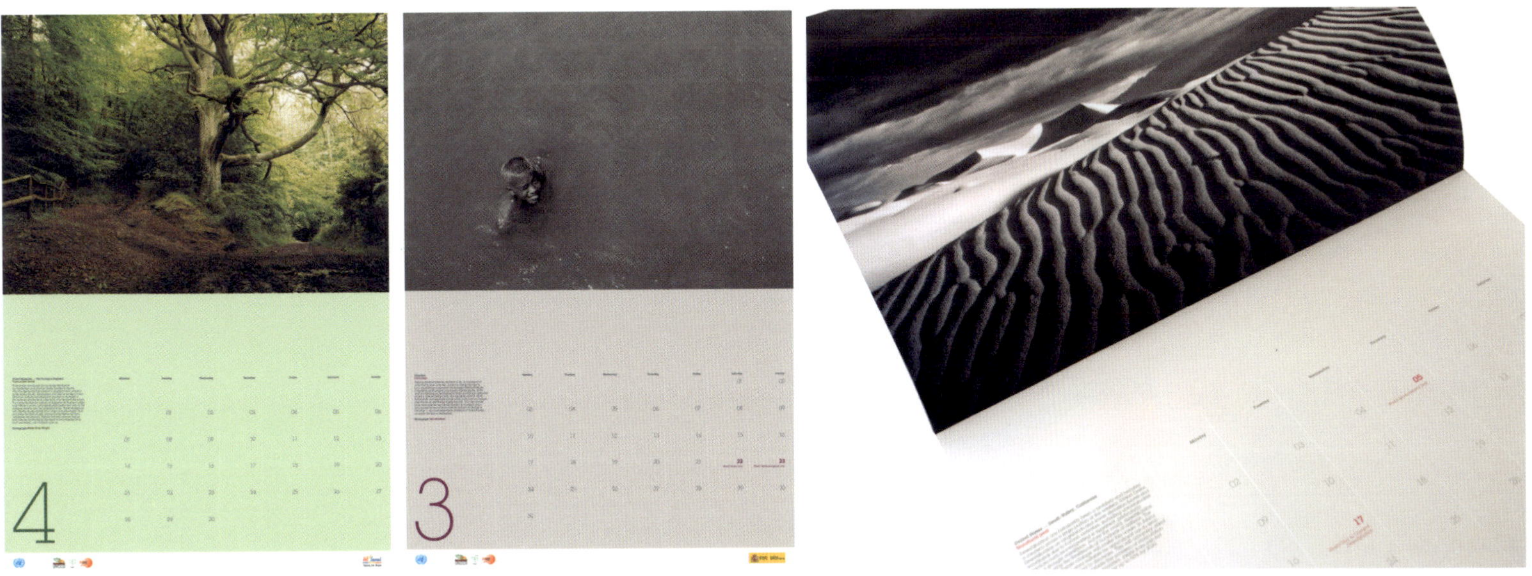

agency/studio: **Deep LLP** / project: Synergy for Sustainable Development Calendar 2008. / client: United Nations / country: United Kingdom

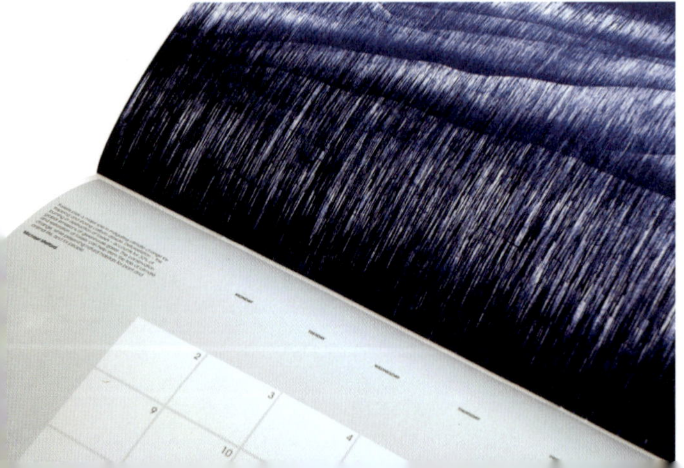

agency/studio: **Deep LLP** / project: UNite to Combat Climate Change Calendar 2009. / client: United Nations / country: United Kingdom

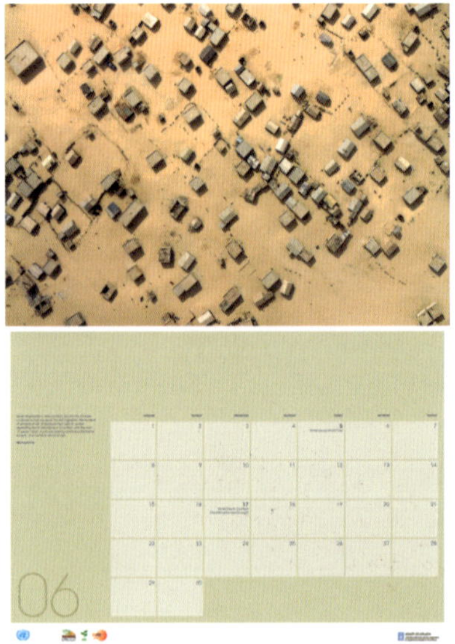

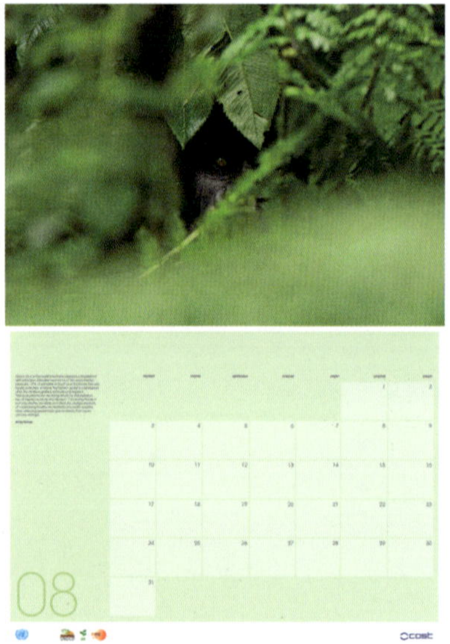

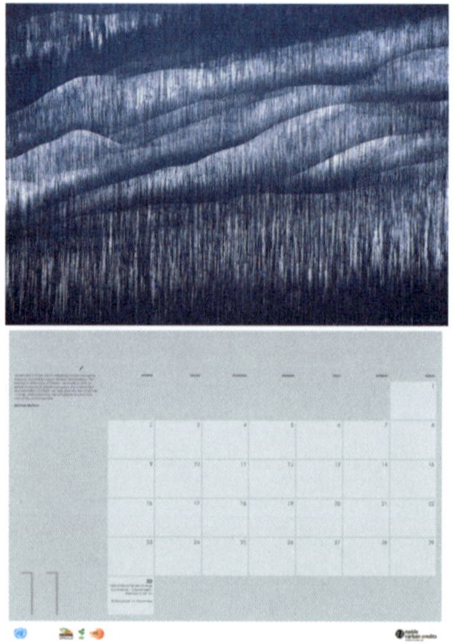

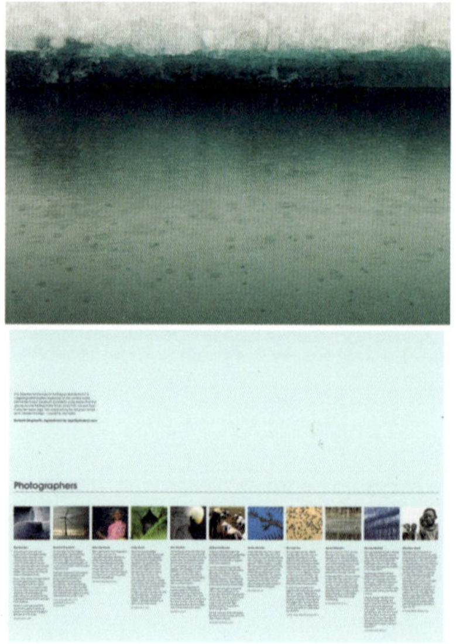

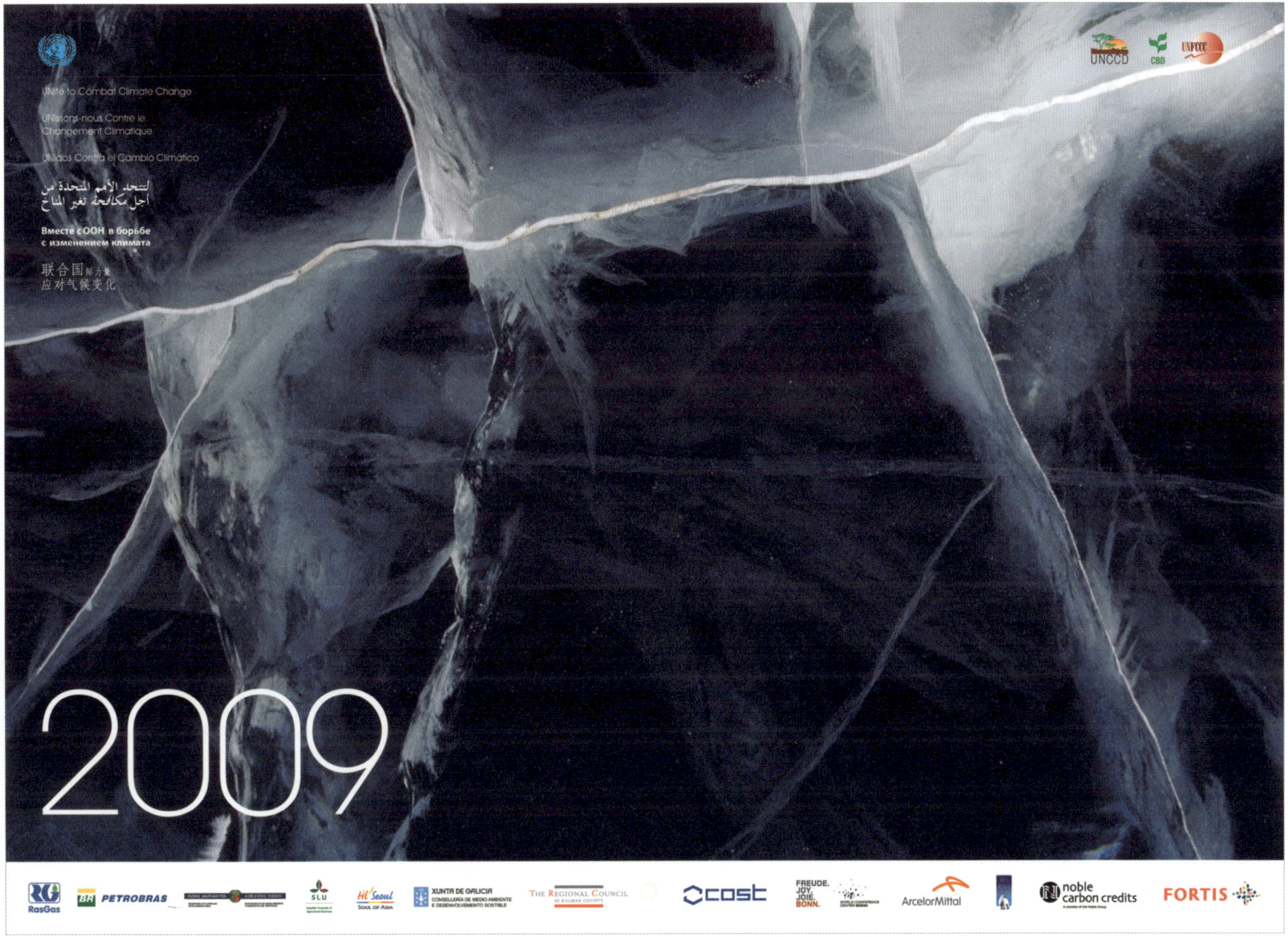

UNCCD
CBD
UNFCCC
UNite to Combat Climate Change
UNissons-nous Contre le
Changement Climatique
UNidos Contra el Cambio Climático
Вместе с ООН в борьбе
с изменением климата
联合国助力量
应对气候变化
2009

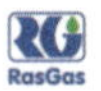 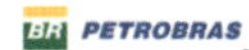 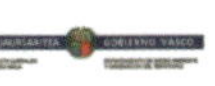 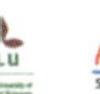 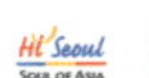 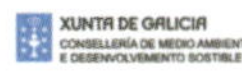 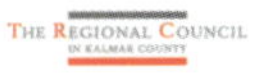 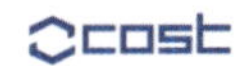 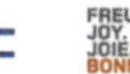 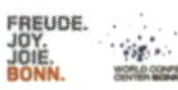 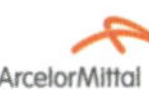  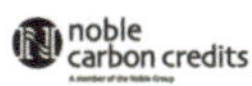 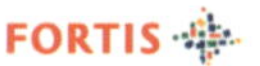
RasGas
BR PETROBRAS
SLU
Hi! Seoul SOUL OF ASIA
XUNTA DE GALICIA
CONSELLERÍA DE MEDIO AMBIENTE E DESENVOLVEMENTO SOSTIBLE
THE REGIONAL COUNCIL IN KALMAR COUNTY
cost
FREUDE. JOY. JOIE. BONN.
ArcelorMittal
noble carbon credits
A member of the Noble Group
FORTIS

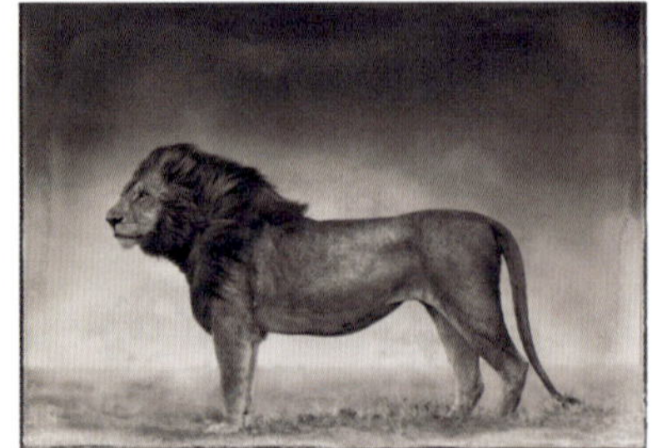

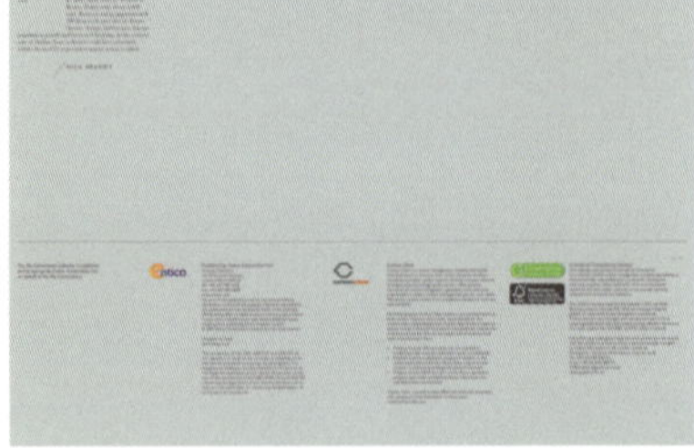

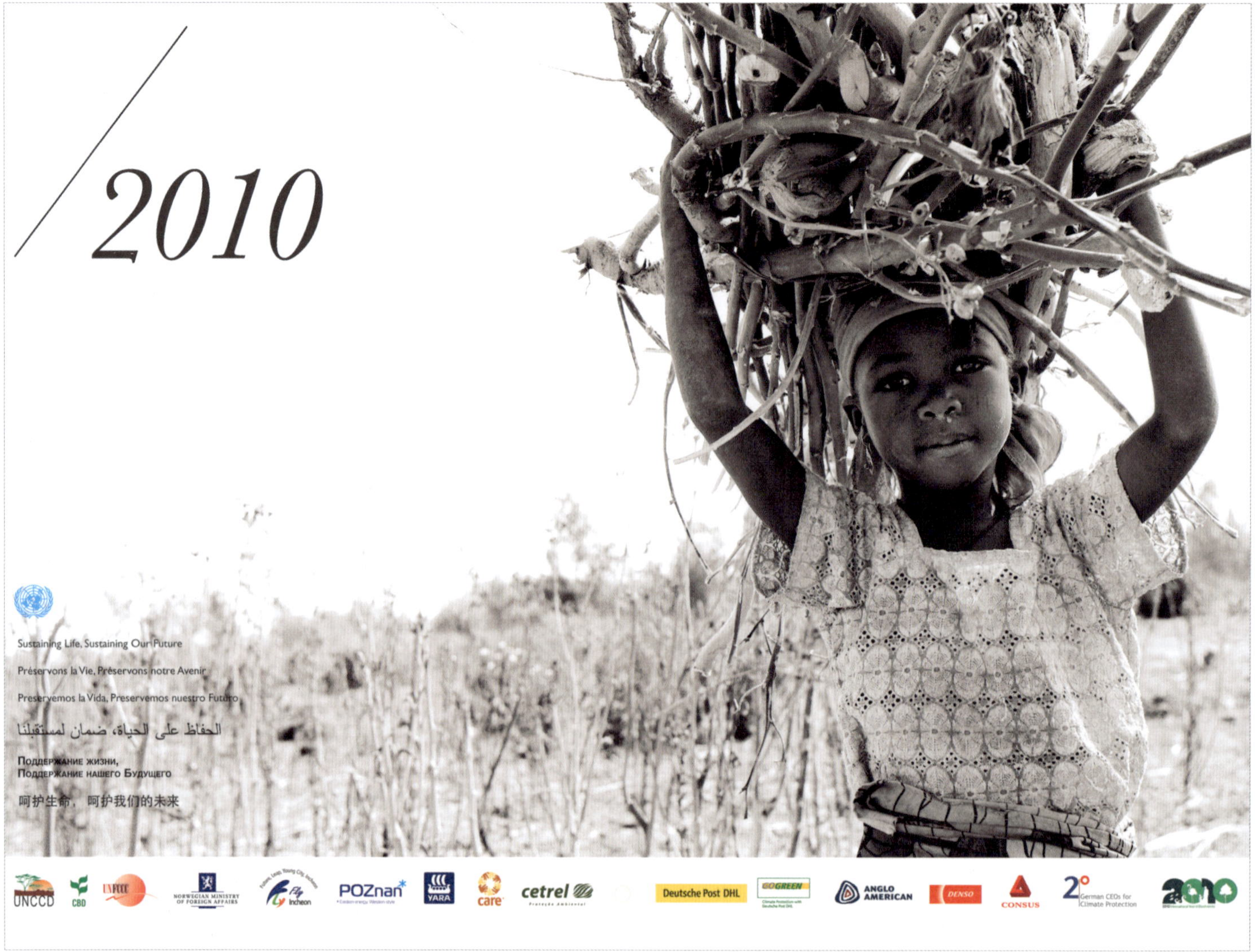

2010
Sustaining Life, Sustaining Our Future
Préservons la Vie, Préservons notre Avenir
Preservemos la Vida, Preservemos nuestro Futuro
الحفاظ على الحياة، ضمان لمستقبلنا
Поддержание жизни, Поддержание нашего Будущего
呵护生命，呵护我们的未来

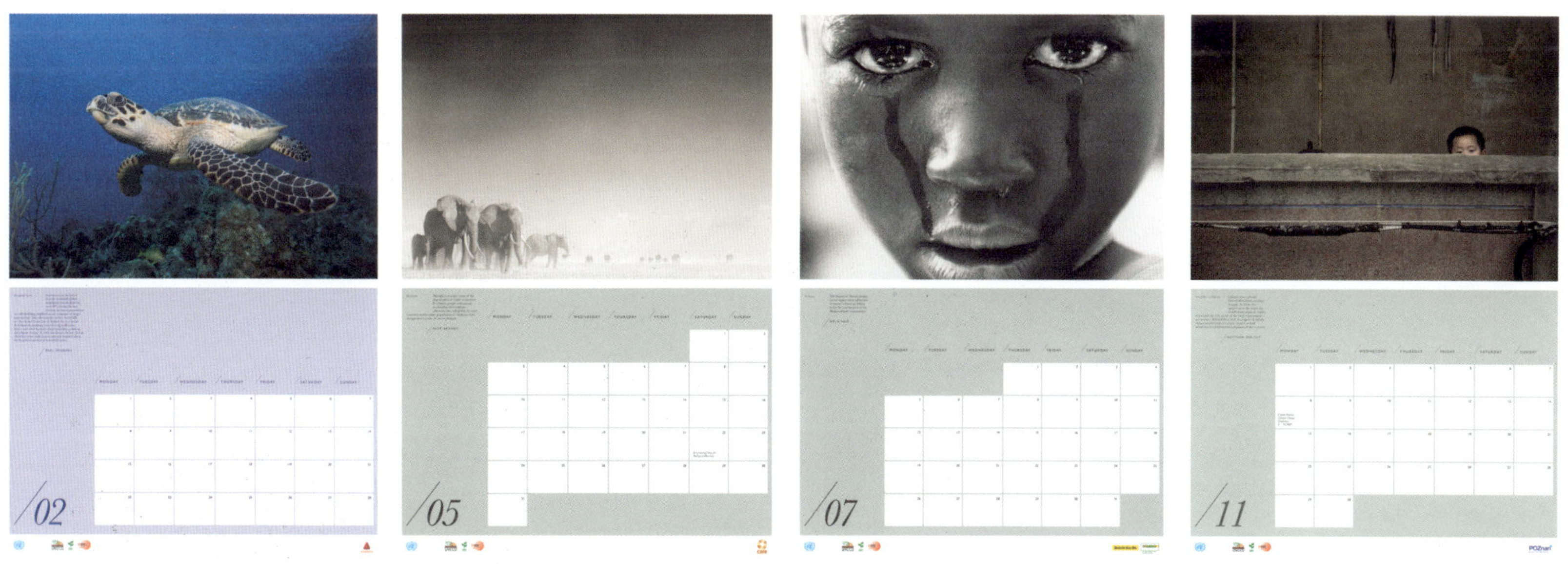

agency/studio: **Deep LLP** / project: Sustaining Life, Sustaining Our Future Calendar 2010. / client: United Nations / country: United Kingdom

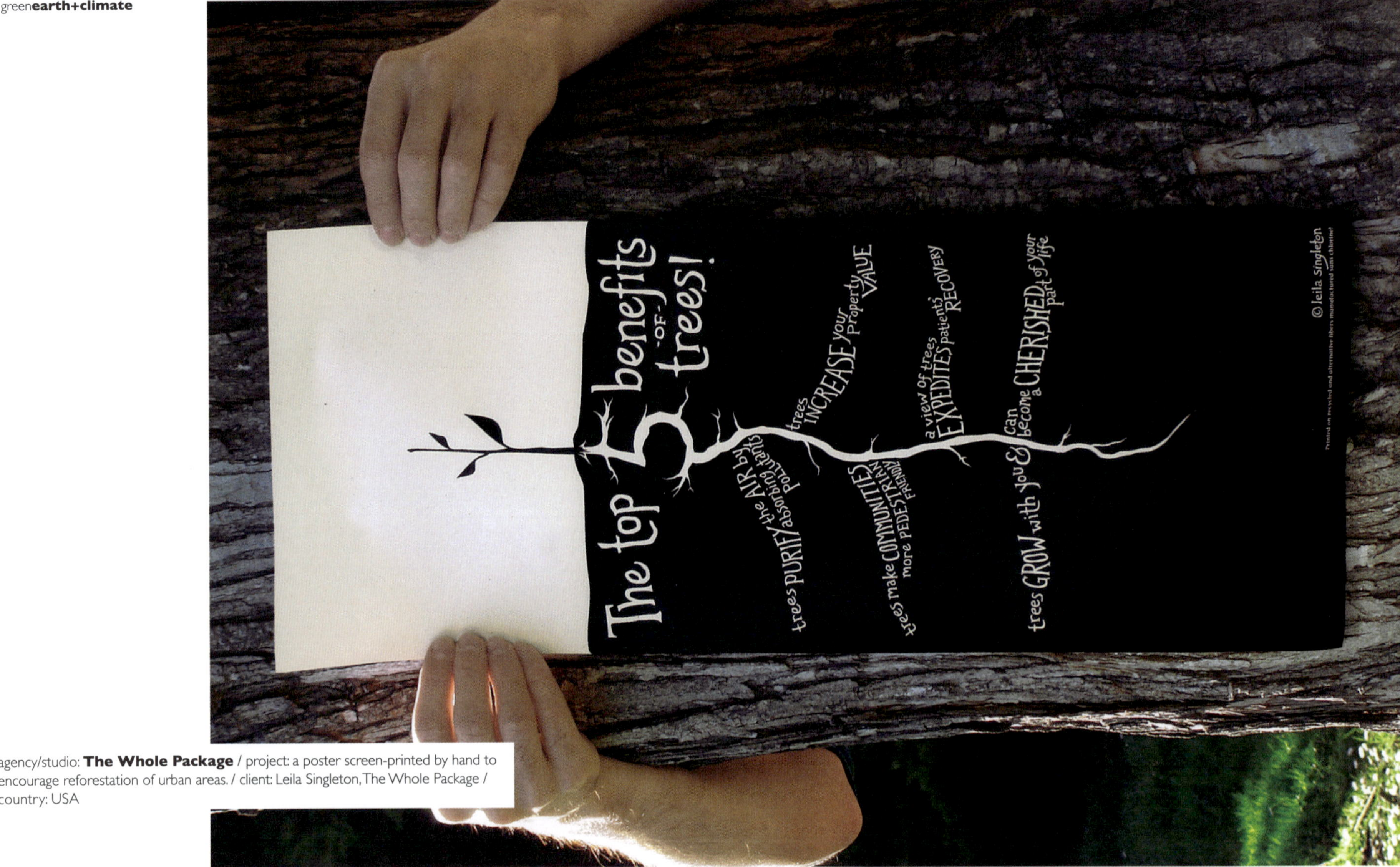

agency/studio: **The Whole Package** / project: a poster screen-printed by hand to encourage reforestation of urban areas. / client: Leila Singleton, The Whole Package / country: USA

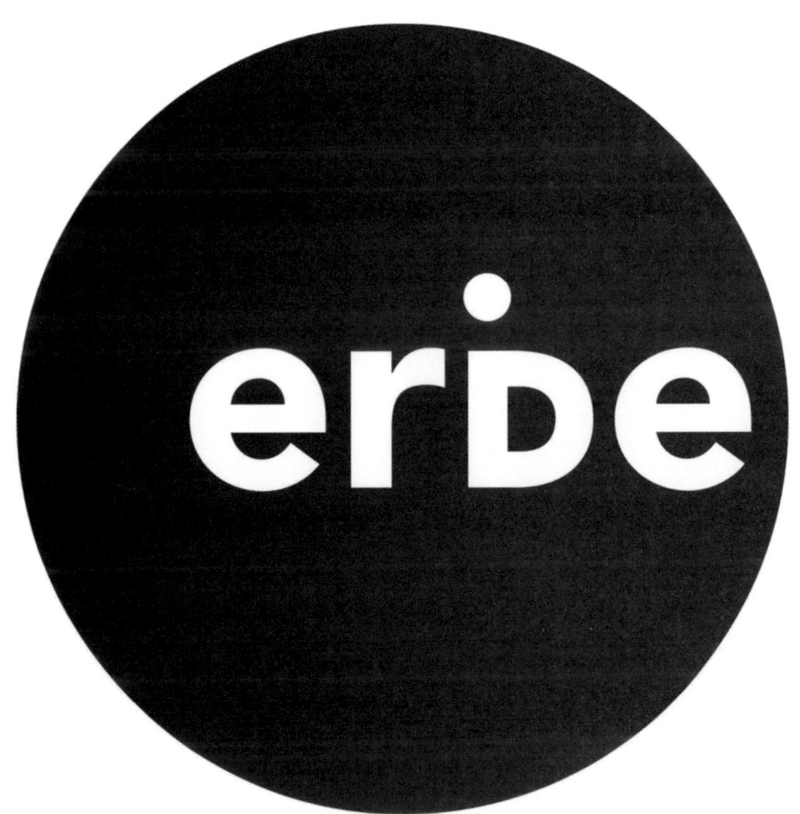

author: **Alexa Gregor** / project: The Earth-is-Heritage logo does not just refer to the protection of our climate but it has become a kind of symbol of the principle of global sustainability. In this context the German words "Erde" and "Erbe" mean "earth" and "heritage". / country: Germany

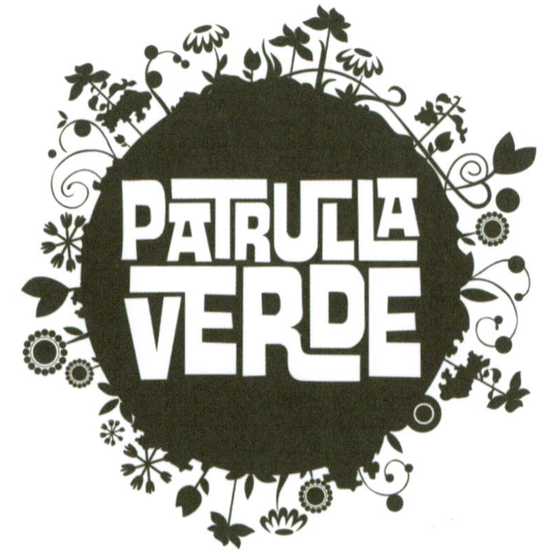

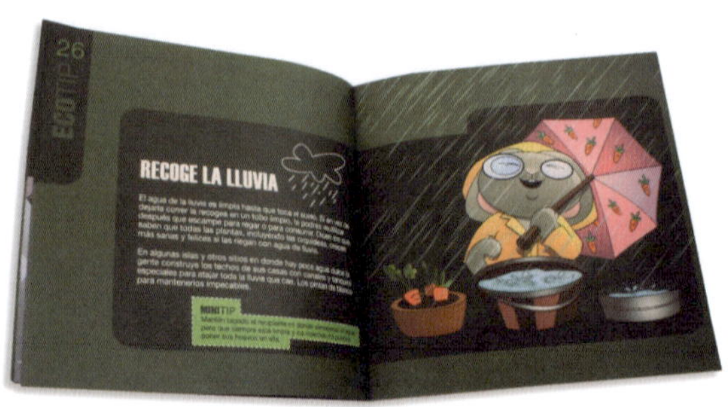

agency/studio: **Musgo Comunicación Visual** / project: illustrated children's book about protecting the environment. / country: Venezuela.

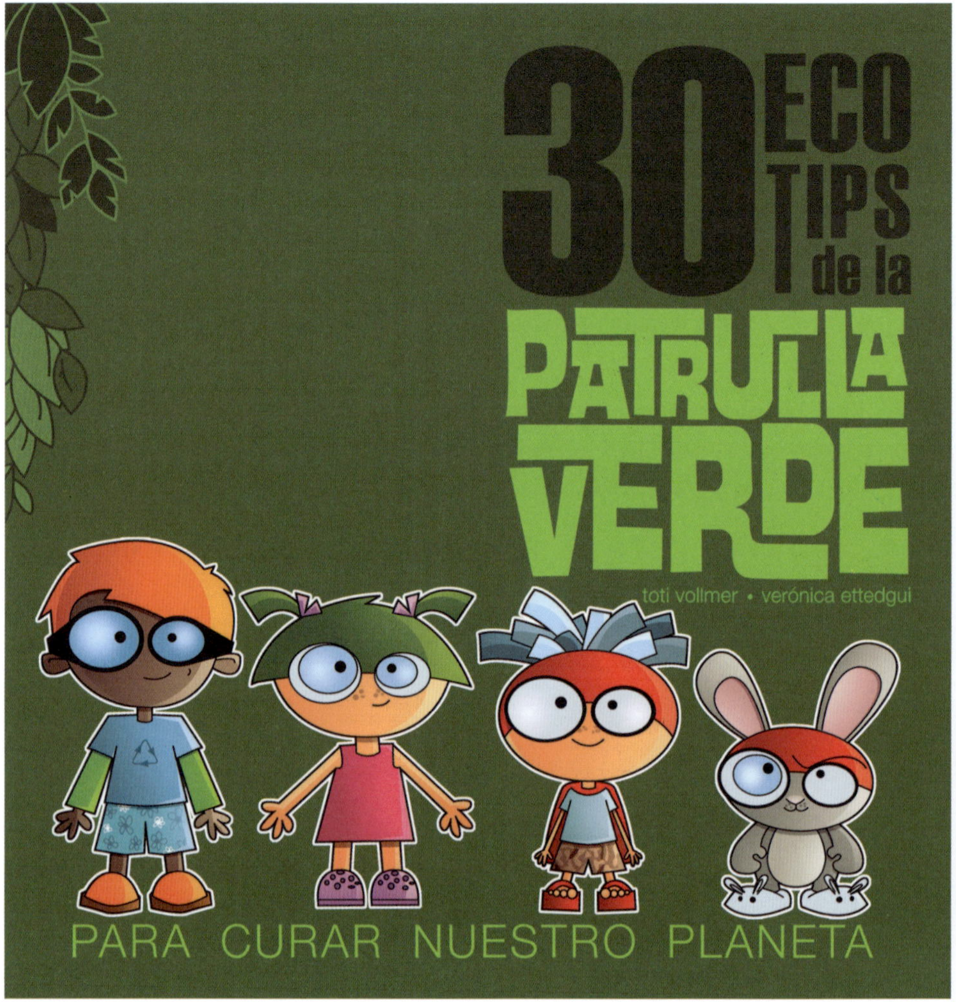

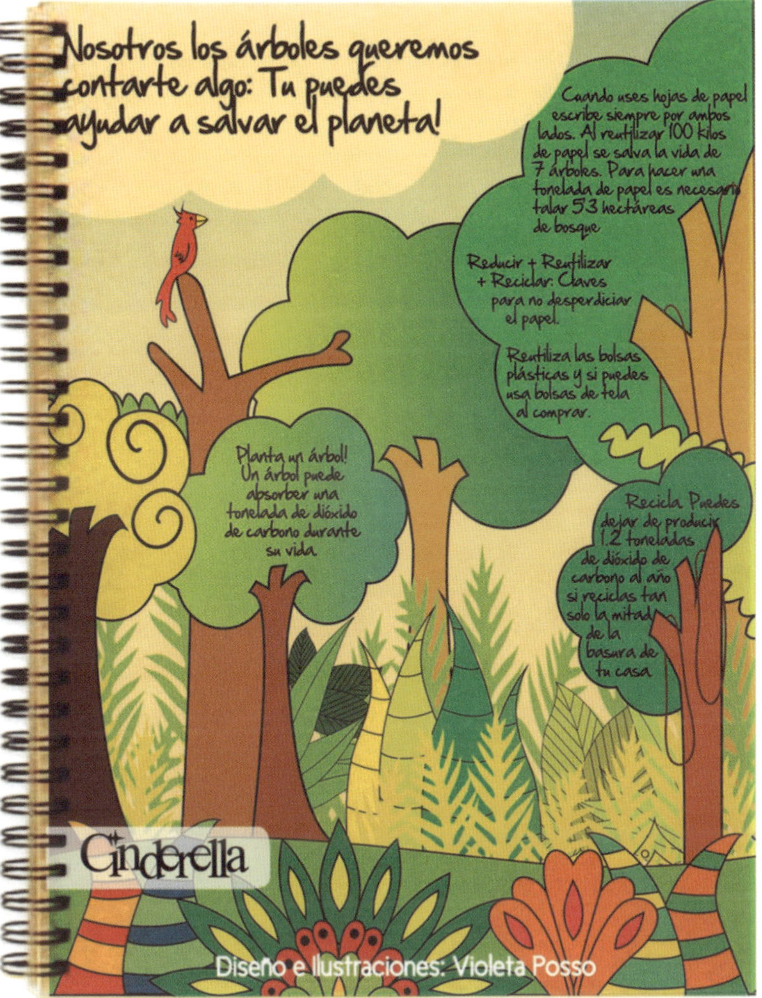

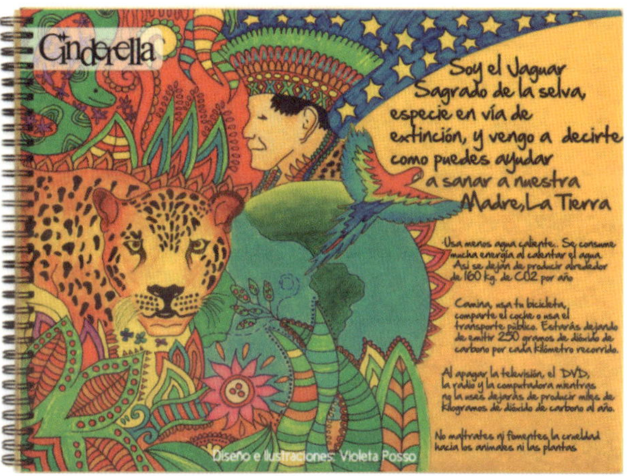

agency/studio: **Cinderella Diseño + Ilustración** / project: eco-friendly exercise books that encourage and educate children to take care of the planet. / country: Colombia

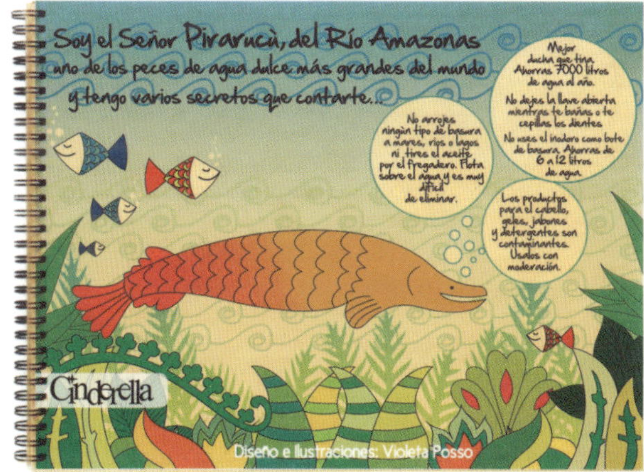

agency/studio: **Nina Levett** / project: bird-protection patterns for glass walls created to prevent birds from crashing into the glass walls of buildings or public spaces. / client: Umweltanwaltschaft Wien / country: Austria

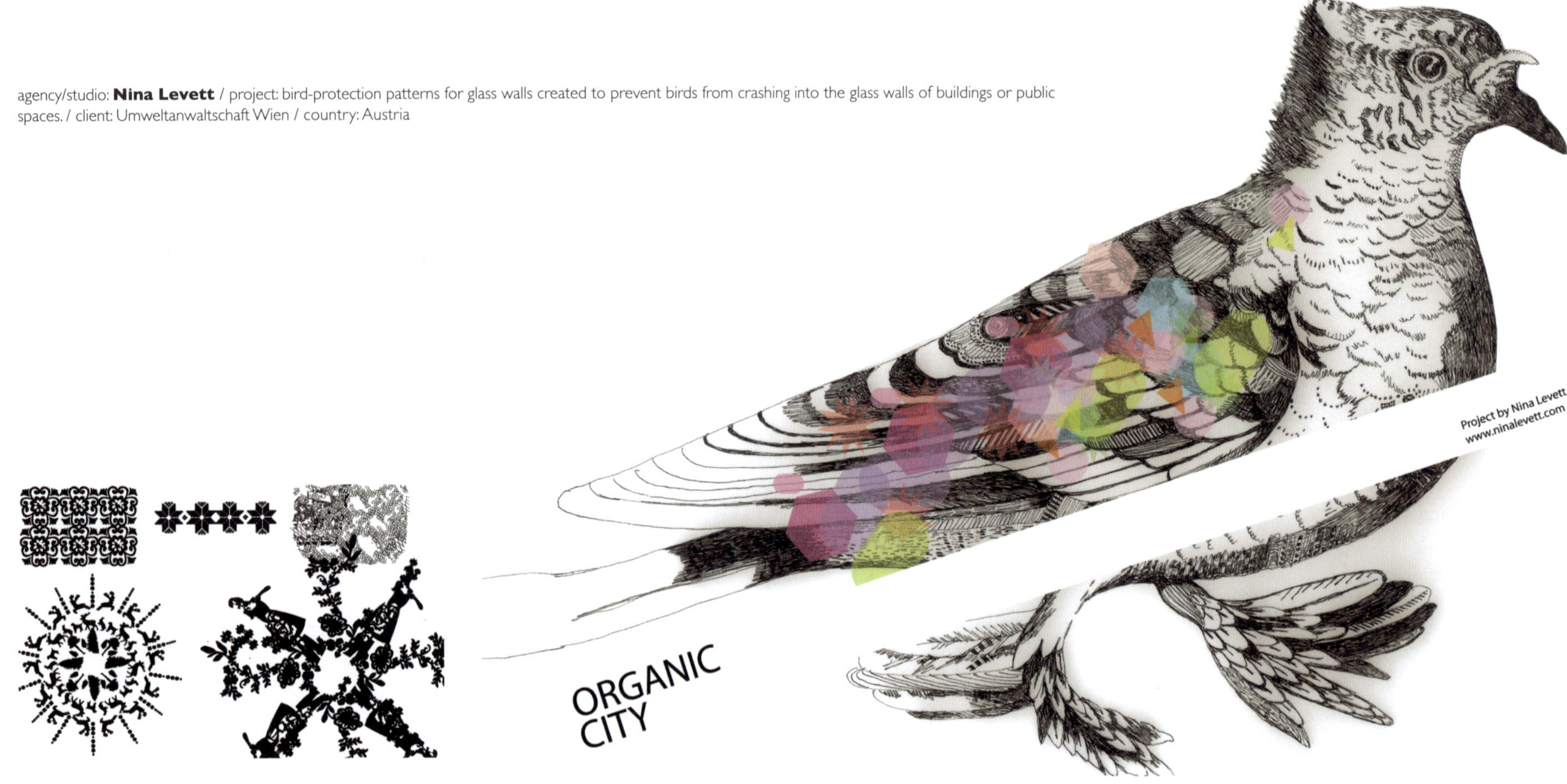

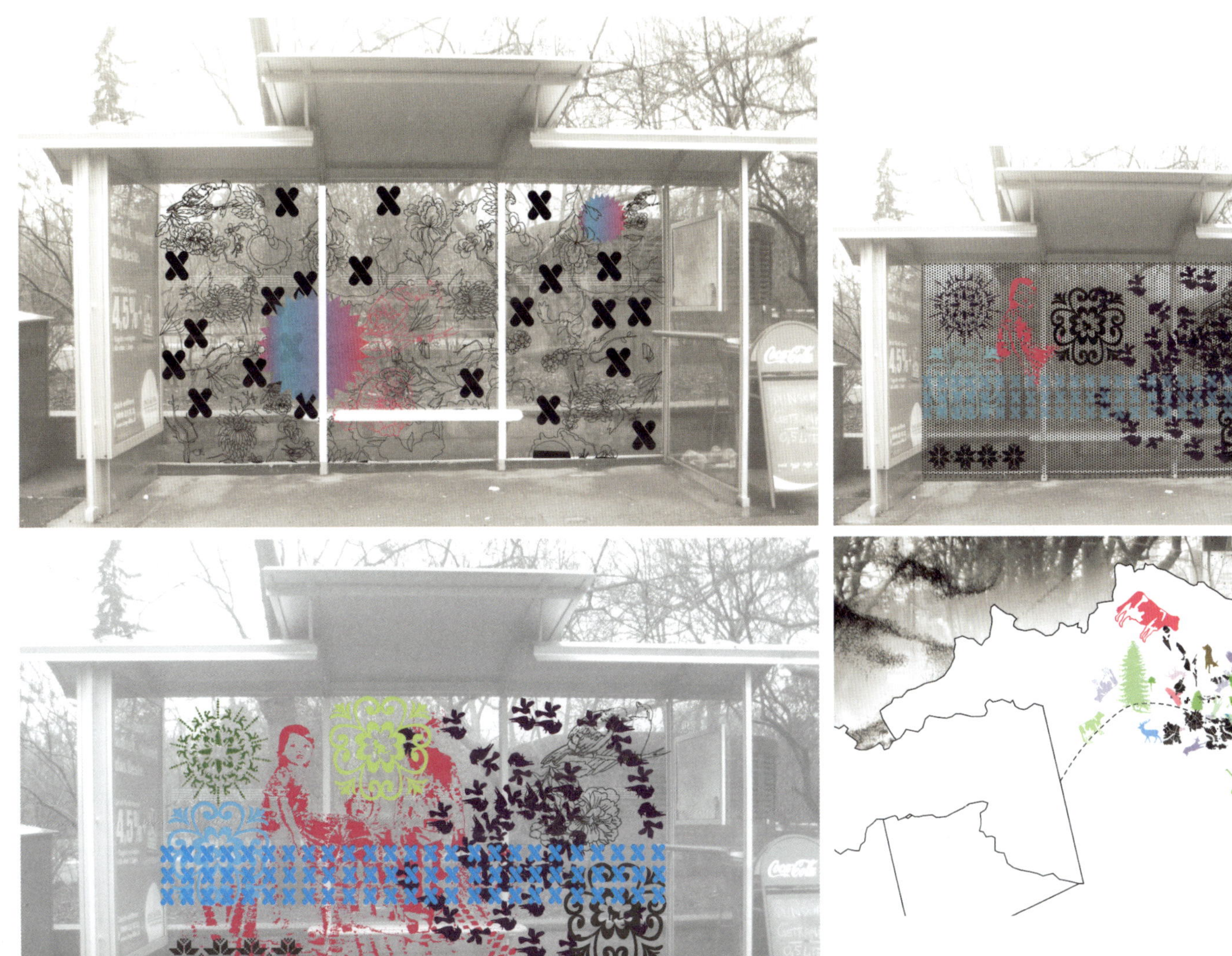

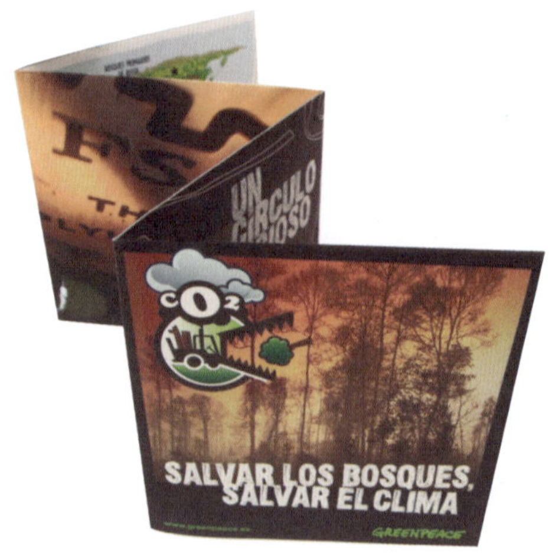

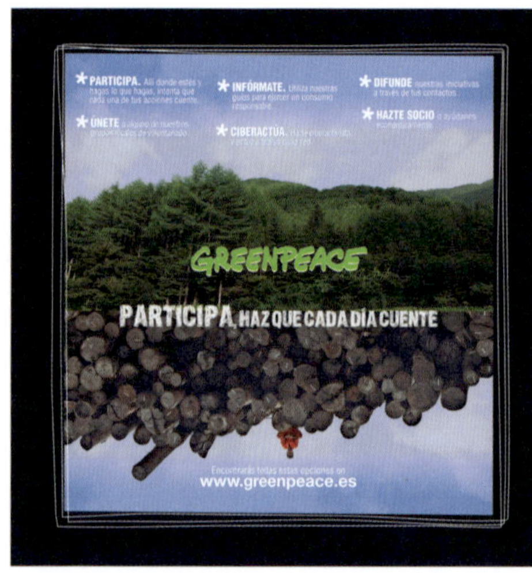

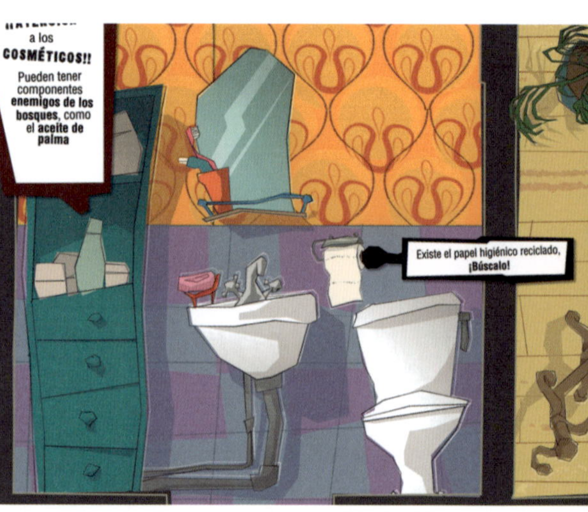

agency/studio: **Zigurat Comunicación Gráfica** / project: Salvar los Bosques Primarios (Save the Primary Forest). Multimedia awareness campaign on the relationship between the destruction of woodland and climate change. / client: Greenpeace España / country: Spain

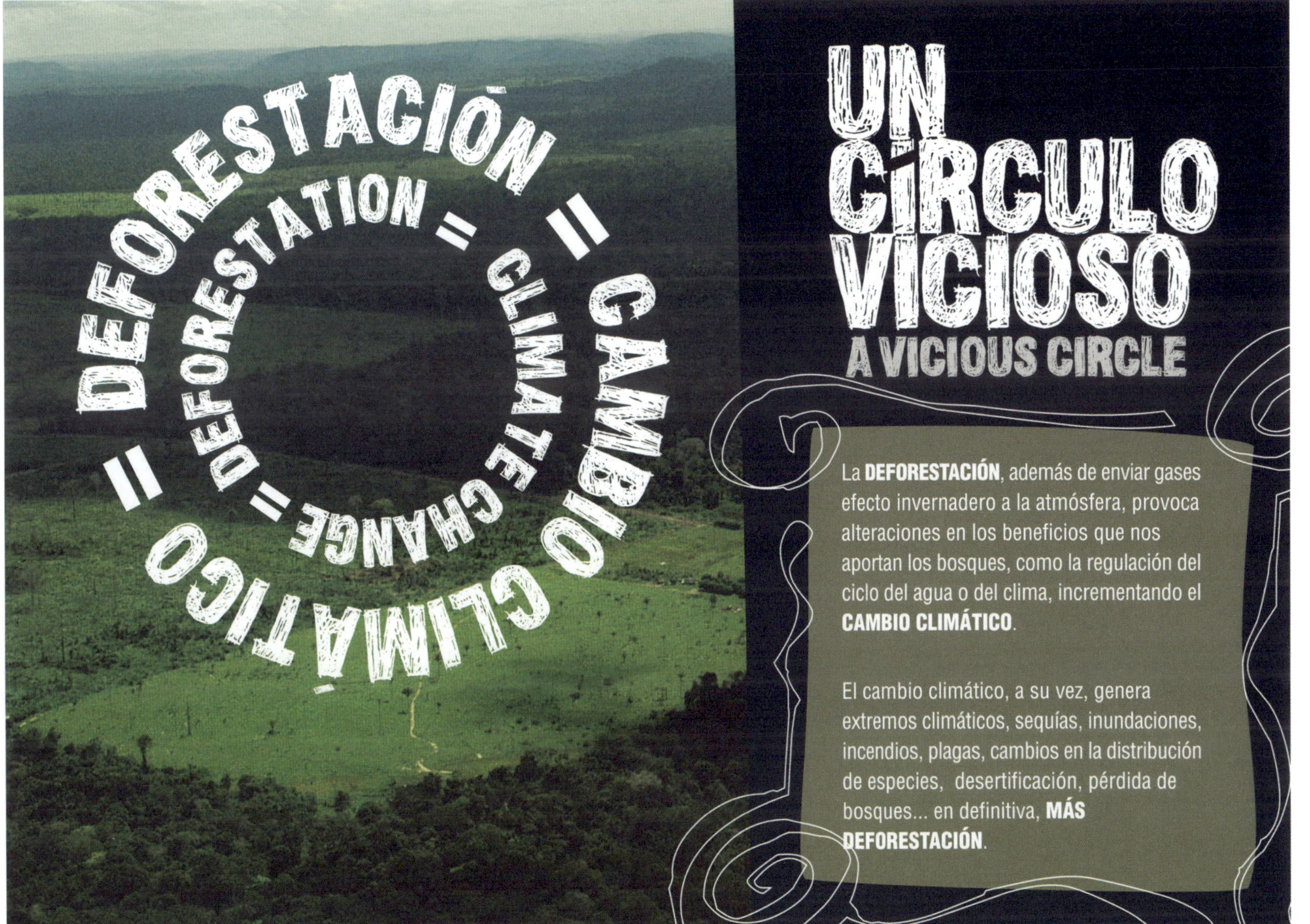

UN CÍRCULO VICIOSO
A VICIOUS CIRCLE

La **DEFORESTACIÓN**, además de enviar gases efecto invernadero a la atmósfera, provoca alteraciones en los beneficios que nos aportan los bosques, como la regulación del ciclo del agua o del clima, incrementando el **CAMBIO CLIMÁTICO**.

El cambio climático, a su vez, genera extremos climáticos, sequías, inundaciones, incendios, plagas, cambios en la distribución de especies, desertificación, pérdida de bosques... en definitiva, **MÁS DEFORESTACIÓN**.

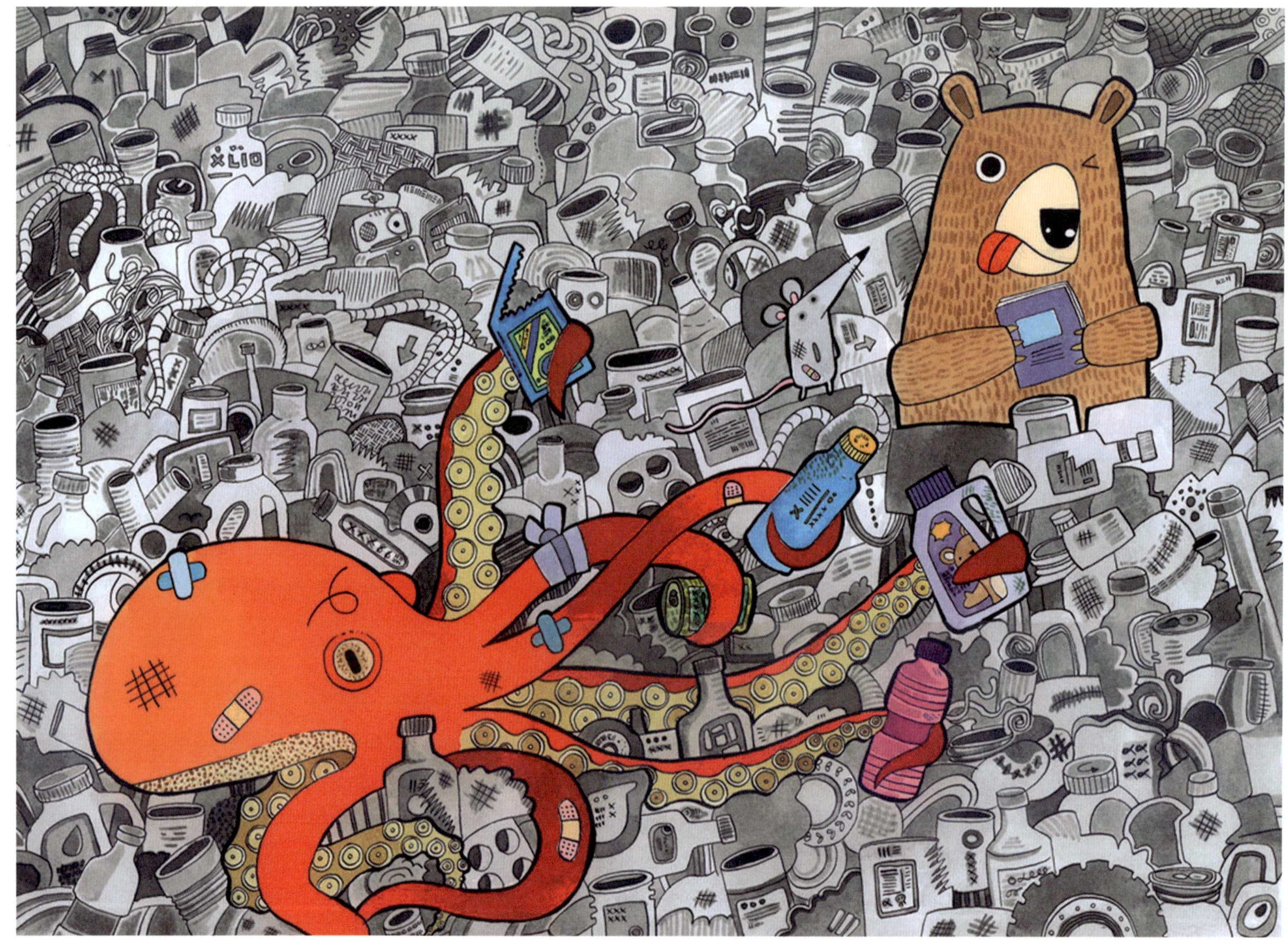

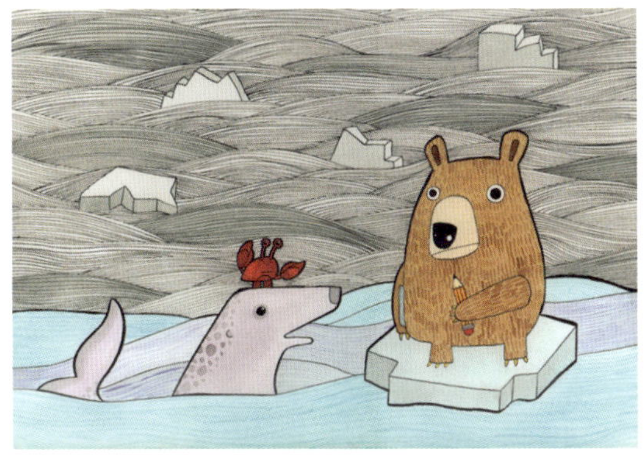

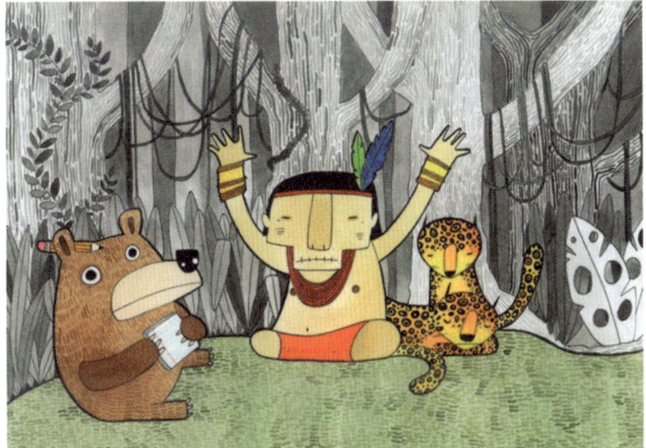

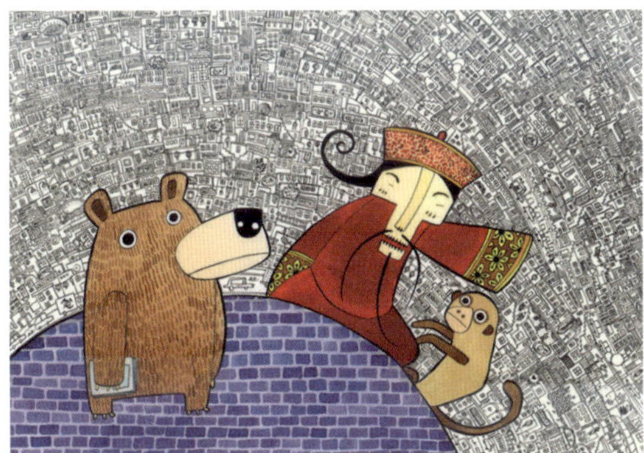

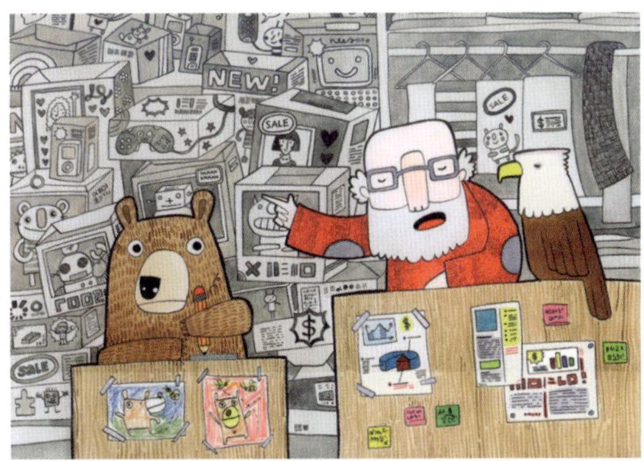

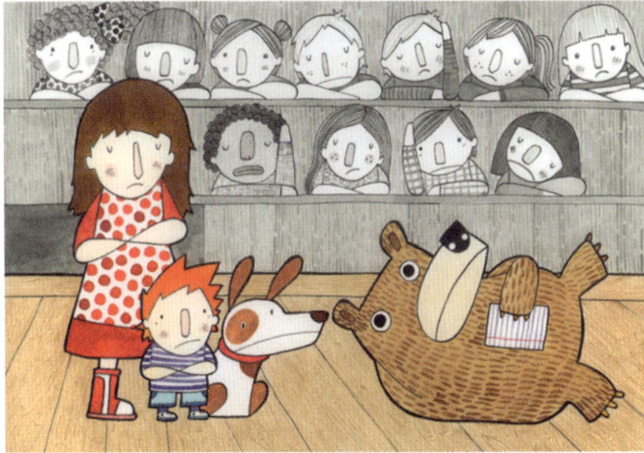

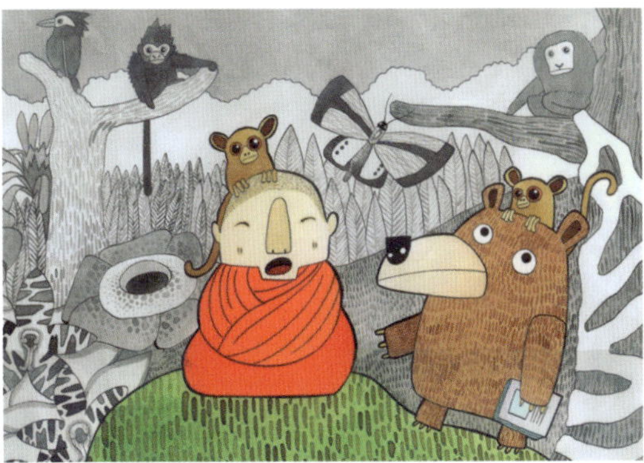

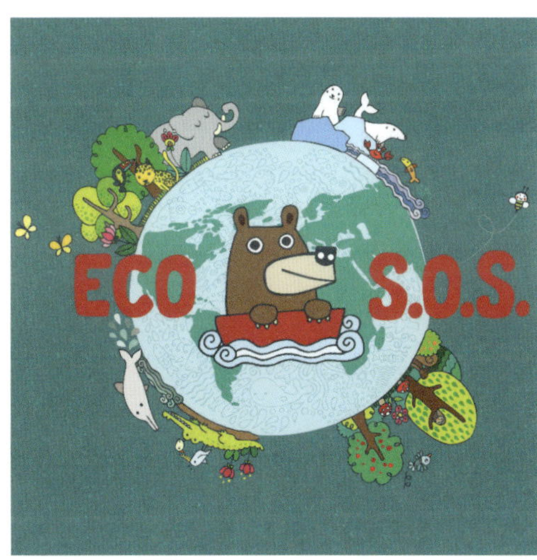

agency/studio: **Laura Osorno** / project: ECO S.O.S. is an illustrated book that gives children the opportunity to receive a complete environmental education that will help them adopt a lifestyle that is pro-active with the environment and the planet Earth. / text writers: Maria Villegas, Jennie Kent / publisher: Villegas Editores / country: Colombia

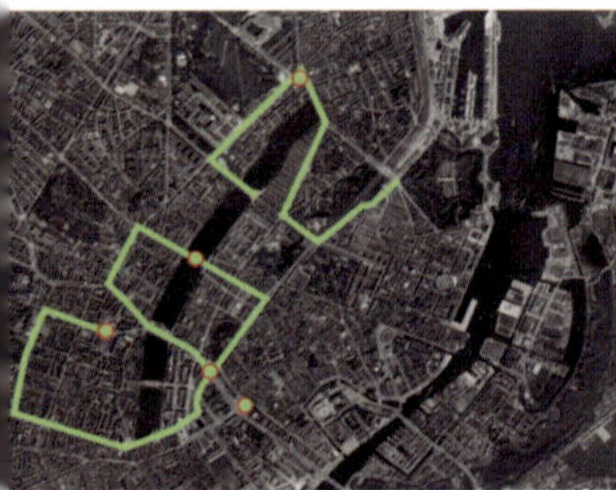
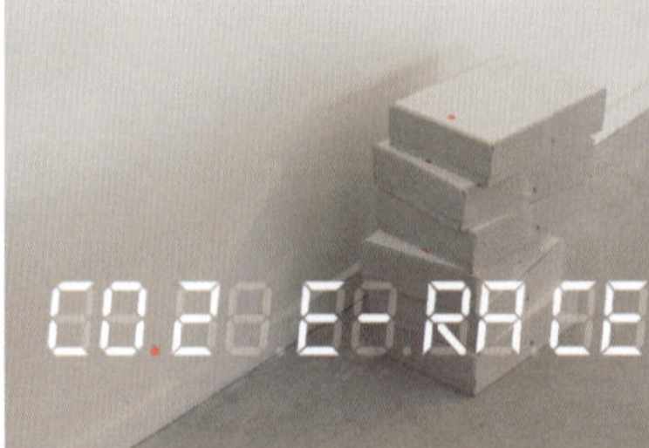

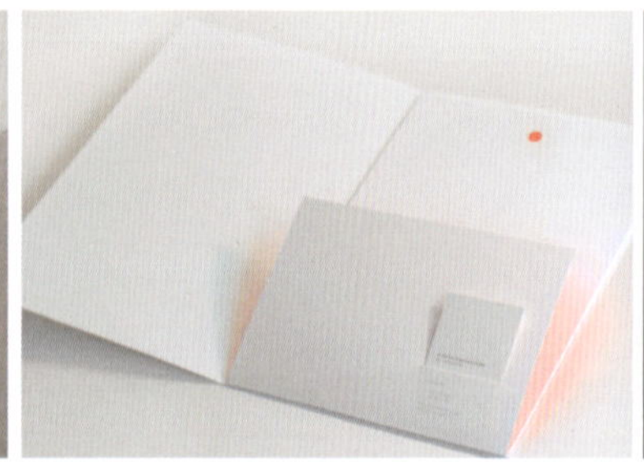
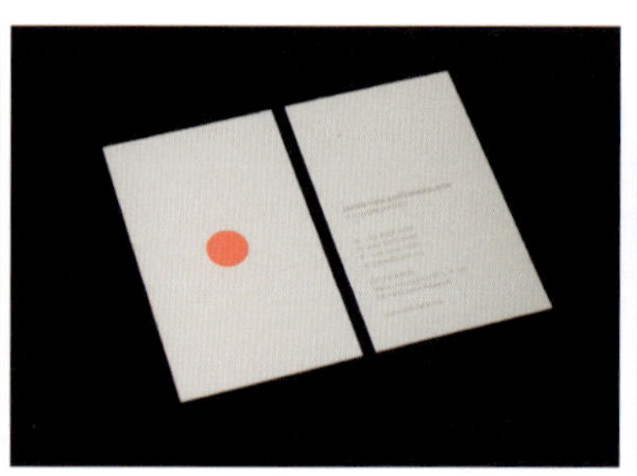
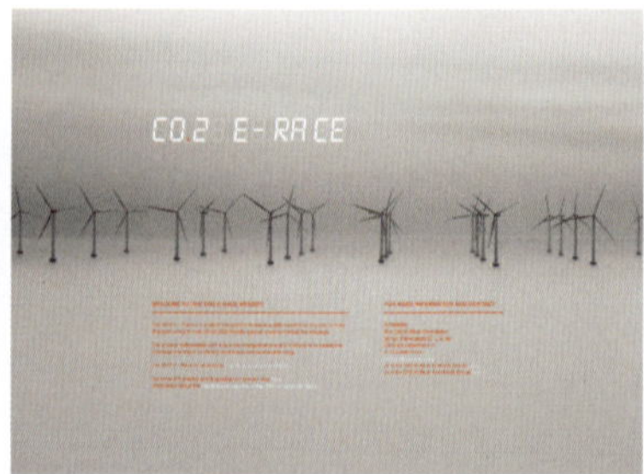

agency/studio: **Re-public** / project: The CO2 E Race is a project designed to increase public awareness of global climate change using the vehicle of CO2-friendly cars as a way to spread the message. The project collaborates with a number of organisations and institutions to spread the message and intent of climate awareness and sustainable living. The CO2 E - Race was initiated by The Danish Cultural Institute. / client: CO2 E - Race / country: Denmark

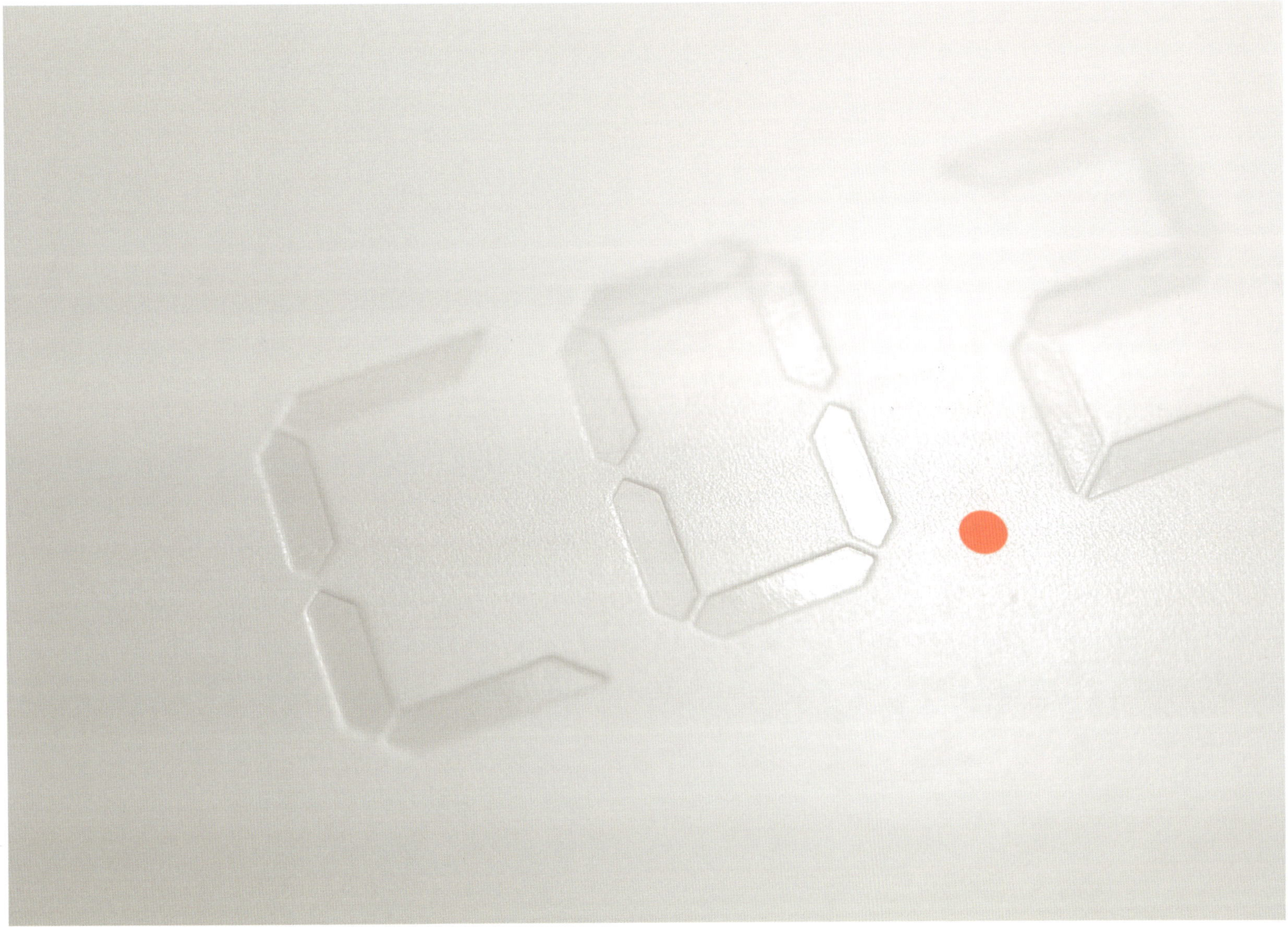

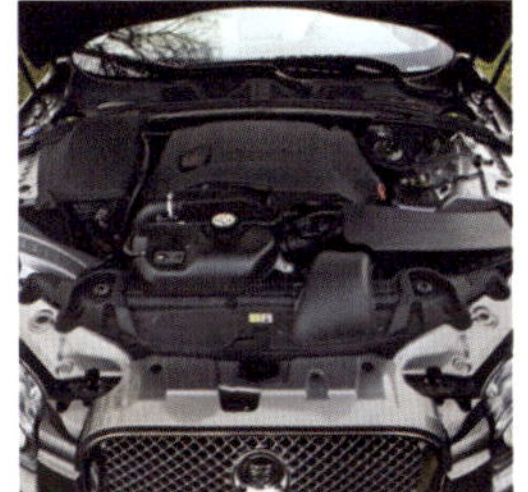

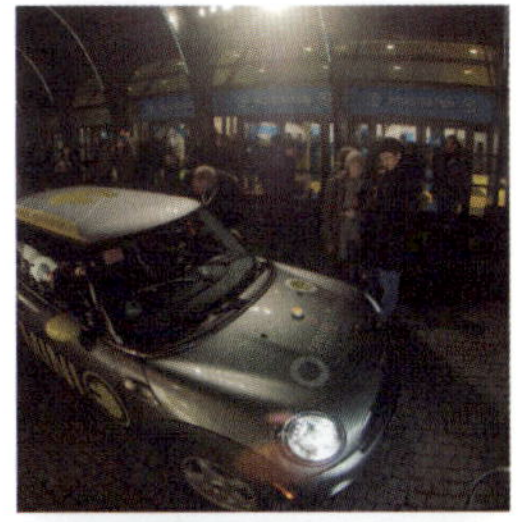

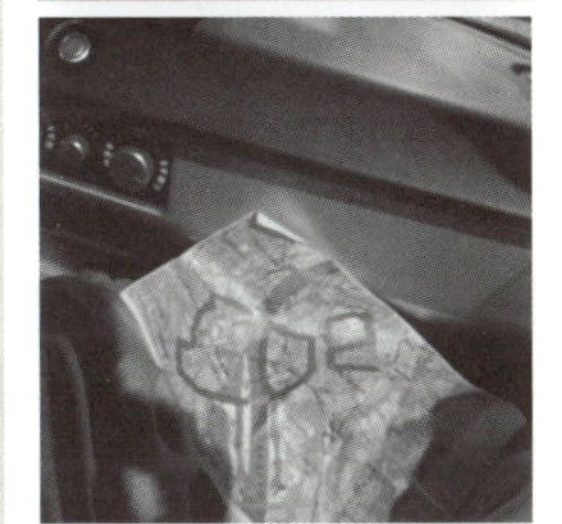

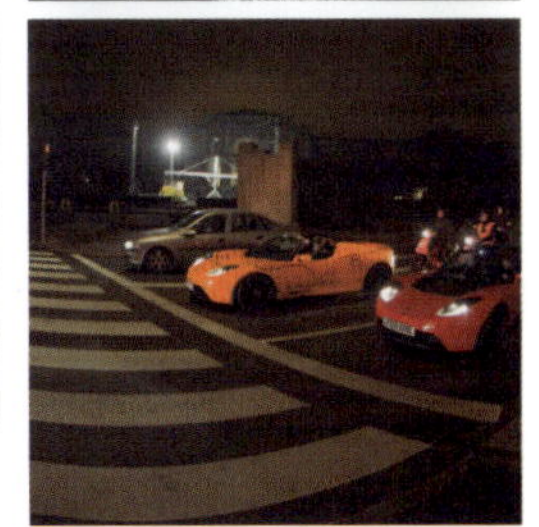

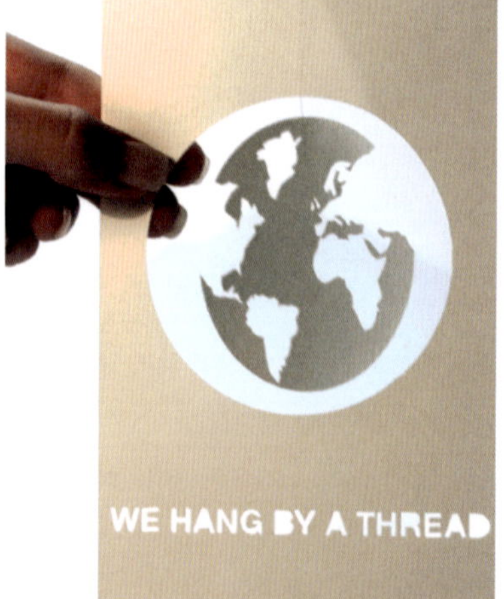

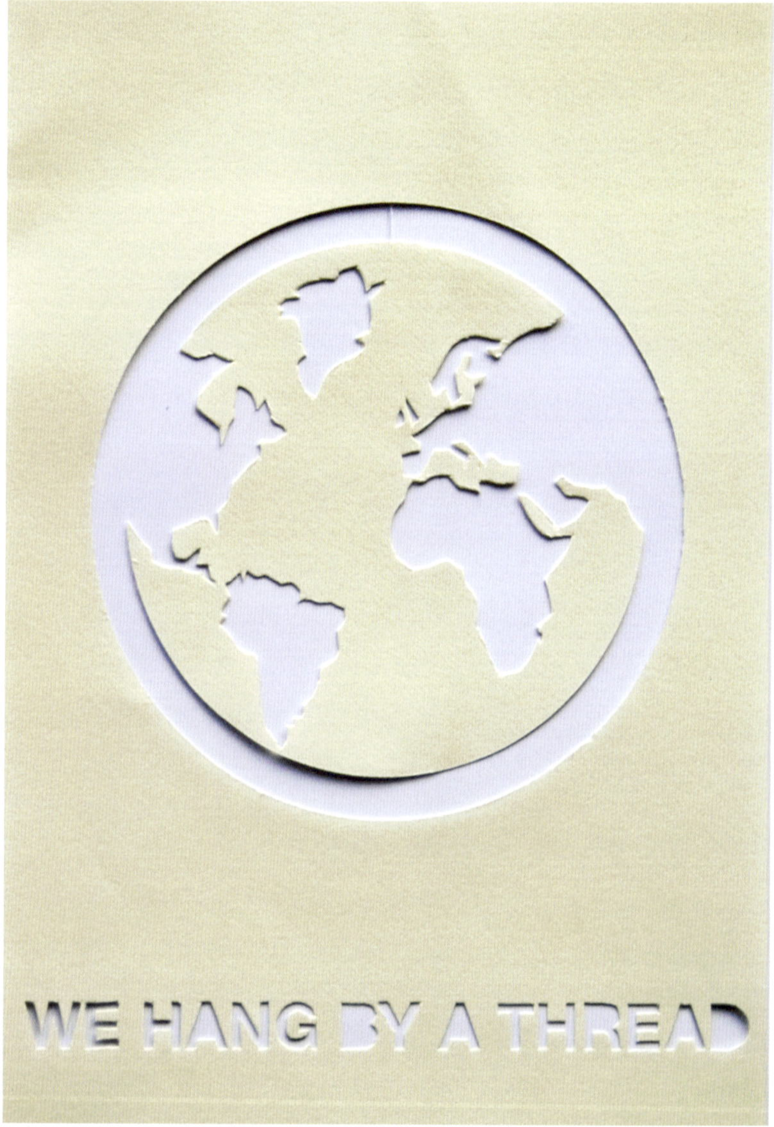

agency/studio: **Metakitrina** / project: we hang by a thread. An ecological awareness postcard that is die-cut, unprinted and made from 100% cotton ecological paper. / country: Spain

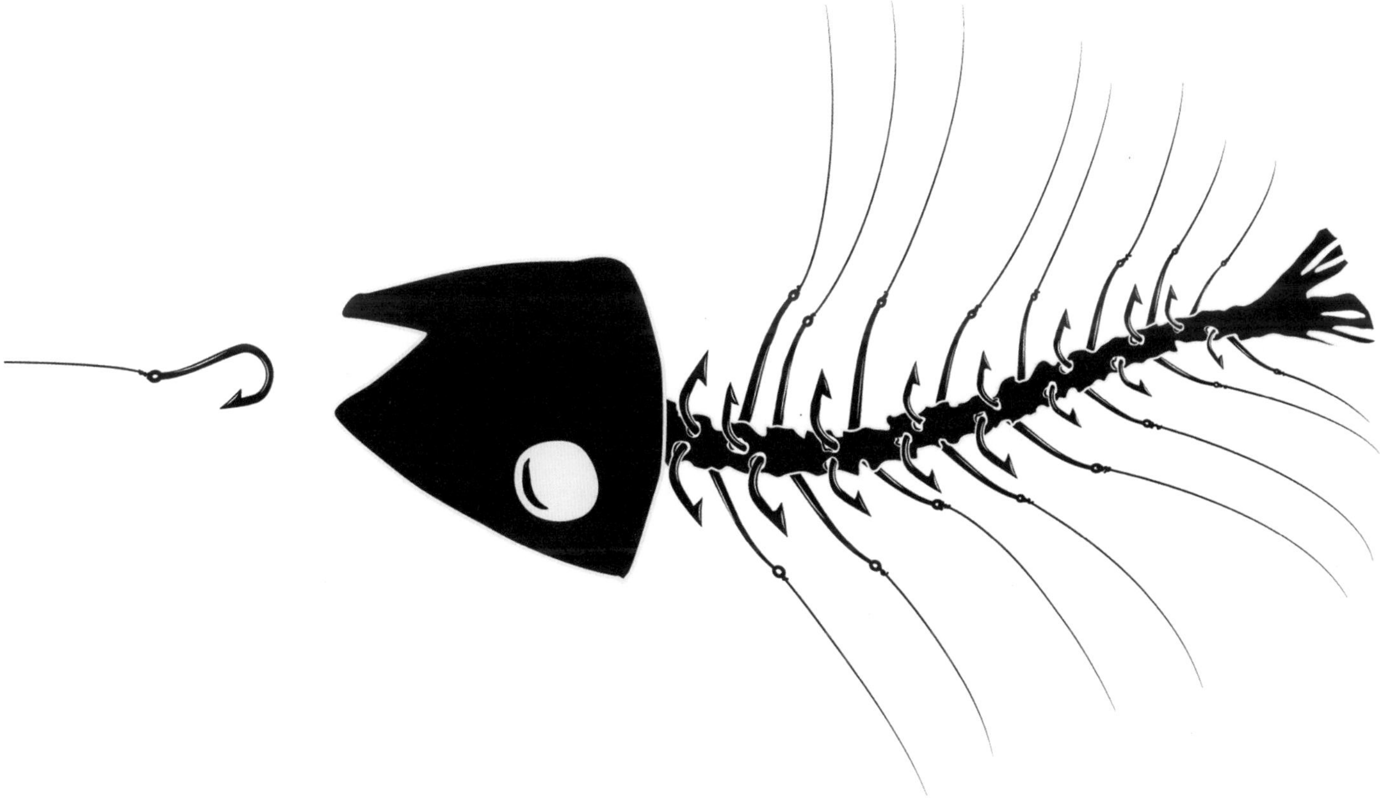

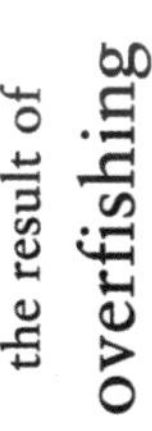

agency/studio: **Wolfgang Steinbauer** / project: the result of overfishing. / client: Greenpeace / country: Austria author: **Anatoliy Omelchenko** / project: China produces and discards more than 45 billion pairs of disposable chopsticks and toothpicks every year, cutting down as many as 25 million trees. Another 15 billion pairs are exported to Japan, South Korea and other countries. / country: USA

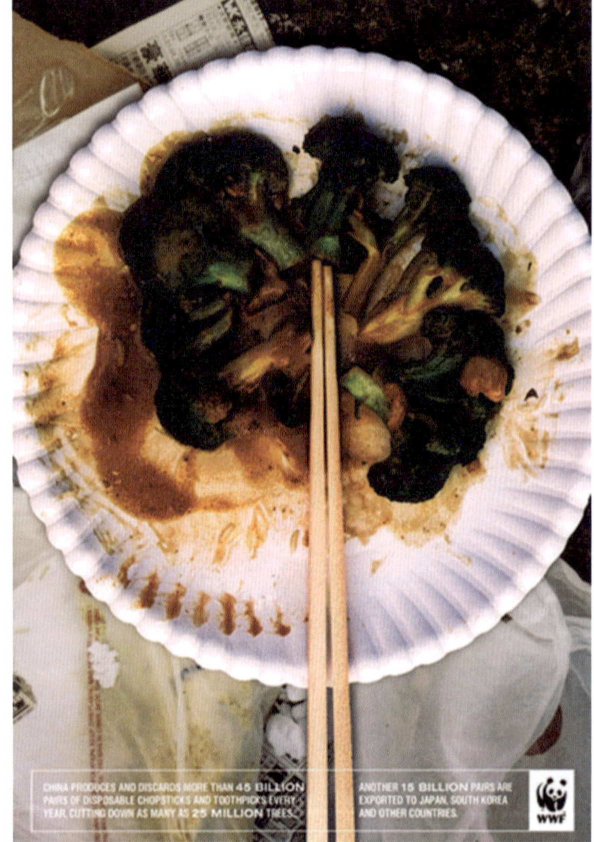

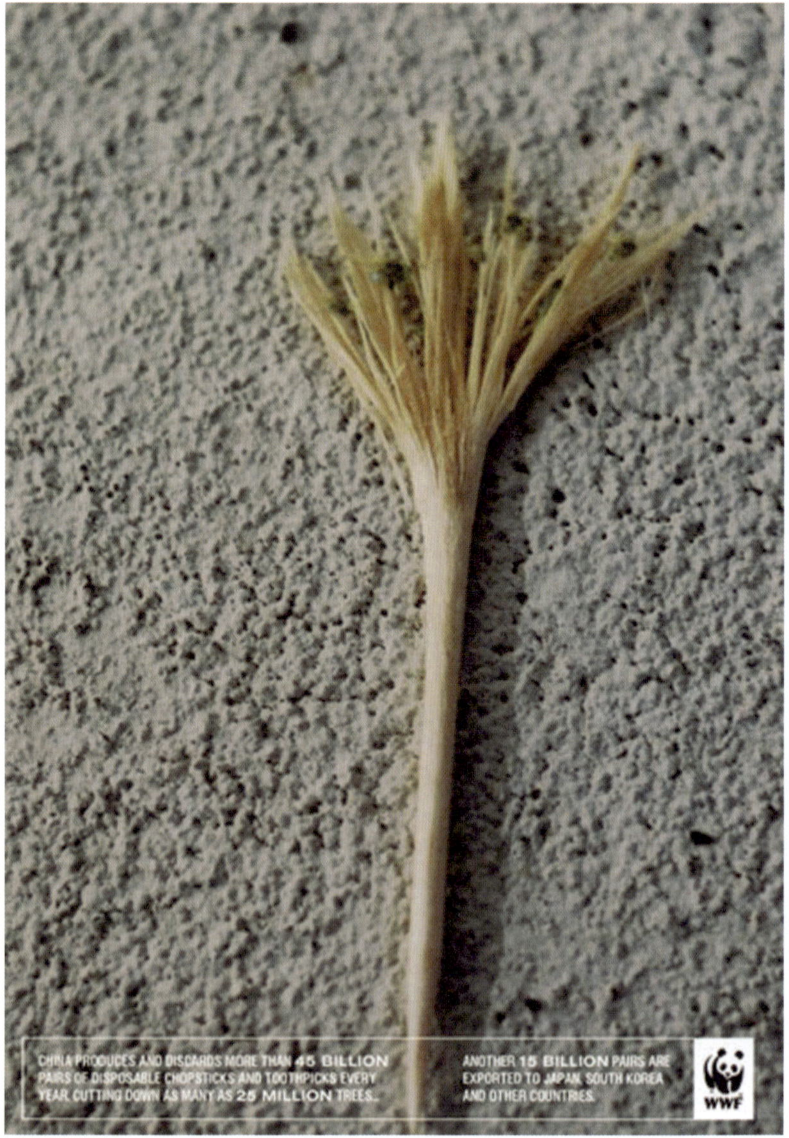

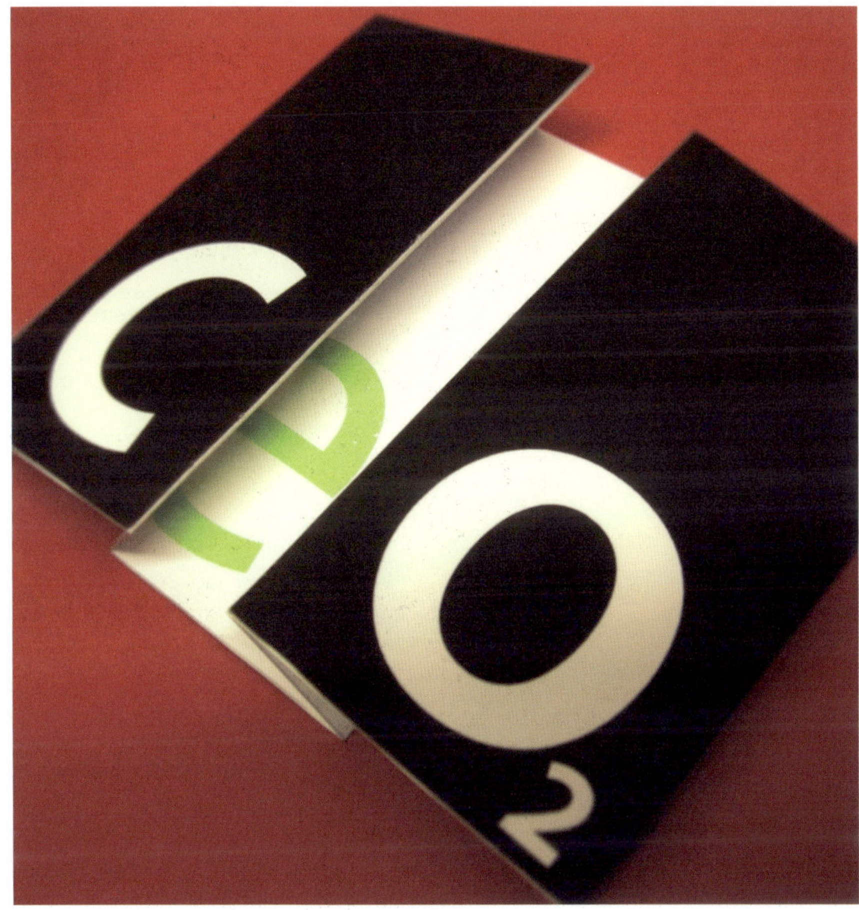

agency/studio: **Alejandro Gallego** / project: CO2 CERO. A folded flyer whose aim is to raise awareness about the danger of CO2 emissions and make people realise that change is possible and that change is in their hands. It depends on them. / client: IED Madrid / country: Spain

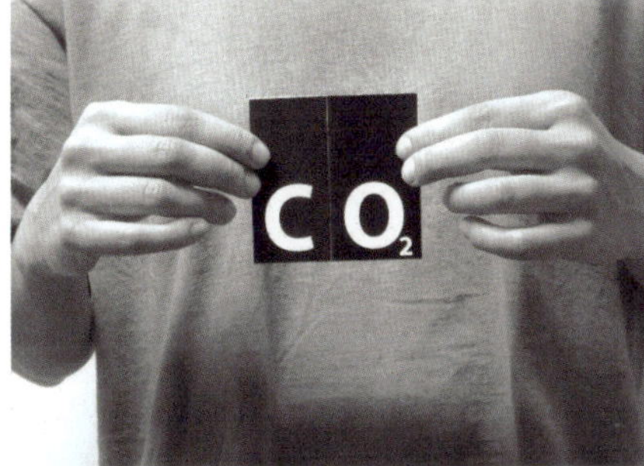

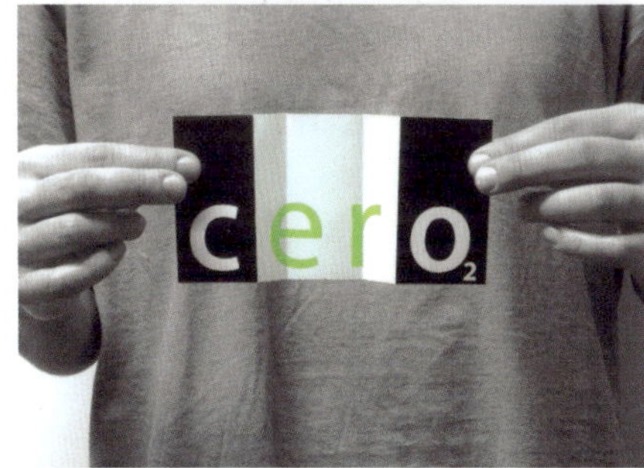

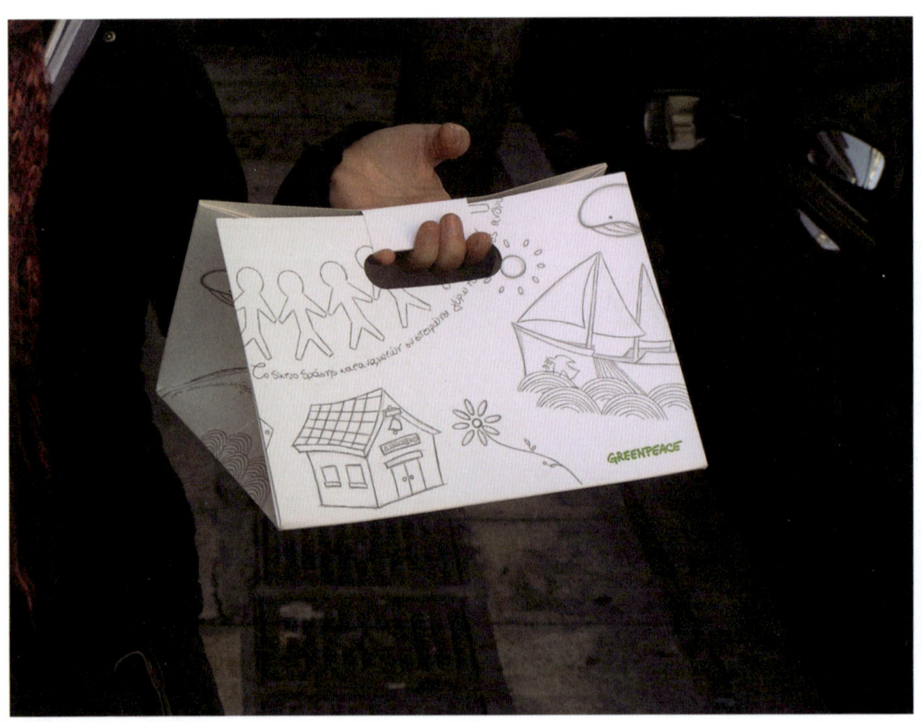

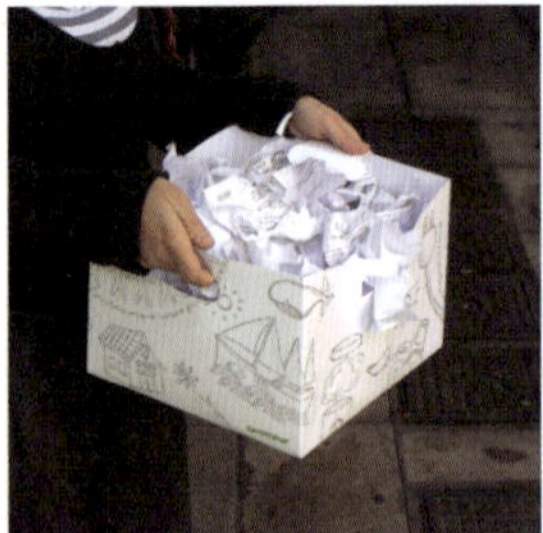

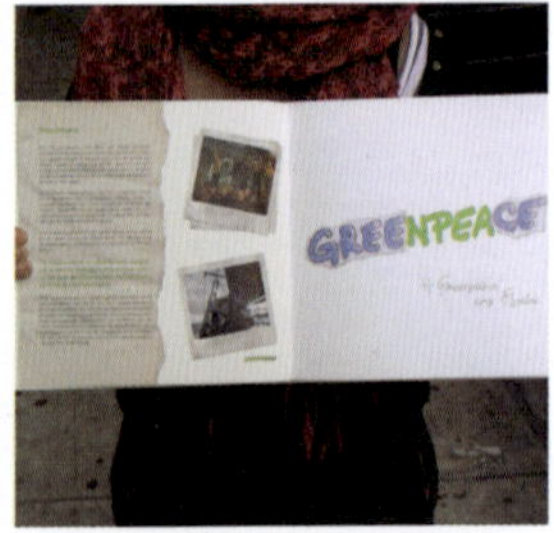

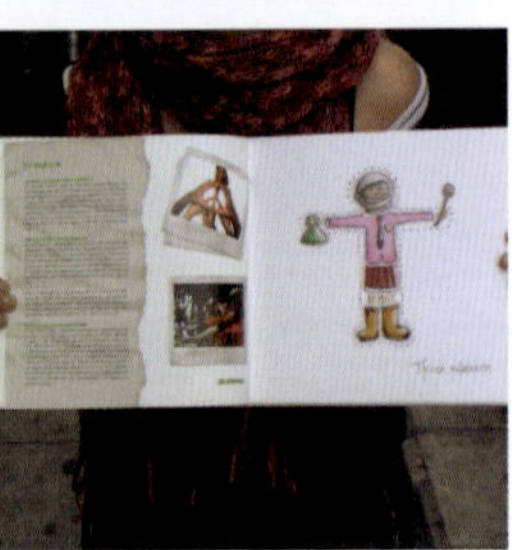

agency/studio: **Myrmigi Design House** / project: Greenpeace Greece's rebranding consists of a corporate brochure, an animated short and a flipbook. These are wrapped in an attractive multi-use bag that becomes a recycling bin. / client: Greenpeace Greece / country: Greece

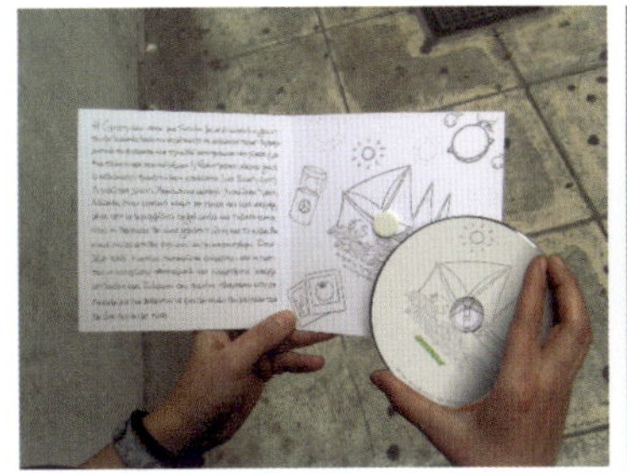

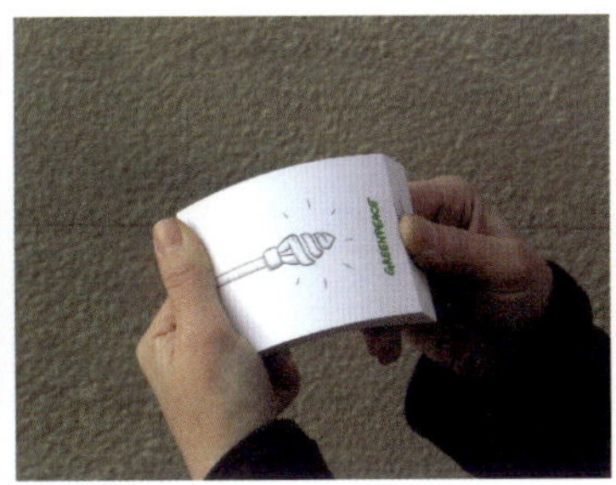

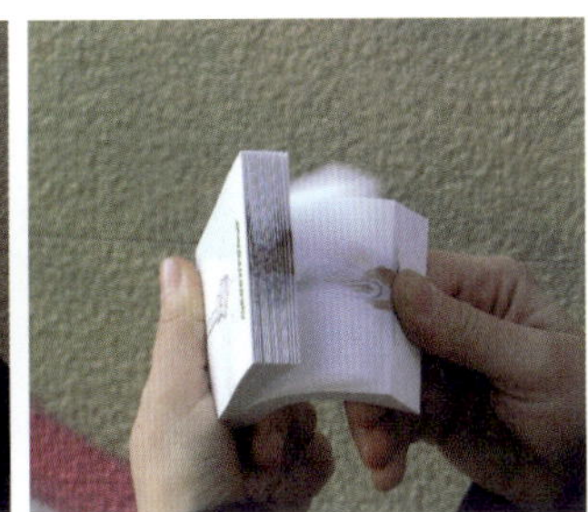

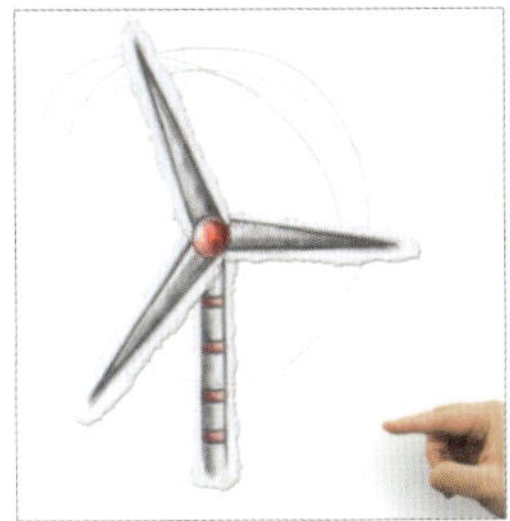

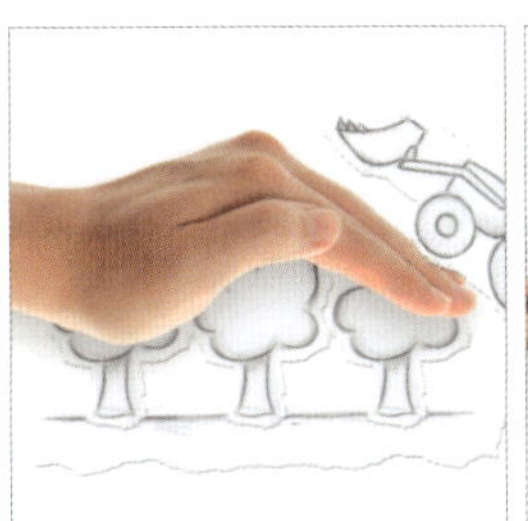

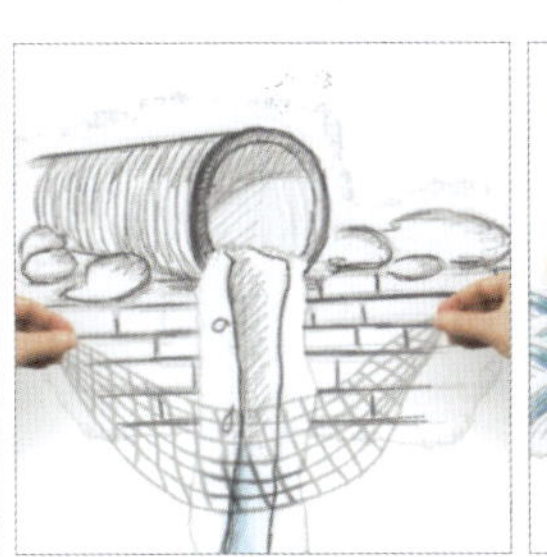

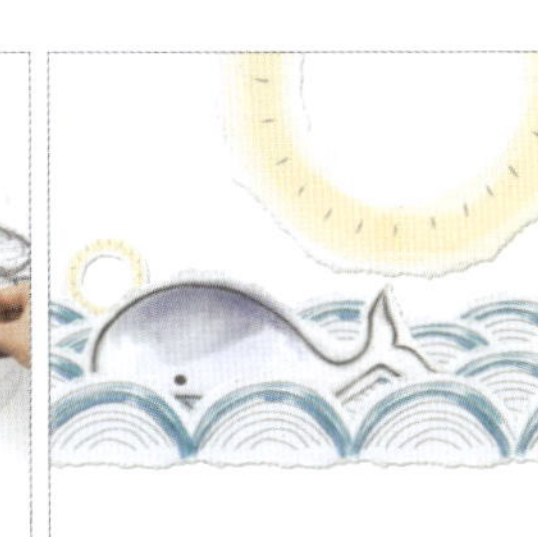

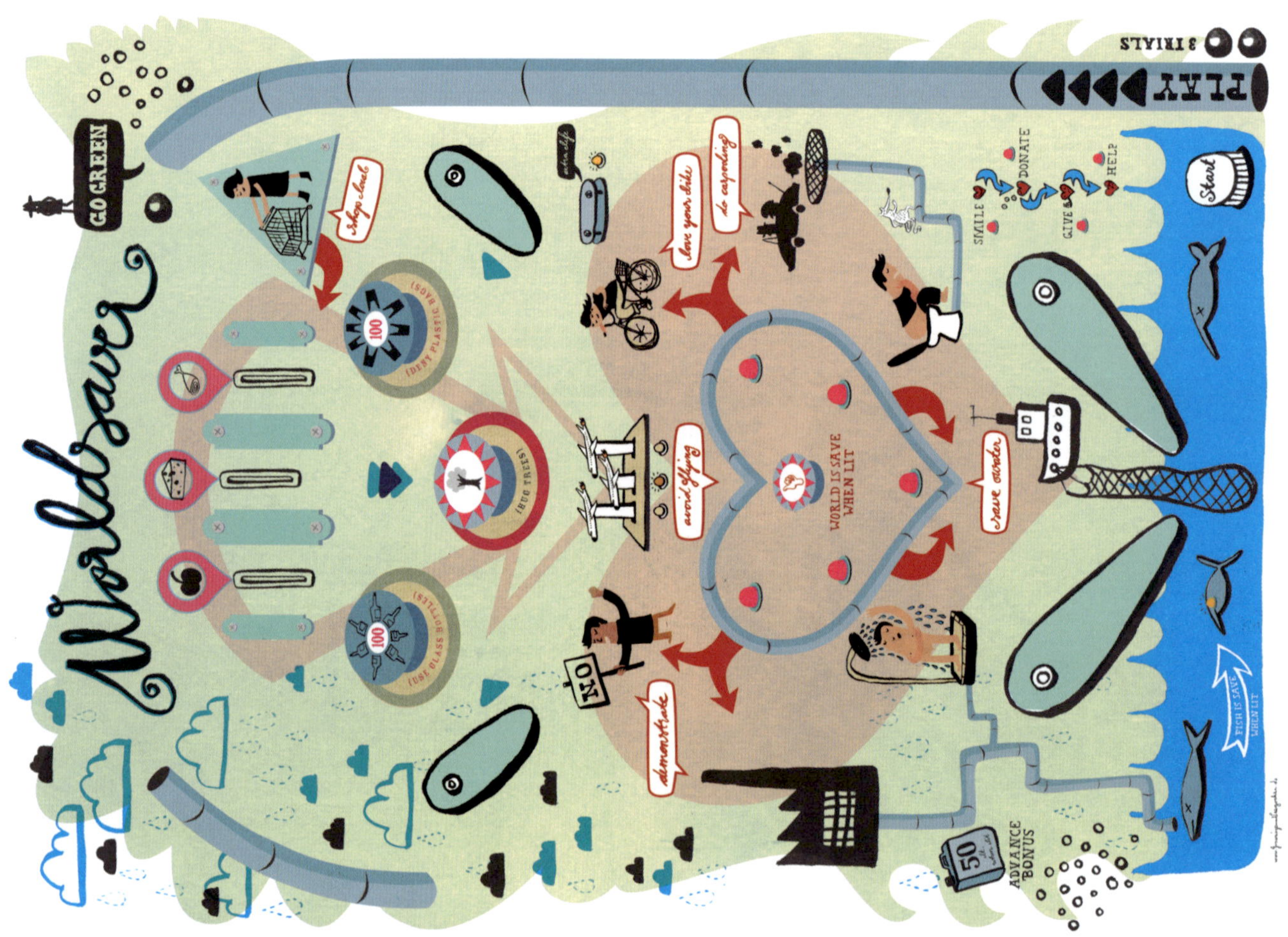

author: **Tine Schulz / Grasziegeundpregochse** / project: Worldsaver poster: how to save the world in a pinball game / country: Germany

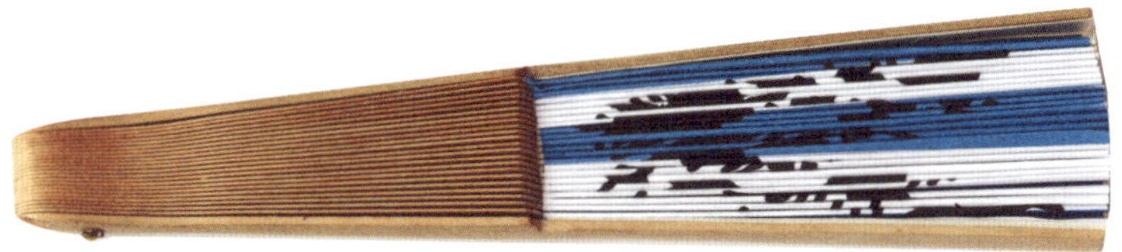

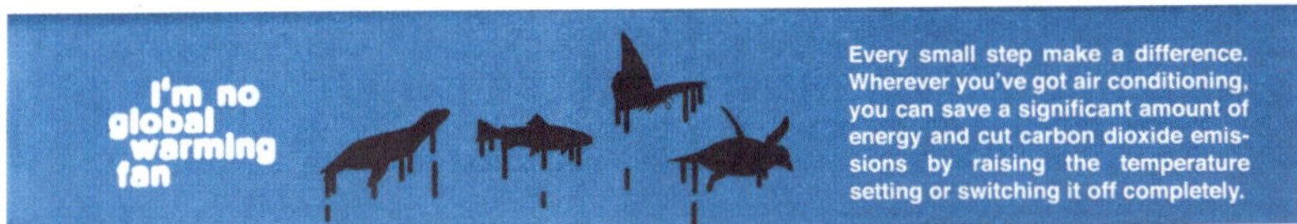

agency/studio: **Pöko Design** / photo by Neckel Sholtus / project: no global warming FAN. A hand fan with an anti-climate-change message. / country: Spain

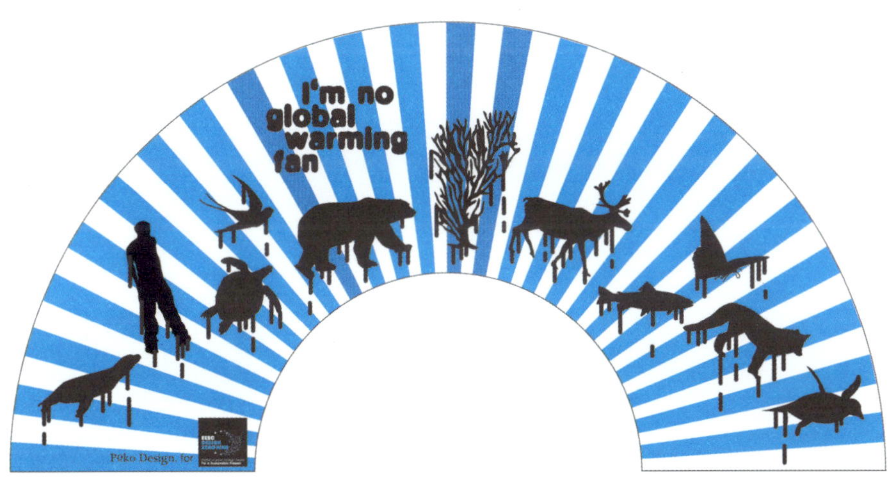

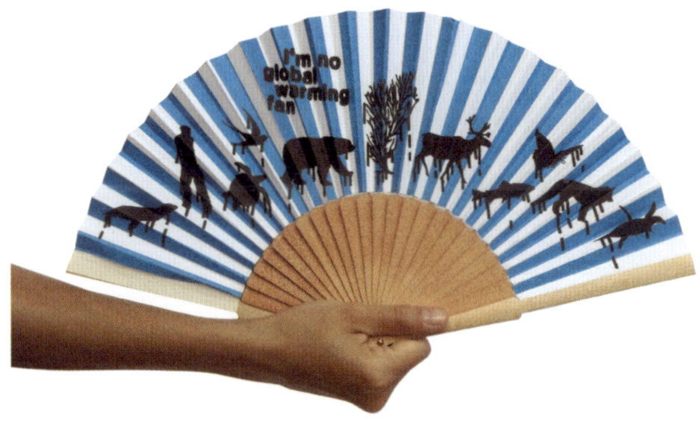

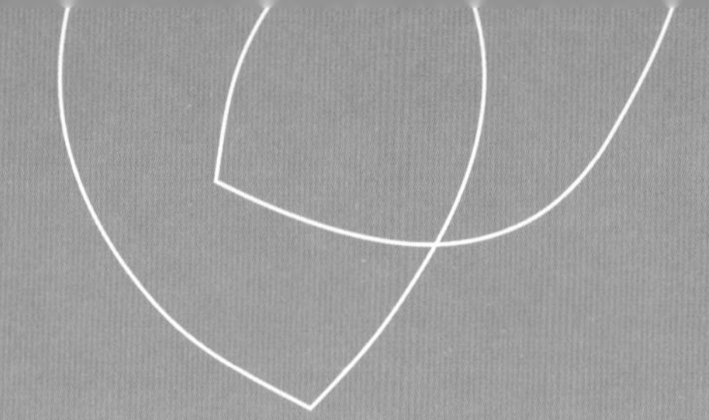
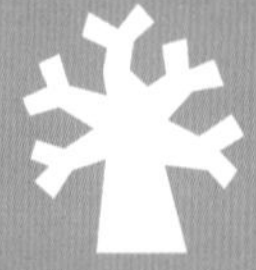

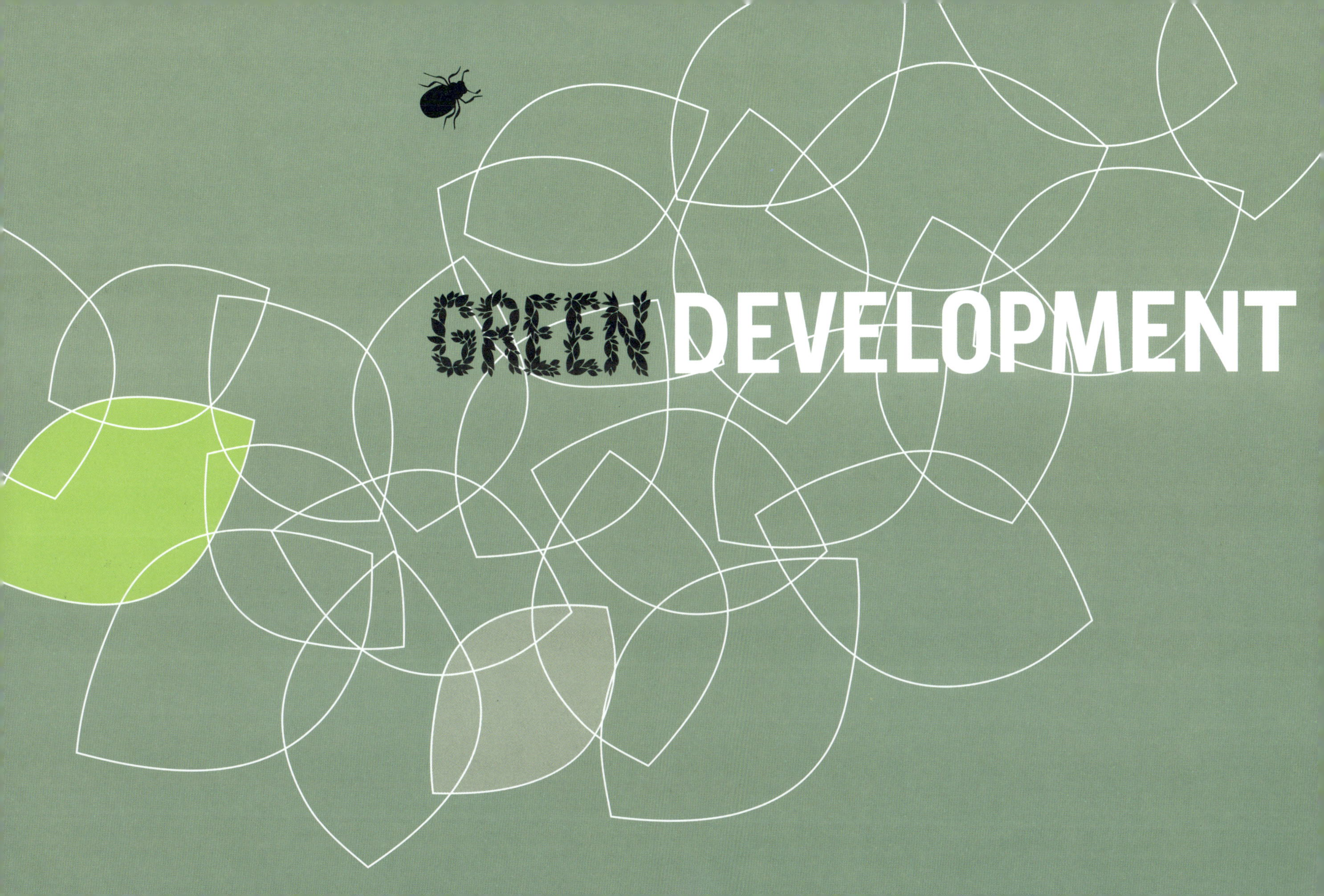
GREEN DEVELOPMENT

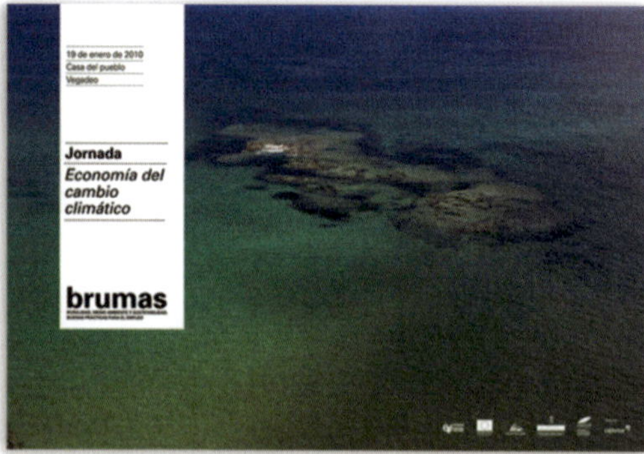

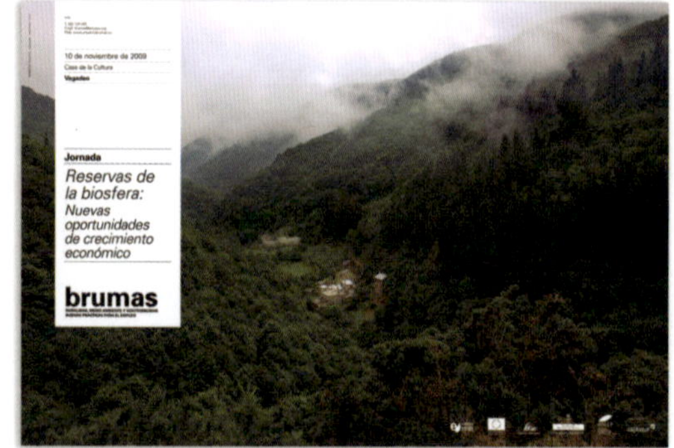

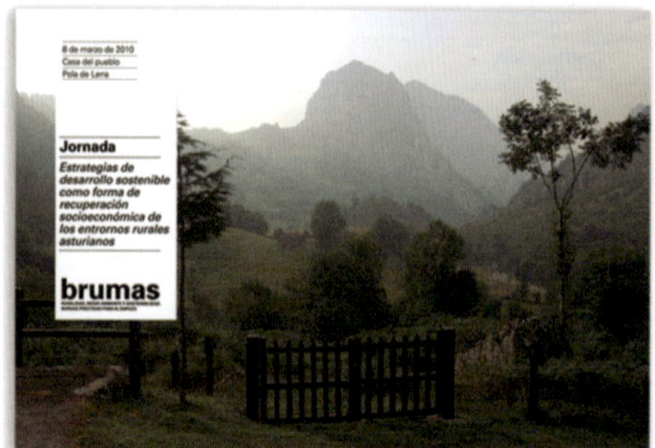

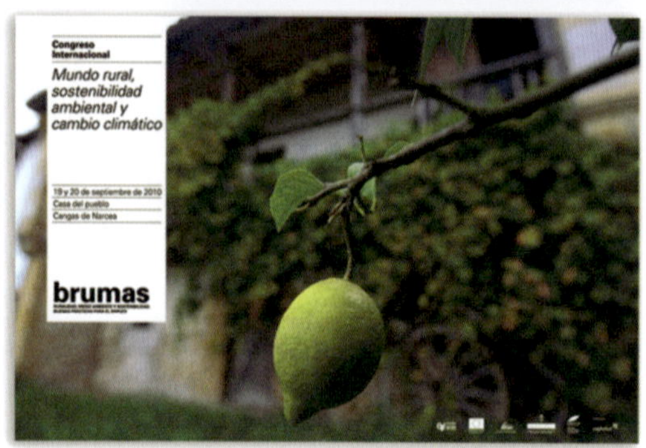

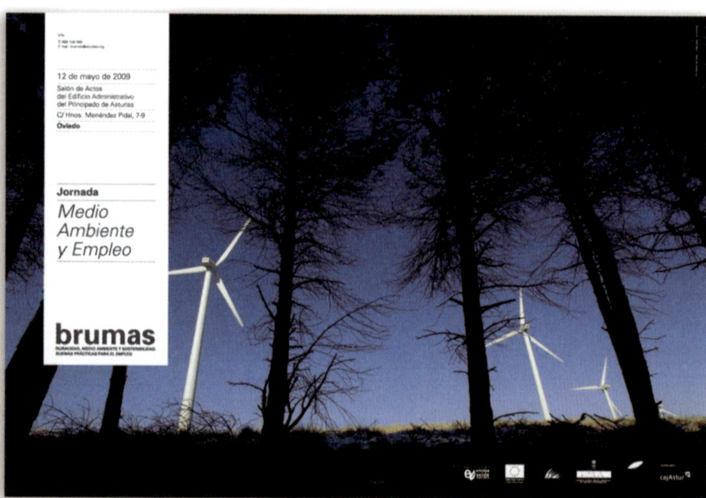

agency/studio: **Jorge Lorenzo Diseño y Comunicación Visual** / project: "Brumas", a campaign for a set of conferences on the environment. / client: Regional government of Asturias / country: Spain

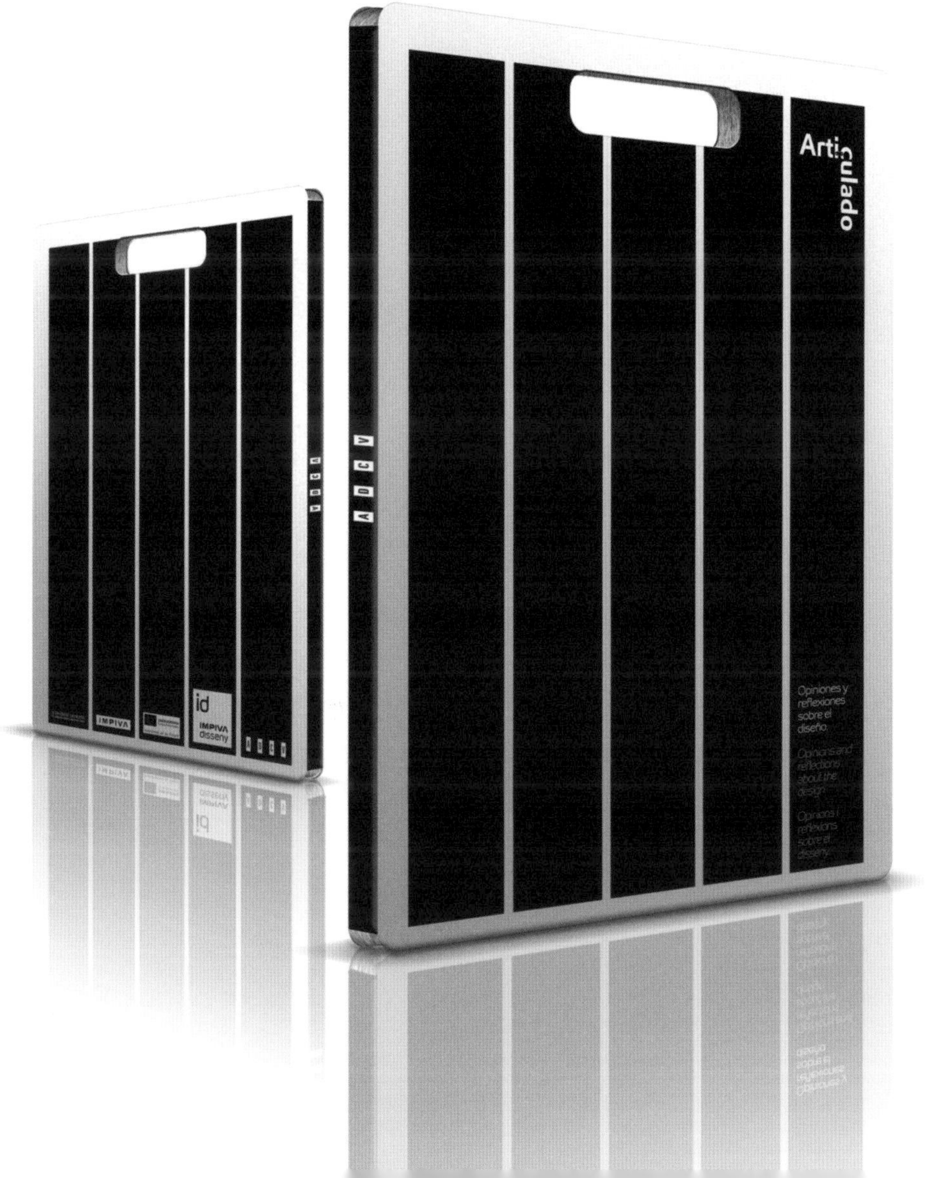

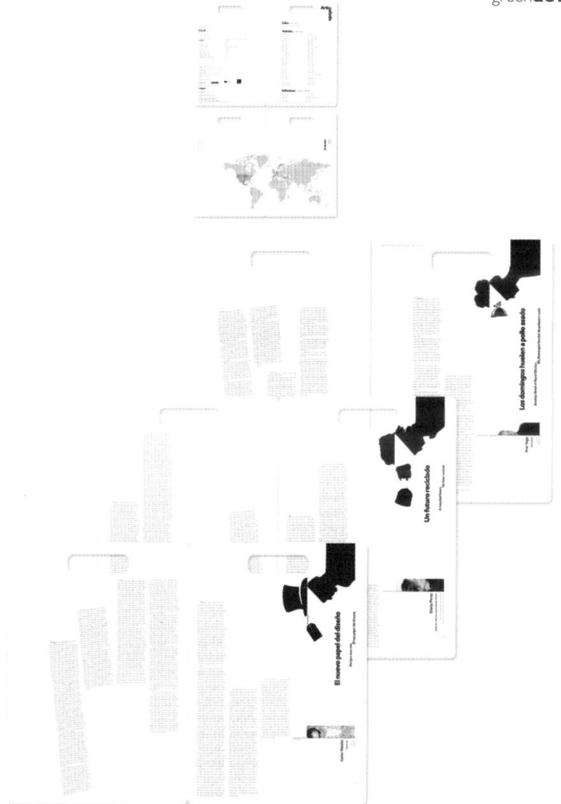

agency/studio: **Sanserif Creatius** / project: the book object "Articulado" is a compilation of opinions of designers from around the world on design, the environment and economics. / client: IMPIVA and ADCV / country: Spain

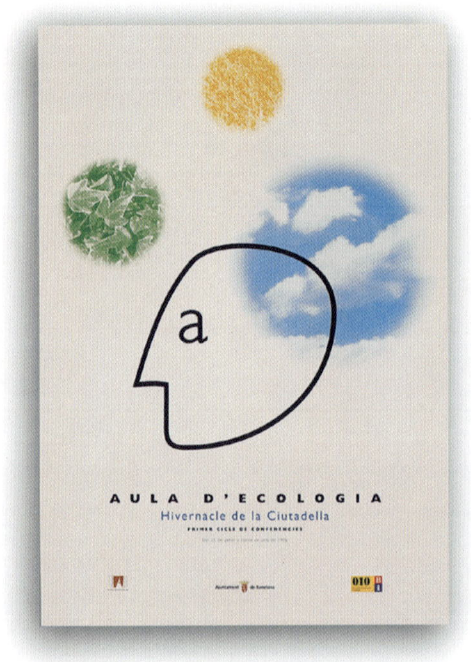

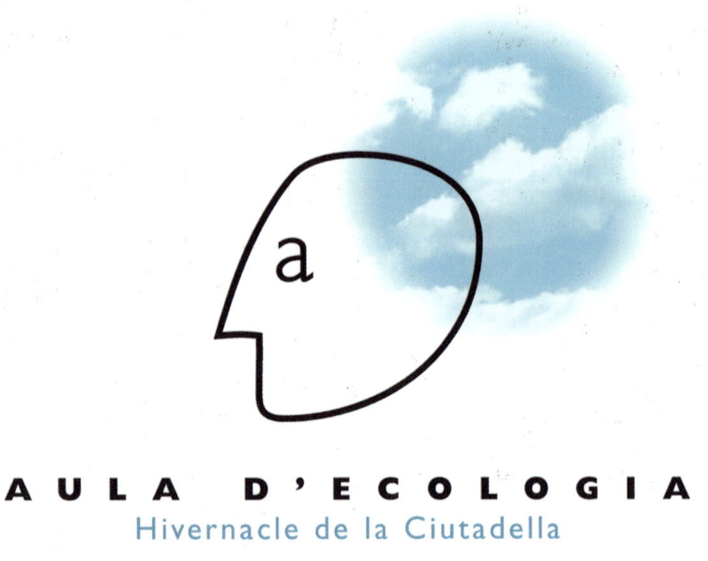

agency/studio: **Sonsoles Llorens** / project: graphic identity for Barcelona City Council's Aula d'Ecologia, which is a crossroads between human reflection and nature. / client: Barcelona City Council / country: Spain

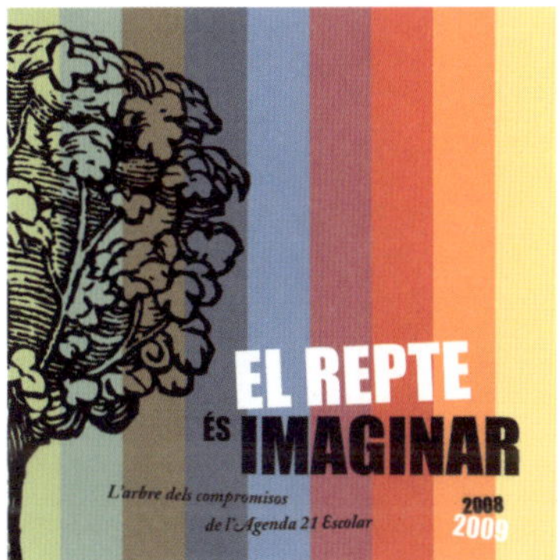

agency/studio: **APS&co** / project: campaign for Barcelona schools adhered to Agenda 21 for Schools. / client: Agenda 21 Escolar Barcelona / country: Spain

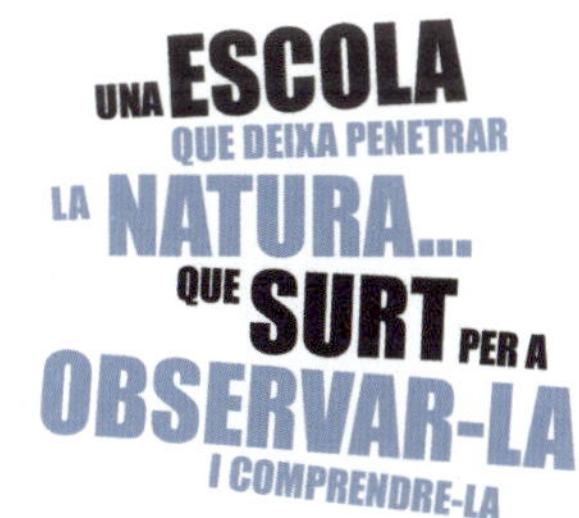

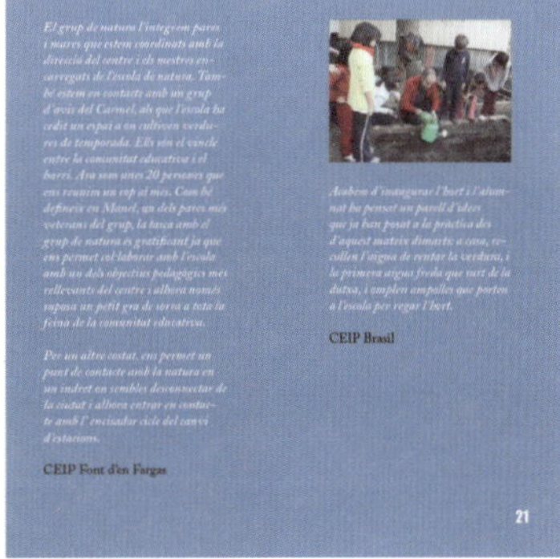

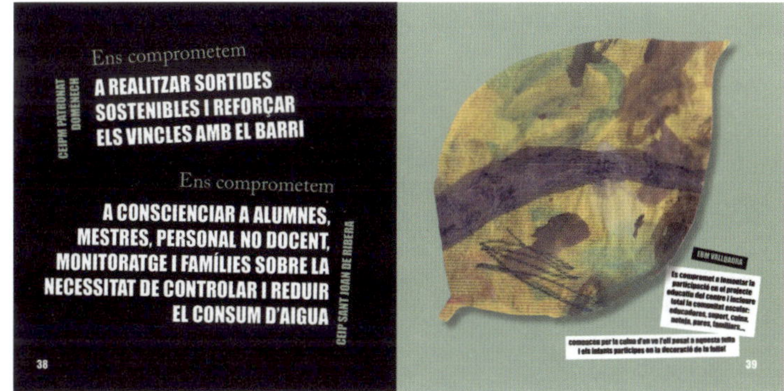

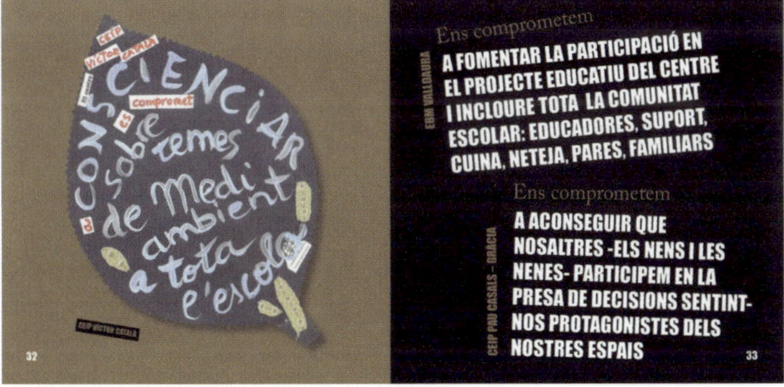

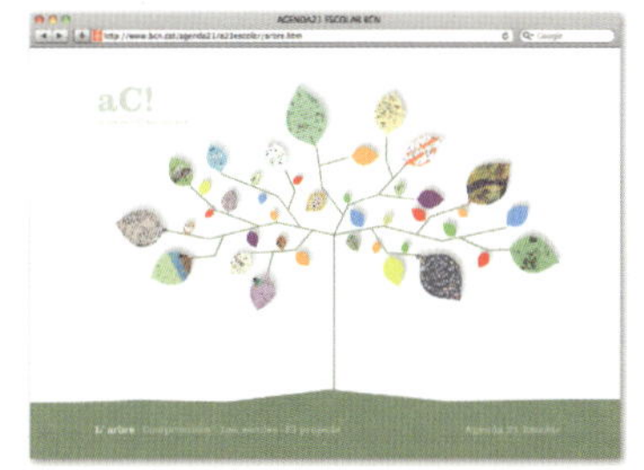

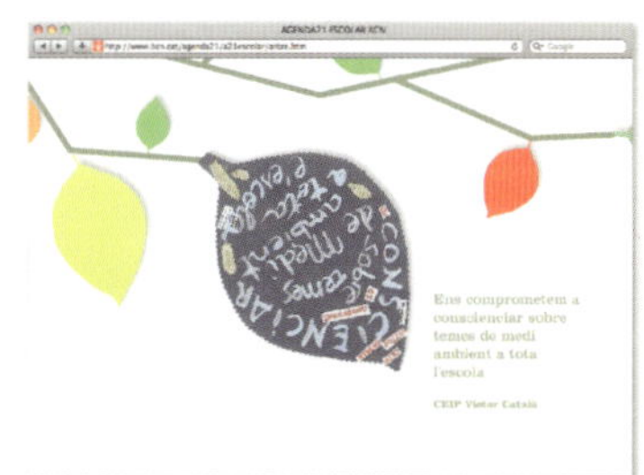

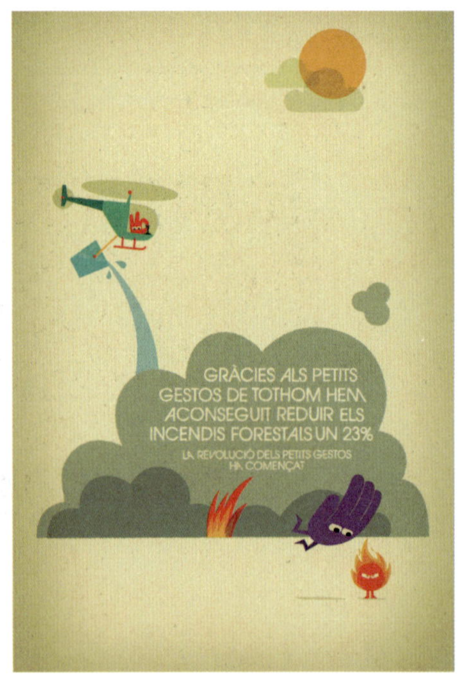
GRÀCIES ALS PETITS
GESTOS DE TOTHOM HEM
ACONSEGUIT REDUIR ELS
INCENDIS FORESTALS UN 23%
LA REVOLUCIÓ DELS PETITS GESTOS
HA COMENÇAT

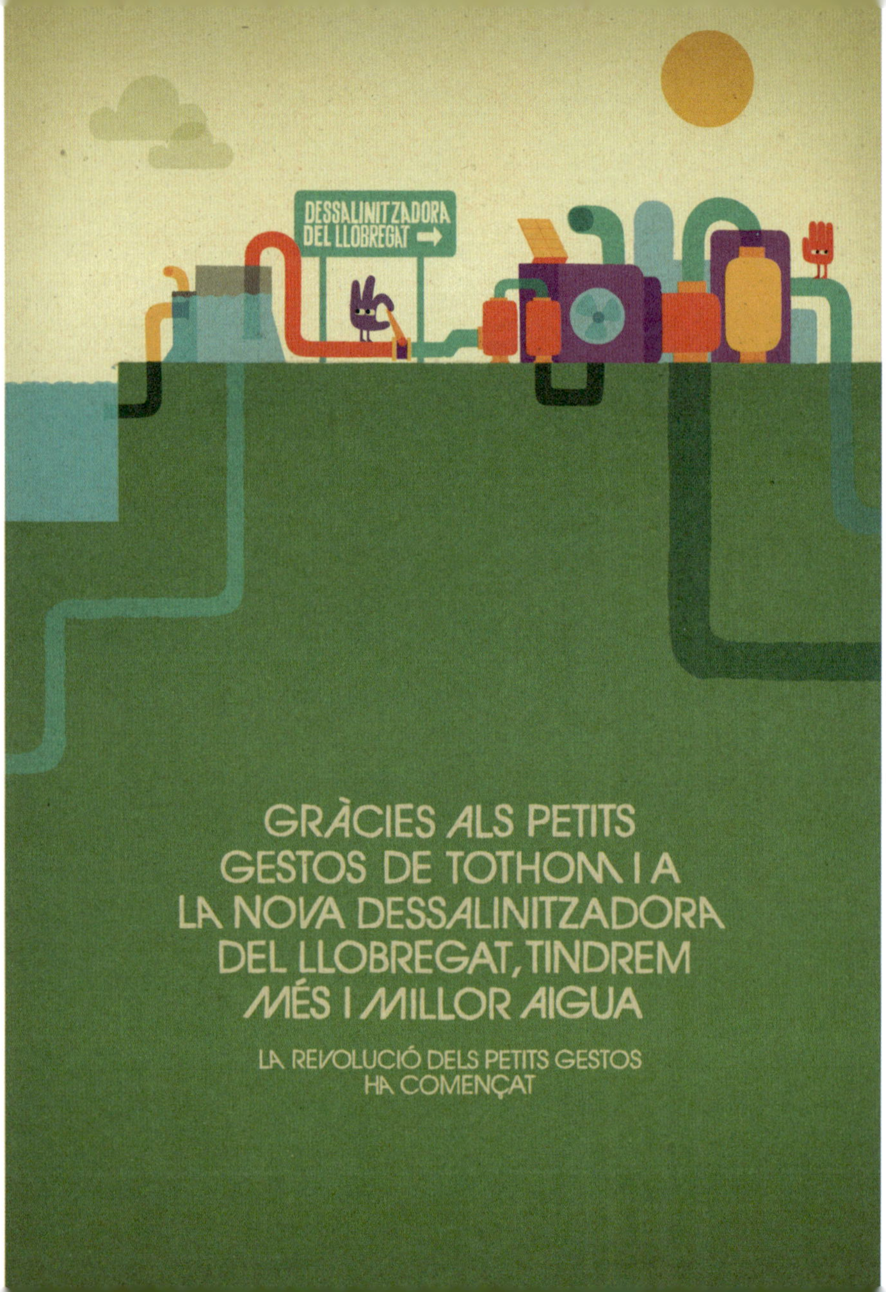

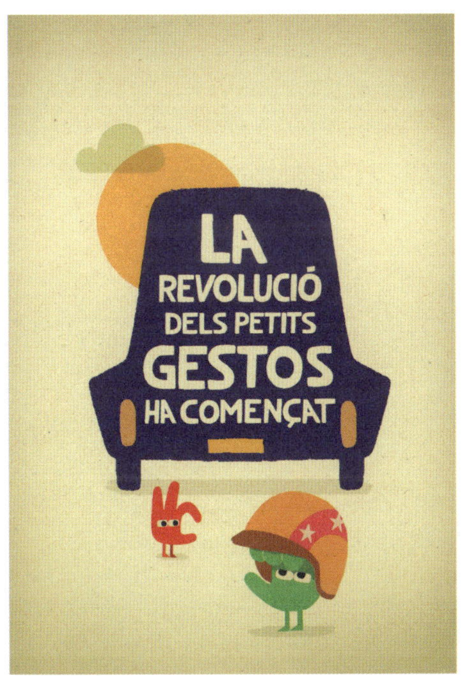

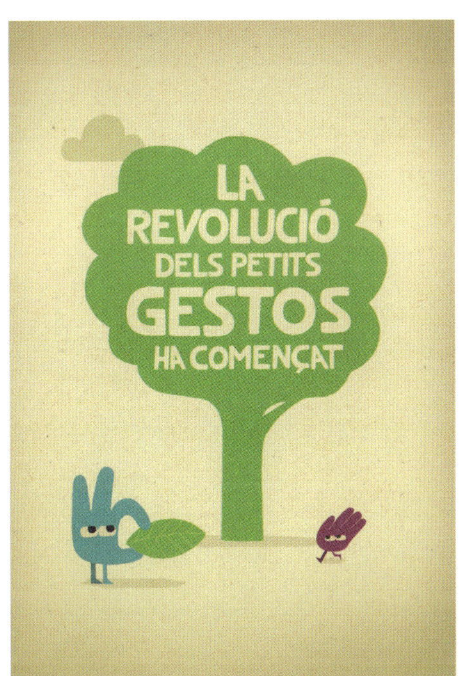

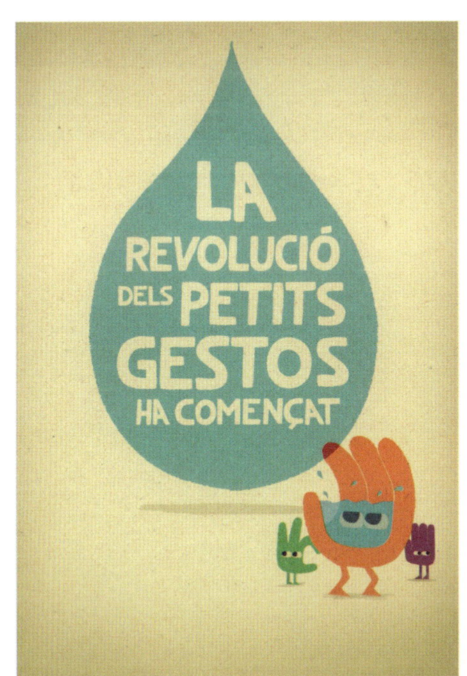

agency/studio: ***S,C,P,F** / project: campaign to promote civic, environmentally friendly practices through posters and television and Internet advertisements. / client: Government of Catalonia / country: Spain

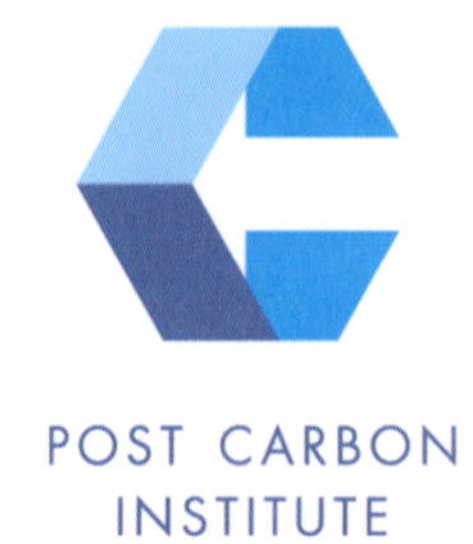

POST CARBON
INSTITUTE

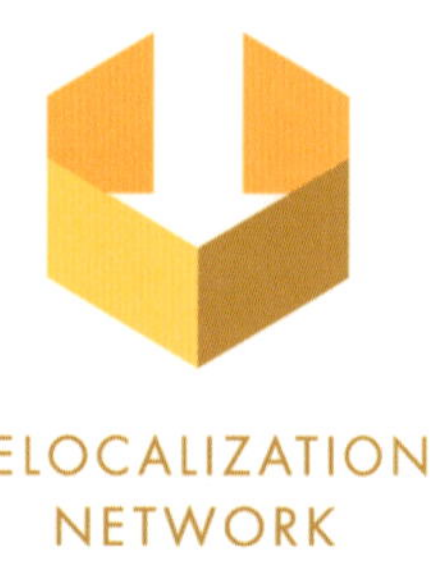

RELOCALIZATION
NETWORK

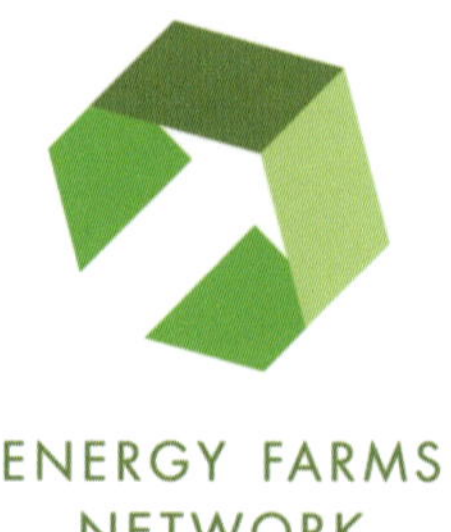

ENERGY FARMS
NETWORK

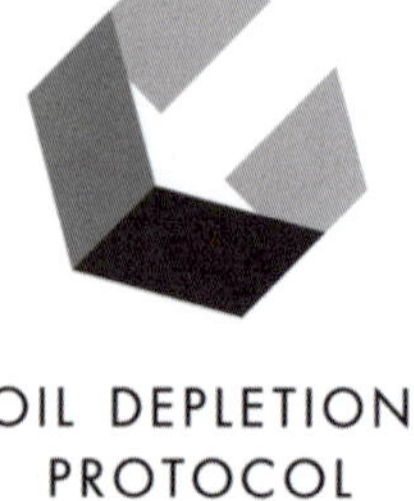

OIL DEPLETION
PROTOCOL

agency/studio: **MINE** / project: Logo for the Post Carbon Institute, an organisation that focuses on solutions to move beyond carbon consumption. The logo can be rotated and the colour changed to make it represent the institute's various initiatives. / client: Post Carbon Institute / country: USA

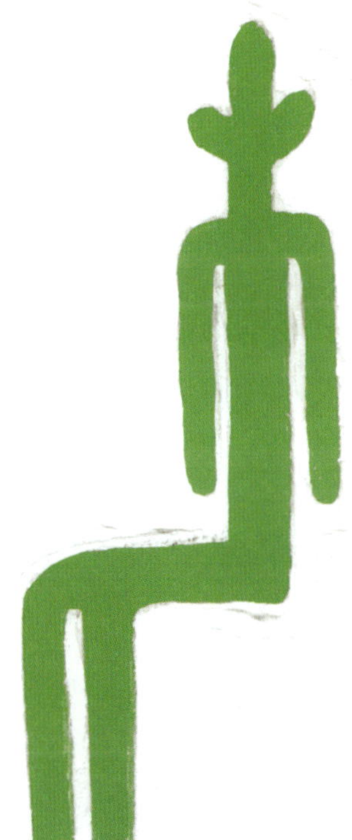

agency/studio: **FORMA** / project: image for the conference and round-table discussions on the position of the University of Oviedo regarding climate change. / client: The University of Oviedo's Espacio Solidario / country: Spain

JORNADA UNIVERSITARIA
POR LA SOSTENIBILIDAD Y EL MEDIO AMBIENTE
18 de diciembre, 2007
Sala de Grados de la Facultad de Biología de la Universidad de Oviedo

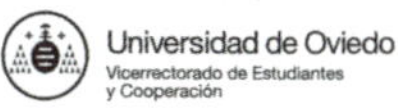

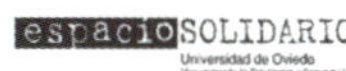

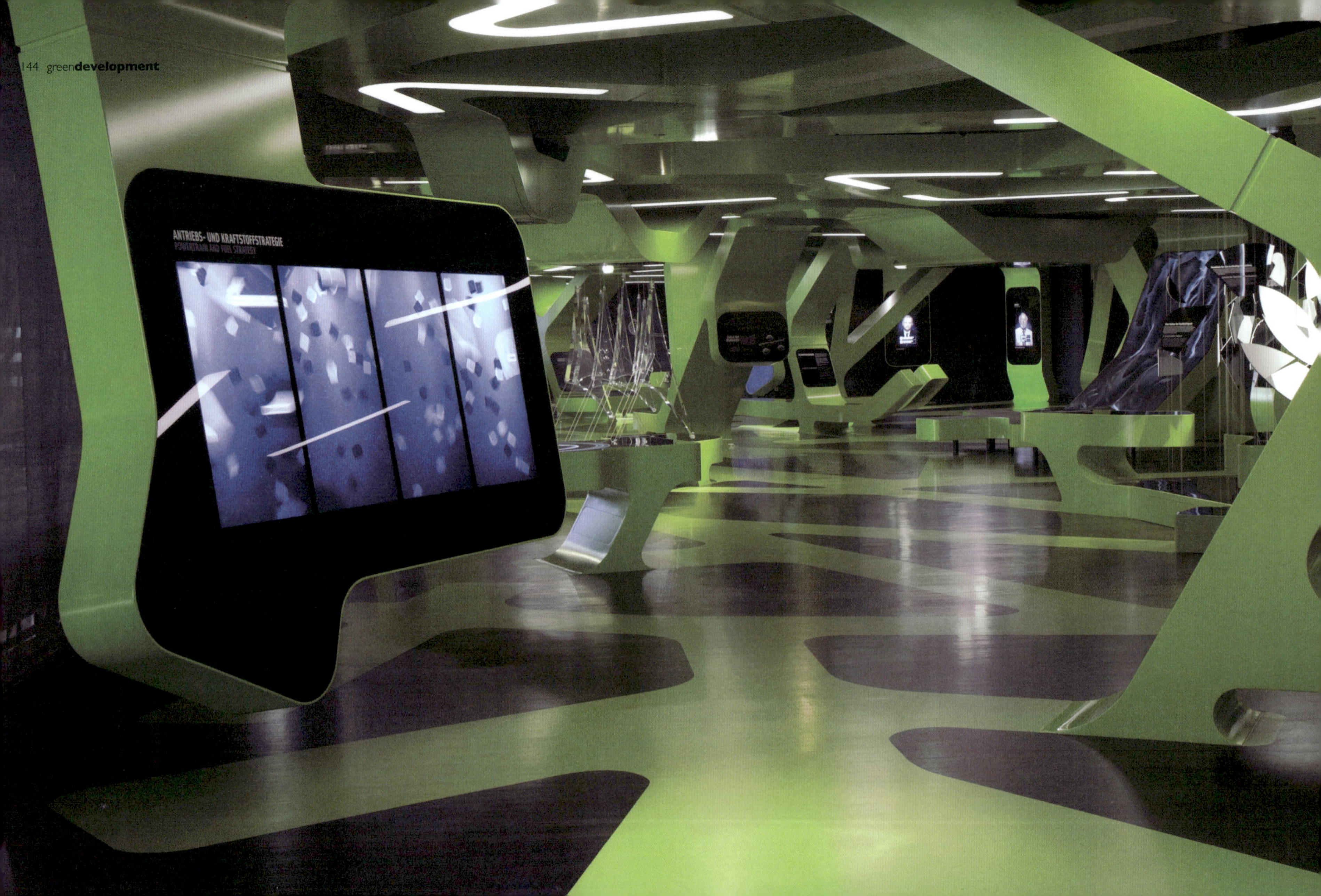
ANTRIEBS- UND KRAFTSTOFFSTRATEGIE
POWERTRAIN AND FUEL STRATEGY

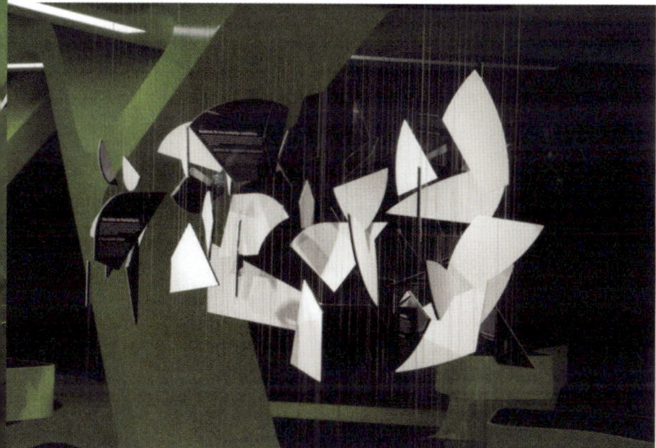

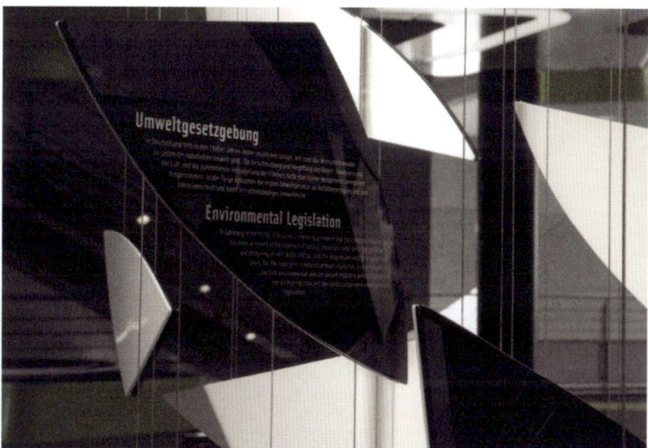

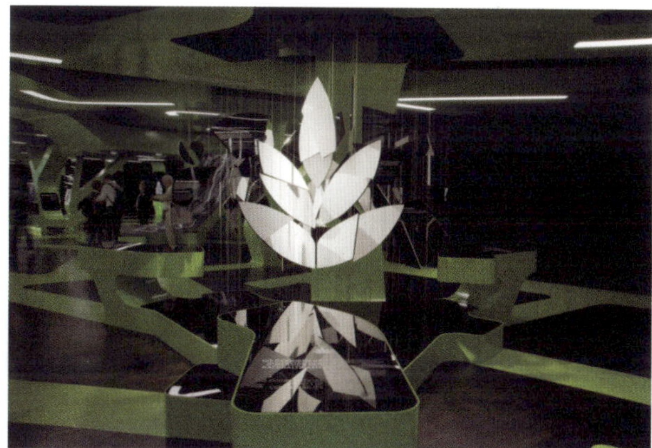

agency/studio: **ART+COM** / project: Level Green: The Idea of Sustainability. Sustainability though ubiquitous in discussions on economics, ecology and society remains an elusive, abstract term. ART+COM translated the topic into the "Level Green" exhibition for Volkswagen's Autostadt complex in Wolfsburg. In six areas containing 25 media exhibits, visitors can learn about the social and economic consequences of climate change, the importance of sustainability for the economy, mobility concepts for the future and Volkswagen's specific approaches towards sustainability. / client: Volkswagen Autostadt Wolfsburg / country: Germany

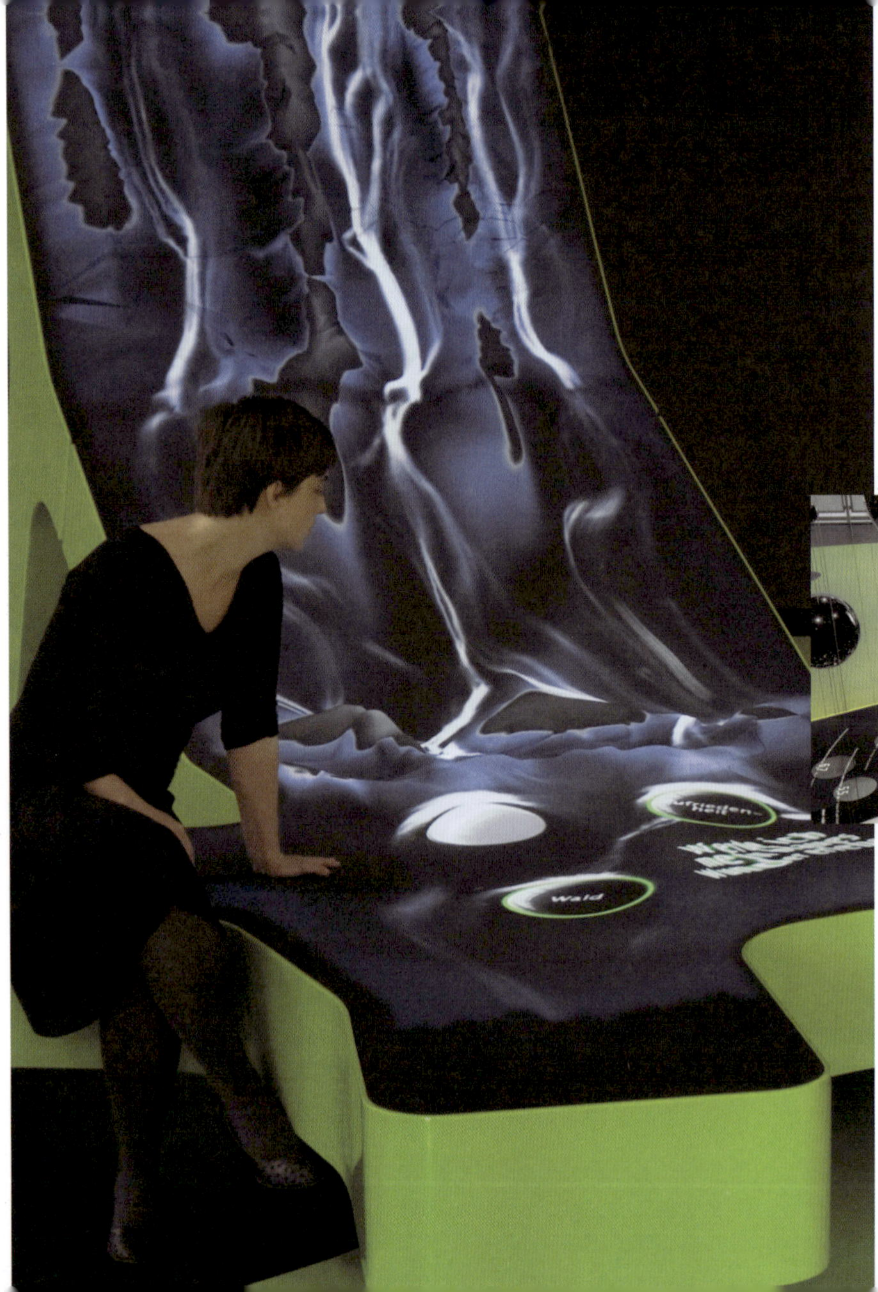

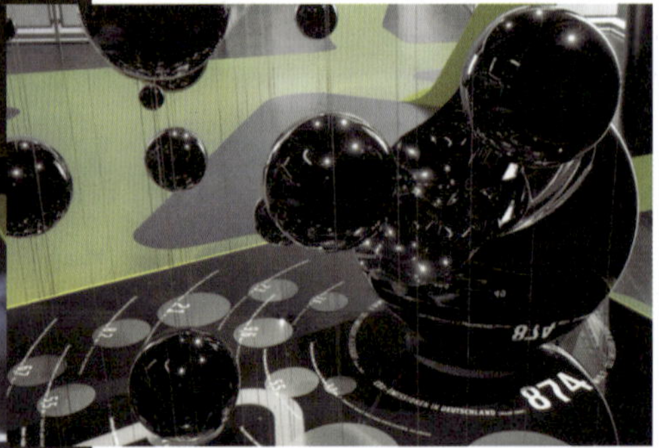

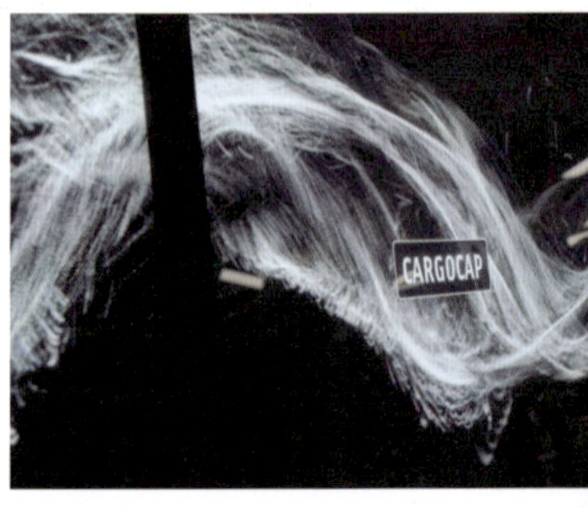

The hands-on arrangement encourages visitors to actively take part in the exhibition and discover the opportunities they can all use for sustainable development.

162 kg

EIN JAHR NUTZUNG
EINES LAPTOPS

Da das Laptop kleiner ist als ein
herkömmlicher Computer und
darüber hinaus über einen inte-
grierten Monitor verfügt, ist sein
ökologischer Rucksack in dieser
Phase rund viermal leichter als
der eines konventionellen Com-
puters mit Monitor.

ROHSTOFF
GEWINNUNG

PRODUKTION

NUTZUNG

ENTSORGUNG

EIN JAHR NUTZU
EINES COMPUTER

ROHSTOFF
GEWINNUNG

PRODUKTION

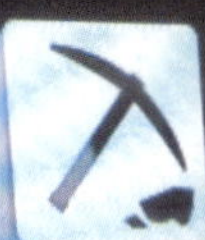

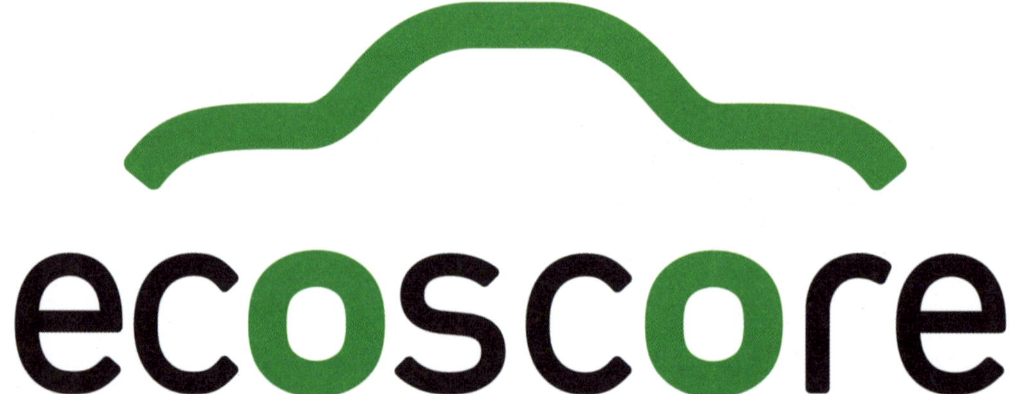

agency/studio: **Gramma** / project: Ecoscore is the label for an institutional website. The ecoscore evaluates the environmental performance of a vehicle by taking into account the vehicle's most important environmental impact factors. / client: Flemish Government / country: Belgium

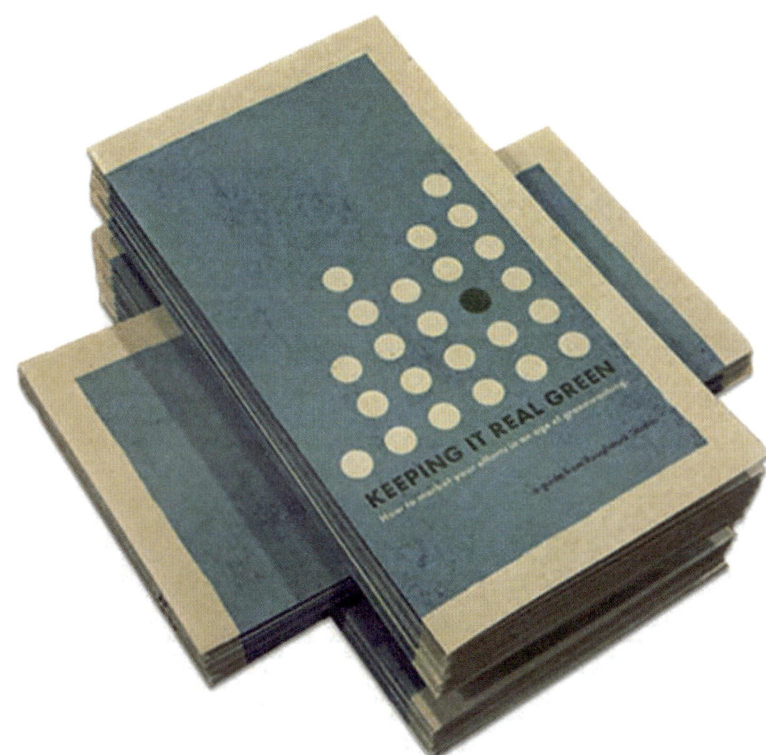

agency/studio: **Jess Sand a.k.a. Roughstock Studios** / project: The "Keeping It Real Green" guide is a foundational overview of responsible green marketing principles. It began as a print-to-order pamphlet, and was converted to a PDF-based e-book for low-environmental-impact distribution. / client: San Francisco Green Business Week / country: USA

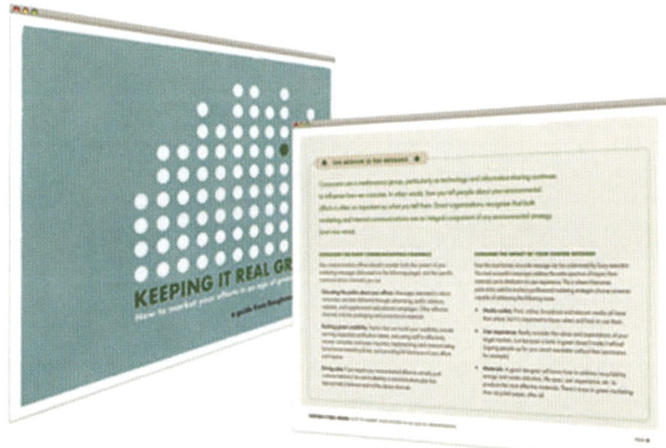

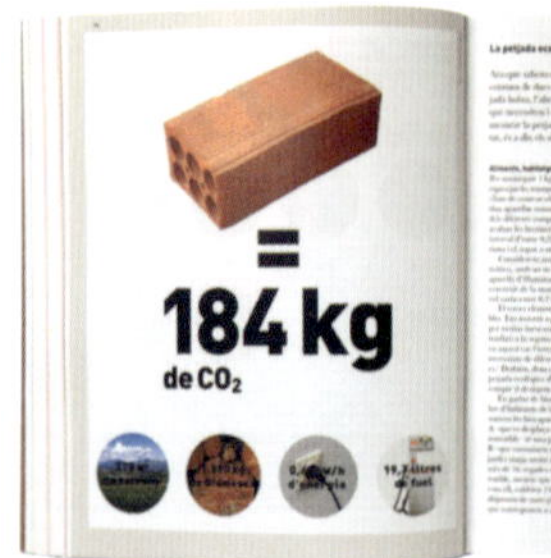
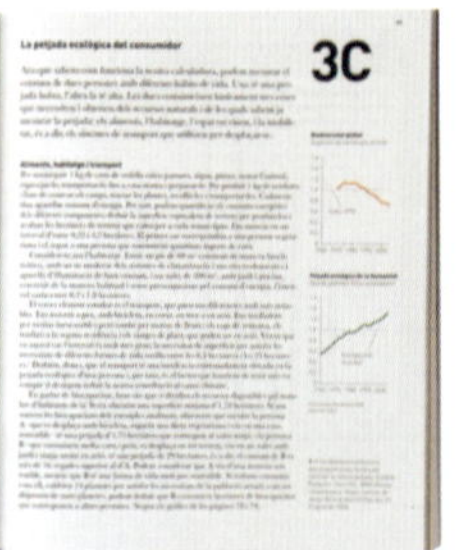

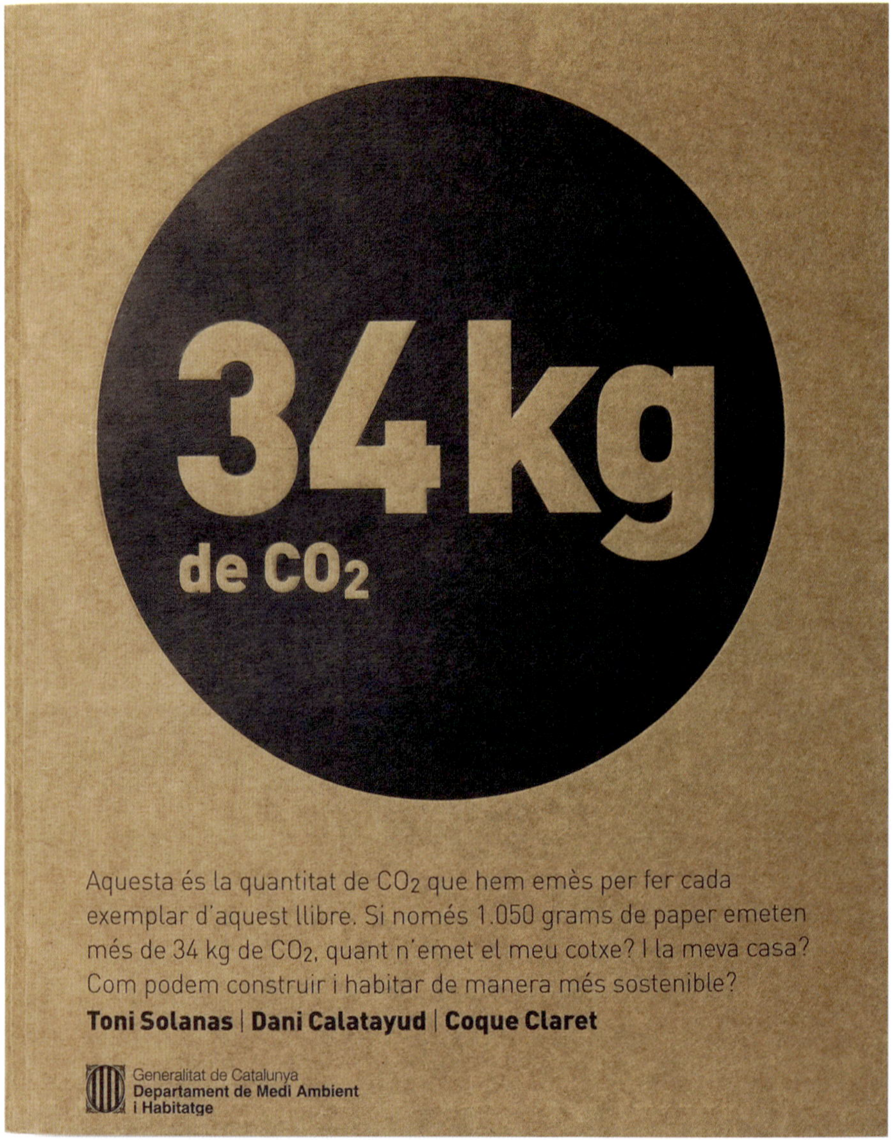

34kg
de CO2

Aquesta és la quantitat de CO2 que hem emès per fer cada exemplar d'aquest llibre. Si només 1.050 grams de paper emeten més de 34 kg de CO2, quant n'emet el meu cotxe? I la meva casa? Com podem construir i habitar de manera més sostenible?

Toni Solanas | Dani Calatayud | Coque Claret

Generalitat de Catalunya
Departament de Medi Ambient i Habitatge

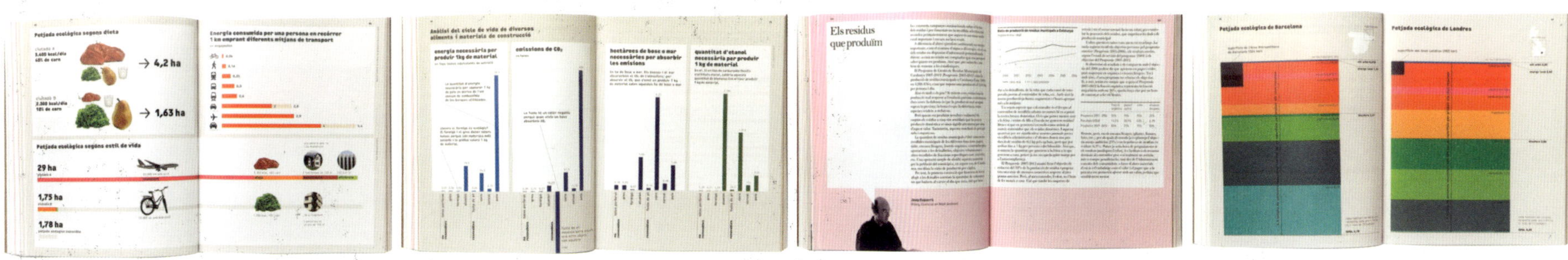

agency/studio: **Pau de Riba + Guillem Cardona** / project: production of this book on architecture and sustainability generated 34 kg of CO2 per copy. / client: Government of Catalonia / country: Spain

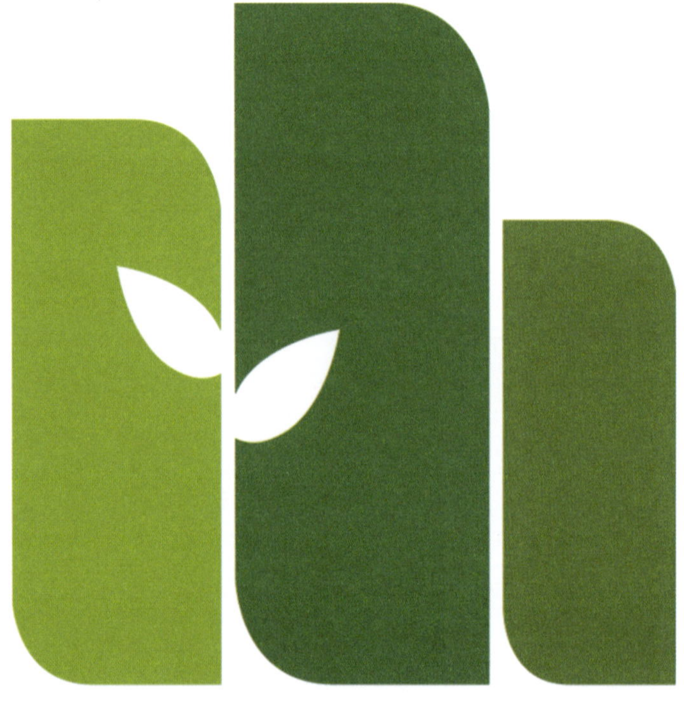

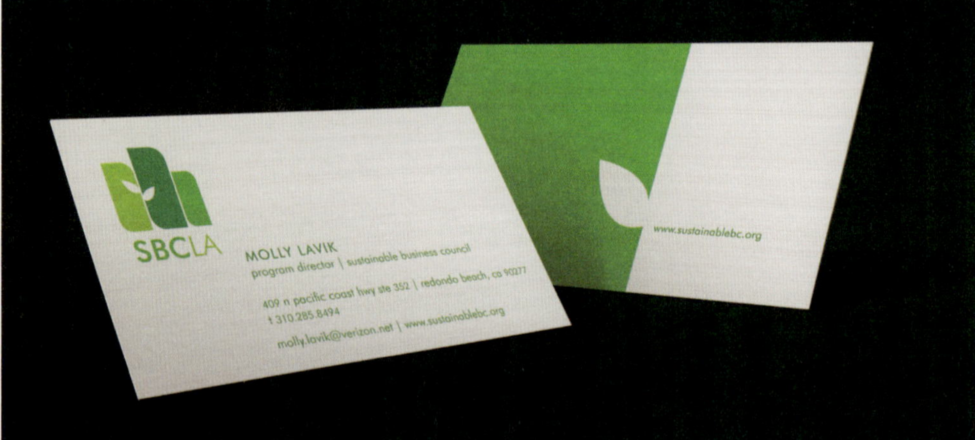

agency/studio: **Evenson Design Group** / project: Identity programme and packaging for the Sustainable Business Council of Los Angeles. Founded by a group of business executives, this non-profit organisation is dedicated to spreading the higher standards of the global sustainability movement. / client: Sustainable Business Council of Los Angeles / country: USA agency/studio: **Burkhardthauke – Büro für Gestaltung** / project: Sustainable Cities green (de)sign. Buildings in big cities are become more and more widespread. Nature, symbolised by a leaf, is replaced by more buildings, shops, industry, etc. / client: Toronto Society of Architects / country: Germany agency/studio: **Deep LLP** / project: Walk the Walk: Putting Sustainability into Practice. Brochure to promote sustainability at the company's head office in London. / client: Lend Lease / country: United Kingdom

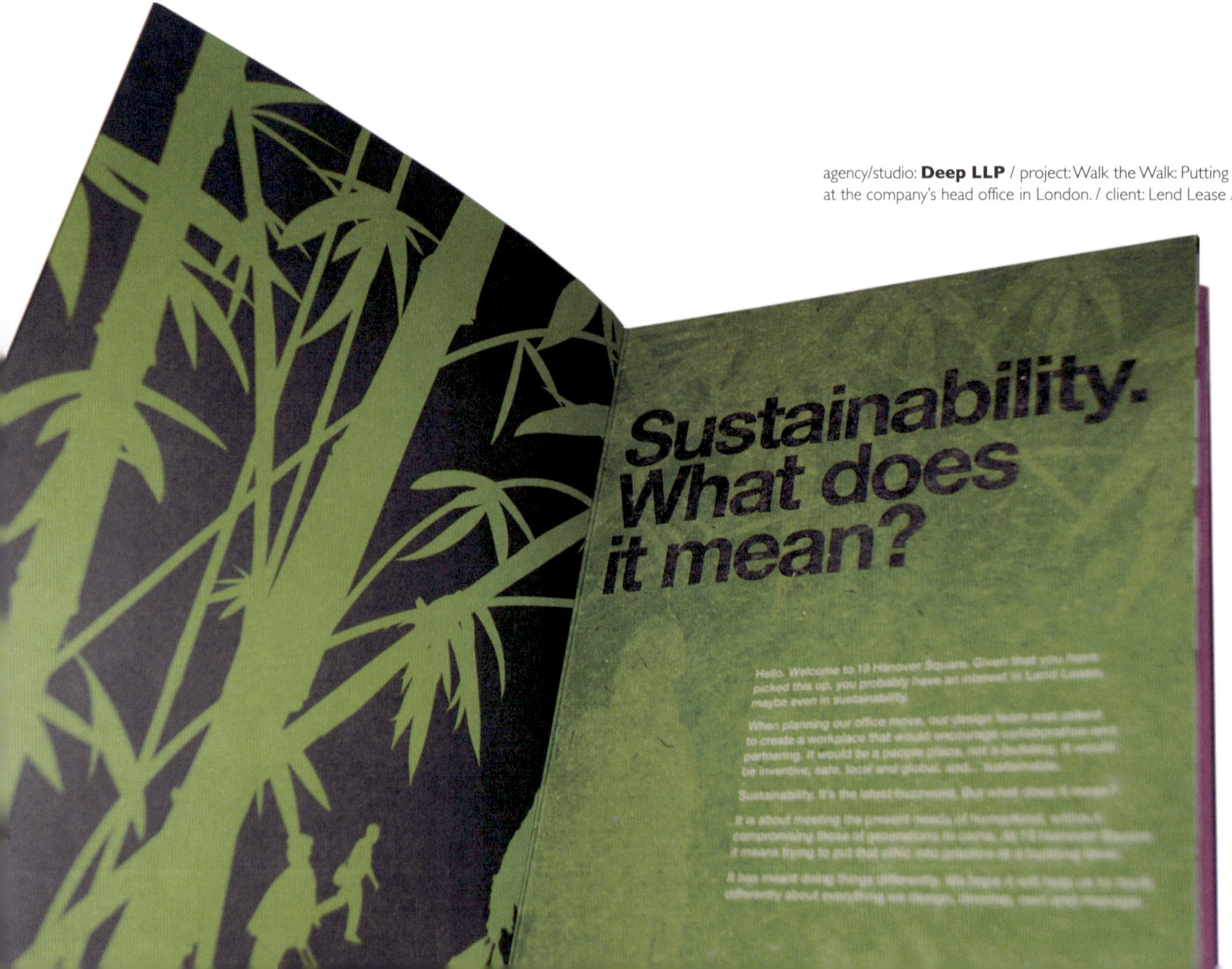

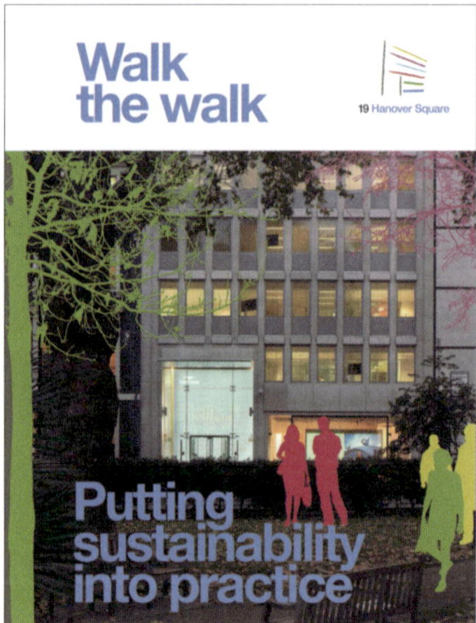

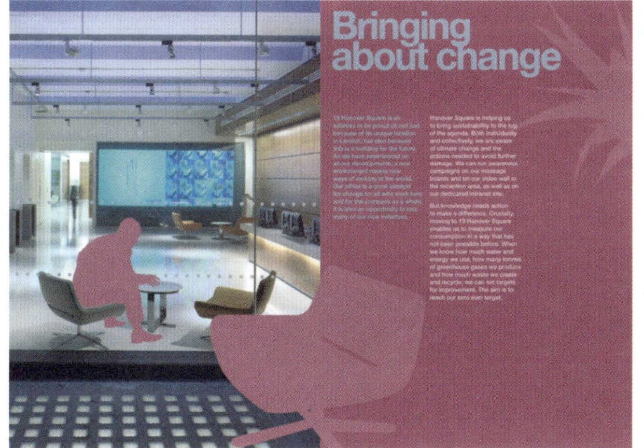

Bringing about change

19 Hanover Square is an address to be proud of, not just because of its unique location in London, but also because this is a building for the future. As we have experienced on all our developments, a new environment means new ways of looking at the world. Our office is a great catalyst for change for all who work here and for the company as a whole. It is also an opportunity to kick many of our new initiatives.

Hanover Square is helping us to bring sustainability to the top of the agenda. Both individually and collectively, we are aware of climate change and the actions needed to avoid further damage. We can run awareness campaigns on our message boards and on our video wall in the reception area, as well as on our dedicated intranet site.

But knowledge needs action to make a difference. Crucially, moving to 19 Hanover Square enables us to measure our consumption in a way that has not been possible before. When we know how much water and energy we use, how many tonnes of greenhouse gases we produce and how much waste we create and recycle, we can set targets for improvement. The aim is to reach our zero sum target.

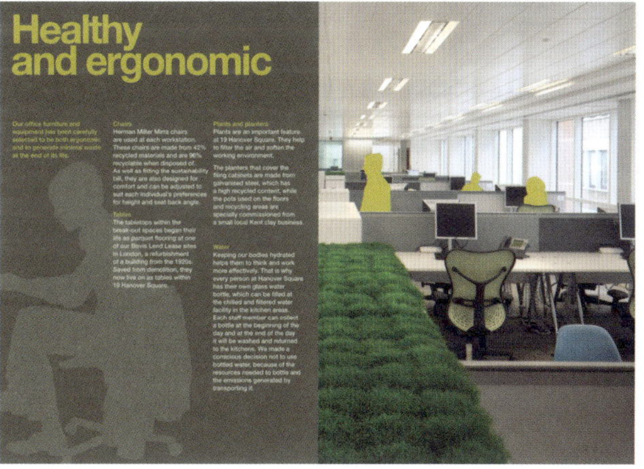

Healthy and ergonomic

Our office furniture and equipment has been carefully selected to be both ergonomic and to generate minimal waste at the end of its life.

Chairs
Herman Miller Mirra chairs are used at each workstation. These chairs are made from 42% recycled materials and are 96% recyclable when disposed of. As well as fitting the sustainability bill, they are also designed for comfort and can be adjusted to suit each individual's preferences for height and seat back angle.

Tables
The tabletops within the break-out spaces began their life as parquet flooring at one of our Bovis Lend Lease sites in London, a refurbishment of a building from the 1920s. Saved from demolition, they now live on as tables within 19 Hanover Square.

Plants and planters
Plants are an important feature at 19 Hanover Square. They help to filter the air and soften the working environment.

The planters that cover the filing cabinets are made from galvanised steel, which has a high recycled content, while the pots used on the floors and recycling areas are specially commissioned from a small local Kent clay business.

Water
Keeping our bodies hydrated helps them to think and work more effectively. That is why every person at Hanover Square has their own glass water bottle, which can be filled at the chilled and filtered water facility in the kitchen areas. Each staff member can collect a bottle at the beginning of the day and at the end of the day it will be washed and returned to the kitchens. We made a conscious decision not to use bottled water, because of the resources needed to bottle and the emissions generated by transporting it.

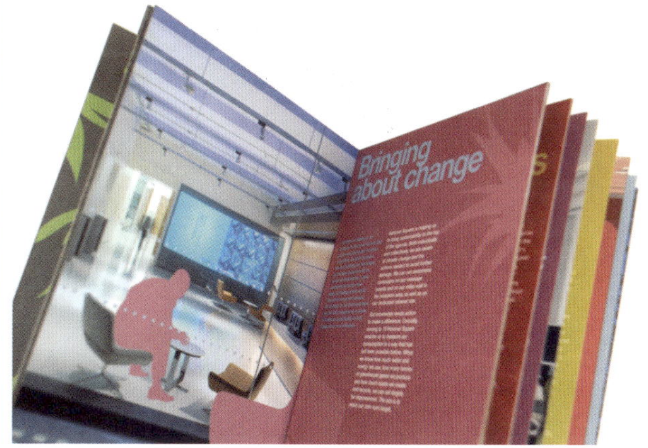

Bringing about change

durable**s**
ustainabl**e**desir
abl**e**architectur
edurabl**e**souten
abl**e**désirabl**e**ar
chitectur**e**dura
bl**e**sustainabl**e**d
esirabl**e**archite
ctur**e**

agency/studio: **Florian Mewes** / project: durable - sustainable - desirable. Graphic image for a conference on architecture and sustainable development in Bordeaux (France). / client: European Forum for Architectural Policies / country: Netherlands.

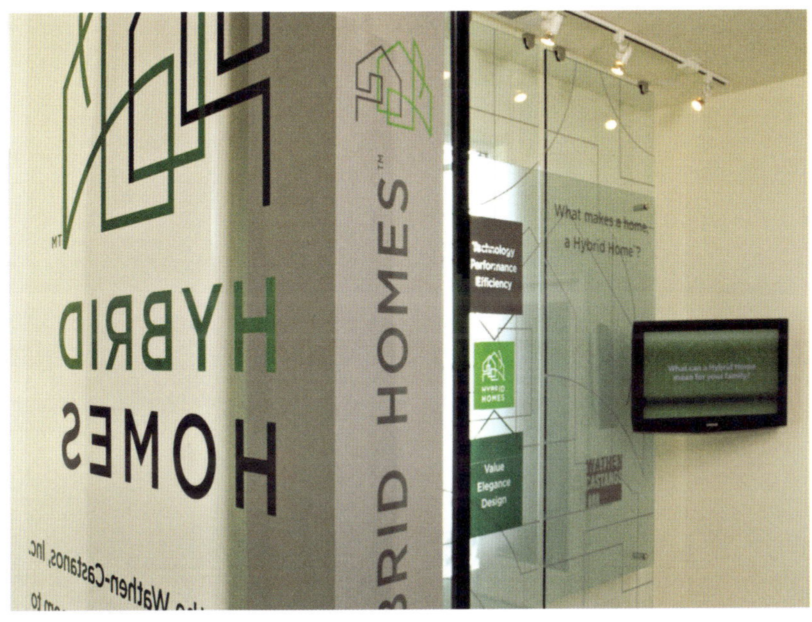

agency/studio: **Five Creative Group** / project: the Hybrid Room is a room inside a model home. It is an interactive experience to present a company that builds energy-efficient homes. / client: Wathen-Castanos, Inc. / country: USA

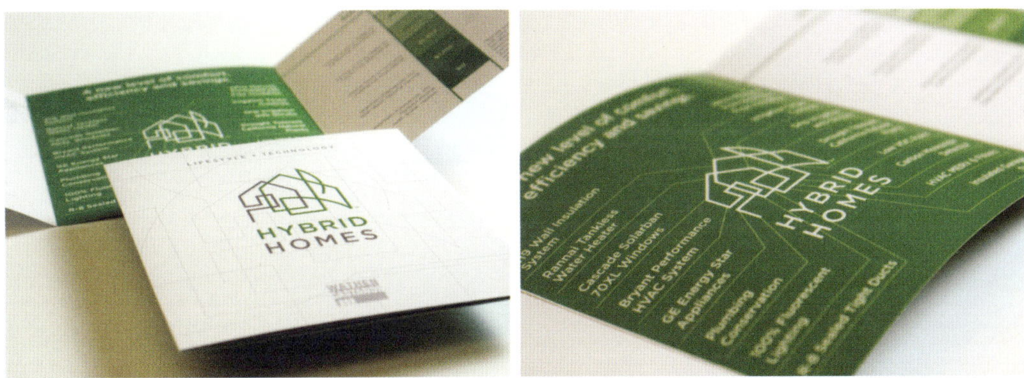

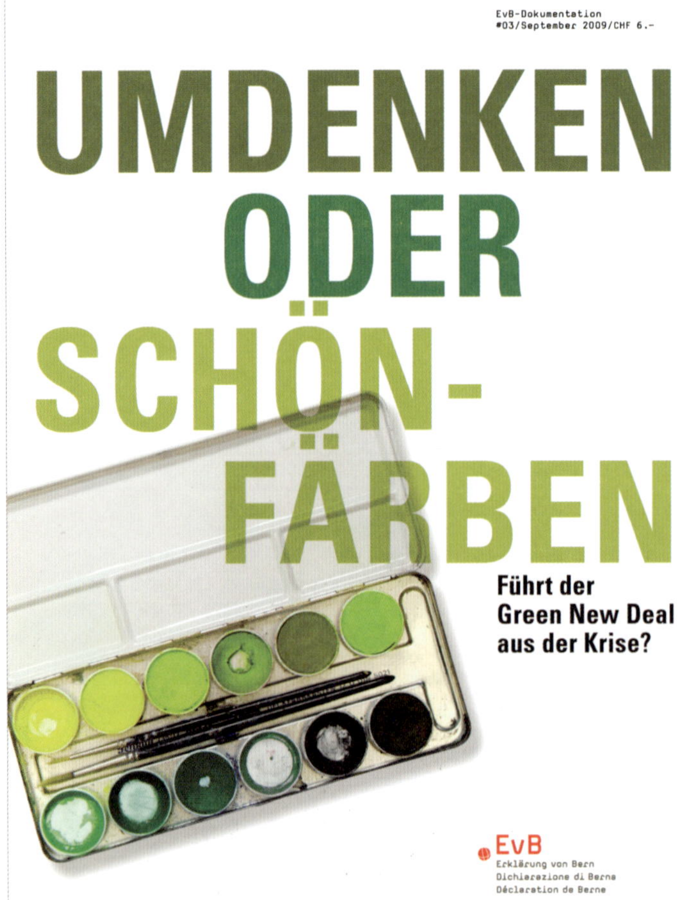

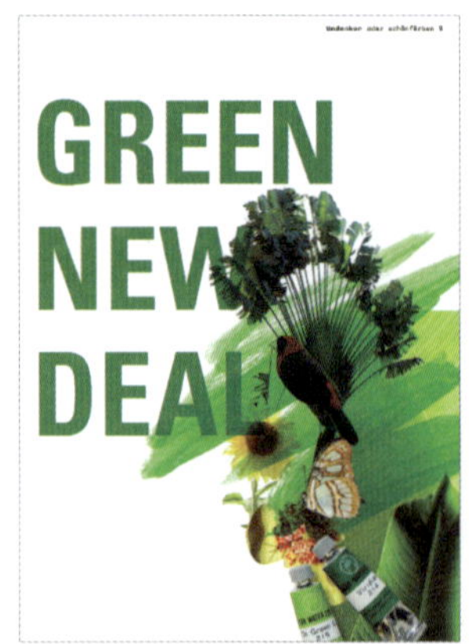

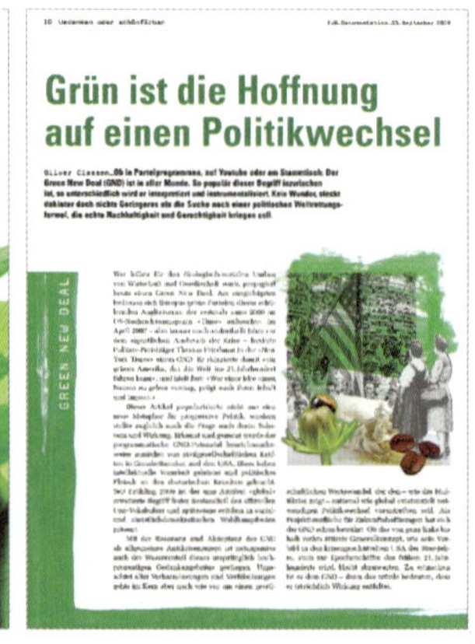

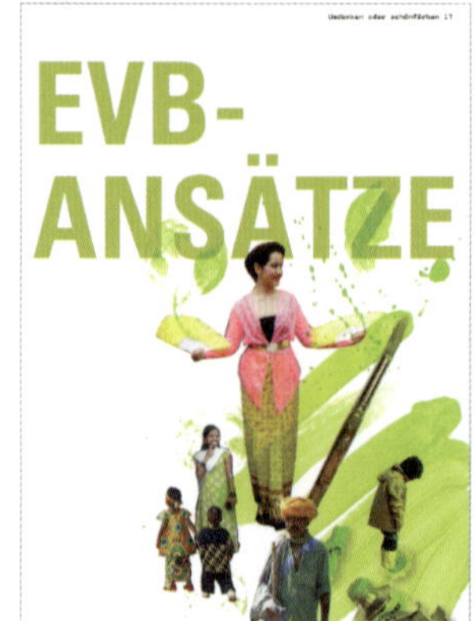

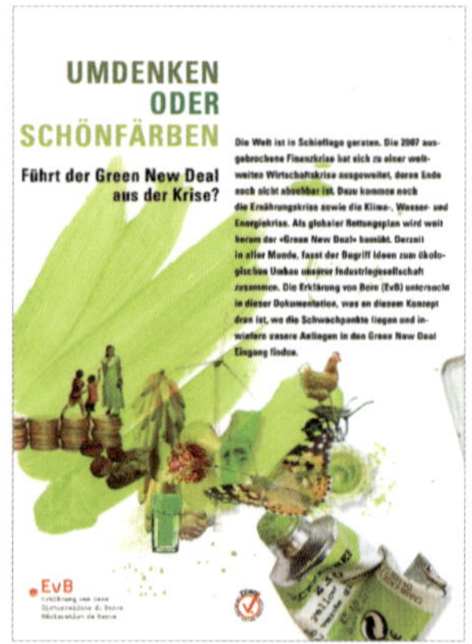

agency/studio: **Clerici Partner AG** / project: membership magazine of BD, a Swiss NGO that promotes more equitable, sustainable and democratic North-South relations. / client: The Berne Declaration (BD) / country: Switzerland

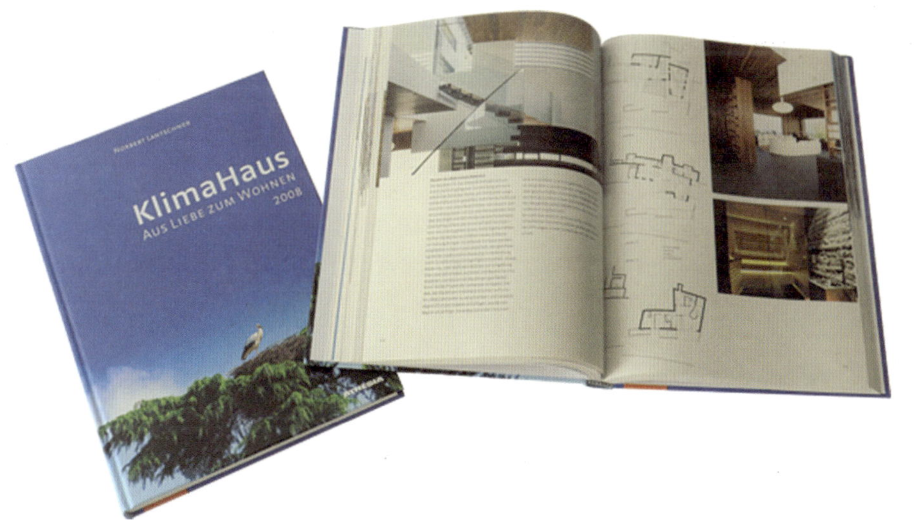

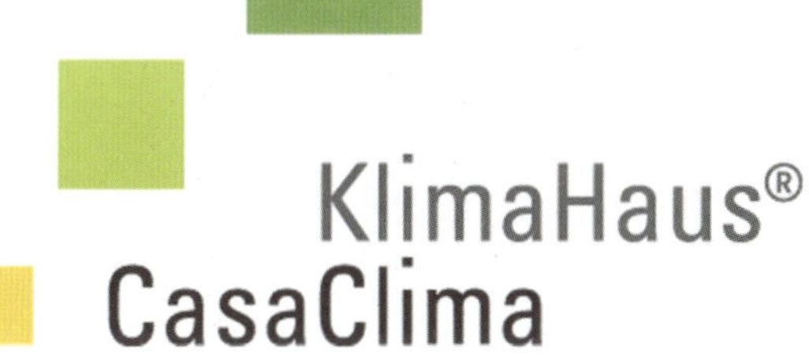

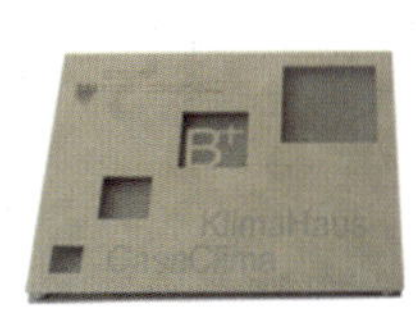

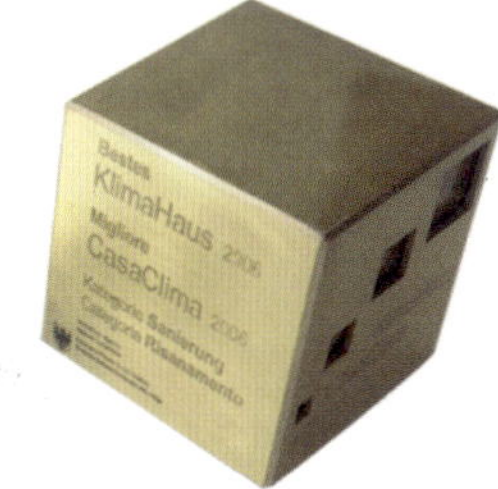

agency/studio: **helios** / project: Identity programme for the KlimaHaus agency. KlimaHaus was presented at the 2006 World Climate Conference in Montreal as one of the ten best projects for reducing CO2 emissions. KlimaHaus (meaning "Climate House") is a term that was coined to describe energy-saving construction and dynamic living. / client: Autonomous Province of South Tyrol, KlimaHaus agency / country: Italy.

agency/studio: **Landor Associates** / project: visual identity for the Green Brands, Global Insight Forum, an annual event about the development of green concerns and brands in the marketplace. / client: Cohn & Wolfe, Landor Associates, Penn, Schoen & Berland Associates and Esty Environmental Partners / country: USA

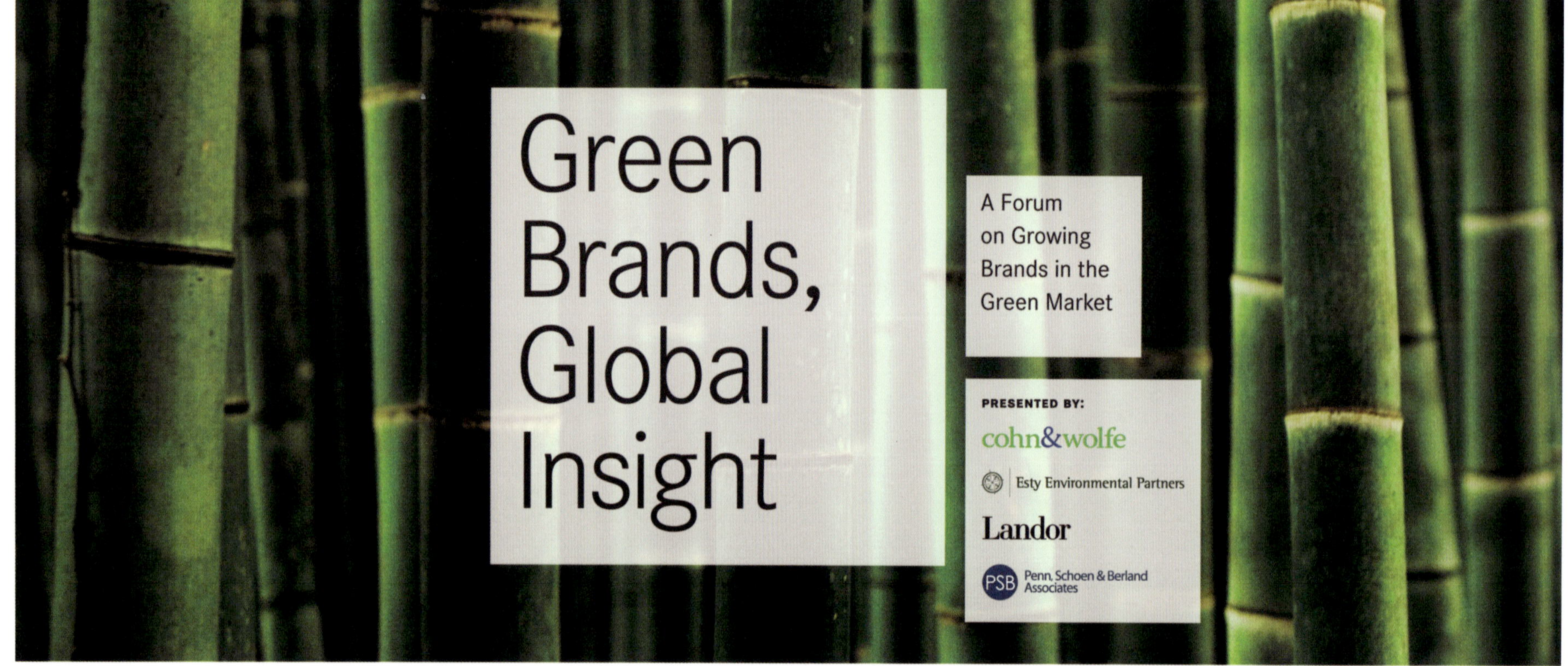

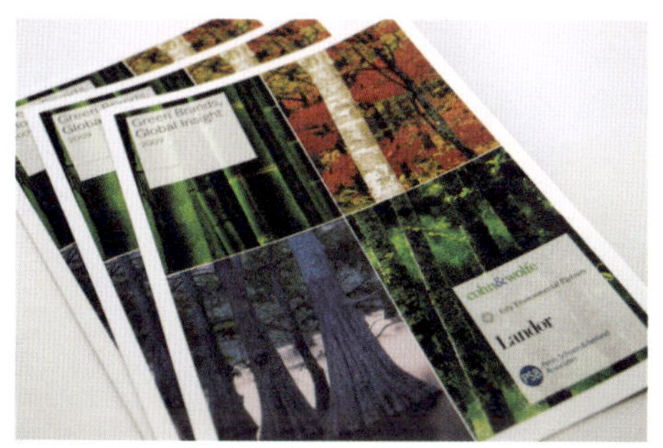

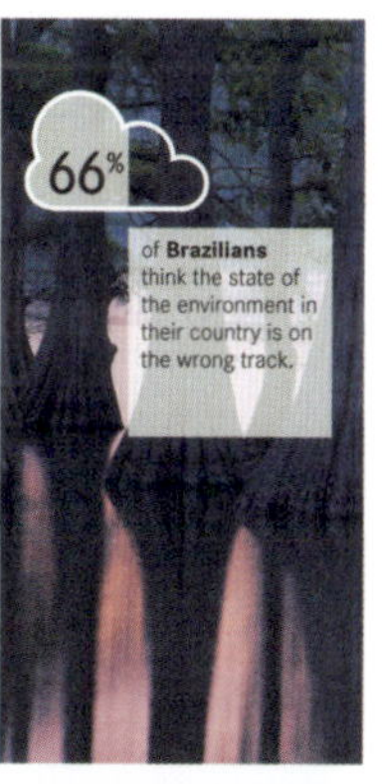
66%
of **Brazilians** think the state of the environment in their country is on the wrong track.

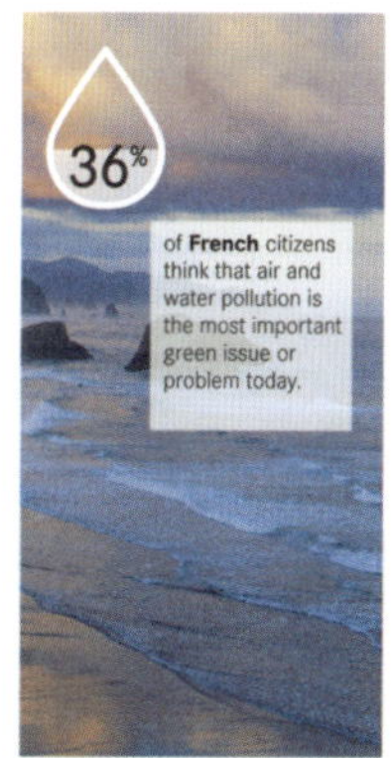
36%
of **French** citizens think that air and water pollution is the most important green issue or problem today.

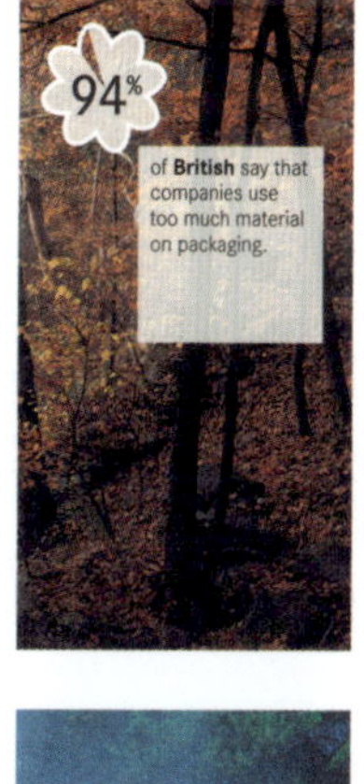
94%
of **British** say that companies use too much material on packaging.

80%
of **Germans** are familiar with the term "Carbon-neutral."

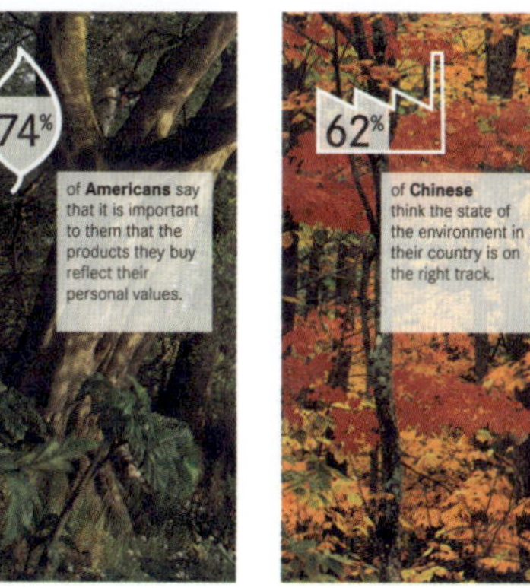
74%
of **Americans** say that it is important to them that the products they buy reflect their personal values.

62%
of **Chinese** think the state of the environment in their country is on the right track.

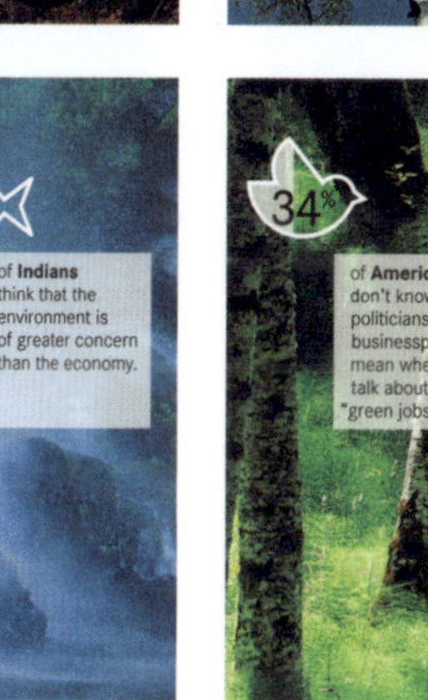
53%
of **Indians** think that the environment is of greater concern than the economy.

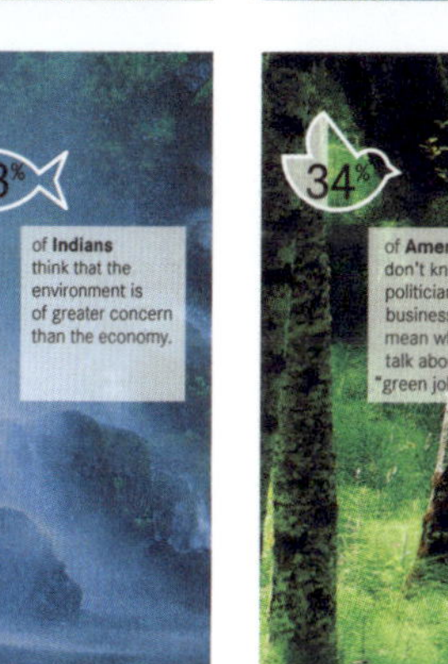
34%
of **Americans** don't know what politicians and businesspeople mean when they talk about "green jobs."

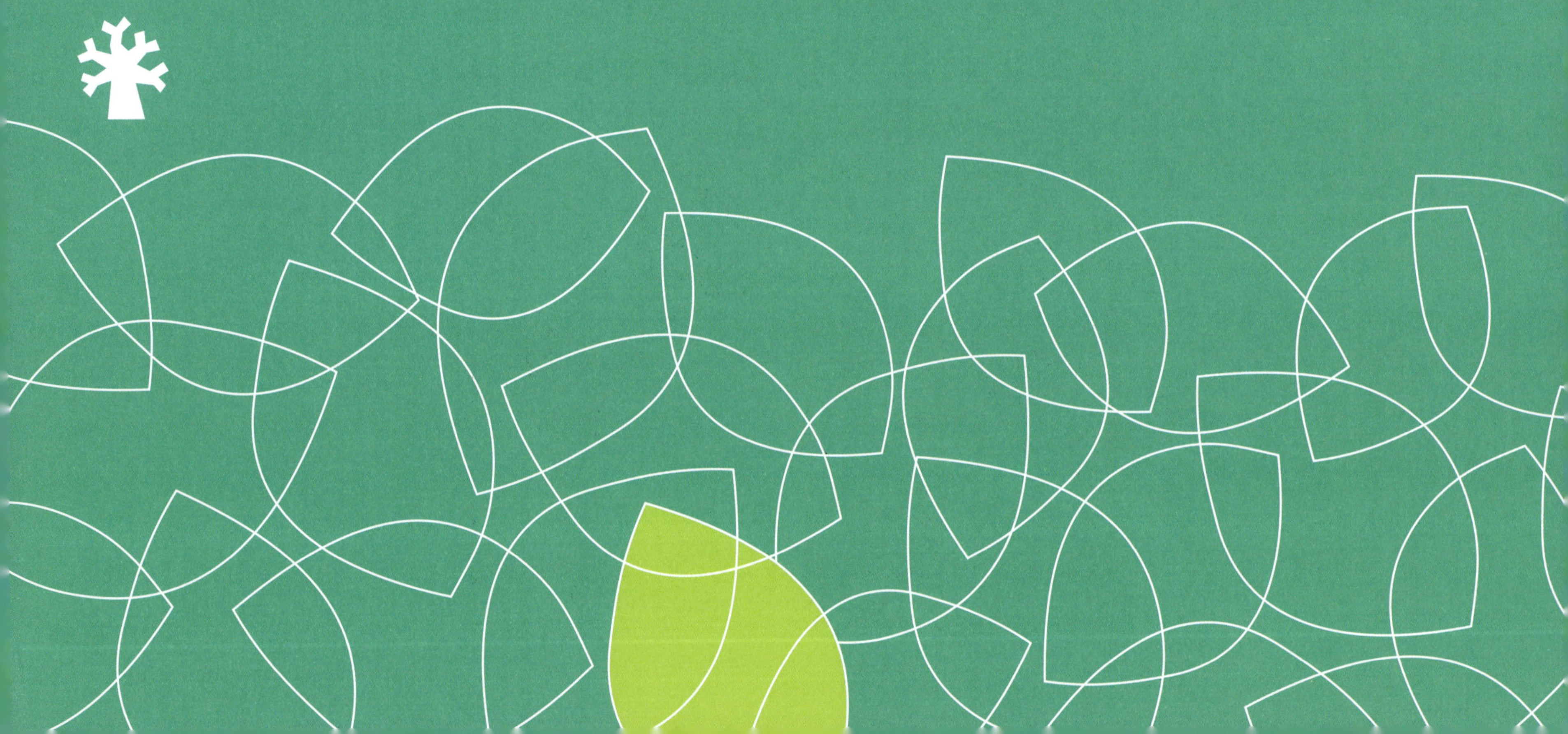

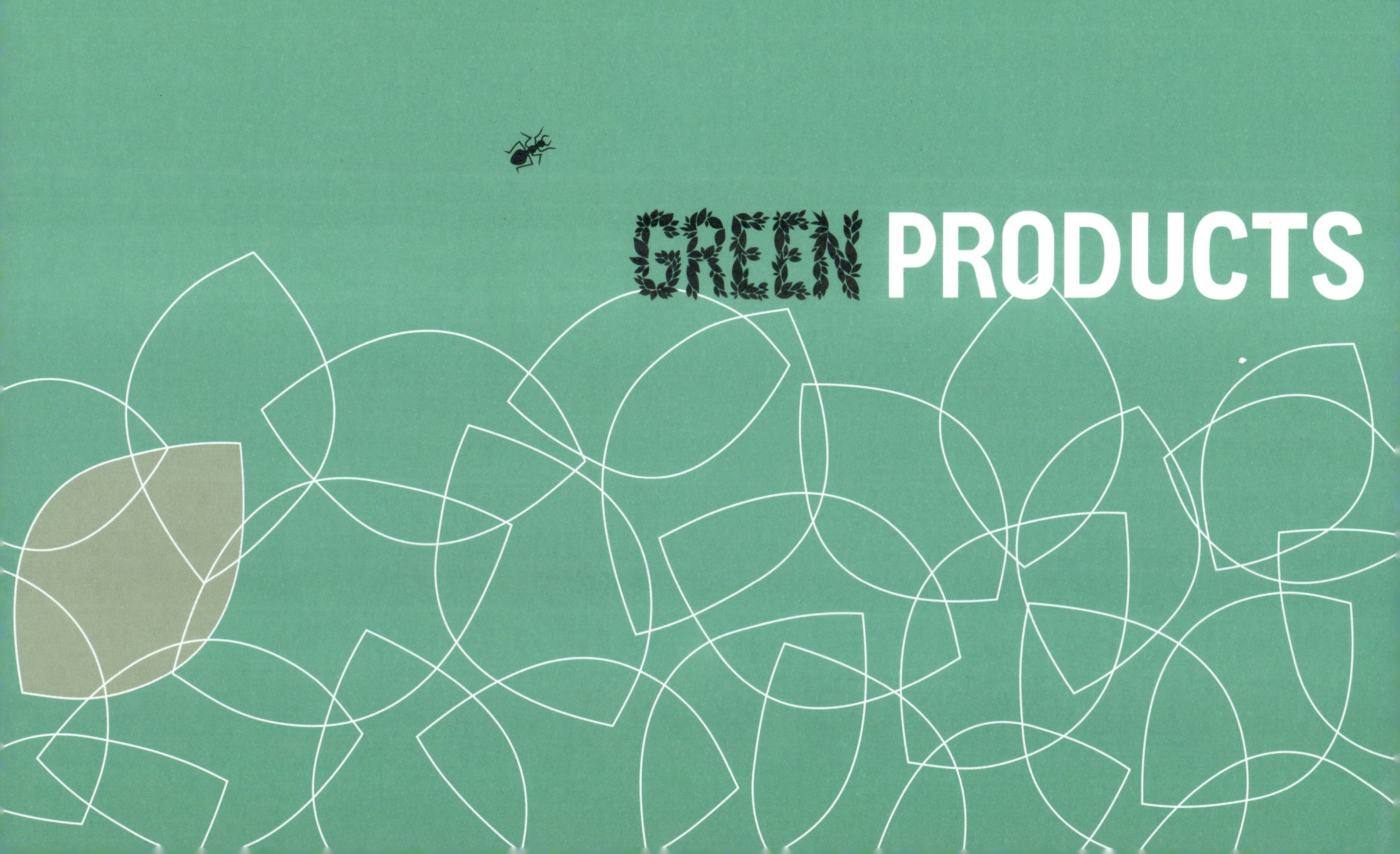
GREEN PRODUCTS

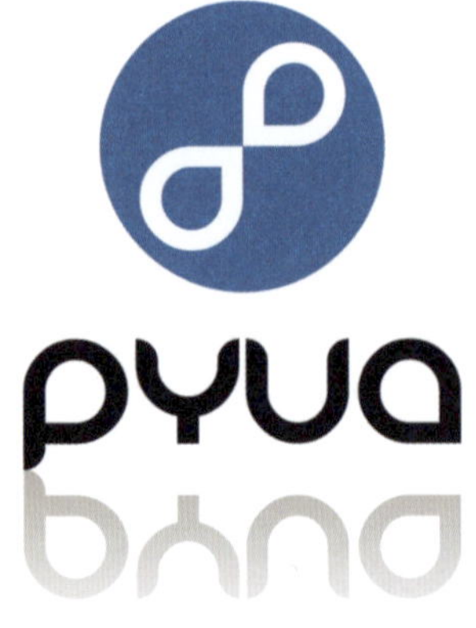

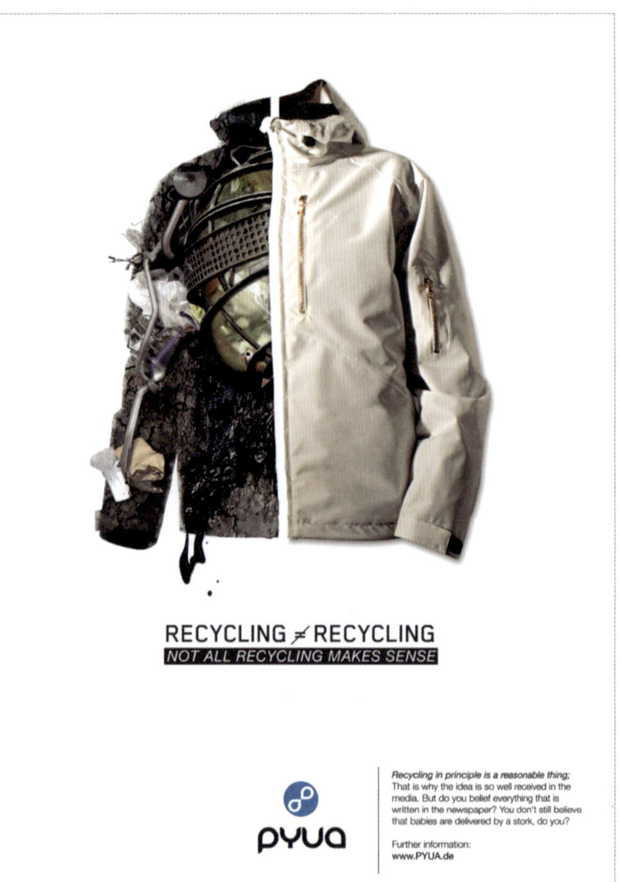

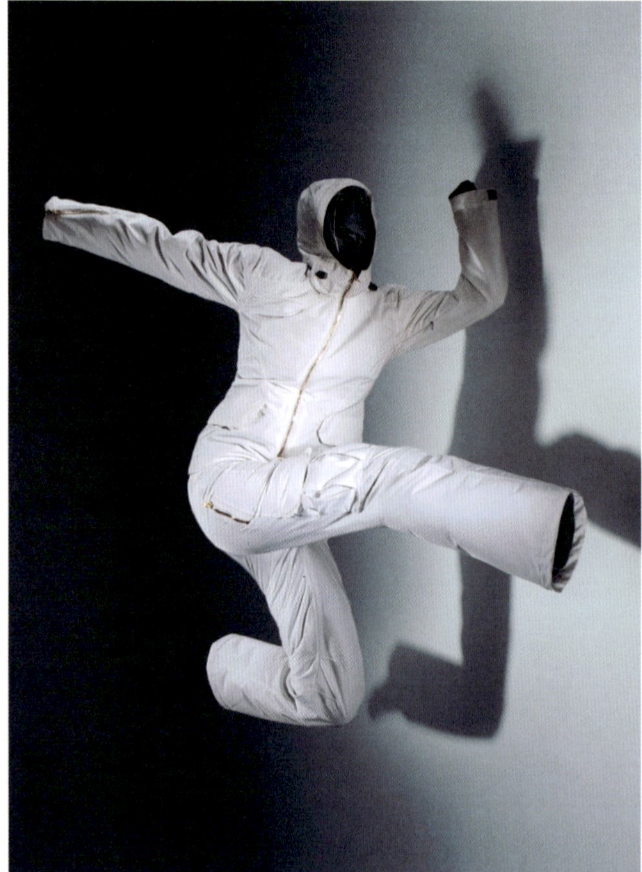

agency/studio: **Melville Brand Design** / project: complete brand design for PYUA, the world's first fully recyclable (closed-loop-recycled functional textiles) ski and outdoor wear collection. / client: PYUA / country: Germany

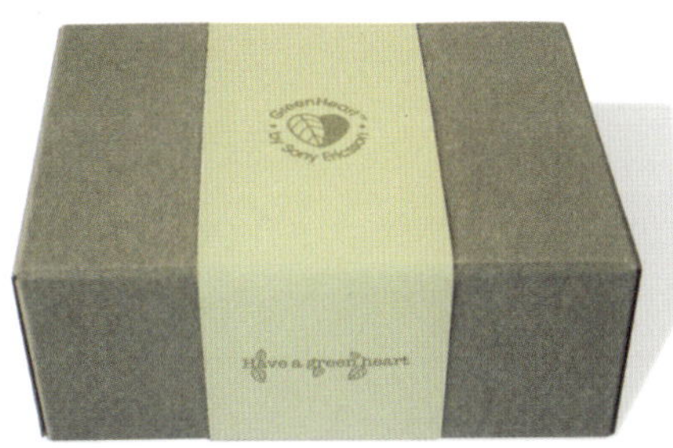
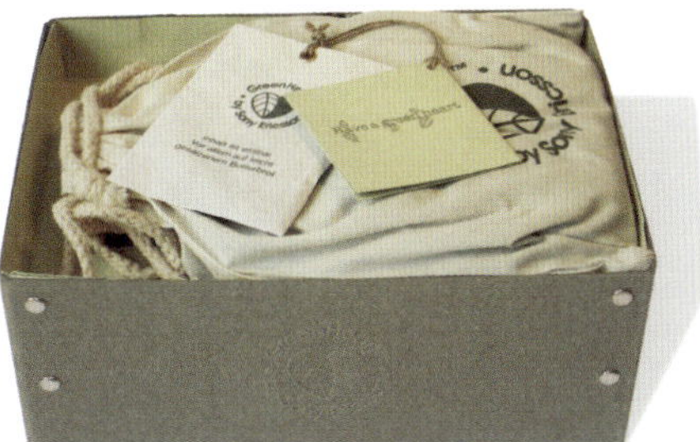
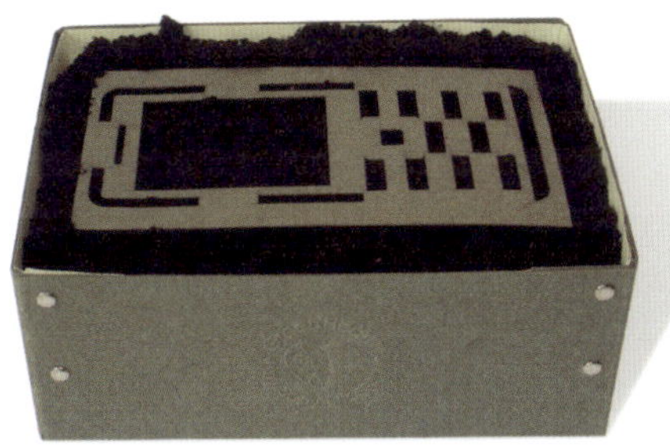
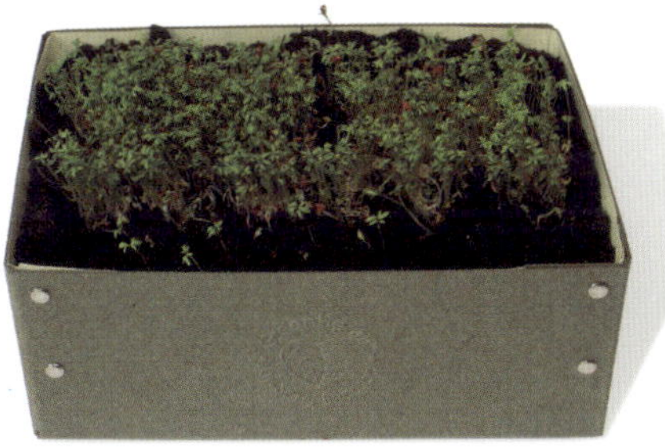

agency/studio: **Melville Brand Design** / project: sustainable mailing for Sony Ericsson's Naite GreenHeart mobile phone aimed to draw the attention of opinion leaders and journalists to Sony Ericsson's sustainability programme. / client: Sony Ericsson / country: Germany

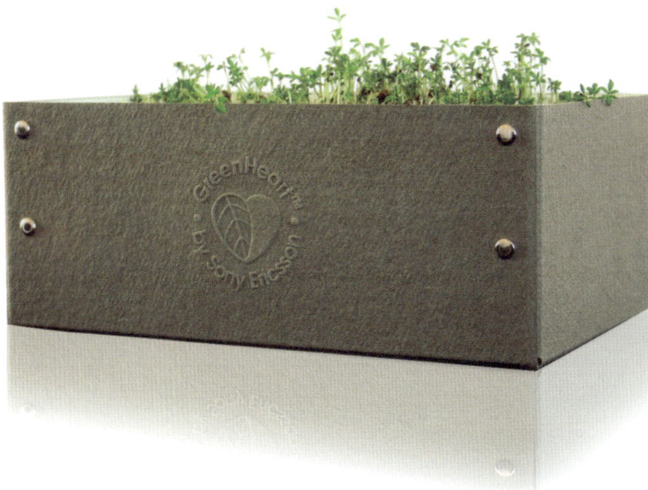

agency/studio: **Isabela Serta** / project: Brand for a small market that promotes sustainable local agriculture. The typography was created following research on small markets, which found that at such markets the products are traditionally written in chalk on a blackboard, in large separated letters. This project was developed for IED Milan's design competition and won the packaging category. / country: Brazil

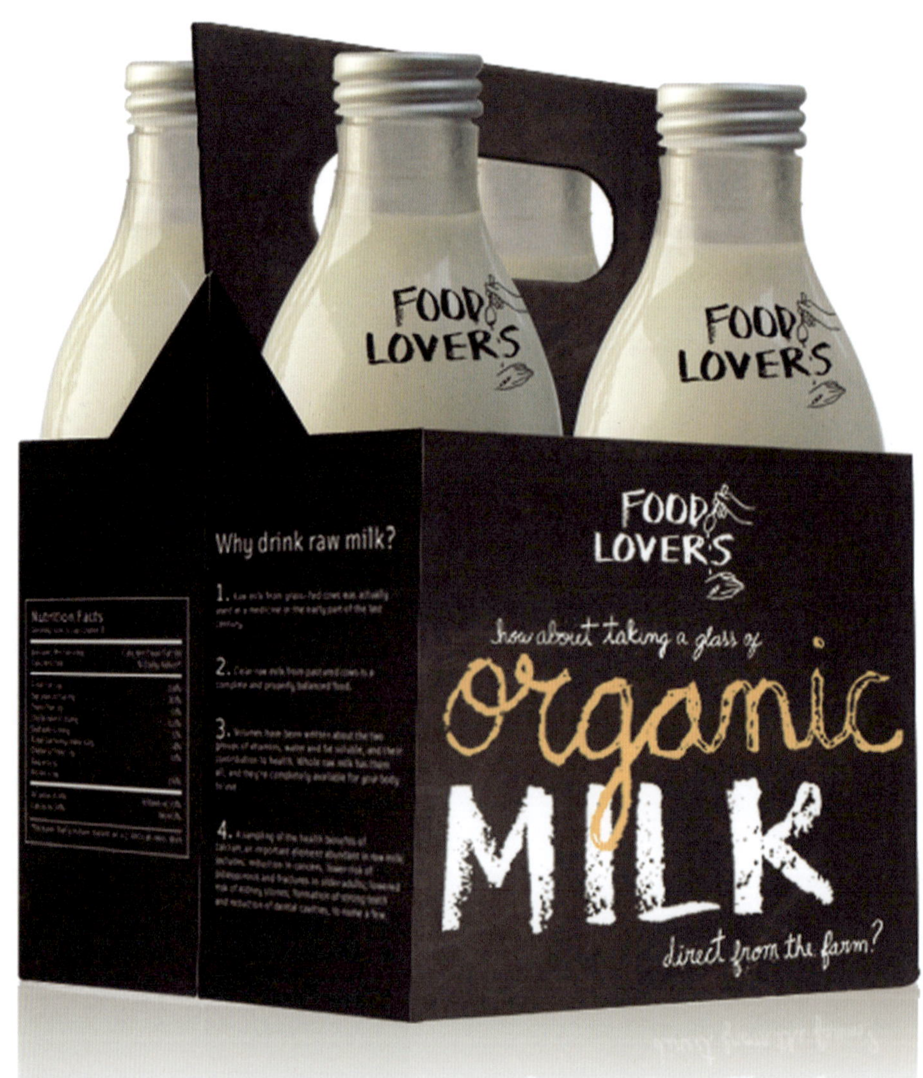

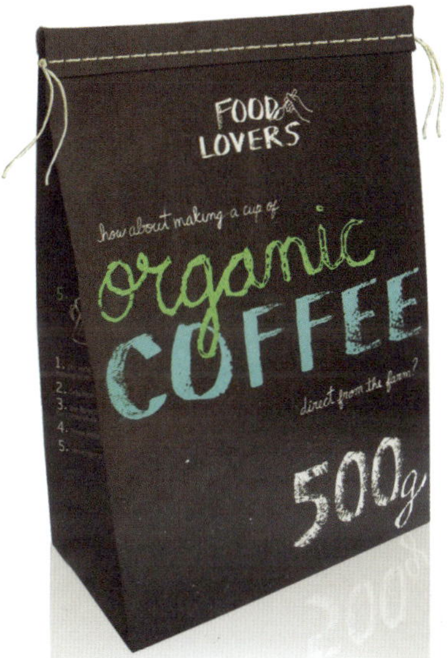
FOOD
LOVERS
how about making a cup of
organic
COFFEE
direct from the farm?
500g

FOOD
LOVERS

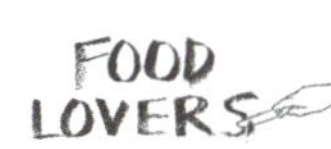
FOOD
LOVERS

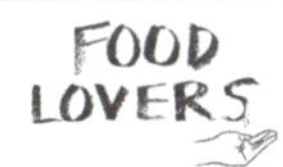
FOOD
LOVERS

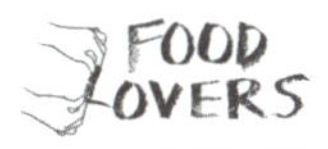
FOOD
LOVERS

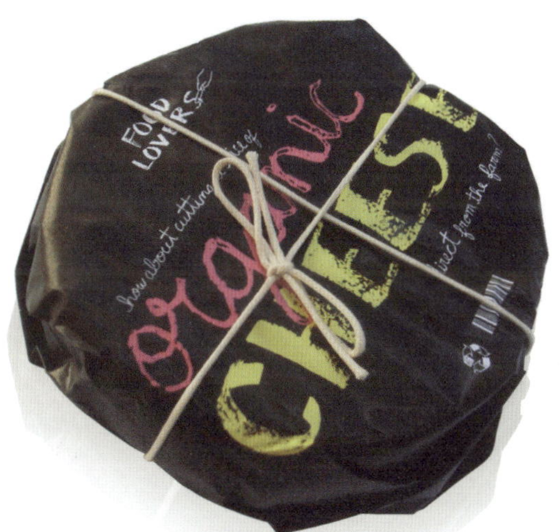
FOOD
LOVERS
how about making a cup of
organic
CHEESE
direct from the farm?

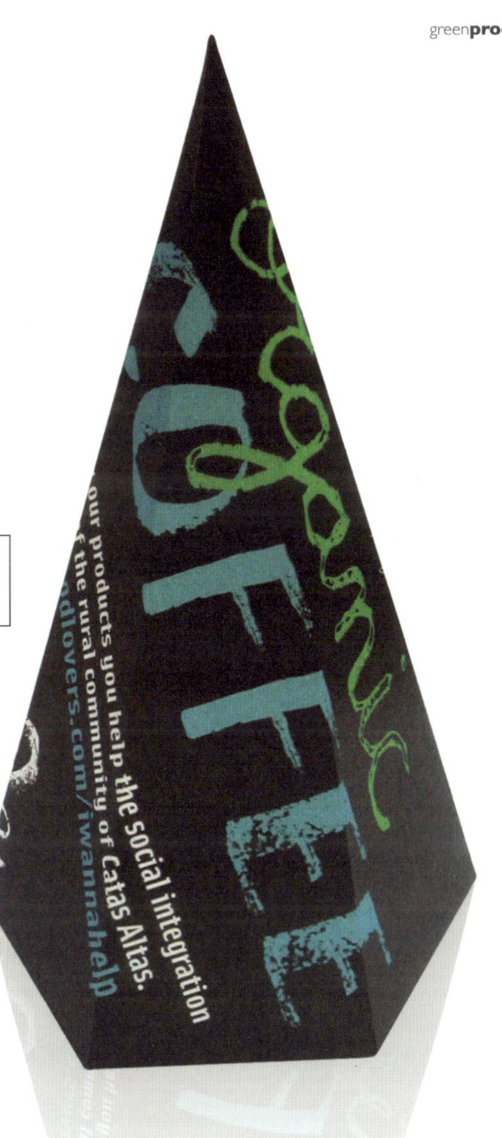
organic
COFFEE
our products you help the social integration
of the rural community of Catas Altas.
dlovers.com/iwannahelp

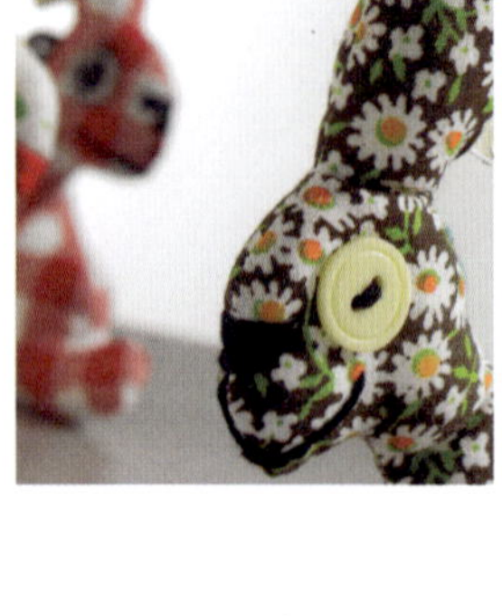

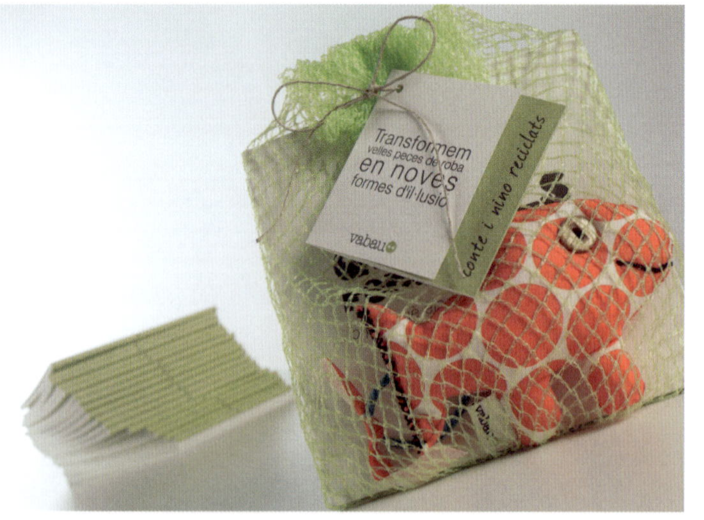
Transformem
velles peces de roba
en noves
formes d'il·lusió
vabau
conte i nino reciclats

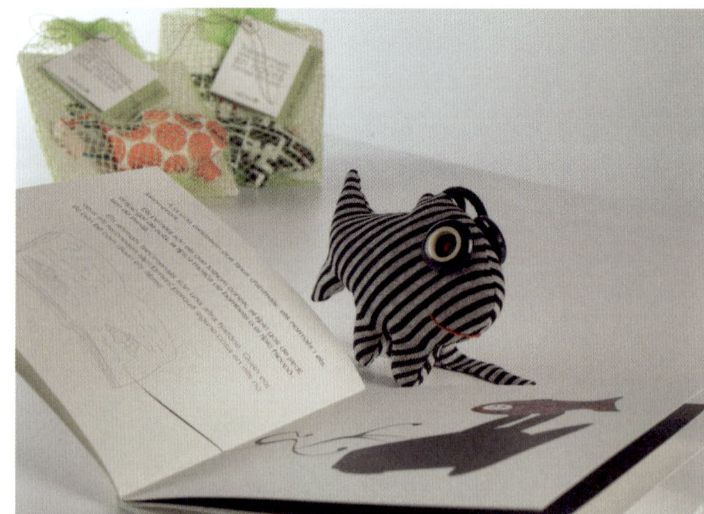

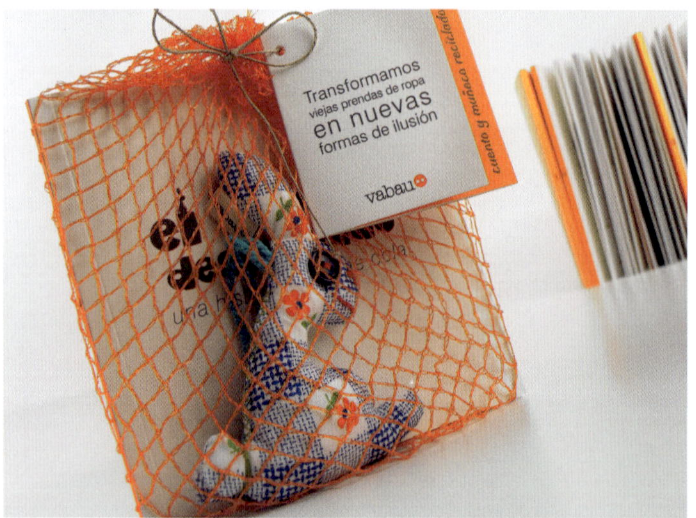
Transformamos
viejas prendas de ropa
en nuevas
formas de ilusión
vabau
cuento y muñeca reciclados

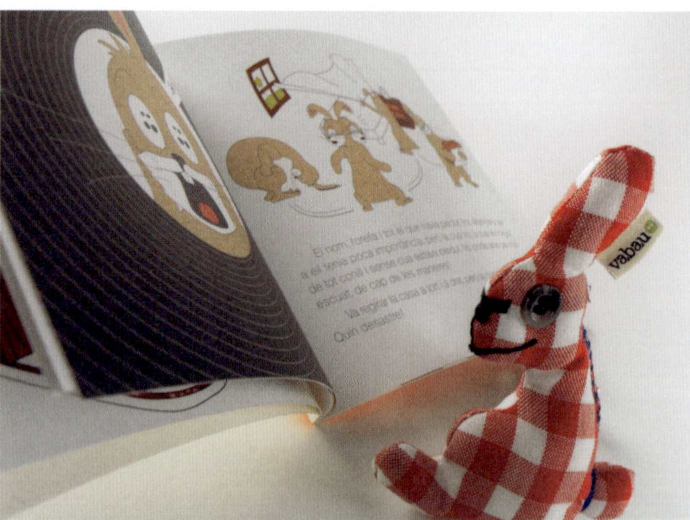

agency/studio: **vabau** / project: Children's stories as part of a recycling-based initiative. The stories are printed on recycled paper and are accompanied by its protagonist made from recycled rags and clothes and other recycled materials. / client: vabau / country: Spain

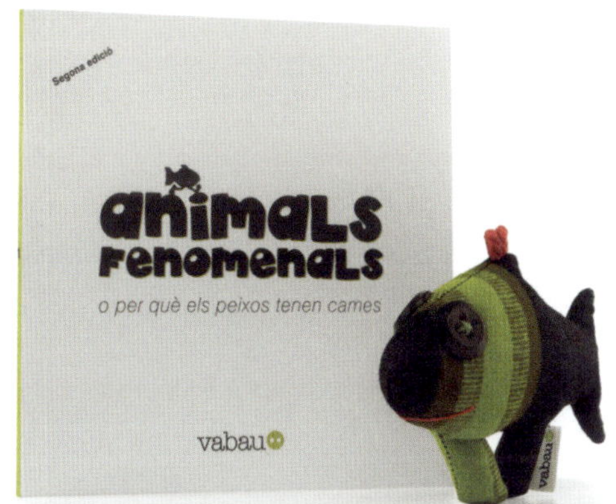

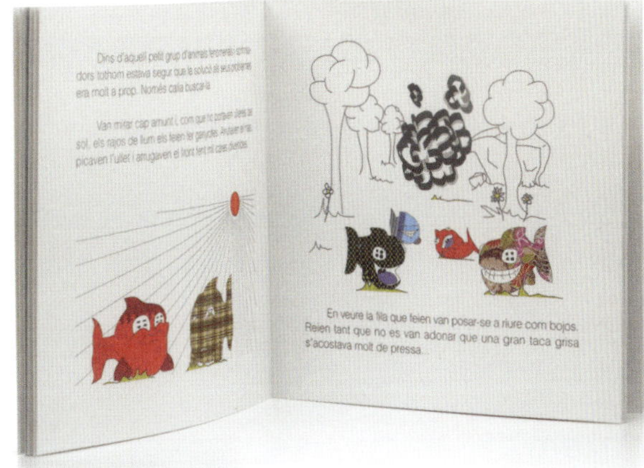

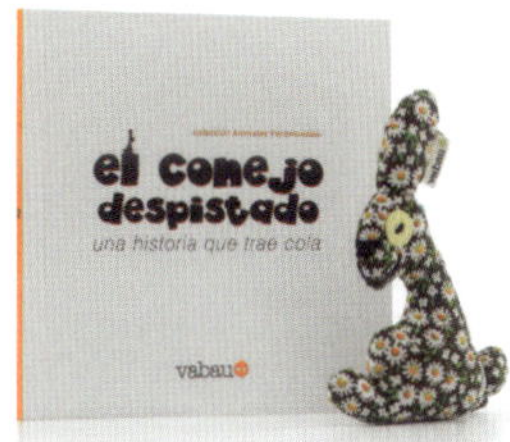

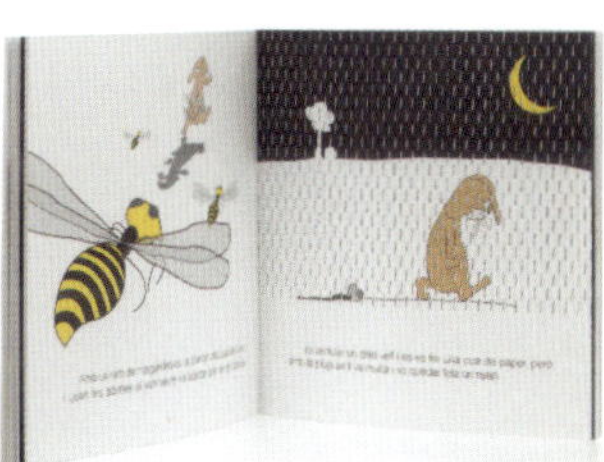

agency/studio: **Flaflaf Editions** / photos by Cristina Reche / project: concepts and design of the board games "Who recycles faster", "Bio-Cycle" and "Eco-House". / clients: Sant Pol de Mar Town Council, Abacus cooperativa, lavola, Abertis and Caldes d'Estrac Town Council / country: Spain

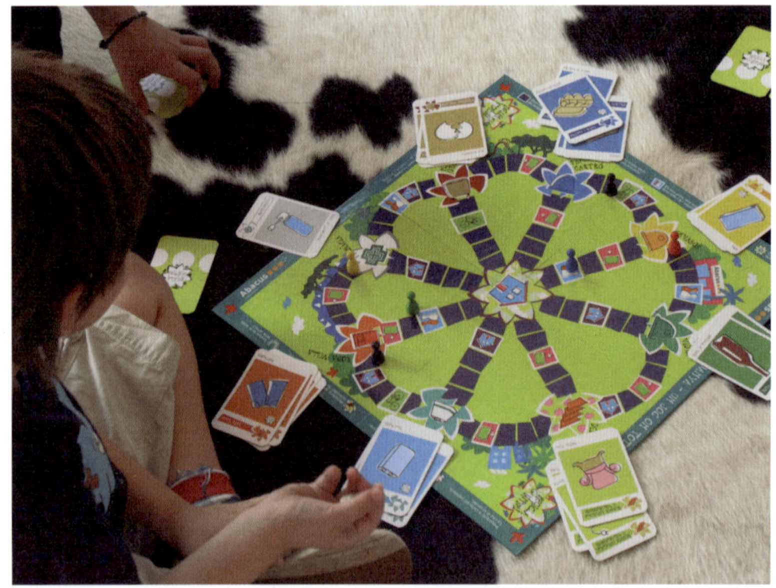

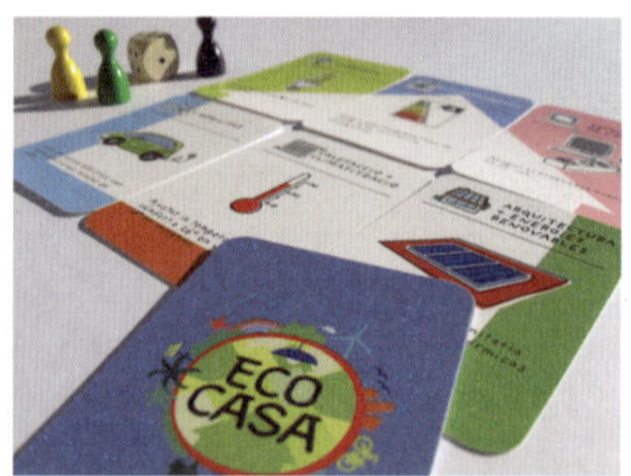

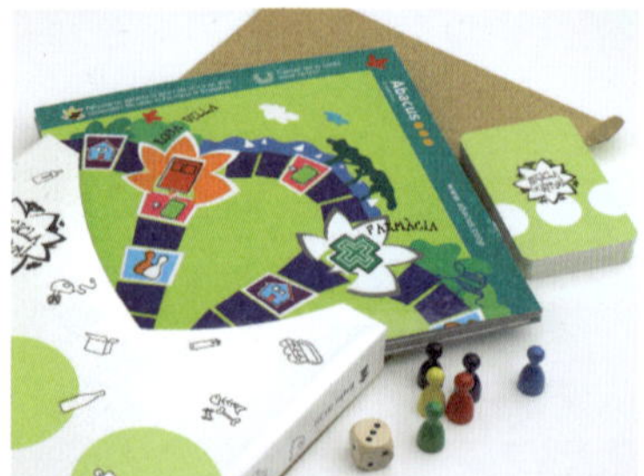

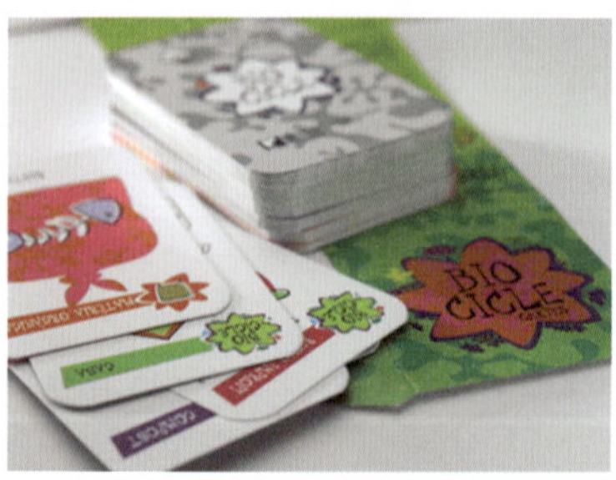

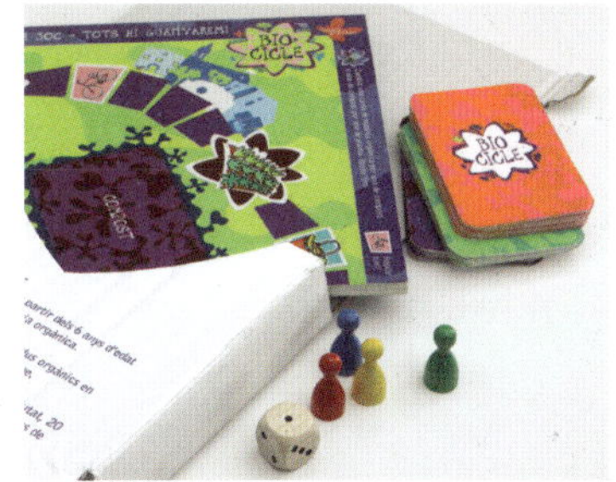

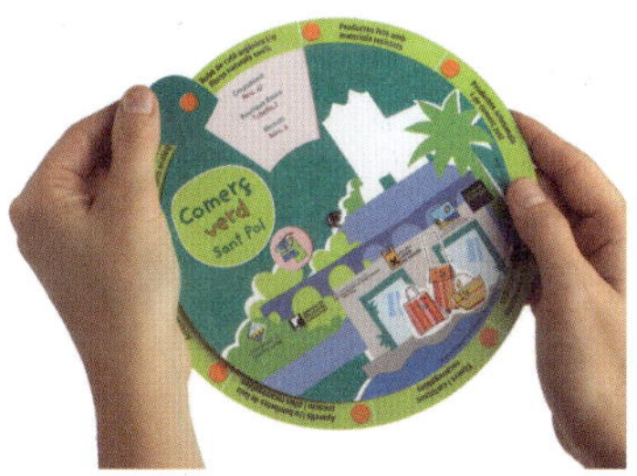

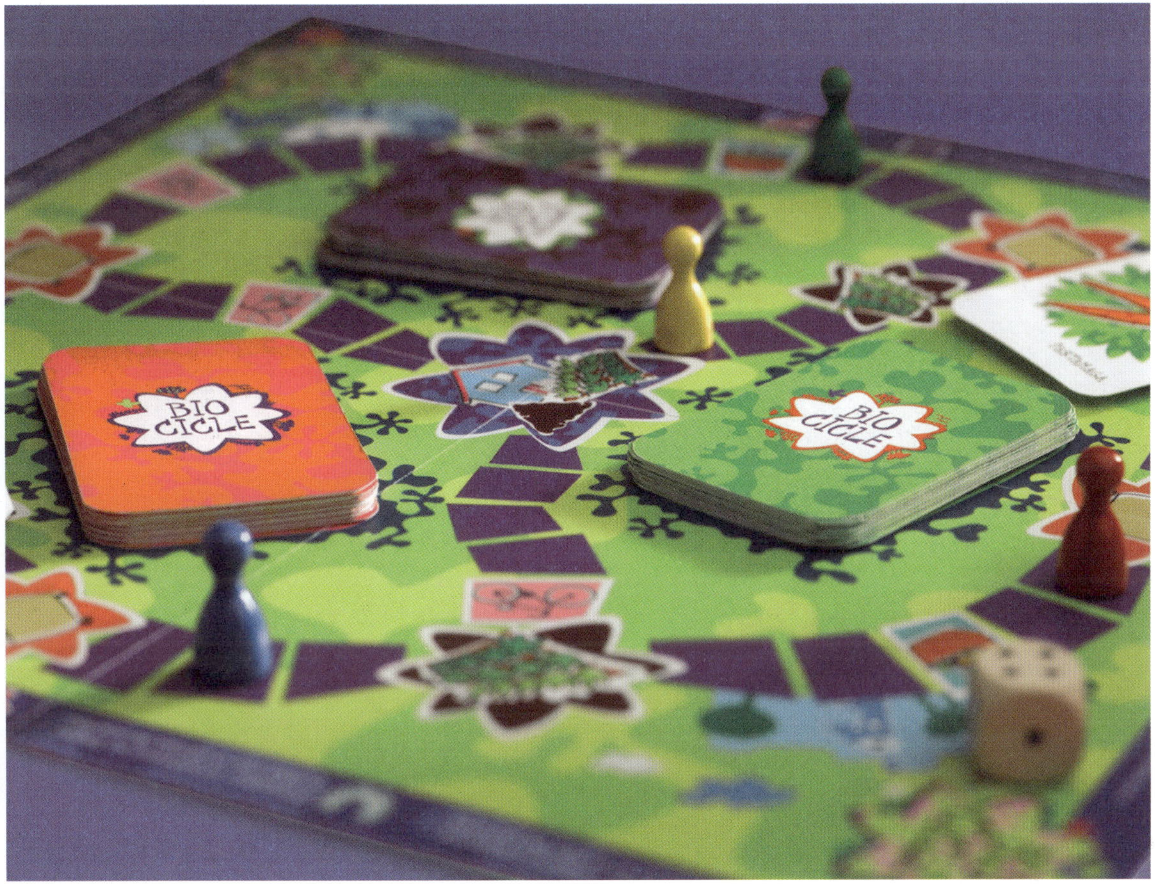

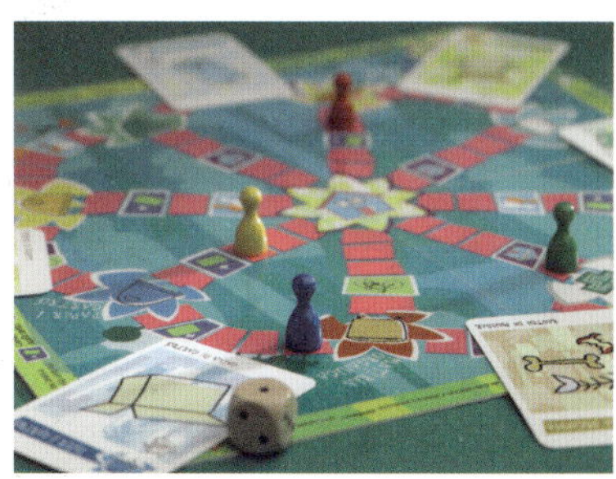

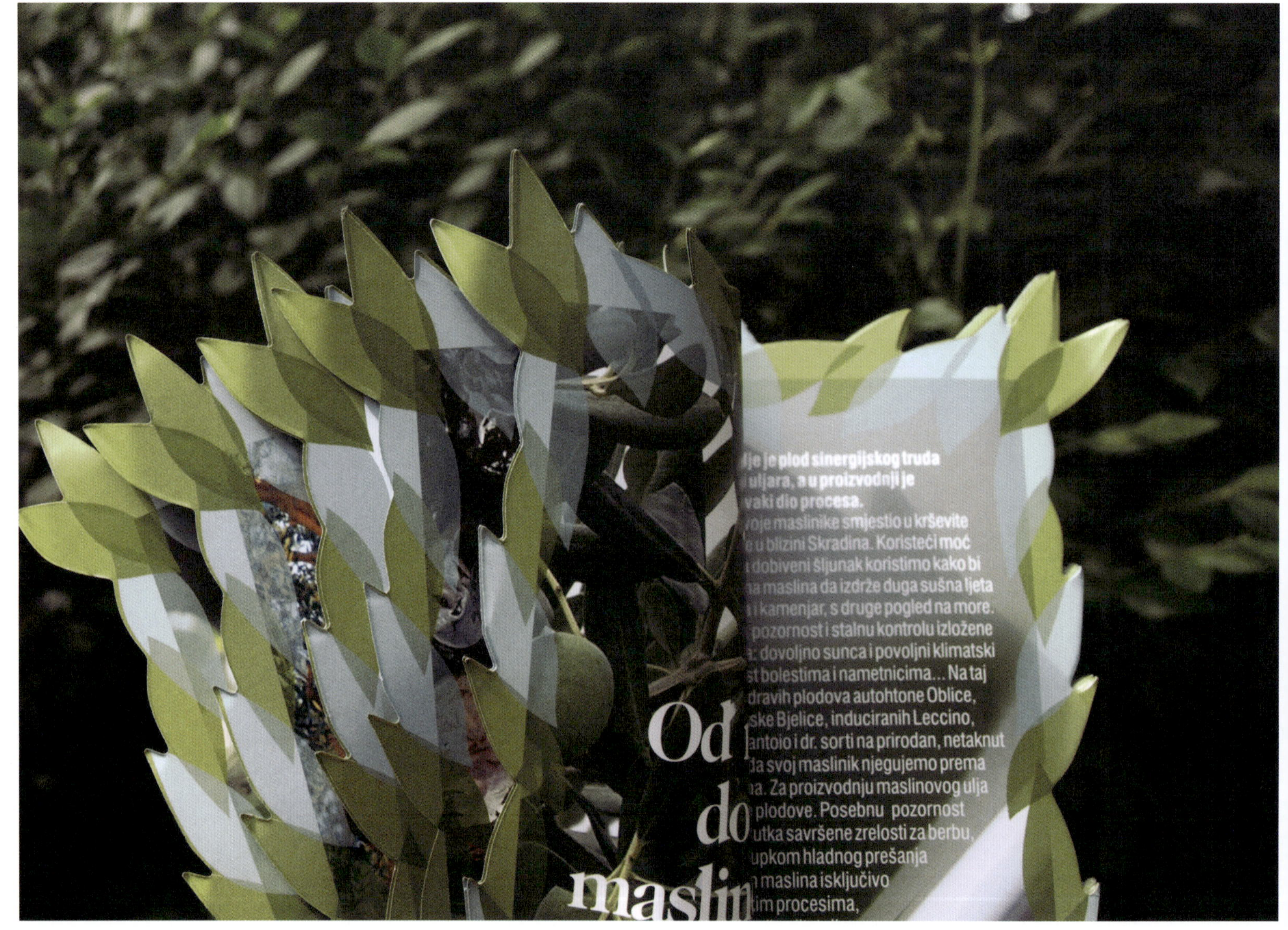
Od
do
maslin
dje je plod sinergijskog truda
uljara, a u proizvodnji je
vaki dio procesa.
voje maslinike smjestio u krševite
u blizini Skradina. Koristeći moć
dobiveni šljunak koristimo kako bi
na maslina da izdrže duga sušna ljeta
kamenjar, s druge pogled na more.
pozornost i stalnu kontrolu izložene
dovoljno sunca i povoljni klimatski
bolestima i nametnicima… Na taj
dravih plodova autohtone Oblice,
ske Bjelice, induciranih Leccino,
antolo i dr. sorti na prirodan, netaknut
da svoj maslinik njegujemo prema
a. Za proizvodnju maslinovog ulja
plodove. Posebnu pozornost
utka savršene zrelosti za berbu,
upkom hladnog prešanja
maslina isključivo
tim procesima,

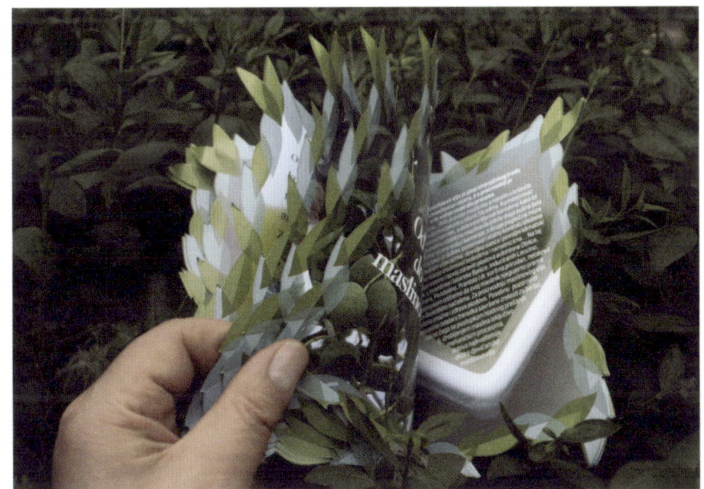

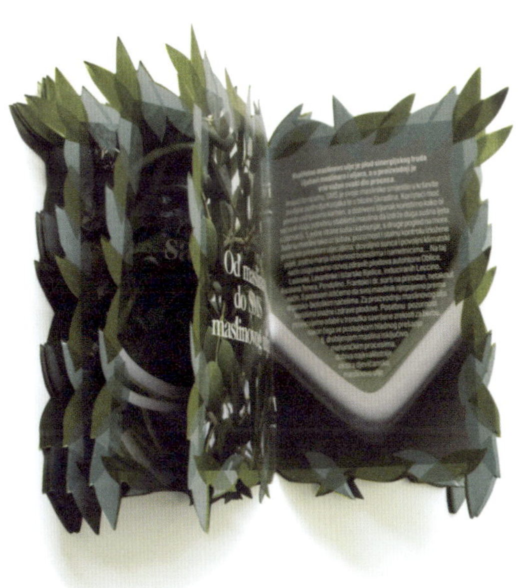

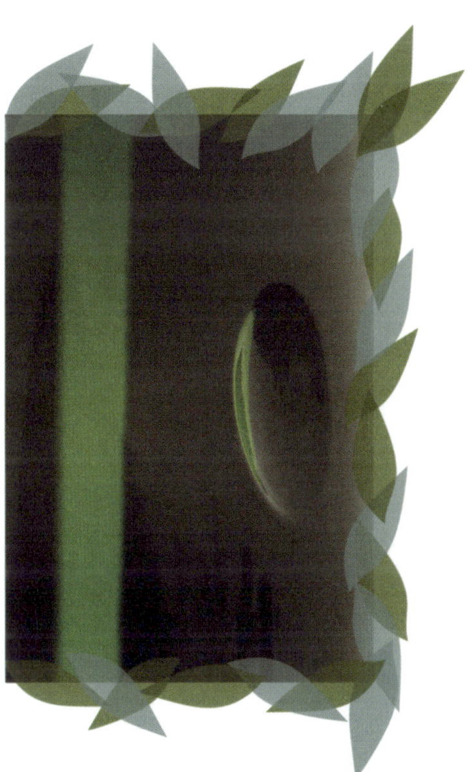

agency/studio: **Studio International** (Boris Ljubicic) / project: promotional booklet about the production of organic olive oil. / client: SMS food factory / country: Croatia

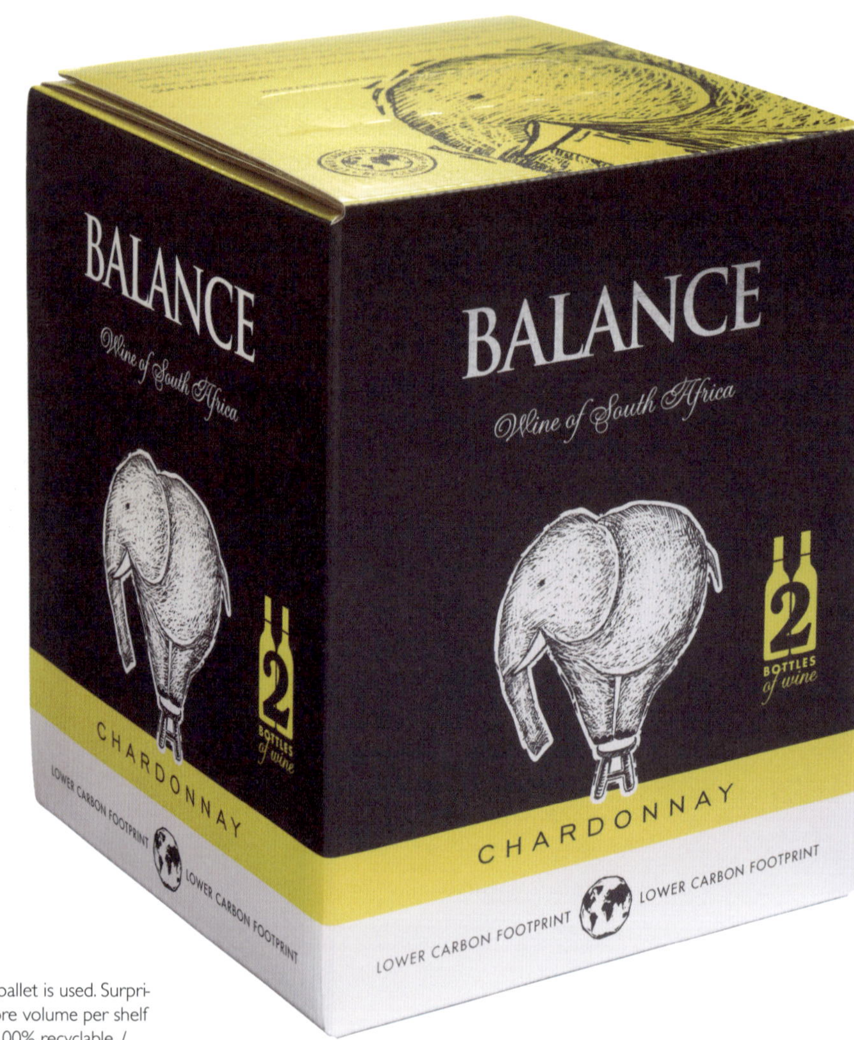

agency/studio: **Dare!** / project: 1.5 litre "Balance" box. A format designed to ensure the maximum number of bottles per pallet is used. Surprisingly, the box contains two 750ml bottles of wine, but with a significant reduction in weight/transit. Retailers can stock more volume per shelf than with regular bottles and once opened, the wine stays fresher for longer. Made from 80% recycled material, it is itself 100% recyclable. / client: Kingsland Wines & Spirits / country: United Kingdom

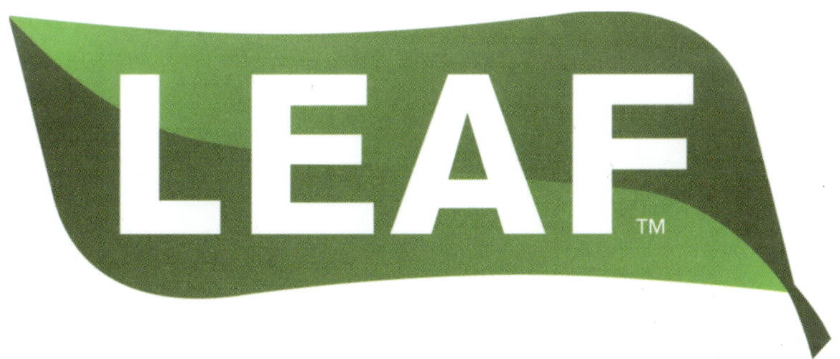

agency/studio: **The Jones Group** / project: Trademark for a family of adhesive products that reduce formaldehyde emissions from chipboard, fibreboard insulation, glass mat and other industrial materials. / client: Georgia-Pacific / country: USA author: **Amanda Mocci** / project: This tea packaging comes in five fruit flavours that are all assembled in one package made from 100% organic canvas. The fruit is dried and packaged in small cotton pouches. / country: Canada

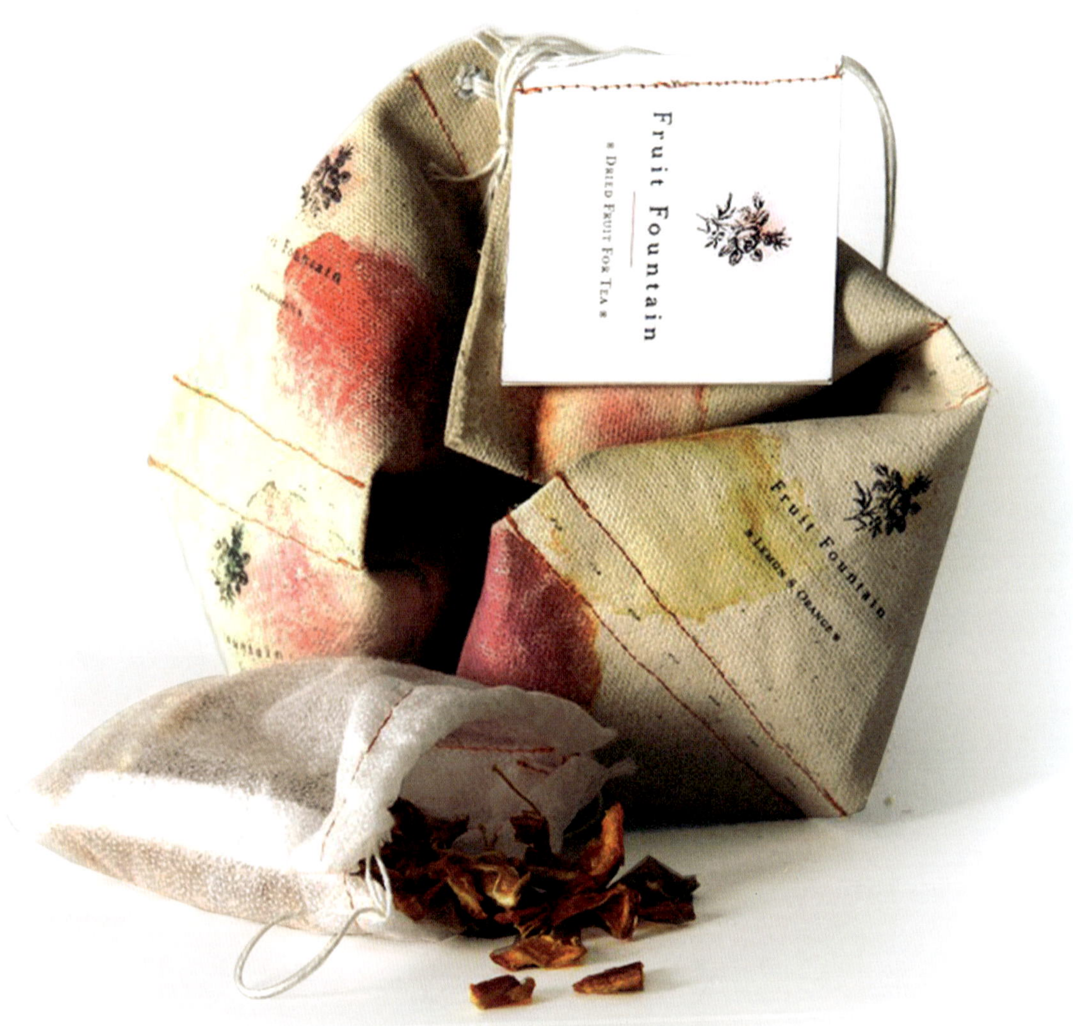

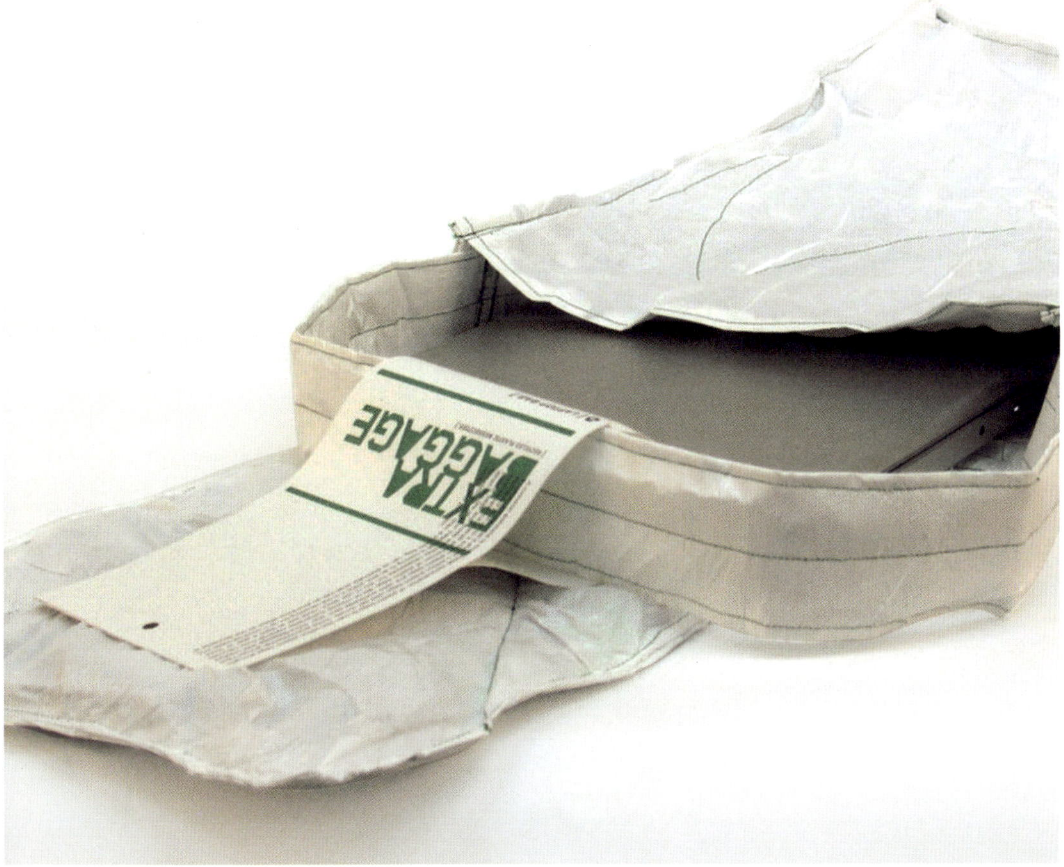

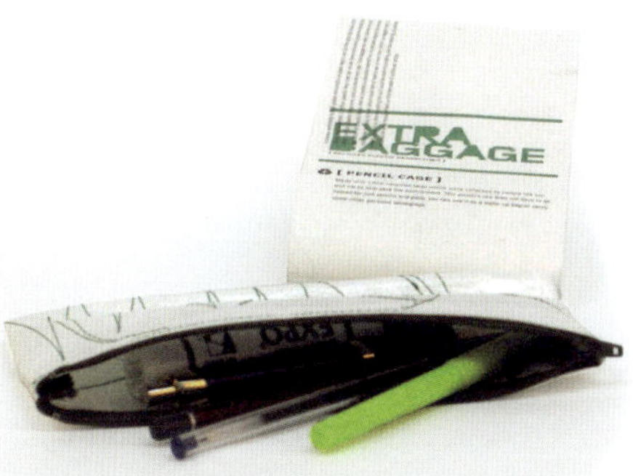

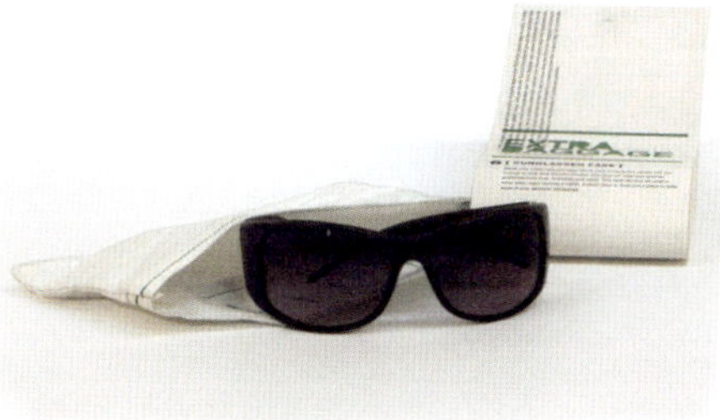

author: **Amanda Mocci** / project: Extra Baggage is a collection of bags, sleeves and cases made out of fused used plastic bags / country: Canada

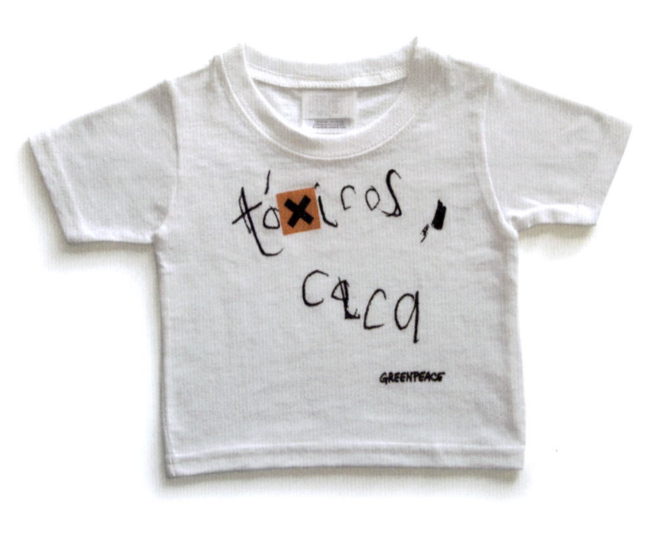

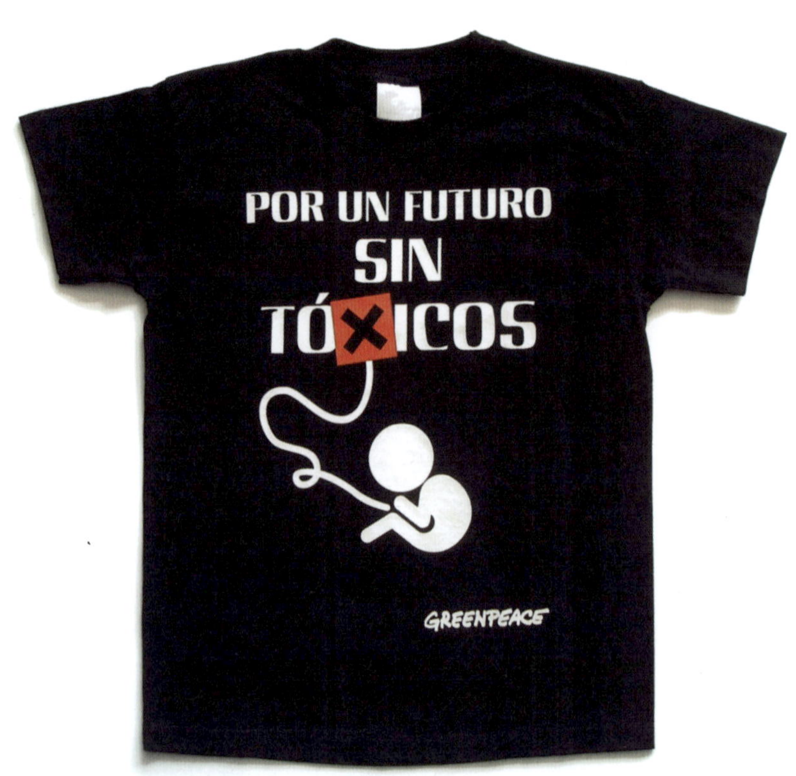

agency/studio: **Hola Por Qué** / project: design and screen printing of t-shirts for a campaign against clothing made from toxic products. / client: Greenpeace / country: Spain

POR UN FUTURO
SIN
TÓXICOS
GREENPEACE

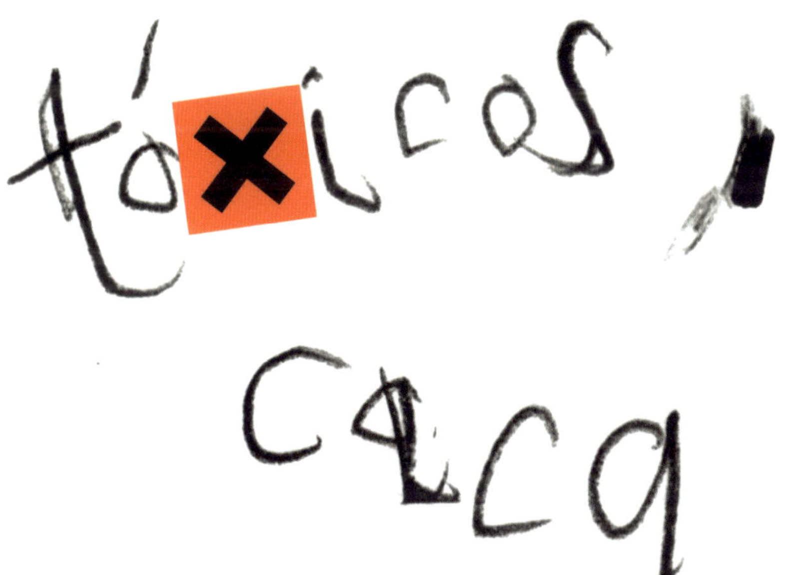
tóxicos,
caca
GREENPEACE

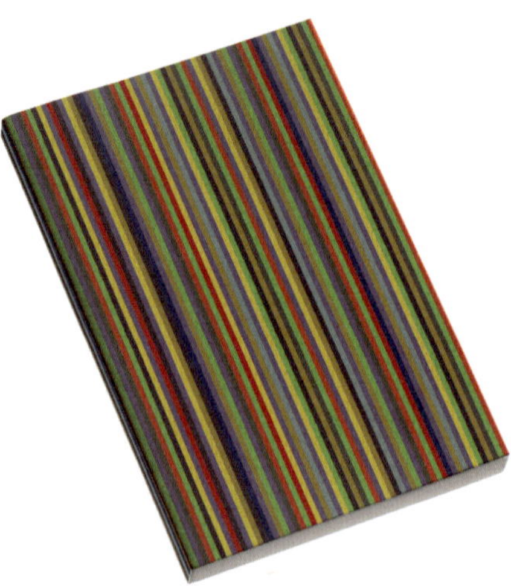

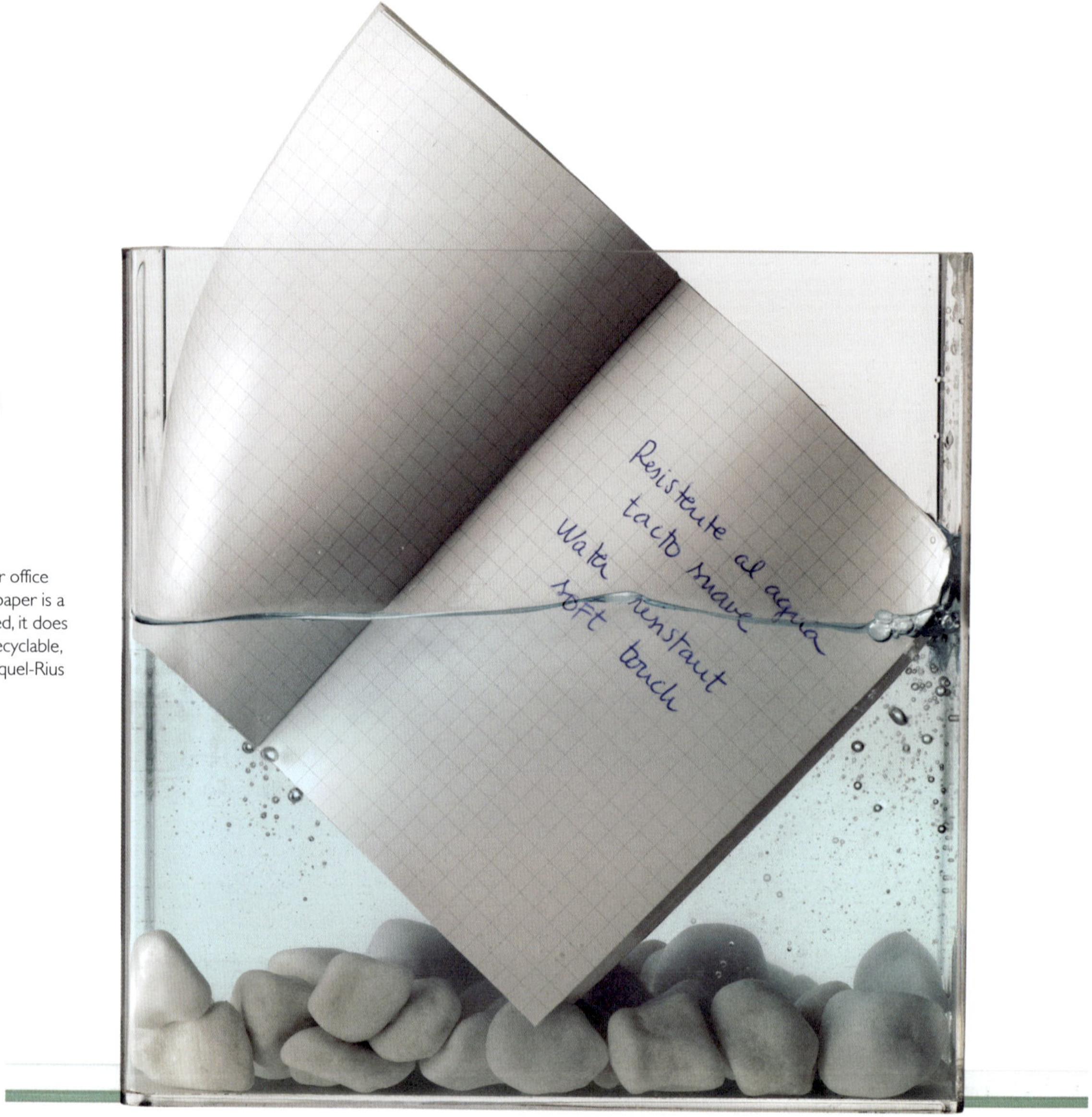

agency/studio: **MIQUEL-RIUS 1839** / project: Stonepaper is the first collection of paper office supplies in Europe to be made from paper made from stone (TerraSkin). This new type of paper is a combination of mineral powder and non-toxic resin. No wood is needed, no water is wasted, it does not pollute, no bleaching is required and 50% less energy is used to produce it. It is 100% recyclable, can be re-used infinitely and degrades when exposed to the sun for 3-9 months. / client: Miquel-Rius 1839 / country: Spain

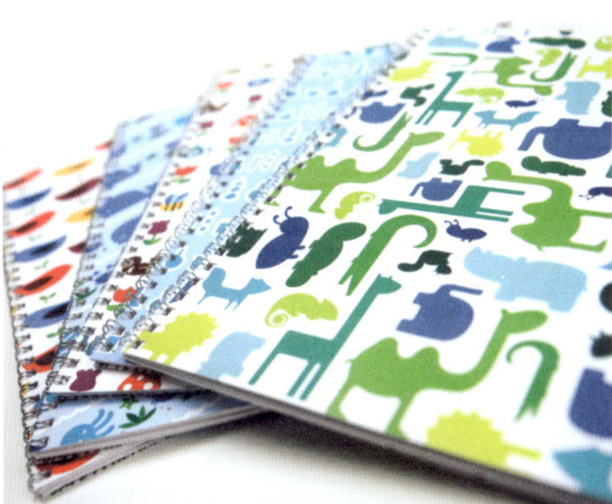

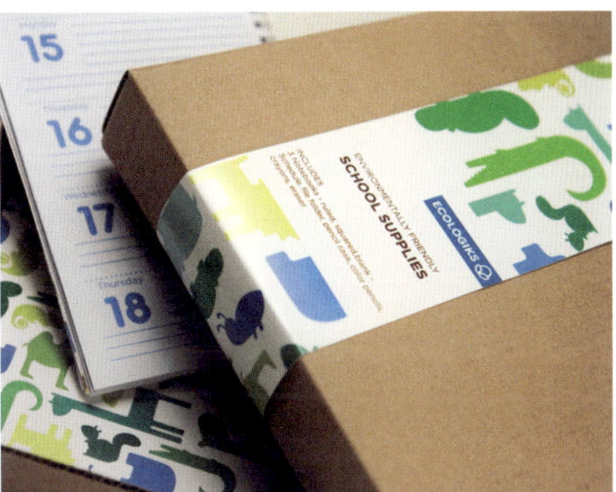

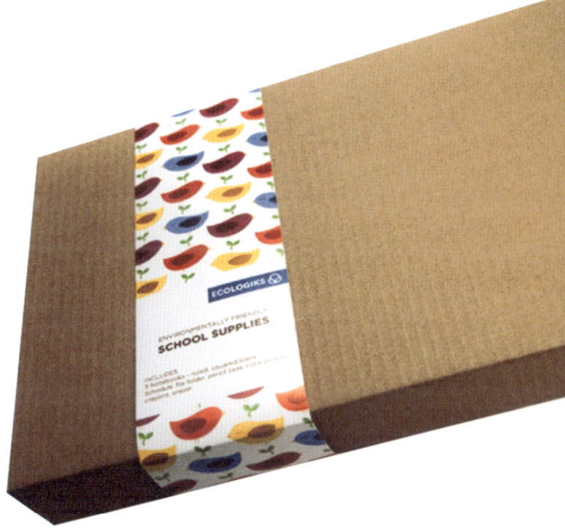

agency/studio: **One Little Tree** / project: Ecologiks is a brand of environmentally friendly school supplies and stationery manufactured for use by children. It is made with recycled post-consumer materials. / country: Canada

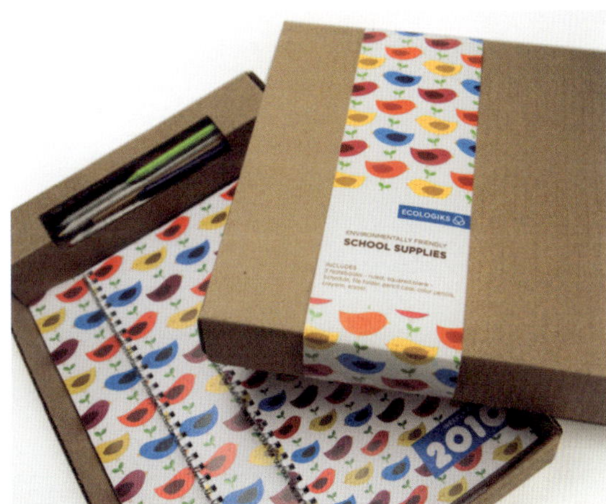

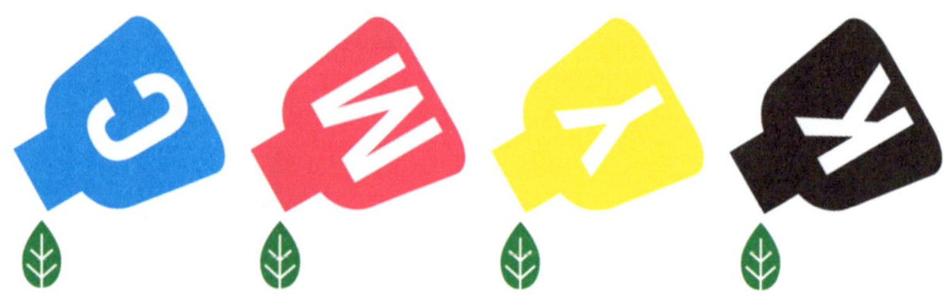

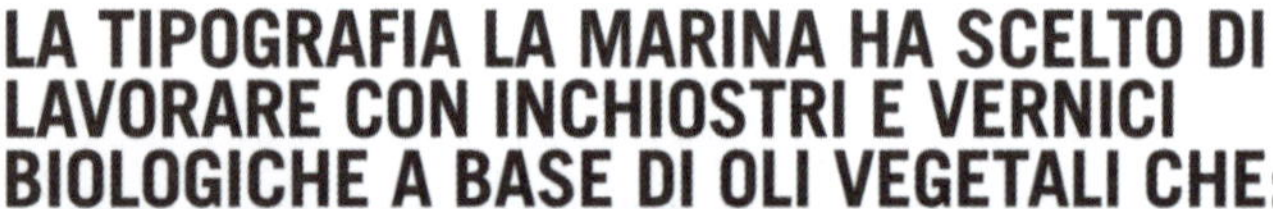

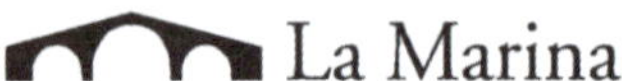

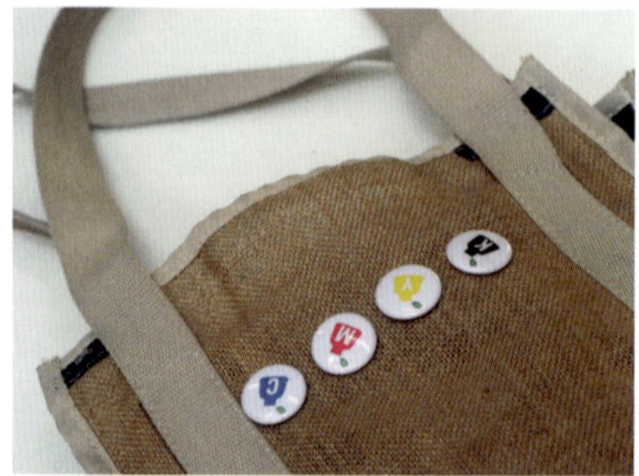

agency/studio: **Frush [design sostenibile]** / project: e-card and badges to promote the use of vegetable-based inks. / client: La Marina (printer) / country: Italy

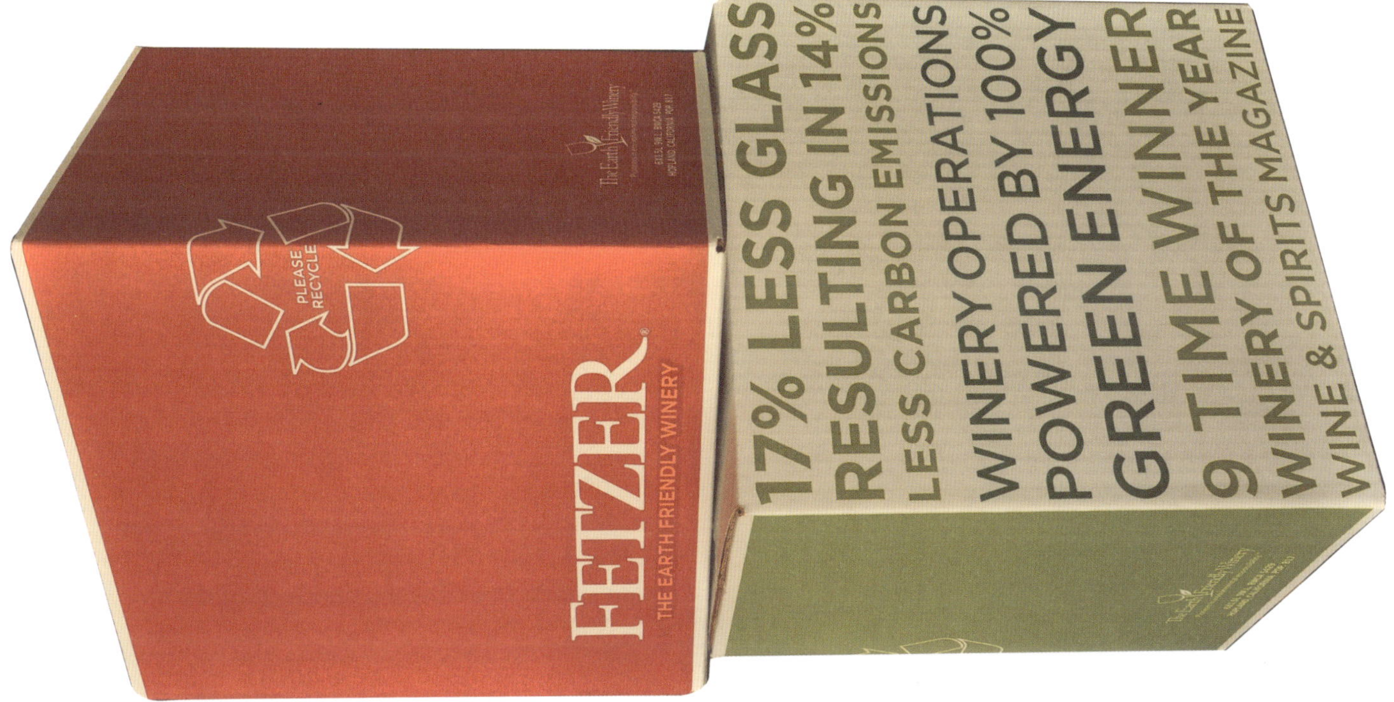

agency/studio: **CF Napa Brand Design** / project: For years, Fetzer has been recognised for its role in pioneering the movement in the wine industry that today is referred to as sustainability. The challenge was to reposition the brand to better leverage its rich history. / client: Brown-Forman / country: USA

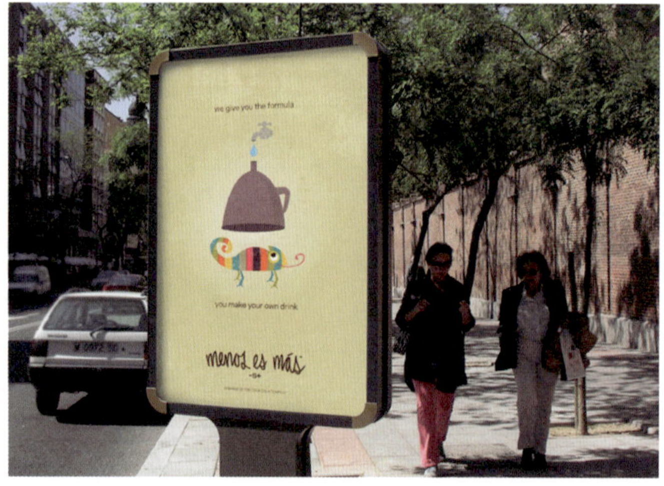
we give you the formula
you make your own drink
menos es más
-S+

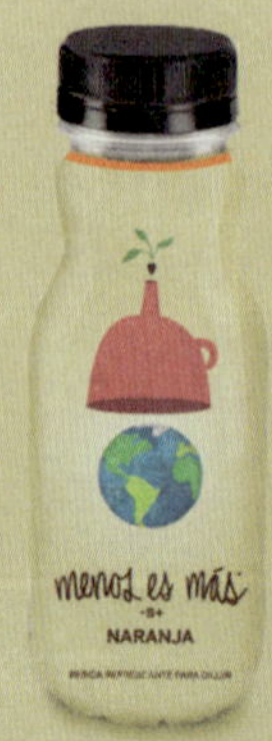
MENOS
COCHES
MÁS
BICICLETAS
Hay refrescos que te prometen ser más guapo, más
alto o tener una casa más grande. menos es más™ te
cuenta las cosas tal y como son, es sencillo y fácil de
entender, sin rollos.
menos es más
-S+
NARANJA
menos es más™ es una marca de THE COCA-COLA COMPANY

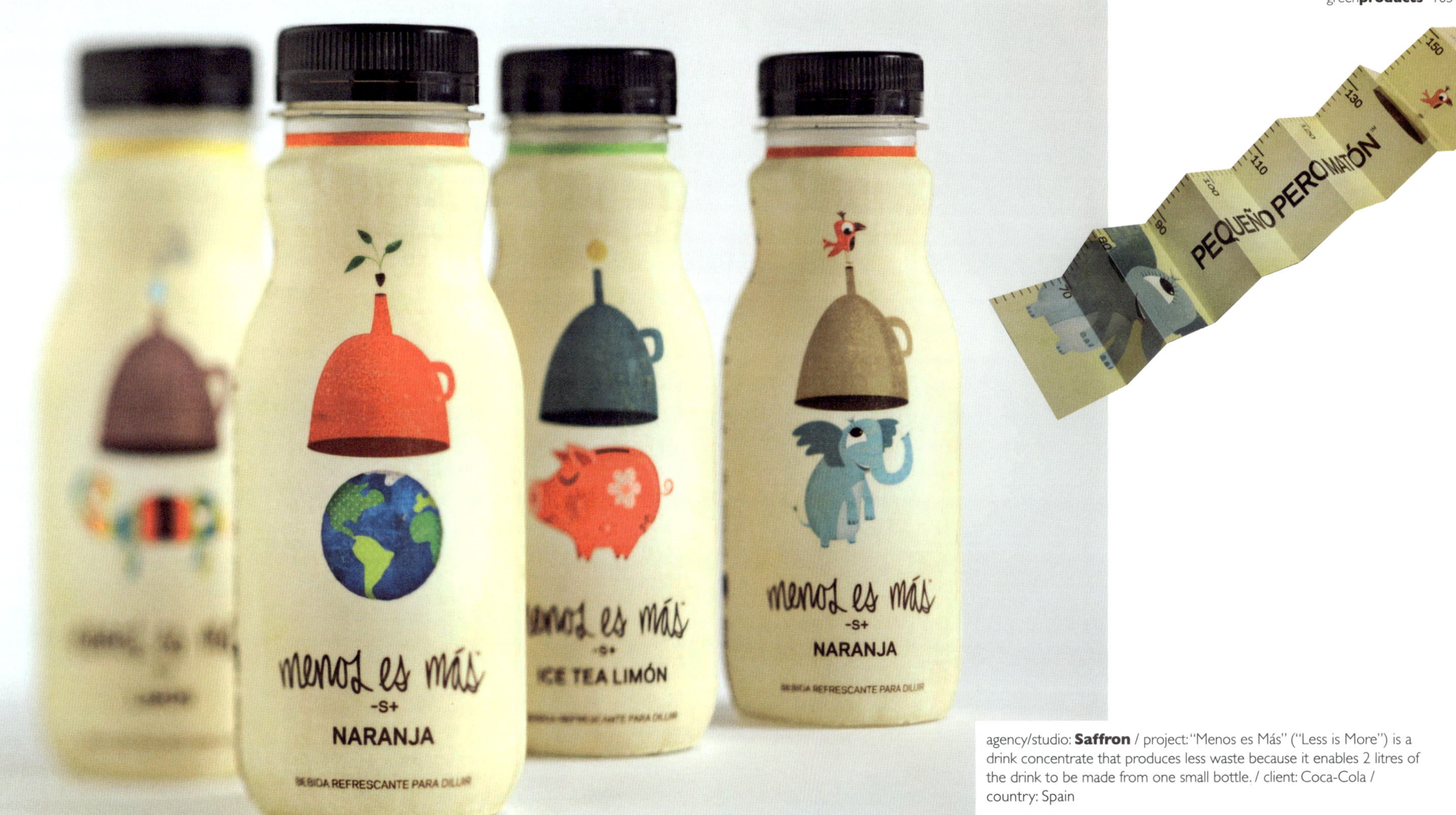

agency/studio: **Saffron** / project: "Menos es Más" ("Less is More") is a drink concentrate that produces less waste because it enables 2 litres of the drink to be made from one small bottle. / client: Coca-Cola / country: Spain

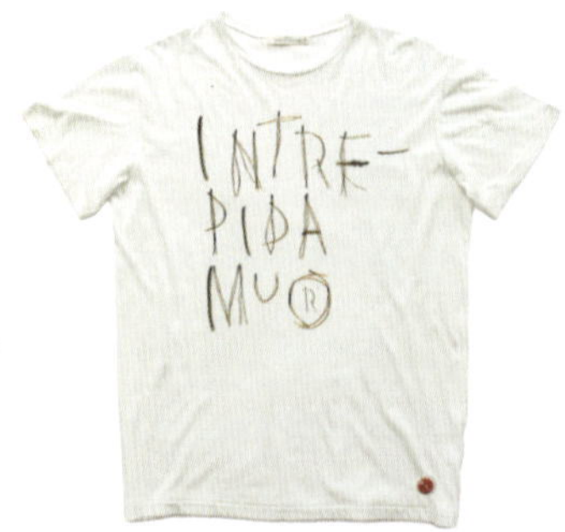
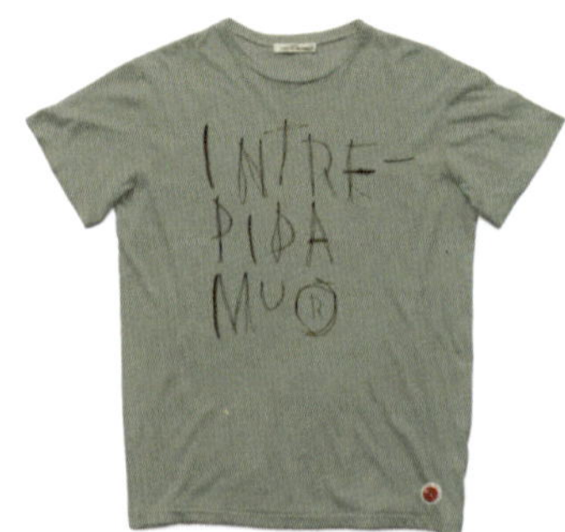

agency/studio: **Borja Garmendia - Pensando en Blanco**™ / project: Typography created using pine needles found in Mediterranean forests. Intrépida Mu is the leading brand in Spain working to support fair trade and the use of certified organic cotton. / client: Intrépida Mu / country: Spain

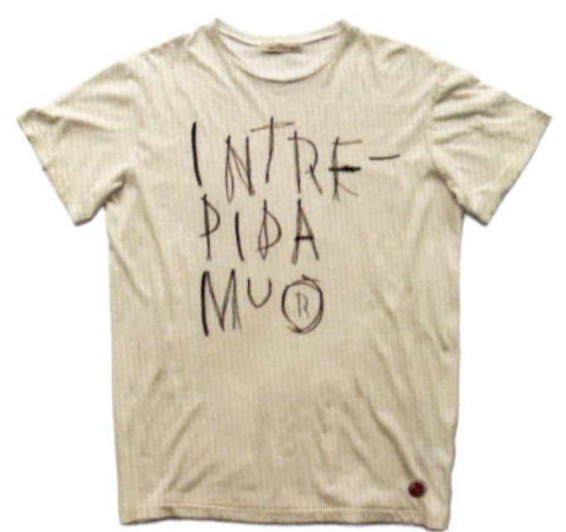
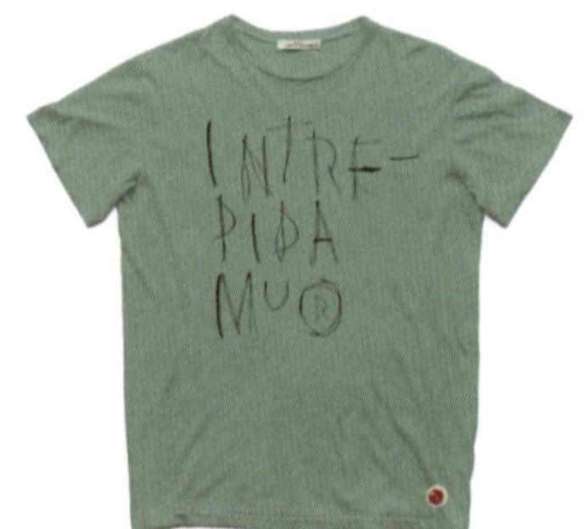

ERM-Type Outline
ERM- es una tipografía creada a partir de maravillosos paseos por los paisajes y bosques del Baix Empordá. Su carácter natural, hace de esta tipografía el elemento para una aplicaciones libres de cualquier norma tipográfica. Se presenta en 3 versiónes, ERM- Type Regular, ERM- Type Bitmap y ERM- Type Outline.

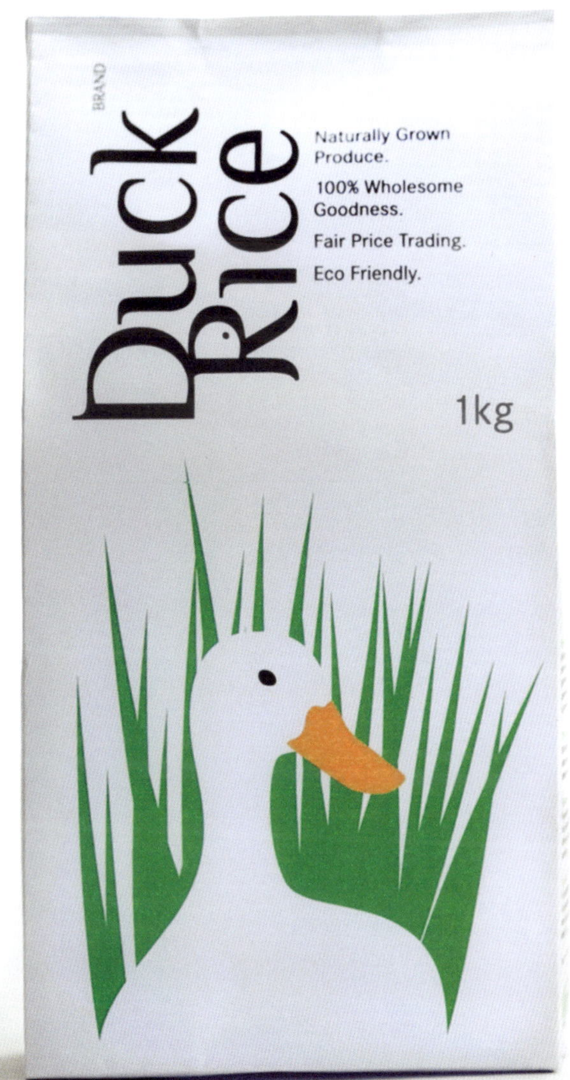

agency/studio: **Design Positive** / project: Duck Rice is a type of rice grown as naturally as possible. Ducks live in the paddies and their everyday habits keep the crop fertilised and free of pests. / client: Xanh / country: Vietnam

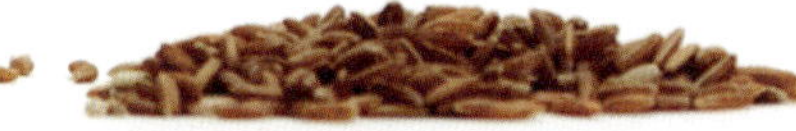

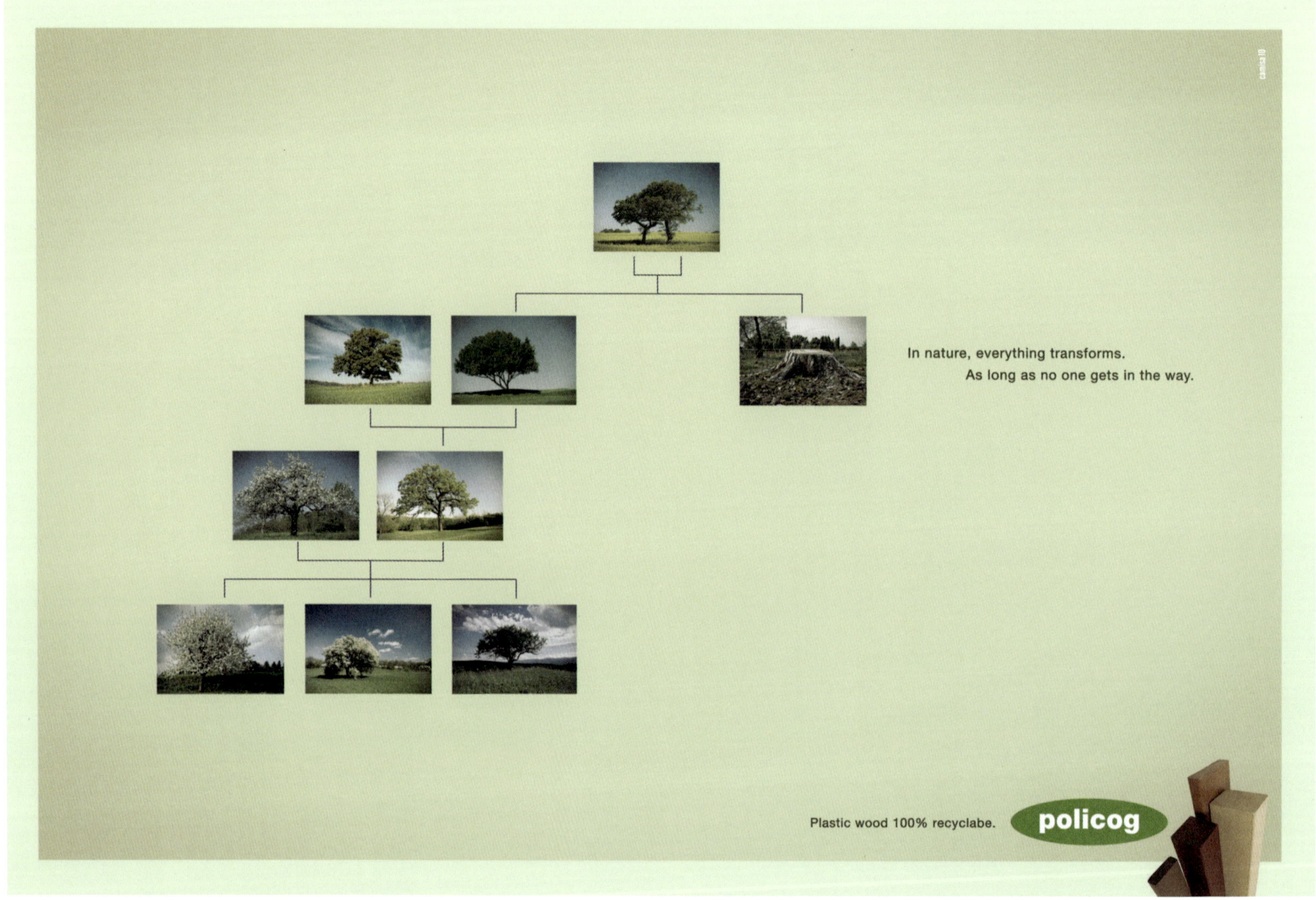

agency/studio: **Camisa 10** / project: Policog is an innovative, environmentally friendly wood imitation created from recycled plastic waste. / client: Cogumelo / country: Brazil

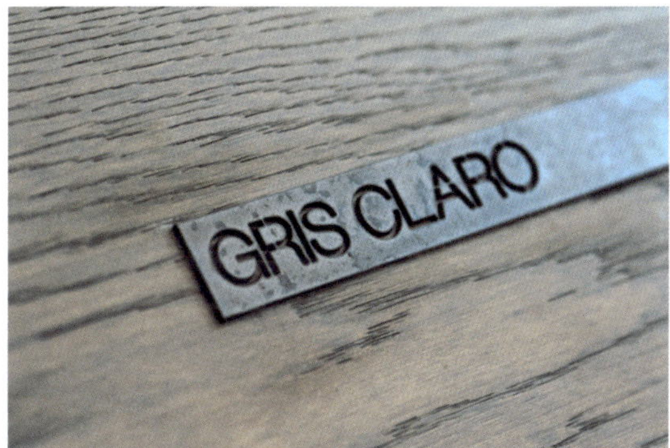

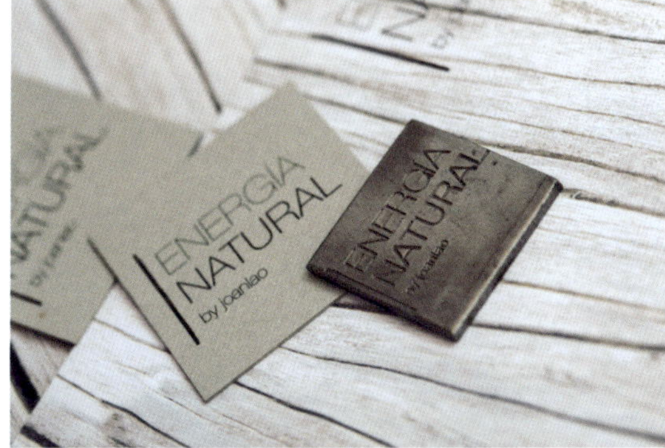

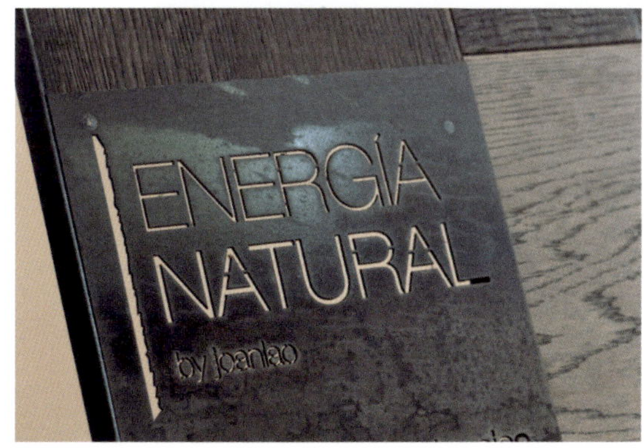

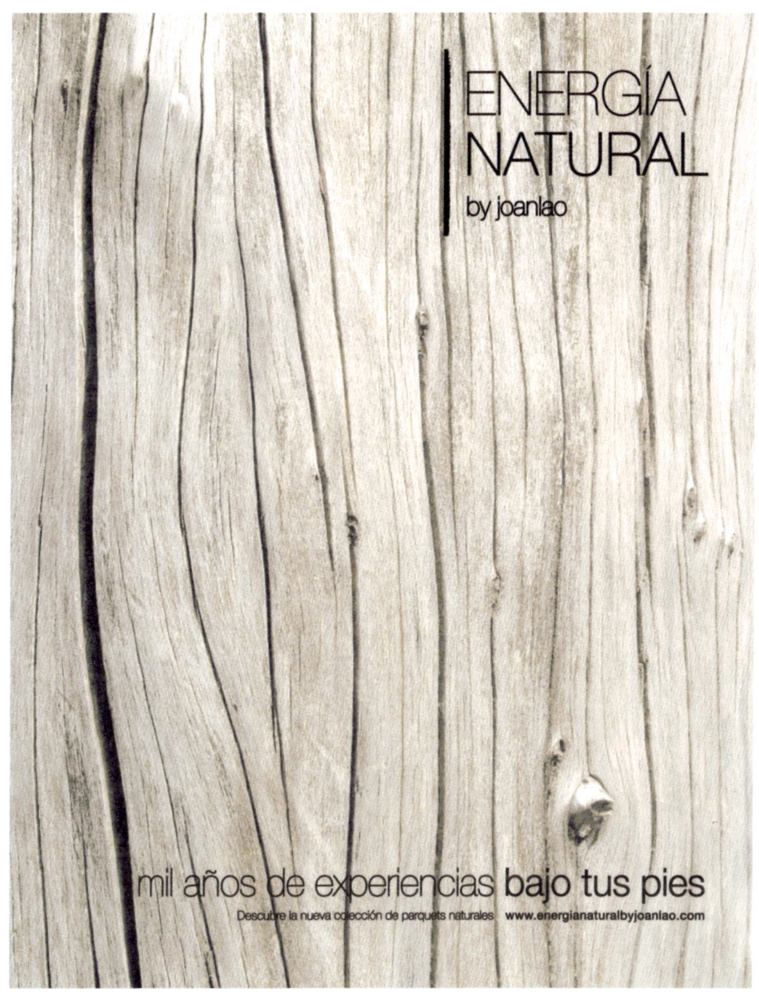

agency/studio: **Cienpies Diseño y Comunicación** / project: global launch of the "Energía Natural by Joan Lao"
collection: flooring produced using wood from sustainable forests. / client: MH Parquets & Joan Lao / country: Spain

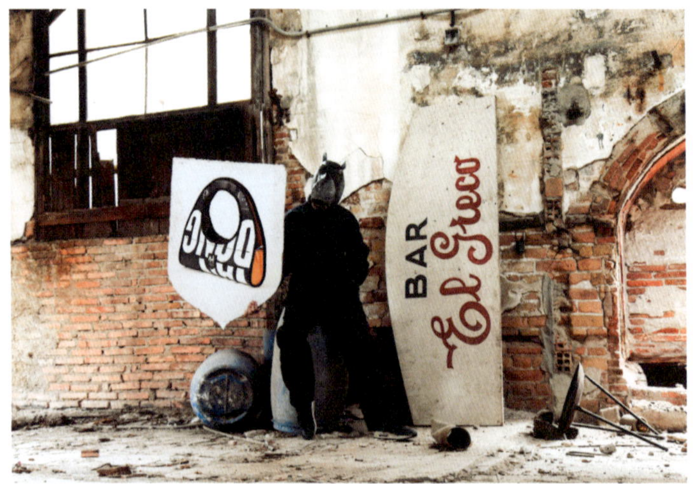

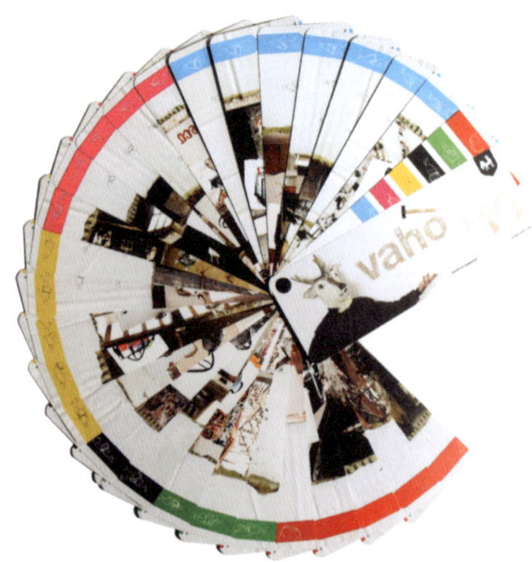

agency/studio: **Maria Molsosa** / project: catalogues, cards and shop graphics for Vaho, a company that makes bags with an exclusive design from used advertising banners. / client: vaho works / country: Spain

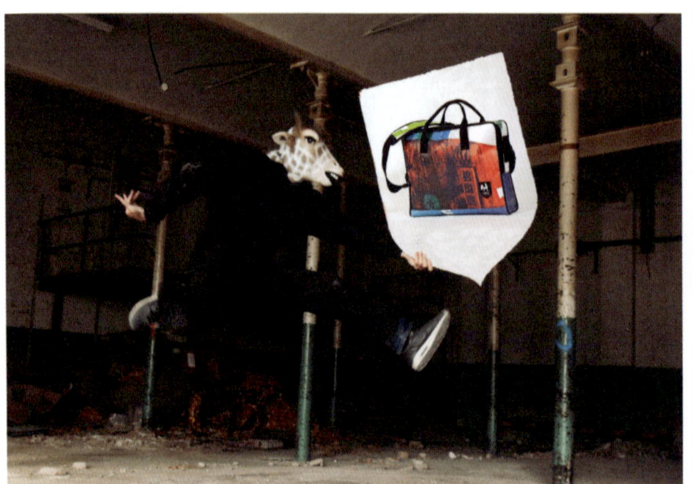

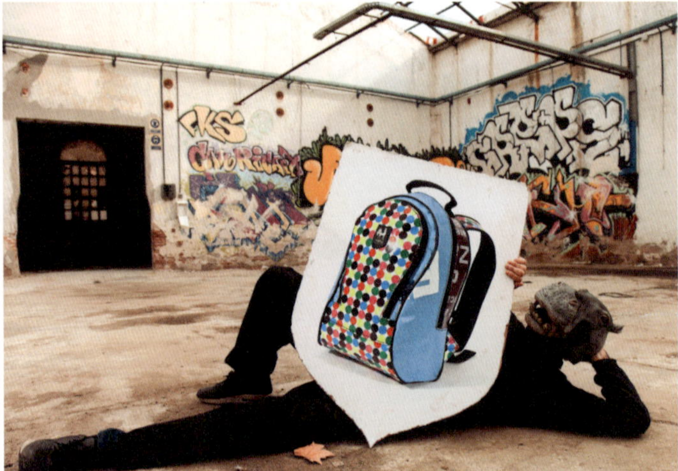

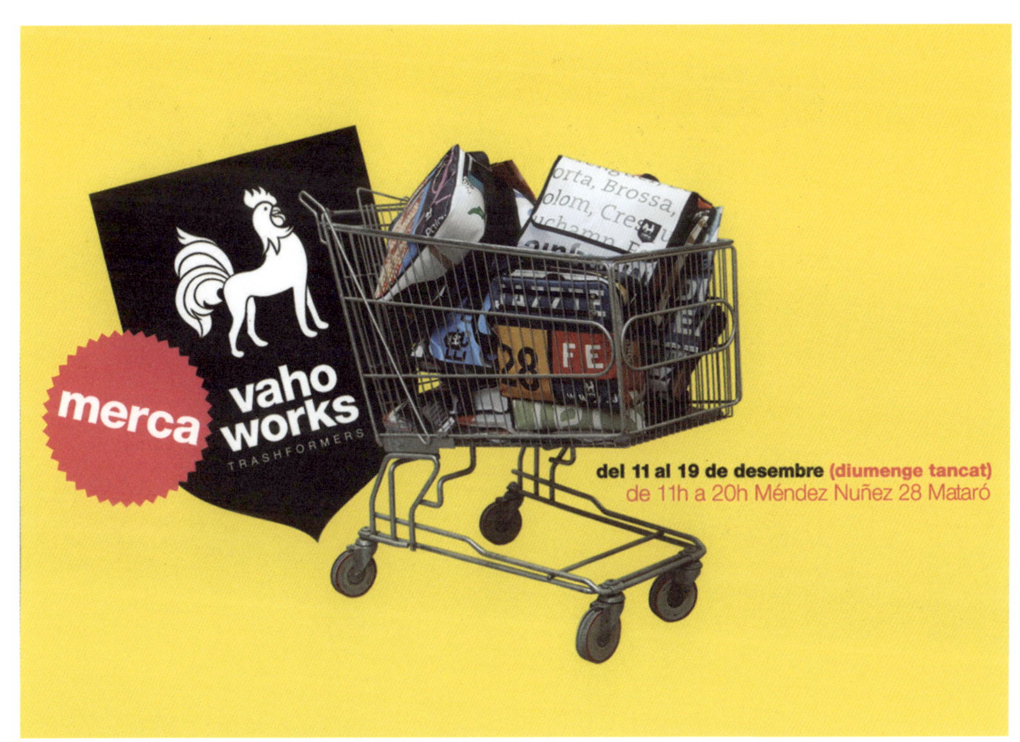
merca
vaho
works
TRASHFORMERS
del 11 al 19 de desembre (diumenge tancat)
de 11h a 20h Méndez Nuñez 28 Mataró

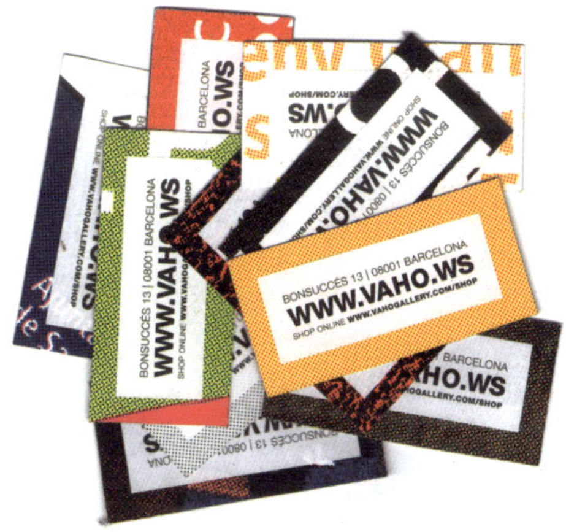
BONSUCCÉS 13 | 08001 BARCELONA
WWW.VAHO.WS
SHOP ONLINE WWW.VAHOGALLERY.COM/SHOP

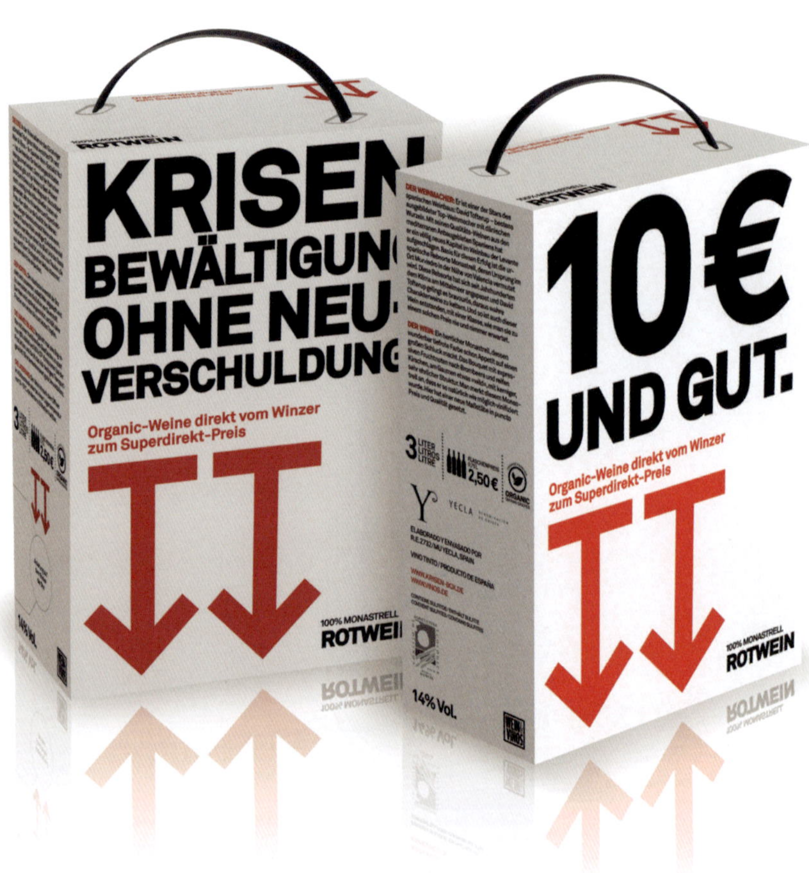

agency/studio: **Ruska, Martín, Associates** / project: The "crisis-box" is a type of eco-friendly, cheap wine packaging. It has an eco-balance that reduces CO2 emissions by 55% compared to traditional glass-and-cork packaging due to its 3-litre capacity, light weight and separable, recyclable materials (outside a carton, inside a foil tube). / client: Wein & Vinos / country: Germany

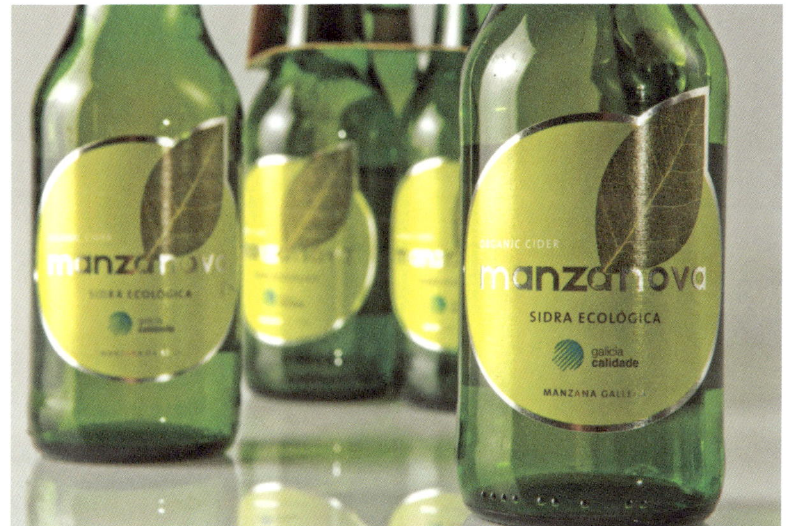

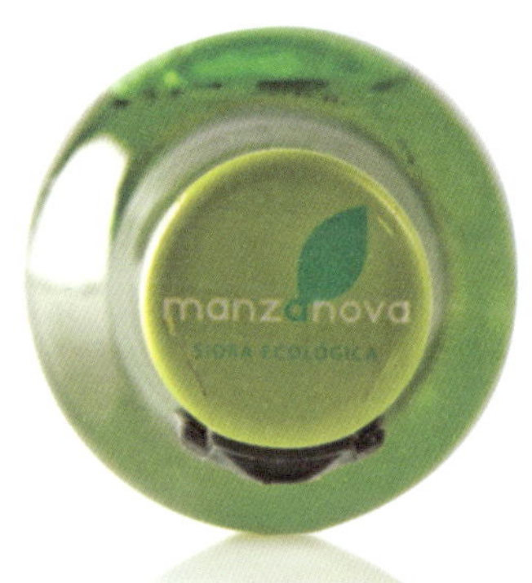

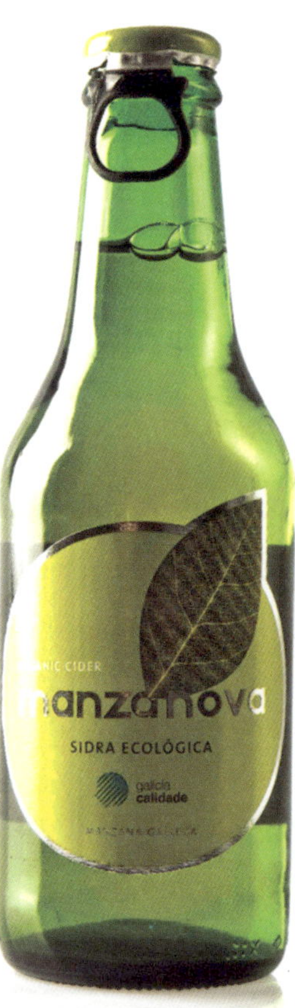

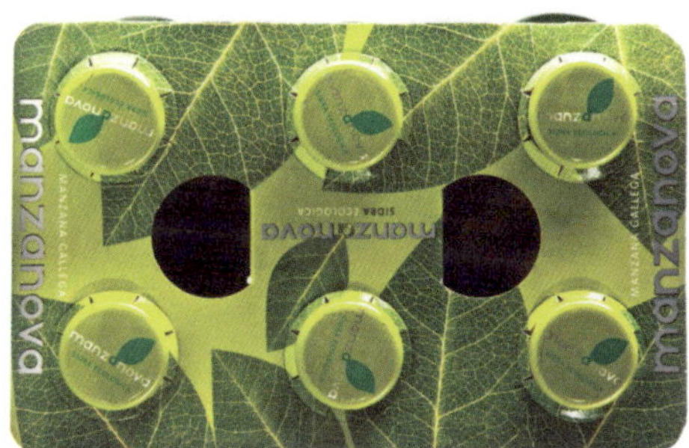

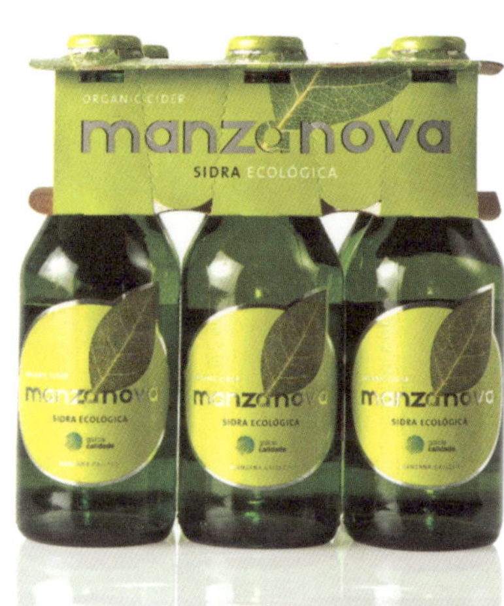

agency/studio: **Grow: The Design Consultancy** / project: updated brand design and packaging for the organic cider Manzanova. / client: Customdrinks / country: Spain

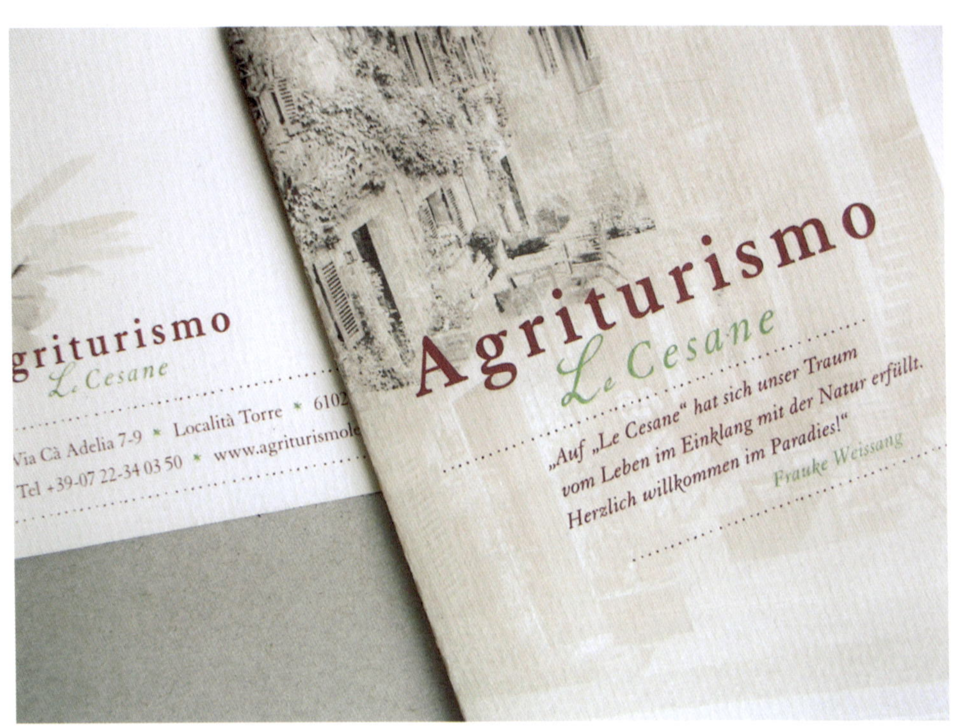

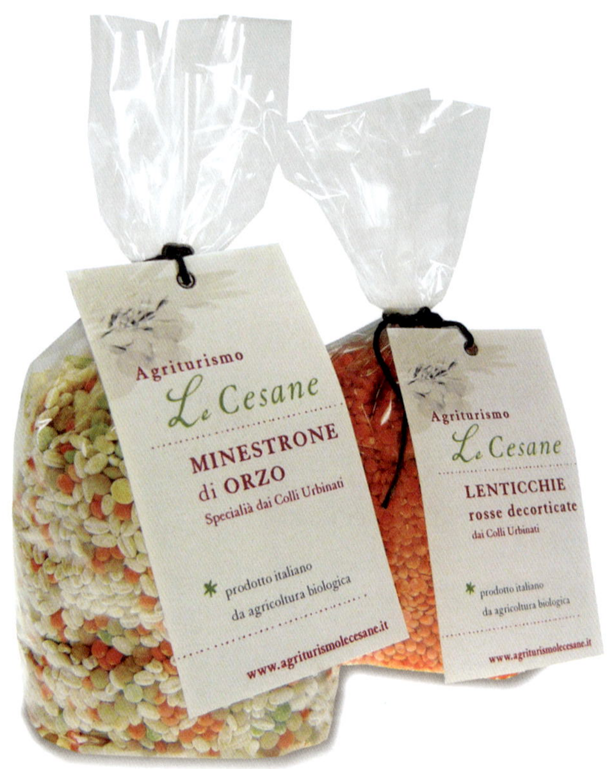

agency/studio: **mërz punkt** / project: packaging for the Italian company Le Cesane, which cultivates and produces its own organic food in the Marche region. / client: Agriturismo Le Cesane / country: Germany agency/studio: **El Cejas** / project: these refillable olive-oil bottles for the restaurants and gourmet stores of Enrique Olvera, one of the best Mexican chefs, are sandblasted to avoid the use of inks. / client: Cooperativa Olvera / country: Mexico

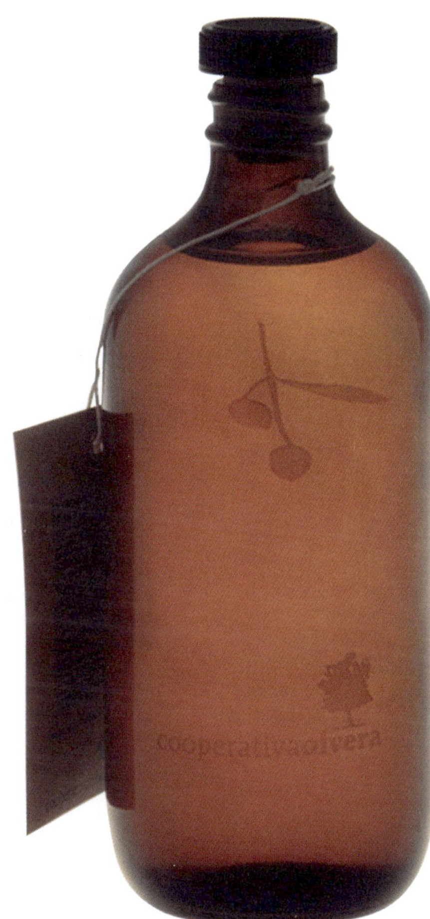

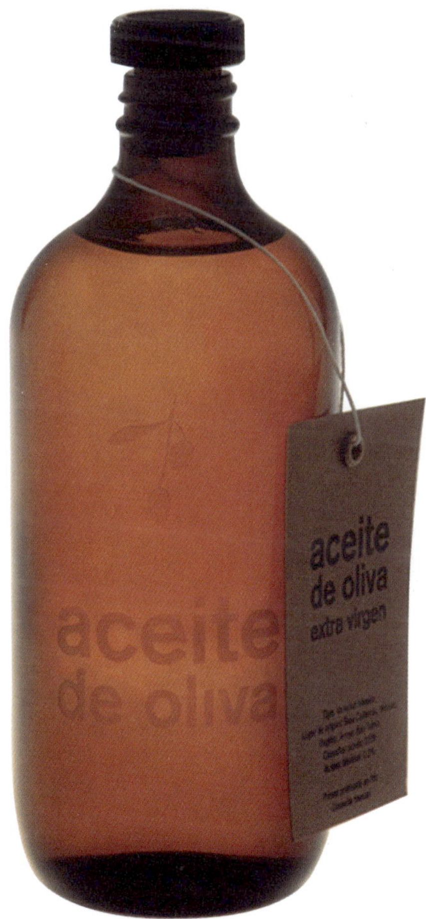

agency/studio: **Nate Williams** / project: shopping bags made of 95 % recycled woven polypropylene. / client: Blue Q / country: USA

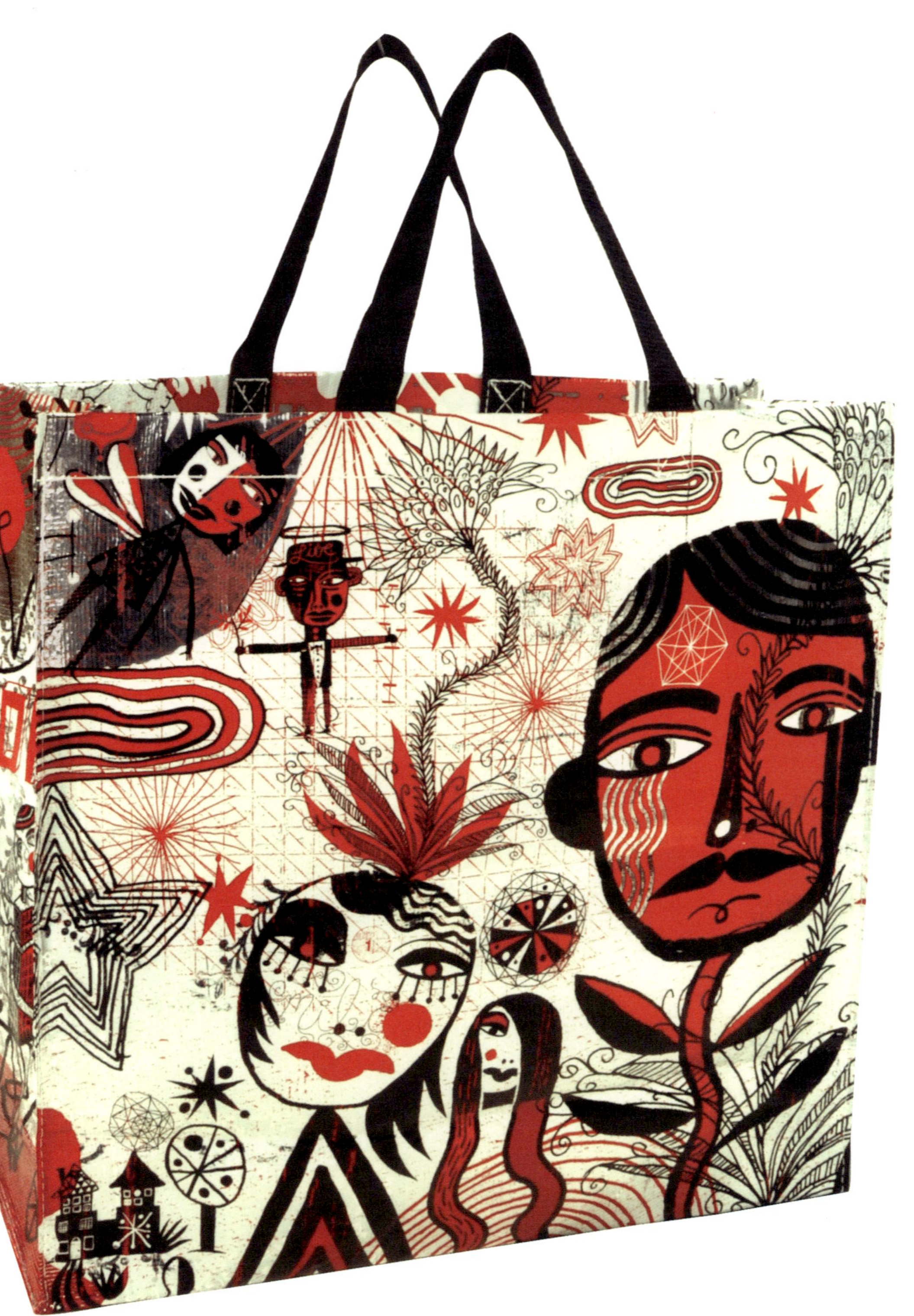

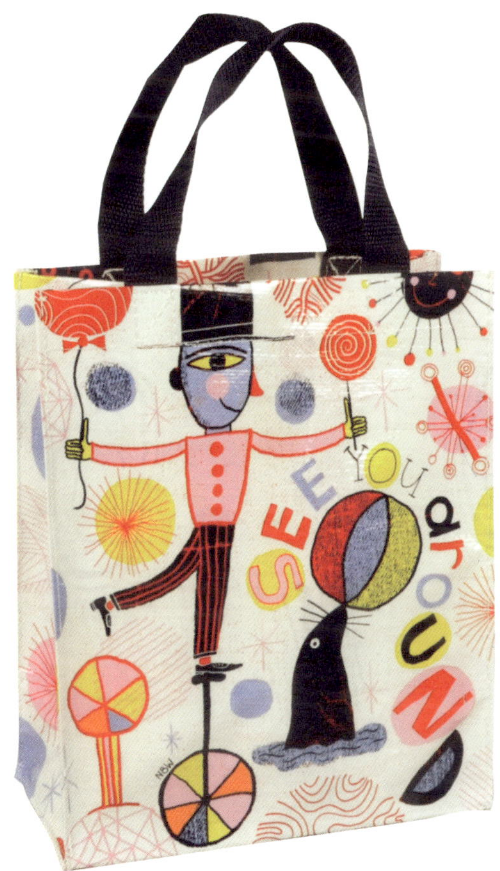

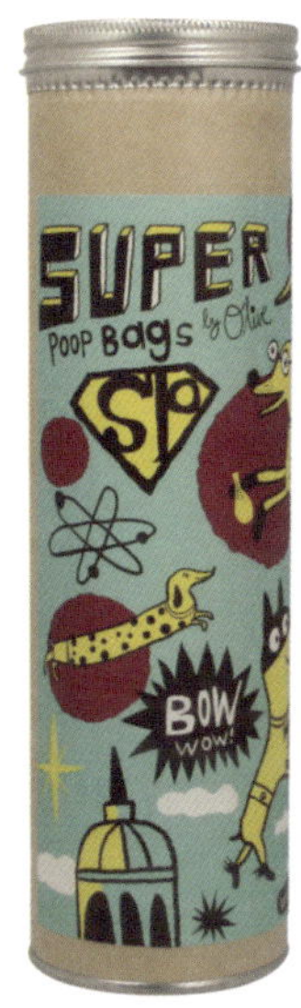

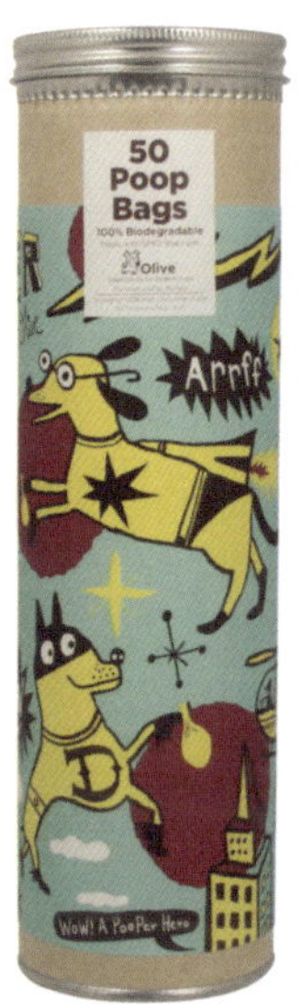

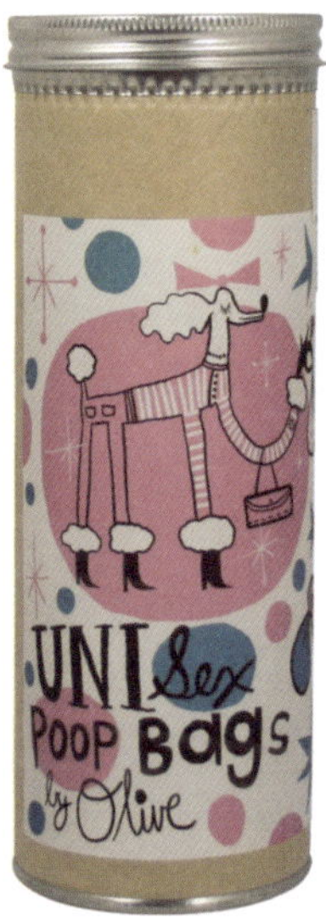

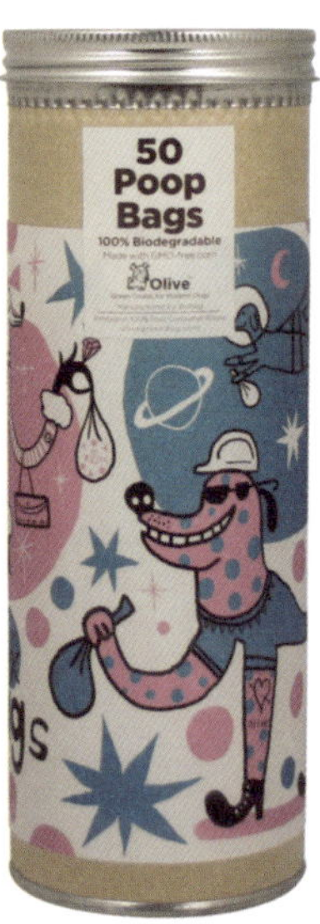

agency/studio: **Nate Williams** / project: Super Poop Bags and Unisex Poop Bags. Packaging for dog poop bags that are made naturally from GMO-free corn starch and vegetable oil. Certified 100% biodegradable and will turn into compost in only 40 days. / client: Olive Green Dog / country: USA

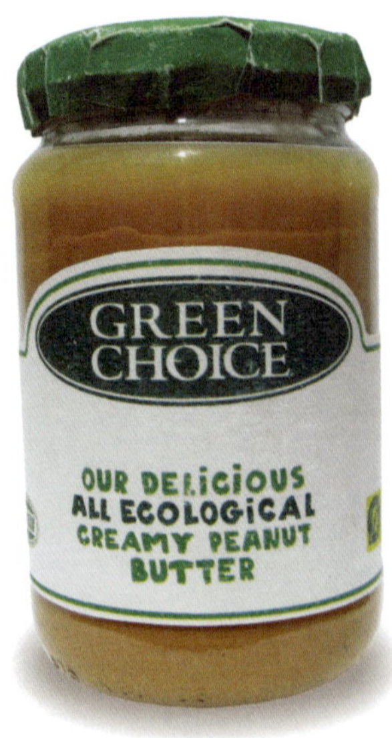

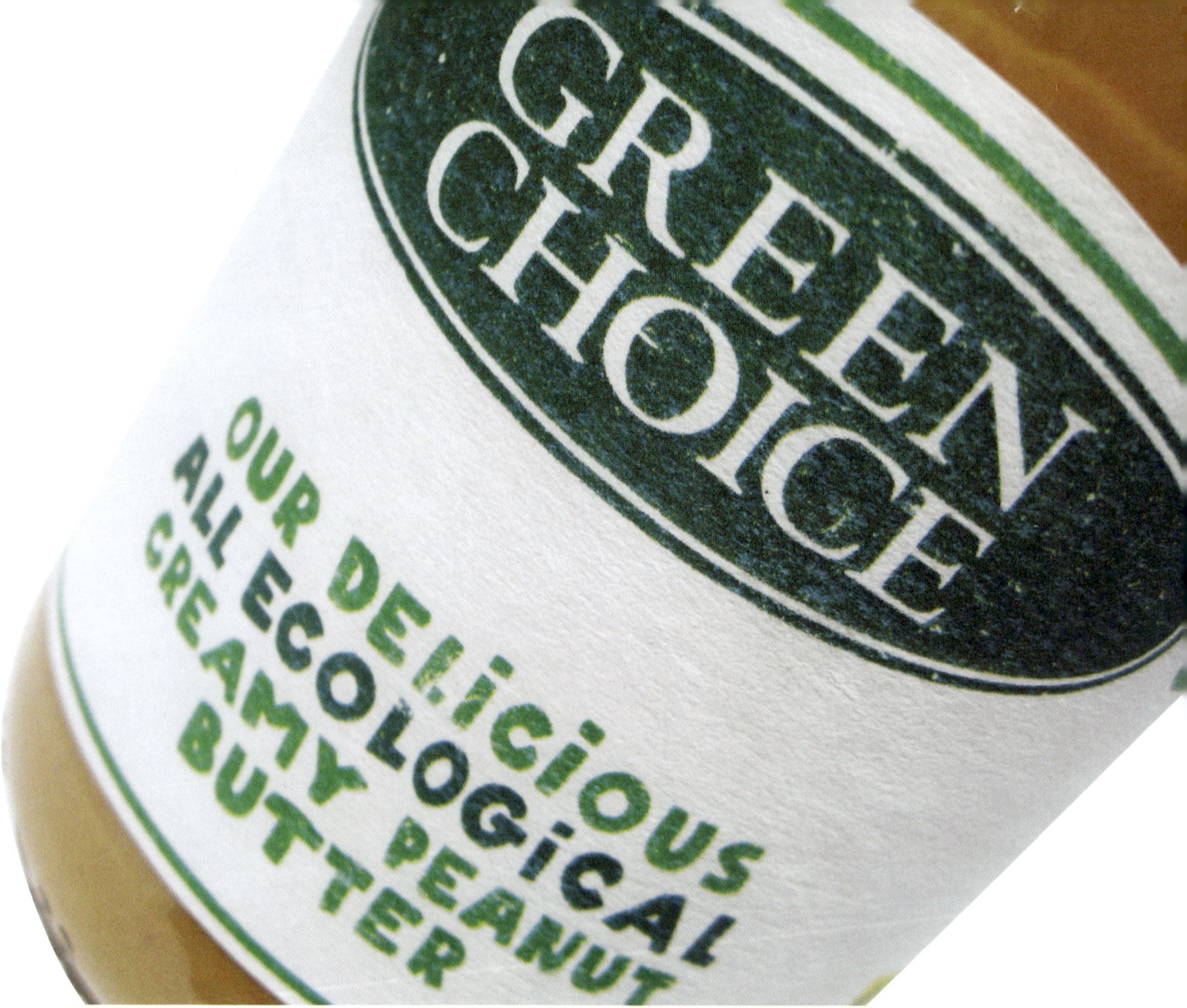

author: **Anna Magnussen** / project: packaging design for the organic peanut butter Greenchoice (student project). / country: Denmark

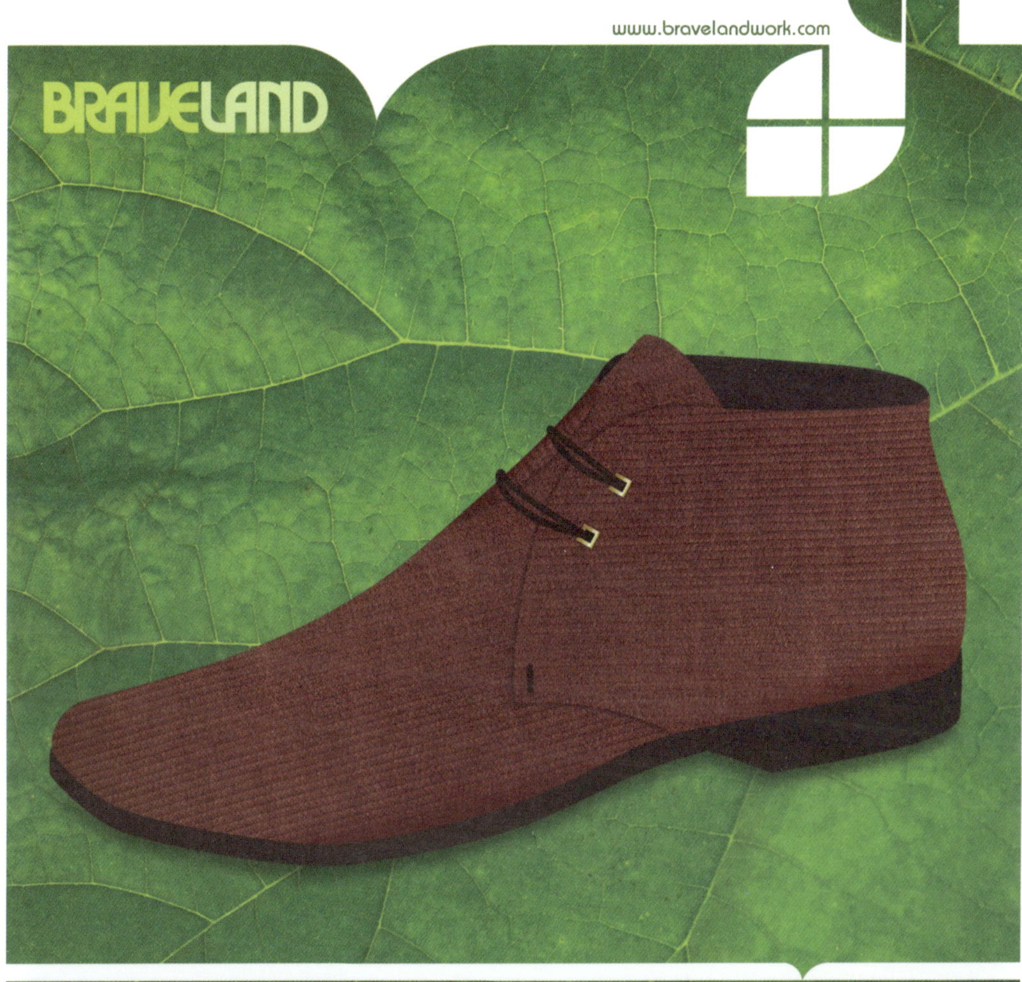

agency/studio: **Braveland** / project: Print advertisement that promotes animal-cruelty-free, environmentally conscious footwear. The shoes are made from natural, recyclable materials such as corduroy, faux suede, canvas and denim to create an affordable, sustainable shoe for a healthier foot. / client: Braveland / country: USA

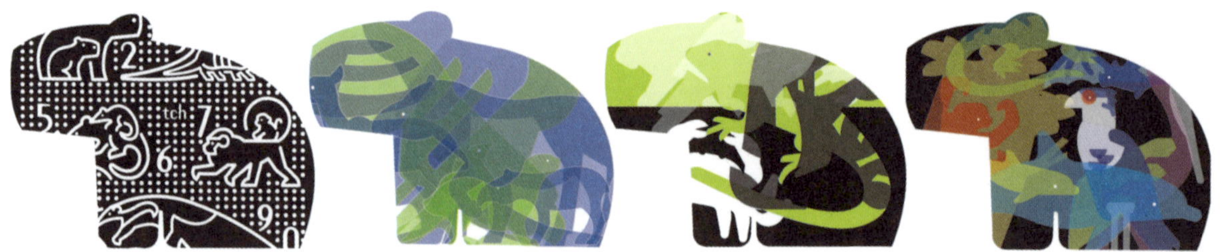

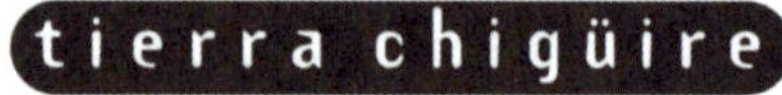
tierra chigüire
Caracas / Venezuela

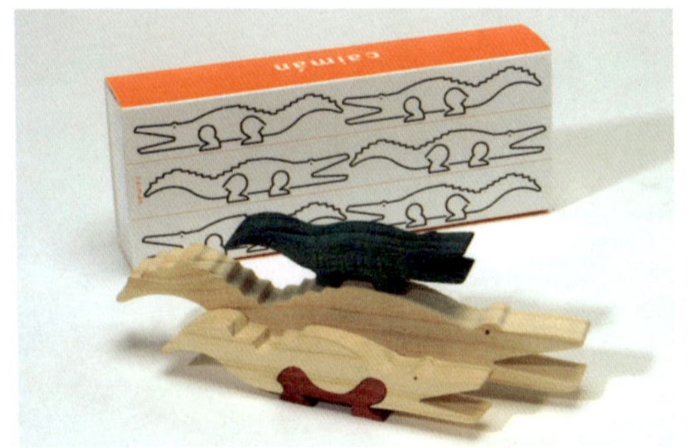

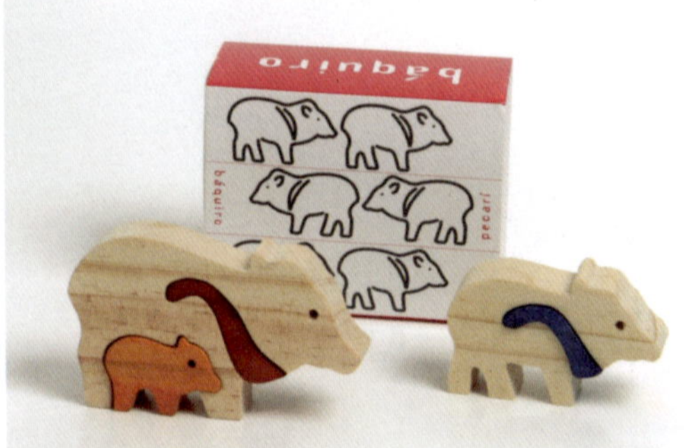

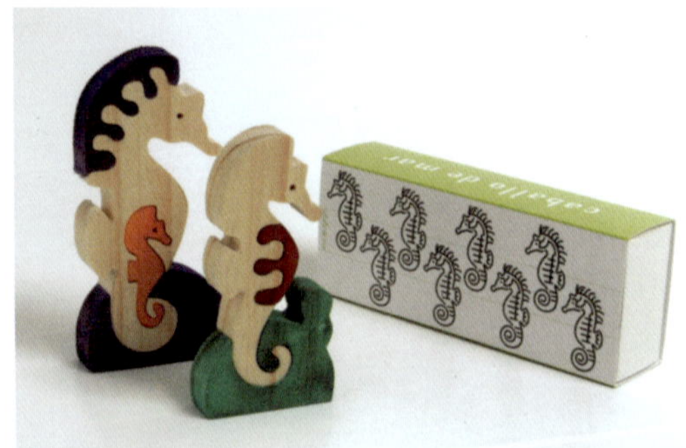

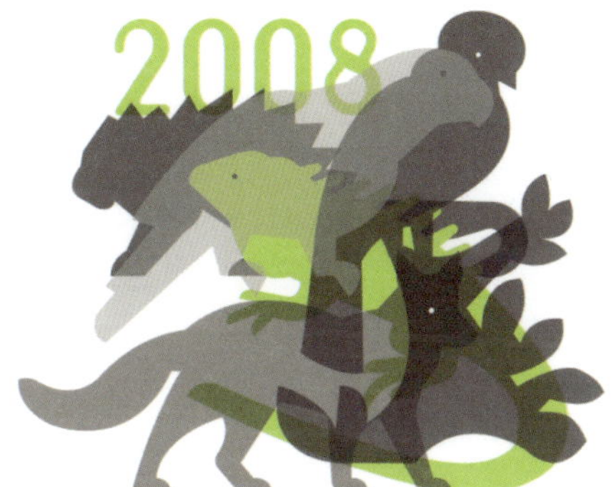

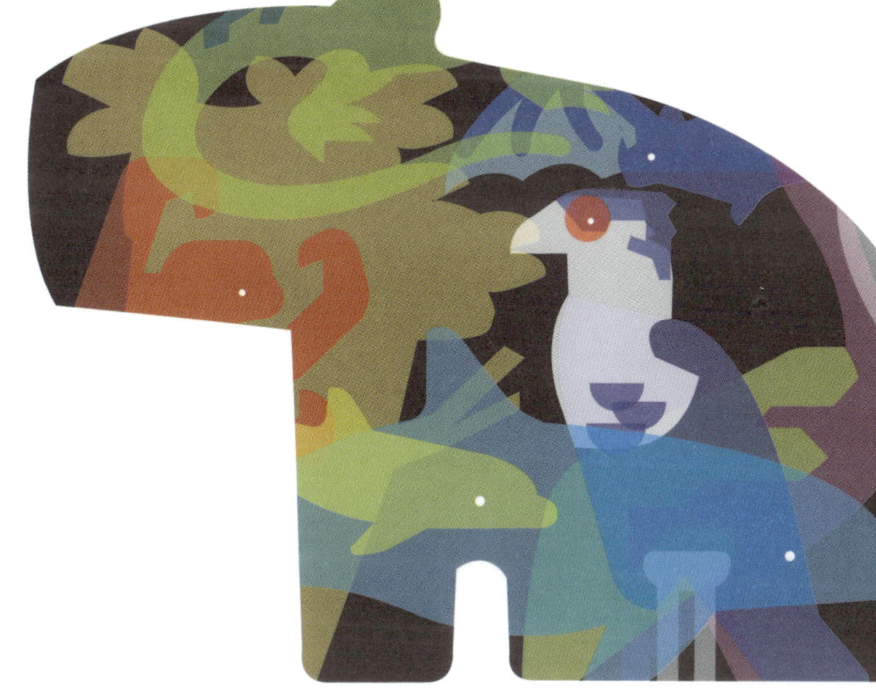

agency/studio: **Annella Armas / Tierra Chigüire** / project: design of the brand and teaching material for children and teenagers about Venezuela's wildlife and natural resources and how to preserve them. / client: Tierra Chigüire / country: Venezuela

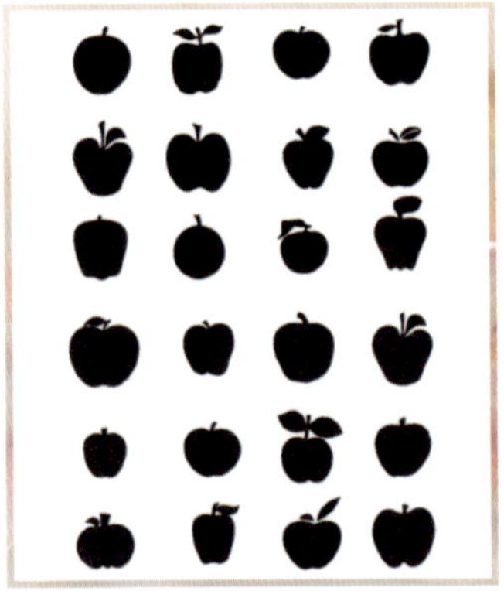

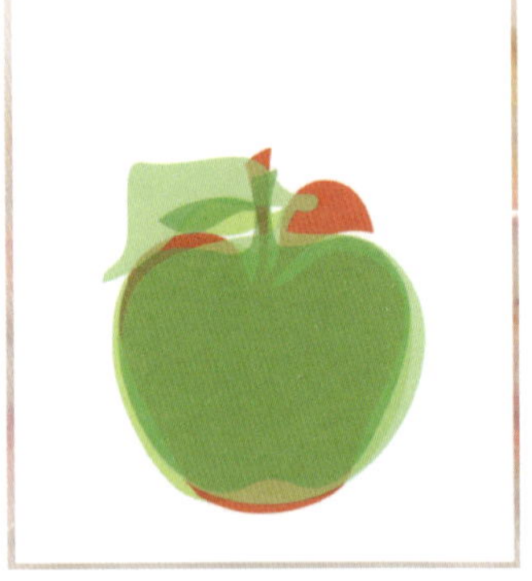

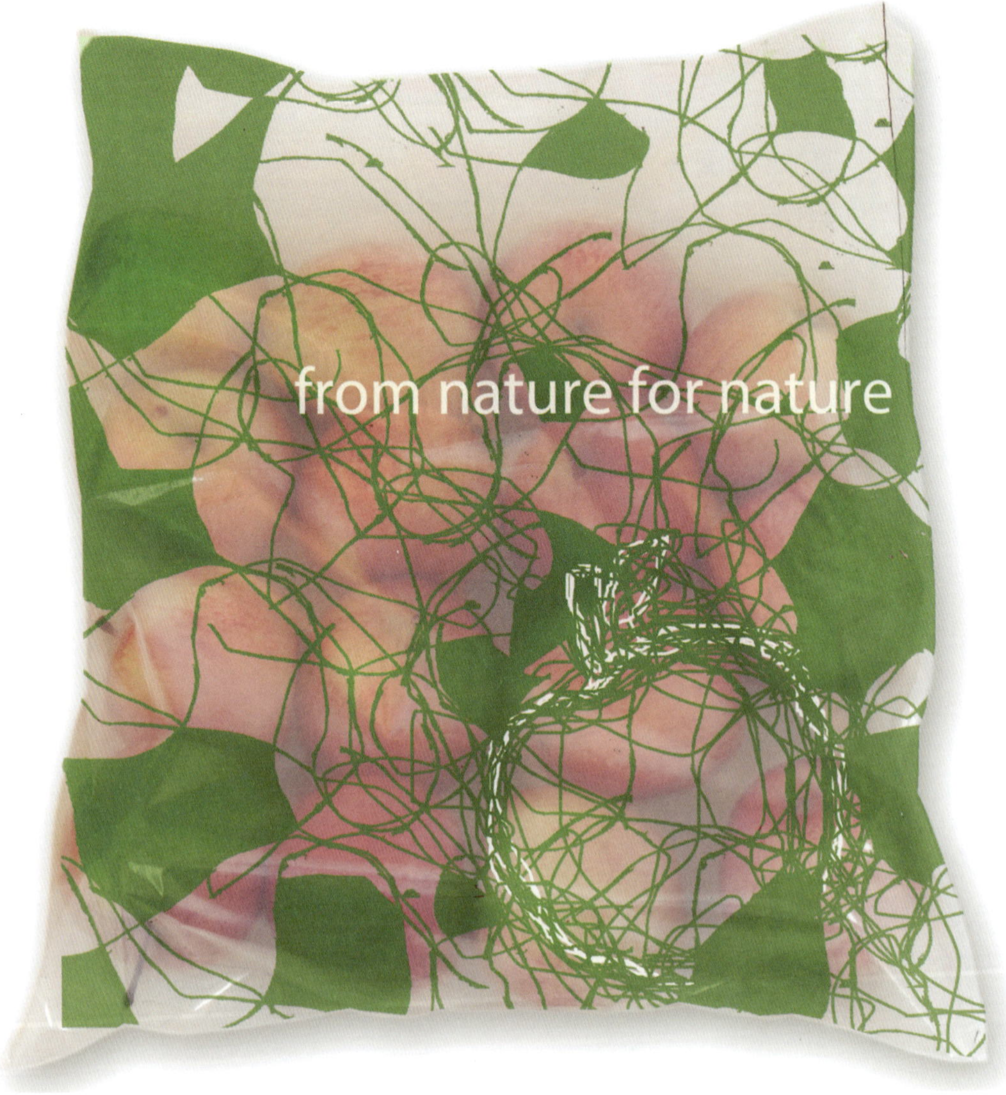

from nature for nature

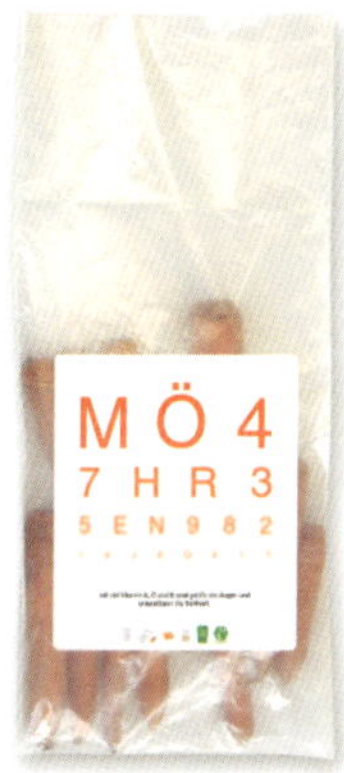
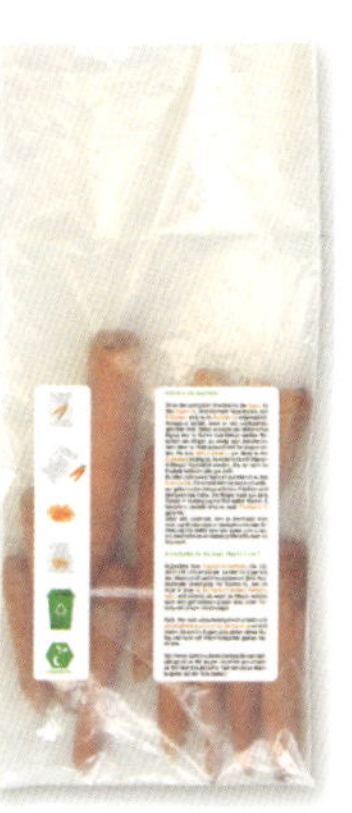
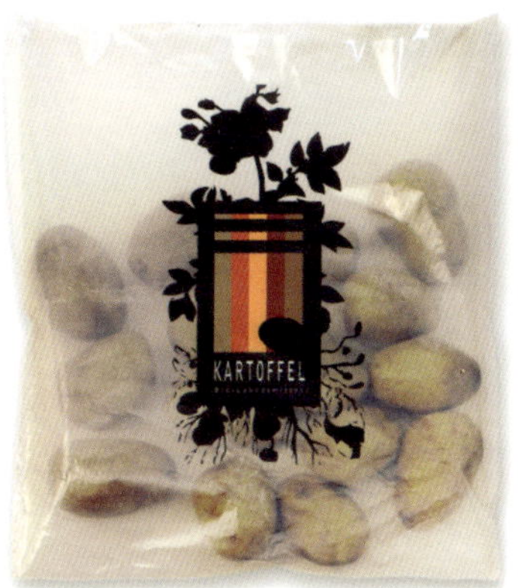
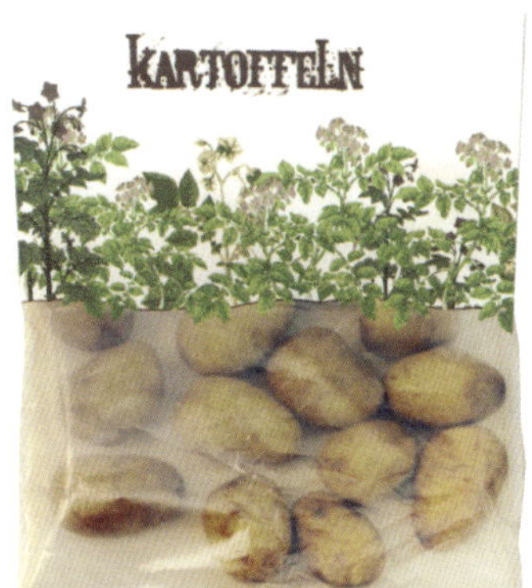
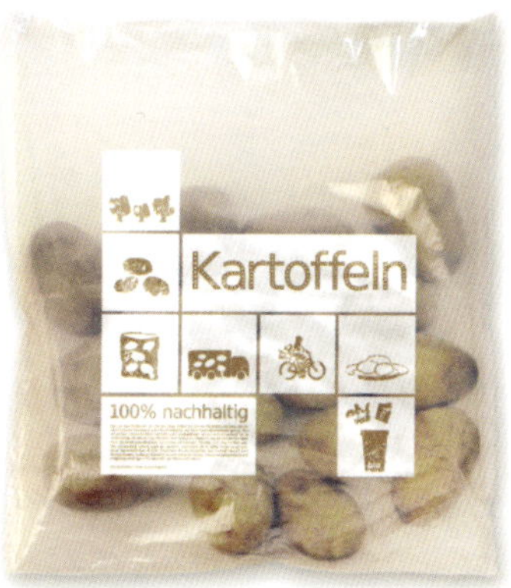

authors: students of **Aachen University of Applied Sciences** (Jann de Vries, Kathrin Corinna Böhm, Karoline Karrenbrock, Alexandra Lazinski, Janina Schmitz, Artur Wied) / project: sustainable packaging design for fruit and vegetable bags made from compostable biofilm. / client: alesco GmbH / country: Germany

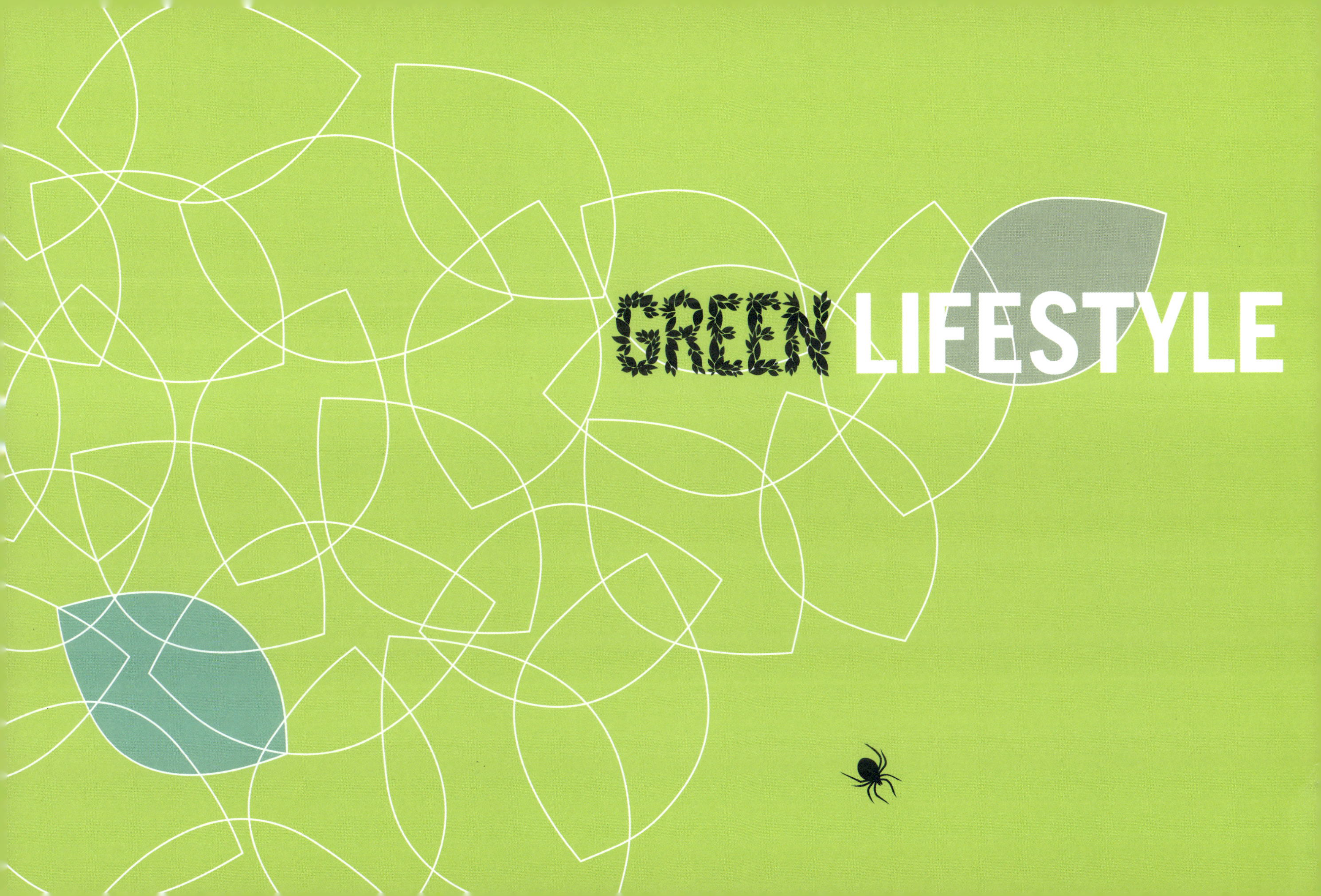

GREEN LIFESTYLE

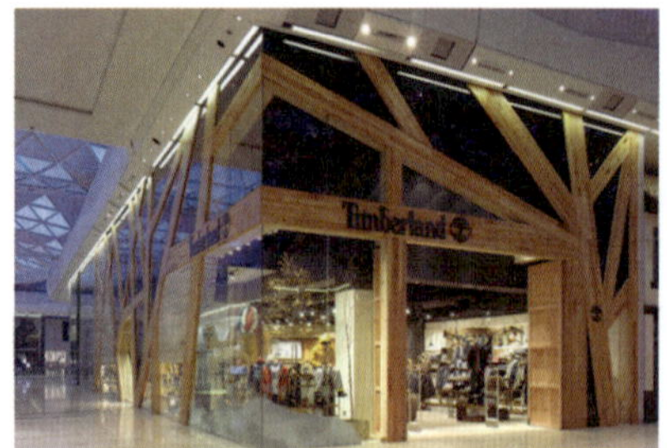 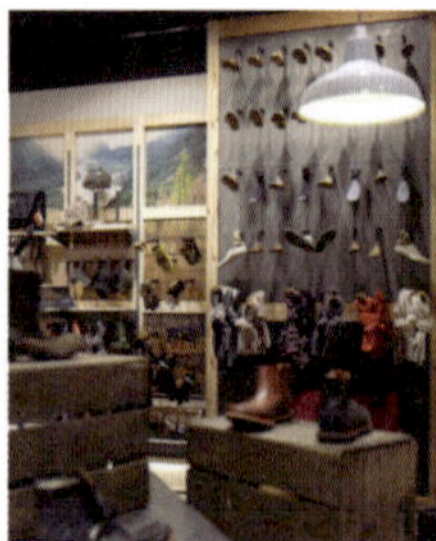 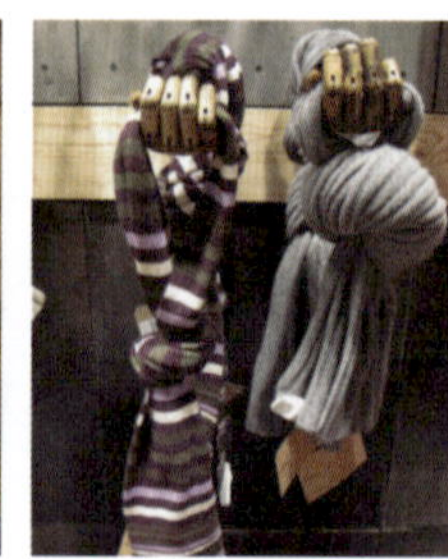 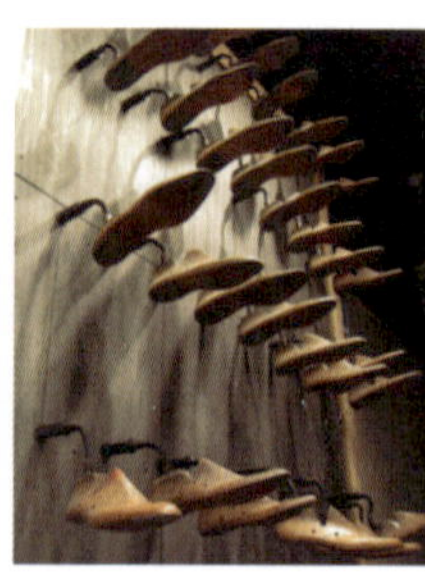

agency/studio: **Checkland Kindleysides** / project: Design of a new Timberland store, including a "Store Content" board showing the eco-friendly, reclaimed products used to build the store. More than 85% of the materials in the store have served other purposes in a previous life, with salvaged props and wood from reclaimed or sustainable sources used in the flooring and merchandising furniture. / client: Timberland / country: United Kingdom

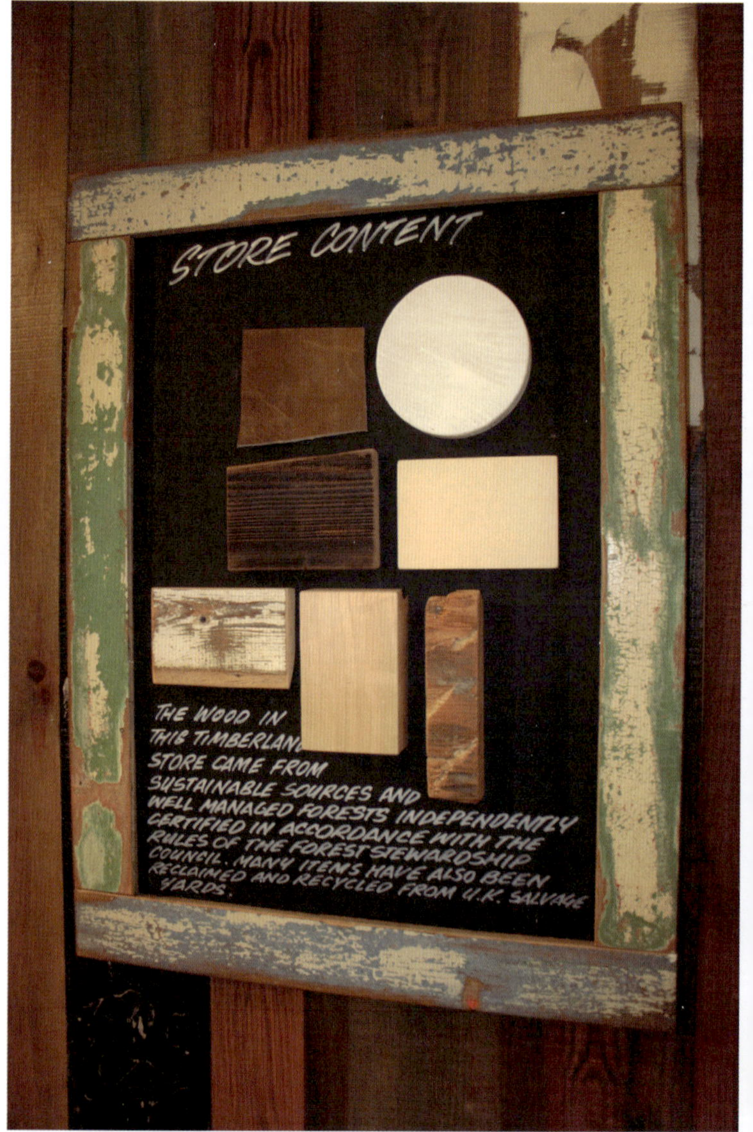

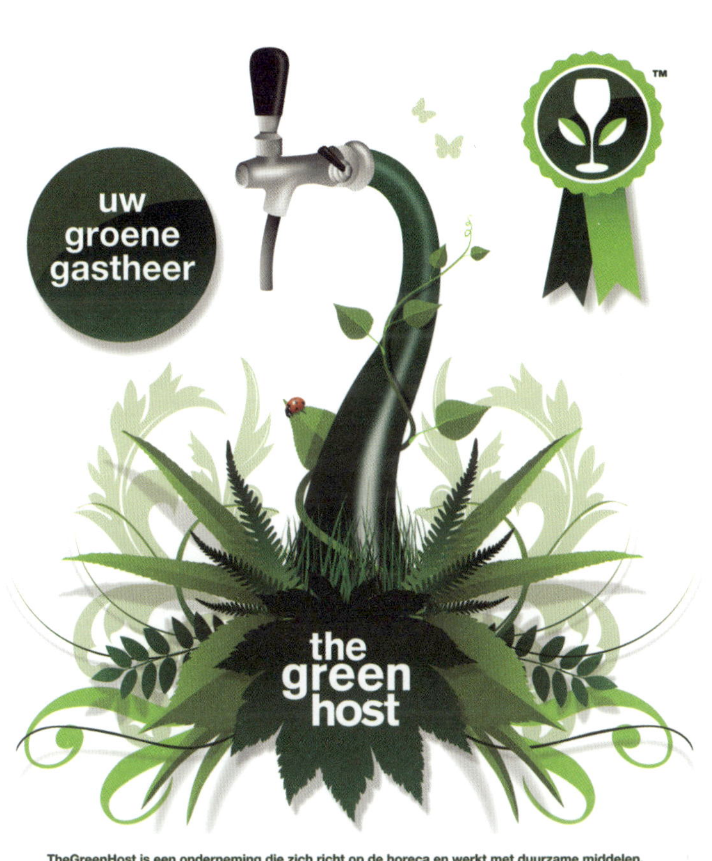

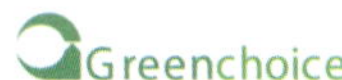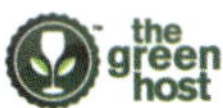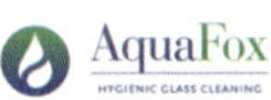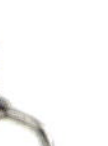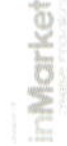

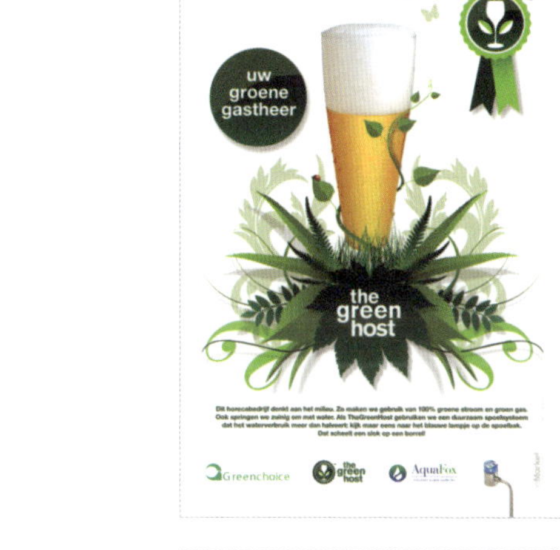

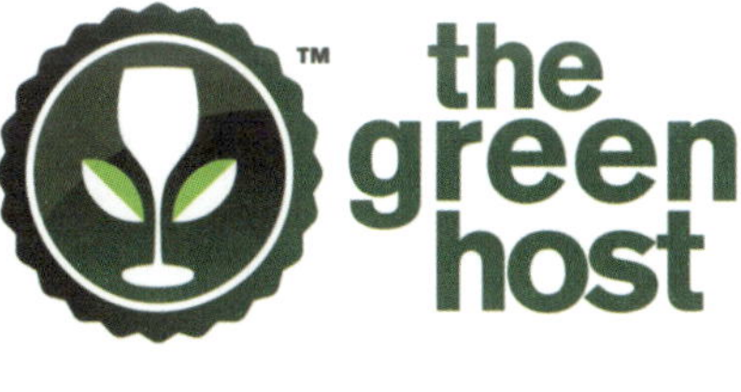

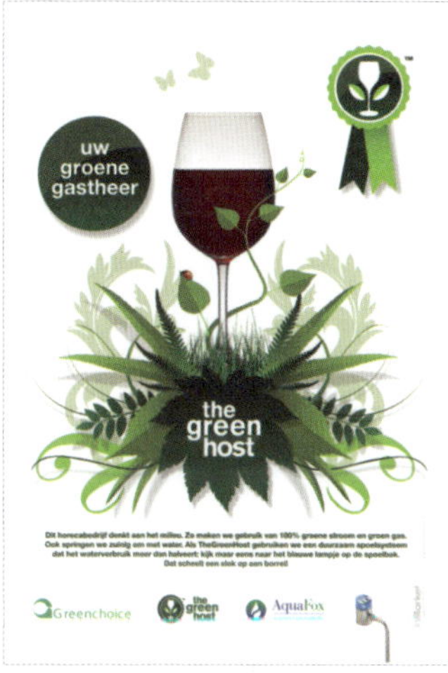

agency/studio: **Studio Piraat** / project: Identity and poster series "The Green Host", a campaign to identify bars, restaurants and clubs in the Netherlands that work according to sustainability criteria, offering natural products while maximising energy efficiency and minimising water use. / client: InMarket / country: Netherlands

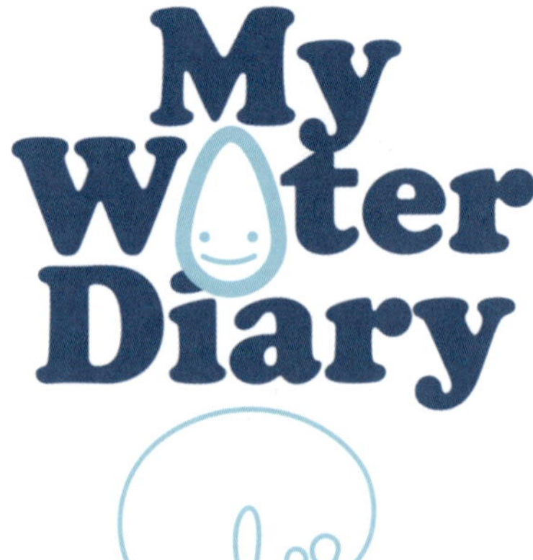

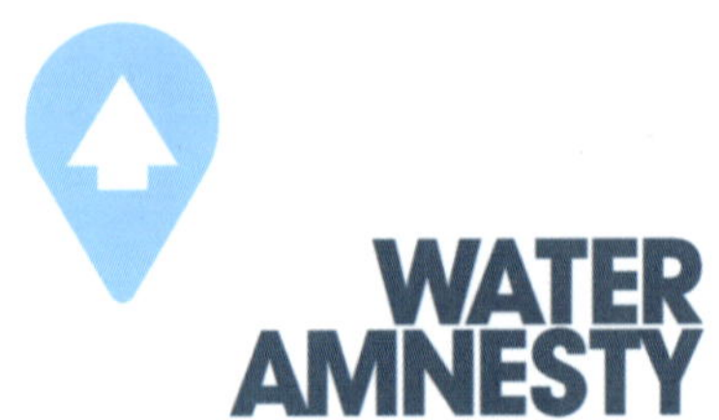

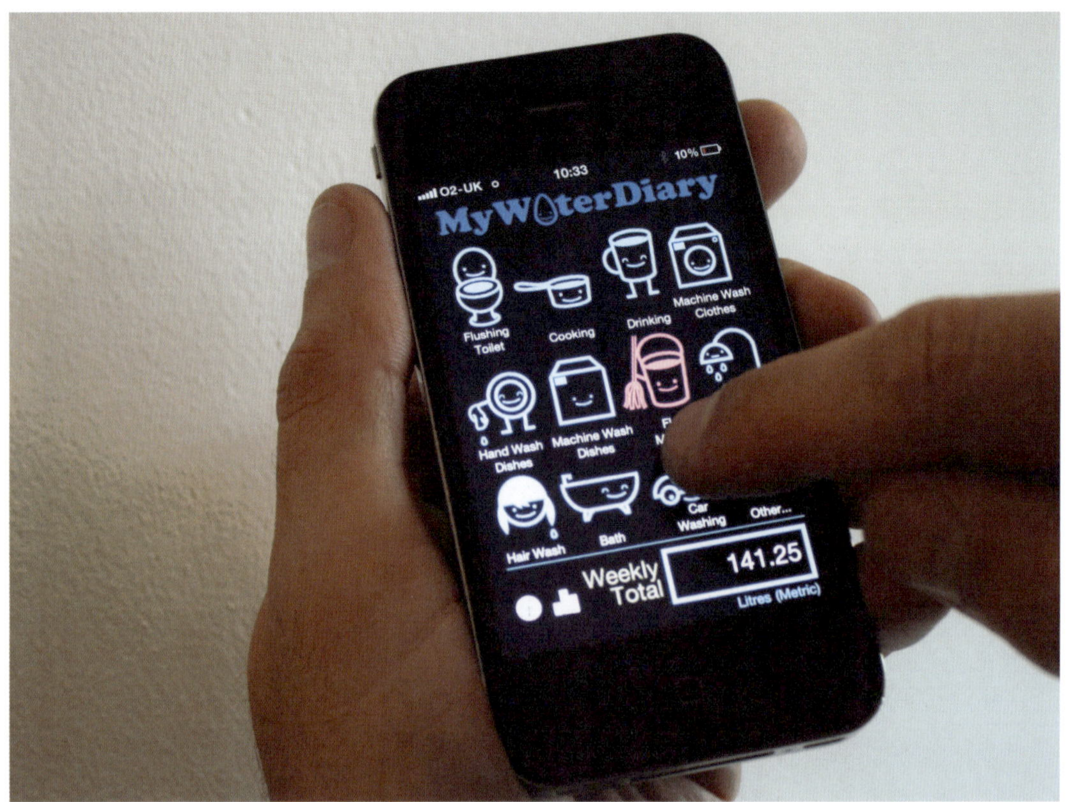

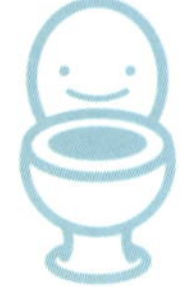   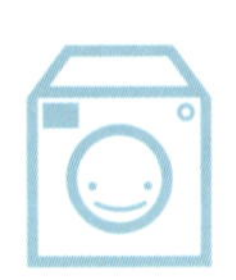 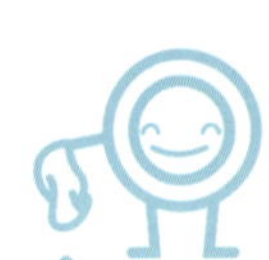 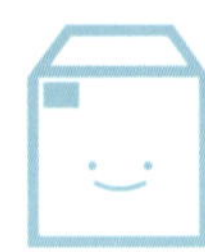  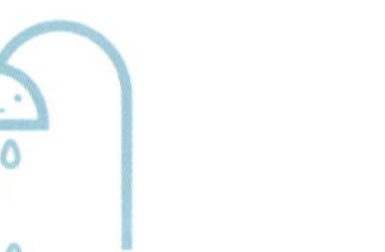  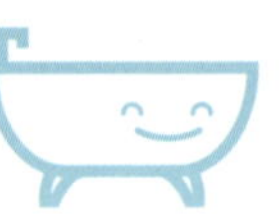  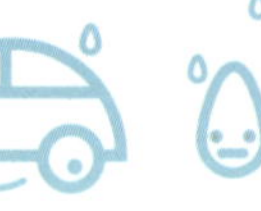

agency/studio: **DED Associates** / project: My Water Diary is an iPhone app that allows users to track their water usage and aims to reduce their consumption. / client: Free Radicals / country: United Kingdom

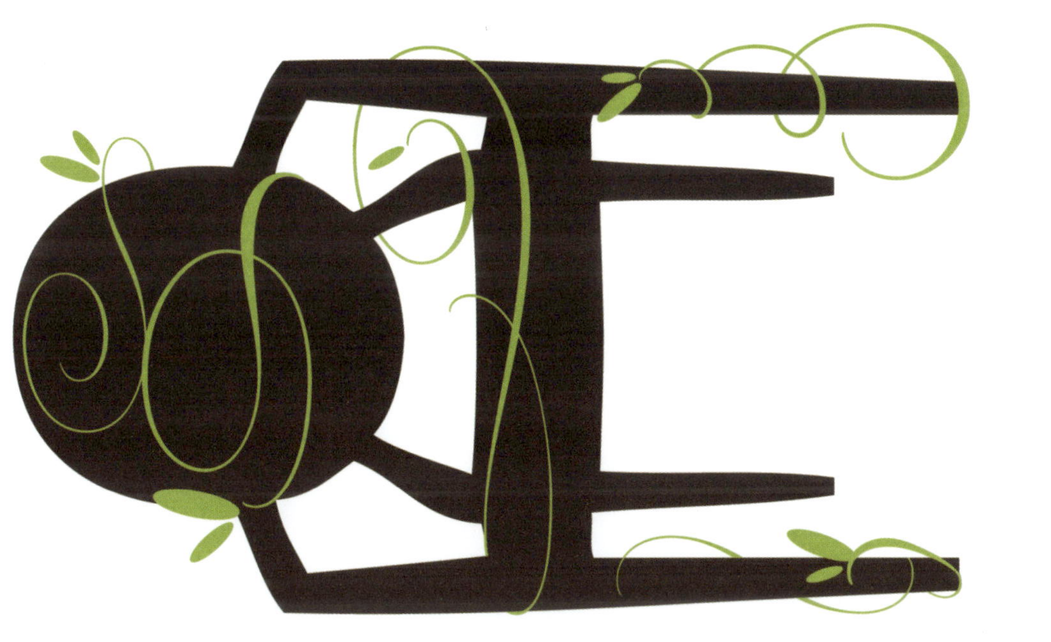

green**JOY**

agency/studio: **Evenson Design Group** / project: identity programme for GreenJoy, a company specialising in sustainable interior design. / client: GreenJoy / country: USA

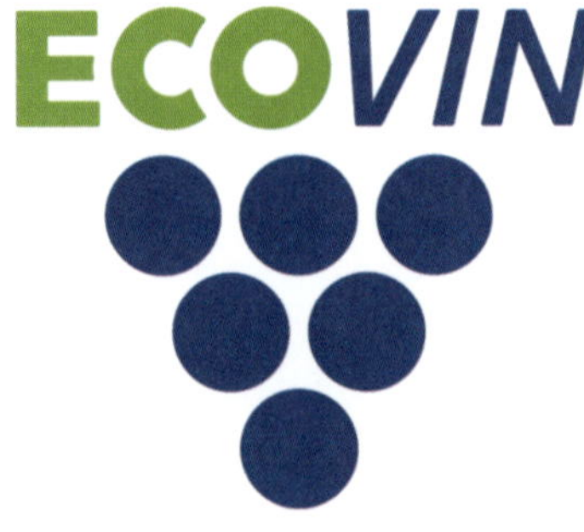

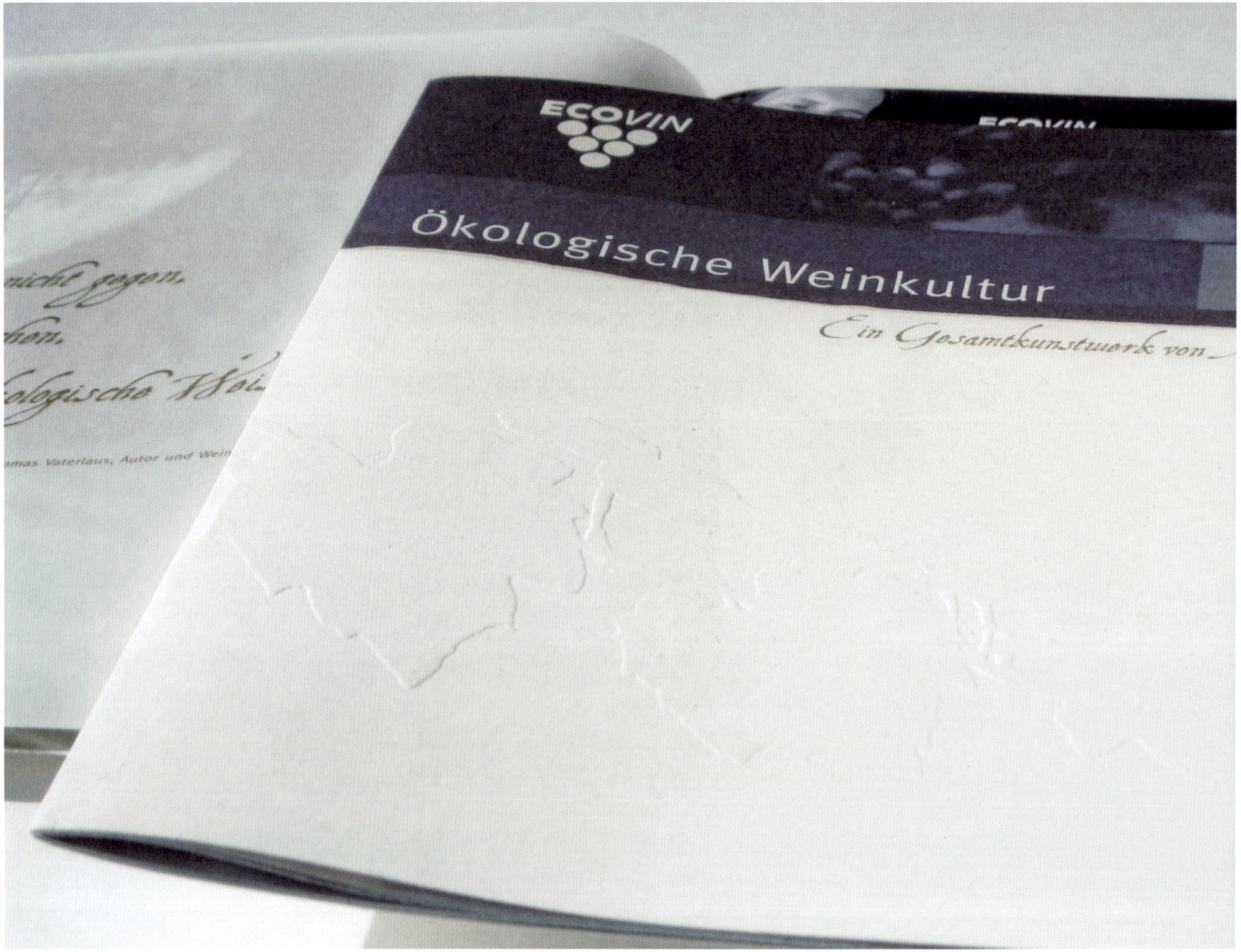

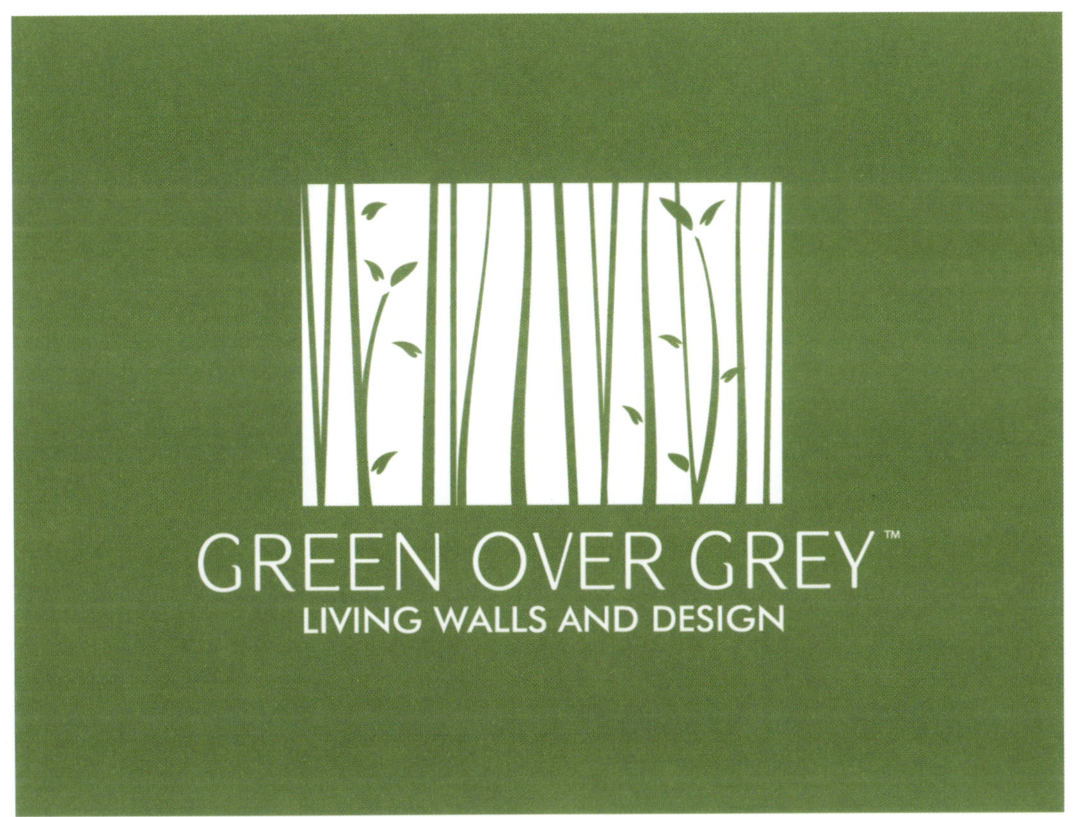

agency/studio: **UneekGrafix** / project: a brand for a new boutique design firm specialising in living green walls and vertical gardens. / client: Green over Grey/ country: USA

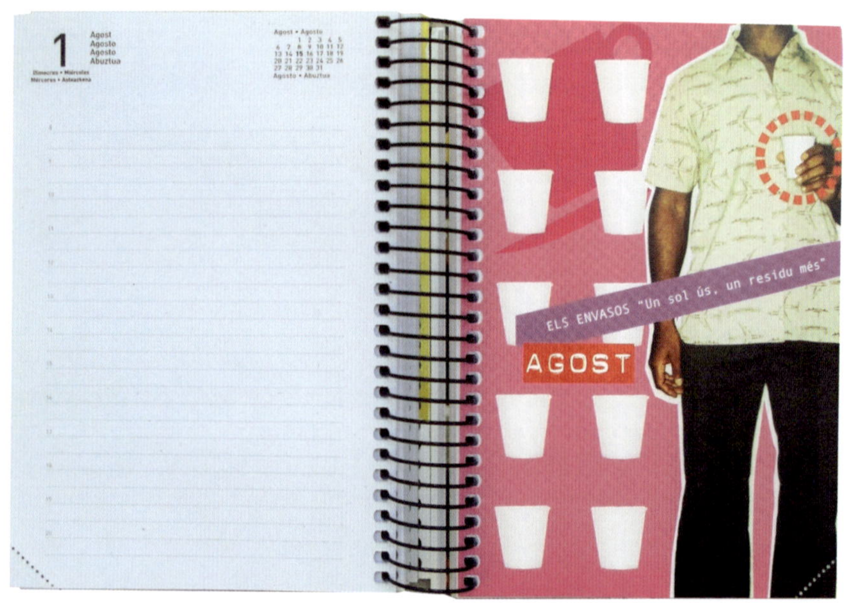
1 Agost
Agosto
Agosto
Abuztua
Dimecres • Miércoles
Mércores • Asteazkena
Agost • Agosto
1 2 3 4 5
4 7 8 9 10 11 12
13 14 15 16 17 18 19
20 21 22 23 24 25 26
27 28 29 30 31
Agosto • Abuztua
ELS ENVASOS "Un sol ús, un residu més"
AGOST

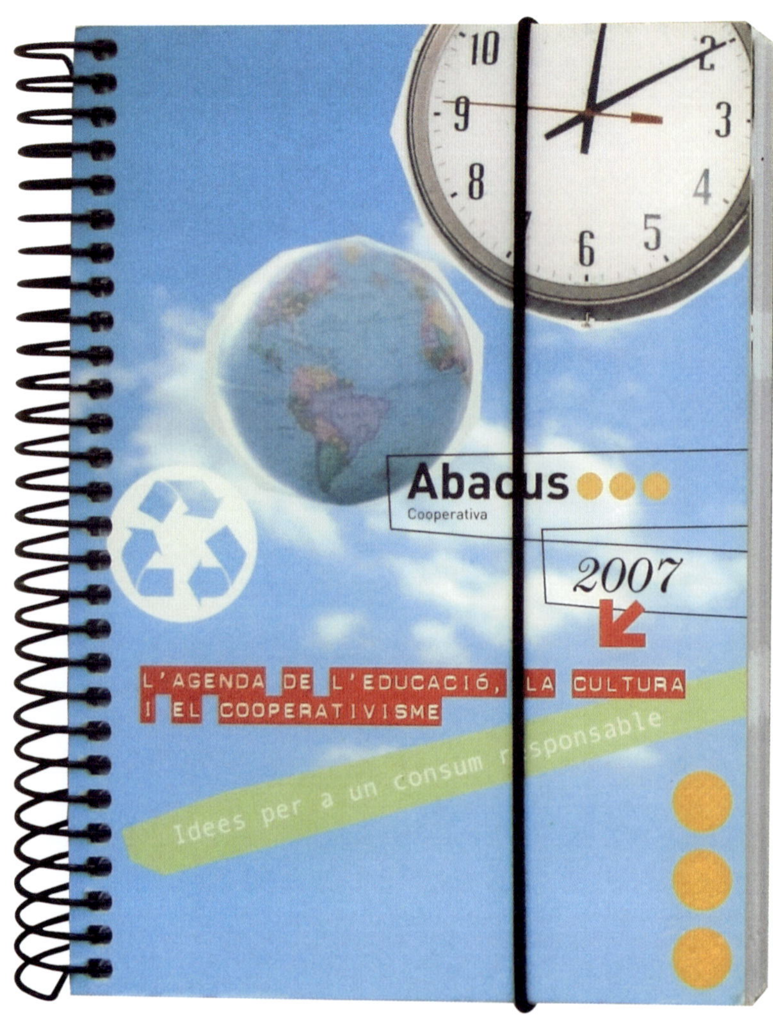
Abacus
Cooperativa
2007
L'AGENDA DE L'EDUCACIÓ, LA CULTURA
I EL COOPERATIVISME
Idees per a un consum responsable

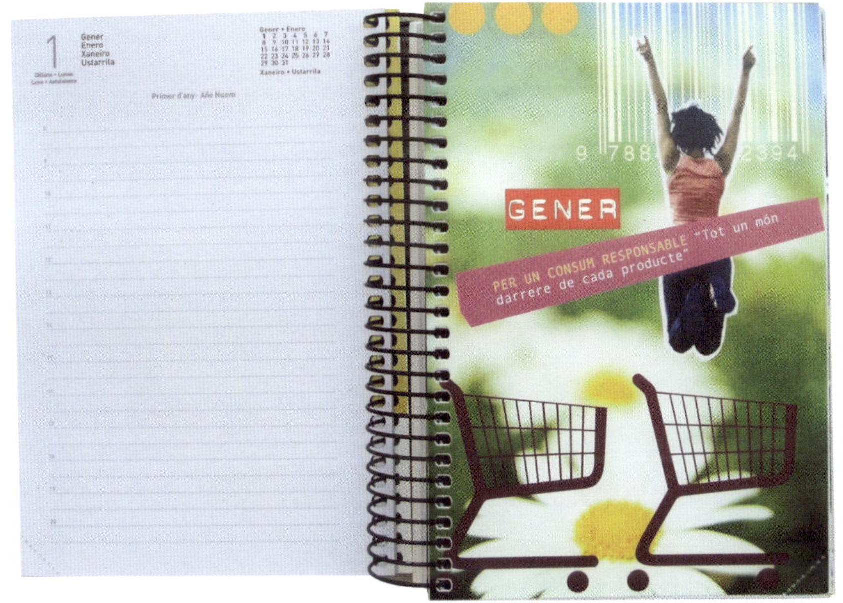

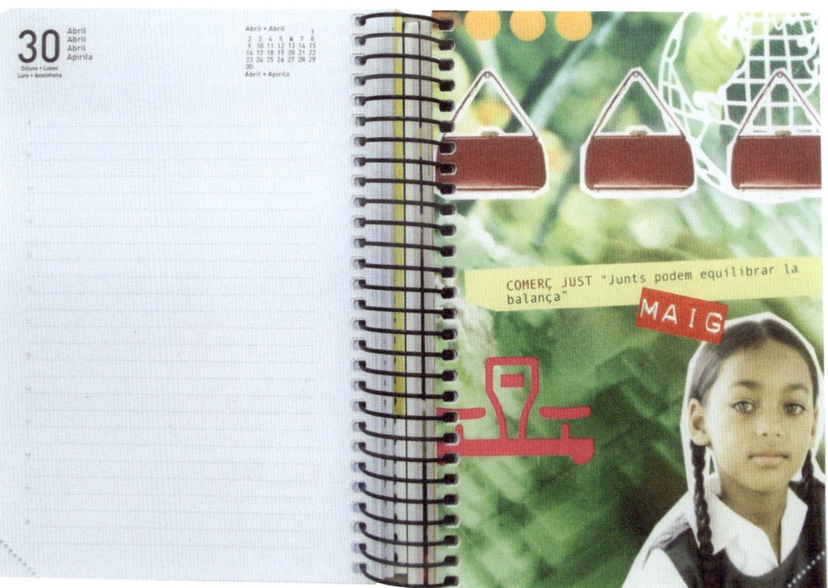

agency/studio: **Eggeassociats** / project: school diary design themed around responsible consumption. / client: Abacus / country: Spain

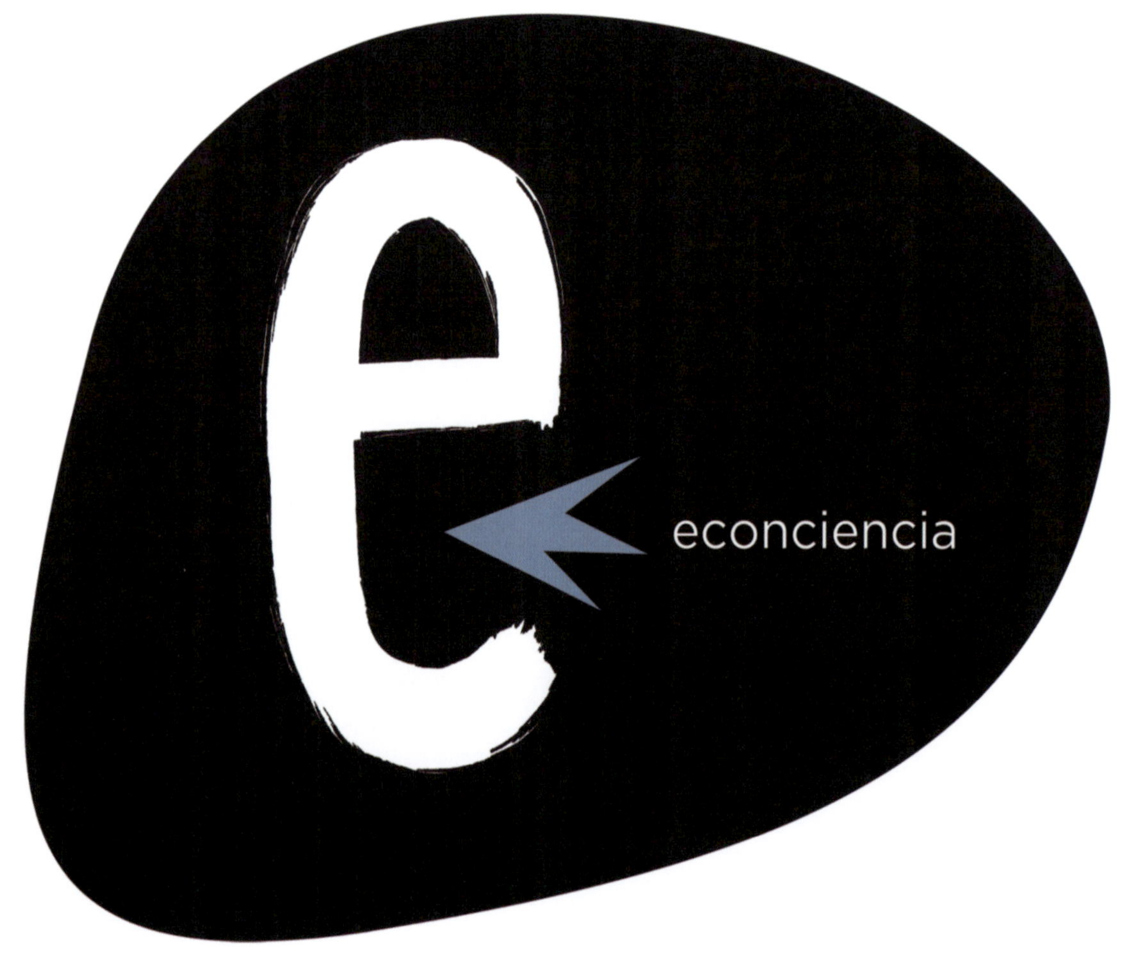

agency/studio: **Mónica Muñoz** / project: logo for the Econciencia exhibition space at the Casa Pasarela design fair for home trends. / client: Casa Pasarela / country: Spain

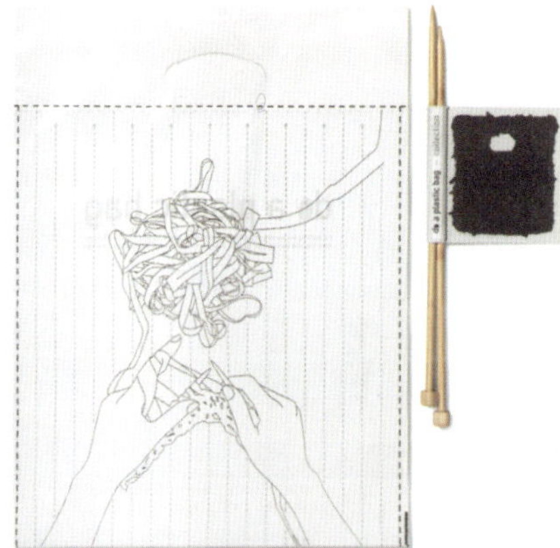

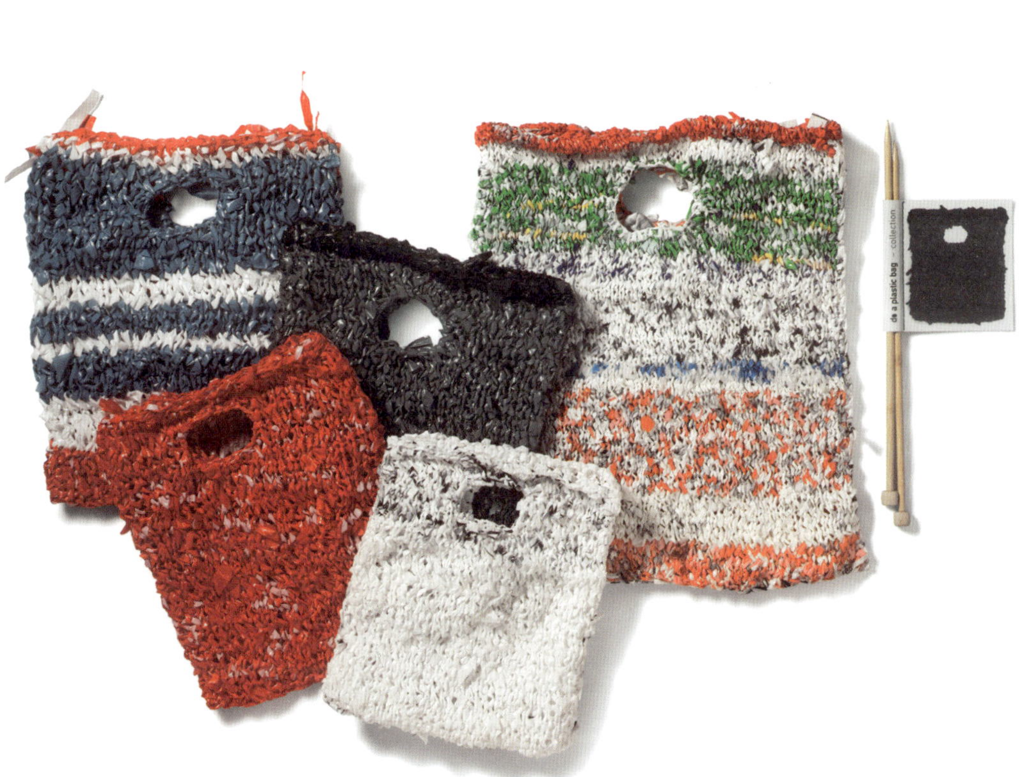

agency/studio: **KesselsKramer** (design by Jennifer Skupin) / project: "do" invites you to create your own custom-designed plastic bag to keep some plastic in use a little longer than usual. / "do" is an initiative by KesselsKramer / country: Netherlands

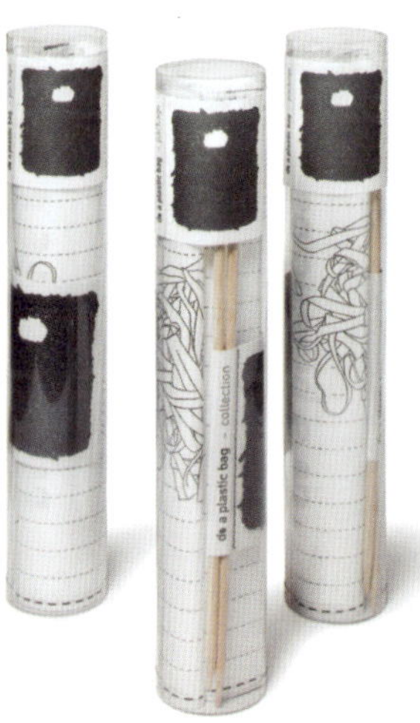

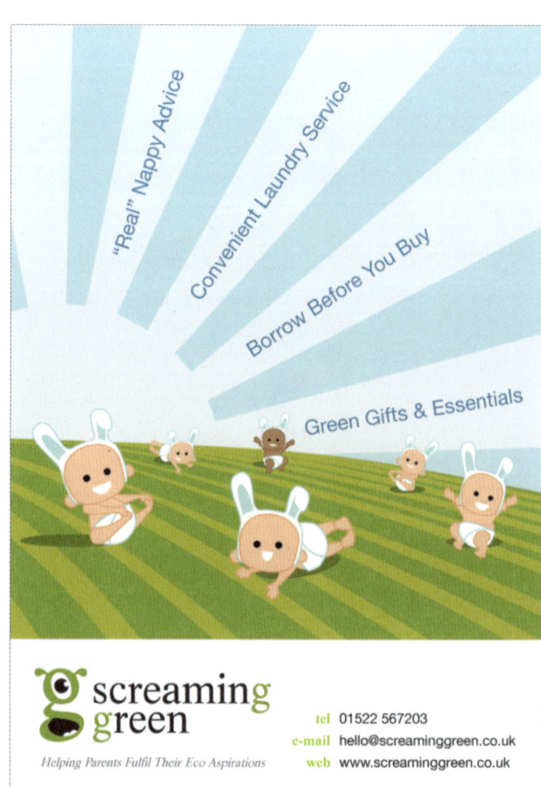

agency/studio: **Root Studio** / project: a logo design for an eco-parenting company. / client: Screaming Green / country: United Kingdom

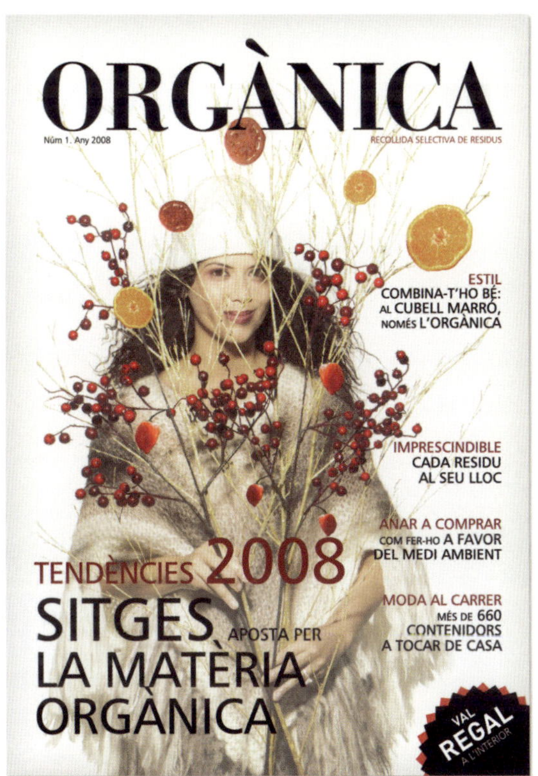

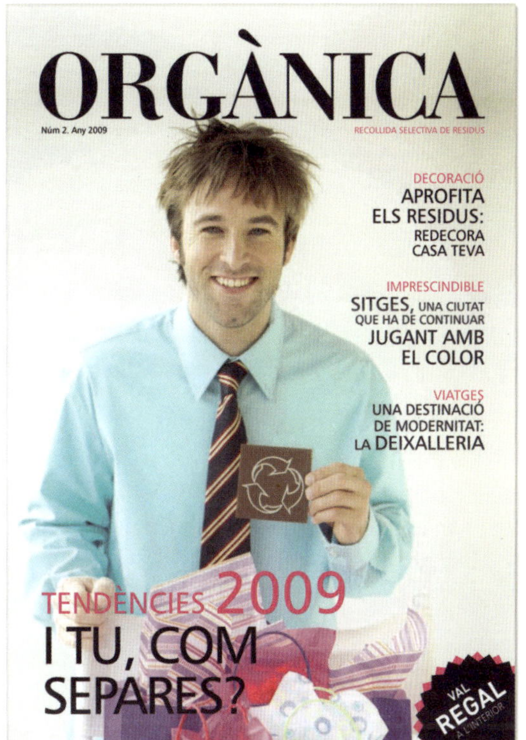

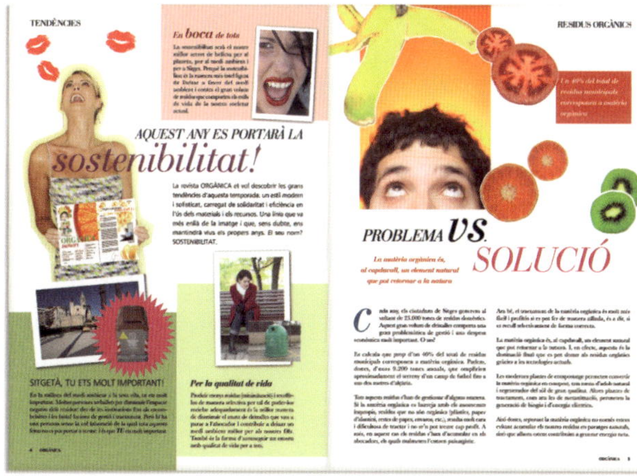

agency/studio: **lavola** / project: Orgànica is a free magazine about separate waste collection, but with a design and approach like that of a fashion and trends magazine. The magazine is the main element of a campaign for the separate collection of organic waste in the Catalan town of Sitges. / client: Sitges Town Council, CESPA / country: Spain

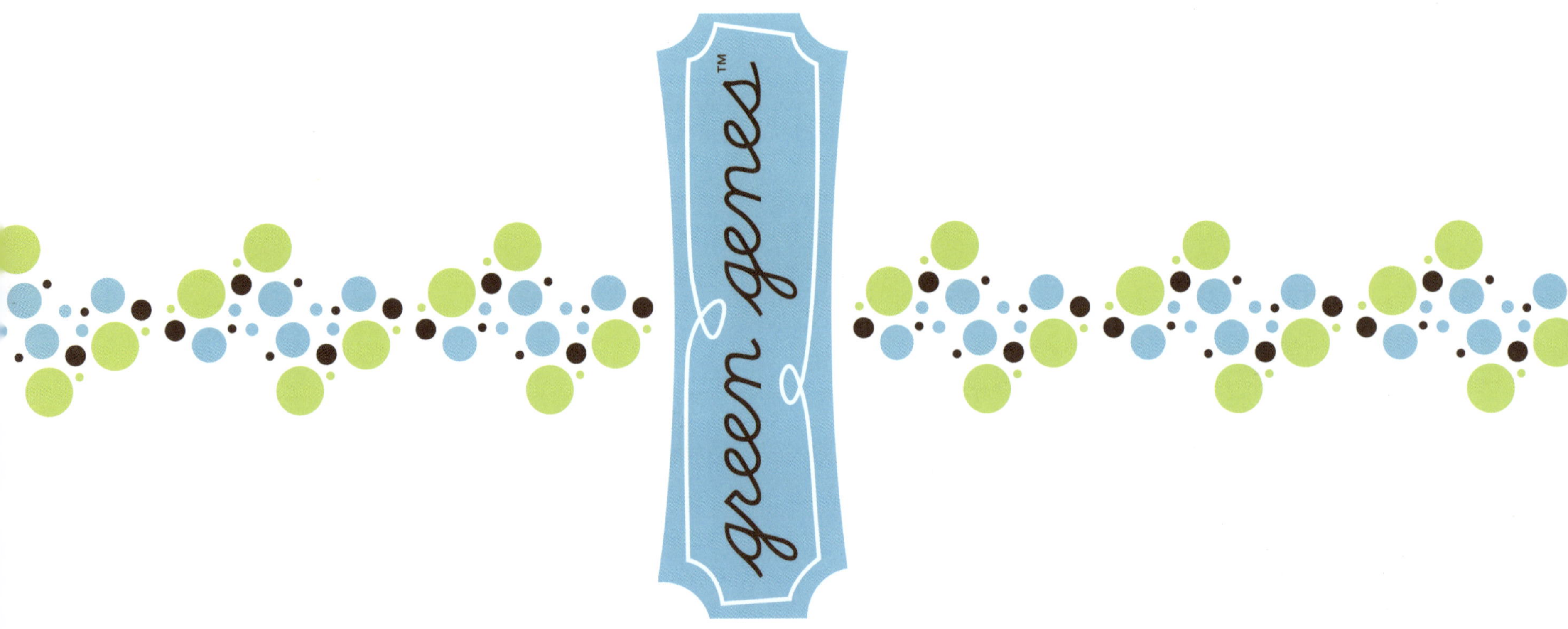

agency/studio: **Funnel: Eric Kass** / project: Green Genes is an eco-friendly boutique specialising in organic and natural products through fair trade and sustainable production. / client: Green Genes / country: USA

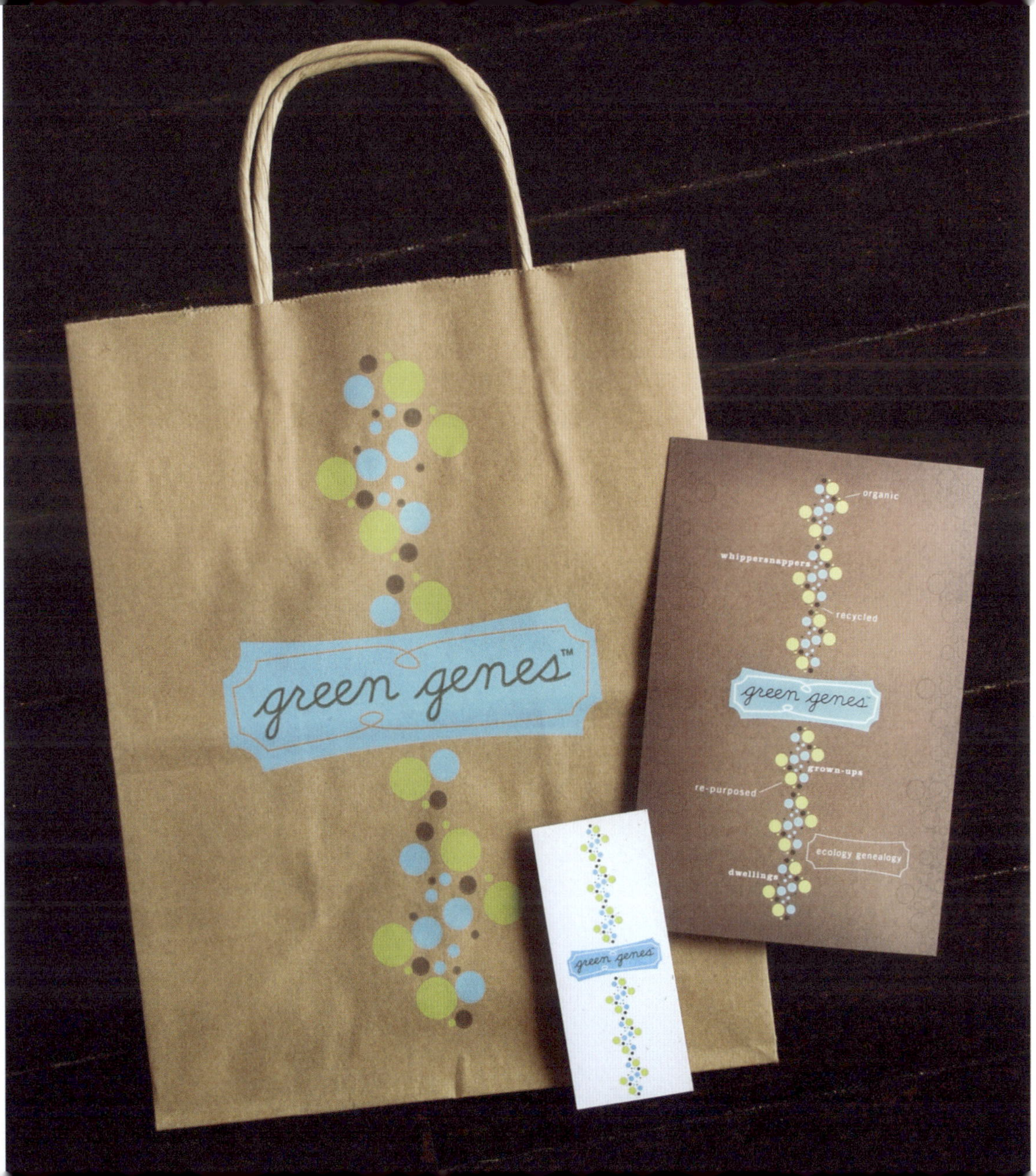

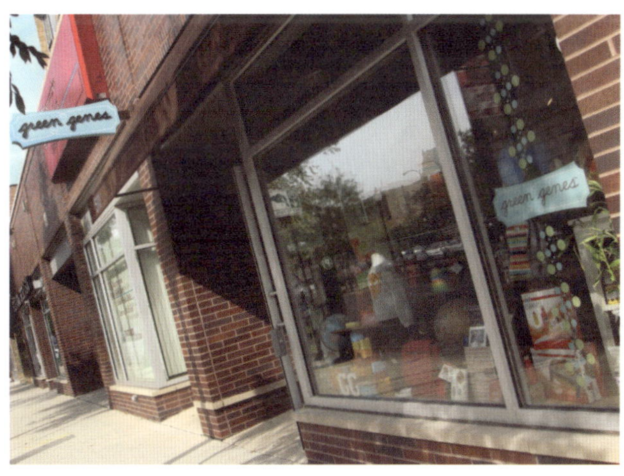

green genes
green genes

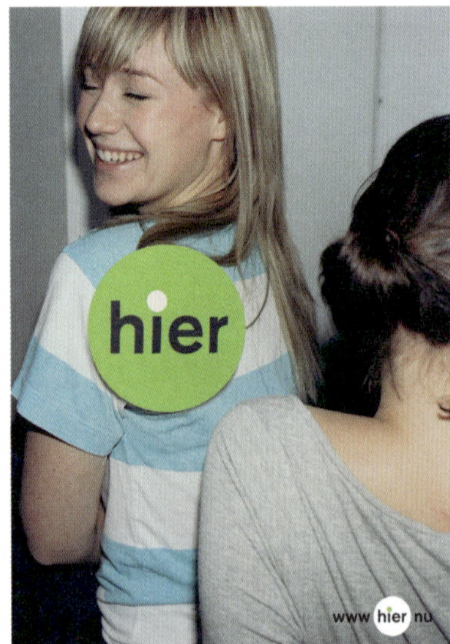

hier
www hier nu

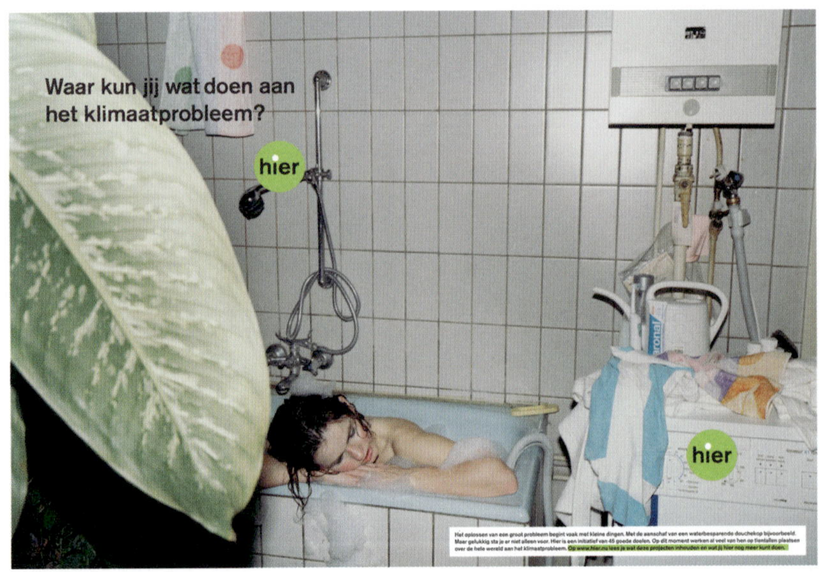

Waar kun jij wat doen aan
het klimaatprobleem?
hier
hier

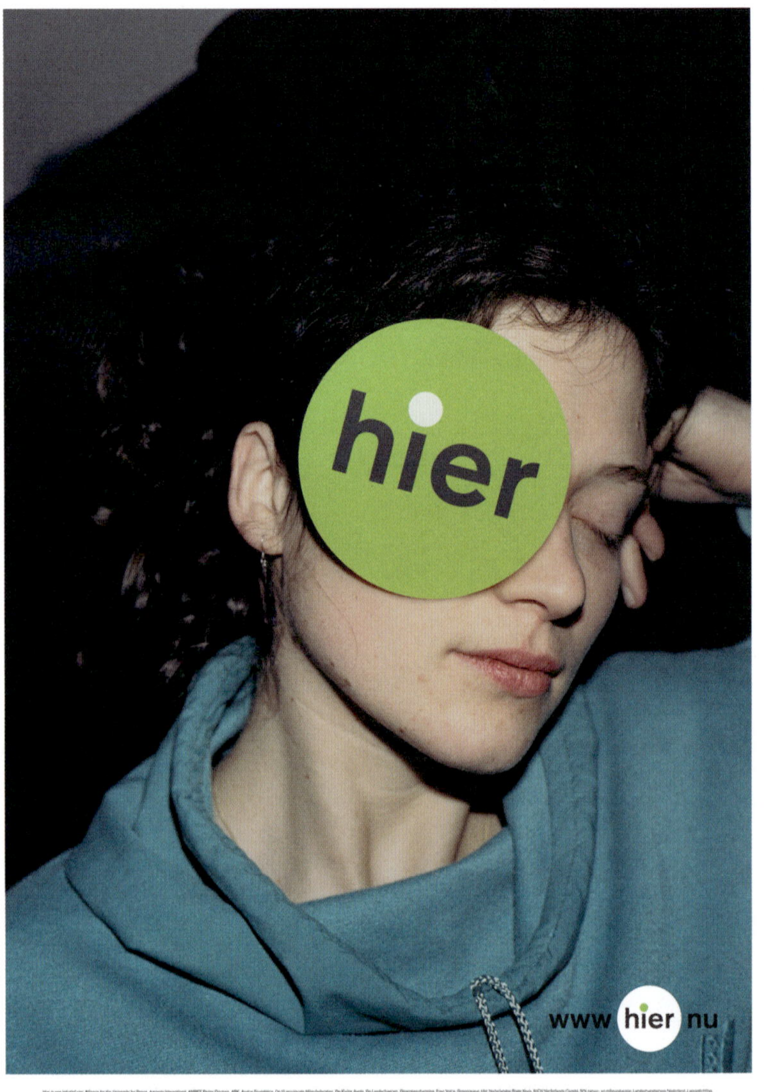

hier
www hier nu

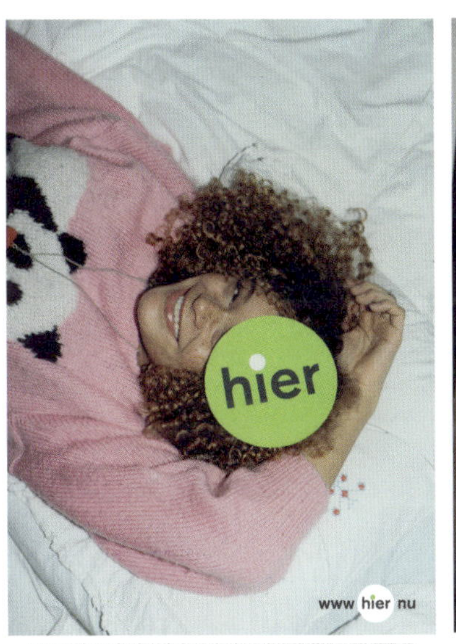

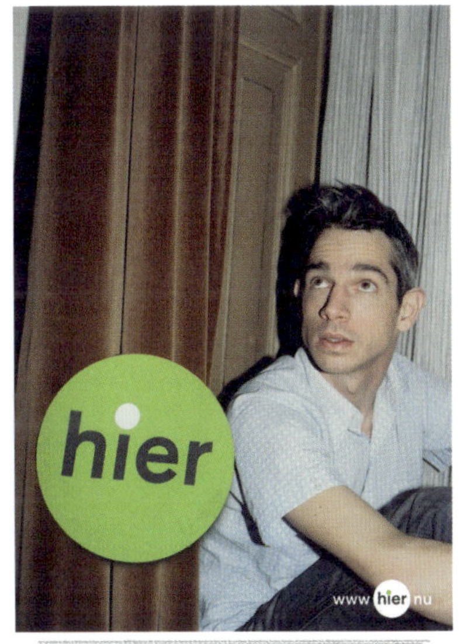

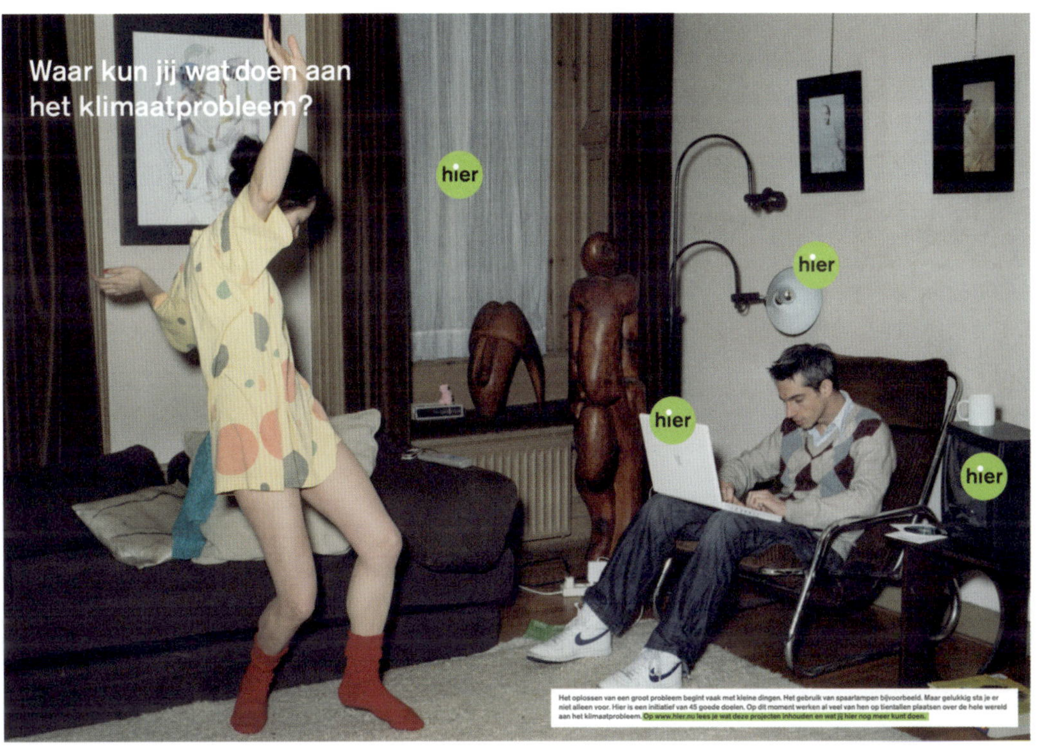

agency/studio: **KesselsKramer** / project: Climate change is a global problem, and yet each one of us has the power to make a difference. Even small changes in our daily behaviour can help. Start here. 'Hier' is a campaign organised by several foundations in the Netherlands that want to encourage climate awareness in people's daily lives. / Hier is an initiative launched by KesselsKramer / country: Netherlands agency/studio: **Greteman Group** / project: The Nuts for Nature kit - a fun, informative book packaged with bird and squirrel seeds and nuts - is supposed to encourage the creation of backyard habitats populated by birds, butterflies, blooms and all manner of friendly beasts. / client: Greteman Group. A gift is also sold, with a portion of the proceeds going to Roots and Shoots, a programme run by the Jane Goodall Institute / country: USA

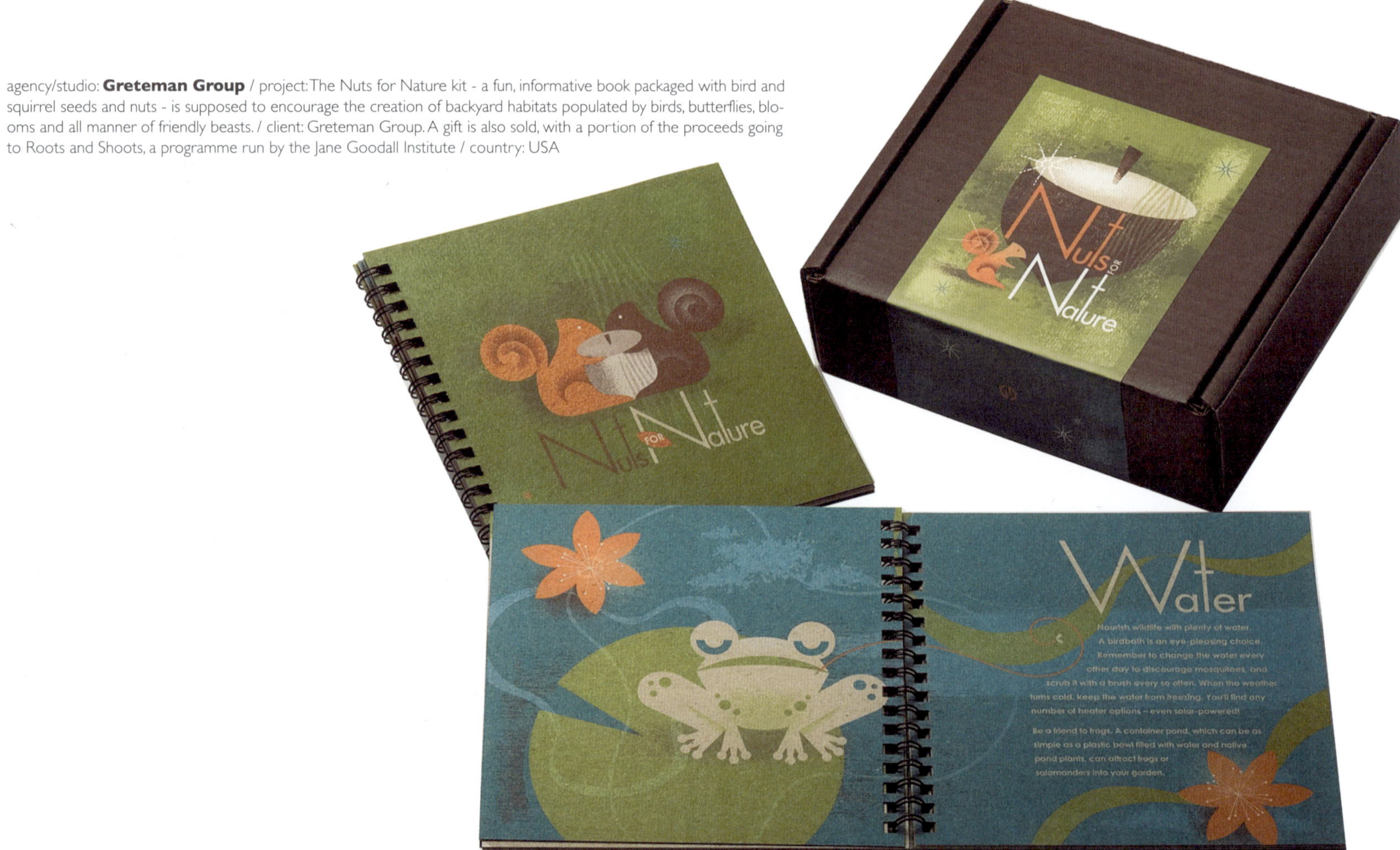

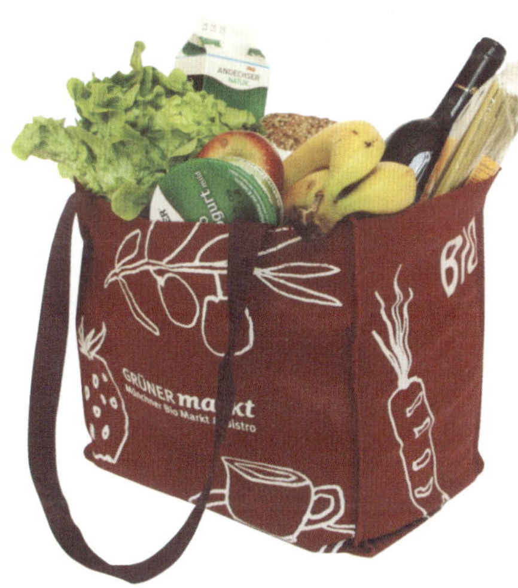

agency/studio: **mërz punkt** / project: corporate design for Grüner Markt (green market), a Munich-based chain of organic whole food stores./ client: Grüner Markt / country: Germany

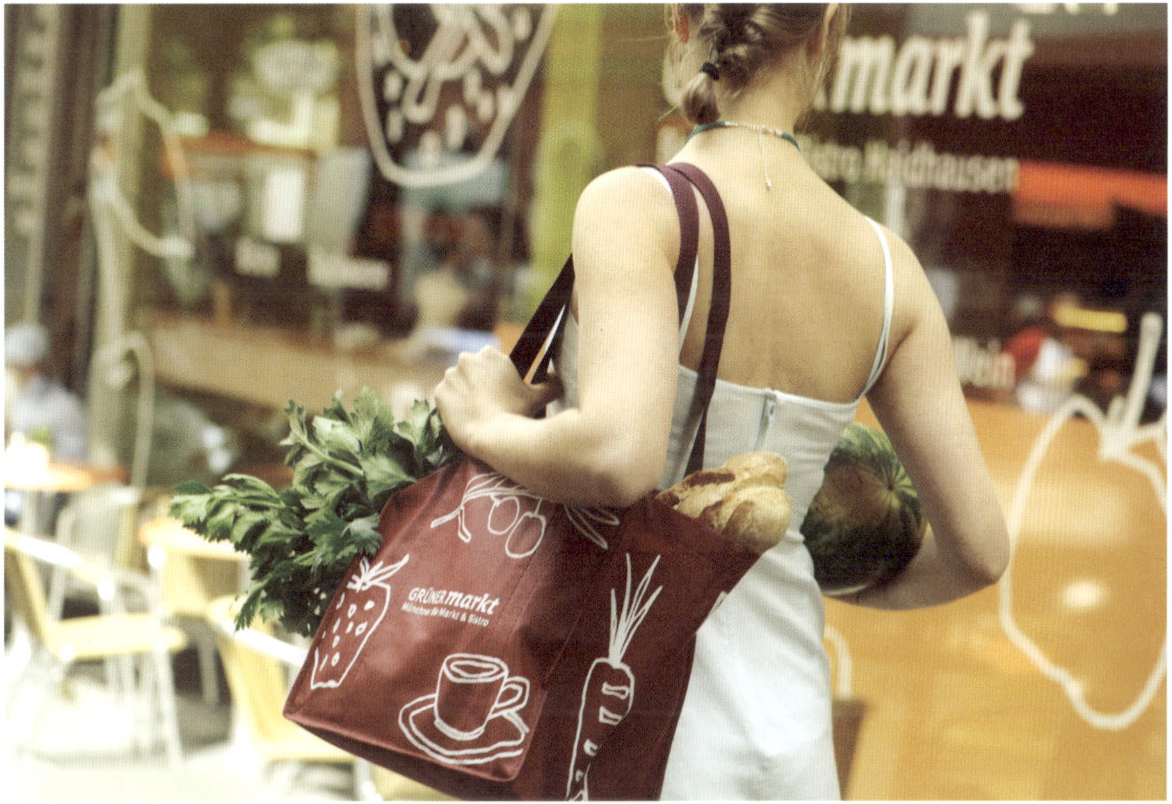

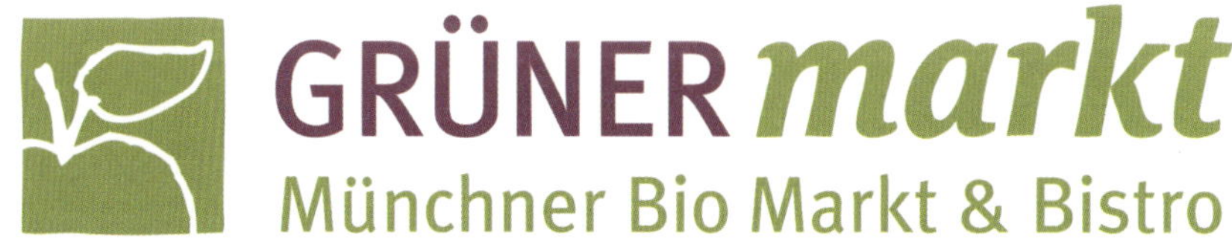

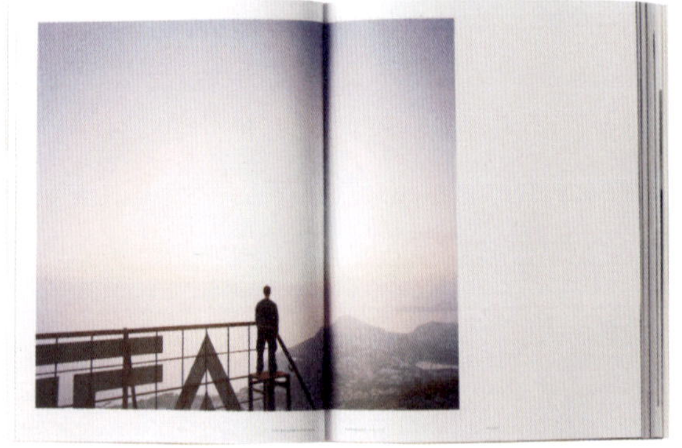

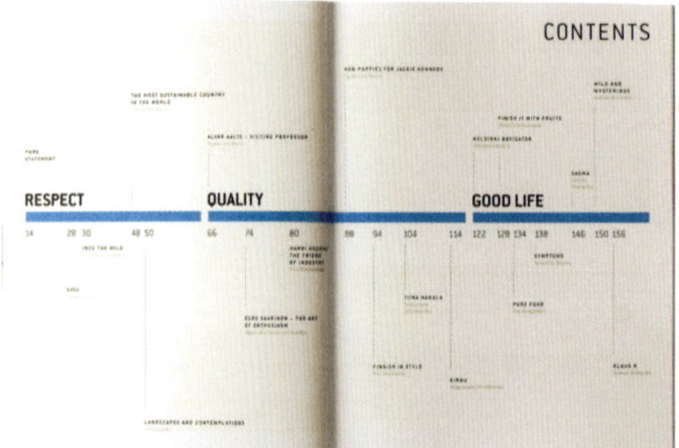

CONTENTS

RESPECT   QUALITY   GOOD LIFE

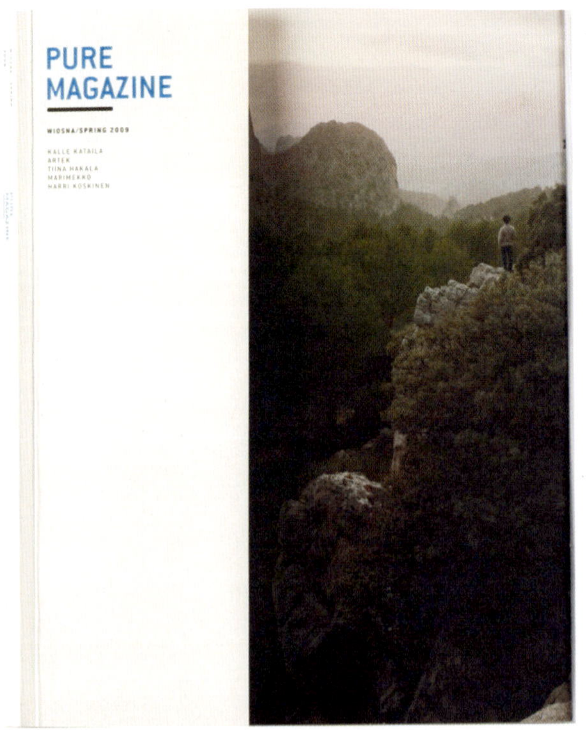

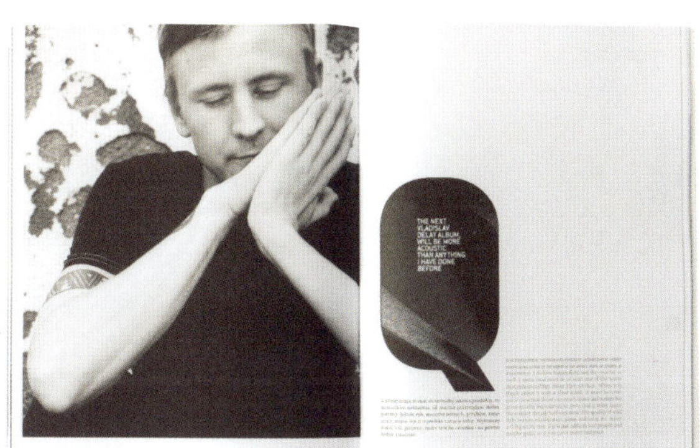
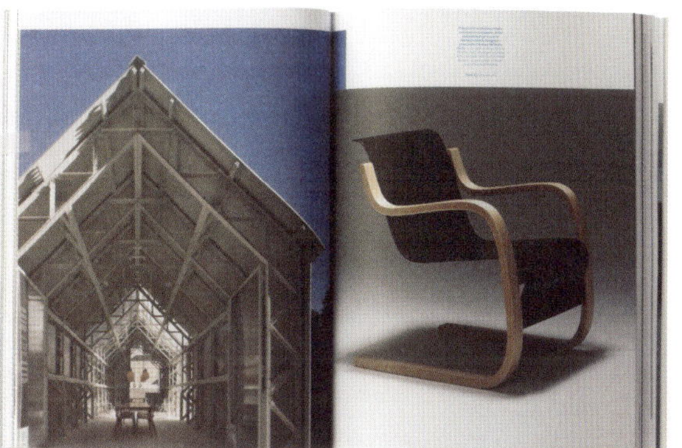
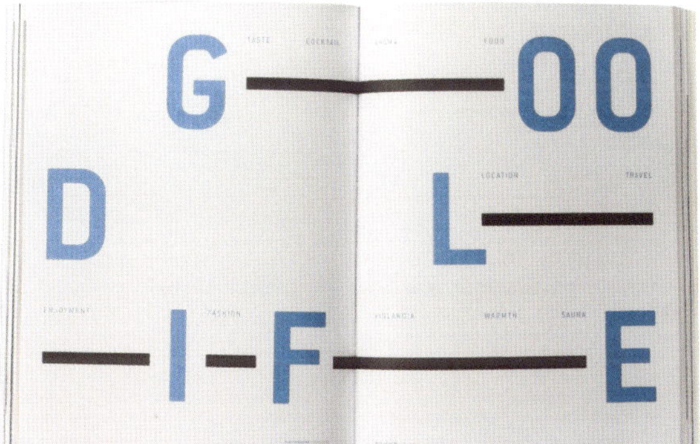

agency/studio: **Edgar Bak** / project: PURE Magazine. A magazine about sustainable ways of communicating the core national values of such countries as Finland. Healthy food, green design and relations. / client: Finlandia Vodka / country: Poland

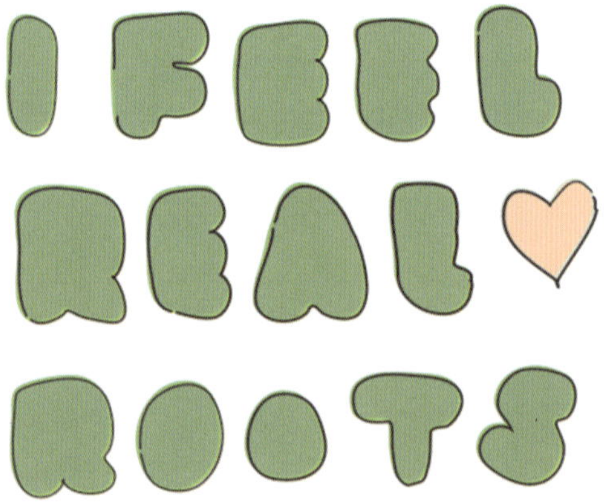

I FEEL REAL ♥ ROOTS

agency/studio: **Peach** / project: I feel real roots. A company idea and guerilla-style campaign to promote indoor plants in the urban home. / country: United Kingdom

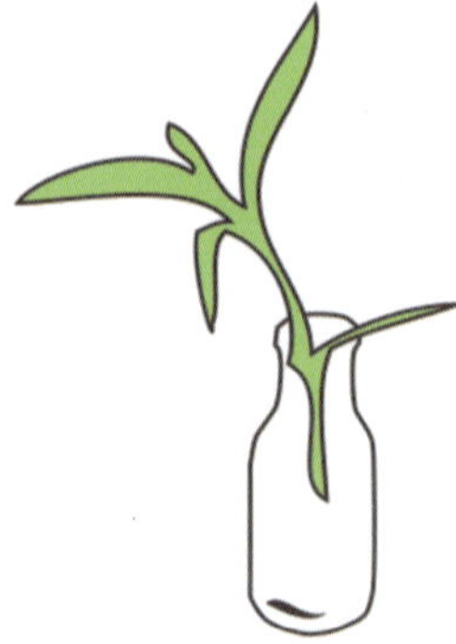

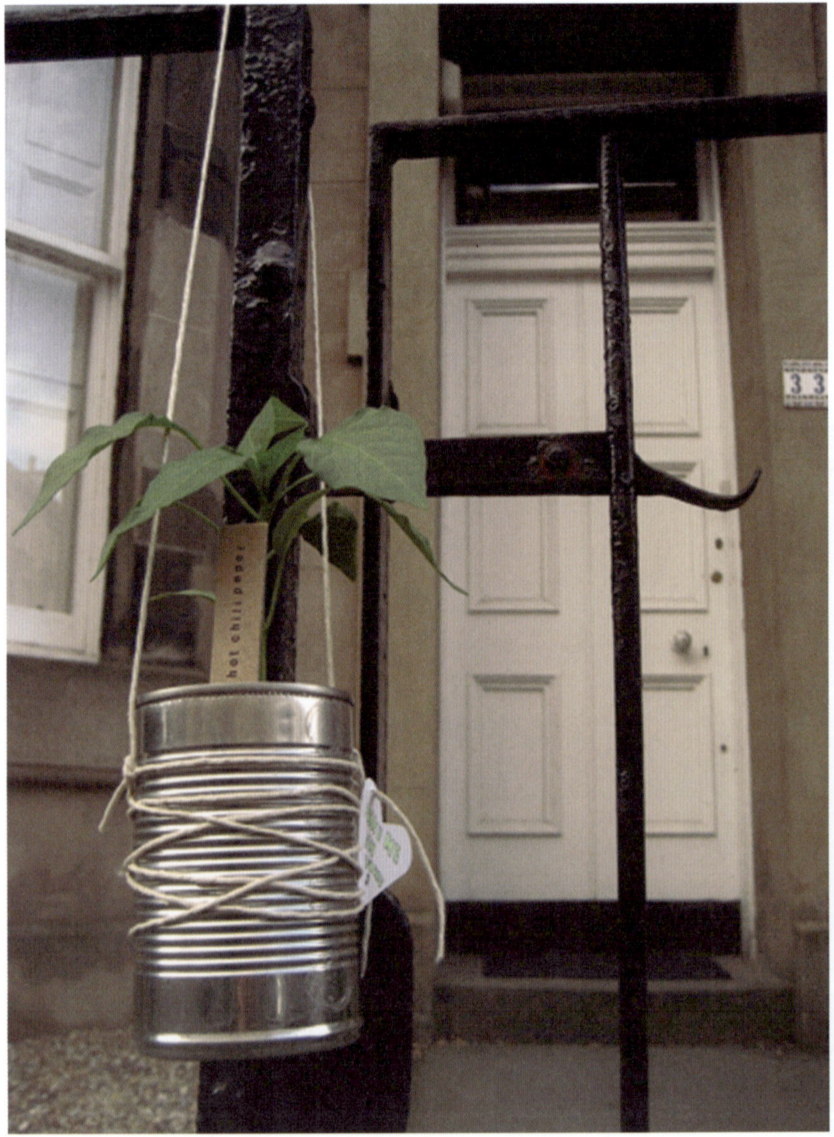

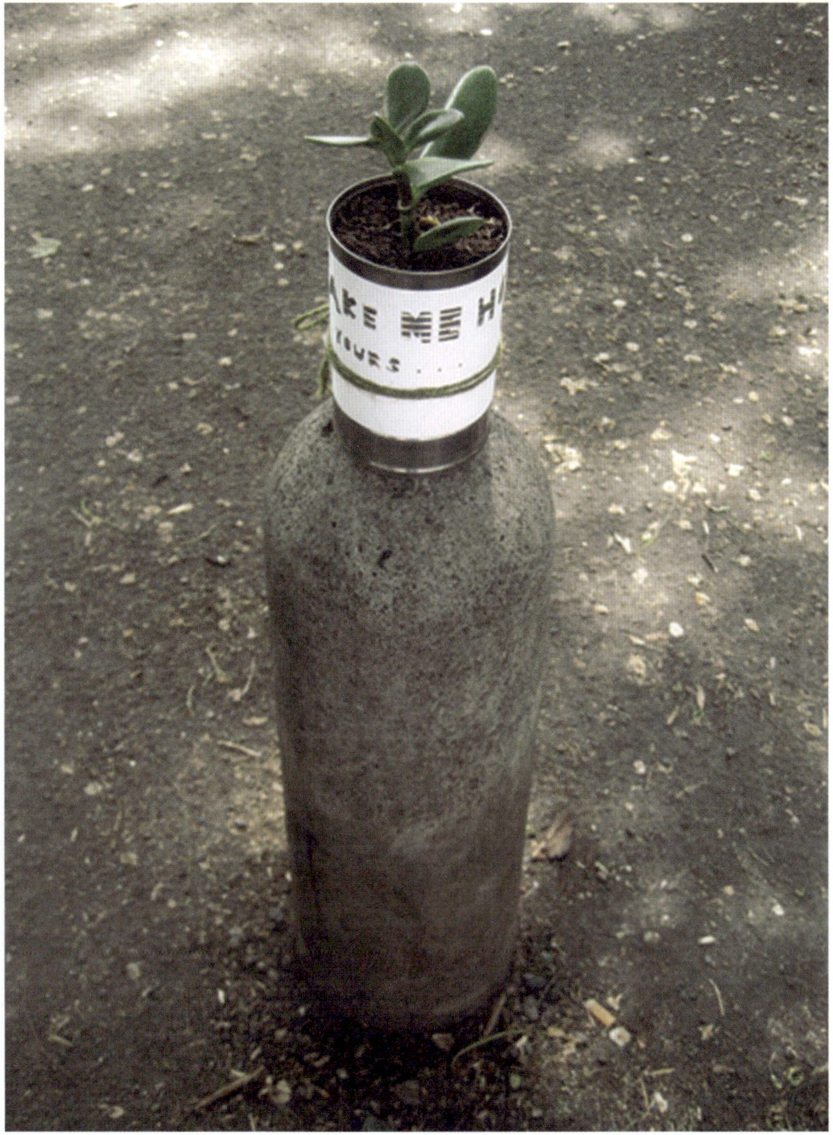

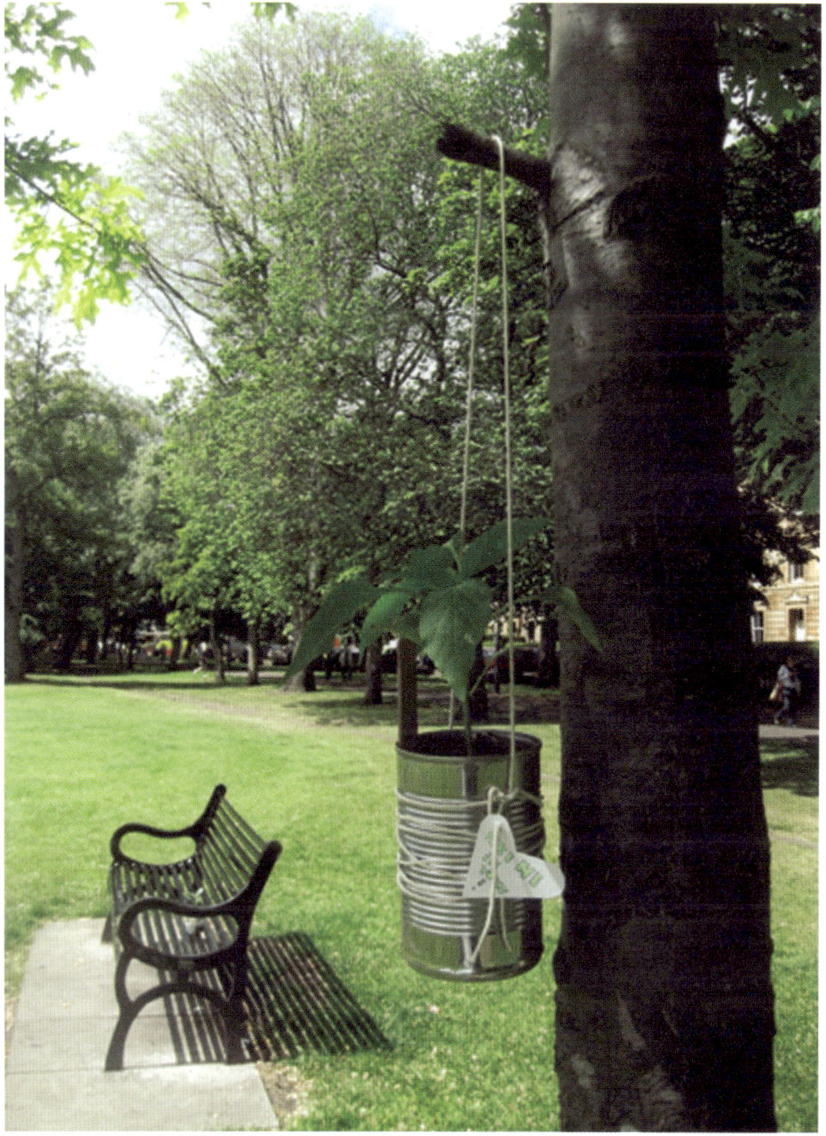

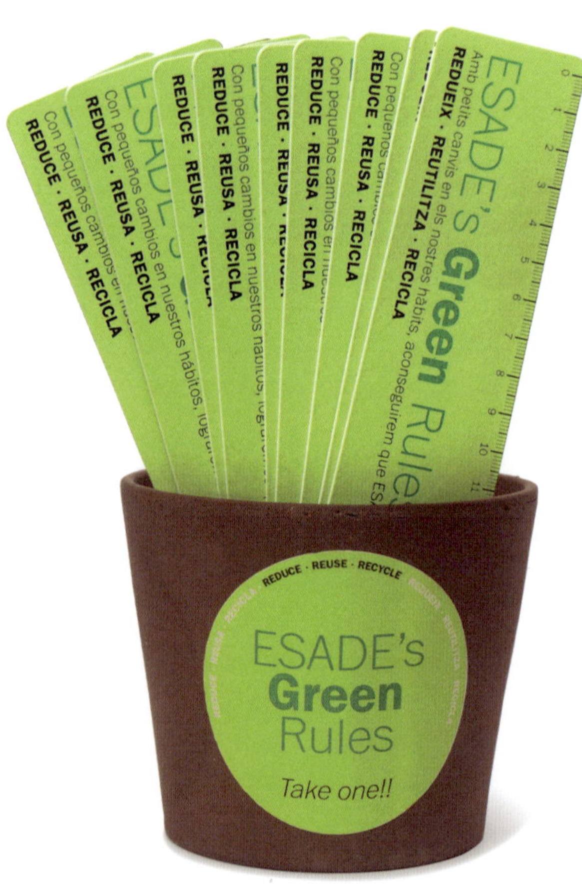

agency/studio: **Cosmic** - Juan Dávila, João Alves / project: ESADE's Green Rules. Campaign on good practices to foster sustainability in different areas of companies. / client: Esade / country: Spain

ESADE's Green Rules

0 1 2 3 4 5 6 7 8 9 10 11 12 13 14 15 16 17 18 19 20

- Evitemos el uso innecesario del papel.
- Reutilicemos y alarguemos la vida útil del material de trabajo.
- Colaboremos en el reciclado selectivo de residuos.
- Aprovechemos la luz natural y optimicemos la artificial.
- Apaguemos los ordenadores al finalizar su uso.
- Racionalicemos el uso de la calefacción y aire acondicionado.
- Reduzcamos el uso del agua sanitaria.
- Bebamos antes el agua de los dispensadores que la envasada.
- Caminemos o desplacémonos en bicicleta o transporte público.
- Respetemos y cuidemos los espacios comunes.

ESADE
Universitat Ramon Llull

Impreso en papel reciclado al 100%, siguiendo un proceso de fabricación sin cloro y sin blanqueantes ópticos. Recíclalo al finalizar su uso.

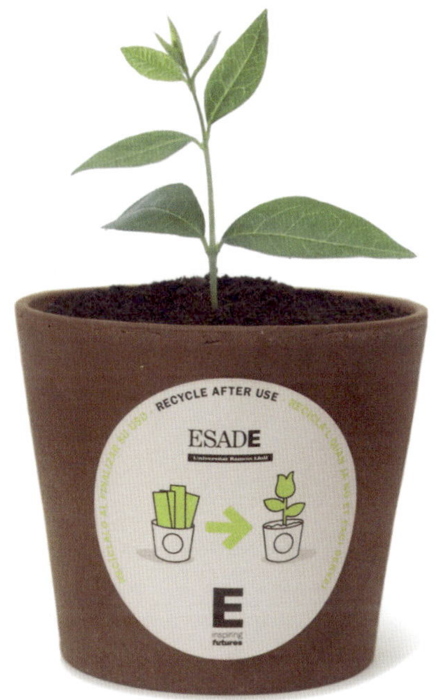

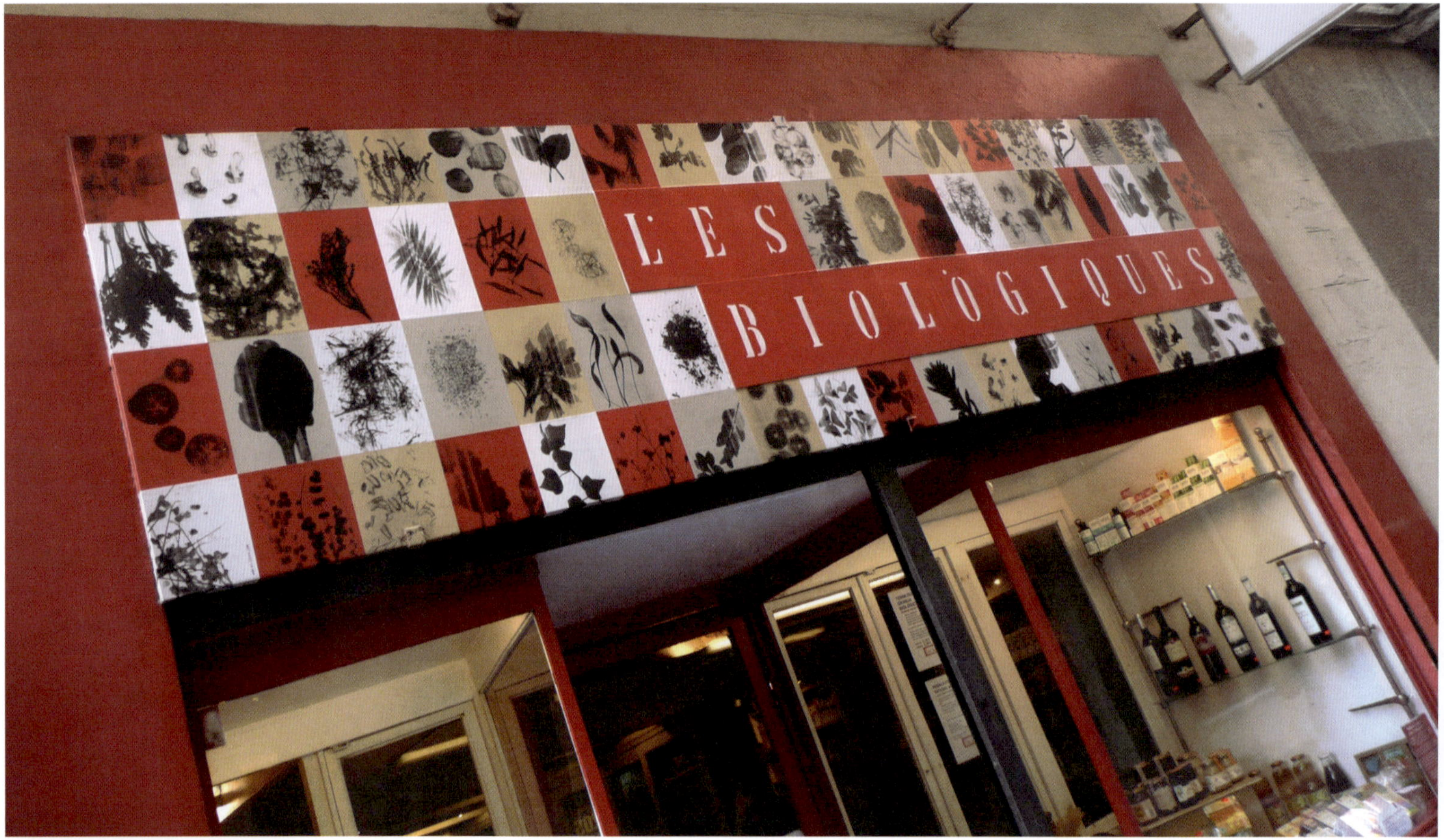

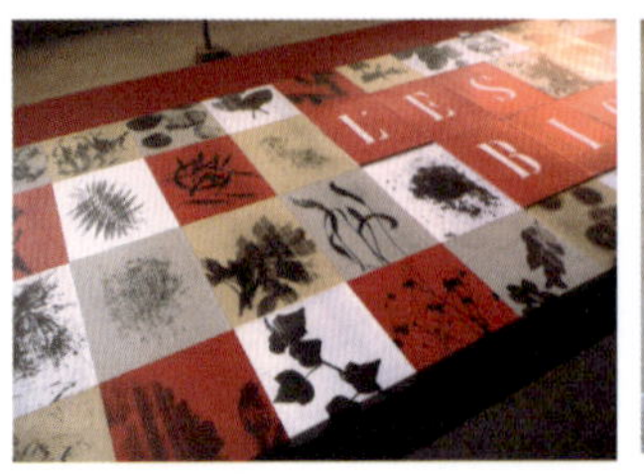

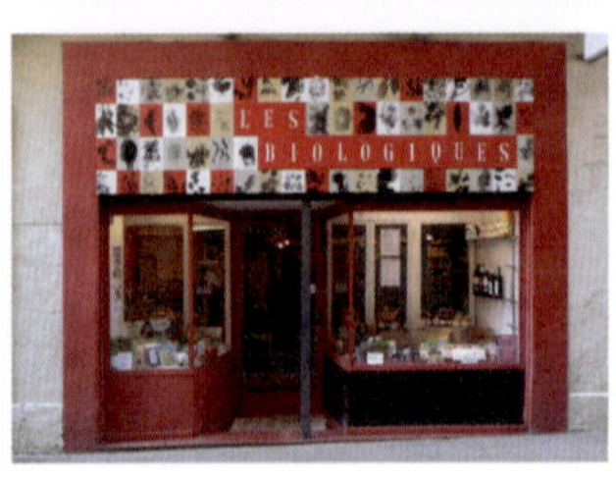

agency/studio: **el-lince** - Solange Dalannais & Carol van Waart / project: image for the herbarium of an organic food store. / client: Les Biològiques / country: Spain

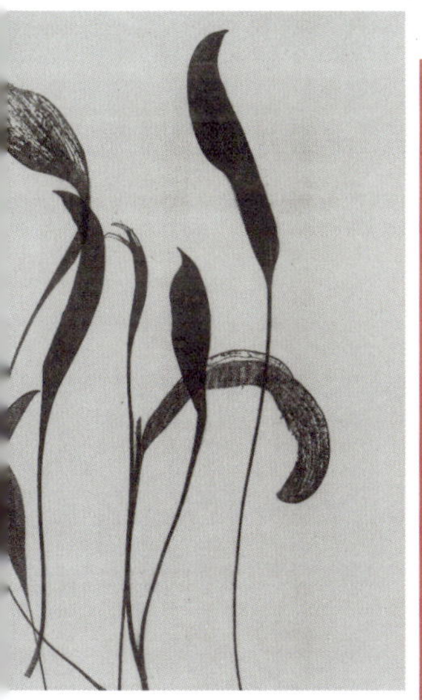
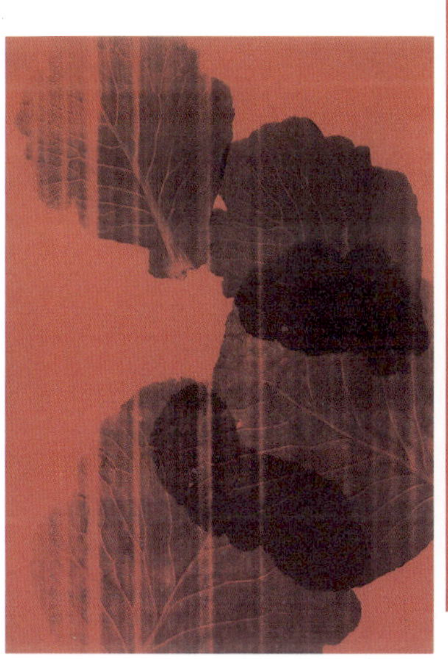
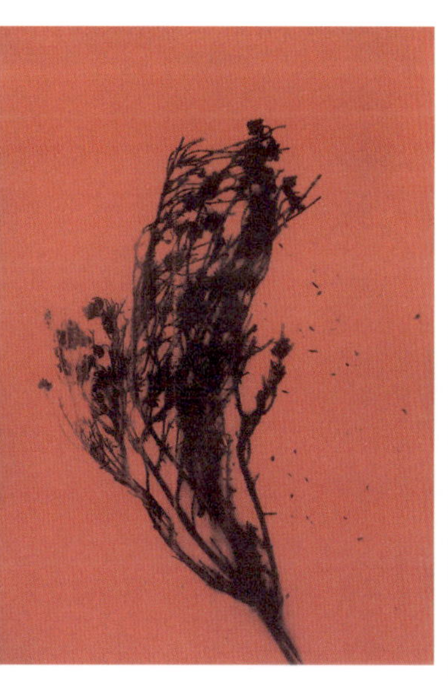
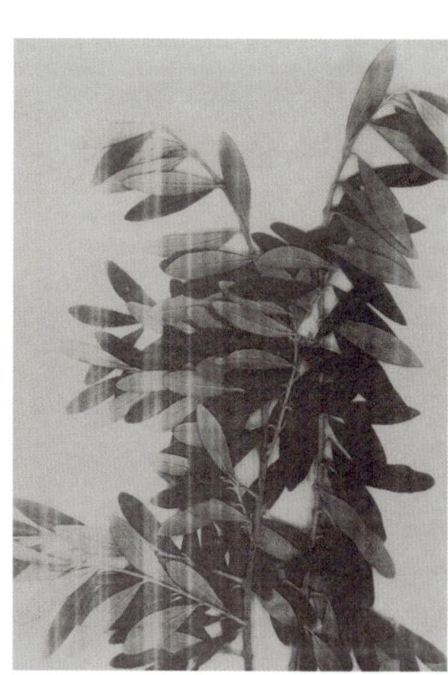
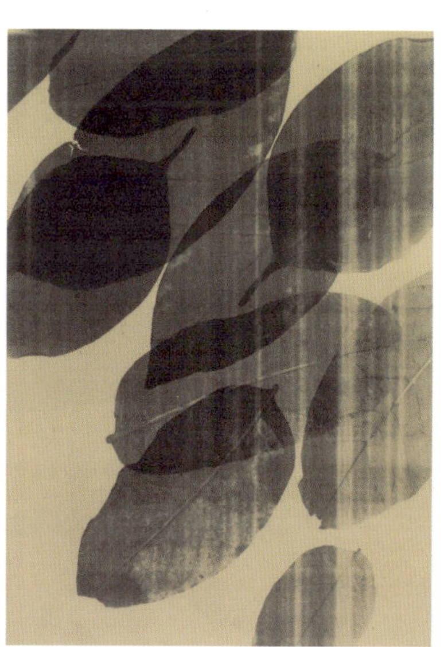

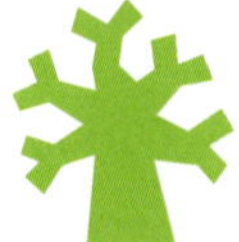

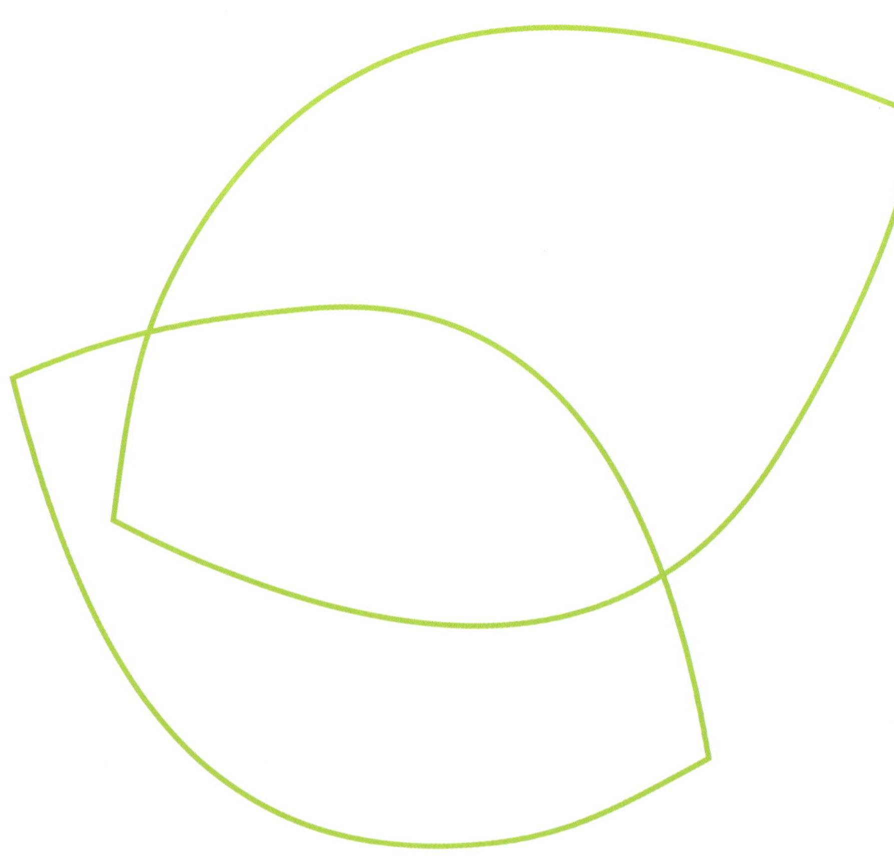

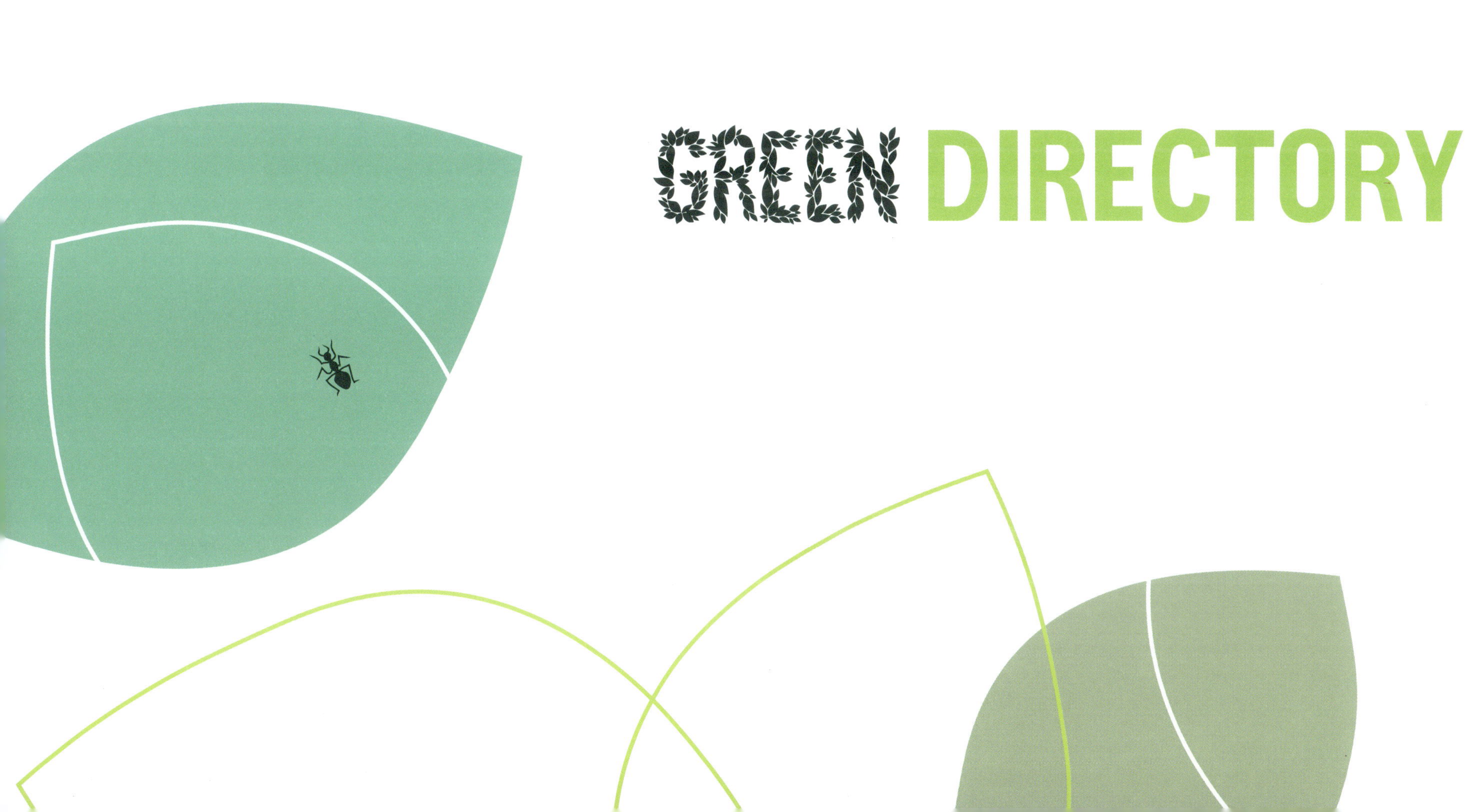

GREEN DIRECTORY

THE AUTHORS

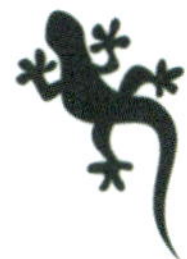

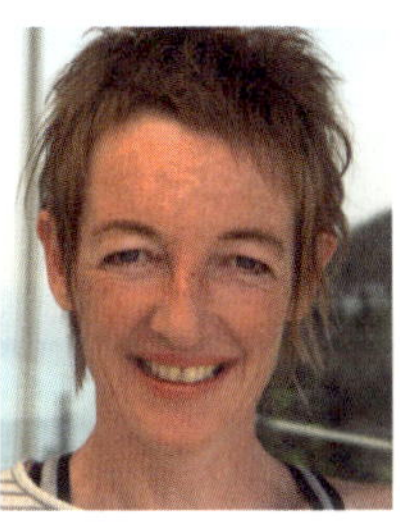

Vicky Eckert

Schwäbisch Hall, Germany -1965
Vicky Eckert has a degree in Visual Communication (FH Darmstadt, Germany). After five years working in graphic design and teaching the subject in Cali, Colombia, she moved to Barcelona in 1996, where she set up Estudio Eckert + Zúñiga. In 2008 she created the publishing house Flaflafeditions, for which she invents, designs and produces board games related to the environment and culture.

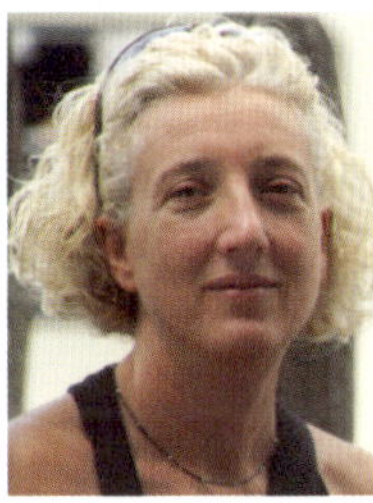

Ana Freixas

Barcelona, Spain - 1964
Ana Freixas has a diploma in Graphic Design. She studied at the Escola Massana and the Escola Llotja in Barcelona. For many years she participated in various design studies as a freelancer, while teaching at Tracor and Mac Escola.
Since 1997, she has been responsible for production and design for Difusión Ediciones, a publishing house working in the sport sector.

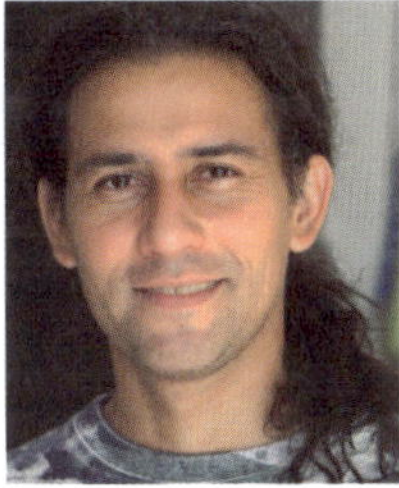

Efrén Zúñiga

Tuluá, Colombia - 1969
Efrén Zúñiga graduated with honours in Graphic Design from the Instituto Departamental de Bellas Artes in Cali, Colombia, where he later worked as a teacher.
He then studied at the Escola Massana in Barcelona, before teaming up with Vicky Eckert in 1997 to create Estudio Eckert + Zúñiga. Since 2008 he has also been part of Flaflafeditions.